1,001 GMAT®
Practice Questions

A Wiley Brand

1,001 GMAT® Practice Questions

by Sandra Luna McCune, PhD, and Shannon Reed, MA, MFA

A Wiley Brand

1,001 GMAT® Practice Questions For Dummies®

Published by: **John Wiley & Sons, Inc.,** 111 River Street, Hoboken, NJ 07030-5774, www.wiley.com

Copyright © 2018 by John Wiley & Sons, Inc., Hoboken, New Jersey

Published simultaneously in Canada

For general information on our other products and services, please contact our Customer Care Department within the U.S. at 877-762-2974, outside the U.S. at 317-572-3993, or fax 317-572-4002. For technical support, please visit https://hub.wiley.com/community/support/dummies.

Wiley publishes in a variety of print and electronic formats and by print-on-demand. Some material included with standard print versions of this book may not be included in e-books or in print-on-demand. If this book refers to media such as a CD or DVD that is not included in the version you purchased, you may download this material at http://booksupport.wiley.com. For more information about Wiley products, visit www.wiley.com.

Library of Congress Control Number: 2017949589

ISBN 978-1-119-36312-5 (pbk); ISBN 978-1-119-36313-2 (ebk); ISBN 978-1-119-36314-9 (ebk)

Manufactured in the United States of America

10 9 8 7 6 5 4 3 2 1

Contents at a Glance

Table of Contents

Introduction

Welcome to *1,001 GMAT Practice Questions For Dummies.* Pay no mind to the *dummies* part of the title. Obviously, if you're gearing up to tackle an MBA program, you're no dummy. You've already successfully finished high school and college, and you might even have a master's degree. Now you're ready to take your education to a higher level.

What you have probably learned after skimming through admissions requirements is that many MBA programs include scores from the Graduate Management Admissions Test (GMAT) as an admissions requirement. So how do you prepare for such a rigorous exam? Clearly, you need to become familiar with the topics covered and the types of questions you'll be faced with. You need practice accompanied by pointers on how best to answer the questions. This book provides all the guidance you need. Along with its 1,001 relevant practice opportunities, this book gives answers and detailed explanations that show simple and effective ways to solve the often challenging GMAT questions.

What You'll Find

This book serves as comprehensive, standalone preparation for the GMAT, or you can use it in conjunction with the latest edition of *GMAT For Dummies* (Wiley). Either way, this book helps you identify question types and content areas you need to work on. The practice questions are constructed to closely resemble the actual exam questions in both format and level of difficulty so that you will know what to expect when you take your exam. The abundance of questions gives you ample opportunity to practice until you're feeling confident and prepared on the big day.

If you miss a question, read the answer explanation and try to figure out where you went wrong. Go back and solve it again, this time avoiding your earlier mistake. Read the answer explanations for the questions you get right as well. Often, the answer explanation will reveal not only the solution to the question but also how to answer it most efficiently. This strategy helps you internalize concepts and skills.

Whatever you do, keep a positive spirit. This book contains challenging questions not unlike those you might encounter on the GMAT. These questions are not meant to discourage you but rather to show you *how* to solve and master them.

How the Questions Are Organized

This book has two parts. The first part contains 1,001 practice questions divided among seven chapters. These chapters are organized around the four sections of the GMAT: Analytical Writing

Assessment (AWA), Integrated Reasoning (IR), Quantitative, and Verbal. The second part of the book contains the answers and detailed answer explanations.

The AWA requires you to write an analytical critique of a presented argument. The IR questions require you to apply analytical reasoning and math skills to various data-intensive scenarios. The Quantitative section consists of problem solving and data sufficiency questions. These questions test your knowledge and understanding of arithmetic, basic probability and statistics, algebra, and geometry. The Verbal section consists of reading comprehension, sentence correction, and critical reasoning questions. These questions test your ability to read and comprehend unfamiliar written material, to recognize and apply the basic rules of standard written English, and to use logical reasoning and critical thinking.

Beyond the Book

Your purchase of this book gives you so much more than a thousand (and one) questions you can work on to improve your GMAT performance. It comes also with a free, one-year subscription to hundreds of practice questions online. Not only can you access this digital content anytime you want, on whichever device is available to you, but you can also track your progress and view personalized reports that show you which concepts you need to study the most.

What you'll find online

The online practice that comes free with this book offers the same 1,001 questions and answers that are available here. The benefit of the online questions is that you can customize your online practice to focus on the topics that give you the most trouble. You get to choose the types of questions and the number of questions you want to practice. The online program tracks how many questions you answer correctly versus incorrectly so that you can monitor your progress and spend time studying exactly what you need.

This product also comes with an online Cheat Sheet that helps you increase your odds of performing well on the GMAT. To get the Cheat Sheet, go to www.dummies.com and type "1,001 GMAT Practice Questions For Dummies cheat sheet" in the search box. (No access code required. You can benefit from this info before you register.)

How to register

To gain access to the online version of all 1,001 practice questions in this book, all you have to do is register. Just follow these simple steps:

1. Find your PIN access code:

    Print-book users: If you purchased a print copy of this book, turn to the inside front cover of the book to find your access code.

    E-book users: If you purchased this book as an e-book, you can get your access code by registering your e-book at www.dummies.com/go/getaccess. Go to this website, find your book and click it, and answer the security questions to verify your purchase. You'll receive an email with your access code.

2. Go to Dummies.com and click *Activate Now*.

3. Find your product (*1,001 GMAT Practice Questions For Dummies*) and then follow the on-screen prompts to activate your PIN.

That's all there is to it! You can come back to the online program again and again. Simply log in with the username and password you chose during your initial login. No need to use the access code a second time.

For Technical Support, please visit `http://wiley.custhelp.com` or call Wiley at 1-800-762-2974 (U.S.) or +1-317-572-3994 (International).

Where to Go for Additional Help

The solutions to the practice problems in this book are meant to walk you through how to get the right answers. They're not meant to teach the material. If certain concepts are unfamiliar to you, you can find help at `www.dummies.com`. Just type "GMAT" into the search box to turn up GMAT-related information.

If you need more detailed instruction, check out the previously mentioned *GMAT For Dummies*.

1

The Questions

IN THIS PART . . .

Practice analytical writing questions.

Answer integrated reasoning questions.

Work on quantitative questions involving problem solving and data sufficiency.

Tackle reading comprehension and sentence correction questions.

Practice critical reasoning questions.

Chapter **1**

Analytical Writing Assessment

The Analytical Writing Assessment on the GMAT is one question, presented at the beginning of your test. You are given the question prompt and then a reading passage of several paragraphs that presents an argument. Your task is to write a response to that passage that analyzes the logic presented in the passage. You need to agree or disagree with the argument's logic and explain why the flaws you see in the argument are problematic.

The Problems You'll Work On

When working through the Analytical Writing Assessment questions presented here, be prepared to do the following:

>> Read a longer passage than at any other point on the GMAT. It will present an argument, often around something related to business, education, or science, and that argument will contain flaws.

>> Analyze the argument for logical flaws and outline a response.

>> Write a four- to six-paragraph essay based on your outline in which you agree or disagree with the argument, and analyze the flaws within it.

>> Proofread the essay carefully before submitting it.

What to Watch Out For

To increase your chances of scoring well, make sure to do the following:

>> Firmly agree or disagree with the argument.

>> Give yourself enough time to plan, write, and proofread your essay.

>> Don't get drawn into an entirely personal response. Your essay must show logic and intelligence.

1. A speaker at a role playing games event made the following statement:

   "Although role playing games — or RPGs — such as Dungeons & Dragons have been widely criticized for having a negative effect on our youth, encouraging them to be 'nerds without social skills' as one reporter put it, this is not a valid viewpoint. If we look at a survey from last year, more young adults who play RPGs value social skills and courtesy than ever before by almost a 2 to 1 margin compared to the same survey from 10 years ago. This evidence suggests that RPGs are actually promoting social interaction and friendship among the young adults playing them. More people should play them."

   Discuss how well-reasoned you find this argument. In your discussion, be sure to analyze the line of reasoning and the use of evidence in the argument. For example, you may need to consider what questionable assumptions underlie the thinking and what alternative examples or counterexamples might weaken the conclusion. You can also discuss what sort of evidence would strengthen or refute the argument, what changes in argument would make it more logically sound, and what, if anything, would help you better evaluate its conclusion.

2. The following appeared in a promotional mailing sent by the publishers of a community directory, encouraging local businesses to buy an ad in the next edition:

   "One of the best ways to reach new customers is also one of the cheapest. That's why it makes sense to purchase an ad in the Stipeville Business Directory! Local business owners who have purchased an ad in years past will tell you the same thing! Did you know that three of our town's top-ten doctors, two of our top-five caterers, and several of our top pet groomers bought ads last year? And we don't want to name names, but a local hairdresser forgot to place her ad before our deadline last year, and she reports that her business dropped by 5%! Well, she's buying an ad this year, and so should you! The Stipesville Business Directory is a must-buy for all local businesses!"

   Discuss how well-reasoned you find this argument. In your discussion, be sure to analyze the line of reasoning and the use of evidence in the argument. For example, you may need to consider what questionable assumptions underlie the thinking and what alternative examples or counterexamples might weaken the conclusion. You can also discuss what sort of evidence would strengthen or refute the argument, what changes in argument would make it more logically sound, and what, if anything, would help you better evaluate its conclusion.

3. A school board member recently made the following statement at a meeting:

"I'm concerned about how poorly the students at Richmeade Senior High School are scoring on their standardized tests. Their math tests scores were, in particular, dreadful, scoring about 20 points lower than the students at Richmeade Prep School, which you all know is just down the road. I've been investigating what the Prep School does differently and noticed that in April, they do not offer any extracurricular or special activities, including school field trips, dances, and shows, before the tests are given. They also require all students to take the exam in order to graduate. Therefore, I propose that we also ban extracurricular and special activities for the month of May since we give the test in June. That should help our students focus."

Discuss how well-reasoned you find this argument. In your discussion, be sure to analyze the line of reasoning and the use of evidence in the argument. For example, you may need to consider what questionable assumptions underlie the thinking and what alternative examples or counterexamples might weaken the conclusion. You can also discuss what sort of evidence would strengthen or refute the argument, what changes in argument would make it more logically sound, and what, if anything, would help you better evaluate its conclusion.

4. A recent column in a conventional cosmetic industry newsletter noted:

"Many customers buy organic makeup products because they are concerned about the consequences of the widespread use of chemical class Zbt in the conventional cosmetics industry. It's part of our job to convince those customers that they're misinformed. You might begin by pointing out that while chemical class Zbt has been shown — in very high dosages — to cause scarring in animal studies, no study has ever show that its presence causes scarring on human test subjects. You can conclude by noting that there is clearly no reason for even the most concerned customer to waste her money on organic makeup products. Perfectly safe makeup, you can say, is available without the hassle of searching out organic cosmetics."

Discuss how well-reasoned you find this argument. In your discussion, be sure to analyze the line of reasoning and the use of evidence in the argument. For example, you may need to consider what questionable assumptions underlie the thinking and what alternative examples or counterexamples might weaken the conclusion. You can also discuss what sort of evidence would strengthen or refute the argument, what changes in argument would make it more logically sound, and what, if anything, would help you better evaluate its conclusion.

5. A banking executive recently made the following comments in an address to shareholders:

> "North Bank was once run out of a single storefront on Main Street. Now we have five satellite locations around North Town. However, North Bank was more profitable when it only had that single storefront than it is today with 6 locations. Therefore, I'm proposing that we close our five satellite locations and move all of our business to our original location. This will improve our profitability and customers will enjoy the nostalgic feel of doing their business at a single location."

Discuss how well-reasoned you find this argument. In your discussion, be sure to analyze the line of reasoning and the use of evidence in the argument. For example, you may need to consider what questionable assumptions underlie the thinking and what alternative examples or counterexamples might weaken the conclusion. You can also discuss what sort of evidence would strengthen or refute the argument, what changes in argument would make it more logically sound, and what, if anything, would help you better evaluate its conclusion.

Chapter **2**

Integrated Reasoning

The GMAT Integrated Reasoning (IR) section consists of 12 multiple-part questions that must be completed in 30 minutes. Your answers for each of the multiple parts of an IR question must all be correct to get credit for the question. You have access to an onscreen calculator for this section of the test. The IR questions require you to apply critical reasoning and math skills to various data-intensive scenarios. The questions are presented in the following four different formats:

>> **Table Analysis** questions present data in sortable tables. You use the data to choose one of two opposing answer choices for each of three statements.

>> **Two-Part Analysis** questions present a short written explanation of a situation or math problem in which two portions of related information are unknown. You are asked to make two choices, one for each of the unknown portions.

>> **Graphics Interpretation** questions present information in a graph or other visual image. You must complete two missing pieces of information in one or two statements by choosing from drop-down menus.

>> **Multi-Source Reasoning** questions present several sources of information, such as text material, graphs, diagrams, charts, and tables. You must synthesize the information and draw logical conclusions to answer three questions. Two of the questions are multiple-part questions. For these two questions, you choose one of two opposing answer choices for each of three statements. The other question is a five-option multiple-choice question, for which you must select the one best answer choice.

The Problems You'll Work On

When working through the IR questions in this chapter, be prepared to

>> Read and understand graphical or visual representations of information.

>> Recognize cause and effect.

>> Identify relationships in information.

What to Watch Out For

Don't make these mistakes:

>> Being confused because questions present excess data that you don't need.

>> Answering questions based on your personal knowledge instead of on the information given.

>> Failing to pace yourself so that you can answer all the questions in the given timeframe.

6. The table shows data from the U.S. Census Bureau, Manufacturing and Trade Inventories and Sales, May 12, 2017, report on estimated sales, inventories, and inventories-to-sales ratios for domestic activities of retailers in the U.S. To make it easier to observe underlying trends and other non-seasonal movements, the data are adjusted for seasonal variations and, in the case of sales, for trading-day differences and holiday variations. The inventories to sales ratios show the relationship of the end-of-month values of inventory to the monthly sales. These ratios can be interpreted as indicating the number of months of inventory that are on hand. For example, a ratio of 2.5 indicates that a business has enough merchandise on hand to cover two and a half months of sales (Source: U.S. Bureau of the Census, Merchant Wholesalers: Inventories to Sales Ratio).

On the actual exam, the table is interactive, and you can sort it in ascending order by selecting the column title you want to sort by from the drop-down menu above the table. The table below is shown sorted by different column titles to simulate the exam.

Sorted by Kind of Business (Column 1)

Kind of Business	Sales			Inventories			Inventories/Sales Ratios		
	Mar. 2017	Feb. 2017	Mar. 2016	Mar. 2017	Feb. 2017	Mar. 2016	Mar. 2017	Feb. 2017	Mar. 2016
Building materials, and garden equipment & supplies	30,864	31,402	29,628	54,188	54,139	52,195	1.76	1.72	1.76
Clothing stores	21,504	21,111	21,242	53,190	53,096	52,790	2.47	2.52	2.49
Food & beverage stores	59,583	59,157	57,406	46,812	46,841	45,797	0.79	0.79	0.80
Furniture, home furnishings, and electrical, & appliance stores	17,618	17,306	17,278	27,400	27,527	27,459	1.56	1.59	1.59
General merchandise stores	56,466	56,605	56,337	81,027	82,403	52,790	1.43	1.43	1.46
Motor vehicle & parts dealers	96,423	96,895	92,140	219,709	217,850	203,835	2.28	2.25	2.21

© John Wiley & Sons, Inc.

Sorted by Inventories March 2017 (Column 5)

Kind of Business	Sales			Inventories			Inventories/Sales Ratios		
	Mar. 2017	Feb. 2017	Mar. 2016	Mar. 2017	Feb. 2017	Mar. 2016	Mar. 2017	Feb. 2017	Mar. 2016
Furniture, home furnishings, and electrical, & appliance stores	17,618	17,306	17,278	27,400	27,527	27,459	1.56	1.59	1.59
Food & beverage stores	59,583	59,157	57,406	46,812	46,841	45,797	0.79	0.79	0.80
Clothing stores	21,504	21,111	21,242	53,190	53,096	52,790	2.47	2.52	2.49
Building materials, and garden equipment & supplies	30,864	31,402	29,628	54,188	54,139	52,195	1.76	1.72	1.76
General merchandise stores	56,466	56,605	56,337	81,027	82,403	52,790	1.43	1.43	1.46
Motor vehicle & parts dealers	96,423	96,895	92,140	219,709	217,850	203,835	2.28	2.25	2.21

Sorted by Inventories/Sales Ratios March 2017 (Column 8)

Kind of Business	Sales			Inventories			Inventories/Sales Ratios		
	Mar. 2017	Feb. 2017	Mar. 2016	Mar. 2017	Feb. 2017	Mar. 2016	Mar. 2017	Feb. 2017	Mar. 2016
Food & beverage stores	59,583	59,157	57,406	46,812	46,841	45,797	0.79	0.79	0.80
General merchandise stores	56,466	56,605	56,337	81,027	82,403	52,790	1.43	1.43	1.46
Furniture, home furnishings, and electrical, & appliance stores	17,618	17,306	17,278	27,400	27,527	27,459	1.56	1.59	1.59
Building materials, and garden equipment & supplies	30,864	31,402	29,628	54,188	54,139	52,195	1.76	1.72	1.76
Motor vehicle & parts dealers	96,423	96,895	92,140	219,709	217,850	203,835	2.28	2.25	2.21
Clothing stores	21,504	21,111	21,242	53,190	53,096	52,790	2.47	2.52	2.49

For each of the following statements, select *Yes* if the statement is true based solely on the information in the table. Otherwise, select *No*.

	Yes	No	
6.1	(A)	(B)	The percent change in sales for the combined domestic activities of retailer businesses from March 2016 to March 2017 is approximately 3.1.
6.2	(A)	(B)	The business that has the highest March 2017 inventory also has the highest March 2017 Inventories/Sales Ratio.
6.3	(A)	(B)	The business that is likely to have less than enough merchandise on hand to cover one month of sales is general merchandise stores.

7. The following table shows stock quotations for 20 companies at the end of a particular trading day in 2018. The table contains the following information: 52-Wk High, the highest price at which a stock has traded over the previous 52 weeks; 52-Wk Low, the lowest price at which a stock has traded over the previous 52 weeks; Stock, the name of the company; Volume (100s), the total number of 100 shares traded that day; High, the highest price of the stock for the day; Low, the lowest price of the stock for the day; Close, the last recorded price of the day when the market closed; and Net Change, the difference between the closing prices of the day and the previous trading day.

On the actual exam, the table is interactive, and you can sort it in ascending order by selecting the column title you want to sort by from the drop-down menu above the table. The table below is shown sorted by different column titles to simulate the exam.

Sorted by Stock (Column 3)

52-Wk High	52-Wk Low	Stock	Volume (100s)	High	Low	Close	Net Change
164.50	107.62	Company A	6,221	154.75	152.60	154.63	1.84
72.62	36.45	Company B	2,315	56.45	56.45	56.45	0.83
27.62	20.00	Company C	154	24.32	23.75	24.05	−0.56
16.25	8.25	Company D	11,872	9.78	8.94	9.05	−0.09
119.25	89.00	Company E	3,475	101.75	99.78	100.25	1.77
22.12	15.25	Company F	4,289	18.23	18.20	18.23	0.86
53.70	41.00	Company G	329	42.79	39.65	39.65	0.05
96.78	35.12	Company H	2,186	88.41	85.38	86.75	1.29
52.24	38.27	Company I	25	50.27	50.00	50.00	0.67
46.50	25.43	Company J	308	25.59	24.75	24.75	0.05
51.86	30.76	Company K	1,097	32.99	30.23	32.55	−0.02
33.18	17.91	Company L	2,086	20.24	20.24	20.24	0.23
220.37	124.30	Company M	2,290	186.15	184.74	186.15	−1.45
136.09	80.39	Company N	9,875	96.94	96.91	96.93	2.00
127.56	101.20	Company O	380	109.67	107.73	108.90	1.01
4.26	2.50	Company P	10,764	3.25	3.21	3.21	0.03
98.73	41.78	Company Q	2,712	61.48	61.45	61.45	3.35
83.00	42.65	Company R	3,612	55.27	55.20	55.27	0.02
88.95	74.67	Company S	1,087	79.65	78.54	78.52	1.15
187.95	122.34	Company T	2,877	180.69	178.52	179.45	0.32

© *John Wiley & Sons, Inc.*

Sorted by Volume (Column 4)

52-Wk High	52-Wk Low	Stock	Volume (100s)	High	Low	Close	Net Change
52.24	38.27	Company I	25	50.27	50.00	50.00	0.67
27.62	20.00	Company C	154	24.32	23.75	24.05	−0.56
46.50	25.43	Company J	308	25.59	24.75	24.75	0.05
53.70	41.00	Company G	329	42.79	39.65	39.65	0.05
127.56	101.20	Company O	380	109.67	107.73	108.90	1.01
88.95	74.67	Company S	1,087	79.65	78.54	78.52	1.15
51.86	30.76	Company K	1,097	32.99	30.23	32.55	−0.02
33.18	17.91	Company L	2,086	20.24	20.24	20.24	0.23
96.78	35.12	Company H	2,186	88.41	85.38	86.75	1.29
220.37	124.30	Company M	2,290	186.15	184.74	186.15	−1.45
72.62	36.45	Company B	2,315	56.45	56.45	56.45	0.83
98.73	41.78	Company Q	2,712	61.48	61.45	61.45	3.35
187.95	122.34	Company T	2,877	180.69	178.52	179.45	0.32
119.25	89.00	Company E	3,475	101.75	99.78	100.25	1.77
83.00	42.65	Company R	3,612	55.27	55.20	55.27	0.02
22.12	15.25	Company F	4,289	18.23	18.20	18.23	0.86
164.50	107.62	Company A	6,221	154.75	152.60	154.63	1.84
136.09	80.39	Company N	9,875	96.94	96.91	96.93	2.00
4.26	2.50	Company P	10,764	3.25	3.21	3.21	0.03
16.25	8.25	Company D	11,872	9.78	8.94	9.05	−0.09

Sorted by Close (Column 7)

52-Wk High	52-Wk Low	Stock	Volume (100s)	High	Low	Close	Net Change
4.26	2.50	Company P	10,764	3.25	3.21	3.21	0.03
16.25	8.25	Company D	11,872	9.78	8.94	9.05	−0.09
22.12	15.25	Company F	4,289	18.23	18.20	18.23	0.86
33.18	17.91	Company L	2,086	20.24	20.24	20.24	0.23
27.62	20.00	Company C	154	24.32	23.75	24.05	−0.56
46.50	25.43	Company J	308	25.59	24.75	24.75	0.05
51.86	30.76	Company K	1,097	32.99	30.23	32.55	−0.02
53.70	41.00	Company G	329	42.79	39.65	39.65	0.05
52.24	38.27	Company I	25	50.27	50.00	50.00	0.67
83.00	42.65	Company R	3,612	55.27	55.20	55.27	0.02
72.62	36.45	Company B	2,315	56.45	56.45	56.45	0.83
98.73	41.78	Company Q	2,712	61.48	61.45	61.45	3.35
88.95	74.67	Company S	1,087	79.65	78.54	78.52	1.15
96.78	35.12	Company H	2,186	88.41	85.38	86.75	1.29
136.09	80.39	Company N	9,875	96.94	96.91	96.93	2.00
119.25	89.00	Company E	3,475	101.75	99.78	100.25	1.77
127.56	101.20	Company O	380	109.67	107.73	108.90	1.01
164.50	107.62	Company A	6,221	154.75	152.60	154.63	1.84
187.95	122.34	Company T	2,877	180.69	178.52	179.45	0.32
220.37	124.30	Company M	2,290	186.15	184.74	186.15	−1.45

Sorted by Net Change (Column 8)

52-Wk High	52-Wk Low	Stock	Volume (100s)	High	Low	Close	Net Change
220.37	124.30	Company M	2,290	186.15	184.74	186.15	−1.45
27.62	20.00	Company C	154	24.32	23.75	24.05	−0.56
16.25	8.25	Company D	11,872	9.78	8.94	9.05	−0.09
51.86	30.76	Company K	1,097	32.99	30.23	32.55	−0.02
83.00	42.65	Company R	3,612	55.27	55.20	55.27	0.02
4.26	2.50	Company P	10,764	3.25	3.21	3.21	0.03
46.50	25.43	Company J	308	25.59	24.75	24.75	0.05
53.70	41.00	Company G	329	42.79	39.65	39.65	0.05
33.18	17.91	Company L	2,086	20.24	20.24	20.24	0.23
187.95	122.34	Company T	2,877	180.69	178.52	179.45	0.32
52.24	38.27	Company I	25	50.27	50.00	50.00	0.67
72.62	36.45	Company B	2,315	56.45	56.45	56.45	0.83
22.12	15.25	Company F	4,289	18.23	18.20	18.23	0.86
127.56	101.20	Company O	380	109.67	107.73	108.90	1.01
88.95	74.67	Company S	1,087	79.65	78.54	78.52	1.15
96.78	35.12	Company H	2,186	88.41	85.38	86.75	1.29
119.25	89.00	Company E	3,475	101.75	99.78	100.25	1.77
164.50	107.62	Company A	6,221	154.75	152.60	154.63	1.84
136.09	80.39	Company N	9,875	96.94	96.91	96.93	2.00
98.73	41.78	Company Q	2,712	61.48	61.45	61.45	3.35

Each of the following options consists of a stock and a quote category. For each option, select *Less than median* if, based on the information in the table, the value of the stock's quote is less than the median of the 20 stocks for that quote category on this day. Otherwise, select *Greater than or equal to median.*

	Less than median	Greater than or equal to median	
7.1	(A)	(B)	Company B, Volume (100s)
7.2	(A)	(B)	Company G, Close
7.3	(A)	(B)	Company L, Net Change

8. The following table shows first quarter sales information from 15 retail stores in a metropolitan area. Each of the 15 stores is open 9 a.m. to 9 p.m., Sunday through Saturday. The table contains monthly sales amounts (in thousands of dollars), and the average number of daily sales for January, February, and March of 2018.

On the actual exam, the table is interactive, and you can sort it in ascending order by selecting the column title you want to sort by from the drop-down menu above the table. The table below is shown sorted by different column titles to simulate the exam.

Sorted by Store (Column 1)

Store	Total sales amount, Jan.	Total sales amount, Feb.	Total sales amount, Mar.	Average number of daily sales, Jan.	Average number of daily sales, Feb.	Average number of daily sales, Mar.
Store A	$ 425,215	$ 326,400	$ 236,160	220	170	123
Store B	$ 108,000	$ 93,000	$ 105,000	144	124	140
Store C	$ 139,200	$ 117,120	$ 145,920	145	122	152
Store D	$ 182,040	$ 145,140	$ 137,760	148	118	112
Store E	$ 224,640	$ 193,440	$ 184,080	144	124	118
Store F	$ 141,570	$ 128,700	$ 193,050	143	130	195
Store G	$ 219,960	$ 190,360	$ 235,560	141	122	151
Store H	$ 255,150	$ 241,920	$ 189,000	135	128	100
Store I	$ 77,220	$ 70,200	$ 89,640	143	130	166
Store J	$ 324,120	$ 254,040	$ 313,170	148	116	143
Store K	$ 120,120	$ 99,120	$ 92,400	143	118	110
Store L	$ 160,950	$ 148,740	$ 127,650	145	134	115
Store M	$ 202,860	$ 182,160	$ 234,600	147	132	170
Store N	$ 261,000	$ 233,160	$ 309,720	150	134	178
Store O	$ 116,580	$ 114,840	$ 89,610	134	132	103

Sorted by Average Number of Daily Sales, Jan. (Column 5)

Store	Total sales amount, Jan.	Total sales amount, Feb.	Total sales amount, Mar.	Average number of daily sales, Jan.	Average number of daily sales, Feb.	Average number of daily sales, Mar.
Store O	$ 116,580	$ 114,840	$ 89,610	134	132	103
Store H	$ 255,150	$ 241,920	$ 189,000	135	128	100
Store G	$ 219,960	$ 190,360	$ 235,560	141	122	151
Store K	$ 120,120	$ 99,120	$ 92,400	143	118	110
Store I	$ 77,220	$ 70,200	$ 89,640	143	130	166
Store F	$ 141,570	$ 128,700	$ 193,050	143	130	195
Store E	$ 224,640	$ 193,440	$ 184,080	144	124	118
Store B	$ 108,000	$ 93,000	$ 105,000	144	124	140
Store L	$ 160,950	$ 148,740	$ 127,650	145	134	115
Store C	$ 139,200	$ 117,120	$ 145,920	145	122	152
Store M	$ 202,860	$ 182,160	$ 234,600	147	132	170
Store D	$ 182,040	$ 145,140	$ 137,760	148	118	112
Store J	$ 324,120	$ 254,040	$ 313,170	148	116	143
Store N	$ 261,000	$ 233,160	$ 309,720	150	134	178
Store A	$ 425,215	$ 326,400	$ 236,160	220	170	123

Sorted by Average Number of Daily Sales, Mar. (Column 7)

Store	Total sales amount, Jan.	Total sales amount, Feb.	Total sales amount, Mar.	Average number of daily sales, Jan.	Average number of daily sales, Feb.	Average number of daily sales, Mar.
Store H	$ 255,150	$ 241,920	$ 189,000	135	128	100
Store O	$ 116,580	$ 114,840	$ 89,610	134	132	103
Store K	$ 120,120	$ 99,120	$ 92,400	143	118	110
Store D	$ 182,040	$ 145,140	$ 137,760	148	118	112
Store L	$ 160,950	$ 148,740	$ 127,650	145	134	115
Store E	$ 224,640	$ 193,440	$ 184,080	144	124	118
Store A	$ 425,215	$ 326,400	$ 236,160	220	170	123
Store B	$ 108,000	$ 93,000	$ 105,000	144	124	140
Store J	$ 324,120	$ 254,040	$ 313,170	148	116	143
Store G	$ 219,960	$ 190,360	$ 235,560	141	122	151
Store C	$ 139,200	$ 117,120	$ 145,920	145	122	152
Store I	$ 77,220	$ 70,200	$ 89,640	143	130	166
Store M	$ 202,860	$ 182,160	$ 234,600	147	132	170
Store N	$ 261,000	$ 233,160	$ 309,720	150	134	178
Store F	$ 141,570	$ 128,700	$ 193,050	143	130	195

© John Wiley & Sons, Inc.

Sorted by Total Sales Amount, Feb. (Column 3)

Store	Total sales amount, Jan.	Total sales amount, Feb.	Total sales amount, Mar.	Average number of daily sales, Jan.	Average number of daily sales, Feb.	Average number of daily sales, Mar.
Store I	$ 77,220	$ 70,200	$ 89,640	143	130	166
Store B	$ 108,000	$ 93,000	$ 105,000	144	124	140
Store K	$ 120,120	$ 99,120	$ 92,400	143	118	110
Store O	$ 116,580	$ 114,840	$ 89,610	134	132	103
Store C	$ 139,200	$ 117,120	$ 145,920	145	122	152
Store F	$ 141,570	$ 128,700	$ 193,050	143	130	195
Store D	$ 182,040	$ 145,140	$ 137,760	148	118	112
Store L	$ 160,950	$ 148,740	$ 127,650	145	134	115
Store M	$ 202,860	$ 182,160	$ 234,600	147	132	170
Store G	$ 219,960	$ 190,360	$ 235,560	141	122	151
Store E	$ 224,640	$ 193,440	$ 184,080	144	124	118
Store N	$ 261,000	$ 233,160	$ 309,720	150	134	178
Store H	$ 255,150	$ 241,920	$ 189,000	135	128	100
Store J	$ 324,120	$ 254,040	$ 313,170	148	116	143
Store A	$ 425,215	$ 326,400	$ 236,160	220	170	123

© John Wiley & Sons, Inc.

Sorted by Average Number of Daily Sales, Feb. (Column 6)

Store	Total sales amount, Jan.	Total sales amount, Feb.	Total sales amount, Mar.	Average number of daily sales, Jan.	Average number of daily sales, Feb.	Average number of daily sales, Mar.
Store J	$ 324,120	$ 254,040	$ 313,170	148	116	143
Store K	$ 120,120	$ 99,120	$ 92,400	143	118	110
Store D	$ 182,040	$ 145,140	$ 137,760	148	118	112
Store C	$ 139,200	$ 117,120	$ 145,920	145	122	152
Store G	$ 219,960	$ 190,360	$ 235,560	141	122	151
Store B	$ 108,000	$ 93,000	$ 105,000	144	124	140
Store E	$ 224,640	$ 193,440	$ 184,080	144	124	118
Store H	$ 255,150	$ 241,920	$ 189,000	135	128	100
Store I	$ 77,220	$ 70,200	$ 89,640	143	130	166
Store F	$ 141,570	$ 128,700	$ 193,050	143	130	195
Store O	$ 116,580	$ 114,840	$ 89,610	134	132	103
Store M	$ 202,860	$ 182,160	$ 234,600	147	132	170
Store L	$ 160,950	$ 148,740	$ 127,650	145	134	115
Store N	$ 261,000	$ 233,160	$ 309,720	150	134	178
Store A	$ 425,215	$ 326,400	$ 236,160	220	170	123

© John Wiley & Sons, Inc.

For each of the following statements, select *Yes* if the statement is true based solely on the information in the table. Otherwise, select *No*.

	Yes	No	
8.1	(A)	(B)	The median average number of daily sales in January is greater than the median average number of daily sales in March.
8.2	(A)	(B)	The store with the highest total sales in February also had the highest average number of daily sales in February.
8.3	(A)	(B)	More than half the stores reported that the total sales amount in February exceeded the total sales amount in March.

9. Company X currently has 15,000 components in inventory, and company Y currently has 16,000 components in inventory. The number of components produced by company X and the number of components produced by company Y are increasing monthly, each at its own constant rate. Forecasters project that if each company continues to produce an increased number of components at its constant rate, in 20 months both companies will have the same number of components for the first time. Thereafter, in subsequent months, company X will have more components in inventory than company Y.

In the table below, indicate by appropriate selections in the first and second columns which of the rates of increase in the third column is a rate of increase for company X, and which is a rate of increase for company Y that together are consistent with the forecasters' performance projections. Make only two selections, one in each column.

9.1 Company X	9.2 Company Y	Rate of increase (components per month)
(A)	(A)	30
(B)	(B)	50
(C)	(C)	200
(D)	(D)	250
(E)	(E)	280

10. A teacher is selecting from among items 1 through 6 to purchase with school funds for the classroom mathematics center. The principal has stated the following conditions:

(A) At least one item, but no more than five items must be selected.

(B) If item 1 is selected, then either item 3 or item 4 must be selected, but not both.

(C) If item 4 is not selected, then item 2 must be selected.

(D) If item 6 is selected, then item 3 cannot be selected.

(E) If item 5 is selected, then either item 1 or item 6 must be selected, but not both.

In the table below, indicate by appropriate selections in the first and second columns which number of items in the third column is the minimum number of items that must be selected if item 1 is selected, and which number is the maximum possible number of items that can be selected if item 5 is selected. Make only two selections, one in each column.

10.1 Minimum	10.2 Maximum	Number of items
(A)	(A)	one
(B)	(B)	two
(C)	(C)	three
(D)	(D)	four
(E)	(E)	five

11. A chain discount is a series of discounts applied to the list price of an item. Chain discounts of $R\%$ and $P\%$ are equivalent to $100\% - (100\% - R\%)(100\% - P\%)$. Ace Company gives chain discounts of 20 percent and 5 percent on the list price of all tools purchased. Deuce Company gives chain discounts of 15 percent and 10 percent on the list price of all tools purchased. For each of the two companies, how much is saved for a purchase of tools that have list prices totally $500?

In the table below, indicate by appropriate selections in the first and second columns which of the savings amounts in the third column is the savings amount if the purchase is from Ace Company, and which is the savings amount if the purchase is from Deuce Company. Make only two selections, one in each column.

11.1 Ace Company	11.2 Deuce Company	Savings amount
(A)	(A)	$62.50
(B)	(B)	$100.00
(C)	(C)	$117.50
(D)	(D)	$120.00
(E)	(E)	$125.00

12. Aziz: Anyone who does not like swimming must not like the ocean either.

Presley: That's not true. I do not like swimming, but I do like the ocean. I propose that anyone who does not like swimming, does like the ocean.

Aziz: Okay, then I say that anyone who does not like the ocean, does not like swimming.

Presley: And I say liking the ocean is a necessary condition for liking swimming.

Suppose that Aziz's and Presley's statements express their committed beliefs. In the table below, indicate by appropriate selections in the first and second columns which of the statements in the third column is a statement about which Aziz and Presley definitely agree, and which is a statement about which Aziz and Presley definitely disagree. Make only two selections, one in each column.

12.1 Definitely Agree	12.2 Definitely Disagree	Statement
(A)	(A)	Anyone who likes the ocean likes swimming.
(B)	(B)	Anyone who likes swimming does not like the ocean.
(C)	(C)	Liking the ocean is a sufficient condition for not liking swimming.
(D)	(D)	Not liking swimming is a necessary condition for liking the ocean.
(E)	(E)	Anyone who likes swimming likes the ocean.

13. On a credit loan of B dollars, a borrower pays R dollars per month for 30 months. The finance charge, FC, in dollars on the loan is the difference between the sum of payments and the amount borrowed.

In the table below, indicate by appropriate selections in the first and second columns which of the expressions in the third column represents the finance charge for this borrower, and which represents the finance charge per $100 borrowed. Make only two selections, one in each column.

13.1 Finance charge	13.2 Finance charge per $100 borrowed	Expression
(A)	(A)	$B - 30R$
(B)	(B)	$\dfrac{FC \times B}{\$100}$
(C)	(C)	$30R - B$
(D)	(D)	$\dfrac{FC}{B(\$100)}$
(E)	(E)	$\dfrac{FC \times \$100}{B}$

14. Set A consists of X numbers and set B consists of Y numbers. The arithmetic average of the numbers in set A is 30, and the arithmetic average of the numbers in set B is 45. When sets A and B are combined, the arithmetic average of the $X + Y$ numbers is $\dfrac{X(30) + Y(45)}{X + Y}$.

In the table below, indicate by appropriate selections in the first and second columns which of the values in the third column for X and which for Y correspond to an arithmetic average of 35 for the combined sets A and B. Make only two selections, one in each column.

14.1 X	14.2 Y	Value
(A)	(A)	11
(B)	(B)	15
(C)	(C)	18
(D)	(D)	22
(E)	(E)	28

15. Working together, machine X and machine Y can finish a job in 12 hours. Working alone, machine X, the newer model, can finish the same job twice as fast as machine Y, the older model.

In the table below, indicate by appropriate selections in the first and second columns which time (in hours) in the third column for machine X, working alone, and which time (in hours) for machine Y, working alone, are consistent with the information given. Make only two selections, one in each column.

15.1 Machine X	15.2 Machine Y	Time (in hours), working alone
(A)	(A)	14
(B)	(B)	18
(C)	(C)	28
(D)	(D)	36
(E)	(E)	56

16. A small city uses natural gas for heating city buildings. The city manager is interested in investigating the relationship between weekly fuel consumption (measured in millions of cubic feet, abbreviated as MMcf) and weekly average hourly temperature (measured in degrees Fahrenheit) during cold or cool weather in the city. Data are collected for 10 consecutive weeks. The graph below shows a scatter plot of the weekly fuel consumption (MMcf, to the nearest tenth) versus the weekly average hourly temperature (degrees F, to the nearest degree). The solid line is the line of best fit. This line best represents the trend that the points in the scatter plot follow. Its slope is the change in the mean (average) weekly fuel consumption that results from a 1-degree increase in weekly average hourly temperature.

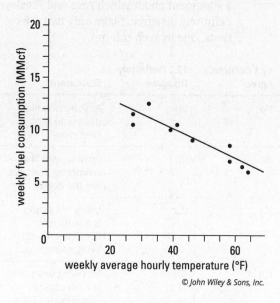

For each of the following statements, select the best answer to fill in the blank based on the data provided in the graph.

16.1 The relationship between weekly fuel consumption and weekly average hourly temperature is best described as

_____.

(A) positive

(B) negative

(C) no relationship

16.2 Using the two data points (39, 10.0) and (46, 9.0) to estimate the slope of the line of best fit, it can be determined that the decrease in the mean (average) weekly fuel consumption, in cubic feet $\left(\text{ft}^3\right)$, when the weekly average hour temperature increases by 1 degree is closest to

_____.

(A) 70,000

(B) 140,000

(C) 280,000

(D) 350,000

(E) 7,000,000

17. Fifty randomly selected customers were asked to provide information about their dining experiences at restaurants A, B, C, and D. Each customer was asked the following three questions:

Question 1: Did you like the service?

Question 2: Did you like the food?

Question 3: Would you recommend this restaurant to your friends?

The graph shows the results of the survey. Each disk represents the summary of the responses from one of the restaurants. The center of a disk marks the intersection of the percentage of customers who responded favorably to question 1 and the percentage of customers who responded favorably to question 2. The area of the disk indicates the percentage of customers who responded in the affirmative that they would recommend the restaurant to a friend.

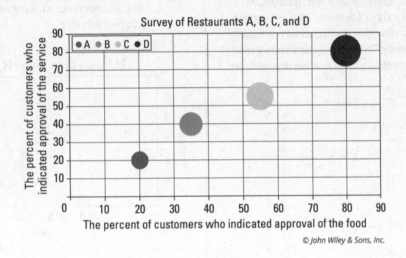

Survey of Restaurants A, B, C, and D

The percent of customers who indicated approval of the service (y-axis)

The percent of customers who indicated approval of the food (x-axis)

© John Wiley & Sons, Inc.

For each of the following statements, select the best answer to fill in the blank based on the information provided in the diagram.

17.1 The percentage of customers at restaurant B who responded favorably to question 2 is _____ times the percentage of customers at restaurant A who responded favorably to question 2.

(A) 1.5

(B) 2

(C) 2.5

(D) 4

17.2 The diameter of disk D is twice the diameter of disk A, indicating that the percentage of customers who would recommend restaurant D to their friends is _____ percent greater than the percentage of customers who would recommend restaurant A to their friends.

(A) 100

(B) 200

(C) 300

(D) 400

18. The probability tree diagram shows probabilities associated with randomly drawing two marbles, one after the other, from two different bags, Bag 1 and Bag 2. Bag 1 contains 10 black, 8 green, and 6 red marbles, all identical except for color. Bag 2 contains 8 black, 2 green, and 2 red marbles, all identical except for color. In the diagram, B represents "the marble drawn is black," G represents "the marble drawn is green," and R represents "the marble drawn is red."

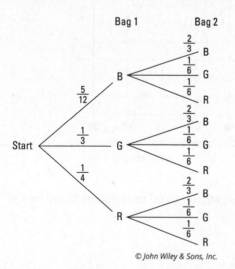

© John Wiley & Sons, Inc.

For each of the following statements, select the best answer to fill in the blank based on the information provided in the diagram.

18.1 The probability that exactly one of the two marbles drawn is red is
_____.

(A) $\frac{1}{6}$

(B) $\frac{3}{8}$

(C) $\frac{1}{3}$

(D) $\frac{2}{3}$

18.2 The probability that both marbles drawn will be the same color is
_____.

(A) $\frac{1}{6}$

(B) $\frac{3}{8}$

(C) $\frac{1}{3}$

(D) $\frac{2}{3}$

19. The following histogram summarizes the scores of 20 students on a 20-question, 100-point chemistry exam. Each question on the exam was scored either 0 points for an incorrect answer or 5 points for a correct answer.

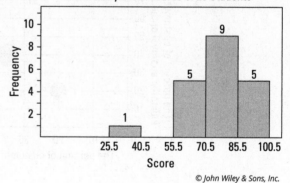

© John Wiley & Sons, Inc.

For each of the following statements, select the best answer to fill in the blank based on the data provided in the graph.

19.1 The mean (arithmetic average) of the 20 exam scores is _____ the median of the 20 exam scores.

(A) greater than

(B) less than

(C) equal to

19.2 The least possible value for the mean (arithmetic average) score on the exam is _____.

(A) 68.25

(B) 68.75

(C) 72.25

(D) 72.75

(E) 75.75

20. A group of 160 senior citizens were asked to provide information about their computer and Wi-Fi access at home. The Venn diagram below shows the survey results. Each symbol represents 10 people in the group of 160 respondents.

Computer and Wi-Fi Access of 160 Senior Citizens, ages 65 years and older

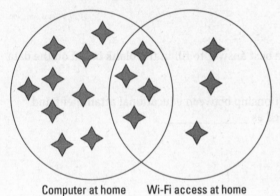

Computer at home   Wi-Fi access at home

◆ = 10 people

© John Wiley & Sons, Inc.

For each of the following statements, select the best answer to fill in the blank based on the data provided in the diagram.

20.1 If one senior citizen is randomly selected from the group, the probability that the person selected has Wi-Fi access at home, given that the person has a home computer, is _____.

(A) $\frac{1}{4}$

(B) $\frac{4}{13}$

(C) $\frac{7}{16}$

(D) $\frac{3}{4}$

20.2 If one senior citizen is randomly selected from the group, the probability that the person selected has Wi-Fi access, but no computer at home, is _____.

(A) $\frac{3}{16}$

(B) $\frac{1}{4}$

(C) $\frac{7}{16}$

(D) $\frac{3}{4}$

21. The following graph shows the median annual earnings of full-time, year-round workers ages 25–34, by educational attainment in 2014. Full-time, year-round workers are those who worked 35 or more hours per week at least 50 weeks in 2014.

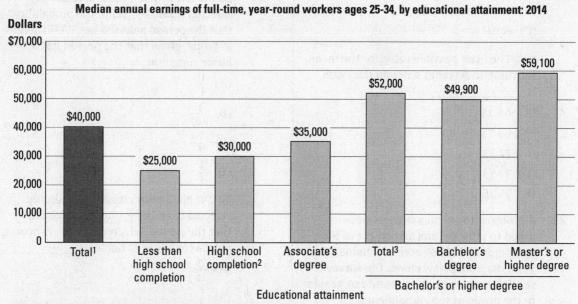

Median annual earnings of full-time, year-round workers ages 25-34, by educational attainment: 2014

[1] Represents median annual earnings of all full-time, year-round workers ages 25-34.
[2] Includes equivalency credentials, such as the GED credential.
[3] Represents median annual earnings of full-time, year-round workers ages 25-34 with a bachelor's or higher degree.
NOTE. *Full-time, year-round workers* are those who worked 35 or more hours per week for 50 or more weeks per year.
SOURCE: U.S. Department of Commerce, Census Bureau, Current Population Survey (CPS), "Annual Social and Economic Supplement," 2015. See *Digest of Education Statistics 2015*, table 502.30.

© *John Wiley & Sons, Inc.*

For each of the following statements, select the best answer to fill in the blank based on the data provided in the graph.

21.1 For full-time workers ages 25–34, the relationship between educational attainment and median annual earnings in 2014 is best described as _____.

(A) positive

(B) negative

(C) no relationship

21.2 For full-time workers ages 25–34, the median annual earnings in 2014 of those whose highest educational attainment was a bachelor's degree were close to _____ percent higher than the median annual earnings in 2014 of those whose highest educational attainment was high school completion.

(A) 43

(B) 49

(C) 66

(D) 73

(E) 100

Analyze the following information to answer Questions 22 through 24.

Incentive Program (Tab 1)

Radio station WXXX is owned by Allmedia Investments, Inc. WXXX generates revenue by selling advertising air time. However, due to competition from the internet, television, newspapers, and other radio stations, bringing in advertising dollars is a competitive challenge for WXXX.

To sustain station profitability, WXXX station manager, Rock Talley, with guidance from Kathy Chen, Allmedia's chief financial officer, created an incentive program to increase annual first-quarter revenues. Under the program, current clients who increase their first-quarter advertising dollars by an additional $25,000 receive an all-expenses-paid 12-day tour of Spain for two people. New clients must purchase $25,000 of advertising to be eligible.

The first quarter of the program ran from January 1 to March 31 of the current year. Throughout the quarter, each client received advertising air time for the $25,000. The cost to WXXX for the trip to Spain was $3,500 for each of the two people, for a total of $7,000 per client.

Talley Memo to Chen (Tab 2)

From: Rock Talley, WXXX Station Manager

To: Kathy Chen, CFO, Allmedia Investments, Inc.

I have two primary concerns about the WXXX advertising incentive program. First, I suspect that clients are purchasing advertising air time that they don't need in order to obtain the paid trip to Spain. One couple, who has a family-owned business, told me pointblank that the station's offer induced them to buy the additional advertising. I'm worried that we may be encouraging clients such as this one, who have small businesses and do not employ a paid financial manager, to make unsound business decisions.

Second, based on the results from the first quarter (see the attached table), the incentive program does not appear to be cost-effective. WXXX pays the full cost of $7,000 for the trip to Spain, and it requires a minimum of $10,000 to cover the advertising air time costs for the time sold in the incentive package to the client. Thus, we need $17,000 in additional monies from each incentive program participant to break even from the program. We should be realizing a net profit of $8,000 per client participant. However, in actuality, because our sales personnel offered reduced rates to current clients that had quarterly contracts, only a few clients paid the full $25,000 that was necessary for program eligibility.

Table 1. First Quarter Incentive Program (Tab 3)

The table shows the business name of each client who participated in the incentive program during the first quarter, the total amount of advertising dollars received from the client upon accepting the station's trip offer, and the amount of these advertising dollars that are additional monies not already accounted for in a quarterly contract with the client.

Client's Business Name	Total Advertising Dollars	Additional Monies
Alltech Electronics	$55,000	$10,000
Apex Auto Repair*	$25,000	$25,000
Beamer's Burger Joint	$25,000	$12,000
Citywide Car Rental	$28,000	$17,000
Fisher's Fine Furniture	$35,000	$15,000
Goldie's Bookstore	$21,000	$10,000
Half-Price Jewelry	$32,000	$18,000
Hub Diner	$26,000	$17,000
JJ's Sporting Goods	$30,000	$14,000
Kishan's Restaurant	$22,000	$14,000
Luxury Motel*	$25,000	$25,000
Patel's Clothing Store	$28,000	$25,000
TOTAL	**$352,000**	**$202,000**

*New client

22. For each of the following statements, select *Yes* if the statement is reasonably inferable from the given information. Otherwise, select *No*.

	Yes	No	
22.1	(A)	(B)	It is of primary importance to Chen that the incentive program yields a net profit.
22.2	(A)	(B)	Talley feels the incentive program is not working as expected and, therefore, should be discontinued.
22.3	(A)	(B)	Talley is uncomfortable with WXXX being involved with clients in the way the incentive program requires.

23. For each of the following statements, select *Yes* if the statement is true based on the given information. Otherwise, select *No*.

	Yes	No	
23.1	(A)	(B)	The advertising incentive program yielded a deficit of $2,000.
23.2	(A)	(B)	Less than half of current clients that participated in the incentive program added sufficient advertising dollars for WXXX to recoup the cost of the incentive program.
23.3	(A)	(B)	The median amount of additional advertising purchased by current clients participating in the incentive program was $16,000.

24. Which of the following statements, if given by Chen in response to Talley's memo, would indicate most clearly that Chen is in favor of continuing the program?

- (A) Acknowledged expenses for the incentive program do not include secondary costs such as car rentals and client gifts while on the trip.
- (B) Positive client relationships are beneficial intangibles whose dollar value cannot be measured.
- (C) Some program participants might turn out to be one-time advertisers, attracted only by the trip to Spain.
- (D) Some clients might start to resent the $25,000 requirement for program eligibility.
- (E) From a business standpoint, offering incentives to advertisers builds solid client relationships.

Analyze the following information to answer Questions 25 through 27.

Memo to district administrators from Superintendent Chewel (Tab 1)

From: Superintendent Chewel, Cityville ISD

To: All district administrators

This memo is to inform you of an exciting initiative that has been approved by the Cityville Independent School District Board of Trustees. The board has established a committee consisting of representative teachers and administrators from across the district, a school board member, parent members, and student representatives to implement a district-wide campaign to increase water consumption by students in Cityville ISD schools. The committee has already received federal and state authorization for the campaign. The campaign will be known as the Drink Water Campaign, or the DW Campaign, for short.

The idea for this campaign came to the board from a local dental hygienist who presented compelling evidence from the U.S. Department of Health and Human Services, the U.S. Centers for Disease Control and Prevention, the American Dental Association, and the American Dental Hygienists Association on the importance of water consumption to the oral health of children. The two main takeaways of the hygienist's presentation are the following:

>> Sugar-sweetened beverages (SSBs), such as soda, provide calories with no beneficial nutrients and are associated with a greater risk of dental caries.

>> Given that 63 percent of youth in the U.S. consume at least one SSB daily, there is a need to motivate children to drink water instead of SSBs.

As across the U.S., the 84,000 students in Cityville ISD schools do not drink enough water, with many preferring instead to drink SSBs, which puts them at risk of dental caries. The primary goal of the DW Campaign is to increase water consumption, while decreasing SSB consumption, by students in Cityville ISD schools for the purpose of improving their oral health.

A logic model and narrative for the campaign are attached.

DW Campaign Logic Model (Tab 2)

DW Campaign Logic Model

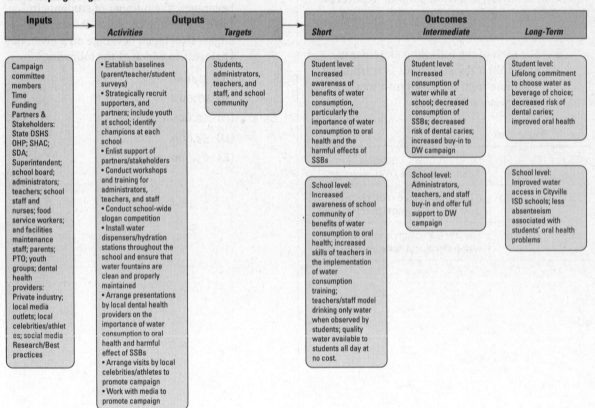

© John Wiley & Sons, Inc.

Logic Model Narrative (Tab 3)

This logic model for the Drink Water (DW) campaign graphically depicts a campaign to increase consumption of water, in lieu of sugar-sweetened beverages (SSBs), by students in Cityville ISD schools for the purpose of improving their oral health. The model shows the logical connections that flow from inputs to outputs to short-, inter-mediate-, and long-term outcomes. Enlisting the support of parents and the parent teacher orga-nization (PTO) is vital to the campaign's success. Also, the assistance of state- and district-level partners/stakeholders including the State Depart-ment of Health Services Oral Health Program (DSHS OHP), the school Health Advisory Council (SHAC), and the State Dental Association (SDA) will increase the likelihood of anticipated out-comes. Evaluation will occur on a yearly basis by analysis of data from parent and teacher surveys regarding student water and other-beverage con-sumption behavior, and from parents' reports of their children's oral health.

25. For each of the following statements, select *Yes* if the statement is reasonably inferable from the given information. Otherwise, select *No*.

	Yes	No	
25.1	(A)	(B)	Superintendent Chewel is supportive of the DW Campaign.
25.2	(A)	(B)	A board of trustee member will chair the DW Campaign committee.
25.3	(A)	(B)	The DW Campaign is in compliance with federal and state policies.

26. The DW Campaign logic model has underlying assumptions that are neces-sary existing conditions for attainment of the campaign's intended outcomes. For each of the following statements, select *Yes* if the statement is a reasonable assumption of the logic model. Otherwise, select *No*.

	Yes	No	
26.1	(A)	(B)	Funding for the campaign can be secured.
26.2	(A)	(B)	Students can and will be motivated to change.
26.3	(A)	(B)	Local celebrities/athletes can be recruited.

27. Assuming the Cityville ISD students follow the national trend with regard to consumption of sugar-sweetened beverages, the number of students in the district who consume at least one sugar-sweetened beverage on a given day is closest to which of the following?

(A) 31,000

(B) 37,000

(C) 42,000

(D) 53,000

(E) 63,000

Chapter **3**

Quantitative: Problem Solving

The Problem Solving questions are mixed in with the Data Sufficiency questions to make up the 37 questions of the GMAT Quantitative section, which must be completed in 75 minutes. (The directions specifically for the question types will be presented each time they appear.) Problem Solving questions are multiple–choice questions with five answer choice options. You must select the one best answer choice. No calculators are permitted during the Quantitative section.

The Problems You'll Work On

When working through the problem solving questions in this chapter, be prepared to answer questions based on your understanding of

>> **Basic math,** including fractions, decimals, ratios and proportions, percents, and exponents.

>> **Probability and Statistics,** including counting techniques, permutations and combinations, basic probability, arithmetic mean, median, mode, and standard deviation.

>> **Algebra,** including polynomials, linear equations and inequalities, quadratic equations, basic function concepts, and systems of linear equations.

>> **Geometry,** including angles, lines, two-dimensional shapes, three-dimensional solids, perimeter, area, surface area, volume, the Pythagorean theorem, and coordinate geometry.

>> **Word problems,** including, percentages, rate-time-distance, consecutive integers, ages, work rate, coins, divisibility, factors, multiples, sequences, and equation setup.

What to Watch Out For

Try to avoid these common mistakes:

> » Writing expressions on the erasable notepad incorrectly, instead of recording carefully.

> » Making careless arithmetic errors, such as adding fractions incorrectly.

> » Making algebra mistakes, such as solving equations incorrectly.

> » Formulating an equation incorrectly because you overlooked something.

> » Failing to answer the question asked in a word problem, such as finding the value of *x* instead of the value of 2*x*.

> » Spending too much time on a question that it is too difficult for you instead of making a guess and moving on.

28. Given $C = \frac{5}{9}(F - 32)$. What is the value of F when $C = 165$?

    (A) 197
    (B) 297
    (C) 319
    (D) 329
    (E) 361

29. Sixty percent of the members of a university orchestra are seniors and 45 percent of those seniors are in the university band. If one member of the university orchestra is randomly selected, what is the probability that the member is a senior band member?

    (A) 0.15
    (B) 0.27
    (C) 0.30
    (D) 0.45
    (E) 0.75

30. What is the value of $\left(\sqrt{4 + \sqrt{6}} - \sqrt{4 - \sqrt{6}} \right)^2$?

    (A) 0
    (B) $8 - 2\sqrt{10}$
    (C) $2\sqrt{6}$
    (D) 12
    (E) $6\sqrt{10}$

31. In a certain youth soccer league, there are 10 teams. Each game in the season is a match between two teams from the league. If each team plays each of the other teams exactly one time, how many games are played in a season?

    (A) 20
    (B) 50
    (C) 45
    (D) 90
    (E) 100

32. A number of students from the same high school graduating class are enrolled at the same regional university in the fall semester. Of these students, 52 are enrolled in a mathematics course, 52 are enrolled in a psychology course, and 64 are enrolled in an English course. None of the students are enrolled in both mathematics and psychology. If 12 of the students are enrolled in both mathematics and English and 22 are enrolled in both psychology and English, how many of the students are in at least one of these three courses?

    (A) 104
    (B) 134
    (C) 142
    (D) 146
    (E) 158

33. If n is a positive integer such that $n!$ is divisible by 840, what is the least possible value of n?

(A) 7

(B) 8

(C) 12

(D) 14

(E) 15

34. Which of the following numbers is the least positive integer that is *not* a prime and is *not* a factor of 15!

(A) 14

(B) 22

(C) 19

(D) 34

(E) 38

35. If $n(n+2)! = n!(n+1)!$, then n could be which of the following values?

(A) 2

(B) 3

(C) 4

(D) 5

(E) 6

36. Kyra and Sage, working together can paint a room in 5 hours. If Melora helps Kyra and Sage paint the room, the three of them can paint the room in 4 hours. What amount of time (in hours) would it take Melora, working alone, to paint the room?

(A) 6

(B) 8

(C) 10

(D) 15

(E) 20

37. The figure shows a triangle inscribed in a semicircle. If $PQ = 16$ and $QR = 12$, what is the length of arc PQR?

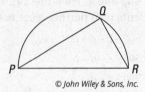

© John Wiley & Sons, Inc.

(A) 10π

(B) 14π

(C) 20π

(D) 24π

(E) 30π

38. The arithmetic average of 20 numbers is A. The arithmetic average of 10 of the number is 16. In terms of A, what is the arithmetic average of the remaining 10 numbers?

(A) $A - 8$

(B) $16 - A$

(C) $16 - 2A$

(D) $2A - 16$

(E) $20A - 16$

39. A family's monthly budget allocates $3,600 for their home mortgage payment plus food and utilities in the ratio of 5:3:1, respectively. What is the dollar amount allocated for food?

(A) $2,000

(B) $1,600

(C) $1,200

(D) $800

(E) $400

40. In a survey of 500 students regarding pet ownership of cats and dogs, c students own at least one cat, d students own at least one dog, and b students own at least one dog and at least one cat. How many students own neither a cat nor a dog?

(A) $500 - c - d + b$

(B) $500 - c - d - b$

(C) $500 - c + d$

(D) $500 - c - d$

(E) $500 - b$

41. One plant grew 6 inches while a second plant grew 250% more than the first plant grew. How much, in inches, did the second plant grow?

(A) 6

(B) 8

(C) 12

(D) 15

(E) 21

42. Which of the following numbers is a factor of $15! + 13$?

I.   11

II. 13

III. 15

(A) I only

(B) II only

(C) I and II only

(D) II and III only

(E) I, II, and III

43. Given p is an integer and $(0.00005)(0.0005)(0.005) \times 10^p$ is an integer, what is the least possible value of p?

(A) -12

(B) -9

(C) 0

(D) 9

(E) 12

44. In the xy-plane, what is the slope of the line that is perpendicular to the line with equation $2x + 5y = 7$?

(A) -2.5

(B) -0.4

(C) -2

(D) 0.4

(E) 2.5

45. The attendance on the first day of a 3-day festival was 20% greater than the attendance on the final day of the festival. If the attendance on the first day was 11,418, what was the attendance on the final day of the festival?

(A) 3,806

(B) 5,190

(C) 9,134

(D) 9,515

(E) 11,194

46. One inlet pipe can fill an empty cistern to $\frac{1}{3}$ of its capacity in 3 hours. A second inlet pipe can fill the empty cistern to $\frac{3}{4}$ of its capacity in 4.5 hours. If both pipes are opened simultaneously, how long, in hours, will it take to fill the cistern?

(A) 4.75

(B) 4.25

(C) 3.75

(D) 3.6

(E) 3.25

47. One-half of the marbles in a box are blue, $\frac{1}{3}$ are red, and $\frac{1}{10}$ are green. If the remaining 6 are yellow, how many marbles are in the box?

(A) 50

(B) 70

(C) 90

(D) 120

(E) 150

48. A rectangular flower garden is twice as long as it is wide. If its perimeter is 180 feet, what is the garden's length, in feet?

(A) 60

(B) 70

(C) 80

(D) 90

(E) 100

49. If $\left(2 - 2\dfrac{4}{5}\right)x = 1$, then $x =$

(A) −125

(B) −1.25

(C) −12.5

(D) 1.25

(E) 125

50. Which of the following expressions in simplified form is a rational number?

I. $\dfrac{\sqrt{46}\,\sqrt{46}}{\left(46\right)^{2}}$

II. $\left(\sqrt{46} + \sqrt{46}\right)^{2}$

III. $46\sqrt{46}$

(A) I only

(B) II only

(C) III only

(D) I and II only

(E) II and III only

51. Given $(562)(9k) = N$, which of the following equals $(562)(9k+1)$?

(A) $N+1$

(B) $N+562$

(C) $N+563$

(D) $N+9k$

(E) $N+(9k+1)$

52. Thirty plants are needed for an experiment. If the plant seeds have a germination rate of 60%, the number of seeds planted should be at least how many?

(A) 40

(B) 42

(C) 48

(D) 50

(E) 60

53. Ninety percent of a large field is cleared for planting. Of the cleared land, 50% is planted with blueberry plants and 40% is planted with strawberry plants. If the remaining 360 acres of cleared land is planted with gooseberry plants, what is the size, in acres, of the original field?

(A) 2,916

(B) 3,240

(C) 3,600

(D) 4,000

(E) 8,000

54. $\dfrac{1}{\left(\dfrac{1}{2}-2\right)} + \dfrac{1}{\left(\dfrac{4}{3}\right)} =$

(A) $-\dfrac{1}{6}$

(B) $-\dfrac{1}{12}$

(C) $\dfrac{1}{12}$

(D) $\dfrac{1}{6}$

(E) $\dfrac{1}{3}$

55. The number of squares is 4 times the number of circles, and the number of circles is twice the number of triangles. What is the ratio of the number of squares to the number of triangles?

(A) 8:1

(B) 4:1

(C) 1:2

(D) 1:4

(E) 1:8

56. In a survey of 600 students, 75% indicated they like orange juice, 40% indicated they like apple juice, and 30% indicated they like grape juice. If all of the survey participants like at least one of these juices and 35% of them like exactly two of these juices, how many survey participants like only one of these juices?

(A) 210

(B) 250

(C) 260

(D) 360

(E) 390

57. The simultaneous solution of $(2x+1)(4x-1)=0$ and $(5x-1)\left(x-\frac{1}{4}\right)=0$ is $x =$

(A) $-\frac{1}{2}$

(B) $-\frac{1}{4}$

(C) $\frac{1}{5}$

(D) $\frac{1}{4}$

(E) $\frac{1}{2}$

58. Last year, the ratio of nonfiction to fiction books in a home library was 1 to 30. This year, the number of nonfiction books increased by 5 and the number of fiction books increased by 50, making the ratio of nonfiction to fiction books 1 to 25. What was the number of nonfiction books last year?

(A) 15

(B) 12

(C) 10

(D) 8

(E) 5

59. If $f(x)=\left(\frac{x-1}{x+1}\right)^2$, $x \neq -1$, which of the following expressions is equivalent to $f\left(\frac{1}{a}\right)$, $a \neq 0$?

(A) $-\dfrac{a^2-1}{a^2+1}$

(B) $-\left(\dfrac{a-1}{a+1}\right)^2$

(C) $\left(\dfrac{1-a}{1+a}\right)^2$

(D) $\dfrac{1-a^2}{1+a^2}$

(E) $\dfrac{a^2-1}{a^2+1}$

60. If k is a positive integer such that $5,880k$ is a perfect square, what is the least possible value of k?

(A) 2

(B) 6

(C) 15

(D) 30

(E) 140

61. The figure shown is a rhombus in which the measure of $\angle A = 120°$. What is the ratio of the length of $\overline{AC}$ to the length of $\overline{DB}$?

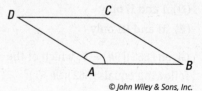

(A) $1:2\sqrt{3}$

(B) $1:2\sqrt{2}$

(C) $1:2$

(D) $1:\sqrt{3}$

(E) $1:\sqrt{2}$

62. If n is an integer such that $15 < n < 250$, for how many possible values of n is $\frac{n}{5}$ the square of a prime number?

(A) Two

(B) Three

(C) Four

(D) Five

(E) Six

63. Students are playing a guessing game in which a player must randomly guess which of five options is correct. After each guess, a new set of five options is presented. A player's turn continues as long as the player answers correctly. A player's turn ends the first time the player guesses incorrectly. What is the probability a player's will end after the player guesses three times?

(A) 0.008

(B) 0.032

(C) 0.128

(D) 0.488

(E) 0.512

64. The probability that team A will not win the tournament is 80% and the probability that team B will not win the tournament is 60%. If there is only one tournament winner, what is the probability that either team A or team B wins the tournament?

(A) 20%

(B) 40%

(C) 48%

(D) 60%

(E) 80%

65. What is the greatest integer p, for which 3^p is a factor of 21!?

(A) 8

(B) 9

(C) 10

(D) 11

(E) 12

66. If $\sqrt{\frac{x}{3}} = 3$, then $x =$

(A) $\frac{1}{9}$

(B) $\sqrt{3}$

(C) 6

(D) 9

(E) 27

67. In the figure shown, $x + y =$

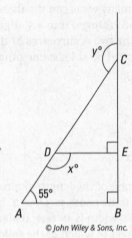

© John Wiley & Sons, Inc.

(A) 230

(B) 250

(C) 260

(D) 270

(E) 290

68. A black and white drawing shows four circles of equal radius. Three of the circles are each divided into k equal parts, where $k > 5$. The fourth circle is divided into $k - 4$ equal parts. A child colors one of the k parts in each of the three circles, and one of the $k - 4$ parts in the fourth circle. What part of a whole circle did the child color?

(A) $\dfrac{4k - 12}{k(k-4)}$

(B) $\dfrac{4k - 8}{k(k-4)}$

(C) $\dfrac{4k - 4}{k(k-4)}$

(D) $\dfrac{2k - 4}{k(k-4)}$

(E) $\dfrac{k + 4}{k(k-4)}$

69. How many ways can the five digits 3, 3, 4, 5, 6 be arranged into a 5-digit number so that the two occurrences of the digit 3 are separated by at least one other digit?

(A) 48

(B) 36

(C) 24

(D) 18

(E) 12

70. The ratio of the length of a rectangular patio to its width is 3.5 to 2. If the rectangle's width is 18 feet, its length, in feet, is closest to which of the following?

(A) 14

(B) 22

(C) 26

(D) 32

(E) 52

71. The distribution of the scores on a standardized test is bell-shaped and is symmetric about its mean, M, with a standard deviation, S. If 68% of the scores fall between $M - S$ and $M + S$, what percent of the scores are greater than $M + S$?

(A) 4%

(B) 8%

(C) 16%

(D) 32%

(E) 34%

72. A painter was paid $800 as labor cost for painting the exterior of the front of a house. This amount was the painter's estimated labor cost based on a regular rate of R, in dollars per hour, for an estimated time T, in hours. However, the actual time it took for the painter to do the job was 4 hours longer than the estimated time, thereby reducing the hourly rate for the job by $10 per hour. What is R, the painter's regular rate, in dollars per hour?

(A) 20

(B) 30

(C) 40

(D) 50

(E) 60

73. What is the least integer p for which $27^p > 3^{18}$?

(A) 6

(B) 7

(C) 8

(D) 9

(E) 18

74. Consider the binary operation $\oplus$ defined by $a \oplus b = 10a + b$, where the operations on the right side of the equal sign denote the standard arithmetic operations. Suppose $M = x \oplus y$ and $N = y \oplus x$, where x and y are positive integers, which of the following must be a factor of $M + N$?

(A) 14

(B) 11

(C) 10

(D) 9

(E) 6

75. Which of the following is the value of $\sqrt{\sqrt{0.00000625}}$?

(A) 0.0025

(B) 0.005

(C) 0.025

(D) 0.05

(E) 0.5

76. A mother, who is 37 years old, and her son, who is 9 years old, have the same birthday anniversary month and day. In how many years from now will the mother be twice as old as her son?

(A) 11

(B) 15

(C) 19

(D) 23

(E) 28

77. Lupita and Vin both swam in the indoor pool at the same gym today. Lupita swims at that gym every 12 days. Vin swims there every 15 days. If both continue with their regular swimming schedules at the gym, the next time both will swim there on the same day is in how many days?

(A) 12

(B) 15

(C) 30

(D) 45

(E) 60

78. If $xy \neq 0$, then $\dfrac{5}{x} + \dfrac{3}{y} =$

(A) $\dfrac{3x + 5y}{xy}$

(B) $\dfrac{5x + 3y}{xy}$

(C) $\dfrac{3x + 5y}{x + y}$

(D) $\dfrac{8}{x + y}$

(E) $\dfrac{8}{xy}$

79. Which of the following expressions is equivalent to $(s^2 + 9)^{-\frac{1}{2}}$?

(A) $-\dfrac{s^2 + 9}{2}$

(B) $-\dfrac{1}{\sqrt{s^2 + 9}}$

(C) $-\sqrt{s^2 + 9}$

(D) $\dfrac{1}{s + 3}$

(E) $\dfrac{1}{\sqrt{s^2 + 9}}$

80. $10^k + 5^k =$

(A) $5\left(2^k + 1^k\right)$

(B) $5^k\left(2^k + 1\right)$

(C) $5^k\left(3^k\right)$

(D) 15^k

(E) 15^{2k}

81. The positive integer m is three times the positive integer n. Which of the following could be the value of $m + n$?

I.   216

II.   314

III. 1,048

(A) I only

(B) II only

(C) I and II only

(D) I and III only

(E) II and III only

82. In the figure shown, $\overline{CE}$ has length 40 feet, $\overline{EA}$ has length 20 feet, and $\overline{DE}$ is perpendicular to $\overline{AC}$ and has length 10 feet. What is the area, in feet^2, of $\triangle ABC$?

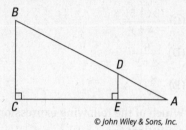

© John Wiley & Sons, Inc.

(A) 225

(B) 450

(C) 900

(D) 1,800

(E) 3,600

83. A length of wire is attached to the top of a 16-foot vertical pole. The wire is anchored 12 feet from the base of the pole. What is the length, in feet, of the wire?

(A) 14

(B) 18

(C) 20

(D) 28

(E) 30

84. Solution X contains 4×10^{-2} grams of sugar. Solution Y contains 8×10^{2} grams of sugar. The number of grams of sugar in solution Y is how many times the number of grams of sugar in solution X?

(A) 0.0002

(B) 0.002

(C) 200

(D) 2,000

(E) 20,000

85. How many different arrangements to seat four spectators in four of seven empty stadium seats that are all in the same row are possible?

(A) 12

(B) 24

(C) 28

(D) 35

(E) 840

86. The data in the table show cell phone ownership status by grade level of 300 middle school students. If one of the 300 students is randomly selected, what is the probability that the student owns a cell phone, given that the student is a seventh grader?

Grade Level	Owns a Cell Phone	Does not own a Cell Phone	Totals
Sixth	30	70	100
Seventh	55	45	100
Eighth	78	22	100
Totals	163	137	300

(A) $\frac{11}{60}$

(B) $\frac{11}{100}$

(C) $\frac{163}{300}$

(D) $\frac{55}{163}$

(E) $\frac{11}{20}$

87. The partially completed probability tree diagram shows the chances of an outdoor concert taking place or being canceled when rain might or might not occur. What is the probability that the concert takes place given that it rains?

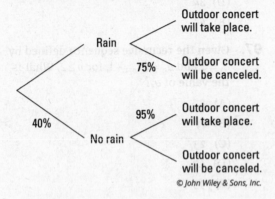

© John Wiley & Sons, Inc.

(A) 2%

(B) 15%

(C) 25%

(D) 38%

(E) 85%

88. If both letters and digits can repeat, which of the following computations can be used to determine how many different license plate alphanumeric codes consisting of two uppercase letters of the English alphabet followed by four digits are possible?

(A) $(2 \cdot 26)(4 \cdot 10)$

(B) $(2!)(4!)$

(C) $\left(\dfrac{26!}{2!24!}\right)\left(\dfrac{10!}{4!6!}\right)$

(D) $(26^2)(10^4)$

(E) $(26+10)^6$

89. A small motor uses $3\frac{3}{8}$ gallons of gasoline every 15 hours. What is the motor's fuel consumption rate, in gallons per day?

(A) 0.225

(B) 1.6

(C) 4.8

(D) 5.2

(E) 5.4

90. Set M consists of all positive integers that are multiples of 4. Set N consists of all positive integers less than 100 that have a units digit of 8. How many integers do sets M and N have in common?

(A) Three

(B) Four

(C) Five

(D) Six

(E) Seven

91. The mean of a list of six different positive integers is 68. Four of the integers in the list are 38, 57, 65, and 86. What is the maximum possible value of the greatest of the six integers?

(A) 86

(B) 87

(C) 123

(D) 161

(E) 162

92. According to a survey of 200 students at a community college, 75 are enrolled in a science course and 52 are enrolled in a sociology course. Of those surveyed, 34 are enrolled in a science course, but not in a sociology course. How many students are enrolled in neither a science course nor a sociology course?

(A) 114

(B) 107

(C) 93

(D) 86

(E) 73

93. In the figure shown, $\overline{QS}$ is an altitude of right triangle PQR, $PS = 16$, and $RS = 4$. Find the perimeter of $\triangle PQR$.

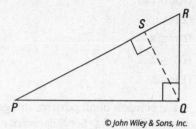

© John Wiley & Sons, Inc.

(A) $20 + 4\sqrt{5}$

(B) $20 + 6\sqrt{5}$

(C) $20 + 8\sqrt{5}$

(D) $20 + 12\sqrt{5}$

(E) $32\sqrt{5}$

94. The enrollment at a local private school for the new school year is 10% more than the enrollment at this time last year. The number of female students increased by 5%, and the number of male students increased by 20%. Female students make up what fraction of the current enrollment at the private school?

(A) $\dfrac{1}{5}$

(B) $\dfrac{4}{11}$

(C) $\dfrac{1}{2}$

(D) $\dfrac{7}{11}$

(E) $\dfrac{4}{5}$

95. If $\frac{1}{4}x < 150 < \frac{1}{3}x$, which of the following numbers could be a value of x?

I.   500

II. 600

III. 700

(A) I only

(B) I and II only

(C) III only

(D) I and III only

(E) II and III only

96. If $\dfrac{1}{5^n} = \dfrac{1}{5^k} + \dfrac{1}{5^k} + \dfrac{1}{5^k} + \dfrac{1}{5^k} + \dfrac{1}{5^k}$, then n expressed in terms of k is

(A) $k - 1$

(B) $k + 1$

(C) $1 - k$

(D) $3k$

(E) k^5

97. Given the recursive sequence defined by $a_1 = 5$ and $a_n = 2a_{n-1} + 1$, for $n \geq 2$. What is the value of a_4?

(A) 8

(B) 11

(C) 23

(D) 47

(E) 95

98. A certain car model averages 25 miles per gallon of gasoline. A certain truck model averages 12 miles per gallon of gasoline. If each vehicle is driven 1,200 miles, how much more gasoline (in gallons) will the truck use than the car?

(A) 26

(B) 32

(C) 48

(D) 52

(E) 68

99. If $x, y,$ and z are positive integers and $x < y < z$, which of the following statements must be true?

I. $\dfrac{y}{z} < \dfrac{y}{x}$

II. $xz > xy$

III. $z > x + y$

(A) I only

(B) II only

(C) III only

(D) I and II only

(E) II and III only

100. What is the probability that a randomly selected integer from a list of consecutive integers from 101 to 500 will have a hundreds digit of 3?

(A) $\frac{1}{5}$

(B) $\frac{1}{4}$

(C) $\frac{1}{3}$

(D) $\frac{2}{5}$

(E) $\frac{3}{4}$

101. Eight boxes, weighing an average of 12.75 kilograms, and 12 boxes, weighing an average of 15.25 kilograms, are shipped to the same location. What is the average weight, in kilograms, of the 20 boxes shipped to the location?

(A) 13

(B) 13.25

(C) 14

(D) 14.25

(E) 15

102. A collection of U.S. coins consists of pennies, nickels, dimes, and quarters, in the ratio 2:3:5:6, respectively. If the number of coins of one of the denominations is 30, which of the following CANNOT be the total number of coins in the collection?

(A) 80

(B) 96

(C) 112

(D) 160

(E) 240

103. A furniture store reduces the retail price of a sofa from $800 to $600. By what percent is the price of the sofa reduced?

(A) 25%

(B) 30%

(C) 35%

(D) 60%

(E) 75%

104. In the xy-plane, which of the following points must lie on the line $mx + 4y = 8$ for every possible value of m?

I. $(2,0)$

II. $(2,2)$

III. $(0,2)$

(A) I only

(B) II only

(C) III only

(D) I and III only

(E) I, II, and III

105. The range of the six numbers 20, 6, 14, 8, 28, and K is 24. The greatest possible value of K is how much greater than the least possible value of K?

(A) 4

(B) 24

(C) 26

(D) 30

(E) 34

106. If a and b are positive numbers such that $a + b = 2$, which of the following could be a value of $50a - 100b$?

I.   150

II. 100

III. 50

(A) I only

(B) II only

(C) III only

(D) I and III only

(E) II and III only

107. If A, B, C, and D are positive numbers such that the ratio of A to B is 3 to 4, the ratio of B to D is 8 to 5, and the ratio of C to D is 3 to 2, what is the ratio of A to C?

(A) 4 to 5

(B) 5 to 4

(C) 5 to 9

(D) 9 to 5

(E) 16 to 5

108. A thrift shop sells pre-owned hardcover books for $7 each and pre-owned paperback books for $5 each. A customer makes a purchase of both hardcover books and paperback books. Before taxes, the total purchase price of the books is $56. How many total books did the customer purchase?

(A) 7

(B) 8

(C) 9

(D) 10

(E) 11

109. In the xy-plane, find the area of a circle that has center $(-4,1)$ and passes through the point $(2,-5)$?

(A) 12π

(B) 20π

(C) 40π

(D) 52π

(E) 72π

110. In a high school election in which only seniors and juniors could vote, one candidate, a high school senior, received 400 of the votes cast by the seniors and 10% of the total votes cast by the juniors. If V is the total number of votes cast in the election and 40% of the total votes were cast by seniors, which of the following expressions represents the number of votes that the candidate received?

(A) $320 + 0.06V$

(B) $400 + 0.06V$

(C) $720 + 0.10V$

(D) $400 + 0.40V$

(E) $400 + 0.70V$

111. A restaurant chef always mixes 6 ounces of red quinoa with every 16 ounces of white quinoa. How many ounces of red quinoa does the chef put in a 110-ounce mixture of the two grain-like seeds?

(A) 10

(B) 16

(C) 30

(D) 60

(E) 80

112. The number 3,080 has how many distinct prime factors?

(A) Two

(B) Three

(C) Four

(D) Five

(E) Six

113. In a list of K consecutive integers, the median is 240. If K is an odd number, what is the greatest integer in the list?

(A) $239 + \dfrac{K-1}{2}$

(B) $240 + \dfrac{K-1}{2}$

(C) $239 + \dfrac{K}{2}$

(D) $240 + \dfrac{K+1}{2}$

(E) $120 + K$

114. If $X = 0.\overline{81}$, where the bar over the 2-digit sequence 81 indicates the sequence repeats indefinitely, what is the value of $99\,X$?

(A) $80.\overline{19}$

(B) 80.19

(C) 81

(D) 81.81

(E) $81.\overline{81}$

115. The length, width, and height of a rectangular box are in the ratio of 6:4:5, respectively. Express the height of the box in terms of its volume V.

(A) $\frac{1}{2}\sqrt[3]{\frac{V}{3}}$

(B) $\frac{5}{6}\sqrt[3]{\frac{V}{15}}$

(C) $2\sqrt[3]{\frac{V}{15}}$

(D) $\frac{5}{2}\sqrt[3]{\frac{V}{15}}$

(E) $3\sqrt[3]{\frac{V}{15}}$

116. Sofi has S game cards, which is half as many as her older brother has, and three times as many as her younger sister has. In terms of S, how many game cards do the three siblings have altogether?

(A) $\frac{4}{3}S$

(B) $2\frac{1}{3}S$

(C) $3\frac{1}{3}S$

(D) $3\frac{1}{2}S$

(E) $5\frac{1}{2}S$

117. The mean of a list of K numbers is 100. If the number 180 is appended to the list of K numbers, the new list of $K+1$ numbers has a mean of 110. What is the value of K?

(A) 7

(B) 9

(C) 10

(D) 18

(E) 30

118. Suppose $a_1, a_2, a_3, \ldots$ is a sequence of integers such that $a_{n+1} = 10a_n$. How many times greater is a_8 than a_3?

(A) 10^4

(B) 10^5

(C) 10^6

(D) 10^9

(E) $8^{10} - 3^{10}$

119. If x and y are positive integers such that $x < y$, which of the following expressions must be less than 1?

I. $\sqrt{\frac{y}{x}}$

II. $\frac{x^2 - 100}{y^2 - 100}$

III. $\frac{x}{y}$

(A) I only

(B) II only

(C) III only

(D) I and II only

(E) II and III only

120. What is the difference between the mean and the median of the positive numbers, $k, k+3, k+4, k+8, k+9, k+12$?

(A) 0

(B) 1

(C) 6

(D) $2k$

(E) $5k$

121. What amount (in milliliters) of a 1% sulfuric acid solution must be added to 60 milliliters of a 6% sulfuric acid solution to yield a 5% sulfuric acid solution?

(A) 12

(B) 15

(C) 18

(D) 20

(E) 45

122. Two vehicles leave the same location at the same time. The first vehicle travels due east at 70 miles per hour. The other vehicle travels due west at 60 miles per hour. Assuming they continue at their respective speeds without stopping, how long (in hours) will it take for the two vehicles to be 455 miles apart?

(A) 2.75

(B) 3.5

(C) 4.25

(D) 4.75

(E) 5.5

123. $\dfrac{5}{16} + \dfrac{\left(\dfrac{3}{8}\right)\left(\dfrac{2}{3}\right)}{4} - \dfrac{3}{8} =$

(A) 0

(B) $\dfrac{9}{13}$

(C) $\dfrac{3}{4}$

(D) $\dfrac{15}{16}$

(E) $\dfrac{19}{16}$

124. Which of the following is a prime factor of $5^8 - 2^8$?

I. 2

II. 3

III. 7

(A) I only

(B) III only

(C) I and II only

(D) II and III only

(E) I, II, and III

125. The length (in feet) of a rectangle is 4 more than twice its width. The area of the rectangle is 70 feet^2. What is the length (in feet) of the rectangle?

(A) 5

(B) 7

(C) 10

(D) 12

(E) 14

126. If $x = -\dfrac{1}{20}$, which of the following is true?

I. $x < x^2 < x^3$

II. $x^2 < x < x^3$

III. $x < x^3 < x^2$

(A) I. only

(B) II. only

(C) III only

(D) I and II only

(E) II and III only

127. Initially, Loyce and Tiara together have $278 for a shopping trip. Loyce spends $8 on a bag of fresh apples at the Farmer's Market, at which point, she has twice as much money as Tiara, who has not yet spent any money. How much money does Loyce have initially?

(A) 188

(B) 147

(C) 139

(D) 135

(E) 131

128. A rectangular crate is packed to capacity with 216 3-inch cubes. What is the volume, in cubic inches, of the crate?

(A) 24

(B) 72

(C) 648

(D) 1,944

(E) 5,832

129. Merida and Jude join two different gyms. Merida joins a gym that has a one-time enrollment fee of $70 and $18 per month of membership, including the first month. Jude joins a gym that has a one-time enrollment fee of $40 and $20 per month of membership, including the first month. After how many months of membership will Merida and Jude have paid the same total amount to their respective gyms?

(A) 15

(B) 20

(C) 25

(D) 30

(E) 35

130. The line plot shows the minutes waited in line by 20 customers at a coffee shop. What is the difference, in minutes, between the median and the mean of the data?

Times Waited in Line by 20 Customers

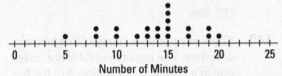

Number of Minutes

© John Wiley & Sons, Inc.

(A) −0.8

(B) −0.2

(C) 0

(D) 0.2

(E) 0.8

131. A sequence of consecutive integers begins with 60 and ends with 100. If one integer is randomly selected from the sequence, what is the probability that the integer is even?

(A) $\frac{20}{41}$

(B) $\frac{1}{2}$

(C) $\frac{19}{40}$

(D) $\frac{21}{41}$

(E) $\frac{21}{40}$

132. Bag 1 contains 10 blue, 8 gold, and 6 red chips, all identical except for color. Bag 2 contains 8 blue, 2 gold, and 2 red chips, also all identical except for color. Two chips, one from each bag, are randomly drawn, one after the other. What is the probability that neither chip will be gold?

(A) $\frac{5}{18}$

(B) $\frac{4}{9}$

(C) $\frac{1}{2}$

(D) $\frac{5}{9}$

(E) $\frac{2}{3}$

133. A field that measures 18 by 30 feet is divided into equal-sized square plots with no land left over. What is the greatest area, in square feet, for each of the square plots?

(A) 4

(B) 9

(C) 16

(D) 25

(E) 36

134. What is the units digit of 2^{99}?

(A) 0

(B) 2

(C) 4

(D) 6

(E) 8

135. A recipe for a mulled cranberry punch calls for $2\frac{3}{4}$ cups of cranberry juice, $1\frac{1}{2}$ cups of white grape juice, $2\frac{1}{3}$ cup of water, and $\frac{1}{4}$ cup of cinnamon sugar.

What is the ratio of the total amount, in cups, of fruit juice to the total amount, in cups, of water and cinnamon sugar in the recipe?

(A) 51 to 31

(B) 31 to 12

(C) 31 to 17

(D) 31 to 51

(E) 12 to 31

136. $\frac{m}{n} = 10$ and $\frac{n}{p} = 5$, where $mn \neq 0$. What is the value of $\frac{m}{n+p}$?

(A) $\frac{25}{6}$

(B) $\frac{25}{3}$

(C) $\frac{5}{3}$

(D) 10

(E) 12

137. The perimeter of the rectangle shown is 18 feet. What is the area, in square feet, of the rectangle?

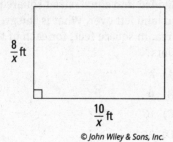

$\frac{8}{x}$ ft

$\frac{10}{x}$ ft

© John Wiley & Sons, Inc.

(A) 9

(B) 10

(C) 20

(D) 30

(E) 40

138. An appliance store owner ordered 50 countertop microwave ovens to be sold for $144 each, which represents a 20 percent markup over the store owner's initial cost for each microwave. Of the microwave ovens ordered, 5 were never sold. These ovens were returned for a refund of 50 percent of the owner's initial cost. What was the owner's profit or loss as a percent of the initial cost of the 50 microwave ovens?

(A) 15% loss

(B) 13% loss

(C) 10% profit

(D) 13% profit

(E) 15% profit

139. If $X = 625{,}000$, how many nonzero digits are in the decimal representation of $\frac{1}{X}$?

(A) One

(B) Two

(C) Three

(D) Four

(E) Five

140. Three of 12 remote controls in a box are defective. The remote controls are tested one at a time and not replaced in the box after testing. What is the probability that neither of the first two remote controls tested is defective?

(A) $\frac{1}{6}$

(B) $\frac{2}{9}$

(C) $\frac{6}{11}$

(D) $\frac{9}{16}$

(E) $\frac{3}{4}$

141. Richard works as a waiter in an elegant downtown restaurant. His average (arithmetic mean) gratuity per day over the past 10 workdays is $200. If Richard's average gratuity per day for the first six of the past 10 workdays was $180, what was his average gratuity per day for the last four of the past 10 workdays?

(A) $210

(B) $220

(C) $225

(D) $230

(E) $240

142. If $x^{-2} = \frac{1}{4}$, then $x^{-4} =$

(A) −16

(B) $-\frac{1}{16}$

(C) $\frac{1}{16}$

(D) 4

(E) 16

143. What is the units digit of $(13)^{25}(17)^{25}$?

(A) 0

(B) 1

(C) 3

(D) 7

(E) 9

144. Twenty people had dinner together at a restaurant. The cost of the meal plus an automatic gratuity of 18% for a large party was $531.00, before sales tax was added. What was the average price of the meal per person NOT INCLUDING the gratuity or sales tax?

(A) $21.77

(B) $22.50

(C) $26.55

(D) $30.50

(E) $36.55

145. What is the greatest value of the positive integer p such that 2^p is a factor of 80^{50}?

(A) 4

(B) 10

(C) 50

(D) 100

(E) 200

146. The circle shown is tangent to both the x- and y-axes. If the length of the segment from the circle's center C to the origin, O, is 6, what is the circle's radius?

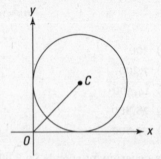

© John Wiley & Sons, Inc.

(A) 6

(B) $3\sqrt{2}$

(C) $2\sqrt{3}$

(D) 3

(E) 2

147. The figure shows the paths from point A to point E in a video game. How many different ways can a player move from point A to point E and then back from point E to point A without retracing a previous path taken?

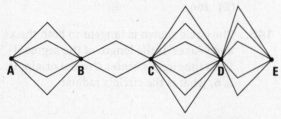

© John Wiley & Sons, Inc.

(A) 300

(B) 7,200

(C) 14,400

(D) 28,800

(E) 57,600

148. If a government spends $9.8 billion on a population of 1.4 million. What is the government's per capita expenditure?

(A) $70

(B) $700

(C) $7,000

(D) $70,000

(E) $700,000

149. Which of the following inequalities is an algebraic expression for the graph shown?

© John Wiley & Sons, Inc.

(A) $\left|x - \frac{1}{2}\right| < \frac{7}{2}$

(B) $\left|x - \frac{1}{2}\right| > \frac{7}{2}$

(C) $\left|x - \frac{1}{2}\right| \leq \frac{7}{2}$

(D) $\left|x - \frac{1}{2}\right| \geq \frac{7}{2}$

(E) $\left|2x - 1\right| > \frac{7}{2}$

150. An online bookstore reported total sales of $768 million for the first quarter of the current year. If the total sales for the first quarter of the previous year was $640 million, what is the percent increase in total sales?

(A) 5%

(B) 15%

(C) 17%

(D) 20%

(E) 80%

151. Everyone who attended the pre-wedding party was either a friend of the bride or a friend of the bridegroom, or both. If 62 percent of those who attended were friends of the bride and 47 percent were friends of the bridegroom, what percent of the attendees were friends of the bride, but not friends of the bridegroom?

(A) 15%

(B) 34%

(C) 44%

(D) 53%

(E) 62%

152. If $xy \neq 0$ and 20 percent of x equals $33\frac{1}{3}$ percent of y, what is the value of $15\left(\frac{x}{y}\right)$?

(A) $\frac{15}{8}$

(B) 3

(C) 5

(D) 9

(E) 25

153. Amiel enrolled in a weight loss program. He lost $\frac{1}{2}$ pound every week for 30 weeks. What percent of his original weight of 240 pounds did Amiel lose during this period?

(A) 0.0625%

(B) 0.625%

(C) 6.25%

(D) 0.16%

(E) 16%

154. The quantity $\sqrt{6.4 \times 10^7}$ equals which of the following?

(A) 800

(B) 3,200

(C) 4,000

(D) 8,000

(E) 80,000

155. Given that $m^2 - 2m - 15 = 0$ and $n^2 - 3n - 10 = 0$, where $m \neq n$, what is the product of m and n?

(A) −15

(B) −10

(C) −6

(D) 6

(E) 15

156. If $\dfrac{1}{x} = \dfrac{1}{2} + \dfrac{2}{5} + \dfrac{1}{3} - \dfrac{5}{6} + \dfrac{1}{4} - \dfrac{9}{20}$, then $3x =$

(A) $\dfrac{3}{5}$

(B) $\dfrac{21}{5}$

(C) 9

(D) 15

(E) 21

157. A crate contains C cases. Each case contains 12 boxes for which the profit is P cents per box. What is the total profit, in cents, for N crates?

(A) $\dfrac{12CP}{N}$

(B) $\dfrac{12NP}{C}$

(C) $12NP$

(D) NCP

(E) $12NCP$

158. In driving a round trip from City A to City B, a motorist drives to City B and, on the way back to City A, by the same route, stops at a service station at a location that is 10 percent of the distance to City A from City B. When the motorist stops at the service station, what percent of the round trip is completed?

(A) 40%

(B) 45%

(C) 55%

(D) 60%

(E) 65%

159. The graph shown is symmetric about the vertical line at $x = 3$. According to the graph, when $x = 5$, $y =$

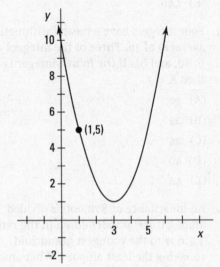

© John Wiley & Sons, Inc.

(A) 2

(B) 3

(C) 4

(D) 5

(E) 6

160. What is the difference between $\frac{1}{10}$ of $2,500 and $\frac{1}{10}$% of $2,500?

(A) −$247.50

(B) −$225.00

(C) $0

(D) $225.00

(E) $247.50

161. A jar contains 640 U. S. coins, each with a face value of either 25 cents or 10 cents. If the total face value of the coins is $94, how many 25-cent coins are in the jar?

(A) 120

(B) 200

(C) 280

(D) 360

(E) 440

162. Four integers have a mean (arithmetic average) of 36. Three of the integers are 6, 30, and 64. If the fourth integer is 2K, then K =

(A) 20

(B) 22

(C) 24

(D) 40

(E) 44

163. An inheritance of $78,000 is divided among three grandchildren in the ratio 3:4:6 with the youngest grandchild receiving the least amount. What amount did the youngest grandchild receive?

(A) $5,200

(B) $6,000

(C) $13,000

(D) $18,000

(E) $24,000

164. The enrollment at a middle school increased by 15 percent from the previous year. If the school's present enrollment is 920 students, how many students were enrolled the previous year?

(A) 782

(B) 800

(C) 820

(D) 846

(E) 890

165. Each year for three years, an investment increases by 2 percent over the preceding year. The value, in dollars, of the investment at the end of the third year is S. In terms of S, what is the amount of the initial investment at the beginning of the three-year period?

(A) $\dfrac{S}{(1.06)}$

(B) $\dfrac{S}{(1.02)^3}$

(C) $\dfrac{S}{(1.02)^2}$

(D) $\dfrac{S}{1.02}$

(E) $3\left(\dfrac{S}{1.02}\right)$

166. An author receives 10% of the publisher's net receipts in royalties on the first 10,000 copies of the author's book sold, 12% on the next 15,000 copies sold, and 15% on all copies sold thereafter. By what percent does the ratio of the royalty percentage to number of copies decrease from the first 10,000 copies to the next 15,000 copies?

(A) 2%

(B) 10%

(C) 15%

(D) 20%

(E) 25%

167. If X is 60 percent more than Y and Y is 40 percent less than Z, then what percent of Z is X?

(A) 64%

(B) 80%

(C) 96%

(D) 120%

(E) 124%

168. While traveling on a 100-mile trip to a weekend destination, Finn had to drive on a dirt road for X% of the trip's total distance at an average speed of 30 miles per hour. The rest of the trip, Finn drove on a paved highway at an average speed of 60 miles per hour. In terms of X, what was the total time, in hours, for the trip?

(A) $\dfrac{X+100}{60}$

(B) $\dfrac{100-2X}{60}$

(C) $\dfrac{100-X}{30}$

(D) $\dfrac{X+200}{90}$

(E) $\dfrac{3X+100}{60}$

169. What is the sum of the first 50 multiples of a positive integer K?

(A) 1,225K

(B) 1,275K

(C) 2,450K

(D) 2,550K

(E) 1,326K

170. Together Ari and Izy have less than P colored markers. Ari has $P-2$ colored markers and Izy has $P-20$ colored markers. If each girl has at least one colored marker, what is the value of P?

(A) 21

(B) 22

(C) 22

(D) 24

(E) 25

171. Only one of ten pens in a box is defective. Three pens are randomly drawn from the box, one at a time. If none of those three pens is defective, what is the probability that the next pen randomly drawn is defective?

(A) $\dfrac{1}{10}$

(B) $\dfrac{1}{7}$

(C) $\dfrac{7}{10}$

(D) $\dfrac{6}{7}$

(E) $\dfrac{9}{10}$

172. For which of the following expression is $a+b$ a factor?

I. a^2+b^2

II. $ac+ad+bc+bd$

III. $a+b(c+d)$

(A) I only

(B) II only

(C) III only

(D) I and II only

(E) II and III only

173. If $4m=10-5n$ and $2m=3n+16$, what is the value of n?

(A) –5

(B) –2

(C) 0

(D) 2

(E) 5

174. A student is trying to achieve an overall average of at least 90.0 to earn a grade of A in a college course. In determining the overall average for the course grade, the instructor calculates a weighted average based on the four major, 100-point exams in the course. The mean (arithmetic average) of the scores on the first three exams counts as 60 percent of the overall average, and the fourth (and final) exam counts as 40 percent of the overall average. The student has scores of 80, 95, and 92 on the first three major exams. Which of the following scores on the fourth major exam would result in an overall average that would earn the student an A in the course?

I.   90

II. 91

III. 92

(A) I only

(B) II only

(C) III only

(D) II and III only

(E) I, II, and III

175. In the figure shown, lines m and n are parallel and $x = 5y$. What is the value of x?

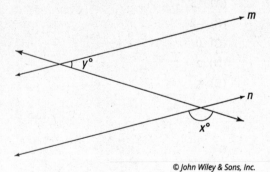

© John Wiley & Sons, Inc.

(A) 30

(B) 36

(C) 60

(D) 150

(E) 225

176. To estimate the population of horned lizards in a national park, a team from the park service captures and tags 25 horned lizards and then releases the tagged lizards back into the park. Two weeks later, the team returns and captures 20 horned lizards, 4 of which bear tags that identify them as being among the previously captured lizards. If all the tagged lizards have dispersed throughout the park and are still active when the second group of lizards is captured, what is the best estimate of the horned lizard population in the park, based on the information obtained through this capture-tag-recapture strategy?

(A) 250

(B) 125

(C) 100

(D) 80

(E) 75

177. A school district's food and nutrition director asks a panel of high school students for recommendations for changes in the menu options in the school cafeteria. After implementing student recommendations that were in compliance with state nutrition guidelines, the director surveys 100 randomly selected students in the high school to assess their satisfaction with the revised cafeteria menu, on a scale of 1 (indicating "Extremely Dissatisfied") to 7 (indicating "Extremely Satisfied"). The graph shown displays the students' responses to the survey. What is the ratio of the number of students who chose 5 or higher as a response to the number of students who chose 3 or lower as a response?

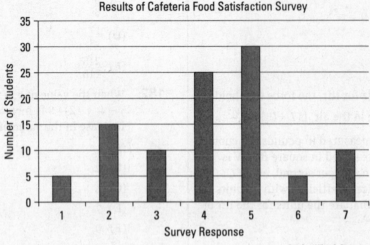

© John Wiley & Sons, Inc.

(A) $\dfrac{9}{11}$

(B) $\dfrac{3}{4}$

(C) $\dfrac{3}{2}$

(D) $\dfrac{9}{4}$

(E) $\dfrac{10}{1}$

178. During the end-of-year sale at an appliance store, 76 customers bought a washer, a dryer, or both of these appliances. In checking the sales records, the store manager found that 47 washers and 40 dryers were sold to these 76 customers. How many of them bought both a washer and a dryer?

(A) 0

(B) 11

(C) 29

(D) 36

(E) 65

179. The formula for lift, the force that holds an airplane in the air, is $L = C_L \left(\dfrac{dAV^2}{2} \right)$.

When d is measured in pounds per cubic feet, A is measured in square feet, V is measured in feet per second, and if C_L is a numerical coefficient with no units attached, what are the units for the lift of an airplane?

(A) $\dfrac{\text{lb} \cdot \text{ft}}{\text{sec}^2}$

(B) $\dfrac{\text{lb}}{\text{sec}^2}$

(C) $\dfrac{\text{lb} \cdot \text{ft}}{\text{sec}}$

(D) $\dfrac{\text{lb} \cdot \text{ft}^2}{\text{sec}^2}$

(E) $\dfrac{\text{lb}^2 \cdot \text{ft}^2}{\text{sec}^2}$

180. The lengths of two sides of a triangle are 14 and 31. Which of the following could be the length of the third side?

I. 17.1

II. 27.8

III. 44.9

(A) I only

(B) II only

(C) I and II only

(D) II and III only

(E) I, II, and III

181. A number cube with six faces, numbered 10, 20, 30, 40, 50, and 60, is tossed three times in a row. What is the probability that the number 50 will appear on the up face on at least one of the three tosses?

(A) $\dfrac{91}{216}$

(B) $\dfrac{125}{216}$

(C) $\dfrac{5}{6}$

(D) $\dfrac{17}{18}$

(E) $\dfrac{215}{216}$

182. When the value of x in the equation $y = 4(x-2) + 9$ is increased by 1, the increase in the value of y is

(A) 1

(B) 2

(C) 4

(D) 7

(E) 9

183. The original price of an antique armoire was 30 percent less than the armoire's suggested retail price of $1,500. The price at which the armoire was sold was 30 percent more than the original price. What is the price at which the armoire was sold?

(A) $1,050

(B) $1,275

(C) $1,365

(D) $1,500

(E) $1,950

184. A prime number n is a factor of both $(14k+13)$ and $(7k+1)$, where k is a positive integer. What is the value of n?

(A) 2

(B) 3

(C) 7

(D) 11

(E) 13

185. Given the equation $4x^2 + 12x + c = (2x + k)^2$, where c and k are real numbers, what is the value of c?

(A) 1

(B) 3

(C) 4

(D) 9

(E) 12

186. If the rectangular prism shown is completely submerged in paint, what fraction of the small cubes that compose the prism will not have any paint on them?

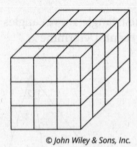

© John Wiley & Sons, Inc.

(A) $\dfrac{1}{18}$

(B) $\dfrac{1}{12}$

(C) $\dfrac{1}{9}$

(D) $\dfrac{2}{9}$

(E) $\dfrac{1}{6}$

187. A bag contains 48 tokens, all identical except for color. There are twice as many red as green tokens and twice as many white tokens as black tokens. There are 6 more black tokens than green tokens. If one token is randomly drawn from the bag, what is the probability that the token is red or black?

(A) $\dfrac{5}{16}$

(B) $\dfrac{7}{16}$

(C) $\dfrac{9}{16}$

(D) $\dfrac{11}{16}$

(E) $\dfrac{1}{3}$

188. What is the least positive integer p such that $5^{-p} < 0.0025$?

(A) 3

(B) 4

(C) 5

(D) 6

(E) 7

189. How many positive factors does the number 1,000 have?

(A) 12

(B) 13

(C) 14

(D) 15

(E) 16

190. The units digit of a 3-digit number is $\frac{1}{3}$ times the hundreds digit and twice the tens digit. What is the number?

(A) 126

(B) 216

(C) 312

(D) 612

(E) 621

191. An operation e is defined as $aeb = \dfrac{1}{b} - \dfrac{1}{a}$, for all a and b such that $ab \neq 0$. Determine $(4e3)e(5e4)$.

(A) –8

(B) $-\dfrac{1}{30}$

(C) 2

(D) $\dfrac{1}{30}$

(E) 8

192. Given positive integers $w, x, y,$ and z. If the remainder when w is divided by x is 9 and the remainder when z is divided by y is 7, what is the least value of $x + y$?

(A) 14

(B) 15

(C) 16

(D) 17

(E) 18

193. The line segment between points A and B has endpoints $6\frac{1}{4}$ and $6\frac{1}{2}$. The line segment between points C and D has endpoints $\frac{5\sqrt{2}}{4}$ and $\frac{3\sqrt{2}}{2}$. What is the ratio of AB to CD?

(A) $-\sqrt{2}$

(B) $-\frac{1}{\sqrt{2}}$

(C) 1

(D) $\frac{1}{\sqrt{2}}$

(E) $\sqrt{2}$

194. $\left(2x^2+7x+3\right)\left(2x^2-3x-2\right)^{-1}\left(x^2-9\right)^{-1}\left(x^2-x-2\right)=$

(A) $\frac{x+1}{x-3}$

(B) $\frac{x-1}{x-3}$

(C) $\frac{x-1}{x+3}$

(D) $\frac{2x+1}{x+3}$

(E) $\frac{2x+1}{x-3}$

195. It takes 6 hours for a water tank to fill to capacity when the input valve is open and the output valve is closed. When the same water tank is full to capacity, it takes 10 hours to empty the tank if the input valve is closed and the output valve is open. How long, in hours, will it take to fill the tank to capacity if both valves are open?

(A) 4

(B) $3\frac{3}{4}$

(C) 4

(D) 8

(E) 15

196. A realtor selling houses located in a gated community determines that the probability that a model home will be sold is 0.5, the probability that the house next door to the model home will be sold is 0.4, and the probability that at least one of the two houses will be sold is 0.8. What is the probability that the house next door will be sold if the model home is sold first?

(A) 0.15

(B) 0.2

(C) 0.25

(D) 0.3

(E) 0.4

197. In the triangle shown angles 1 and 2 are congruent. Determine x.

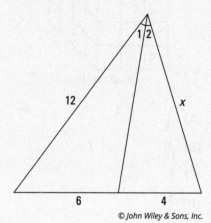

© John Wiley & Sons, Inc.

(A) 6

(B) 7

(C) 8

(D) 9

(E) 10

198. The square root of the product of the positive integers *a* and *b* is 14, which of the following could equal $a + b$?

I.   35
II. 53
III. 100

(A) I only

(B) II only

(C) I and II only

(D) II and III only

(E) I, II, and III

199. Children are playing a game using two identical spinners that have four equal sections numbered 10, 20, 30, and 40. A child spins the two spinners and computes the product of the two numbers that result from the two spins. Which of the following products is most likely to occur?

(A) 400

(B) 600

(C) 800

(D) 1,200

(E) 1,600

200. Which of the following equations have both 2 and –2 in the solution set?

I. $x = \sqrt{4}$
II. $x^2 = 4$
III. $x^4 = 16$

(A) I only

(B) II only

(C) III only

(D) II and III only

(E) I, II, and III

201. The table shows the results of a poll of 320 library patrons who were asked what genre of books they read most often. What is the ratio of the number of patrons who chose nonfiction genres to the number who chose fiction genres?

Genre	Number of Patrons
Biography/Historical Nonfiction	44
Historical Fiction	58
Mystery Fiction	64
Science/Nature Nonfiction	50
Science Fiction/Fantasy	104
Total	320

(A) $\dfrac{47}{320}$

(B) $\dfrac{47}{160}$

(C) $\dfrac{47}{113}$

(D) $\dfrac{113}{160}$

(E) $\dfrac{113}{47}$

202. Working alone at its constant rate, Machine A can produce 1,050 electrical components in 5 hours. Machine B, working alone, can produce 1,050 electrical components in $7\frac{1}{2}$ hours. If the two machine work simultaneously for *T* hours and produce 1,050 electrical components, how many electrical components has Machine B produced at the end of *T* hours?

(A) 140

(B) 210

(C) 420

(D) 525

(E) 630

203. In the figure shown, $\overline{PQ}$ is perpendicular to $\overline{QR}$ and $\overline{ST}$ is parallel to $\overline{QR}$. The measure of $\angle SQR$ is 45°; the measure of $\angle TQR$ is 30°; and $QS = 50$. What is the perimeter of triangle SQT?

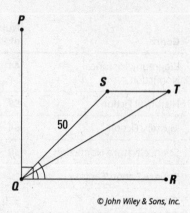

© John Wiley & Sons, Inc.

(A) $25\left(2 + \sqrt{6} + \sqrt{2}\right)$

(B) $25\left(2 + \sqrt{8}\right)$

(C) $25\left(2 + 2\sqrt{3}\right)$

(D) $50\left(2 + \sqrt{8}\right)$

(E) $50\left(2 + \sqrt{3} + \sqrt{2}\right)$

204. If x is an integer, what is the least possible value of $|19 - 3x|$?

(A) 0

(B) 1

(C) 2

(D) 3

(E) 4

205. While on a family vacation in a national park, Carson, who is training for a long distance running race, leaves the family RV, runs 6 miles to a ranger camp, rests for a while, then runs 8 more miles. At this point, which of the following could be Carson's distance, in miles, from the family RV?

I. 12

II. 14

III. 16

(A) I only

(B) II only

(C) I and II only

(D) I and III only

(E) II and III only

206. Katie, Ace, and Rory interviewed for jobs at companies A, B, and C, respectively. The probability that Katie will get a job offer from company A is $\frac{1}{4}$; the probability that Ace will get a job offer from company B is $\frac{1}{2}$; and the probability that Rory will get a job offer from company C is $\frac{5}{8}$. The three companies have no connections to one another, so the job offers are mutually independent. What is the probability that Katie and Ace will get job offers, but not Rory?

(A) $\frac{3}{64}$

(B) $\frac{5}{64}$

(C) $\frac{1}{8}$

(D) $\frac{3}{8}$

(E) $\frac{9}{8}$

207. What is the maximum value of $P = 2x + 5y$ subject to the constraints $x \leq y$, $3x - y \geq 1$, and $3x + y \leq 5$?

(A) 3.5

(B) 8.75

(C) 12

(D) 12.25

(E) 14

208. Consider $ab = c$, where $a > 0$, $b > 0$, and c is a positive constant. If b increases by 50%, then what percent change in a should occur, so that the equation remains true?

(A) 25% decrease

(B) $33\frac{1}{3}\%$ decrease

(C) 25% increase

(D) 50% increase

(E) $66\frac{2}{3}\%$ increase

209. In the figure, the circle circumscribed about square $ABCD$ has a circumference of 16π. The length of a side of square $ABCD$ is s. What is the square's area?

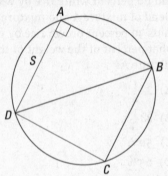

© John Wiley & Sons, Inc.

(A) $8\sqrt{2}$

(B) 128

(C) 256

(D) 128π

(E) 256π

210. Given the graphs of $y = \dfrac{x^2 - 3x - 10}{x + 2}$ and $y = 3x - 1$ in the xy-plane. Which of the following can be the number of points of intersection of the two graphs?

I.   0

II. 1

III. 2

(A) I only

(B) II only

(C) I and II only

(D) II and III only

(E) I, II, and III

211. Game coins in a board game are placed at locations A, B, C, D, and E, in the ratio 1:2:3:4:5, respectively. To win the game, a player must acquire at least 50 percent of the coins in each of three or more of the five locations. What minimum percent of the total coins must a player acquire to win the game?

(A) 10%

(B) 20%

(C) 30%

(D) 40%

(E) 50%

212. If p and q are positive integers such that their greatest common factor is 6 and their least common multiple is 120. What is the product of p and q?

(A) 60

(B) 72

(C) 120

(D) 360

(E) 720

213. If two identical machines can complete a job in 40 hours, how long, in hours, will it take five such machines to complete the same job?

(A) 4

(B) 8

(C) 10

(D) 16

(E) 20

214. A teacher has 120 pens, consisting of 72 black pens and 48 red pens. The teacher wants to put together packets for her students in which she uniformly distributes the black and red pens among the packets so that none of the pens are left over and all the packets have the same ratio of black pens to red pens. What is the greatest number of packets the teacher can make?

(A) 8

(B) 12

(C) 16

(D) 24

(E) 30

215. For how many values of x is the equation $y = \dfrac{x^4 - 81}{x^2 + x - 12}$ undefined?

(A) Zero

(B) One

(C) Two

(D) Four

(E) Six

216. 400 consecutive multiples of 5 and 600 consecutive multiples of 4 are selected. What is the ratio of odd to even numbers in the selected numbers?

(A) 1 to 5

(B) 1 to 4

(C) 4 to 1

(D) 5 to 16

(E) 5 to 17

217. What is the ratio of $\dfrac{2^{-16} + 2^{-17} + 2^{-18} + 2^{-19}}{\frac{1}{4}(5)}$ to 2^{-17}?

(A) 3 to 2

(B) 5 to 2

(C) 3 to 1

(D) 4 to 1

(E) 5 to 1

218. If $0 < a < b < c < d$ and $y = \left(x^2 - ax - bx + ab\right)\left(x^2 - cx - dx + cd\right)$, in which of the following intervals is $y < 0$?

I. $a < x < b$

II. $b < x < c$

III. $c < x < d$

(A) I only

(B) II only

(C) I and II only

(D) I and III only

(E) II and III only

219. Rice mixture A is 25 percent brown rice and 75 percent wild rice by weight; and rice mixture B is 40 percent brown rice and 60 percent white rice by weight. If a blend of mixture A and mixture B contains 30 percent brown rice by weight, what percent of the weight of the blend is mixture A?

(A) $32\frac{1}{2}\%$

(B) $33\frac{1}{3}\%$

(C) 50%

(D) 65%

(E) $66\frac{2}{3}\%$

220. If a is a positive integer, then $\left(\dfrac{1}{a}\right)^{-3}\left(\dfrac{1}{a^2}\right)^{-2}\left(\dfrac{1}{a^4}\right)^{-1}$ is equivalent to which of the following?

(A) $\left(\dfrac{1}{a}\right)^{-48}$

(B) $\left(\dfrac{1}{a}\right)^{-11}$

(C) $\left(\dfrac{1}{a}\right)^{-6}$

(D) $\left(\dfrac{1}{a^3}\right)^{-11}$

(E) $\left(\dfrac{1}{a^3}\right)^{-6}$

221. If a, b, and x are nonzero numbers such that $\dfrac{1}{a}+\dfrac{1}{b}=\dfrac{1}{x}$, then $x =$

(A) ab

(B) $a+b$

(C) $\dfrac{1}{a+b}$

(D) $\dfrac{ab}{a+b}$

(E) $\dfrac{a+b}{ab}$

222. If the digits of a two–digit number are interchanged, the resulting integer is 18 more than the original number. What is the difference between the tens digit and the units digit of the original number?

(A) –2

(B) –1

(C) 1

(D) 2

(E) 3

223. A moving van starts out from a house at 8 a.m., traveling at an average speed of 50 miles per hour. One hour and 30 minutes later a car starts out from the same house traveling in the same direction as the van at an average speed of 70 miles per hour. If both vehicles continue at their respective average speeds without making any stops, at what clock time will the car overtake the van?

(A) 9:30 a.m.

(B) 10:30 a.m.

(C) 10:45 a.m.

(D) 11:45 a.m.

(E) 1:15 p.m.

224. In the xy-plane, the triangle AOB shown has area of 48. What is the value of a?

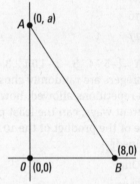

(A) 6

(B) 12

(C) 18

(D) 24

(E) 48

225. In a 3-digit code, the first digit must be chosen from the digits 2, 3, 4, 5, 6, 7, 8, and 9; the second digit must be 0 or 1; and the third digit cannot be 0. How many different such codes are possible?

(A) 128

(B) 144

(C) 160

(D) 576

(E) 1000

226. The remainder when positive integer N is divided by 2 is 1, when divided by 3 is 2, when divided by 4 is 3, and when divided by 5 is 4. What is the sum of the digits of the least possible value of N?

(A) 11

(B) 13

(C) 14

(D) 16

(E) 17

227. Set A = $\{-5,-4,-3,-2,-1,0,1,2,3,4,5\}$. If 10 integers are randomly chosen from A, with repetitions allowed, how many different ways, can the least possible value of the product of the 10 integers be obtained?

(A) One

(B) Two

(C) Three

(D) Four

(E) Five

228. Seven positive integers have an arithmetic average of 34 and a median of 42. If the greatest of these integers is 7 more than 2 times the least of the integers, what is the maximum possible value of the greatest integer?

(A) 42

(B) 49

(C) 70

(D) 52

(E) 91

229. Mani saves money in a jar at home for six months. The first month he saves S dollars. Each month thereafter, Mani saves $\frac{1}{2}$ of what he has saved the previous month. If Mani's total savings at the end of the six months is $393.75, how much money does he save the sixth month?

(A) $6.25

(B) $7.50

(C) $12.50

(D) $18.75

(E) $25.00

230. Rose read a novel that has 208 pages in four days. Each day she read 20 more pages than she read the previous day. How many pages did Rose read on the first day?

(A) 20

(B) 22

(C) 24

(D) 26

(E) 28

231. If x is an integer such that $|2x+1| < 3$, then which of the following is a possible value of $x^3 + 2x^2 + 5x + 10$?

I. 0

II. 6

III. 10

(A) I only

(B) II only

(C) I and II only

(D) II and III only

(E) I, II, III

232. The integer $K = 3a^2 + 6b^2$, where a and b are positive integers such that their greatest common factor is 2. What is the greatest even number that must be a factor of K?

(A) 3

(B) 4

(C) 6

(D) 12

(E) 24

233. Twenty-five percent of the 4,800 students in an urban school district. ride the bus to school. If $33\frac{1}{3}$ percent of the bus riders transfer to a different school district and no other changes occur, what portion of the students remaining at the first school district are bus riders?

(A) $\frac{1}{12}$

(B) $\frac{2}{7}$

(C) $\frac{2}{11}$

(D) $\frac{1}{6}$

(E) $\frac{2}{5}$

234. The scoring formula for a timed, 50-question test is $S = C - \frac{1}{4}B$, where S is the score on the test, C is the number of questions answered correctly and B is the number of questions that were left unanswered. A student answers 42 questions and leaves 8 questions unanswered. Which of the following could be the student's score?

I.   −2

II. 40

III. 41

(A) I only

(B) II only

(C) III only

(D) I and II only

(E) I and III only

235. If $Z = N\left(\dfrac{1}{1+N^{-1}}\right)^{-1}$, then $\dfrac{10Z}{N+1} =$

(A) 5

(B) 10

(C) $\dfrac{10}{N}$

(D) $\dfrac{10}{N+1}$

(E) $10(N+1)^2$

236. In the figure shown, parallel lines m and n are cut by a transversal t. What is the value of y?

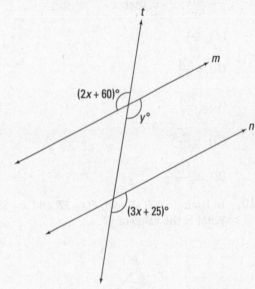

© John Wiley & Sons, Inc.

(A) 100

(B) 115

(C) 120

(D) 125

(E) 130

237. The positive integer N is not divisible by 2 or 4. What is the sum of the possible remainders when N is divided by 8?

(A) 9

(B) 11

(C) 13

(D) 15

(E) 16

238. The original price of a jacket is reduced by 15 percent for a one-day sale at an online store. After the sale ends, the sale price of the jacket is increased by 20 percent. The final price of the jacket is what percent of its original price?

(A) 120%

(B) 105%

(C) 102%

(D) 98%

(E) 95%

239. If A is a positive integer such that $y = \dfrac{6A}{5x^2}$, $x \neq 0$, then $x =$

(A) $\dfrac{6A}{5y}$

(B) $\pm\dfrac{6A}{5y}$

(C) $\sqrt{\dfrac{6A}{5y}}$

(D) $\pm\sqrt{\dfrac{6A}{5y}}$

(E) $\pm\sqrt{\dfrac{6Ay}{5}}$

240. In triangle PQR shown, $PQ = PR$ and $x = 50$. What is the value of y?

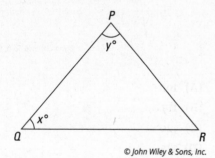

© John Wiley & Sons, Inc.

(A) 45

(B) 50

(C) 65

(D) 80

(E) 90

241. A solution of salt and water is 10 percent salt by weight. After a period of time under pressure and heat, a portion of the water evaporates so that the solution is 40 percent salt by weight. What is the ratio of the initial weight of water to the final weight of water in the solution?

(A) 1 to 6

(B) 1 to 4

(C) 1 to 3

(D) 4 to 1

(E) 6 to 1

242. As shown in the following figure, a *space diagonal* in a rectangular prism is a line that goes from a vertex of the prism, through the center of the prism to the opposite vertex. What is the length of the space diagonal of a 3 by 4 by 12 rectangular prism?

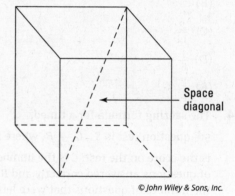

© John Wiley & Sons, Inc.

(A) 25

(B) 15

(C) 13

(D) 11

(E) 5

243. What is the area of an equilateral triangle that has an altitude of length 24?

(A) $24\sqrt{3}$

(B) $48\sqrt{3}$

(C) $96\sqrt{3}$

(D) $192\sqrt{3}$

(E) $384\sqrt{3}$

244. A chord of a circle is 15 centimeters from the circle's center. If the circle's radius is 17 centimeters, what is the chord's length, in centimeters?

(A) 7.5

(B) 8

(C) 9.5

(D) 12

(E) 16

245. The price of season tickets this year is 25% more than the price last year. Last year's price is what percent of this year's price?

(A) 75%

(B) 80%

(C) 90%

(D) 120%

(E) 125%

246. Two consecutive angles of a parallelogram have angle measures, in degrees, of $2x - 30$ and $x + 60$. What is the measure, in degrees, of the smaller angle?

(A) 50

(B) 60

(C) 70

(D) 100

(E) 110

247. If K is a positive integer such that the remainder when 17 is divided by K is 2, what is the sum of all the possible values of K?

(A) 8

(B) 18

(C) 20

(D) 23

(E) 25

248. How many different meal combinations consisting of one entrée, one vegetable side dish, one nonalcoholic beverage, and one dessert are possible from a selection of 10 entrées, 12 vegetable side dishes, 5 nonalcoholic beverages, and 6 desserts?

(A) 3,600

(B) 720

(C) 600

(D) 300

(E) 33

249. Jayma has applied to graduate programs at both university A and university B. The probability that Jayma will receive an acceptance letter from university A is 0.45; the probability she will receive an acceptance letter from university B is 0.36; and the probability she will receive an acceptance letter from both universities is 0.17. What is the probability that Jayma will receive an acceptance letter from at least one of the two universities?

(A) 0.26

(B) 0.41

(C) 0.64

(D) 0.81

(E) 0.98

250. Five people are to be seated in five identical chairs that are placed in a circular pattern. How many different seating arrangements of the five people (relative to each other) are possible?

(A) 10

(B) 24

(C) 25

(D) 60

(E) 120

251. If $a \geq 0$, then $\left(\sqrt[4]{\sqrt[3]{\sqrt{a}}} \right)^{18} =$

(A) $a^{\frac{39}{2}}$

(B) $a^{\frac{9}{4}}$

(C) $a^{\frac{4}{3}}$

(D) $a^{\frac{3}{4}}$

(E) $a^{\frac{2}{3}}$

252. How many integers n satisfy the absolute value inequality $|4n - 3| \leq 2$

(A) One

(B) Two

(C) Three

(D) Four

(E) Five

253. If $x \neq 0$, then $\left(\dfrac{x^{-7}}{x^{-11}} \right)^{-\frac{1}{2}} =$

(A) $\dfrac{1}{x}$

(B) $\dfrac{1}{x^2}$

(C) x^2

(D) x^4

(E) x^9

254. If $\sqrt{2x-1} = \sqrt{2x} - 1$, then $2x =$

(A) $-\dfrac{1}{2}$

(B) -1

(C) 0

(D) 1

(E) $\dfrac{1}{2}$

255. If $\left(4^x \right)\left(8^y \right) = 128$, what is the value of x when $y = 3$?

(A) -2

(B) $-\dfrac{3}{2}$

(C) -1

(D) 0

(E) $\dfrac{1}{2}$

256. In circle K shown, chords $\overline{AB}$ and $\overline{CD}$ intersect at point E within the circle. What is the value of x?

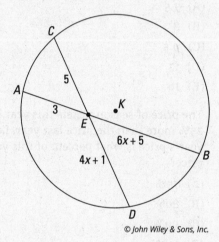

© John Wiley & Sons, Inc.

(A) 3

(B) 5

(C) 10

(D) 21

(E) 35

257. In a survey of students at a certain college, participants were asked two questions. If $\frac{2}{3}$ of those surveyed responded "Strongly Agree" to the first question, and of those respondents, $\frac{1}{5}$ answered "Strongly Agree" to the second question, what portion of the survey participants did not answer "Strongly Agree" to both questions?

(A) $\frac{13}{15}$

(B) $\frac{5}{6}$

(C) $\frac{3}{4}$

(D) $\frac{3}{5}$

(E) $\frac{2}{15}$

258. Babia has seven more marbles than three times the number of marbles that Joe has. If Babia has B marbles and Joe has J marbles, which of the following is a possible value for B?

I.   10

II. 18

III. 49

(A) I only

(B) II only

(C) III only

(D) I and III only

(E) I, II, and III

259. In the figure shown, what is the value of z?

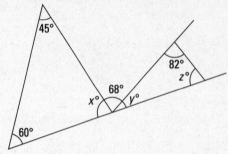

(A) 37

(B) 47

(C) 51

(D) 61

(E) 75

260. When positive integer N is divided by 7, the remainder is x, and when positive integer M is divided by 11, the remainder is y. What is the greatest value for $x + y$?

(A) 14

(B) 15

(C) 16

(D) 17

(E) 18

261. If 3 is one root of the quadratic equation $2x^2 - 5x + k = 2$, where k is a constant, what is the equation's other root?

(A) –3

(B) $-\frac{1}{2}$

(C) –1

(D) $\frac{1}{2}$

(E) 3

Chapter **4**

Quantitative: Data Sufficiency

The Data Sufficiency questions are mixed in with the Problem Solving questions to make up the 37 questions of the GMAT Quantitative section, which must be completed in 75 minutes. (The directions for the specific question types will be presented each time they appear.) Data Sufficiency questions are exclusive to the GMAT. Each Data Sufficiency question poses a question, followed by two statements. Your task is to evaluate the statements to determine at what point there is or is not sufficient information to answer the question. Unlike the Problem Solving questions, you do not actually have to answer the question posed. Instead, you select one of five fixed answer choices that offer different options about the sufficiency of the information provided in the two statements. *Remember:* The five answer choices are exactly the same and in the same order for each question. No calculators are permitted during the Quantitative section.

The Problems You'll Work On

When working through the Data Sufficiency questions in this chapter, be prepared to select your answer choice based on your understanding of

>> **Basic math,** including fractions, decimals, ratios and proportions, percent, and exponents.

>> **Probability and Statistics,** including counting techniques, permutations and combinations, basic probability, arithmetic mean, median, mode, and standard deviation.

>> **Algebra,** including polynomials, linear equations and inequalities, quadratic equations, basic function concepts, and systems of linear equations.

>> **Geometry,** including angles, lines, two-dimensional shapes, three-dimensional solids, perimeter, area, surface area, volume, the Pythagorean theorem, and coordinate geometry.

>> **Word problems,** including percentages, rate-time-distance, consecutive integers, ages, work rate, coins, mixtures, divisibility, factors, sequences, and equation setup.

What to Watch Out For

Don't make these mistakes:

>> Failing to memorize the five fixed answer choices so you don't have to refer to them.

>> Failing to check whether the second statement is sufficient when the first statement is determined to be sufficient.

>> When the question posed is a yes or no question, carelessly deciding about sufficiency without ensuring that a *definite* yes or no answer is possible.

>> Spending too much time on a question that it is too difficult for you, instead of making a guess and moving on.

262. If x and y are both positive integers, is $xy \geq 250$?

   (1) $x = 300$

   (2) $50 < y < 100$

   (A) Statement (1) ALONE is sufficient, but statement (2) alone is not sufficient to answer the question asked.

   (B) Statement (2) ALONE is sufficient, but statement (1) alone is not sufficient to answer the question asked.

   (C) Both statements TOGETHER are sufficient, but NEITHER statement ALONE is sufficient to answer the question asked.

   (D) Each statement ALONE is sufficient to answer the question asked.

   (E) Statements (1) and (2) TOGETHER are NOT sufficient to answer the question asked.

263. A vehicle averaged x miles per hour for $1\frac{1}{2}$ hours and y miles per hour for $2\frac{1}{2}$ hours on a nonstop trip of d miles. What was the average speed, in miles per hour, for the entire trip?

   (1) $x = y + 10$

   (2) $d = 255$

   (A) Statement (1) ALONE is sufficient, but statement (2) alone is not sufficient to answer the question asked.

   (B) Statement (2) ALONE is sufficient, but statement (1) alone is not sufficient to answer the question asked.

   (C) Both statements TOGETHER are sufficient, but NEITHER statement ALONE is sufficient to answer the question asked.

   (D) Each statement ALONE is sufficient to answer the question asked.

   (E) Statements (1) and (2) TOGETHER are NOT sufficient to answer the question asked.

264. If x, y, and z are integers, is $xz < 0$?

(1) $xy > 0$

(2) $yz < 0$

(A) Statement (1) ALONE is sufficient, but statement (2) alone is not sufficient to answer the question asked.

(B) Statement (2) ALONE is sufficient, but statement (1) alone is not sufficient to answer the question asked.

(C) Both statements TOGETHER are sufficient, but NEITHER statement ALONE is sufficient to answer the question asked.

(D) Each statement ALONE is sufficient to answer the question asked.

(E) Statements (1) and (2) TOGETHER are NOT sufficient to answer the question asked.

265. If $n > 1$, does the integer n have a prime factor k?

(1) $1 < k < n$

(2) $10! + 2 \le n \le 10! + 10$

(A) Statement (1) ALONE is sufficient, but statement (2) alone is not sufficient to answer the question asked.

(B) Statement (2) ALONE is sufficient, but statement (1) alone is not sufficient to answer the question asked.

(C) Both statements TOGETHER are sufficient, but NEITHER statement ALONE is sufficient to answer the question asked.

(D) Each statement ALONE is sufficient to answer the question asked.

(E) Statements (1) and (2) TOGETHER are NOT sufficient to answer the question asked.

266. A campus organization is selling tee shirts to raise money for a charity. What amount does the organization expect to donate to the charity?

(1) The organization expects to sell 1,000 tee shirts.

(2) The organization sells 500 more tee shirts than expected, for a total donation of $30,000 to the charity.

(A) Statement (1) ALONE is sufficient, but statement (2) alone is not sufficient to answer the question asked.

(B) Statement (2) ALONE is sufficient, but statement (1) alone is not sufficient to answer the question asked.

(C) Both statements TOGETHER are sufficient, but NEITHER statement ALONE is sufficient to answer the question asked.

(D) Each statement ALONE is sufficient to answer the question asked.

(E) Statements (1) and (2) TOGETHER are NOT sufficient to answer the question asked.

267. Viggo has 25 hardcover books that he is arranging upright on the top shelf of a bookcase. Will the 25 books fit on the top shelf?

  (1) The top shelf of Viggo's bookcase has a length of 36 inches.

  (2) The average (arithmetic mean) thickness of the 25 books is at most $1\frac{1}{2}$ inches.

  (A) Statement (1) ALONE is sufficient, but statement (2) alone is not sufficient to answer the question asked.

  (B) Statement (2) ALONE is sufficient, but statement (1) alone is not sufficient to answer the question asked.

  (C) Both statements TOGETHER are sufficient, but NEITHER statement ALONE is sufficient to answer the question asked.

  (D) Each statement ALONE is sufficient to answer the question asked.

  (E) Statements (1) and (2) TOGETHER are NOT sufficient to answer the question asked.

268. How many dolls does Josephine currently have?

  (1) If Josephine gets 2 more dolls for her birthday, she will have a least 14 dolls.

  (2) If Josephine donates 3 of her dolls to a toy drive, she will have less than 10 dolls.

  (A) Statement (1) ALONE is sufficient, but statement (2) alone is not sufficient to answer the question asked.

  (B) Statement (2) ALONE is sufficient, but statement (1) alone is not sufficient to answer the question asked.

  (C) Both statements TOGETHER are sufficient, but NEITHER statement ALONE is sufficient to answer the question asked.

  (D) Each statement ALONE is sufficient to answer the question asked.

  (E) Statements (1) and (2) TOGETHER are NOT sufficient to answer the question asked.

269. Is x a negative number?

  (1) $-x^3 > 0$

  (2) $-3x > 0$

  (A) Statement (1) ALONE is sufficient, but statement (2) alone is not sufficient to answer the question asked.

  (B) Statement (2) ALONE is sufficient, but statement (1) alone is not sufficient to answer the question asked.

  (C) Both statements TOGETHER are sufficient, but NEITHER statement ALONE is sufficient to answer the question asked.

  (D) Each statement ALONE is sufficient to answer the question asked.

  (E) Statements (1) and (2) TOGETHER are NOT sufficient to answer the question asked.

270. A garden contains 32 tomato plants. How many pepper plants does the garden contain?

  (1) The ratio of the number of tomato plants to the number of pepper plants is 8 to 3.

  (2) If the number of tomato plants is increased by 4, and the number of pepper plants stays the same, the ratio of the number of tomato plants to the number of pepper plants is 3 to 1.

  (A) Statement (1) ALONE is sufficient, but statement (2) alone is not sufficient to answer the question asked.

  (B) Statement (2) ALONE is sufficient, but statement (1) alone is not sufficient to answer the question asked.

  (C) Both statements TOGETHER are sufficient, but NEITHER statement ALONE is sufficient to answer the question asked.

  (D) Each statement ALONE is sufficient to answer the question asked.

  (E) Statements (1) and (2) TOGETHER are NOT sufficient to answer the question asked.

271. A grocer sells avocados for $1.50 each and pineapples for $2.00 each. How many avocados did the grocer sell today?

(1) The number of avocados sold today is 20 more than twice the number of pineapples sold.

(2) Today the grocer received a total of $155 from the sale of avocados and pineapples.

(A) Statement (1) ALONE is sufficient, but statement (2) alone is not sufficient to answer the question asked.

(B) Statement (2) ALONE is sufficient, but statement (1) alone is not sufficient to answer the question asked.

(C) Both statements TOGETHER are sufficient, but NEITHER statement ALONE is sufficient to answer the question asked.

(D) Each statement ALONE is sufficient to answer the question asked.

(E) Statements (1) and (2) TOGETHER are NOT sufficient to answer the question asked.

272. A box contains only black, green, and red chips, all identical except for color. How many red chips are in the box?

(1) The box contains 48 chips, 16 of which are black.

(2) The probability is $\frac{1}{2}$ that a chip randomly drawn from the box is green.

(A) Statement (1) ALONE is sufficient, but statement (2) alone is not sufficient to answer the question asked.

(B) Statement (2) ALONE is sufficient, but statement (1) alone is not sufficient to answer the question asked.

(C) Both statements TOGETHER are sufficient, but NEITHER statement ALONE is sufficient to answer the question asked.

(D) Each statement ALONE is sufficient to answer the question asked.

(E) Statements (1) and (2) TOGETHER are NOT sufficient to answer the question asked.

273. If $a > 0$, what is the value of $a^{\frac{1}{2}}$?

(1) $a^{\frac{1}{8}} = 16$

(2) $a^{\frac{1}{32}} = 2$

(A) Statement (1) ALONE is sufficient, but statement (2) alone is not sufficient to answer the question asked.

(B) Statement (2) ALONE is sufficient, but statement (1) alone is not sufficient to answer the question asked.

(C) Both statements TOGETHER are sufficient, but NEITHER statement ALONE is sufficient to answer the question asked.

(D) Each statement ALONE is sufficient to answer the question asked.

(E) Statements (1) and (2) TOGETHER are NOT sufficient to answer the question asked.

274. What is the value of 20 percent of B?

(1) 15 percent of B is 375.

(2) B is 40 percent of 6,250.

(A) Statement (1) ALONE is sufficient, but statement (2) alone is not sufficient to answer the question asked.

(B) Statement (2) ALONE is sufficient, but statement (1) alone is not sufficient to answer the question asked.

(C) Both statements TOGETHER are sufficient, but NEITHER statement ALONE is sufficient to answer the question asked.

(D) Each statement ALONE is sufficient to answer the question asked.

(E) Statements (1) and (2) TOGETHER are NOT sufficient to answer the question asked.

275. In the figure shown, what is the value of z?

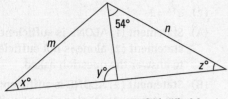

© John Wiley & Sons, Inc.

(1) m = n

(2) y = 88

(A) Statement (1) ALONE is sufficient, but statement (2) alone is not sufficient to answer the question asked.

(B) Statement (2) ALONE is sufficient, but statement (1) alone is not sufficient to answer the question asked.

(C) Both statements TOGETHER are sufficient, but NEITHER statement ALONE is sufficient to answer the question asked.

(D) Each statement ALONE is sufficient to answer the question asked.

(E) Statements (1) and (2) TOGETHER are NOT sufficient to answer the question asked.

276. Parallel lines p and q have equal slope m. Is m < 0?

(1) The line p intercepts the y-axis at the point (0,3).

(2) The line q intercepts the x-axis at the point (3,0).

(A) Statement (1) ALONE is sufficient, but statement (2) alone is not sufficient to answer the question asked.

(B) Statement (2) ALONE is sufficient, but statement (1) alone is not sufficient to answer the question asked.

(C) Both statements TOGETHER are sufficient, but NEITHER statement ALONE is sufficient to answer the question asked.

(D) Each statement ALONE is sufficient to answer the question asked.

(E) Statements (1) and (2) TOGETHER are NOT sufficient to answer the question asked.

277. Do at least 40 percent of the students enrolled at Sunshine Elementary School ride the bus to school?

(1) 10 percent of the students enrolled at Sunshine Elementary School walk to school.

(2) The number of students enrolled at Sunshine Elementary School who ride the bus to school is three times the number of students who do not ride the bus.

(A) Statement (1) ALONE is sufficient, but statement (2) alone is not sufficient to answer the question asked.

(B) Statement (2) ALONE is sufficient, but statement (1) alone is not sufficient to answer the question asked.

(C) Both statements TOGETHER are sufficient, but NEITHER statement ALONE is sufficient to answer the question asked.

(D) Each statement ALONE is sufficient to answer the question asked.

(E) Statements (1) and (2) TOGETHER are NOT sufficient to answer the question asked.

278. Is k an even integer?

(1) $5k + 2$ is even.

(2) $k^2 + 1$ is odd.

(A) Statement (1) ALONE is sufficient, but statement (2) alone is not sufficient to answer the question asked.

(B) Statement (2) ALONE is sufficient, but statement (1) alone is not sufficient to answer the question asked.

(C) Both statements TOGETHER are sufficient, but NEITHER statement ALONE is sufficient to answer the question asked.

(D) Each statement ALONE is sufficient to answer the question asked.

(E) Statements (1) and (2) TOGETHER are NOT sufficient to answer the question asked.

279. If Hollis's gross hourly pay is increased by $2 per hour, how many fewer hours per week could Hollis work to earn the same gross weekly pay that she currently receives for working 40 hours per week?

(1) A pay increase of $2 per hour will result in a new gross hourly pay that is $1\frac{1}{9}$ of Hollis's current gross hourly pay.

(2) Hollis's current gross weekly pay is $720.

(A) Statement (1) ALONE is sufficient, but statement (2) alone is not sufficient to answer the question asked.

(B) Statement (2) ALONE is sufficient, but statement (1) alone is not sufficient to answer the question asked.

(C) Both statements TOGETHER are sufficient, but NEITHER statement ALONE is sufficient to answer the question asked.

(D) Each statement ALONE is sufficient to answer the question asked.

(E) Statements (1) and (2) TOGETHER are NOT sufficient to answer the question asked.

280. Does $b = (ac)^{-1}$?

(1) $abc = 1$

(2) $(abc)^{-1} = 1$

(A) Statement (1) ALONE is sufficient, but statement (2) alone is not sufficient to answer the question asked.

(B) Statement (2) ALONE is sufficient, but statement (1) alone is not sufficient to answer the question asked.

(C) Both statements TOGETHER are sufficient, but NEITHER statement ALONE is sufficient to answer the question asked.

(D) Each statement ALONE is sufficient to answer the question asked.

(E) Statements (1) and (2) TOGETHER are NOT sufficient to answer the question asked.

281. If k is an integer and M and D are the least common multiple and the greatest common factor of $9k + 8$ and $6k + 5$, respectively, is $M = 54k^2 + 93k + 40$?

(1) $D = 1$

(2) D is a factor of $3k + 3$

(A) Statement (1) ALONE is sufficient, but statement (2) alone is not sufficient to answer the question asked.

(B) Statement (2) ALONE is sufficient, but statement (1) alone is not sufficient to answer the question asked.

(C) Both statements TOGETHER are sufficient, but NEITHER statement ALONE is sufficient to answer the question asked.

(D) Each statement ALONE is sufficient to answer the question asked.

(E) Statements (1) and (2) TOGETHER are NOT sufficient to answer the question asked.

282. What is the value of $\frac{4a-3b}{a-2b}$?

(1) $\frac{3a-b}{a-2b} = 1$

(2) $a - b = 3$

(A) Statement (1) ALONE is sufficient, but statement (2) alone is not sufficient to answer the question asked.

(B) Statement (2) ALONE is sufficient, but statement (1) alone is not sufficient to answer the question asked.

(C) Both statements TOGETHER are sufficient, but NEITHER statement ALONE is sufficient to answer the question asked.

(D) Each statement ALONE is sufficient to answer the question asked.

(E) Statements (1) and (2) TOGETHER are NOT sufficient to answer the question asked.

283. If K is a positive integer, what is the units digit of K?

(1) The units digit of $2K$ is 6.

(2) The hundreds digit of $100K$ is 8.

(A) Statement (1) ALONE is sufficient, but statement (2) alone is not sufficient to answer the question asked.

(B) Statement (2) ALONE is sufficient, but statement (1) alone is not sufficient to answer the question asked.

(C) Both statements TOGETHER are sufficient, but NEITHER statement ALONE is sufficient to answer the question asked.

(D) Each statement ALONE is sufficient to answer the question asked.

(E) Statements (1) and (2) TOGETHER are NOT sufficient to answer the question asked.

284. If m and n are both positive integers is $\sqrt[6]{m+n^4}$ an integer?

(1) $m = n^4 + n^5$

(2) $m = n^4(n^2 - 1)$

(A) Statement (1) ALONE is sufficient, but statement (2) alone is not sufficient to answer the question asked.

(B) Statement (2) ALONE is sufficient, but statement (1) alone is not sufficient to answer the question asked.

(C) Both statements TOGETHER are sufficient, but NEITHER statement ALONE is sufficient to answer the question asked.

(D) Each statement ALONE is sufficient to answer the question asked.

(E) Statements (1) and (2) TOGETHER are NOT sufficient to answer the question asked.

285. If m and n are positive integers, is $\frac{m}{n} < \frac{3}{7}$?

(1) $\frac{m}{n} < 0.42$

(2) $\left(\frac{m}{n}\right)^{-1} > 2.5$

(A) Statement (1) ALONE is sufficient, but statement (2) alone is not sufficient to answer the question asked.

(B) Statement (2) ALONE is sufficient, but statement (1) alone is not sufficient to answer the question asked.

(C) Both statements TOGETHER are sufficient, but NEITHER statement ALONE is sufficient to answer the question asked.

(D) Each statement ALONE is sufficient to answer the question asked.

(E) Statements (1) and (2) TOGETHER are NOT sufficient to answer the question asked.

286. A sales clerk in an electronics store earns commission on total weekly sales. What amount, in dollars, did the sales clerk earn as commission on last week's total sales?

(1) The electronic store pays sales personnel a commission rate of 2 percent on total weekly sales.

(2) The amount of the sales clerk's total weekly sales last week was $500 more than the sales clerk's total weekly sales the previous week.

(A) Statement (1) ALONE is sufficient, but statement (2) alone is not sufficient to answer the question asked.

(B) Statement (2) ALONE is sufficient, but statement (1) alone is not sufficient to answer the question asked.

(C) Both statements TOGETHER are sufficient, but NEITHER statement ALONE is sufficient to answer the question asked.

(D) Each statement ALONE is sufficient to answer the question asked.

(E) Statements (1) and (2) TOGETHER are NOT sufficient to answer the question asked.

287. Amari, Belen, and Chiaki all make purchases from the same vendor at an outdoor market. The vendor sells fruits and vegetables priced at a certain amount for each one. How much does Chiaki pay for 1 banana and 2 navel oranges?

(1) Amari bought four bananas for $1.00.

(2) Belen bought 3 bananas and 6 navel oranges for $6.15.

(A) Statement (1) ALONE is sufficient, but statement (2) alone is not sufficient to answer the question asked.

(B) Statement (2) ALONE is sufficient, but statement (1) alone is not sufficient to answer the question asked.

(C) Both statements TOGETHER are sufficient, but NEITHER statement ALONE is sufficient to answer the question asked.

(D) Each statement ALONE is sufficient to answer the question asked.

(E) Statements (1) and (2) TOGETHER are NOT sufficient to answer the question asked.

288. What is the area of the right triangle shown?

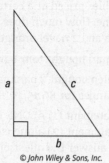

© John Wiley & Sons, Inc.

(1) $a + b = 14$

(2) $c^2 = a^2 + 36$

(A) Statement (1) ALONE is sufficient, but statement (2) alone is not sufficient to answer the question asked.

(B) Statement (2) ALONE is sufficient, but statement (1) alone is not sufficient to answer the question asked.

(C) Both statements TOGETHER are sufficient, but NEITHER statement ALONE is sufficient to answer the question asked.

(D) Each statement ALONE is sufficient to answer the question asked.

(E) Statements (1) and (2) TOGETHER are NOT sufficient to answer the question asked.

289. If $A = \dfrac{7x}{5y}$, with $y \neq 0$, what is the value of A?

(1) $x = 10y$

(2) $x = \dfrac{5}{7}$

(A) Statement (1) ALONE is sufficient, but statement (2) alone is not sufficient to answer the question asked.

(B) Statement (2) ALONE is sufficient, but statement (1) alone is not sufficient to answer the question asked.

(C) Both statements TOGETHER are sufficient, but NEITHER statement ALONE is sufficient to answer the question asked.

(D) Each statement ALONE is sufficient to answer the question asked.

(E) Statements (1) and (2) TOGETHER are NOT sufficient to answer the question asked.

290. If the mean (arithmetic average) of eight numbers is 60, how many of the eight numbers equal 60?

(1) None of the eight numbers is less than 60.

(2) None of the eight numbers is greater than 60.

(A) Statement (1) ALONE is sufficient, but statement (2) alone is not sufficient to answer the question asked.

(B) Statement (2) ALONE is sufficient, but statement (1) alone is not sufficient to answer the question asked.

(C) Both statements TOGETHER are sufficient, but NEITHER statement ALONE is sufficient to answer the question asked.

(D) Each statement ALONE is sufficient to answer the question asked.

(E) Statements (1) and (2) TOGETHER are NOT sufficient to answer the question asked.

291. Do at least 20 percent of the organization members who are over 40 have college degrees?

(1) Among the member of the organization who are over 40, 24 percent of the female members and 16 percent of the male members have college degrees.

(2) Female members constitute 55 percent of the organization's membership.

(A) Statement (1) ALONE is sufficient, but statement (2) alone is not sufficient to answer the question asked.

(B) Statement (2) ALONE is sufficient, but statement (1) alone is not sufficient to answer the question asked.

(C) Both statements TOGETHER are sufficient, but NEITHER statement ALONE is sufficient to answer the question asked.

(D) Each statement ALONE is sufficient to answer the question asked.

(E) Statements (1) and (2) TOGETHER are NOT sufficient to answer the question asked.

292. On a number line, $0 < A < B$, is $|20 - A| < |20 - B|$?

(1) $A + 20 < 2B$

(2) $B = 3A$

(A) Statement (1) ALONE is sufficient, but statement (2) alone is not sufficient to answer the question asked.

(B) Statement (2) ALONE is sufficient, but statement (1) alone is not sufficient to answer the question asked.

(C) Both statements TOGETHER are sufficient, but NEITHER statement ALONE is sufficient to answer the question asked.

(D) Each statement ALONE is sufficient to answer the question asked.

(E) Statements (1) and (2) TOGETHER are NOT sufficient to answer the question asked.

293. If N is an integer, is $\frac{36}{N}$ an integer?

(1) N is a multiple of 9.

(2) $9 < N < 27$

(A) Statement (1) ALONE is sufficient, but statement (2) alone is not sufficient to answer the question asked.

(B) Statement (2) ALONE is sufficient, but statement (1) alone is not sufficient to answer the question asked.

(C) Both statements TOGETHER are sufficient, but NEITHER statement ALONE is sufficient to answer the question asked.

(D) Each statement ALONE is sufficient to answer the question asked.

(E) Statements (1) and (2) TOGETHER are NOT sufficient to answer the question asked.

294. If x and y are both positive numbers, is $\frac{x}{y} > \frac{y}{x}$?

(1) $\frac{4y}{x} = 5$

(2) $x + 4 = y$

(A) Statement (1) ALONE is sufficient, but statement (2) alone is not sufficient to answer the question asked.

(B) Statement (2) ALONE is sufficient, but statement (1) alone is not sufficient to answer the question asked.

(C) Both statements TOGETHER are sufficient, but NEITHER statement ALONE is sufficient to answer the question asked.

(D) Each statement ALONE is sufficient to answer the question asked.

(E) Statements (1) and (2) TOGETHER are NOT sufficient to answer the question asked.

295. If $xy \neq 0$, what is the ratio of $\frac{x}{6}$ to $\frac{y}{7}$?

(1) $7x = 6y$

(2) $x = 6$

(A) Statement (1) ALONE is sufficient, but statement (2) alone is not sufficient to answer the question asked.

(B) Statement (2) ALONE is sufficient, but statement (1) alone is not sufficient to answer the question asked.

(C) Both statements TOGETHER are sufficient, but NEITHER statement ALONE is sufficient to answer the question asked.

(D) Each statement ALONE is sufficient to answer the question asked.

(E) Statements (1) and (2) TOGETHER are NOT sufficient to answer the question asked.

296. In a certain high school, how many seniors are enrolled in both AP calculus and AP statistics?

(1) 45 seniors are enrolled in AP calculus.

(2) 60 seniors are enrolled in either AP calculus or AP statistics or both.

(A) Statement (1) ALONE is sufficient, but statement (2) alone is not sufficient to answer the question asked.

(B) Statement (2) ALONE is sufficient, but statement (1) alone is not sufficient to answer the question asked.

(C) Both statements TOGETHER are sufficient, but NEITHER statement ALONE is sufficient to answer the question asked.

(D) Each statement ALONE is sufficient to answer the question asked.

(E) Statements (1) and (2) TOGETHER are NOT sufficient to answer the question asked.

297. Micah saved $300 of his take-home pay last month. How much was Micah's take-home pay last month?

(1) From last month's take-home pay, Micah paid three times as much in rent as he saved.

(2) Micah spent 50% of his take-home pay on living expenses, and saved 25% of the remainder.

(A) Statement (1) ALONE is sufficient, but statement (2) alone is not sufficient to answer the question asked.

(B) Statement (2) ALONE is sufficient, but statement (1) alone is not sufficient to answer the question asked.

(C) Both statements TOGETHER are sufficient, but NEITHER statement ALONE is sufficient to answer the question asked.

(D) Each statement ALONE is sufficient to answer the question asked.

(E) Statements (1) and (2) TOGETHER are NOT sufficient to answer the question asked.

298. In the figure shown, what is the value of x?

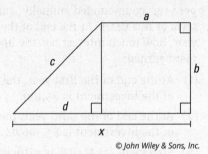

© John Wiley & Sons, Inc.

(1) $a = b = 4$

(2) $c = 4\sqrt{2}$

(A) Statement (1) ALONE is sufficient, but statement (2) alone is not sufficient to answer the question asked.

(B) Statement (2) ALONE is sufficient, but statement (1) alone is not sufficient to answer the question asked.

(C) Both statements TOGETHER are sufficient, but NEITHER statement ALONE is sufficient to answer the question asked.

(D) Each statement ALONE is sufficient to answer the question asked.

(E) Statements (1) and (2) TOGETHER are NOT sufficient to answer the question asked.

299. Given an arithmetic sequence of N terms in which the common difference between terms is 2, what is the value of N?

(1) The first term is 18.

(2) The last term is 70.

(A) Statement (1) ALONE is sufficient, but statement (2) alone is not sufficient to answer the question asked.

(B) Statement (2) ALONE is sufficient, but statement (1) alone is not sufficient to answer the question asked.

(C) Both statements TOGETHER are sufficient, but NEITHER statement ALONE is sufficient to answer the question asked.

(D) Each statement ALONE is sufficient to answer the question asked.

(E) Statements (1) and (2) TOGETHER are NOT sufficient to answer the question asked.

300. A mixture consists of flaxseed and cornmeal in the ratio 1 to 4, respectively. How many cups of flaxseed are used to make the mixture?

(1) There are a total of 15 cups in the mixture.

(2) The ratio of the number of cups of flaxseed to the total number of cups in the mixture is 1 to 5.

(A) Statement (1) ALONE is sufficient, but statement (2) alone is not sufficient to answer the question asked.

(B) Statement (2) ALONE is sufficient, but statement (1) alone is not sufficient to answer the question asked.

(C) Both statements TOGETHER are sufficient, but NEITHER statement ALONE is sufficient to answer the question asked.

(D) Each statement ALONE is sufficient to answer the question asked.

(E) Statements (1) and (2) TOGETHER are NOT sufficient to answer the question asked.

301. What is the fifth term of the geometric sequence?

(1) The second term of the geometric sequence is 12.

(2) The fourth term of the geometric sequence is 432.

(A) Statement (1) ALONE is sufficient, but statement (2) alone is not sufficient to answer the question asked.

(B) Statement (2) ALONE is sufficient, but statement (1) alone is not sufficient to answer the question asked.

(C) Both statements TOGETHER are sufficient, but NEITHER statement ALONE is sufficient to answer the question asked.

(D) Each statement ALONE is sufficient to answer the question asked.

(E) Statements (1) and (2) TOGETHER are NOT sufficient to answer the question asked.

302. What is the value of x^{-4}?

(1) $x^{-2} = 225$

(2) $x^4 = \dfrac{1}{50,625}$

(A) Statement (1) ALONE is sufficient, but statement (2) alone is not sufficient to answer the question asked.

(B) Statement (2) ALONE is sufficient, but statement (1) alone is not sufficient to answer the question asked.

(C) Both statements TOGETHER are sufficient, but NEITHER statement ALONE is sufficient to answer the question asked.

(D) Each statement ALONE is sufficient to answer the question asked.

(E) Statements (1) and (2) TOGETHER are NOT sufficient to answer the question asked.

303. An investor purchases a certificate of deposit with a fixed interest rate of 2% per year, compounded annually, and a term of five years. At the end of the fifth year, how much interest has the investment earned?

(1) At the end of the first year, the value of the investment is $5,100.

(2) At the end of the third year, the value of the investment is $5,306.04.

(A) Statement (1) ALONE is sufficient, but statement (2) alone is not sufficient to answer the question asked.

(B) Statement (2) ALONE is sufficient, but statement (1) alone is not sufficient to answer the question asked.

(C) Both statements TOGETHER are sufficient, but NEITHER statement ALONE is sufficient to answer the question asked.

(D) Each statement ALONE is sufficient to answer the question asked.

(E) Statements (1) and (2) TOGETHER are NOT sufficient to answer the question asked.

304. Is the sum of the roots of the equation, $x^2 + bx + c = 0$, positive?

(1) $b < 0$

(2) $c < 0$

(A) Statement (1) ALONE is sufficient, but statement (2) alone is not sufficient to answer the question asked.

(B) Statement (2) ALONE is sufficient, but statement (1) alone is not sufficient to answer the question asked.

(C) Both statements TOGETHER are sufficient, but NEITHER statement ALONE is sufficient to answer the question asked.

(D) Each statement ALONE is sufficient to answer the question asked.

(E) Statements (1) and (2) TOGETHER are NOT sufficient to answer the question asked.

305. A 500-gallon cistern is filled to half its capacity with water. At what rate, in gallons per minute, is the amount of water in the cistern increasing if both the inlet pipe and outlet pipe are open?

(1) The inlet pipe pumps water into the cistern at a rate of 7 gallons per 30 seconds.

(2) The outlet pipe pumps water out of the cistern at the rate of 12 gallons every 1 minute 30 seconds.

(A) Statement (1) ALONE is sufficient, but statement (2) alone is not sufficient to answer the question asked.

(B) Statement (2) ALONE is sufficient, but statement (1) alone is not sufficient to answer the question asked.

(C) Both statements TOGETHER are sufficient, but NEITHER statement ALONE is sufficient to answer the question asked.

(D) Each statement ALONE is sufficient to answer the question asked.

(E) Statements (1) and (2) TOGETHER are NOT sufficient to answer the question asked.

306. In a fleet of 70 cars that are either black or white. What is the ratio of the number of black cars to the number of white cars in the fleet?

(1) The number of black cars is 10 more than twice the number of white cars.

(2) The ratio of the number of black cars to the number of cars in the fleet is $\frac{3}{7}$ more than the ratio of the number of white cars to the number of cars in the fleet.

(A) Statement (1) ALONE is sufficient, but statement (2) alone is not sufficient to answer the question asked.

(B) Statement (2) ALONE is sufficient, but statement (1) alone is not sufficient to answer the question asked.

(C) Both statements TOGETHER are sufficient, but NEITHER statement ALONE is sufficient to answer the question asked.

(D) Each statement ALONE is sufficient to answer the question asked.

(E) Statements (1) and (2) TOGETHER are NOT sufficient to answer the question asked.

307. What is the value of $m - n$?

(1) $n^2 = 25$

(2) $m^2 = 49$

(A) Statement (1) ALONE is sufficient, but statement (2) alone is not sufficient to answer the question asked.

(B) Statement (2) ALONE is sufficient, but statement (1) alone is not sufficient to answer the question asked.

(C) Both statements TOGETHER are sufficient, but NEITHER statement ALONE is sufficient to answer the question asked.

(D) Each statement ALONE is sufficient to answer the question asked.

(E) Statements (1) and (2) TOGETHER are NOT sufficient to answer the question asked.

308. The sale price of a ceiling fan was $250. After the sale, the price increased. What is the percent increase in the sale price?

(1) The original price of the ceiling fan was $312.50.

(2) The sale price increased by $50.

(A) Statement (1) ALONE is sufficient, but statement (2) alone is not sufficient to answer the question asked.

(B) Statement (2) ALONE is sufficient, but statement (1) alone is not sufficient to answer the question asked.

(C) Both statements TOGETHER are sufficient, but NEITHER statement ALONE is sufficient to answer the question asked.

(D) Each statement ALONE is sufficient to answer the question asked.

(E) Statements (1) and (2) TOGETHER are NOT sufficient to answer the question asked.

309. If p and q are positive integers, is pq a multiple of 36?

(1) $p = 6x$, where x is a prime number.

(2) $q = 15y$, where y is a positive integer.

(A) Statement (1) ALONE is sufficient, but statement (2) alone is not sufficient to answer the question asked.

(B) Statement (2) ALONE is sufficient, but statement (1) alone is not sufficient to answer the question asked.

(C) Both statements TOGETHER are sufficient, but NEITHER statement ALONE is sufficient to answer the question asked.

(D) Each statement ALONE is sufficient to answer the question asked.

(E) Statements (1) and (2) TOGETHER are NOT sufficient to answer the question asked.

310. What is the remainder when the 4-digit positive number, $1{,}000a + 100b + 10c + d$, is divided by 3?

(1) $a + b + c + d = 17$

(2) $(1{,}000a + 100b + 10c + d) - 2$ is divisible by 3.

(A) Statement (1) ALONE is sufficient, but statement (2) alone is not sufficient to answer the question asked.

(B) Statement (2) ALONE is sufficient, but statement (1) alone is not sufficient to answer the question asked.

(C) Both statements TOGETHER are sufficient, but NEITHER statement ALONE is sufficient to answer the question asked.

(D) Each statement ALONE is sufficient to answer the question asked.

(E) Statements (1) and (2) TOGETHER are NOT sufficient to answer the question asked.

311. Is $x^2 > 1$?

(1) $x < 1$

(2) $x > -1$

(A) Statement (1) ALONE is sufficient, but statement (2) alone is not sufficient to answer the question asked.

(B) Statement (2) ALONE is sufficient, but statement (1) alone is not sufficient to answer the question asked.

(C) Both statements TOGETHER are sufficient, but NEITHER statement ALONE is sufficient to answer the question asked.

(D) Each statement ALONE is sufficient to answer the question asked.

(E) Statements (1) and (2) TOGETHER are NOT sufficient to answer the question asked.

312. A pair of athletic shoes that usually sells for $170 is marked down for a clearance sale. If the sales tax rate is 8 percent, how much does the customer pay for the marked-down shoes, including sales tax?

(1) Including sales tax, the customer saves a total of $36.72.

(2) The sales tax on the marked-down price is $10.88.

(A) Statement (1) ALONE is sufficient, but statement (2) alone is not sufficient to answer the question asked.

(B) Statement (2) ALONE is sufficient, but statement (1) alone is not sufficient to answer the question asked.

(C) Both statements TOGETHER are sufficient, but NEITHER statement ALONE is sufficient to answer the question asked.

(D) Each statement ALONE is sufficient to answer the question asked.

(E) Statements (1) and (2) TOGETHER are NOT sufficient to answer the question asked.

313. If n is an integer such that $3 \leq n \leq 7$, what is the unit's digit of n^2?

(1) $(n+1)^2$ has units digit 6.

(2) $(n-1)^2$ has units digit 6.

(A) Statement (1) ALONE is sufficient, but statement (2) alone is not sufficient to answer the question asked.

(B) Statement (2) ALONE is sufficient, but statement (1) alone is not sufficient to answer the question asked.

(C) Both statements TOGETHER are sufficient, but NEITHER statement ALONE is sufficient to answer the question asked.

(D) Each statement ALONE is sufficient to answer the question asked.

(E) Statements (1) and (2) TOGETHER are NOT sufficient to answer the question asked.

314. How old will Mayte be in 5 years?

(1) In 10 years, Mayte will be $1\frac{1}{2}$ times as old as she is now.

(2) Five years ago, Mayte was $\frac{3}{4}$ as old as she is now.

(A) Statement (1) ALONE is sufficient, but statement (2) alone is not sufficient to answer the question asked.

(B) Statement (2) ALONE is sufficient, but statement (1) alone is not sufficient to answer the question asked.

(C) Both statements TOGETHER are sufficient, but NEITHER statement ALONE is sufficient to answer the question asked.

(D) Each statement ALONE is sufficient to answer the question asked.

(E) Statements (1) and (2) TOGETHER are NOT sufficient to answer the question asked.

315. Is $x > y$?

(1) $x = \frac{1}{7}\left(91^{25}\right)$

(2) $y = 13\left(91^{24}\right)$

(A) Statement (1) ALONE is sufficient, but statement (2) alone is not sufficient to answer the question asked.

(B) Statement (2) ALONE is sufficient, but statement (1) alone is not sufficient to answer the question asked.

(C) Both statements TOGETHER are sufficient, but NEITHER statement ALONE is sufficient to answer the question asked.

(D) Each statement ALONE is sufficient to answer the question asked.

(E) Statements (1) and (2) TOGETHER are NOT sufficient to answer the question asked.

316. Three integers A, B, and C are in the ratio 2 to 3 to 5, respectively. What is the sum of the three integers?

(1) $A + B = C$

(2) $C - A = 24$

(A) Statement (1) ALONE is sufficient, but statement (2) alone is not sufficient to answer the question asked.

(B) Statement (2) ALONE is sufficient, but statement (1) alone is not sufficient to answer the question asked.

(C) Both statements TOGETHER are sufficient, but NEITHER statement ALONE is sufficient to answer the question asked.

(D) Each statement ALONE is sufficient to answer the question asked.

(E) Statements (1) and (2) TOGETHER are NOT sufficient to answer the question asked.

317. What is the value of $|x - 3|$?

(1) $x^2 - 6x = 16$

(2) $-3 < x < 9$

(A) Statement (1) ALONE is sufficient, but statement (2) alone is not sufficient to answer the question asked.

(B) Statement (2) ALONE is sufficient, but statement (1) alone is not sufficient to answer the question asked.

(C) Both statements TOGETHER are sufficient, but NEITHER statement ALONE is sufficient to answer the question asked.

(D) Each statement ALONE is sufficient to answer the question asked.

(E) Statements (1) and (2) TOGETHER are NOT sufficient to answer the question asked.

318. The sum of two positive integers is 21. What is the value of the larger integer?

(1) The product of the two integers is 104.

(2) The larger integer is a prime number.

(A) Statement (1) ALONE is sufficient, but statement (2) alone is not sufficient to answer the question asked.

(B) Statement (2) ALONE is sufficient, but statement (1) alone is not sufficient to answer the question asked.

(C) Both statements TOGETHER are sufficient, but NEITHER statement ALONE is sufficient to answer the question asked.

(D) Each statement ALONE is sufficient to answer the question asked.

(E) Statements (1) and (2) TOGETHER are NOT sufficient to answer the question asked.

319. A coin bank contains only dimes and quarters. How many quarters are in the coin bank?

(1) There are twice as many dimes as quarters in the coin bank.

(2) The total face value of the coins in the coin bank is $9.90.

(A) Statement (1) ALONE is sufficient, but statement (2) alone is not sufficient to answer the question asked.

(B) Statement (2) ALONE is sufficient, but statement (1) alone is not sufficient to answer the question asked.

(C) Both statements TOGETHER are sufficient, but NEITHER statement ALONE is sufficient to answer the question asked.

(D) Each statement ALONE is sufficient to answer the question asked.

(E) Statements (1) and (2) TOGETHER are NOT sufficient to answer the question asked.

320. What is the average (arithmetic mean) of R, S, and T?

(1) $R + 2S + 3T = 30$

(2) $3R = 90 - (2S + T)$

(A) Statement (1) ALONE is sufficient, but statement (2) alone is not sufficient to answer the question asked.

(B) Statement (2) ALONE is sufficient, but statement (1) alone is not sufficient to answer the question asked.

(C) Both statements TOGETHER are sufficient, but NEITHER statement ALONE is sufficient to answer the question asked.

(D) Each statement ALONE is sufficient to answer the question asked.

(E) Statements (1) and (2) TOGETHER are NOT sufficient to answer the question asked.

321. Is $x < 0$?

(1) $x^3 + 8 < 0$

(2) $-\left(\frac{1}{4}x + 3\right) > 0$

(A) Statement (1) ALONE is sufficient, but statement (2) alone is not sufficient to answer the question asked.

(B) Statement (2) ALONE is sufficient, but statement (1) alone is not sufficient to answer the question asked.

(C) Both statements TOGETHER are sufficient, but NEITHER statement ALONE is sufficient to answer the question asked.

(D) Each statement ALONE is sufficient to answer the question asked.

(E) Statements (1) and (2) TOGETHER are NOT sufficient to answer the question asked.

322. What is the value of $\left(a\sqrt{5} + b\sqrt{5}\right)^2$?

(1) $a - b = 5$

(2) $a(a + b) = 81 - b(b + a)$

(A) Statement (1) ALONE is sufficient, but statement (2) alone is not sufficient to answer the question asked.

(B) Statement (2) ALONE is sufficient, but statement (1) alone is not sufficient to answer the question asked.

(C) Both statements TOGETHER are sufficient, but NEITHER statement ALONE is sufficient to answer the question asked.

(D) Each statement ALONE is sufficient to answer the question asked.

(E) Statements (1) and (2) TOGETHER are NOT sufficient to answer the question asked.

323. How many hours will it take 6 identical machines, working at their constant rates, to produce 1,200 components?

(1) Each machine produces 200 components.

(2) Two such machines, working at their constant rates, can produce 1,200 components in $4\frac{1}{2}$ hours.

(A) Statement (1) ALONE is sufficient, but statement (2) alone is not sufficient to answer the question asked.

(B) Statement (2) ALONE is sufficient, but statement (1) alone is not sufficient to answer the question asked.

(C) Both statements TOGETHER are sufficient, but NEITHER statement ALONE is sufficient to answer the question asked.

(D) Each statement ALONE is sufficient to answer the question asked.

(E) Statements (1) and (2) TOGETHER are NOT sufficient to answer the question asked.

324. A truck and a van leave the same location at the same time traveling in opposite directions. In how many hours will the two vehicles be 405 miles apart?

(1) The truck travels due east at 70 miles per hour.

(2) The van travels due west at 65 miles per hour.

(A) Statement (1) ALONE is sufficient, but statement (2) alone is not sufficient to answer the question asked.

(B) Statement (2) ALONE is sufficient, but statement (1) alone is not sufficient to answer the question asked.

(C) Both statements TOGETHER are sufficient, but NEITHER statement ALONE is sufficient to answer the question asked.

(D) Each statement ALONE is sufficient to answer the question asked.

(E) Statements (1) and (2) TOGETHER are NOT sufficient to answer the question asked.

325. If $x \neq 0$, what is the value of k?

(1) $\dfrac{3}{4x} + \dfrac{k}{3x} = \dfrac{1}{x}$

(2) $\dfrac{k}{x} = 2$

(A) Statement (1) ALONE is sufficient, but statement (2) alone is not sufficient to answer the question asked.

(B) Statement (2) ALONE is sufficient, but statement (1) alone is not sufficient to answer the question asked.

(C) Both statements TOGETHER are sufficient, but NEITHER statement ALONE is sufficient to answer the question asked.

(D) Each statement ALONE is sufficient to answer the question asked.

(E) Statements (1) and (2) TOGETHER are NOT sufficient to answer the question asked.

326. If $a_n = a_1 + (n-1)d$, what is the value of a_{51}?

(1) $a_{11} = 25$

(2) $a_{21} = 45$

(A) Statement (1) ALONE is sufficient, but statement (2) alone is not sufficient to answer the question asked.

(B) Statement (2) ALONE is sufficient, but statement (1) alone is not sufficient to answer the question asked.

(C) Both statements TOGETHER are sufficient, but NEITHER statement ALONE is sufficient to answer the question asked.

(D) Each statement ALONE is sufficient to answer the question asked.

(E) Statements (1) and (2) TOGETHER are NOT sufficient to answer the question asked.

327. If m and n are positive integers such that $m + n = 9$, what is the value of mn?

(1) $39 < 3m + 5n < 43$

(2) $8 \leq mn \leq 18$

(A) Statement (1) ALONE is sufficient, but statement (2) alone is not sufficient to answer the question asked.

(B) Statement (2) ALONE is sufficient, but statement (1) alone is not sufficient to answer the question asked.

(C) Both statements TOGETHER are sufficient, but NEITHER statement ALONE is sufficient to answer the question asked.

(D) Each statement ALONE is sufficient to answer the question asked.

(E) Statements (1) and (2) TOGETHER are NOT sufficient to answer the question asked.

328. What is the value of $x + y$?

(1) $|x + y| = 11$

(2) $\sqrt{44(x + y)} = 22$

(A) Statement (1) ALONE is sufficient, but statement (2) alone is not sufficient to answer the question asked.

(B) Statement (2) ALONE is sufficient, but statement (1) alone is not sufficient to answer the question asked.

(C) Both statements TOGETHER are sufficient, but NEITHER statement ALONE is sufficient to answer the question asked.

(D) Each statement ALONE is sufficient to answer the question asked.

(E) Statements (1) and (2) TOGETHER are NOT sufficient to answer the question asked.

329. Is $\dfrac{4^{x+5}}{2^{12}} > 1$?

(1) $x > 1$

(2) $2^{2x-2} > 1$

(A) Statement (1) ALONE is sufficient, but statement (2) alone is not sufficient to answer the question asked.

(B) Statement (2) ALONE is sufficient, but statement (1) alone is not sufficient to answer the question asked.

(C) Both statements TOGETHER are sufficient, but NEITHER statement ALONE is sufficient to answer the question asked.

(D) Each statement ALONE is sufficient to answer the question asked.

(E) Statements (1) and (2) TOGETHER are NOT sufficient to answer the question asked.

330. If $\sqrt{x^2 + 4} = x + h$, what is the value of x?

(1) $h = 2$

(2) $h^2 = 4$

(A) Statement (1) ALONE is sufficient, but statement (2) alone is not sufficient to answer the question asked.

(B) Statement (2) ALONE is sufficient, but statement (1) alone is not sufficient to answer the question asked.

(C) Both statements TOGETHER are sufficient, but NEITHER statement ALONE is sufficient to answer the question asked.

(D) Each statement ALONE is sufficient to answer the question asked.

(E) Statements (1) and (2) TOGETHER are NOT sufficient to answer the question asked.

331. What is the range of the 15 numbers?

(1) $\frac{1}{3}$ of the numbers equal 25.

(2) The minimum value of the 15 numbers is $\frac{1}{4}$ the maximum value of the 15 numbers.

(A) Statement (1) ALONE is sufficient, but statement (2) alone is not sufficient to answer the question asked.

(B) Statement (2) ALONE is sufficient, but statement (1) alone is not sufficient to answer the question asked.

(C) Both statements TOGETHER are sufficient, but NEITHER statement ALONE is sufficient to answer the question asked.

(D) Each statement ALONE is sufficient to answer the question asked.

(E) Statements (1) and (2) TOGETHER are NOT sufficient to answer the question asked.

332. Is $xy < 0$?

(1) $-1 < x < 2$

(2) $3 < y < 5$

(A) Statement (1) ALONE is sufficient, but statement (2) alone is not sufficient to answer the question asked.

(B) Statement (2) ALONE is sufficient, but statement (1) alone is not sufficient to answer the question asked.

(C) Both statements TOGETHER are sufficient, but NEITHER statement ALONE is sufficient to answer the question asked.

(D) Each statement ALONE is sufficient to answer the question asked.

(E) Statements (1) and (2) TOGETHER are NOT sufficient to answer the question asked.

333. What is the value of x?

(1) $3^x 4^x = 144$

(2) $\left(10^x\right)^x = 10,000$

(A) Statement (1) ALONE is sufficient, but statement (2) alone is not sufficient to answer the question asked.

(B) Statement (2) ALONE is sufficient, but statement (1) alone is not sufficient to answer the question asked.

(C) Both statements TOGETHER are sufficient, but NEITHER statement ALONE is sufficient to answer the question asked.

(D) Each statement ALONE is sufficient to answer the question asked.

(E) Statements (1) and (2) TOGETHER are NOT sufficient to answer the question asked.

334. If a, b, c, and d are positive integers, is $\frac{a}{b} > \frac{c}{d}$?

(1) $a - c > 0$

(2) $b - d < 0$

(A) Statement (1) ALONE is sufficient, but statement (2) alone is not sufficient to answer the question asked.

(B) Statement (2) ALONE is sufficient, but statement (1) alone is not sufficient to answer the question asked.

(C) Both statements TOGETHER are sufficient, but NEITHER statement ALONE is sufficient to answer the question asked.

(D) Each statement ALONE is sufficient to answer the question asked.

(E) Statements (1) and (2) TOGETHER are NOT sufficient to answer the question asked.

335. What is the value of $\frac{c+d}{c-d}$?

(1) The ratio of c to d is 5 to 1.

(2) $1 < \frac{c+d}{c-d} < 2$

(A) Statement (1) ALONE is sufficient, but statement (2) alone is not sufficient to answer the question asked.

(B) Statement (2) ALONE is sufficient, but statement (1) alone is not sufficient to answer the question asked.

(C) Both statements TOGETHER are sufficient, but NEITHER statement ALONE is sufficient to answer the question asked.

(D) Each statement ALONE is sufficient to answer the question asked.

(E) Statements (1) and (2) TOGETHER are NOT sufficient to answer the question asked.

336. If k is a positive integer, what is the value of k?

   (1) k is a prime number less than 5.

   (2) If f is any positive factor of k, then $f+1$ is even.

   (A) Statement (1) ALONE is sufficient, but statement (2) alone is not sufficient to answer the question asked.

   (B) Statement (2) ALONE is sufficient, but statement (1) alone is not sufficient to answer the question asked.

   (C) Both statements TOGETHER are sufficient, but NEITHER statement ALONE is sufficient to answer the question asked.

   (D) Each statement ALONE is sufficient to answer the question asked.

   (E) Statements (1) and (2) TOGETHER are NOT sufficient to answer the question asked.

337. What is the value of x?

   (1) The mean (arithmetic average) of 14, $6x$, x^2, and 19 is 6.

   (2) The range of 4, 15, x, and 10 is 18.

   (A) Statement (1) ALONE is sufficient, but statement (2) alone is not sufficient to answer the question asked.

   (B) Statement (2) ALONE is sufficient, but statement (1) alone is not sufficient to answer the question asked.

   (C) Both statements TOGETHER are sufficient, but NEITHER statement ALONE is sufficient to answer the question asked.

   (D) Each statement ALONE is sufficient to answer the question asked.

   (E) Statements (1) and (2) TOGETHER are NOT sufficient to answer the question asked.

338. Of a faculty of 90 high school teachers, how many have masters degrees?

   (1) The number of teachers on the faculty who do not have masters degrees is $\frac{1}{5}$ the number who do have masters degrees.

   (2) The number of teachers on the faculty who have masters degrees is 60 more than the number who do not have masters degrees.

   (A) Statement (1) ALONE is sufficient, but statement (2) alone is not sufficient to answer the question asked.

   (B) Statement (2) ALONE is sufficient, but statement (1) alone is not sufficient to answer the question asked.

   (C) Both statements TOGETHER are sufficient, but NEITHER statement ALONE is sufficient to answer the question asked.

   (D) Each statement ALONE is sufficient to answer the question asked.

   (E) Statements (1) and (2) TOGETHER are NOT sufficient to answer the question asked.

339. If $x^2 - 3x + k = -30$, what is the value of k?

   (1) -2 is an element of the solution set of the given equation.

   (2) 5 is an element of the solution set of the given equation.

   (A) Statement (1) ALONE is sufficient, but statement (2) alone is not sufficient to answer the question asked.

   (B) Statement (2) ALONE is sufficient, but statement (1) alone is not sufficient to answer the question asked.

   (C) Both statements TOGETHER are sufficient, but NEITHER statement ALONE is sufficient to answer the question asked.

   (D) Each statement ALONE is sufficient to answer the question asked.

   (E) Statements (1) and (2) TOGETHER are NOT sufficient to answer the question asked.

340. If $N = 100x + 10y + z$ is a three-digit positive integer, is N divisible by 9?

(1) $x + y + z = 18$

(2) $N + 432$ is divisible by 9.

(A) Statement (1) ALONE is sufficient, but statement (2) alone is not sufficient to answer the question asked.

(B) Statement (2) ALONE is sufficient, but statement (1) alone is not sufficient to answer the question asked.

(C) Both statements TOGETHER are sufficient, but NEITHER statement ALONE is sufficient to answer the question asked.

(D) Each statement ALONE is sufficient to answer the question asked.

(E) Statements (1) and (2) TOGETHER are NOT sufficient to answer the question asked.

341. What is the perimeter of the triangle shown?

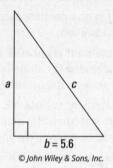

$b = 5.6$

© John Wiley & Sons, Inc.

(1) $c = 7.0$

(2) $a = 4.2$

(A) Statement (1) ALONE is sufficient, but statement (2) alone is not sufficient to answer the question asked.

(B) Statement (2) ALONE is sufficient, but statement (1) alone is not sufficient to answer the question asked.

(C) Both statements TOGETHER are sufficient, but NEITHER statement ALONE is sufficient to answer the question asked.

(D) Each statement ALONE is sufficient to answer the question asked.

(E) Statements (1) and (2) TOGETHER are NOT sufficient to answer the question asked.

342. In the triangle shown, is $x > 2y$?

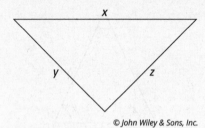

© John Wiley & Sons, Inc.

(1) $y = z$

(2) $0 < x < 10$

(A) Statement (1) ALONE is sufficient, but statement (2) alone is not sufficient to answer the question asked.

(B) Statement (2) ALONE is sufficient, but statement (1) alone is not sufficient to answer the question asked.

(C) Both statements TOGETHER are sufficient, but NEITHER statement ALONE is sufficient to answer the question asked.

(D) Each statement ALONE is sufficient to answer the question asked.

(E) Statements (1) and (2) TOGETHER are NOT sufficient to answer the question asked.

343. A rectangular wall area is tiled with 9-inch-by-9-inch decorative square tiles. What is the perimeter of the wall area?

(1) It takes 48 of the square tiles to cover the wall area.

(2) The number of tiles along each of the horizontal boundaries of the wall area is three times the number of tiles along each of the vertical boundaries of the wall area.

(A) Statement (1) ALONE is sufficient, but statement (2) alone is not sufficient to answer the question asked.

(B) Statement (2) ALONE is sufficient, but statement (1) alone is not sufficient to answer the question asked.

(C) Both statements TOGETHER are sufficient, but NEITHER statement ALONE is sufficient to answer the question asked.

(D) Each statement ALONE is sufficient to answer the question asked.

(E) Statements (1) and (2) TOGETHER are NOT sufficient to answer the question asked.

344. In the figure shown, is $x < 30$?

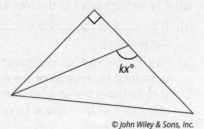

© John Wiley & Sons, Inc.

(1) $k = 6$

(2) $x > 15$

(A) Statement (1) ALONE is sufficient, but statement (2) alone is not sufficient to answer the question asked.

(B) Statement (2) ALONE is sufficient, but statement (1) alone is not sufficient to answer the question asked.

(C) Both statements TOGETHER are sufficient, but NEITHER statement ALONE is sufficient to answer the question asked.

(D) Each statement ALONE is sufficient to answer the question asked.

(E) Statements (1) and (2) TOGETHER are NOT sufficient to answer the question asked.

345. In the triangle shown, what is the value x?

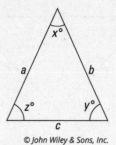

© John Wiley & Sons, Inc.

(1) $a = b$

(2) $y = 65$

(A) Statement (1) ALONE is sufficient, but statement (2) alone is not sufficient to answer the question asked.

(B) Statement (2) ALONE is sufficient, but statement (1) alone is not sufficient to answer the question asked.

(C) Both statements TOGETHER are sufficient, but NEITHER statement ALONE is sufficient to answer the question asked.

(D) Each statement ALONE is sufficient to answer the question asked.

(E) Statements (1) and (2) TOGETHER are NOT sufficient to answer the question asked.

346. Tek has two routes that he normally takes when he drives to work. He always drives the same speed regardless of which route he takes. What is the difference in the distances to and from work between route 1 and route 2?

(1) It takes one hour for Tek to drive round-trip to and from work using route 1.

(2) It takes 40 minutes for Tek to drive round-trip to and from work using route 2.

(A) Statement (1) ALONE is sufficient, but statement (2) alone is not sufficient to answer the question asked.

(B) Statement (2) ALONE is sufficient, but statement (1) alone is not sufficient to answer the question asked.

(C) Both statements TOGETHER are sufficient, but NEITHER statement ALONE is sufficient to answer the question asked.

(D) Each statement ALONE is sufficient to answer the question asked.

(E) Statements (1) and (2) TOGETHER are NOT sufficient to answer the question asked.

347. In a certain neighborhood, 60 percent of the houses have four bedrooms, and 50 percent of the houses are more than 30 years old. If 75 percent of the houses that are more than 30 years old have four bedrooms, how many of the houses 30 years old or under do not have four bedrooms?

(1) The neighborhood has 80 houses that do not have four bedrooms.

(2) Of the houses having four bedrooms, 25 percent are two-story houses that are more than 30 years old.

(A) Statement (1) ALONE is sufficient, but statement (2) alone is not sufficient to answer the question asked.

(B) Statement (2) ALONE is sufficient, but statement (1) alone is not sufficient to answer the question asked.

(C) Both statements TOGETHER are sufficient, but NEITHER statement ALONE is sufficient to answer the question asked.

(D) Each statement ALONE is sufficient to answer the question asked.

(E) Statements (1) and (2) TOGETHER are NOT sufficient to answer the question asked.

348. What is the ratio of r to s?

(1) $r = 3(s+1)$

(2) The ratio of $1.2r$ to $3.6s$ is 3 to 2.

(A) Statement (1) ALONE is sufficient, but statement (2) alone is not sufficient to answer the question asked.

(B) Statement (2) ALONE is sufficient, but statement (1) alone is not sufficient to answer the question asked.

(C) Both statements TOGETHER are sufficient, but NEITHER statement ALONE is sufficient to answer the question asked.

(D) Each statement ALONE is sufficient to answer the question asked.

(E) Statements (1) and (2) TOGETHER are NOT sufficient to answer the question asked.

349. If x, y, and z are three integers such that $0 < x < y < z$, is the range of x, y, and z equal to 2?

(1) The mean (arithmetic average) of x, y, and z is 2.

(2) The median of x, y, and z is 2.

(A) Statement (1) ALONE is sufficient, but statement (2) alone is not sufficient to answer the question asked.

(B) Statement (2) ALONE is sufficient, but statement (1) alone is not sufficient to answer the question asked.

(C) Both statements TOGETHER are sufficient, but NEITHER statement ALONE is sufficient to answer the question asked.

(D) Each statement ALONE is sufficient to answer the question asked.

(E) Statements (1) and (2) TOGETHER are NOT sufficient to answer the question asked.

350. If n is a positive integer, is $n + 425{,}371$ odd?

(1) $n - 268{,}865$ is odd.

(2) $890{,}214n$ is even.

(A) Statement (1) ALONE is sufficient, but statement (2) alone is not sufficient to answer the question asked.

(B) Statement (2) ALONE is sufficient, but statement (1) alone is not sufficient to answer the question asked.

(C) Both statements TOGETHER are sufficient, but NEITHER statement ALONE is sufficient to answer the question asked.

(D) Each statement ALONE is sufficient to answer the question asked.

(E) Statements (1) and (2) TOGETHER are NOT sufficient to answer the question asked.

351. A mixture is composed of ingredients A, B, C, and D. How much more (in grams) of ingredient A than ingredient D is in the mixture?

(1) The ingredients A, B, C, and D are in the ratio 10:5:4:2, respectively.

(2) The amount (in grams) of ingredient B is 4 more than that of ingredient C.

(A) Statement (1) ALONE is sufficient, but statement (2) alone is not sufficient to answer the question asked.

(B) Statement (2) ALONE is sufficient, but statement (1) alone is not sufficient to answer the question asked.

(C) Both statements TOGETHER are sufficient, but NEITHER statement ALONE is sufficient to answer the question asked.

(D) Each statement ALONE is sufficient to answer the question asked.

(E) Statements (1) and (2) TOGETHER are NOT sufficient to answer the question asked.

352. If K is a 5-digit positive integer, is K divisible by 4?

(1) The tens digit and the units digit of K are 3 and 6, respectively.

(2) K is divisible by 12.

(A) Statement (1) ALONE is sufficient, but statement (2) alone is not sufficient to answer the question asked.

(B) Statement (2) ALONE is sufficient, but statement (1) alone is not sufficient to answer the question asked.

(C) Both statements TOGETHER are sufficient, but NEITHER statement ALONE is sufficient to answer the question asked.

(D) Each statement ALONE is sufficient to answer the question asked.

(E) Statements (1) and (2) TOGETHER are NOT sufficient to answer the question asked.

353. Is $x^{x^3} > 0$?

(1) $x < 0$

(2) $x^3 + 64 = 0$

(A) Statement (1) ALONE is sufficient, but statement (2) alone is not sufficient to answer the question asked.

(B) Statement (2) ALONE is sufficient, but statement (1) alone is not sufficient to answer the question asked.

(C) Both statements TOGETHER are sufficient, but NEITHER statement ALONE is sufficient to answer the question asked.

(D) Each statement ALONE is sufficient to answer the question asked.

(E) Statements (1) and (2) TOGETHER are NOT sufficient to answer the question asked.

354. If a and b are positive integers, what is the value of $a - b$?

(1) $36a^2 + 5a + 49b^2 - 5b = (6a)^2 + (7b)^2 + 20$

(2) $\sqrt{a^2 - b^2} = 8$

(A) Statement (1) ALONE is sufficient, but statement (2) alone is not sufficient to answer the question asked.

(B) Statement (2) ALONE is sufficient, but statement (1) alone is not sufficient to answer the question asked.

(C) Both statements TOGETHER are sufficient, but NEITHER statement ALONE is sufficient to answer the question asked.

(D) Each statement ALONE is sufficient to answer the question asked.

(E) Statements (1) and (2) TOGETHER are NOT sufficient to answer the question asked.

355. The value of Brie's heirloom pendant decreased by 50 percent from 2013 to 2015. What was the pendant's value in 2013?

(1) The value of the pendant in 2014 was $3,000.

(2) The value of the pendant increased by 25% from 2015 to 2017, resulting in a value of $3,125 at the end of 2017.

(A) Statement (1) ALONE is sufficient, but statement (2) alone is not sufficient to answer the question asked.

(B) Statement (2) ALONE is sufficient, but statement (1) alone is not sufficient to answer the question asked.

(C) Both statements TOGETHER are sufficient, but NEITHER statement ALONE is sufficient to answer the question asked.

(D) Each statement ALONE is sufficient to answer the question asked.

(E) Statements (1) and (2) TOGETHER are NOT sufficient to answer the question asked.

356. If a is an element of $\{23, 24, 28, 29, 31, 33, 36\}$, what is the value of a?

(1) a is even.

(2) a is divisible by 3.

(A) Statement (1) ALONE is sufficient, but statement (2) alone is not sufficient to answer the question asked.

(B) Statement (2) ALONE is sufficient, but statement (1) alone is not sufficient to answer the question asked.

(C) Both statements TOGETHER are sufficient, but NEITHER statement ALONE is sufficient to answer the question asked.

(D) Each statement ALONE is sufficient to answer the question asked.

(E) Statements (1) and (2) TOGETHER are NOT sufficient to answer the question asked.

357. Is the triangle shown an equilateral triangle?

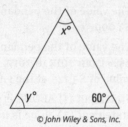

© John Wiley & Sons, Inc.

(1) $x = y$

(2) $x + y = 120$

(A) Statement (1) ALONE is sufficient, but statement (2) alone is not sufficient to answer the question asked.

(B) Statement (2) ALONE is sufficient, but statement (1) alone is not sufficient to answer the question asked.

(C) Both statements TOGETHER are sufficient, but NEITHER statement ALONE is sufficient to answer the question asked.

(D) Each statement ALONE is sufficient to answer the question asked.

(E) Statements (1) and (2) TOGETHER are NOT sufficient to answer the question asked.

358. If m and n are integers such that $mn \neq 0$, what is the value of $\frac{m}{n}$?

(1) $m - n = 8$

(2) $(m + n)(m - n) = 0$

(A) Statement (1) ALONE is sufficient, but statement (2) alone is not sufficient to answer the question asked.

(B) Statement (2) ALONE is sufficient, but statement (1) alone is not sufficient to answer the question asked.

(C) Both statements TOGETHER are sufficient, but NEITHER statement ALONE is sufficient to answer the question asked.

(D) Each statement ALONE is sufficient to answer the question asked.

(E) Statements (1) and (2) TOGETHER are NOT sufficient to answer the question asked.

359. If $xy \neq 0$ and $x \neq y$, what is the value of K?

(1) $Kx + x - Ky - y = 0$

(2) $\left(\dfrac{x}{y}\right)^{K} = \dfrac{y}{x}$

(A) Statement (1) ALONE is sufficient, but statement (2) alone is not sufficient to answer the question asked.

(B) Statement (2) ALONE is sufficient, but statement (1) alone is not sufficient to answer the question asked.

(C) Both statements TOGETHER are sufficient, but NEITHER statement ALONE is sufficient to answer the question asked.

(D) Each statement ALONE is sufficient to answer the question asked.

(E) Statements (1) and (2) TOGETHER are NOT sufficient to answer the question asked.

360. Is the measure of an exterior angle of triangle XYZ equal to 140°?

   (1) The measure of angle Y is 60°.

   (2) The measure of angle Z is 70°.

   (A) Statement (1) ALONE is sufficient, but statement (2) alone is not sufficient to answer the question asked.

   (B) Statement (2) ALONE is sufficient, but statement (1) alone is not sufficient to answer the question asked.

   (C) Both statements TOGETHER are sufficient, but NEITHER statement ALONE is sufficient to answer the question asked.

   (D) Each statement ALONE is sufficient to answer the question asked.

   (E) Statements (1) and (2) TOGETHER are NOT sufficient to answer the question asked.

361. Does $5x - 3y = 0$?

   (1) $xy = 15$

   (2) $20x = 12y$

   (A) Statement (1) ALONE is sufficient, but statement (2) alone is not sufficient to answer the question asked.

   (B) Statement (2) ALONE is sufficient, but statement (1) alone is not sufficient to answer the question asked.

   (C) Both statements TOGETHER are sufficient, but NEITHER statement ALONE is sufficient to answer the question asked.

   (D) Each statement ALONE is sufficient to answer the question asked.

   (E) Statements (1) and (2) TOGETHER are NOT sufficient to answer the question asked.

362. Kwasi has S dollars. The purchase price of a television set that Kwasi wants to buy is P dollars plus 8 percent sales tax. Does Kwasi have enough money to purchase the item?

   (1) P dollars = \$405

   (2) P dollars $= 0.9S$ dollars

   (A) Statement (1) ALONE is sufficient, but statement (2) alone is not sufficient to answer the question asked.

   (B) Statement (2) ALONE is sufficient, but statement (1) alone is not sufficient to answer the question asked.

   (C) Both statements TOGETHER are sufficient, but NEITHER statement ALONE is sufficient to answer the question asked.

   (D) Each statement ALONE is sufficient to answer the question asked.

   (E) Statements (1) and (2) TOGETHER are NOT sufficient to answer the question asked.

363. If $xy < 10$, is $y < 1$?

   (1) $y < 7$

   (2) $x > 10$

   (A) Statement (1) ALONE is sufficient, but statement (2) alone is not sufficient to answer the question asked.

   (B) Statement (2) ALONE is sufficient, but statement (1) alone is not sufficient to answer the question asked.

   (C) Both statements TOGETHER are sufficient, but NEITHER statement ALONE is sufficient to answer the question asked.

   (D) Each statement ALONE is sufficient to answer the question asked.

   (E) Statements (1) and (2) TOGETHER are NOT sufficient to answer the question asked.

364. Is the integer n a prime number?

(1) $n + 95$ is odd.

(2) $2 < n < 12$

(A) Statement (1) ALONE is sufficient, but statement (2) alone is not sufficient to answer the question asked.

(B) Statement (2) ALONE is sufficient, but statement (1) alone is not sufficient to answer the question asked.

(C) Both statements TOGETHER are sufficient, but NEITHER statement ALONE is sufficient to answer the question asked.

(D) Each statement ALONE is sufficient to answer the question asked.

(E) Statements (1) and (2) TOGETHER are NOT sufficient to answer the question asked.

365. Store X has a sale on the store brand of canned tomatoes. A customer buys a six-month supply of the store-brand canned tomatoes. How much money does the customer save?

(1) The customer uses 4 cans of tomatoes every month.

(2) The cans of tomatoes are reduced in price to 4 for $1.

(A) Statement (1) ALONE is sufficient, but statement (2) alone is not sufficient to answer the question asked.

(B) Statement (2) ALONE is sufficient, but statement (1) alone is not sufficient to answer the question asked.

(C) Both statements TOGETHER are sufficient, but NEITHER statement ALONE is sufficient to answer the question asked.

(D) Each statement ALONE is sufficient to answer the question asked.

(E) Statements (1) and (2) TOGETHER are NOT sufficient to answer the question asked.

366. Adwoa drove a distance of 288 miles from city A to city B. At what time did Adwoa leave city A?

(1) Adwoa drove an average speed of 72 miles per hour.

(2) Adwoa arrived in city B at 2 p.m.

(A) Statement (1) ALONE is sufficient, but statement (2) alone is not sufficient to answer the question asked.

(B) Statement (2) ALONE is sufficient, but statement (1) alone is not sufficient to answer the question asked.

(C) Both statements TOGETHER are sufficient, but NEITHER statement ALONE is sufficient to answer the question asked.

(D) Each statement ALONE is sufficient to answer the question asked.

(E) Statements (1) and (2) TOGETHER are NOT sufficient to answer the question asked.

367. In the circular region shown, what portion of the total area is section *A*?

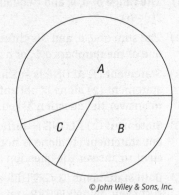

© John Wiley & Sons, Inc.

(1) Sections *A* and *B* account for $\frac{8}{9}$ of the total area.

(2) Section *B* takes up three times as much area as section *C*.

(A) Statement (1) ALONE is sufficient, but statement (2) alone is not sufficient to answer the question asked.

(B) Statement (2) ALONE is sufficient, but statement (1) alone is not sufficient to answer the question asked.

(C) Both statements TOGETHER are sufficient, but NEITHER statement ALONE is sufficient to answer the question asked.

(D) Each statement ALONE is sufficient to answer the question asked.

(E) Statements (1) and (2) TOGETHER are NOT sufficient to answer the question asked.

368. What is the value of $x - z$?

(1) The arithmetic average of *x* and *y* is 55.

(2) The arithmetic average of *y* and *z* is 80.

(A) Statement (1) ALONE is sufficient, but statement (2) alone is not sufficient to answer the question asked.

(B) Statement (2) ALONE is sufficient, but statement (1) alone is not sufficient to answer the question asked.

(C) Both statements TOGETHER are sufficient, but NEITHER statement ALONE is sufficient to answer the question asked.

(D) Each statement ALONE is sufficient to answer the question asked.

(E) Statements (1) and (2) TOGETHER are NOT sufficient to answer the question asked.

369. If *p* is a prime number, what is the value of *p*?

(1) $10 < p - 3 < 16$

(2) $p^2 = 289$

(A) Statement (1) ALONE is sufficient, but statement (2) alone is not sufficient to answer the question asked.

(B) Statement (2) ALONE is sufficient, but statement (1) alone is not sufficient to answer the question asked.

(C) Both statements TOGETHER are sufficient, but NEITHER statement ALONE is sufficient to answer the question asked.

(D) Each statement ALONE is sufficient to answer the question asked.

(E) Statements (1) and (2) TOGETHER are NOT sufficient to answer the question asked.

370. At a youth soccer game in a certain town, $\frac{2}{3}$ of the spectators are residents of the town and the rest are visitors from out-of-town. If $\frac{3}{4}$ of the spectators who are residents of the town are close relatives of players in the game, how many of the town-resident spectators are not close relatives of players in the game?

(1) There are 1,380 spectators at the game.

(2) There are 460 spectators who are visitors from out-of-town at the game.

(A) Statement (1) ALONE is sufficient, but statement (2) alone is not sufficient to answer the question asked.

(B) Statement (2) ALONE is sufficient, but statement (1) alone is not sufficient to answer the question asked.

(C) Both statements TOGETHER are sufficient, but NEITHER statement ALONE is sufficient to answer the question asked.

(D) Each statement ALONE is sufficient to answer the question asked.

(E) Statements (1) and (2) TOGETHER are NOT sufficient to answer the question asked.

371. The greatest of M integers is 400. The least of N integers is 475. What is the median of the $M + N$ integers?

(1) $M = 25$

(2) $N = 24$

(A) Statement (1) ALONE is sufficient, but statement (2) alone is not sufficient to answer the question asked.

(B) Statement (2) ALONE is sufficient, but statement (1) alone is not sufficient to answer the question asked.

(C) Both statements TOGETHER are sufficient, but NEITHER statement ALONE is sufficient to answer the question asked.

(D) Each statement ALONE is sufficient to answer the question asked.

(E) Statements (1) and (2) TOGETHER are NOT sufficient to answer the question asked.

372. If $0 < a < b < c$, does the median of a, b, and c equal the mean of a, b, and c?

(1) The range of a, b, and c equals $2(c - b)$.

(2) The sum of a, b, and c is three times one of the numbers a, b, or c.

(A) Statement (1) ALONE is sufficient, but statement (2) alone is not sufficient to answer the question asked.

(B) Statement (2) ALONE is sufficient, but statement (1) alone is not sufficient to answer the question asked.

(C) Both statements TOGETHER are sufficient, but NEITHER statement ALONE is sufficient to answer the question asked.

(D) Each statement ALONE is sufficient to answer the question asked.

(E) Statements (1) and (2) TOGETHER are NOT sufficient to answer the question asked.

373. If set A is a subset of set B, is the range of set A less than the range of set B?

(1) Set A consists of 4 numbers.

(2) Set B consists of 5 numbers.

(A) Statement (1) ALONE is sufficient, but statement (2) alone is not sufficient to answer the question asked.

(B) Statement (2) ALONE is sufficient, but statement (1) alone is not sufficient to answer the question asked.

(C) Both statements TOGETHER are sufficient, but NEITHER statement ALONE is sufficient to answer the question asked.

(D) Each statement ALONE is sufficient to answer the question asked.

(E) Statements (1) and (2) TOGETHER are NOT sufficient to answer the question asked.

374. Is $(1+0.01r)(1-0.01s)>1$

(1) $r>s$

(2) $0.01rs<r-s$

(A) Statement (1) ALONE is sufficient, but statement (2) alone is not sufficient to answer the question asked.

(B) Statement (2) ALONE is sufficient, but statement (1) alone is not sufficient to answer the question asked.

(C) Both statements TOGETHER are sufficient, but NEITHER statement ALONE is sufficient to answer the question asked.

(D) Each statement ALONE is sufficient to answer the question asked.

(E) Statements (1) and (2) TOGETHER are NOT sufficient to answer the question asked.

375. The circumference of circle X is $\frac{1}{2}$ the circumference of circle Y. What is the area of circle X?

(1) The area of circle Y is 100π ft^2.

(2) The circumference of circle Y is 20π ft.

(A) Statement (1) ALONE is sufficient, but statement (2) alone is not sufficient to answer the question asked.

(B) Statement (2) ALONE is sufficient, but statement (1) alone is not sufficient to answer the question asked.

(C) Both statements TOGETHER are sufficient, but NEITHER statement ALONE is sufficient to answer the question asked.

(D) Each statement ALONE is sufficient to answer the question asked.

(E) Statements (1) and (2) TOGETHER are NOT sufficient to answer the question asked.

376. What is the perimeter of the triangle shown?

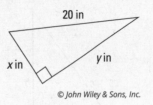

© John Wiley & Sons, Inc.

(1) The area of the triangle is 96 in^2.

(2) $y=x+4$

(A) Statement (1) ALONE is sufficient, but statement (2) alone is not sufficient to answer the question asked.

(B) Statement (2) ALONE is sufficient, but statement (1) alone is not sufficient to answer the question asked.

(C) Both statements TOGETHER are sufficient, but NEITHER statement ALONE is sufficient to answer the question asked.

(D) Each statement ALONE is sufficient to answer the question asked.

(E) Statements (1) and (2) TOGETHER are NOT sufficient to answer the question asked.

377. If $y=ax$ and $x=bz$, what is y when $z=75$?

(1) $x=\frac{1}{2}$ when $z=60$.

(2) $y=2$ when $z=50$.

(A) Statement (1) ALONE is sufficient, but statement (2) alone is not sufficient to answer the question asked.

(B) Statement (2) ALONE is sufficient, but statement (1) alone is not sufficient to answer the question asked.

(C) Both statements TOGETHER are sufficient, but NEITHER statement ALONE is sufficient to answer the question asked.

(D) Each statement ALONE is sufficient to answer the question asked.

(E) Statements (1) and (2) TOGETHER are NOT sufficient to answer the question asked.

378. If the area of the right triangle shown is 24, what is the value of c?

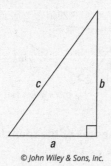

© John Wiley & Sons, Inc.

(1) $b^2 = 225$

(2) $a^2 = \dfrac{256}{25}$

(A) Statement (1) ALONE is sufficient, but statement (2) alone is not sufficient to answer the question asked.

(B) Statement (2) ALONE is sufficient, but statement (1) alone is not sufficient to answer the question asked.

(C) Both statements TOGETHER are sufficient, but NEITHER statement ALONE is sufficient to answer the question asked.

(D) Each statement ALONE is sufficient to answer the question asked.

(E) Statements (1) and (2) TOGETHER are NOT sufficient to answer the question asked.

379. The heights of a certain plant species are normally distributed. What height is 2 standard deviations greater than the arithmetic mean height of the plant species?

(1) The arithmetic mean height is 32.8 centimeters.

(2) The standard deviation of the heights is 2.4 centimeters.

(A) Statement (1) ALONE is sufficient, but statement (2) alone is not sufficient to answer the question asked.

(B) Statement (2) ALONE is sufficient, but statement (1) alone is not sufficient to answer the question asked.

(C) Both statements TOGETHER are sufficient, but NEITHER statement ALONE is sufficient to answer the question asked.

(D) Each statement ALONE is sufficient to answer the question asked.

(E) Statements (1) and (2) TOGETHER are NOT sufficient to answer the question asked.

380. Each day, Sergio feeds his cat a 500-gram mixture of Brand X and Brand Y cat foods. If Sergio's cat eats only this mix of cat food and she consumes 103 grams of fat per day, what is the amount of Brand X cat food that she receives each day?

(1) Brand X cat food consists of 35 percent fat.

(2) Brand Y cat food consists of 11 percent fat.

(A) Statement (1) ALONE is sufficient, but statement (2) alone is not sufficient to answer the question asked.

(B) Statement (2) ALONE is sufficient, but statement (1) alone is not sufficient to answer the question asked.

(C) Both statements TOGETHER are sufficient, but NEITHER statement ALONE is sufficient to answer the question asked.

(D) Each statement ALONE is sufficient to answer the question asked.

(E) Statements (1) and (2) TOGETHER are NOT sufficient to answer the question asked.

381. What is the area of the rectangular floor?

(1) The length of the floor is 4 feet greater than its width.

(2) The perimeter of the floor is 56 feet.

(A) Statement (1) ALONE is sufficient, but statement (2) alone is not sufficient to answer the question asked.

(B) Statement (2) ALONE is sufficient, but statement (1) alone is not sufficient to answer the question asked.

(C) Both statements TOGETHER are sufficient, but NEITHER statement ALONE is sufficient to answer the question asked.

(D) Each statement ALONE is sufficient to answer the question asked.

(E) Statements (1) and (2) TOGETHER are NOT sufficient to answer the question asked.

382. How many vehicles are in the parking lot?

(1) Of the vehicles in the parking lot, five are pickup trucks.

(2) Of the vehicles in the parking lot 60 percent are sedans.

(A) Statement (1) ALONE is sufficient, but statement (2) alone is not sufficient to answer the question asked.

(B) Statement (2) ALONE is sufficient, but statement (1) alone is not sufficient to answer the question asked.

(C) Both statements TOGETHER are sufficient, but NEITHER statement ALONE is sufficient to answer the question asked.

(D) Each statement ALONE is sufficient to answer the question asked.

(E) Statements (1) and (2) TOGETHER are NOT sufficient to answer the question asked.

383. In the triangle shown $y < z$. If $j < x < k$, what is the least value of k?

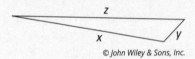
© John Wiley & Sons, Inc.

(1) $y = 5$

(2) $z = 17$

(A) Statement (1) ALONE is sufficient, but statement (2) alone is not sufficient to answer the question asked.

(B) Statement (2) ALONE is sufficient, but statement (1) alone is not sufficient to answer the question asked.

(C) Both statements TOGETHER are sufficient, but NEITHER statement ALONE is sufficient to answer the question asked.

(D) Each statement ALONE is sufficient to answer the question asked.

(E) Statements (1) and (2) TOGETHER are NOT sufficient to answer the question asked.

384. If m and n are positive integers, what is the greatest possible value of n?

(1) $m^5 + n^5 < 1,200$

(2) $m^5 = 0$

(A) Statement (1) ALONE is sufficient, but statement (2) alone is not sufficient to answer the question asked.

(B) Statement (2) ALONE is sufficient, but statement (1) alone is not sufficient to answer the question asked.

(C) Both statements TOGETHER are sufficient, but NEITHER statement ALONE is sufficient to answer the question asked.

(D) Each statement ALONE is sufficient to answer the question asked.

(E) Statements (1) and (2) TOGETHER are NOT sufficient to answer the question asked.

385. A specialty bakery sells decorated one-layer cakes for \$40 and two-layer decorated cakes for \$75. If last month the bakery's total sales for decorated one-layer and two-layer cakes was \$13,900, how many decorated one-layer and two-layer cakes did the bakery sell last month?

(1) Last month, the number of decorated one-layer cakes sold was 40 less than twice the number of decorated two-layer cakes sold.

(2) Last month, the number of decorated two-layer cakes sold was 60 less than the number of decorated one-layer cakes sold.

(A) Statement (1) ALONE is sufficient, but statement (2) alone is not sufficient to answer the question asked.

(B) Statement (2) ALONE is sufficient, but statement (1) alone is not sufficient to answer the question asked.

(C) Both statements TOGETHER are sufficient, but NEITHER statement ALONE is sufficient to answer the question asked.

(D) Each statement ALONE is sufficient to answer the question asked.

(E) Statements (1) and (2) TOGETHER are NOT sufficient to answer the question asked.

386. In a certain high school, there are 31 students who are members of the chess club or the swim team or both. How many students belong to either the chess club or the swim team, but not both?

(1) The chess club has 24 members.

(2) The swim team has 20 members.

(A) Statement (1) ALONE is sufficient, but statement (2) alone is not sufficient to answer the question asked.

(B) Statement (2) ALONE is sufficient, but statement (1) alone is not sufficient to answer the question asked.

(C) Both statements TOGETHER are sufficient, but NEITHER statement ALONE is sufficient to answer the question asked.

(D) Each statement ALONE is sufficient to answer the question asked.

(E) Statements (1) and (2) TOGETHER are NOT sufficient to answer the question asked.

387. If x and y are positive numbers, is $xy < 16$?

(1) $x < 8$ and $y < 3$

(2) $x^3 < 8$ and $y - 8 < 0$

(A) Statement (1) ALONE is sufficient, but statement (2) alone is not sufficient to answer the question asked.

(B) Statement (2) ALONE is sufficient, but statement (1) alone is not sufficient to answer the question asked.

(C) Both statements TOGETHER are sufficient, but NEITHER statement ALONE is sufficient to answer the question asked.

(D) Each statement ALONE is sufficient to answer the question asked.

(E) Statements (1) and (2) TOGETHER are NOT sufficient to answer the question asked.

388. In the figure shown, if $ABCD$ is a parallelogram, what is the value of y?

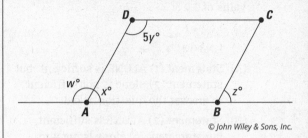

© John Wiley & Sons, Inc.

(1) $w = 125$

(2) $z = 55$

(A) Statement (1) ALONE is sufficient, but statement (2) alone is not sufficient to answer the question asked.

(B) Statement (2) ALONE is sufficient, but statement (1) alone is not sufficient to answer the question asked.

(C) Both statements TOGETHER are sufficient, but NEITHER statement ALONE is sufficient to answer the question asked.

(D) Each statement ALONE is sufficient to answer the question asked.

(E) Statements (1) and (2) TOGETHER are NOT sufficient to answer the question asked.

389. The symbol ◊ represents one of the arithmetic operations: addition, subtraction, multiplication, or division. What is the value of 2 ◊ 5?

(1) $1 ◊ 1 = 1$

(2) $1 ◊ 3 = 3$

(A) Statement (1) ALONE is sufficient, but statement (2) alone is not sufficient to answer the question asked.

(B) Statement (2) ALONE is sufficient, but statement (1) alone is not sufficient to answer the question asked.

(C) Both statements TOGETHER are sufficient, but NEITHER statement ALONE is sufficient to answer the question asked.

(D) Each statement ALONE is sufficient to answer the question asked.

(E) Statements (1) and (2) TOGETHER are NOT sufficient to answer the question asked.

390. How many math majors are in Professor X's physics class?

(1) If Professor X admits 10 more students into the class, and if all the newly admitted students are math majors, then the ratio of non-math majors to math majors would be 5 to 4.

(2) Currently, there are 25 non-math majors in Professor X's class.

(A) Statement (1) ALONE is sufficient, but statement (2) alone is not sufficient to answer the question asked.

(B) Statement (2) ALONE is sufficient, but statement (1) alone is not sufficient to answer the question asked.

(C) Both statements TOGETHER are sufficient, but NEITHER statement ALONE is sufficient to answer the question asked.

(D) Each statement ALONE is sufficient to answer the question asked.

(E) Statements (1) and (2) TOGETHER are NOT sufficient to answer the question asked.

391. How many members are in the photography club?

(1) If the photography club doubles its membership, it will have at least 34 members.

(2) If the photography club loses 5 members, it will have fewer than 13 members.

(A) Statement (1) ALONE is sufficient, but statement (2) alone is not sufficient to answer the question asked.

(B) Statement (2) ALONE is sufficient, but statement (1) alone is not sufficient to answer the question asked.

(C) Both statements TOGETHER are sufficient, but NEITHER statement ALONE is sufficient to answer the question asked.

(D) Each statement ALONE is sufficient to answer the question asked.

(E) Statements (1) and (2) TOGETHER are NOT sufficient to answer the question asked.

392. If $xyz \neq 0$, is $xyz > 0$?

(1) $xz < 0$

(2) $x + y + z = 0$

(A) Statement (1) ALONE is sufficient, but statement (2) alone is not sufficient to answer the question asked.

(B) Statement (2) ALONE is sufficient, but statement (1) alone is not sufficient to answer the question asked.

(C) Both statements TOGETHER are sufficient, but NEITHER statement ALONE is sufficient to answer the question asked.

(D) Each statement ALONE is sufficient to answer the question asked.

(E) Statements (1) and (2) TOGETHER are NOT sufficient to answer the question asked.

393. Is $2k > 13$?

(1) $6 < k - 0.6 < 7$

(2) $k + 0.8$ rounded to the nearest integer is 8.

(A) Statement (1) ALONE is sufficient, but statement (2) alone is not sufficient to answer the question asked.

(B) Statement (2) ALONE is sufficient, but statement (1) alone is not sufficient to answer the question asked.

(C) Both statements TOGETHER are sufficient, but NEITHER statement ALONE is sufficient to answer the question asked.

(D) Each statement ALONE is sufficient to answer the question asked.

(E) Statements (1) and (2) TOGETHER are NOT sufficient to answer the question asked.

394. If k is a positive integer, what is the value of k?

(1) $k^2 < 10$

(2) $k^5 > 30$

(A) Statement (1) ALONE is sufficient, but statement (2) alone is not sufficient to answer the question asked.

(B) Statement (2) ALONE is sufficient, but statement (1) alone is not sufficient to answer the question asked.

(C) Both statements TOGETHER are sufficient, but NEITHER statement ALONE is sufficient to answer the question asked.

(D) Each statement ALONE is sufficient to answer the question asked.

(E) Statements (1) and (2) TOGETHER are NOT sufficient to answer the question asked.

395. A certain species of bacteria doubles its population every m minutes. What will be the population of this bacteria colony in 4 hours?

(1) In one hour, the population of the bacteria colony is 20,000.

(2) In three hours, the population of the bacteria colony is 320,000.

(A) Statement (1) ALONE is sufficient, but statement (2) alone is not sufficient to answer the question asked.

(B) Statement (2) ALONE is sufficient, but statement (1) alone is not sufficient to answer the question asked.

(C) Both statements TOGETHER are sufficient, but NEITHER statement ALONE is sufficient to answer the question asked.

(D) Each statement ALONE is sufficient to answer the question asked.

(E) Statements (1) and (2) TOGETHER are NOT sufficient to answer the question asked.

396. If $y \neq 0$, is $y > 0$?

(1) $|y| > 1$

(2) $\dfrac{y^2 + y}{y^2} > 1$

(A) Statement (1) ALONE is sufficient, but statement (2) alone is not sufficient to answer the question asked.

(B) Statement (2) ALONE is sufficient, but statement (1) alone is not sufficient to answer the question asked.

(C) Both statements TOGETHER are sufficient, but NEITHER statement ALONE is sufficient to answer the question asked.

(D) Each statement ALONE is sufficient to answer the question asked.

(E) Statements (1) and (2) TOGETHER are NOT sufficient to answer the question asked.

397. Is the positive integer n divisible by 24?

(1) n is divisible by 12.

(2) n is even.

(A) Statement (1) ALONE is sufficient, but statement (2) alone is not sufficient to answer the question asked.

(B) Statement (2) ALONE is sufficient, but statement (1) alone is not sufficient to answer the question asked.

(C) Both statements TOGETHER are sufficient, but NEITHER statement ALONE is sufficient to answer the question asked.

(D) Each statement ALONE is sufficient to answer the question asked.

(E) Statements (1) and (2) TOGETHER are NOT sufficient to answer the question asked.

398. Mimi's corner grocery store sells only two kinds of ice cream: Brand X ice cream in 48-ounce containers and Brand Y ice cream in 64-ounce containers. What is the price of one 64-ounce container of Brand Y ice cream?

(1) A customer at Mimi's bought one 64-ounce container of Brand Y ice cream and two 48-ounce containers of Brand X ice cream for $15.

(2) A customer at Mimi's bought a total of 192 ounces of ice cream for $18.

(A) Statement (1) ALONE is sufficient, but statement (2) alone is not sufficient to answer the question asked.

(B) Statement (2) ALONE is sufficient, but statement (1) alone is not sufficient to answer the question asked.

(C) Both statements TOGETHER are sufficient, but NEITHER statement ALONE is sufficient to answer the question asked.

(D) Each statement ALONE is sufficient to answer the question asked.

(E) Statements (1) and (2) TOGETHER are NOT sufficient to answer the question asked.

399. The Venn diagram shows the enrollment of 400 college students in one or more of three classes: mathematics, English, and physics. What percent of the students are taking only mathematics or only physics and no other class?

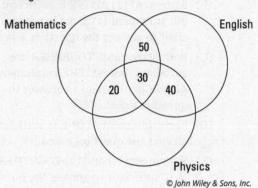

400 College Students

© John Wiley & Sons, Inc.

(1) Of the 400 students, 240 are taking English.

(2) Of the 400 students, 190 are taking mathematics and 140 are taking physics.

(A) Statement (1) ALONE is sufficient, but statement (2) alone is not sufficient to answer the question asked.

(B) Statement (2) ALONE is sufficient, but statement (1) alone is not sufficient to answer the question asked.

(C) Both statements TOGETHER are sufficient, but NEITHER statement ALONE is sufficient to answer the question asked.

(D) Each statement ALONE is sufficient to answer the question asked.

(E) Statements (1) and (2) TOGETHER are NOT sufficient to answer the question asked.

400. What is the value of x?

(1) $x^2 + x - 12 = 0$

(2) $x^2 < 25$

(A) Statement (1) ALONE is sufficient, but statement (2) alone is not sufficient to answer the question asked.

(B) Statement (2) ALONE is sufficient, but statement (1) alone is not sufficient to answer the question asked.

(C) Both statements TOGETHER are sufficient, but NEITHER statement ALONE is sufficient to answer the question asked.

(D) Each statement ALONE is sufficient to answer the question asked.

(E) Statements (1) and (2) TOGETHER are NOT sufficient to answer the question asked.

401. If $0 < p \leq q \leq r$, what is the value of q?

(1) $r - p = 260$

(2) $r - q = 170$

(A) Statement (1) ALONE is sufficient, but statement (2) alone is not sufficient to answer the question asked.

(B) Statement (2) ALONE is sufficient, but statement (1) alone is not sufficient to answer the question asked.

(C) Both statements TOGETHER are sufficient, but NEITHER statement ALONE is sufficient to answer the question asked.

(D) Each statement ALONE is sufficient to answer the question asked.

(E) Statements (1) and (2) TOGETHER are NOT sufficient to answer the question asked.

402. Was Rylon's average speed greater than 55 miles per hour?

(1) Rylon drove 100 miles in 1 hour 48 minutes.

(2) Rylon drove 60 miles at an average speed of 60 miles per hour, and then drove 40 miles at an average speed of 50 miles per hour.

(A) Statement (1) ALONE is sufficient, but statement (2) alone is not sufficient to answer the question asked.

(B) Statement (2) ALONE is sufficient, but statement (1) alone is not sufficient to answer the question asked.

(C) Both statements TOGETHER are sufficient, but NEITHER statement ALONE is sufficient to answer the question asked.

(D) Each statement ALONE is sufficient to answer the question asked.

(E) Statements (1) and (2) TOGETHER are NOT sufficient to answer the question asked.

403. If $0 < x \leq y$, what is the value of x?

(1) $x^2 + 2xy = 12y + 36$

(2) $y(x^3 - 216) = 0$

(A) Statement (1) ALONE is sufficient, but statement (2) alone is not sufficient to answer the question asked.

(B) Statement (2) ALONE is sufficient, but statement (1) alone is not sufficient to answer the question asked.

(C) Both statements TOGETHER are sufficient, but NEITHER statement ALONE is sufficient to answer the question asked.

(D) Each statement ALONE is sufficient to answer the question asked.

(E) Statements (1) and (2) TOGETHER are NOT sufficient to answer the question asked.

404. In a city that has a 6 percent sales tax rate, Vinod purchases a cotton shirt and a cashmere sweater. If the cost of the shirt, excluding sales tax, is $100, what was the total amount that Vinod paid for the shirt and sweater, including sales tax?

(1) The sales tax on the sweater is $19.20.

(2) The total sales tax is $25.20.

(A) Statement (1) ALONE is sufficient, but statement (2) alone is not sufficient to answer the question asked.

(B) Statement (2) ALONE is sufficient, but statement (1) alone is not sufficient to answer the question asked.

(C) Both statements TOGETHER are sufficient, but NEITHER statement ALONE is sufficient to answer the question asked.

(D) Each statement ALONE is sufficient to answer the question asked.

(E) Statements (1) and (2) TOGETHER are NOT sufficient to answer the question asked.

405. If a sequence A has 200 terms, what is the 100th term of A?

(1) The first term of sequence A is –10.

(2) Each term of sequence A after the first term is 15 more than the preceding term.

(A) Statement (1) ALONE is sufficient, but statement (2) alone is not sufficient to answer the question asked.

(B) Statement (2) ALONE is sufficient, but statement (1) alone is not sufficient to answer the question asked.

(C) Both statements TOGETHER are sufficient, but NEITHER statement ALONE is sufficient to answer the question asked.

(D) Each statement ALONE is sufficient to answer the question asked.

(E) Statements (1) and (2) TOGETHER are NOT sufficient to answer the question asked.

406. A survey of seniors and juniors at a small college revealed 50 are seniors who live off-campus. How many students were surveyed?

(1) 80 of the students surveyed are seniors and the rest are juniors.

(2) 120 of the students surveyed live off campus and the rest live on campus.

(A) Statement (1) ALONE is sufficient, but statement (2) alone is not sufficient to answer the question asked.

(B) Statement (2) ALONE is sufficient, but statement (1) alone is not sufficient to answer the question asked.

(C) Both statements TOGETHER are sufficient, but NEITHER statement ALONE is sufficient to answer the question asked.

(D) Each statement ALONE is sufficient to answer the question asked.

(E) Statements (1) and (2) TOGETHER are NOT sufficient to answer the question asked.

407. Is $wz(x+y)$ a negative even integer?

(1) w, x, and y are positive odd integers.

(2) z is a negative even integer.

(A) Statement (1) ALONE is sufficient, but statement (2) alone is not sufficient to answer the question asked.

(B) Statement (2) ALONE is sufficient, but statement (1) alone is not sufficient to answer the question asked.

(C) Both statements TOGETHER are sufficient, but NEITHER statement ALONE is sufficient to answer the question asked.

(D) Each statement ALONE is sufficient to answer the question asked.

(E) Statements (1) and (2) TOGETHER are NOT sufficient to answer the question asked.

408. Is $RX > \$2,000$?

(1) One percent of R times $300,000 is $1,500.

(2) One-fourth percent of X is $12.50.

(A) Statement (1) ALONE is sufficient, but statement (2) alone is not sufficient to answer the question asked.

(B) Statement (2) ALONE is sufficient, but statement (1) alone is not sufficient to answer the question asked.

(C) Both statements TOGETHER are sufficient, but NEITHER statement ALONE is sufficient to answer the question asked.

(D) Each statement ALONE is sufficient to answer the question asked.

(E) Statements (1) and (2) TOGETHER are NOT sufficient to answer the question asked.

409. A square is inscribed in a circle. What is the area of the circle?

(1) The area of the square is 18.

(2) The circumference of the circle is 6π.

(A) Statement (1) ALONE is sufficient, but statement (2) alone is not sufficient to answer the question asked.

(B) Statement (2) ALONE is sufficient, but statement (1) alone is not sufficient to answer the question asked.

(C) Both statements TOGETHER are sufficient, but NEITHER statement ALONE is sufficient to answer the question asked.

(D) Each statement ALONE is sufficient to answer the question asked.

(E) Statements (1) and (2) TOGETHER are NOT sufficient to answer the question asked.

410. What is the ratio of the number of men to the number of women at the ceremony?

(1) There are three times as many women as men at the ceremony.

(2) The number of women is $\frac{3}{4}$ the total of men and women at the ceremony.

(A) Statement (1) ALONE is sufficient, but statement (2) alone is not sufficient to answer the question asked.

(B) Statement (2) ALONE is sufficient, but statement (1) alone is not sufficient to answer the question asked.

(C) Both statements TOGETHER are sufficient, but NEITHER statement ALONE is sufficient to answer the question asked.

(D) Each statement ALONE is sufficient to answer the question asked.

(E) Statements (1) and (2) TOGETHER are NOT sufficient to answer the question asked.

411. An investor invests $10,000 at R percent simple annual interest and a different amount at P percent simple annual interest. What total amount did the investor invest?

(1) The total amount of interest earned by the two investments in one year is $1,800.

(2) $R\% = 6\%$.

(A) Statement (1) ALONE is sufficient, but statement (2) alone is not sufficient to answer the question asked.

(B) Statement (2) ALONE is sufficient, but statement (1) alone is not sufficient to answer the question asked.

(C) Both statements TOGETHER are sufficient, but NEITHER statement ALONE is sufficient to answer the question asked.

(D) Each statement ALONE is sufficient to answer the question asked.

(E) Statements (1) and (2) TOGETHER are NOT sufficient to answer the question asked.

412. If h denotes the hundredths digit of the number $X = 0.4h8$, what digit is h?

(1) The number X rounded to the nearest tenth is 0.5.

(2) The number X rounded to the nearest hundredth is 0.47.

(A) Statement (1) ALONE is sufficient, but statement (2) alone is not sufficient to answer the question asked.

(B) Statement (2) ALONE is sufficient, but statement (1) alone is not sufficient to answer the question asked.

(C) Both statements TOGETHER are sufficient, but NEITHER statement ALONE is sufficient to answer the question asked.

(D) Each statement ALONE is sufficient to answer the question asked.

(E) Statements (1) and (2) TOGETHER are NOT sufficient to answer the question asked.

413. If m and n are positive integers, is the product mn even?

(1) $m + 1$ is odd.

(2) $m + n$ is odd.

(A) Statement (1) ALONE is sufficient, but statement (2) alone is not sufficient to answer the question asked.

(B) Statement (2) ALONE is sufficient, but statement (1) alone is not sufficient to answer the question asked.

(C) Both statements TOGETHER are sufficient, but NEITHER statement ALONE is sufficient to answer the question asked.

(D) Each statement ALONE is sufficient to answer the question asked.

(E) Statements (1) and (2) TOGETHER are NOT sufficient to answer the question asked.

414. The net proceeds increase as the number of tickets sold increases. Did the net proceeds exceed $80,000 on 7,600 tickets sold?

(1) The net proceeds exceeded $40,000 on 4,000 tickets sold.

(2) The net proceeds exceeded $100,000 on $7,000 tickets sold.

(A) Statement (1) ALONE is sufficient, but statement (2) alone is not sufficient to answer the question asked.

(B) Statement (2) ALONE is sufficient, but statement (1) alone is not sufficient to answer the question asked.

(C) Both statements TOGETHER are sufficient, but NEITHER statement ALONE is sufficient to answer the question asked.

(D) Each statement ALONE is sufficient to answer the question asked.

(E) Statements (1) and (2) TOGETHER are NOT sufficient to answer the question asked.

415. If x and y are integers such that $0 < x < y$, what is the value of xy?

(1) $\sqrt{x} + \sqrt{y} = 4$

(2) $x + y = 10$

(A) Statement (1) ALONE is sufficient, but statement (2) alone is not sufficient to answer the question asked.

(B) Statement (2) ALONE is sufficient, but statement (1) alone is not sufficient to answer the question asked.

(C) Both statements TOGETHER are sufficient, but NEITHER statement ALONE is sufficient to answer the question asked.

(D) Each statement ALONE is sufficient to answer the question asked.

(E) Statements (1) and (2) TOGETHER are NOT sufficient to answer the question asked.

416. By what percent was the original price of the computer discounted?

    (1) The original price of the computer is 25 percent greater than the discounted price.

    (2) The computer's discounted price is $148 less than the computer's original price.

    (A) Statement (1) ALONE is sufficient, but statement (2) alone is not sufficient to answer the question asked.

    (B) Statement (2) ALONE is sufficient, but statement (1) alone is not sufficient to answer the question asked.

    (C) Both statements TOGETHER are sufficient, but NEITHER statement ALONE is sufficient to answer the question asked.

    (D) Each statement ALONE is sufficient to answer the question asked.

    (E) Statements (1) and (2) TOGETHER are NOT sufficient to answer the question asked.

417. A retail store sent out a promotional offer to 300 former customers and 700 potential customers. What percent of the total number of people who received the promotional offer gave a favorable response?

    (1) The store received a favorable response from 30 percent of the former customers.

    (2) The store received a favorable response from 20 percent of the potential customers.

    (A) Statement (1) ALONE is sufficient, but statement (2) alone is not sufficient to answer the question asked.

    (B) Statement (2) ALONE is sufficient, but statement (1) alone is not sufficient to answer the question asked.

    (C) Both statements TOGETHER are sufficient, but NEITHER statement ALONE is sufficient to answer the question asked.

    (D) Each statement ALONE is sufficient to answer the question asked.

    (E) Statements (1) and (2) TOGETHER are NOT sufficient to answer the question asked.

418. If A and B are both positive, A is what percent of B?

    (1) $33\frac{1}{3}\% A$ is $25\% B$.

    (2) $A + B = 175$.

    (A) Statement (1) ALONE is sufficient, but statement (2) alone is not sufficient to answer the question asked.

    (B) Statement (2) ALONE is sufficient, but statement (1) alone is not sufficient to answer the question asked.

    (C) Both statements TOGETHER are sufficient, but NEITHER statement ALONE is sufficient to answer the question asked.

    (D) Each statement ALONE is sufficient to answer the question asked.

    (E) Statements (1) and (2) TOGETHER are NOT sufficient to answer the question asked.

419. Machine A and machine B working at their constant respective rates produced 50 components in 20 minutes. How much time, in minutes, would it have taken machine B working alone at its constant rate to produce 50 components?

(1) Machine A produced 10 fewer components than did machine B.

(2) The rate at which machine B works is 50 percent faster than the rate at which machine A works.

(A) Statement (1) ALONE is sufficient, but statement (2) alone is not sufficient to answer the question asked.

(B) Statement (2) ALONE is sufficient, but statement (1) alone is not sufficient to answer the question asked.

(C) Both statements TOGETHER are sufficient, but NEITHER statement ALONE is sufficient to answer the question asked.

(D) Each statement ALONE is sufficient to answer the question asked.

(E) Statements (1) and (2) TOGETHER are NOT sufficient to answer the question asked.

420. What is the least positive value of x for which $\frac{1}{6} + kx^2$ is at least $\frac{5}{6}$?

(1) $k = \frac{1}{5,400}$

(2) $\frac{1}{6} + 900k = \frac{1}{3}$

(A) Statement (1) ALONE is sufficient, but statement (2) alone is not sufficient to answer the question asked.

(B) Statement (2) ALONE is sufficient, but statement (1) alone is not sufficient to answer the question asked.

(C) Both statements TOGETHER are sufficient, but NEITHER statement ALONE is sufficient to answer the question asked.

(D) Each statement ALONE is sufficient to answer the question asked.

(E) Statements (1) and (2) TOGETHER are NOT sufficient to answer the question asked.

421. If x and y are integers, what is the value of xy?

(1) $x^2 - y^2 < 0$

(2) $x^y = \frac{1}{16}$

(A) Statement (1) ALONE is sufficient, but statement (2) alone is not sufficient to answer the question asked.

(B) Statement (2) ALONE is sufficient, but statement (1) alone is not sufficient to answer the question asked.

(C) Both statements TOGETHER are sufficient, but NEITHER statement ALONE is sufficient to answer the question asked.

(D) Each statement ALONE is sufficient to answer the question asked.

(E) Statements (1) and (2) TOGETHER are NOT sufficient to answer the question asked.

422. What is the value of $a + c$?

(1) The arithmetic average of a and b is 55.

(2) The arithmetic average of b and c is 70.

(A) Statement (1) ALONE is sufficient, but statement (2) alone is not sufficient to answer the question asked.

(B) Statement (2) ALONE is sufficient, but statement (1) alone is not sufficient to answer the question asked.

(C) Both statements TOGETHER are sufficient, but NEITHER statement ALONE is sufficient to answer the question asked.

(D) Each statement ALONE is sufficient to answer the question asked.

(E) Statements (1) and (2) TOGETHER are NOT sufficient to answer the question asked.

423. If $xy \neq 0$, what is the value of $\frac{x}{3}$ divided by $\frac{y}{5}$.

(1) $3x = 5y$

(2) $\sqrt{\dfrac{5x}{3y}} = \dfrac{5}{3}$

(A) Statement (1) ALONE is sufficient, but statement (2) alone is not sufficient to answer the question asked.

(B) Statement (2) ALONE is sufficient, but statement (1) alone is not sufficient to answer the question asked.

(C) Both statements TOGETHER are sufficient, but NEITHER statement ALONE is sufficient to answer the question asked.

(D) Each statement ALONE is sufficient to answer the question asked.

(E) Statements (1) and (2) TOGETHER are NOT sufficient to answer the question asked.

424. Of the 220 restaurants in a certain city, how many serve neither shrimp nor crab?

(1) 94 serve shrimp and 72 serve crab.

(2) 42 serve both shrimp and crab.

(A) Statement (1) ALONE is sufficient, but statement (2) alone is not sufficient to answer the question asked.

(B) Statement (2) ALONE is sufficient, but statement (1) alone is not sufficient to answer the question asked.

(C) Both statements TOGETHER are sufficient, but NEITHER statement ALONE is sufficient to answer the question asked.

(D) Each statement ALONE is sufficient to answer the question asked.

(E) Statements (1) and (2) TOGETHER are NOT sufficient to answer the question asked.

425. If b is an integer how many values of b satisfy $a < b < c$?

(1) $a + b$ is an integer.

(2) $c - a = 6.5$.

(A) Statement (1) ALONE is sufficient, but statement (2) alone is not sufficient to answer the question asked.

(B) Statement (2) ALONE is sufficient, but statement (1) alone is not sufficient to answer the question asked.

(C) Both statements TOGETHER are sufficient, but NEITHER statement ALONE is sufficient to answer the question asked.

(D) Each statement ALONE is sufficient to answer the question asked.

(E) Statements (1) and (2) TOGETHER are NOT sufficient to answer the question asked.

426. How much compensation did Nio receive for selling 21 home security systems last month?

(1) For each system that he sells, Nio receives a fee of $25 plus a 15 percent commission on the selling price.

(2) The selling prices of the 21 systems that Nio sold totaled $52,500.

(A) Statement (1) ALONE is sufficient, but statement (2) alone is not sufficient to answer the question asked.

(B) Statement (2) ALONE is sufficient, but statement (1) alone is not sufficient to answer the question asked.

(C) Both statements TOGETHER are sufficient, but NEITHER statement ALONE is sufficient to answer the question asked.

(D) Each statement ALONE is sufficient to answer the question asked.

(E) Statements (1) and (2) TOGETHER are NOT sufficient to answer the question asked.

427. Is X less than $\frac{1}{4}Y$?

(1) $X + 50 = Y - 50$

(2) $X + Y = 1.2Y$

(A) Statement (1) ALONE is sufficient, but statement (2) alone is not sufficient to answer the question asked.

(B) Statement (2) ALONE is sufficient, but statement (1) alone is not sufficient to answer the question asked.

(C) Both statements TOGETHER are sufficient, but NEITHER statement ALONE is sufficient to answer the question asked.

(D) Each statement ALONE is sufficient to answer the question asked.

(E) Statements (1) and (2) TOGETHER are NOT sufficient to answer the question asked.

428. Is integer K even?

(1) The sum of K, $K + 20$, $K + 25$ is even.

(2) The sum of $K - 15$, K, $K + 23$, $K + 24$ is even.

(A) Statement (1) ALONE is sufficient, but statement (2) alone is not sufficient to answer the question asked.

(B) Statement (2) ALONE is sufficient, but statement (1) alone is not sufficient to answer the question asked.

(C) Both statements TOGETHER are sufficient, but NEITHER statement ALONE is sufficient to answer the question asked.

(D) Each statement ALONE is sufficient to answer the question asked.

(E) Statements (1) and (2) TOGETHER are NOT sufficient to answer the question asked.

429. Both Nayeli and Tristan received raises this year. Which one received the greater percent increase over last year's salary?

(1) Nayeli's salary increased from $46,000 to $48,300.

(2) Tristan's salary increased by $2,500 over last year's salary.

(A) Statement (1) ALONE is sufficient, but statement (2) alone is not sufficient to answer the question asked.

(B) Statement (2) ALONE is sufficient, but statement (1) alone is not sufficient to answer the question asked.

(C) Both statements TOGETHER are sufficient, but NEITHER statement ALONE is sufficient to answer the question asked.

(D) Each statement ALONE is sufficient to answer the question asked.

(E) Statements (1) and (2) TOGETHER are NOT sufficient to answer the question asked.

430. What will be a certain country's national debt in 30 days?

(1) The country's national debt increases by $120 million every day.

(2) The country's national debt is currently $50 billion.

(A) Statement (1) ALONE is sufficient, but statement (2) alone is not sufficient to answer the question asked.

(B) Statement (2) ALONE is sufficient, but statement (1) alone is not sufficient to answer the question asked.

(C) Both statements TOGETHER are sufficient, but NEITHER statement ALONE is sufficient to answer the question asked.

(D) Each statement ALONE is sufficient to answer the question asked.

(E) Statements (1) and (2) TOGETHER are NOT sufficient to answer the question asked.

431. In a certain stock fund, 50 percent of the funds is invested in stocks from U.S. companies. What is the total value of the stock fund?

(1) Of the funds invested in U.S. companies, 12.5 percent are invested in Texas companies.

(2) The fund has 20 million dollars invested in Texas companies.

(A) Statement (1) ALONE is sufficient, but statement (2) alone is not sufficient to answer the question asked.

(B) Statement (2) ALONE is sufficient, but statement (1) alone is not sufficient to answer the question asked.

(C) Both statements TOGETHER are sufficient, but NEITHER statement ALONE is sufficient to answer the question asked.

(D) Each statement ALONE is sufficient to answer the question asked.

(E) Statements (1) and (2) TOGETHER are NOT sufficient to answer the question asked.

432. What is the value of integer k?

(1) $k^2 < 16$

(2) $-60 < k^3 < -20$

(A) Statement (1) ALONE is sufficient, but statement (2) alone is not sufficient to answer the question asked.

(B) Statement (2) ALONE is sufficient, but statement (1) alone is not sufficient to answer the question asked.

(C) Both statements TOGETHER are sufficient, but NEITHER statement ALONE is sufficient to answer the question asked.

(D) Each statement ALONE is sufficient to answer the question asked.

(E) Statements (1) and (2) TOGETHER are NOT sufficient to answer the question asked.

433. If t denotes the thousandths digit of the number $X = 0.01t5$, what is the value of X rounded to the nearest hundredth?

(1) The sum of the digits of X is less than 10.

(2) $X > 0.0125$

(A) Statement (1) ALONE is sufficient, but statement (2) alone is not sufficient to answer the question asked.

(B) Statement (2) ALONE is sufficient, but statement (1) alone is not sufficient to answer the question asked.

(C) Both statements TOGETHER are sufficient, but NEITHER statement ALONE is sufficient to answer the question asked.

(D) Each statement ALONE is sufficient to answer the question asked.

(E) Statements (1) and (2) TOGETHER are NOT sufficient to answer the question asked.

434. How many kilometers is the flight from city A to city B?

(1) Traveling at a speed of 270 kilometers per hour, the flight from city A to city B takes $6\frac{2}{3}$ hours.

(2) Traveling at a speed of 300 kilometers per hour, the flight from city A to city B takes 40 minutes less than when traveling at a speed of 270 kilometers per hour.

(A) Statement (1) ALONE is sufficient, but statement (2) alone is not sufficient to answer the question asked.

(B) Statement (2) ALONE is sufficient, but statement (1) alone is not sufficient to answer the question asked.

(C) Both statements TOGETHER are sufficient, but NEITHER statement ALONE is sufficient to answer the question asked.

(D) Each statement ALONE is sufficient to answer the question asked.

(E) Statements (1) and (2) TOGETHER are NOT sufficient to answer the question asked.

435. The total area of the smaller circle is what percent of the total area of the larger circle?

(1) The length of the radius of the larger circle is 300 percent longer than the length of the radius of the smaller circle.

(2) The ratio of the length of the radius of the larger circle to the length of the radius of the smaller circle is 4 to 1.

(A) Statement (1) ALONE is sufficient, but statement (2) alone is not sufficient to answer the question asked.

(B) Statement (2) ALONE is sufficient, but statement (1) alone is not sufficient to answer the question asked.

(C) Both statements TOGETHER are sufficient, but NEITHER statement ALONE is sufficient to answer the question asked.

(D) Each statement ALONE is sufficient to answer the question asked.

(E) Statements (1) and (2) TOGETHER are NOT sufficient to answer the question asked.

436. From 2015 to 2017, the value of products labeled gluten-free sold by a certain grocery store increased by what percent?

(1) In 2015, products labeled gluten-free accounted for 2.4 percent of the value of all products sold in the grocery store.

(2) In 2017, products labeled gluten-free accounted for 7.2 percent of the value of all products sold in the grocery store.

(A) Statement (1) ALONE is sufficient, but statement (2) alone is not sufficient to answer the question asked.

(B) Statement (2) ALONE is sufficient, but statement (1) alone is not sufficient to answer the question asked.

(C) Both statements TOGETHER are sufficient, but NEITHER statement ALONE is sufficient to answer the question asked.

(D) Each statement ALONE is sufficient to answer the question asked.

(E) Statements (1) and (2) TOGETHER are NOT sufficient to answer the question asked.

437. What was Hachi's average number of pages read for 15 days?

(1) Hachi read an average of 22 pages during the first 10 days.

(2) The average number of pages Hachi read during the first 10 days is two more than twice the average number of pages read for the remainder of the days.

(A) Statement (1) ALONE is sufficient, but statement (2) alone is not sufficient to answer the question asked.

(B) Statement (2) ALONE is sufficient, but statement (1) alone is not sufficient to answer the question asked.

(C) Both statements TOGETHER are sufficient, but NEITHER statement ALONE is sufficient to answer the question asked.

(D) Each statement ALONE is sufficient to answer the question asked.

(E) Statements (1) and (2) TOGETHER are NOT sufficient to answer the question asked.

438. If p is a prime number, how many positive factors of Y are not factors of X?

(1) $X = 4p$

(2) $Y = 8p$

(A) Statement (1) ALONE is sufficient, but statement (2) alone is not sufficient to answer the question asked.

(B) Statement (2) ALONE is sufficient, but statement (1) alone is not sufficient to answer the question asked.

(C) Both statements TOGETHER are sufficient, but NEITHER statement ALONE is sufficient to answer the question asked.

(D) Each statement ALONE is sufficient to answer the question asked.

(E) Statements (1) and (2) TOGETHER are NOT sufficient to answer the question asked.

439. If a, b, and c are positive integers, is $a - 2b + 3c > a + 2b - 3c$?

(1) $a < b$

(2) $b < c$

(A) Statement (1) ALONE is sufficient, but statement (2) alone is not sufficient to answer the question asked.

(B) Statement (2) ALONE is sufficient, but statement (1) alone is not sufficient to answer the question asked.

(C) Both statements TOGETHER are sufficient, but NEITHER statement ALONE is sufficient to answer the question asked.

(D) Each statement ALONE is sufficient to answer the question asked.

(E) Statements (1) and (2) TOGETHER are NOT sufficient to answer the question asked.

440. At company X, do at least 40 percent of the workers over the age of 40 years have 401(k) accounts?

(1) At company X, 16 percent of the workers age 40 years and younger have 401(k) accounts and 29 percent of all workers at the company have 401(k) accounts.

(2) At company X, there are more workers age 40 years of age and younger than workers over the age of 40.

(A) Statement (1) ALONE is sufficient, but statement (2) alone is not sufficient to answer the question asked.

(B) Statement (2) ALONE is sufficient, but statement (1) alone is not sufficient to answer the question asked.

(C) Both statements TOGETHER are sufficient, but NEITHER statement ALONE is sufficient to answer the question asked.

(D) Each statement ALONE is sufficient to answer the question asked.

(E) Statements (1) and (2) TOGETHER are NOT sufficient to answer the question asked.

441. If r is greater than 120 percent of s, is $r > 70$?

(1) $60 < s < 80$

(2) $r - s = 40$

(A) Statement (1) ALONE is sufficient, but statement (2) alone is not sufficient to answer the question asked.

(B) Statement (2) ALONE is sufficient, but statement (1) alone is not sufficient to answer the question asked.

(C) Both statements TOGETHER are sufficient, but NEITHER statement ALONE is sufficient to answer the question asked.

(D) Each statement ALONE is sufficient to answer the question asked.

(E) Statements (1) and (2) TOGETHER are NOT sufficient to answer the question asked.

442. Initially, how many black chips are in a box containing only red chips and black chips, all identical except for color?

(1) Initially, the ratio of red chips to black chips in the box is $\frac{3}{25}$.

(2) If 12 red chips and 80 black chips are removed from the box, the probability of randomly drawing a red chip from the box is $\frac{1}{11}$.

(A) Statement (1) ALONE is sufficient, but statement (2) alone is not sufficient to answer the question asked.

(B) Statement (2) ALONE is sufficient, but statement (1) alone is not sufficient to answer the question asked.

(C) Both statements TOGETHER are sufficient, but NEITHER statement ALONE is sufficient to answer the question asked.

(D) Each statement ALONE is sufficient to answer the question asked.

(E) Statements (1) and (2) TOGETHER are NOT sufficient to answer the question asked.

443. Does the line defined by $y = mx + b$ contain the point $(3,1)$?

(1) The line is perpendicular to $y = -5x$.

(2) The line contains the point $\left(0, \frac{2}{5}\right)$.

(A) Statement (1) ALONE is sufficient, but statement (2) alone is not sufficient to answer the question asked.

(B) Statement (2) ALONE is sufficient, but statement (1) alone is not sufficient to answer the question asked.

(C) Both statements TOGETHER are sufficient, but NEITHER statement ALONE is sufficient to answer the question asked.

(D) Each statement ALONE is sufficient to answer the question asked.

(E) Statements (1) and (2) TOGETHER are NOT sufficient to answer the question asked.

444. A jar contains 100 glass beads, of which 56 are pink and 44 are blue. If 24 beads are removed from the jar, how many of the beads remaining are blue?

(1) After the 24 beads are removed, the number of pink beads remaining in the bag equals the number of blue beads remaining in the bag.

(2) Of the beads removed, the ratio of the number of pink beads to the number of blue beads is 3 to 1.

(A) Statement (1) ALONE is sufficient, but statement (2) alone is not sufficient to answer the question asked.

(B) Statement (2) ALONE is sufficient, but statement (1) alone is not sufficient to answer the question asked.

(C) Both statements TOGETHER are sufficient, but NEITHER statement ALONE is sufficient to answer the question asked.

(D) Each statement ALONE is sufficient to answer the question asked.

(E) Statements (1) and (2) TOGETHER are NOT sufficient to answer the question asked.

445. Cerenity and Jas rented a jet ski for an afternoon. The rental fee for the first hour is more than for each additional hour. If Cerenity and Jas paid $16.50 when they returned the jet ski, for how many hours did they rent the jet ski?

(1) Cerenity and Jas paid $10.50 for the first 2 hours.

(2) Cerenity and Jas paid $9.00 for the last 3 hours.

(A) Statement (1) ALONE is sufficient, but statement (2) alone is not sufficient to answer the question asked.

(B) Statement (2) ALONE is sufficient, but statement (1) alone is not sufficient to answer the question asked.

(C) Both statements TOGETHER are sufficient, but NEITHER statement ALONE is sufficient to answer the question asked.

(D) Each statement ALONE is sufficient to answer the question asked.

(E) Statements (1) and (2) TOGETHER are NOT sufficient to answer the question asked.

446. If k is a prime number, what is the value of k?

(1) $3k$ is a common factor of 24 and 36.

(2) k is a factor of 6.

(A) Statement (1) ALONE is sufficient, but statement (2) alone is not sufficient to answer the question asked.

(B) Statement (2) ALONE is sufficient, but statement (1) alone is not sufficient to answer the question asked.

(C) Both statements TOGETHER are sufficient, but NEITHER statement ALONE is sufficient to answer the question asked.

(D) Each statement ALONE is sufficient to answer the question asked.

(E) Statements (1) and (2) TOGETHER are NOT sufficient to answer the question asked.

447. The cost of all items of type 1 is exactly the same, and the cost of all items of type 2 is exactly the same. Is the cost of one item of type 1 less than the cost of one item of type 2?

(1) The total cost of 6 items of type 1 and 4 items of type 2 is less than the total cost of 4 items of type 1 and 8 items of type 2.

(2) The total cost of 5 items of type 1 and 4 items of type 2 is less than the total cost of 4 items of type 1 and 5 items of type 2.

(A) Statement (1) ALONE is sufficient, but statement (2) alone is not sufficient to answer the question asked.

(B) Statement (2) ALONE is sufficient, but statement (1) alone is not sufficient to answer the question asked.

(C) Both statements TOGETHER are sufficient, but NEITHER statement ALONE is sufficient to answer the question asked.

(D) Each statement ALONE is sufficient to answer the question asked.

(E) Statements (1) and (2) TOGETHER are NOT sufficient to answer the question asked.

448. The arithmetic average cost of the three items that Emma purchased from a grocery store is $25. No sales tax was charged on any item that cost less than $40. A sales tax of 8 percent was charged on any item that cost $40 or more. What is the sales tax on the three items that Emma purchased?

(1) The most costly item that Emma purchased was $50.

(2) The least costly item that Emma purchased was $5.

(A) Statement (1) ALONE is sufficient, but statement (2) alone is not sufficient to answer the question asked.

(B) Statement (2) ALONE is sufficient, but statement (1) alone is not sufficient to answer the question asked.

(C) Both statements TOGETHER are sufficient, but NEITHER statement ALONE is sufficient to answer the question asked.

(D) Each statement ALONE is sufficient to answer the question asked.

(E) Statements (1) and (2) TOGETHER are NOT sufficient to answer the question asked.

449. Harper interviewed for a job with company A and with company B. What is the probability that Harper will get job offers from both companies?

(1) The probability that Harper will get a job offer from exactly one of the companies is 0.6.

(2) The probability that Harper will get a job offer from neither company is 0.1.

(A) Statement (1) ALONE is sufficient, but statement (2) alone is not sufficient to answer the question asked.

(B) Statement (2) ALONE is sufficient, but statement (1) alone is not sufficient to answer the question asked.

(C) Both statements TOGETHER are sufficient, but NEITHER statement ALONE is sufficient to answer the question asked.

(D) Each statement ALONE is sufficient to answer the question asked.

(E) Statements (1) and (2) TOGETHER are NOT sufficient to answer the question asked.

450. If x and y are the standard deviations of two different data sets, is $x > y$?

(1) x is the standard deviation of the data set 50, 50, 50, 50, 50, 50, 50, 50 50, 50, 50.

(2) y is the standard deviation of the data set 40, 42, 44, 46, 48, 50, 52, 54 56, 58, 60.

(A) Statement (1) ALONE is sufficient, but statement (2) alone is not sufficient to answer the question asked.

(B) Statement (2) ALONE is sufficient, but statement (1) alone is not sufficient to answer the question asked.

(C) Both statements TOGETHER are sufficient, but NEITHER statement ALONE is sufficient to answer the question asked.

(D) Each statement ALONE is sufficient to answer the question asked.

(E) Statements (1) and (2) TOGETHER are NOT sufficient to answer the question asked.

451. A bag contains 24 chips, each of which is black, blue, green, or red, all identical except for color. If a chip is randomly drawn from the bag, what is the probability that the chip drawn is black or blue?

(1) The probability that the chip drawn will be green or red is $\frac{1}{2}$.

(2) The probability that the chip drawn is black is $\frac{1}{3}$.

(A) Statement (1) ALONE is sufficient, but statement (2) alone is not sufficient to answer the question asked.

(B) Statement (2) ALONE is sufficient, but statement (1) alone is not sufficient to answer the question asked.

(C) Both statements TOGETHER are sufficient, but NEITHER statement ALONE is sufficient to answer the question asked.

(D) Each statement ALONE is sufficient to answer the question asked.

(E) Statements (1) and (2) TOGETHER are NOT sufficient to answer the question asked.

452. In the parallelogram shown, what is the value of a?

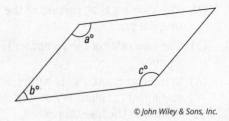

© John Wiley & Sons, Inc.

(1) $a = 3b$

(2) $a + c = 270$

(A) Statement (1) ALONE is sufficient, but statement (2) alone is not sufficient to answer the question asked.

(B) Statement (2) ALONE is sufficient, but statement (1) alone is not sufficient to answer the question asked.

(C) Both statements TOGETHER are sufficient, but NEITHER statement ALONE is sufficient to answer the question asked.

(D) Each statement ALONE is sufficient to answer the question asked.

(E) Statements (1) and (2) TOGETHER are NOT sufficient to answer the question asked.

453. The original price of a certain computer has increased. The increase is what percent of the new price?

(1) The increase is 25 percent of the original price.

(2) The new price of the computer is $1,200.

(A) Statement (1) ALONE is sufficient, but statement (2) alone is not sufficient to answer the question asked.

(B) Statement (2) ALONE is sufficient, but statement (1) alone is not sufficient to answer the question asked.

(C) Both statements TOGETHER are sufficient, but NEITHER statement ALONE is sufficient to answer the question asked.

(D) Each statement ALONE is sufficient to answer the question asked.

(E) Statements (1) and (2) TOGETHER are NOT sufficient to answer the question asked.

454. What is Makayla's current age?

(1) If Makayla were twice her current age, she would be two years younger than Gilbert is now.

(2) In four years, Makayla will be Gilbert's current age.

(A) Statement (1) ALONE is sufficient, but statement (2) alone is not sufficient to answer the question asked.

(B) Statement (2) ALONE is sufficient, but statement (1) alone is not sufficient to answer the question asked.

(C) Both statements TOGETHER are sufficient, but NEITHER statement ALONE is sufficient to answer the question asked.

(D) Each statement ALONE is sufficient to answer the question asked.

(E) Statements (1) and (2) TOGETHER are NOT sufficient to answer the question asked.

455. If $x = \dfrac{a}{2} = 3b$, what is the value of $a^2 - b^2$?

(1) $\dfrac{x^3}{27} = -1$

(2) $|x| = 3$

(A) Statement (1) ALONE is sufficient, but statement (2) alone is not sufficient to answer the question asked.

(B) Statement (2) ALONE is sufficient, but statement (1) alone is not sufficient to answer the question asked.

(C) Both statements TOGETHER are sufficient, but NEITHER statement ALONE is sufficient to answer the question asked.

(D) Each statement ALONE is sufficient to answer the question asked.

(E) Statements (1) and (2) TOGETHER are NOT sufficient to answer the question asked.

456. If t denotes the thousandths digit of the number $N = 0.56t8$, what digit is t?

(1) If N is rounded to the nearest hundredth, the result would be 0.57.

(2) If N is rounded to the nearest thousandth, the result would be 0.568.

(A) Statement (1) ALONE is sufficient, but statement (2) alone is not sufficient to answer the question asked.

(B) Statement (2) ALONE is sufficient, but statement (1) alone is not sufficient to answer the question asked.

(C) Both statements TOGETHER are sufficient, but NEITHER statement ALONE is sufficient to answer the question asked.

(D) Each statement ALONE is sufficient to answer the question asked.

(E) Statements (1) and (2) TOGETHER are NOT sufficient to answer the question asked.

457. If r and s are positive integers, what is the value of $\frac{r}{s}$?

(1) $rs = 15$

(2) $r + s = 8$

(A) Statement (1) ALONE is sufficient, but statement (2) alone is not sufficient to answer the question asked.

(B) Statement (2) ALONE is sufficient, but statement (1) alone is not sufficient to answer the question asked.

(C) Both statements TOGETHER are sufficient, but NEITHER statement ALONE is sufficient to answer the question asked.

(D) Each statement ALONE is sufficient to answer the question asked.

(E) Statements (1) and (2) TOGETHER are NOT sufficient to answer the question asked.

458. A car and a van are traveling at different constant speeds on a straight highway. If the car is now 4 miles ahead of the van, how much time, in hours, will it take for the car to be 10 miles ahead of the van?

(1) The car is traveling 70 miles per hour and the truck is traveling 65 miles per hour.

(2) One hour ago, the car was 1 mile behind the van.

(A) Statement (1) ALONE is sufficient, but statement (2) alone is not sufficient to answer the question asked.

(B) Statement (2) ALONE is sufficient, but statement (1) alone is not sufficient to answer the question asked.

(C) Both statements TOGETHER are sufficient, but NEITHER statement ALONE is sufficient to answer the question asked.

(D) Each statement ALONE is sufficient to answer the question asked.

(E) Statements (1) and (2) TOGETHER are NOT sufficient to answer the question asked.

459. A total of 83 occupants live in a college apartment complex. If there are 40 apartments and each apartment has at least two occupants, how many apartments have more than two occupants?

(1) Only one apartment has more than three occupants.

(2) The apartment manager lives in one of the apartments with her husband and two children.

(A) Statement (1) ALONE is sufficient, but statement (2) alone is not sufficient to answer the question asked.

(B) Statement (2) ALONE is sufficient, but statement (1) alone is not sufficient to answer the question asked.

(C) Both statements TOGETHER are sufficient, but NEITHER statement ALONE is sufficient to answer the question asked.

(D) Each statement ALONE is sufficient to answer the question asked.

(E) Statements (1) and (2) TOGETHER are NOT sufficient to answer the question asked.

460. If $X = \frac{a}{2^2} + \frac{b}{2^3} + \frac{c}{2^5}$, can $X = \frac{5}{16}$?

(1) a, b, and c are each either 0 or 1.

(2) The greatest possible value of X is $\frac{13}{32}$.

(A) Statement (1) ALONE is sufficient, but statement (2) alone is not sufficient to answer the question asked.

(B) Statement (2) ALONE is sufficient, but statement (1) alone is not sufficient to answer the question asked.

(C) Both statements TOGETHER are sufficient, but NEITHER statement ALONE is sufficient to answer the question asked.

(D) Each statement ALONE is sufficient to answer the question asked.

(E) Statements (1) and (2) TOGETHER are NOT sufficient to answer the question asked.

461. What is the value of $k - 4$?

(1) $(k - 2)^2 = 64$

(2) $(k + 2)^2 = 144$

(A) Statement (1) ALONE is sufficient, but statement (2) alone is not sufficient to answer the question asked.

(B) Statement (2) ALONE is sufficient, but statement (1) alone is not sufficient to answer the question asked.

(C) Both statements TOGETHER are sufficient, but NEITHER statement ALONE is sufficient to answer the question asked.

(D) Each statement ALONE is sufficient to answer the question asked.

(E) Statements (1) and (2) TOGETHER are NOT sufficient to answer the question asked.

462. If $\frac{p}{q}$ is $\frac{2}{5}$, $\frac{1}{4}$, or $\frac{4}{17}$, what is the value of $\frac{p}{q}$?

(1) $\frac{p}{q} < 0.5$

(2) $\frac{p}{q} > 0.25$

(A) Statement (1) ALONE is sufficient, but statement (2) alone is not sufficient to answer the question asked.

(B) Statement (2) ALONE is sufficient, but statement (1) alone is not sufficient to answer the question asked.

(C) Both statements TOGETHER are sufficient, but NEITHER statement ALONE is sufficient to answer the question asked.

(D) Each statement ALONE is sufficient to answer the question asked.

(E) Statements (1) and (2) TOGETHER are NOT sufficient to answer the question asked.

463. Is $4x$ less than y?

(1) $4x + 7 > y$

(2) $y > 15$

(A) Statement (1) ALONE is sufficient, but statement (2) alone is not sufficient to answer the question asked.

(B) Statement (2) ALONE is sufficient, but statement (1) alone is not sufficient to answer the question asked.

(C) Both statements TOGETHER are sufficient, but NEITHER statement ALONE is sufficient to answer the question asked.

(D) Each statement ALONE is sufficient to answer the question asked.

(E) Statements (1) and (2) TOGETHER are NOT sufficient to answer the question asked.

464. If $6 < X < 7$, is the tenths digit of the decimal representation of X greater than 6?

(1) X rounded up to the nearest integer is 7.

(2) $X + 0.28 > 7$

(A) Statement (1) ALONE is sufficient, but statement (2) alone is not sufficient to answer the question asked.

(B) Statement (2) ALONE is sufficient, but statement (1) alone is not sufficient to answer the question asked.

(C) Both statements TOGETHER are sufficient, but NEITHER statement ALONE is sufficient to answer the question asked.

(D) Each statement ALONE is sufficient to answer the question asked.

(E) Statements (1) and (2) TOGETHER are NOT sufficient to answer the question asked.

465. If $x^3 = y^4$, what is the value of x?

    (1) $y^3 = -64$

    (2) $y^2 = 16$

    (A) Statement (1) ALONE is sufficient, but statement (2) alone is not sufficient to answer the question asked.

    (B) Statement (2) ALONE is sufficient, but statement (1) alone is not sufficient to answer the question asked.

    (C) Both statements TOGETHER are sufficient, but NEITHER statement ALONE is sufficient to answer the question asked.

    (D) Each statement ALONE is sufficient to answer the question asked.

    (E) Statements (1) and (2) TOGETHER are NOT sufficient to answer the question asked.

466. In the figure shown, what is the value of x?

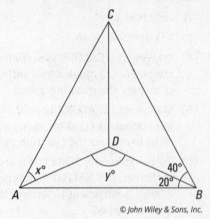

© John Wiley & Sons, Inc.

    (1) $AD = BD = CD$

    (2) $y = 140$

    (A) Statement (1) ALONE is sufficient, but statement (2) alone is not sufficient to answer the question asked.

    (B) Statement (2) ALONE is sufficient, but statement (1) alone is not sufficient to answer the question asked.

    (C) Both statements TOGETHER are sufficient, but NEITHER statement ALONE is sufficient to answer the question asked.

    (D) Each statement ALONE is sufficient to answer the question asked.

    (E) Statements (1) and (2) TOGETHER are NOT sufficient to answer the question asked.

467. If k is an integer such that $224 < k < 256$, what is the value of $\frac{k}{16}$?

(1) $\sqrt{k} < 16$

(2) k is divisible by 16.

(A) Statement (1) ALONE is sufficient, but statement (2) alone is not sufficient to answer the question asked.

(B) Statement (2) ALONE is sufficient, but statement (1) alone is not sufficient to answer the question asked.

(C) Both statements TOGETHER are sufficient, but NEITHER statement ALONE is sufficient to answer the question asked.

(D) Each statement ALONE is sufficient to answer the question asked.

(E) Statements (1) and (2) TOGETHER are NOT sufficient to answer the question asked.

468. If m is a positive integer, is $\sqrt{m}$ an integer?

(1) $\sqrt{49m}$ is an integer.

(2) $\sqrt{7m}$ is not an integer.

(A) Statement (1) ALONE is sufficient, but statement (2) alone is not sufficient to answer the question asked.

(B) Statement (2) ALONE is sufficient, but statement (1) alone is not sufficient to answer the question asked.

(C) Both statements TOGETHER are sufficient, but NEITHER statement ALONE is sufficient to answer the question asked.

(D) Each statement ALONE is sufficient to answer the question asked.

(E) Statements (1) and (2) TOGETHER are NOT sufficient to answer the question asked.

469. Is x a negative number?

(1) $-5x^{99}$ is positive.

(2) $-5x^{100}$ is negative.

(A) Statement (1) ALONE is sufficient, but statement (2) alone is not sufficient to answer the question asked.

(B) Statement (2) ALONE is sufficient, but statement (1) alone is not sufficient to answer the question asked.

(C) Both statements TOGETHER are sufficient, but NEITHER statement ALONE is sufficient to answer the question asked.

(D) Each statement ALONE is sufficient to answer the question asked.

(E) Statements (1) and (2) TOGETHER are NOT sufficient to answer the question asked.

470. A total of $5,600 in bonuses was given to three member of the sales team this month. How large was Benjamin's bonus?

(1) Sian and Lin's bonuses were the same amount.

(2) Benjamin's bonus was $\frac{1}{3}$ the amount of Sian's bonus.

(A) Statement (1) ALONE is sufficient, but statement (2) alone is not sufficient to answer the question asked.

(B) Statement (2) ALONE is sufficient, but statement (1) alone is not sufficient to answer the question asked.

(C) Both statements TOGETHER are sufficient, but NEITHER statement ALONE is sufficient to answer the question asked.

(D) Each statement ALONE is sufficient to answer the question asked.

(E) Statements (1) and (2) TOGETHER are NOT sufficient to answer the question asked.

471. If k is a positive integer, is k odd?

(1) For integer m, $m^k < 0$.

(2) $4k - 5$ is odd.

(A) Statement (1) ALONE is sufficient, but statement (2) alone is not sufficient to answer the question asked.

(B) Statement (2) ALONE is sufficient, but statement (1) alone is not sufficient to answer the question asked.

(C) Both statements TOGETHER are sufficient, but NEITHER statement ALONE is sufficient to answer the question asked.

(D) Each statement ALONE is sufficient to answer the question asked.

(E) Statements (1) and (2) TOGETHER are NOT sufficient to answer the question asked.

472. If x and y are positive integers, what is the value of $x + y$?

(1) $xy = 36$

(2) $y \geq x + 6$

(A) Statement (1) ALONE is sufficient, but statement (2) alone is not sufficient to answer the question asked.

(B) Statement (2) ALONE is sufficient, but statement (1) alone is not sufficient to answer the question asked.

(C) Both statements TOGETHER are sufficient, but NEITHER statement ALONE is sufficient to answer the question asked.

(D) Each statement ALONE is sufficient to answer the question asked.

(E) Statements (1) and (2) TOGETHER are NOT sufficient to answer the question asked.

473. If $a, b,$ and c are positive integers and $a^2 + b^2 = c^2$, what is the value of $\frac{a}{c}$?

(1) $a = 3$

(2) $c = 5$

(A) Statement (1) ALONE is sufficient, but statement (2) alone is not sufficient to answer the question asked.

(B) Statement (2) ALONE is sufficient, but statement (1) alone is not sufficient to answer the question asked.

(C) Both statements TOGETHER are sufficient, but NEITHER statement ALONE is sufficient to answer the question asked.

(D) Each statement ALONE is sufficient to answer the question asked.

(E) Statements (1) and (2) TOGETHER are NOT sufficient to answer the question asked.

474. In a random sample of 160 homeowners in a certain neighborhood, how many of the homeowners have lived in their current home for at least 10 years?

    (1) In the sample, the number of homeowners who have <u>not</u> lived in their current home for at least 10 years is three times the numbers who have lived in their current home for at least 10 years.

    (2) In the sample, the number of homeowners who have <u>not</u> lived in their current home for at least 10 years is 80 more than the number who have lived in their current home for at least 10 years.

    (A) Statement (1) ALONE is sufficient, but statement (2) alone is not sufficient to answer the question asked.

    (B) Statement (2) ALONE is sufficient, but statement (1) alone is not sufficient to answer the question asked.

    (C) Both statements TOGETHER are sufficient, but NEITHER statement ALONE is sufficient to answer the question asked.

    (D) Each statement ALONE is sufficient to answer the question asked.

    (E) Statements (1) and (2) TOGETHER are NOT sufficient to answer the question asked.

475. Piper bought three shirts. The three shirts cost $210 in total, not including sales tax. What was the cost of the most expensive shirt?

    (1) One shirt was twice as expensive as exactly one of the other shirts.

    (2) One shirt cost one-half as much as exactly one of the other shirts.

    (A) Statement (1) ALONE is sufficient, but statement (2) alone is not sufficient to answer the question asked.

    (B) Statement (2) ALONE is sufficient, but statement (1) alone is not sufficient to answer the question asked.

    (C) Both statements TOGETHER are sufficient, but NEITHER statement ALONE is sufficient to answer the question asked.

    (D) Each statement ALONE is sufficient to answer the question asked.

    (E) Statements (1) and (2) TOGETHER are NOT sufficient to answer the question asked.

476. If $xy \neq 0$, what is the value of $\frac{x}{y}$?

    (1) $xy = 3x^2$

    (2) The ratio of $\frac{1}{4}x$ to $2y$ is 1 to 24.

    (A) Statement (1) ALONE is sufficient, but statement (2) alone is not sufficient to answer the question asked.

    (B) Statement (2) ALONE is sufficient, but statement (1) alone is not sufficient to answer the question asked.

    (C) Both statements TOGETHER are sufficient, but NEITHER statement ALONE is sufficient to answer the question asked.

    (D) Each statement ALONE is sufficient to answer the question asked.

    (E) Statements (1) and (2) TOGETHER are NOT sufficient to answer the question asked.

477. In triangle ABC shown what is the value of $a^2 + b^2$?

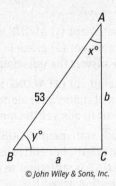

© John Wiley & Sons, Inc.

(1) $2(x + y) = 180$

(2) $x = y$

(A) Statement (1) ALONE is sufficient, but statement (2) alone is not sufficient to answer the question asked.

(B) Statement (2) ALONE is sufficient, but statement (1) alone is not sufficient to answer the question asked.

(C) Both statements TOGETHER are sufficient, but NEITHER statement ALONE is sufficient to answer the question asked.

(D) Each statement ALONE is sufficient to answer the question asked.

(E) Statements (1) and (2) TOGETHER are NOT sufficient to answer the question asked.

478. If x, y, and z are positive integers and $x \neq z$, is $x = \dfrac{y^2}{x - z}$?

(1) $(x - y)(x + y) = xz$

(2) $y^2 \geq x - z$

(A) Statement (1) ALONE is sufficient, but statement (2) alone is not sufficient to answer the question asked.

(B) Statement (2) ALONE is sufficient, but statement (1) alone is not sufficient to answer the question asked.

(C) Both statements TOGETHER are sufficient, but NEITHER statement ALONE is sufficient to answer the question asked.

(D) Each statement ALONE is sufficient to answer the question asked.

(E) Statements (1) and (2) TOGETHER are NOT sufficient to answer the question asked.

479. If p, q, and r are positive integers, what is the least possible value of $p + q + r$?

(1) $p = 2q$

(2) $4q = 11r$

(A) Statement (1) ALONE is sufficient, but statement (2) alone is not sufficient to answer the question asked.

(B) Statement (2) ALONE is sufficient, but statement (1) alone is not sufficient to answer the question asked.

(C) Both statements TOGETHER are sufficient, but NEITHER statement ALONE is sufficient to answer the question asked.

(D) Each statement ALONE is sufficient to answer the question asked.

(E) Statements (1) and (2) TOGETHER are NOT sufficient to answer the question asked.

480. A large barrel is $\frac{1}{4}$ full of water. How many gallons of water did Tajiri add to the barrel?

(1) The barrel's capacity is twice as many gallons as Tajiri added.

(2) Tajiri added twice as many gallons as were already in the barrel.

(A) Statement (1) ALONE is sufficient, but statement (2) alone is not sufficient to answer the question asked.

(B) Statement (2) ALONE is sufficient, but statement (1) alone is not sufficient to answer the question asked.

(C) Both statements TOGETHER are sufficient, but NEITHER statement ALONE is sufficient to answer the question asked.

(D) Each statement ALONE is sufficient to answer the question asked.

(E) Statements (1) and (2) TOGETHER are NOT sufficient to answer the question asked.

481. A group of 9 teachers from the same middle school went to a teachers' convention and split up into two groups to attend two different workshops. What percent of the 9 teachers were math teachers?

(1) Two math teachers from the group attended the workshop on fractions.

(2) Seven teachers from the group attended the workshop on classroom management.

(A) Statement (1) ALONE is sufficient, but statement (2) alone is not sufficient to answer the question asked.

(B) Statement (2) ALONE is sufficient, but statement (1) alone is not sufficient to answer the question asked.

(C) Both statements TOGETHER are sufficient, but NEITHER statement ALONE is sufficient to answer the question asked.

(D) Each statement ALONE is sufficient to answer the question asked.

(E) Statements (1) and (2) TOGETHER are NOT sufficient to answer the question asked.

482. Is $x^2 < y^2$?

(1) $x^2 + y^2 = 169$

(2) $y - x = 7$

(A) Statement (1) ALONE is sufficient, but statement (2) alone is not sufficient to answer the question asked.

(B) Statement (2) ALONE is sufficient, but statement (1) alone is not sufficient to answer the question asked.

(C) Both statements TOGETHER are sufficient, but NEITHER statement ALONE is sufficient to answer the question asked.

(D) Each statement ALONE is sufficient to answer the question asked.

(E) Statements (1) and (2) TOGETHER are NOT sufficient to answer the question asked.

483. How many people in a group of 100 own neither a dog nor a cat?

(1) The total number of people in the group who own either a dog or a cat or both is less than 100.

(2) The total number of people in the group who own both a dog and a cat is 30.

(A) Statement (1) ALONE is sufficient, but statement (2) alone is not sufficient to answer the question asked.

(B) Statement (2) ALONE is sufficient, but statement (1) alone is not sufficient to answer the question asked.

(C) Both statements TOGETHER are sufficient, but NEITHER statement ALONE is sufficient to answer the question asked.

(D) Each statement ALONE is sufficient to answer the question asked.

(E) Statements (1) and (2) TOGETHER are NOT sufficient to answer the question asked.

484. What is the value of x^{-6}?

(1) $x^{-2} = \dfrac{1}{36}$

(2) $x^6 = 46,656$

(A) Statement (1) ALONE is sufficient, but statement (2) alone is not sufficient to answer the question asked.

(B) Statement (2) ALONE is sufficient, but statement (1) alone is not sufficient to answer the question asked.

(C) Both statements TOGETHER are sufficient, but NEITHER statement ALONE is sufficient to answer the question asked.

(D) Each statement ALONE is sufficient to answer the question asked.

(E) Statements (1) and (2) TOGETHER are NOT sufficient to answer the question asked.

485. If m and n are positive integers, what is the value of $m + n$?

(1) $5m - mn = 3$

(2) $m(m + 2n) + 4 = 13 - n^2$

(A) Statement (1) ALONE is sufficient, but statement (2) alone is not sufficient to answer the question asked.

(B) Statement (2) ALONE is sufficient, but statement (1) alone is not sufficient to answer the question asked.

(C) Both statements TOGETHER are sufficient, but NEITHER statement ALONE is sufficient to answer the question asked.

(D) Each statement ALONE is sufficient to answer the question asked.

(E) Statements (1) and (2) TOGETHER are NOT sufficient to answer the question asked.

486. If the sequence G has 100 terms, what is the 51st term of the sequence?

(1) The first term of the sequence G is 5.

(2) The 7th term of the sequence G is 320, and each term of G after the first is 2 times the preceding term.

(A) Statement (1) ALONE is sufficient, but statement (2) alone is not sufficient to answer the question asked.

(B) Statement (2) ALONE is sufficient, but statement (1) alone is not sufficient to answer the question asked.

(C) Both statements TOGETHER are sufficient, but NEITHER statement ALONE is sufficient to answer the question asked.

(D) Each statement ALONE is sufficient to answer the question asked.

(E) Statements (1) and (2) TOGETHER are NOT sufficient to answer the question asked.

487. Is ab negative?

(1) $ab^8 < 0$

(2) $a + b^8 = 12$

(A) Statement (1) ALONE is sufficient, but statement (2) alone is not sufficient to answer the question asked.

(B) Statement (2) ALONE is sufficient, but statement (1) alone is not sufficient to answer the question asked.

(C) Both statements TOGETHER are sufficient, but NEITHER statement ALONE is sufficient to answer the question asked.

(D) Each statement ALONE is sufficient to answer the question asked.

(E) Statements (1) and (2) TOGETHER are NOT sufficient to answer the question asked.

488. At the beginning of the summer, swim team A and swim team B each had m members, and no one was a member of both teams. At the end of the summer 6 members left swim team A and 4 members left swim team B. How many members did swim team A have at the beginning of the summer?

(1) The ratio of the total number of members who left the two teams at the end of the year to the total number of members at the beginning of the year is $\frac{1}{5}$.

(2) At the end of the summer 21 members remained on swim team B.

(A) Statement (1) ALONE is sufficient, but statement (2) alone is not sufficient to answer the question asked.

(B) Statement (2) ALONE is sufficient, but statement (1) alone is not sufficient to answer the question asked.

(C) Both statements TOGETHER are sufficient, but NEITHER statement ALONE is sufficient to answer the question asked.

(D) Each statement ALONE is sufficient to answer the question asked.

(E) Statements (1) and (2) TOGETHER are NOT sufficient to answer the question asked.

489. What is the tenth's digit in the decimal representation of the positive number X?

(1) $X < \frac{1}{2}$

(2) $X > \frac{1}{3}$

(A) Statement (1) ALONE is sufficient, but statement (2) alone is not sufficient to answer the question asked.

(B) Statement (2) ALONE is sufficient, but statement (1) alone is not sufficient to answer the question asked.

(C) Both statements TOGETHER are sufficient, but NEITHER statement ALONE is sufficient to answer the question asked.

(D) Each statement ALONE is sufficient to answer the question asked.

(E) Statements (1) and (2) TOGETHER are NOT sufficient to answer the question asked.

490. If $x, y,$ and z are three odd integers such that $x < y < z$ and $x + y + z = 45$, what is the value of z?

(1) $z - x = 4$

(2) $x, y,$ and z are consecutive odd integers.

(A) Statement (1) ALONE is sufficient, but statement (2) alone is not sufficient to answer the question asked.

(B) Statement (2) ALONE is sufficient, but statement (1) alone is not sufficient to answer the question asked.

(C) Both statements TOGETHER are sufficient, but NEITHER statement ALONE is sufficient to answer the question asked.

(D) Each statement ALONE is sufficient to answer the question asked.

(E) Statements (1) and (2) TOGETHER are NOT sufficient to answer the question asked.

491. Is $r + s^{10}$ a positive number?

(1) $r^3 > 0$

(2) $s > 0$

(A) Statement (1) ALONE is sufficient, but statement (2) alone is not sufficient to answer the question asked.

(B) Statement (2) ALONE is sufficient, but statement (1) alone is not sufficient to answer the question asked.

(C) Both statements TOGETHER are sufficient, but NEITHER statement ALONE is sufficient to answer the question asked.

(D) Each statement ALONE is sufficient to answer the question asked.

(E) Statements (1) and (2) TOGETHER are NOT sufficient to answer the question asked.

492. If a and b are both positive, is $a < 5 < b$?

(1) $a < b$ and $ab = 25$

(2) $a^2 < 25 < b^2$

(A) Statement (1) ALONE is sufficient, but statement (2) alone is not sufficient to answer the question asked.

(B) Statement (2) ALONE is sufficient, but statement (1) alone is not sufficient to answer the question asked.

(C) Both statements TOGETHER are sufficient, but NEITHER statement ALONE is sufficient to answer the question asked.

(D) Each statement ALONE is sufficient to answer the question asked.

(E) Statements (1) and (2) TOGETHER are NOT sufficient to answer the question asked.

493. Does the sum of the prices, not including sales tax, of three chairs exceed $600?

(1) The price of the most expensive chair exceeds $300.

(2) The price of the least expensive chair exceeds $200.

(A) Statement (1) ALONE is sufficient, but statement (2) alone is not sufficient to answer the question asked.

(B) Statement (2) ALONE is sufficient, but statement (1) alone is not sufficient to answer the question asked.

(C) Both statements TOGETHER are sufficient, but NEITHER statement ALONE is sufficient to answer the question asked.

(D) Each statement ALONE is sufficient to answer the question asked.

(E) Statements (1) and (2) TOGETHER are NOT sufficient to answer the question asked.

494. How many total tokens do Blake and Kylie have?

(1) Blake has $1\frac{1}{2}$ times as many tokens as Kylie has.

(2) The total number of tokens that Blake and Kylie have is greater than 19 but less than 25.

(A) Statement (1) ALONE is sufficient, but statement (2) alone is not sufficient to answer the question asked.

(B) Statement (2) ALONE is sufficient, but statement (1) alone is not sufficient to answer the question asked.

(C) Both statements TOGETHER are sufficient, but NEITHER statement ALONE is sufficient to answer the question asked.

(D) Each statement ALONE is sufficient to answer the question asked.

(E) Statements (1) and (2) TOGETHER are NOT sufficient to answer the question asked.

495. Machine A, machine B, and machine C, working together at their respective constant rates, can complete a certain job in 24 hours. How many hours would it take machine A, working alone at its constant rate, to complete the same job?

(1) Machines B and C, working together at their respective constant rates, can complete the job in 36 hours.

(2) Machines A and C, working together at their respective constant rates, can complete the job in 48 hours.

(A) Statement (1) ALONE is sufficient, but statement (2) alone is not sufficient to answer the question asked.

(B) Statement (2) ALONE is sufficient, but statement (1) alone is not sufficient to answer the question asked.

(C) Both statements TOGETHER are sufficient, but NEITHER statement ALONE is sufficient to answer the question asked.

(D) Each statement ALONE is sufficient to answer the question asked.

(E) Statements (1) and (2) TOGETHER are NOT sufficient to answer the question asked.

Chapter 5

Verbal: Reading Comprehension

The Reading Comprehension portion of the GMAT is about 12 questions (more or less) in the Verbal section of the GMAT. These questions will be mixed in with the Sentence Correction and Critical Reasoning questions, but the directions specifically for each type of question will be presented each time they appear. In Reading Comprehension, you are shown a reading passage of one to three paragraphs, along with between two and six questions about each passage. You are able to refer to the passage while you answer each question about it.

The Problems You'll Work On

When working through the Reading Comprehension questions presented here, be prepared to

>> Read the question first to determine what information you will need to look for in the passage.

>> Recognize that questions that ask for titles for the passage are essentially asking for the main idea of the passage, a frequent type of question.

>> Identify the tone and style of the author, as well as why he or she might have structured a passage or included certain information.

>> Scan the passage for factual information.

>> Consider the information in the passage to make logical, small inferences.

What to Watch Out For

The following may cause you some problems:

>> Inference questions that play to your assumptions instead of your ability to think logically.

>> Factual questions that are more complicated than they seem.

>> The urge to choose an answer that seems correct instead of reviewing the passage to make sure it is.

Literature in the second half of the twentieth century in the United States bears only a faint resemblance to the writing accomplished between 1900 and 1950. Early in the century, arguments as to what distinguished American literature from British led to the emphasis on plain character and plain language that marked the writing done in both realism and naturalism. Then, with the modernist sweep to overthrow most existing literary traditions (always using Ezra Pound's rationale that making it new was to be primary), the innovation that made American poetry, fiction, and drama of keen interest to the world settled in.

By 1950, however, traditional aesthetic innovation was wearing thin. The United States had endured the Great Depression, a long decade of hardship that not only dampened the promise of the American dream but changed literary methods to a surprising extent. The amalgam of cryptic modernist innovation and almost sentimental proselytizing that characterized the collective, proletarian novel and the speech-lined poems of the Depression gave rise to incredible variety: despite the paper shortages of World War II, published writing in the United States continued to be influential. It is in the aftermath of the war, once people had righted their perceptions about causation and blame, and had admitted again the atrocity of war itself (as well as of the Holocaust and the atomic bomb), that literature — whether called contemporary or postmodern — began to change.

A History of American Literature, 1950 to the Present by Linda Wagner-Martin

496. Which of the following statements most accurately captures the main point of the passage?

(A) By the middle of the 20th century, American literature needed to change.

(B) Literature in the United States changed dramatically in the second half of the 20th century.

(C) American literature was considerably better in the second half of the 20th century.

(D) World War II profoundly affected American literature.

(E) The style of American literature is not as standardized as some many think.

497. In the last sentence of the passage, to what does the author attribute the turning point for the change in literature?

(A) The aftermath of the war.

(B) People had righted the perceptions about causation and blame.

(C) People admitted the atrocity of war.

(D) People admitted the horrors of the atomic bomb.

(E) People recognized the horrors of the Holocaust.

498. According to the passage, in what ways was American literature distinguished from British literature in the first part of the century?

(A) World War I

(B) The way the Holocaust was incorporated

(C) The way true aesthetic innovation was wearing thin

(D) An emphasis on plain character and plain language

(E) The arrival of the Great Depression

499. It can be inferred that American and British literature diverged after the mid-part of the century because . . .?

(A) . . . historical events in each country radically changed their writers in non-analogous ways.

(B) . . . America suffered a paper shortage after World War II.

(C) . . . World War II was not fought on American soil.

(D) . . . the United Kingdom was no longer the former colonizer of America.

(E) . . . American and British writers felt differently about the second half of the 20th century.

500. Which of the following definitions most closely resembles how *distinguished* is used in the passage (first paragraph)?

(A) Elite, commanding respect

(B) Native-born

(C) Snuffed out, ended

(D) Made conspicuous, usually by achievement

(E) To recognize as different or unique

501. The second paragraph plays what role in the passage?

(A) It provides further information to back up the thesis of the first paragraph.

(B) It reverses the premise of the first paragraph, to prove why it is not true.

(C) It introduces the topic of the passage.

(D) It provides a turn from the topic of the first paragraph, clarifying what the purpose of the passage will be.

(E) It is an anecdote, used to prove the first paragraph.

Questions 502 through 506 are based on the following passage.

Incandescent lamps, like the sun, produce light by burning; the light they emit is a by-product of heat. Only a tiny percentage — 5 percent or less — of the energy used by an incandescent lamp produces light. The balance of the energy used produces heat, so incandescent lamps are supremely inefficient. But, like the sun, incandescent sources emit the visible wavelengths as a continuous band. Candlelight, firelight, and incandescent lamplight are sensed as familiar and comforting because they provide light in the same way the sun does. The apparent whiteness of the light given off by an incandescent lamp depends on the temperature at which it burns, called its color temperature.

Understanding Color: An Introduction for Designers by Linda Holtzschue

502. What can be inferred about incandescent lamplight from the passage?

(A) So far, humanity has not been able to develop an electric source of light that is more efficient than lamplight.

(B) While incandescent lamps may produce heat, many people will continue use them because the light is familiar and comforting.

(C) Incandescent lights burn energy in the same way the sun does.

(D) Incandescent lamplight, a fire, and candlelight produce virtually the same emotional response.

(E) It would beneficial to find a way to harvest and keep the heat produced by incandescent lamplight.

503. Which role does the final sentence in the passage play?

(A) It concludes the passage by restating the main idea.

(B) It gives a hint as to why incandescent light sources remain popular, despite their inefficiency.

(C) It provides anecdotal proof of the main assertion of the passage.

(D) It provides additional factual information about the topic of the passage.

(E) It reveals the author's opinion of the topic of the passage.

504. How much is the energy of an incandescent lamp spent on tasks other than giving off light?

(A) About 5 percent

(B) About 10 percent

(C) About 95 percent

(D) About half

(E) About 85 percent

505. Which of the following statements most clearly captures the main idea of the passage?

(A) Incandescent lamps should be replaced because they are hugely inefficient.

(B) Incandescent lamps give off a very white light.

(C) Despite their inefficiencies, there are reasons why incandescent lamps remain popular.

(D) If you use incandescent lamps, you like to waste energy.

(E) Incandescent lamps are hiding a dirty little secret.

506. Which of the following is the best definition for the word "apparent" as used in the passage (last sentence)?

(A) Visible, obvious

(B) False, misleading

(C) Incorrectly perceived

(D) Lifelike, realistic

(E) As father to child

> *Questions 507 through 510 are based on the following passage.*

In 1971, Robert James Fischer (nicknamed Bobby) shocked the chess world by winning 19 consecutive games against an extremely high level of competition. This feat has been compared to throwing back-to-back no-hitters in major league baseball. During his peak playing period, from the mid 1960s into the early '70s, players spoke of "Fischer Fever," where they felt ill just having to play against him. Just as with José Rail Capablanca, Fischer had an aura of invincibility — which wasn't far from the truth. Fischer was head and shoulders above the best players of his day.

His abrupt withdrawal from chess was tragic. Rumors of Fischer sightings were rampant, and the public was often tantalized by stories of his impending reemergence. Unfortunately, Fischer waited more than 20 years before playing in public again. His behavior, always intense, became increasingly odd over the years and prevented him from ever again competing at the highest level.

Chess For Dummies by James Eade

507. Which of the following most accurately describes the structure of the passage?

   (A) The opening paragraph describes a person who was prominent in the world of chess, and the second paragraph describes some of his strategies in the game.

   (B) The first paragraph is a description of Fischer's physicality, while the second paragraph describes his emotional and mental characteristics.

   (C) The first paragraph describes a problem Fischer faced, and the second provides further details about that problem.

   (D) The first paragraph describes Fischer's reputation, and the second describes his ultimate fate.

   (E) The first paragraph describes Fischer's prowess in chess at the height of his career, and the second paragraph describes the fall he experienced.

508. Which of the following best describes the author's attitude toward the subject of the passage?

   (A) He feels a deep sadness that Fischer was so unhinged by the events of his life.

   (B) He finds Fischer's ultimate fate tragic, but also finds fault with Fischer.

   (C) He feels Fischer was overrated, and attempt to prove his opinion with facts.

   (D) Fischer was a misunderstood genius who lacked for companionship, the author feels.

   (E) The author thinks Fischer should have made more of an effort to curb his ego.

509. Which of the following statements most accurately describes a reasonable inference from the passage?

   (A) Fischer could have benefitted from more intense therapy.

   (B) Chess is best understood through metaphors from another sport, such as baseball.

   (C) A man of Fischer's talents is almost certain to face tragedy.

   (D) José Rail Capablanca was also a successful chess player with a high degree of self-confidence.

   (E) Chess is a very complicated game.

510. According to the passage, what would be a symptom of "Fischer Fever"?

   (A) A temperature of over 100 degrees

   (B) Inability to focus on playing the match

   (C) Anxiety about playing a match against Fischer that was so extreme that it causes physical illness

   (D) Viewers' intense excitement at seeing Fischer play

   (E) Forgetting the most basic rules of chess

Questions 511 through 514 are based on the following passage.

The world of Minecraft is made of cubic blocks, materials such as dirt or stone that you can break down and rebuild into houses or craft into useful items. A block made of a material such as sand is referred to as a sand block. Because the side length of every block measures 1 meter, most distances are measured in blocks as well: If you read about an object that's located "three blocks up," it's the distance from the ground to the top of a stack of three blocks. In addition to building and crafting, you have to defend against monsters and eventually face them head-on. As the game progresses, your goal becomes less about surviving and more about building structures, gathering resources, and facing challenges to gain access to more blocks and items.

Building a Minecraft City by Sarah Guthals

511. According to the passage, what are some of the tasks associated with playing Minecraft?

(A) Killing characters who attack your compound.

(B) Crafting characters and structures, and gathering resources.

(C) Gathering resources and strategizing about how to build wealth.

(D) Surviving and cooking.

(E) Protecting against monsters and designing clothing.

512. The passage can best be described as which of the following?

(A) An exploration of the possible meaning behind a popular computer game.

(B) A look at the individuals who play Minecraft, and how it shapes them.

(C) The author's attempt to explain her unique game strategy to a group of seasoned players.

(D) An overview of the game of Minecraft, aimed at those who might want to try playing it.

(E) An opinion column from a newspaper about the dangers of online games.

513. What is implied in the last sentence of the passage?

(A) Minecraft is a game that allows players to change in their focus the more they play it.

(B) Minecraft becomes easier the more you play it.

(C) Minecraft is a game that does not justify an intense interest in it.

(D) People who play Minecraft are introverts who may enjoy controlled, limited interactions with others.

(E) There is a version of Minecraft for everyone.

514. Which of the following most closely matches the meaning of *crafting* as used in the passage?

(A) Knit or crocheted

(B) Creating a physical object or a representation of a physical object

(C) Writing

(D) Programming, as in computer code

(E) Sculpting

> *Questions 515 through 519 are based on the following passage.*

The "morning star" isn't a star; it's always a planet. And sometimes two Morning Stars appear at once, such as Mercury and Venus. **The same idea applies to the "evening star": You're seeing a planet, and you may see more than one. "Shooting stars" and "falling stars" are misnomers, too. These "stars" are meteors — the flashes of light caused by small meteoroids falling through Earth's atmosphere.** Many of the "superstars" you see on television may be just flashes in the pan, but they at least get 15 minutes of fame.

Astronomy For Dummies by Stephen P. Maran

515. Which of the following titles would be the most appropriate for the contents of this passage?

(A) 15 Minutes of Celestial Fame

(B) What Was That Flash?

(C) Explaining the Evening Star

(D) Don't Wish on the Morning Star!

(E) Some Stars Aren't What You Think!

516. According to the passage, which two planets often masquerade as the Morning Star?

(A) Earth and Mars

(B) Mercury and Venus

(C) Mercury and Earth

(D) Venus and Neptune

(E) Jupiter and Mercury

517. Which of the following is a statement that it can be reasonably be inferred that the author would agree with?

(A) The lack of astronomical knowledge is one of our most embarrassing national problems.

(B) Astronomy is an unappreciated science.

(C) Americans are far too interested in celebrities.

(D) Many Americans have ideas about the sky that show their interest but lack of understanding about astronomy.

(E) People need to look up from their phones more often.

518. Which of the following situations is most similar to that described in the bolded section?

(A) A group of teenagers identifying the constellations in the sky based on what they learned in their freshman year science class.

(B) A couple looks through a telescope to try to see Jupiter's rings but the sky is too cloudy.

(C) A group of people on a boat spot what they think is a pack of dolphins in the ocean in the distance, but the captain informs them they're actually looking at buoys bouncing in the water.

(D) A man thinks he won the city marathon but he actually misread his time and came in second.

(E) A group of friends follow what they think is the sound of a band playing, and end up dancing the night away at a club.

519. Which of the following provides the best meaning *misnomer* as used in the passage?

(A) Mistakes

(B) Misleading

(C) Mercurial

(D) Metaphors

(E) Wrong names

Questions 520 through 525 are based on the following passage.

The United States Constitution is the oldest, continuous, national republican document in existence today. It was not the first. Republics, or mixed regimes as they are also known, existed long before the Americans crafted theirs in 1787. Most did not last very long. **In the ancient world, the Roman republic collapsed when it degenerated into empire. During the Renaissance, the Florentine republic in Italy survived a mere 14 years, from 1498 to 1512. It dissolved when the powerful Medici family, which had once ruled Florence, re-established a dictatorship.**

According to the classical republican tradition, republics were fragile political organizations, because the critical balance between the various branches of government could easily crumble when one or two dominated the others. The Americans modeled their constitution on the British government with its one-person executive and two-part legislature. The British failed to create a true republic, because a hereditary monarch led the executive branch and hereditary aristocrats controlled the upper house, the unelected House of Lords. Large landowners controlled the House of Commons and only a few men possessed the right to vote. Americans believed that after separating from the British Empire, they could create a true republican structure where citizens participated in decision-making and enjoyed peaceful transitions of power.

American Constitutional History by Jack Fruchtman

520. According to the passage, it is safe to assume that American most likely saw one of the major flaws of the British government to be which of the following?

(A) Maintaining a monarchy.

(B) Failing to give women the right to vote.

(C) Allowing one of the branch of the government to be tied to a hereditary monarch and aristocrats.

(D) Failing to outlaw a dictatorship.

(E) Not distributing land equally among the citizens.

521. Which of the following best describes the author's tone in the passage?

(A) Accusatory and irate

(B) Wistful and yearning

(C) Provocative and probing

(D) Factual and learned

(E) Reflective and erudite

522. What role does the bolded portion play in the passage?

(A) It introduces the main idea of the passage.

(B) It raises a question that the rest of the passage will attempt to answer.

(C) It is a series of suggestions that the author feels readers should contemplate.

(D) It provides historical proof of the assertion the author has made earlier.

(E) It is the thesis of the argument that the author tries to put forward.

523. Which of the following statements most accurately captures the main point of the passage?

(A) America rebelled against Britain by refusing to set up their government in the same way.

(B) The American who set up the country's government tried to do something uniquely long-lasting yet based in the historical example of republics that came before.

(C) The Ancient Greeks could've learned a lot about governing from Americans.

(D) Republics are a popular but short-lived type of government.

(E) Setting up a government is much harder than it might at first appear.

524. According to the passage, what form of government followed the brief Florentine republic in Italy in the late 1400s?

(A) A monarchy

(B) A republic

(C) A constitution

(D) A dictatorship

(E) A rebellion

525. According to the passage, who controlled the House of Commons in Britain?

(A) The monarch

(B) Americans

(C) Noblemen

(D) Peasants

(E) Landowners

Questions 526 through 530 are based on the following passage.

Video has become a common element that you should consider in the design of your website. The soaring popularity of YouTube, its influence in search engine rankings, and the amount of times it is shared through social media have contributed to the widespread acceptance and use of online video for all sorts of purposes. For some sites, this capability becomes an intricate design element. For others, it may be considered only as a marketing tool. Research supports the idea that video increases customer engagement (how the customer interacts with your site and brand) and can increase product sales (when using video for product reviews or testimonials, for example). You must weigh the pros and cons of video and decide where and when it will be used across your site, along with how to use it in a way that supports, rather than detracts, from your site's usability.

Starting an Online Business by Shannon Belew & Joel Elad

526. Which of the following statements most accurately captures the main point of the passage?

(A) Building a website is an important part of running a business.

(B) Including video on your website is an absolute must.

(C) Don't build a website without researching.

(D) Including video elements in a website is increasingly common, and may be a good choice for your site.

(E) YouTube has popularized video across the internet.

527. Which of the following is the most likely intended audience for this passage?

(A) Small business owners trying to decide whether they should have an online presence.

(B) Researchers interested in new ways that media is developing.

(C) Business owners who are deciding what elements to include in their web pages.

(D) Older adults who would like to learn more about the internet.

(E) People who want to learn more about popular social media apps.

528. According to the passage, what is the effect of video on a website to customer engagement?

(A) It increases.

(B) It decreases.

(C) There is no change.

(D) Research is not clear.

(E) Research has not been conducted.

529. What can we infer about the use of video from the conclusion of the passage?

(A) Video is a necessity on any decent website.

(B) Any use of video on a website will drive up viewership.

(C) Only certain types of businesses should use video on their websites.

(D) Video should be used carefully on a website, as it can work against the site's accessibility and enjoyment.

(E) Use video sparingly on a website.

530. Which of the following phrases could best substitute for the phrase "The soaring popularity of YouTube" in the passage?

(A) The lyrical nature of YouTube

(B) The ubiquity of YouTube

(C) The inevitable likelihood of YouTube

(D) The ever-increasing interest in YouTube

(E) The far-reaching trendiness of YouTube

Questions 531 through 536 are based on the following passage.

A more serious hazard associated with canned food is botulism, the potentially fatal form of food poisoning that may result if the food is not heated for a sufficient period of time to a temperature high enough to kill all Clostridium botulinum (or C. botulinum) spores. C. botulinum is an anaerobic (an = without; aerobic = air) organism that thrives in the absence of oxygen, a condition nicely fulfilled by a sealed can. If a low-acid food (such as green beans or peas or potatoes) is incorrectly canned, botulinum spores not destroyed by high heat during the canning process may produce a toxin that can kill by paralyzing muscles, including the heart muscle and the muscles that enable you to breathe.

To avoid potentially hazardous canned food, don't buy, store, or use any can that is:

- Swollen: The swelling suggests that bacteria are growing inside and producing gas.

- Damaged, rusted, or deeply dented along the seam: A break in the can permits air to enter and may promote the growth of organisms other than C. botulinum.

Nutrition For Dummies by Carol Ann Rinzler

531. What two characteristics should customers buying food packaged in metal cans for consumption avoid?

    (A) Heated and lacking in oxygen

    (B) Swollen and damaged

    (C) Rusted and heated

    (D) Swollen and boiled

    (E) Exposed to oxygen and damaged

532. The bulleted points in this passage play what role?

    (A) They provide anecdotal evidence to support the main paragraph.

    (B) They contradict the main paragraph.

    (C) They provide an alternative to the main paragraph.

    (D) They present the same evidence as what's in the main paragraph.

    (E) They provide a helpful list of characteristics to look for that is drawn from the main paragraph.

533. Which of the following statements most accurately captures the main point of the passage?

    (A) Botulism is a serious health hazard, but there are steps you can take to avoid the risk of mistakenly consuming it.

    (B) Food must be heated to a high enough temperature to kill botulism spores.

    (C) C. Botulism is one of the greatest threats facing our collective health today.

    (D) Canned food is deadly and should be avoided.

    (E) Never buy a can that is swollen.

534. Use the information in the passage to choose the word that most likely means something close to *without or lacking water.*

    (A) By hydration

    (B) Unhydration

    (C) Anhydration

    (D) Hydrationless

    (E) Innohydration

535. Which of the following would be the best substitute for the word *toxic* as used in the passage?

    (A) Destabilizer

    (B) Germ

    (C) Adhesive

    (D) Deferral

    (E) Poison

536. Based on the information in this passage, what would be the safest approach to consuming food in cans?

(A) Do not consume food in cans.

(B) Boil all food packaged in cans before consuming it.

(C) Carefully check cans for swelling, damage, rust or deep dents, and do not consumer the food therein if you notice any of these.

(D) Do not consume canned low-acid foods such as potatoes.

(E) There's no way to detect botulism, so all you can do is hope you don't happen upon a can that contains it.

Questions 537 through 541 are based on the following passage.

Just as individual stock prices can plummet, so can individual real estate property prices. In California during the 1990s, for example, earthquakes rocked the prices of properties built on landfills. These quakes highlighted the dangers of building on poor soil. In the decade prior, real estate values in the communities of Times Beach, Missouri, and Love Canal, New York, plunged because of carcinogenic toxic waste contamination. (Ultimately, many property owners in these areas received compensation for their losses from the federal government as well as from some real estate agencies that didn't disclose these known contaminants.)

Investing For Dummies by Eric Tyson

537. Which of the following would be the best title for the passage?

(A) Don't Build Your House in an Earthquake Zone

(B) The Story of Love Canal, New York

(C) Personal Real Estate Is Not a Foolproof Investment

(D) There's No Point in Investing in Real Estate

(E) A Guide to Individual Stock Purchases

538. Why did the value of real estate plummet in Love Canal and Times Beach, according to the passage?

(A) Both communities were in earthquake zones.

(B) Real estate agencies did not disclose know contaminants.

(C) They were filled with noxious gases.

(D) Both towns were sites of carcinogenic toxic waste contamination.

(E) Both towns were located on contaminated shore fronts.

539. Based on the passage, it can be inferred that the former land-owning citizens of Love Canal and Times Beach most likely did what?

(A) Fled both towns.

(B) Pursued legal action against the real estate agencies that did not disclose known contaminants to them before selling them property in the towns.

(C) Suffered from diseases caused by the contaminants.

(D) Sold their properties in the town at a loss.

(E) Wished that they had bought property in an earthquake zone.

540. The author's attitude towards purchasing individual real estate as an investment could best be described as which of the following?

(A) Cautious and factual

(B) Aggrieved and petulant

(C) Knowing and allusive

(D) Skeptical and discouraging

(E) Rhetorical and questioning

541. The parenthetical sentence at the end plays what role in this passage?

(A) It adds anecdotal information that may be of interest to the reader.

(B) It suggests a counter-argument to the main argument of the passage.

(C) It refers to another way of calculating the percentages shown in the passage.

(D) It clarifies that some property owners were eventually compensated for their losses.

(E) It is a citation.

Questions 542 through 547 are based on the following passage.

To the uninitiated, the world of intellectual property often appears an impenetrable collision of legal, scientific and economic themes. Indeed, the study of intellectual property draws from these three disciplines in a way that our educational and philosophical systems struggle to reconcile. Technically-expert lawyers, scientists and economists find it equally difficult to adopt a **holistic** overview and to look beyond their specialized field. Whilst Patent Offices have recently intensified their efforts to be more accessible, publishing readable introductions to the very basic terms of intellectual property, and guides to initial patent application, these laudable efforts fail to penetrate the heart of the problem as we see it: the connection of legal procedure, beyond its mere application, with technological development and the business strategy that drives it.

Intellectual Property Management by Claas Junghaus & Adam Levy

542. Which of the following most accurately describes the structure of the passage?

(A) It summarizes what "intellectual property" can be.

(B) It briefly explains the process of applying for a patent.

(C) It suggests further reading about patent law.

(D) It reveals the ways in which the legal, scientific, and economic themes are at work in intellectual property.

(E) It summarizes attempts to fix a problem before asserting that the problem is not yet fixed.

543. According to the passage, what is one of the ways Patent Offices have tried to be more accessible?

(A) By combing the legal, scientific and economic themes of their work.

(B) By producing guides to initial patent application.

(C) By better explaining their legal procedures.

(D) By accepting that they are part of intellectual property laws.

(E) By improving economic development.

544. Which of the following statements best captures the main point of the passage?

(A) The world of intellectual property is very complicated.

(B) Intellectual property is an important field of study.

(C) More Patent Offices should publish guides to their application processes.

(D) Intellectual property management must do a better job of connecting legal procedure with technological development and business strategy.

(E) Without a business strategy, intellectual property management is inert.

545. Which of the following most closely matches the meaning of *holistic* (in bold) as used in the passage?

   (A) Wholistic

   (B) Organic

   (C) Of a whole, more than the sum of its parts

   (D) Reductive, of a smaller number

   (E) Unusual

546. What can we infer about the authors' objective in writing this passage?

   (A) They feel most intellectual property lawyers should be re-trained into a different area of practice.

   (B) They feel that Patent Offices have made no real attempts to be helpful to outsiders.

   (C) They see intellectual property management as a worthless field.

   (D) They will have further suggestions about how intellectual property management can be approached.

   (E) They feel that most intellectual property managers are incompetent.

547. Which of the following most closely resembles the organization used in the passage?

   (A) Zoos are not very well understood. Zookeepers, administrators, and veterinarians have to work together at a zoo, but often they are unable to see how their efforts appear to visitors to the zoo, even after making efforts to make the zoo accessible. Their efforts need to be combined better.

   (B) People who file for patents often do not understand the process for doing so, even when supplied with information about how to go about it. The information provided must be improved.

   (C) A good education for a teenager is the result of teachers, administrators, and the student him- or herself working together to understand how best to move forward.

   (D) Many people who feel that they understand the practice of law quite well are, in fact, deluded. The American legal system is extraordinarily complex, and most Americans have not even made the basic effort to understand it.

   (E) The well-being of beach-goers depends on the efforts of lifeguards, the police patrolling, and the intelligence of the beach-goers themselves. However, in an emergency situation on the beach, the lifeguard is always the first to respond and his or her authority must be accepted.

You can't chop vegetables, slice meat, or whip up a cake batter if you can't even fit a cutting board or a mixing bowl on your counter, so take a good look at your countertops. What's on them? **Coffee-makers, blenders, food processors, racks of spice jars or canisters of flour and sugar, stacks of bills, permission slips, and grade school art projects?** Is your countertop doubling as a magazine rack, plant holder, or wine rack? Consider this: Your kitchen counters aren't meant to be storage units. They are meant to be food preparation areas. A clean, clear counter space can inspire the creation of a great meal. A cluttered one is more likely to inspire a call to the pizza delivery guy.

If your kitchen counter is cluttered with paraphernalia beyond usefulness, that's a problem you can fix. The ultimate test for whether something should be allowed valuable countertop real estate is how often you use it. If you use an appliance or food ingredient (like coffee or flour) almost every day, then go ahead and give it hallowed ground. Otherwise, stow it. Be ruthless. Put away the mixer, the food processor, the bread machine, and the rice cooker. Away with the herb and spice rack, the bottles of nut oil and fancy vinegar. Find a better spot for the mail and the bills. As you rid your counters of this clutter, you also get rid of your excuses for not having the space to cook dinner.

Cooking Basics For Dummies by Bryan Miller & Marie Rama

548. The bolded sentence in the passage is included for what likely purpose?

(A) The author is suggesting appropriate items to keep on your countertop.

(B) The author is mocking American capitalism and the overwhelming amount of stuff many people own.

(C) The author is pointing out common safety hazards in the kitchen.

(D) The author is gently teasing readers about the items that they might be storing on their kitchen counters instead of using the counters for cooking.

(E) The author has created a list of unneeded items that should be disposed of immediately.

549. Which of the following would be the best title for this passage?

(A) Here Are the Basics You Need to Start Cooking

(B) Coffee and Flour are the Building Blocks of the Kitchen

(C) Cleaning Off Your Counter Gets Your Ready to Cook!

(D) No One Considers the Lowly Kitchen Counter

(E) Let's Get Your House Organized!

550. The second paragraph of the passage would be most likely to be helpful to someone who is . . .

(A) Trying to give up coffee.

(B) Unsure about whether to keep their deep fryer on their kitchen counter, even though it is only used once a month.

(C) Looking for an organizational system to corral all of their loose papers.

(D) Remodeling their kitchen.

(E) Not sure if they want to cook at home more often or not.

551. Based on the passage, it can reasonably be inferred that the authors approve of which of the following ideas?

   (A) Planning a monthly menu.

   (B) Shopping for produce and other ingredients locally.

   (C) Keeping a kitchen spice collection down to a half-dozen instead of twenty or more spices.

   (D) Encouraging families to cook together.

   (E) Maintaining a clutter-free kitchen so it is usable whenever cooking inspiration strikes.

552. According to the passage, where do the mail and bills belong?

   (A) On the kitchen counter

   (B) On the dining room table

   (C) Neatly sorted

   (D) Not specified, but not on a kitchen counter

   (E) They should be recycled as soon as possible

Questions 553 through 558 are based on the following passage.

High-level programming languages must be converted to low-level programming languages using an interpreter or compiler, depending on the language. Interpreted languages are considered more portable than compiled languages, while compiled languages execute faster than interpreted languages. However, the speed advantage compiled languages have is starting to fade in importance as improving processor speeds make performance differences between interpreted and compiled languages negligible.

High-level programming languages like JavaScript, Python, and Ruby are interpreted. For these languages the interpreter executes the program directly, translating each statement one line at a time into machine code. High-level programming languages like C++, COBOL, and Visual Basic are compiled. For these languages, after the code is written a compiler translates all the code into machine code, and an executable file is created. This executable file is then distributed via the internet, CD-ROMs, or other media and run. Software you install on your computer, like Microsoft Windows or Mac OS X, are coded using compiled languages, usually C or C++.

Coding for Dummies by Nikhail Abraham

553. According to the passage, which type of language is your home computer or laptop most likely to use?

   (A) An interpreted language.

   (B) A native language.

   (C) A computer code.

   (D) An internet language.

   (E) A compiled language.

554. Based on the passage, what can we infer about how frequently compiled and interpreted languages will be used five years from now?

   (A) Most likely, there will be little change.

   (B) Compiled languages will continue to offer benefits in speed.

   (C) As the speed advantage that compiled languages have continues to decline, both languages will offer equal incentives to be used.

   (D) Interpreted languages are likely to be far more frequently employed.

   (E) Another form of language will overtake both interpreted and compiled languages to be the most used language.

555. Which of the following statements most accurately captures the central idea of the passage?

(A) Coding for computers is complicated but anyone can learn it.

(B) There are two types of programming languages, and each offers advantages and disadvantages.

(C) You may not even be aware that your home computer is using a programming language right now.

(D) The program C++ is a compiled high-level programming language.

(E) Only professionals should use high-level programming languages which run the risk of destroying your computer.

556. Which of the following most accurately describes the author's attitude towards high-level programming languages?

(A) Dismissive and uninterested

(B) Inquiring and trying to understand

(C) Factual and helpful

(D) Intrigued and curious

(E) Rote and disinterested

557. According to the passage, how is an executable file built and then distributed?

(A) The computer runs the file and distributes in manually.

(B) A programming language builds the executable file and a CD-ROM is distributed to all users.

(C) A computer translates the code into an executable file, and then it is distributed via the internet, CD-ROMs, or other media.

(D) It is built by programmers and run by the internet.

(E) A computer programmer translates the file into code, which is then distributed.

558. Which of the following answer choices is a list of high-level programming languages as mentioned in the passage?

(A) C++, C−, Aereus

(B) JavaScript, Python, MacApple

(C) Ruby, Elementary, Javascript

(D) Javascript, Ruby, and C++

(E) There are no high-level programming languages mentioned in the passage.

Questions 559 through 564 are based on the following passage.

Any gardener recognizes the value of pollinating insects. Various insects perform an essential service in the production of seed and fruit. The survival of plants depends on pollination. You may not have thought much about the role honey bees play in our everyday food supply. It is estimated that in North America around 30 percent of the food we consume is produced from bee-pollinated plants. Bees also pollinate crops, such as clover and alfalfa that cattle feed on, making bees important to our production and consumption of meat and dairy. The value of pollination by bees is estimated at around $16 billion in the United States alone.

These are more than interesting facts; these are realities with devastating consequences if bees were to disappear. And sadly, the health of honey bees has been **compromised** in recent years. Indeed a spring without bees could endanger our food supply and impact our economy. It's a story that has become headline news in the media.

Beekeeping For Dummies by Howland Blackiston

559. Which of the following statements most accurately captures the purpose of the first paragraph in the passage?

(A) The first paragraph introduces the concern that the author has about the decline of bees.

(B) The first paragraph builds the author's case that bees are in decline with statistical analysis.

(C) The first paragraph is an anecdotal look at what will happen if bees decline.

(D) The first paragraph presents the counter-argument that the second paragraph undercuts.

(E) The first paragraph provides an over-view of how beneficial bees are to our world, so as to make the impact of losing them clearer when presented later.

560. According to the passage, which two types of food might be impacted if the bee population in the United States declined?

(A) Pork and produce

(B) Beef and dairy

(C) Ice cream and milk

(D) Grains and produce

(E) Chickens and dairy

561. What can be reasonably inferred about the decline in bees from the second paragraph?

(A) The health of honey bees has been so compromised in recent years that a spring without them is a possibility.

(B) Honeybees are often needlessly slaughtered.

(C) Honeybees produce 30 percent of the food we consume.

(D) Honeybees are our most valuable insect.

(E) Honeybees are on the brink of extinction.

562. The author's attitude toward the possible decline in bee population could best be characterized as which of the following?

(A) Hysterical disbelief

(B) Easy-going acceptance

(C) Concerned and alert

(D) Realistically accepting

(E) Deviously scheming

563. Which of the following statements might best summarize the author's suggestion for what should next be done about the declining bee population?

(A) A twenty-year study, noting the declining numbers, should be undertaken.

(B) The nations of the world must band together to do everything in their power to keep the bees from further declining.

(C) There's nothing to be done; the decline is already happening.

(D) Scientists who have been study-ing bees should provide suggestions about how the rest of us can help, including keeping hives.

(E) Bees should be kept only by those who are licensed and trained to do so.

564. Which of the following is the best substi-tute for the word *compromised* (in bold) as used in the passage?

(A) Made up of

(B) Vowed to

(C) An agreement made by previously antagonistic parties, in which each changes their position in order to reach consensus

(D) A binding agreement.

(E) To expose to danger in some way

Step outside on a clear night and look at the sky. If you're a city dweller or live in a cramped suburb, you see dozens, maybe hundreds, of twinkling stars. Depending on the time of the month, you may also see a full Moon and up to five of the eight planets that revolve around the Sun. A shooting star or "meteor" may appear overhead. What you actually see is the flash of light from a tiny piece of comet dust streaking through the upper atmosphere. Another pinpoint of light moves slowly and steadily across the sky. Is it a space satellite, such as the Hubble Space Telescope, or just a high-altitude airliner? If you have a pair of binoculars, you may be able to see the difference. Most airliners have running lights, and their shapes may be perceptible. If you live in the country — on the seashore away from resorts and developments, on the plains, or in the mountains far from any floodlit ski slope — you can see thousands of stars. The Milky Way appears as a beautiful pearly swath across the heavens. **What you're seeing is the cumulative glow from millions of faint stars, individually indistinguishable with the naked eye**. At a great observation place, such as Cerro Tololo in the Chilean Andes, you can see even more stars. They hang like brilliant lamps in a coal black sky, often not even twinkling, like in van Gogh's "Starry Night" painting.

Astronomy For Dummies by Stephen P. Maran

565. According to the passage, which of the following places would be the best for an astronomer to live?

(A) Cerro Tololo in the Chilean Andes

(B) A seashore far from resorts and developments

(C) The mountains, away from any floodlit ski slopes

(D) The suburbs of any medium-sized American city

(E) A large city

566. Which of the following statements most accurately captures the main point of the passage?

(A) Light pollution is ruining stargazing for many Americans.

(B) Satellites and airliners can be differentiated with the use of good binoculars.

(C) The sky is a busy place, and no matter where you watch it from, you can see interesting things.

(D) The Andes Mountains provide unparalleled star-gazing opportunities.

(E) Astrology and astronomy are not the same thing.

567. According the passage, what might be mistaken for an airliner traveling across the night sky?

(A) A shooting star

(B) The Hubble Space Telescope

(C) One of the planets

(D) A comet

(E) The moon

568. What role does the sentence in bold play in the rest of the passage?

(A) It is the introduction to the passage.

(B) It is one of a list of examples in the passage.

(C) It explains the phenomenon mentioned in the sentence before it.

(D) It is the main idea of the passage.

(E) It is evidence that supports the argument of the passage.

569. What can you infer about van Gogh's "Starry Night" from the passage?

(A) "Starry Night" was painted before the arrival of airliners.

(B) "Starry Night" is a painting of comets and meteors.

(C) "Starry Night" may have been painted in an area that the author would deem a "great observation place" like Cerro Tololo.

(D) Van Gogh must have been an amateur astronomer.

(E) "Starry Night" is a realistic painting.

570. Which of the following most accurately describes the likely intended audience for this passage?

(A) A group of astronomers, interested in sharing their findings from studying the night sky

(B) Amateur astrologers

(C) Students in an intermediate astronomy class at a local college

(D) A group of preschoolers learning the names of the planets

(E) Average adults interested in learning more about the night sky

Questions 571 through 575 are based on the following passage.

The Constitution created a democratic republic, not a democracy. In a democracy, citizens vote directly on government policies, while in a republic, they elect representatives to develop policies on their behalf. Vestiges of democracy remain in America. They include the New England town meeting when residents directly vote on issues, such as whether the town should purchase a new police cruiser. The ballot initiative, also called the referendum, exists in over 40 states, allowing voters to make specific policies, such as whether a state should repeal its capital punishment law. **Most laws in the United States today, however, are passed by representatives elected by the citizens.** This system comprises the republic.

American Constitutional History by Jack Fruchtman

571. Which of the following would make the best title for this passage?

(A) What is the Ballot Initiative?

(B) Town Meetings, A New England Tradition

(C) No More Democracies!

(D) The American Democracy Is a Lie!

(E) America's Democratic Republic System

572. According to the passage, New England town meetings operate under what political system?

(A) They are democracies.

(B) They are republics.

(C) They are republican democracies.

(D) They are representative democracies.

(E) They are representative republics.

573. Which of the following best describes the role of the sentence in bold in the passage?

(A) It introduces the main idea.

(B) It is the conclusion.

(C) It is a part of a group of sentences listing examples to prove the main point of the passage.

(D) It turns the paragraph back to the main topic after a series of sentences that provided exceptions to the topic under discussion.

(E) It refutes the thesis of the passage.

574. According to the passage, what is another term for "ballot initiative" and what kind of government is it an example of?

(A) Referral; Democracy

(B) Referendum; Democracy

(C) Rehabilitation; Democratic republic

(D) Rebuttal; Democracy

(E) Realignment; Republic

575. According to the passage, what would be another example of a democratic republic form of governing?

(A) An entire student body votes on the next school president.

(B) A CEO chooses the best candidate from several dozen applicants.

(C) The Board of Trustees, chosen by election, vote on the next steps for an insurance company.

(D) A group of people decide to choose a leader from within their ranks.

(E) The government decides who should lead the military.

Questions 576 through 580 are based on the following passage.

Color temperature in light sources is a measurement of heat in degrees Kelvin (K). Color temperatures over 5,000 K, the hottest, are sensed as sharp, clear blue-white. **In contradictory language** the color of light delivered by this hot radiation is referred to as "cool." Temperatures around 2,700–3,000 K, actually cooler, are perceived as warm in color, tilting toward yellow and red. The heat-light- color relationship is recognized in **colloquial language;** something that is "white- hot" is dangerously hotter than something "red- hot."

Understanding Color: An Introduction for Designers by Linda Holtzschue

576. The author uses the phrase *In contradictory language* (in bold) in the passage in order to do what?

(A) To alert readers to the fact that something strange is about to be noted.

(B) To point out a discrepancy in the mathematical equation that follows.

(C) To attribute an error to the source of the information and not herself.

(D) To alert readers that something paradoxical has been noted.

(E) To reveal the truth about an assertion.

577. According to the passage, temperatures in the 2700–3000 K range are likely to appear in which of the following colors?

(A) Blue

(B) Green

(C) White

(D) Grey

(E) Yellow

578. Which of the following can we best infer about colloquial language used about color from the passage?

(A) The colloquial language used about light is unrelated to actual observations about light.

(B) Colloquial language about light often reflects actual observation about the color of hot things.

(C) Colloquial language about the color of light is very poetic.

(D) Most people who use colloquial language do not understand the scientific heat-light-color relationship.

(E) The heat-light-color relationship is not expressible in colloquial language (in bold).

579. Which of the following statements most accurately captures the central idea of the passage?

(A) There is a relationship between heat and color.

(B) Kelvin is a unit of measurement for heat.

(C) We have developed a great deal of colloquial language to express how hot something is.

(D) The relationship between heat, light, and color is sometimes counter-intuitive.

(E) Heat is very dangerous.

580. According to the passage, which is hotter?

    (A) Metal burning "red-hot."

    (B) Metal burning "white-hot."

    (C) Wood burning "blue-hot."

    (D) Brick burning "red-hot."

    (E) All things burning hot are equally dangerous.

Questions 581 through 586 are based on the following passage.

Huey Long was a traveling salesman, a lawyer, and a world-class demagogue. He was elected governor of Louisiana in 1928 on a populist platform, **and he actually did some good things for the state,** such as making school text-books free and improving roads and highways. But he also ran a corrupt administration that was not above roughing up, blackmailing, or slandering those who opposed him. By 1930, the "Kingfish" was as close to an absolute dictator as there was in the country. He controlled the legislature and, after winning a U.S. Senate seat, refused to promptly vacate the governor's office, thus holding both jobs for a while.

Originally an FDR supporter, Long broke with the White House mostly for egotistical reasons. He proposed a "Share Our Wealth" program that called for confiscating family fortunes of more than $5 million and annual incomes over $1 million and guaranteeing every family $2,500 a year, a homestead, and a car. Long had a national following and announced he would run against FDR at the head of a third party in 1936. Private polls showed he might garner 4 million votes, enough to tip the election to the Republicans. But he never got the chance. In September 1935, Long was shot to death on the steps of the Louisiana capitol by a man whose family he had ruined.

U.S. History For Dummies, 3rd Edition, by Steve Wiegand

581. The passage can best be described as which of the following?

    (A) An overview of the danger of demagogues in American politics.

    (B) A look at a distinctive regional political story in America.

    (C) A brief biography of a memorable American.

    (D) A cautionary tale about the dangers of democracy.

    (E) A polemic against radicalism.

582. According to the passage, why might the Democratic party have been worried about Long's possible run for the White House in 1936?

    (A) He might have run as a Republican.

    (B) He refused to give FDR his formal endorsement.

    (C) His death made him ineligible to run.

    (D) Polls showed he would secure enough of the Democratic vote to swing the election to the Republican party.

    (E) He was a demagogue.

583. The last sentence of the passage most likely points to which of the following?

    (A) Long's policies hurt some of the people who he was supposed to represent as an elected official.

    (B) Long did not know how to defend himself in an attack.

    (C) Private security forces were not as common in the 1930s as they are now.

    (D) The man who shot Long was probably ruined by the Great Depression.

    (E) People always get what's coming to them.

584. According to the passage, what was a popular nickname for Huey Long?

    (A) "Huey"

    (B) "FDR"

    (C) "Demagogue"

    (D) "Share Our Wealth"

    (E) "Kingfish"

585. The bolded section in the passage plays what role in the first paragraph?

    (A) Reveals the author's shock that Long did worthwhile things.

    (B) Pivots to the type of activities Long usually engaged in.

    (C) Reminds or informs readers that Long did some good things on the way to his eventual demagoguery.

    (D) Reveals that Long was really a good person underneath his bluster.

    (E) Hints as to why some people may have been slow to recognize Long's true nature.

586. Based on the passage, which of the following groups of people could reasonably be assumed to be most against Huey Long's presidential run?

    (A) The Republican Party

    (B) The people of Louisiana

    (C) Economically disadvantaged people

    (D) Wealthy people with annual incomes of over $1,000,000

    (E) Women

Questions 587 through 592 are based on the following passage.

Of course, it doesn't hurt that everyone from consumers to investors now recognizes the legitimacy of online businesses. It was once considered risky to shop online. But an Internet-based business model has proven to be a worthwhile investment time and time again, with the same potential risks and rewards as any other type of business. Add to the mix that technology has also come a long way, and shopping online using everything from a desktop computer or laptop, to a tablet or a web-enabled mobile phone (smartphone) is as easy as ever. **And individuals are not the only ones spending more on online transactions.** Increasingly, businesses of all sizes are also buying products and services online. Those same companies are also spending money to advertise on the Internet and reach their customers through traditional websites and social media sites. All these interactions represent a business opportunity by which people earn a living on the Internet. Why shouldn't one of those people be you?

Starting an Online Business by Shannon Belew & Joel Elad

587. The authors' attitude towards starting an online business can best be characterized as which of the following?

    (A) Prophetic and stern

    (B) Eager and over-accommodating

    (C) Enthusiastic and supportive

    (D) Doubtful and cautioning

    (E) World-weary and accepting

588. Which of the following statements most accurately explains the role of the bolded sentence in the passage?

(A) It provides a counter-argument which will be refuted.

(B) It is the thesis of the passage.

(C) It provides a list of examples that support the passage.

(D) It shows a pivot in the passage away from the main point to a subsidiary point.

(E) It develops the main idea beyond the initial example to show another way it applies.

589. Which of the following would be the best title for the passage?

(A) Technology Has Come a Long Way

(B) More and More People Shop Online

(C) Are You Interested in Using the Internet?

(D) Consider Starting an Online Business

(E) The Internet Changes Rapidly

590. According to the passage, what is one technological development which has contributed to the ease of shopping online?

(A) Cell phones

(B) Smart televisions

(C) The rise of computer coding as a hobby

(D) Smartphones

(E) Broadband internet

591. The last sentence plays what role in this passage?

(A) It asks a rhetorical question.

(B) It poses a challenge to the reader.

(C) It reveals the authors' true purpose in writing the passage.

(D) It lends a sense of mystery or suspense.

(E) It invites readers to give an Internet-based business a try.

592. According to the passage, who or what has joined the individual consumer as a major purchaser via online sites?

(A) Individual consumers

(B) Websites

(C) Social media

(D) Businesses of all sizes

(E) The government

Questions 593 through 599 are based on the following passage.

Slide an apple pie in the oven, and soon the kitchen fills with an aroma that makes your mouth water and your digestive juices flow. But boil some cabbage and — what is that awful smell? It's sulfur, the same chemical you smell in rotten eggs. Cruciferous vegetables (the name comes from *crux*, the Latin word meaning cross, a reference to their x-shape blossoms), such as broccoli, Brussels sprouts, cauliflower, kale, kohlrabi, mustard seed, radishes, rutabaga, turnips, and watercress, all contain stinky sulfur compounds such as sulforaphane glucosinolate (SGSD), glucobrassicin, gluconapin, gluconasturtin, neoglucobrassicin, and sinigrin whose aromas are liberated when the food is heated.

Nutrition For Dummies by Carol Ann Rinzler

593. The author likely begins the passage with the sentence in bold for what reason?

(A) To set up a contrast between the appealing smell of apple pie baking and the less pleasant smell of cruciferous vegetables being cooked.

(B) To urge readers to consider baking an apple pie instead of boiling cabbage.

(C) To discourage boiling as a means of preparing cruciferous vegetables.

(D) To build a case that apples are part of the cruciferous family.

(E) To suggest that baking an apple pie is a task achievable by most inexperienced cooks.

594. Which of the following would be a good title for this passage?

(A) Don't Boil the Cabbage!

(B) Everyone Should Know How to Bake an Apple Pie.

(C) Sulfur Is the Smell of Cruciferous Vegetables Cooking

(D) Cabbages and Radishes are Related

(E) Freeing the Stink

595. According to the passage, all of the following are sulfur compounds released by cooking except for which one?

(A) Glucobrassicin

(B) Gluconasturtin

(C) Sinigrin

(D) Plexin

(E) Sulforaphane glucosinolate (SGSD)

596. The meaning of *crux*, as presented in the passage, would be most helpful in determining the meaning for which of the following bolded words in phrases?

(A) The *crux* of the matter.

(B) The *crucifix* at the front of the sanctuary.

(C) The day *cruise* leaves at 9 AM.

(D) The *crucial* point.

(E) The *crocus* in bloom.

597. The author's attitude towards cruciferous vegetables in the passage could best be described as which of the following?

(A) Disgusted by them

(B) Discouraging to readers who might try to cook them

(C) Dismissive of them, preferring apple pie

(D) Interested in one of their distinctive characteristics

(E) Fervent in appreciation for them

598. Which of the following statements can you most safely infer from the passage's information?

(A) When you boil cruciferous vegetables, you will release as sulforaphane glucosinolate (SGSD), glucobrassicin, gluconapin, gluconasturtin, neoglucobrassicin, and sinigrin simultaneously.

(B) Broccoli, Brussels sprouts, cauliflower, kale, kohlrabi, mustard seed, radishes, rutabaga, turnips, and watercress is a comprehensive listing of all cruciferous vegetables.

(C) The sulfuric smell from cooking cruciferous vegetables is very difficult to get rid of.

(D) Cooking an apple with cruciferous vegetables will help tame the sulfurous smell.

(E) The smell of sulfurous compounds in cruciferous vegetables is heightened by heat.

599. According to the passage, which of the following is not a cruciferous vegetable?

(A) Watercress

(B) Kale

(C) Kohlrabi

(D) Carrots

(E) Radishes

Questions 600 through 606 are based on the following passage.

The largest part of the brain, which is what you actually see when you look at a brain from above or the side, is the neocortex. The neocortex is really a 1.5 square foot sheet of cells wadded up a bit to fit inside the head. The neurons in the neocortex form a complex neural circuit that is repeated millions of times across the cortical surface. This repeated neural circuit is called a minicolumn.

The brain contains many specialized areas associated with particular senses (vision versus **audition,** for example) and other areas mediating particular motor outputs (like moving the leg versus the tongue). The function of different brain areas depends not on any particular structure of the minicolumns within it, but its inputs and outputs. So even though the cell types and circuits in the auditor cortex are similar to those in the visual and motor cortices, the auditory cortex is the auditory cortex because it receives inputs from the cochlea (a part of the ear) and because it sends output to areas associated with processing auditory information and using it to guide behavior.

Neuroscience For Dummies by Frank Amthor

600. Which of the following statements most accurately captures the main point of the passage?

(A) The human brain is complex and misunderstood.

(B) Most people have minicolumns in their brains.

(C) The brain's minicolumns are key to how it works, as are the inputs it receives.

(D) The brain understands auditory and visual inputs in different ways.

(E) The neocortex is what most of us think of as "the brain."

601. Which of the following statements is the most specific definition of a minicolumn, according to the passage?

(A) A repeated neural circuit in the brain

(B) A less-than-full-sized column

(C) The auditory cortex input pattern

(D) A part of the brain

(E) The feedback loop between the neocortex and the rest of the brain

602. The second paragraph plays what role in this passage?

(A) It refutes the argument about the neocortex presented in the first paragraph.

(B) It clarifies a broad opinion about the human brain stated in the first paragraph.

(C) It presents a series of examples that prove the first paragraph's thesis about the brain is correct.

(D) It supplies further details and information about a general concept presented in the first paragraph.

(E) It concludes the argument presented in the first paragraph by restating it using an anecdote about the neocortex.

603. The bolded word *audition* in the passage could best be replaced with which of the following words or phrases?

(A) Try-out

(B) A hearing

(C) A competition

(D) Decibel level

(E) Auditory

604. Which situation is most similar to the brain function described in the second paragraph?

(A) A sewer system is created with specific pipes for different kinds of waste being carried through it.

(B) A phone system is built out of a single type of wire which adjusts to respond to the location of the call being placed.

(C) A man keeps a capsule wardrobe which has outfits appropriate for many different occasions.

(D) The military maintains several different divisions for peace-keeping in a variety of terrains.

(E) A woman decides to use the same color of paint throughout very room in her house.

605. Based on the passage, it can be inferred that a minicolumn would be most likely to do which of the following?

(A) Remain securely in the vision function of the brain if used there.

(B) Receive input and output from a variety of senses.

(C) Control the neocortex.

(D) Respond differently to different inputs from vision or hearing.

(E) Calcify if not used on a daily basis.

606. Which of the following statements most accurately captures the author's attitude towards the brain, based on this passage?

(A) Full of wonder, uncomprehending

(B) Aggrieved that it's not better understood

(C) Reflective and poetic

(D) Factual and explanatory

(E) Eager to convince, winning

Questions 607 through 611 are based on the following passage.

David Packard, co-founder of Hewlett-Packard, said, "You are likely to die not of starvation for opportunities, but of indigestion of opportunities." Most small businesses succeed in keeping their owners more than busy — in some cases, too busy. If you provide needed products or services at a fair price, customers will beat a path to your door. Your business will grow and be busier than you can personally handle. You may need to start hiring people. I know small-business owners who work themselves into a frenzy by putting in 70 or more hours a week.

If you enjoy your work so much that it's not really work and you end up putting in long hours because you enjoy it, terrific! **But success in your company can cause you to put less energy into other important aspects of your life that perhaps don't come as easily.**

Investing For Dummies by Eric Tyson

607. Which of the following sentences would most likely follow the bolded sentence in the passage?

(A) Balance is over-rated.

(B) It's important to find a balance between your work life and your personal life.

(C) We all know someone who never worked a day in their life and still was very happy.

(D) This is no way to raise children. I have a better idea.

(E) Of course, the phrase "sleep when you're dead" resonates, too.

608. The author incorporates a quote at the beginning of this passage for what likely purpose?

(A) To show that he has the backing and approval of David Packard.

(B) To capture the interest of readers who own Hewlett-Packard products.

(C) To introduce in an interesting way an idea the author intends to develop.

(D) To show the he's not afraid to stand up to an authority like David Packard.

(E) To bolster a weak argument with a famous name.

609. Based on the passage, it can be inferred that the author finds working 70 hours a week to be . . .

(A) The correct amount of time a small business owner should expect to work.

(B) An excessive amount of time for a small-business owner to work.

(C) A sign that the small business owner who works that much is not managing his or her business well.

(D) The minimum amount of time a successful small business owner should expect to work a week.

(E) A sign that a small business owner is out of his or her depth in running their business.

610. Which of the following is a suggestion that the author makes to small business owners in the passage?

(A) Expect to work over 70 hours a week.

(B) Even if you run a great business, you may need to build clientele slowly.

(C) The only way to make sure a business is run correctly is to do everything yourself.

(D) Hiring a good accountant is a key part of running a business.

(E) You may want to consider hiring an employee to help with the business.

611. The passage can best be described as which of the following?

(A) A polemic discouraging readers from starting small businesses.

(B) The survey results from a poll of small business owners.

(C) A collection of inspiring quotes for small business owners.

(D) Suggestions for improving readers' family lives.

(E) A thoughtful exploration about finding a balance between a rewarding small business and a personal life.

Questions 612 through 615 are based on the following passage.

Kale is a strong winter green that's increasingly finding its way to the summer table. Although it's traditionally sautéed, baked, or simmered in stews and soups, **inventive** cooks have found that treating it to a massage turns this tough cookie of a green into one that's soft and silky. You'll find two kinds of kale at your market: curly and lacinato, also known as Tuscan or dinosaur kale ("dino" for short). Lacinato is less fibrous and grassy tasting than curly kale, and we recommend it over curly kale for making salads.

Cooking Basics For Dummies by Bryan Miller & Marie Rama

612. Which of the following best substitutes for the word *inventive*, which is bolded in the passage?

(A) New technology

(B) Intelligent

(C) Enterprising

(D) Unique

(E) Gifted at creating new products

613. According to the passage, a restaurant that serves kale in more traditional ways would be most like to prepare it how?

(A) In a salad

(B) Raw

(C) Boiled

(D) Baked

(E) Flambéed

614. Which of the following statements most accurately captures the main point of the passage?

(A) Kale should no longer be served in traditional ways.

(B) There are two kinds of kale.

(C) Lacinato kale should be used for salads.

(D) Inventive cooks have paved the way for many innovations in food.

(E) Kale, which has several types, can be prepared in a myriad of ways, including an innovative new form.

615. Which of the following statements most accurately explains why the authors recommend lacinato kale in a salad?

(A) It is less fibrous and grassy tasting that curly kale.

(B) It is easier to massage than regular kale.

(C) It contains more dietary fiber than regular kale.

(D) It is less curly than regular kale, making it easier to chop.

(E) It has a higher concentration of Vitamin A than curly kale.

Questions 616 through 620 are based on the following passage.

Some kids gravitate toward individual competitions, whereas others prefer tournaments. Competition can prove stressful, so be sure your child can handle it. Even a well-prepared child has to learn to face disappointment. Some have trouble coping with defeat. Crying is the most obvious sign of distress. Some parents think that crying is a sign that their child isn't ready for competition. But it is a natural response to loss. Even adults have been known to shed tears after an especially excruciating defeat. Chess is good way to help children deal with these issues. They learn that they cannot always win, but that giving their best effort is worthwhile in its own right. Kids begin competing at all ages. When a child is ready for individual or team competition depends upon many factors. These factors are best weighed and evaluated by attentive parents.

Chess For Dummies by James Eade

616. The author's attitude toward children competing in chess tournaments can best be summed up by which of the following statements?

(A) Children are naturally too delicate to compete in chess tournaments and should not be allowed to do so.

(B) Chess tournaments are for children who are exceptionally good at chess.

(C) A child can compete in chess tournaments up to the point he begins to cry; then he should no longer be allowed to compete.

(D) Competing in a chess tournament can be emotionally grueling for children, but doing so can also teach them resilience and other valuable lessons.

(E) Chess competitions at any level or for any age group are inappropriate.

617. According to the passage, at what age is a child ready for competitive chess?

(A) 8 years old

(B) At any age so long as the child wishes to compete

(C) 13

(D) Children should not play competitive chess.

(E) The author does not believe in competitive chess at any age.

618. Which of the following best describes the author's tone in this passage?

(A) Straightforward, gently leading

(B) Suggestive, provocative

(C) Laissez-faire, individualistic

(D) Hectoring, demanding

(E) Unscrupulous, conniving

619. Based on the information in this passage, what should a parent recognize about their child's tears after losing a chess competition?

(A) The child is unready to compete in chess.

(B) The child is most likely not very talented at chess.

(C) The child is reacting to a loss in a natural way.

(D) Losing may be too much for the child; she should be allowed to quit chess.

(E) The child was most likely bullied by her competitor.

620. Which of the following would be the best title for this passage?

(A) Toughen Up Your Kid Through Chess

(B) Chess Is Not for Wimps

(C) Delicate Children Play Chess

(D) Chess Will Teach Children Valuable, If Sometimes Painful, Lessons

(E) First, Know Which Pieces Are Which!

Questions 621 through 625 are based on the following passage.

Sunflowers are made up of two families, and they provide the bees with both pollen and nectar. Each family is readily grown from seed, but you may find some nurseries that carry them as potted plants. When you start sunflowers early in the season, make sure you use peat pots. They are rapid growers that transplant better when you leave their roots undisturbed by planting the entire pot. *Helianthus annuus* include the well-known giant sunflower as well as many varieties of dwarf and multi-branched types. Sunflowers no longer are only tall and yellow. They come in a wide assortment of sizes (from 2 to 12 feet) as well as a range of colors (from white to rust). **There are several varieties with a mixture of colors. Watch out for the hybrid that is pollenless because it is of little use to the bees.** Several varieties will easily self-seed, even in the cold Northeast.

Beekeeping For Dummies by Howland Blackiston

621. According to the passage, why should some hybrid sunflowers be avoided?

(A) They are difficult to grow from seed.

(B) They do not self-seed as regularly as other varieties.

(C) They do not produce pollen and thus do not attract bees.

(D) They do not look like more typical sunflowers.

(E) Their color variation is broad and unpredictable.

622. Which of the following statements most accurately captures the main point of the passage?

(A) Sunflowers do not always produce pollen.

(B) Everyone should grow a variety of sunflowers in their garden.

(C) Sunflowers are no longer only tall and yellow.

(D) The widely-loved sunflower is more complex than you may know.

(E) Sunflowers are easy to grow.

623. Based on the information given in this passage, it can reasonably be inferred that the author would most like agree with which of the following statements?

(A) Gardens should feature a wide variety of plants.

(B) A principal reason for maintaining a garden is to provide pollen for bees.

(C) No garden is complete without sunflowers.

(D) Gardeners should know the Latin names and other characteristics of flowers they grow.

(E) Hybrid plants are an environmental hazard.

624. Based on the sentences in bold, which of the following could be inferred about the author's attitude towards bees?

(A) The author feels that they are an important part of the ecosystem.

(B) The author dislikes bees and would like to see them eliminated.

(C) The author has no particular animus towards bees but is aware that many people are deeply allergic to their stings.

(D) The author feels that bees are more important than human beings.

(E) The author esteems bees.

625. Which of the following is the most likely reason the author included this advice: "When you start sunflowers early in the season, make sure you use peat pots."?

(A) The author has a sponsorship deal with the makers of peat pots.

(B) The author's experience in trying to transplant sunflowers has taught him that using peat pots is a smart move.

(C) Most readers will never have heard of a peat pot.

(D) Peat pots have been around for hundreds of years; older ways are usually best.

(E) Peat pots often cost twice what a clay pot costs.

Questions 626 through 630 are based on the following passage.

Early republics defined citizens as only male property owners and excluded all others. Landowning citizens possessed a stake in society; they were public spirited and had the desire and qualifications to participate in decision-making. No one held office for a long period of time, because when citizens rotate in and out of office they avoid corrupting influences. The great Renaissance theorist Niccolo Machiavelli argued in his *Discourses on Livy* that this public spiritedness promoted virtue the highest ideal a republican citizen could achieve. Rooted in the Latin *res publica*, the term republic literally means the "public thing." In the eighteenth century, the American Constitution framers used the word republic, or *res publica*, to refer to the "common good," the "public good," or the "good of all."

American Constitutional History by Jack Fruchtman

626. The author incorporates the Latin phrase *res publica* to what likely purpose?

(A) To show the depth of his knowledge and education.

(B) To show how the founders of America were in thrall to Latin ideas.

(C) To show how the concept of a republic is an ancient ideal.

(D) To prove that America's founders misunderstood the phrase.

(E) To build a case for a return to the ideals of ancient Rome.

627. Which of the following statements most accurately captures the main point of the passage?

(A) Machiavelli created the idea of a republic.

(B) The word *republic* comes from the Latin term *res publica*.

(C) America stole the idea of "a republic."

(D) The concept of a republic now used in America has been developed for thousands of years.

(E) Many people do not understand the fundamentals of how government works in a republic.

628. According to the passage, why, in early republics, did no citizens hold office for short periods of time?

(A) As landowners, they had other important matters to attend to.

(B) Only male property owners could be citizens.

(C) Shorter terms of office were more compatible with the agrarian lifestyle of the time.

(D) It was difficult to convince people to hold office at all.

(E) It was felt that short terms of office reduced the likelihood of corruption.

629. According to the theorist Niccolo Machiavelli, what was the highest idea a republican citizen could achieve?

(A) Virtue

(B) A republic

(C) To be a land-owner

(D) The "good of all"

(E) The "public thing"

630. Which of the following statements is one the author would most likely agree with?

(A) Niccolo Machiavelli is greatly misunderstood today.

(B) More people should learn to read Latin.

(C) The American republic grew out of a number of historical precedents.

(D) The American republic perfected prior ideas about governing.

(E) It is wrong for only land-holding men to be allowed to vote.

Questions 631 through 634 are based on the following passage.

You may already be familiar with the Big Dipper, an asterism in Ursa Major. An asterism is a named star pattern that's not identical to one of the 88 recognized constellations. An asterism may be wholly within a single constellation or may include stars from more than one constellation. For example, the four corners of the Great Square of Pegasus, a large asterism, are marked by three stars of the Pegasus constellation and a fourth from Andromeda.

Astronomy For Dummies by Stephen P. Maran

631. Which of the following statements would be the most accurate title for the passage?

(A) The Big Dipper Is an Asterism!

(B) Learn About the Great Square of Pegasus

(C) Stars Are Unknowable

(D) What Is an Asterism?

(E) Astronomy Is the Study of the Sky

632. The first sentence plays what role in this passage?

(A) It provides an example so that readers can relate to the main idea of the passage.

(B) It reveals a cultural truism before revoking its status.

(C) It reminds readers that they are all already aware of the information that will be explained in the passage.

(D) It provides the thesis that will be proved by the rest of the passage.

(E) It debunks a commonly held belief about the night sky.

633. According to the passage, what is an asterism?

(A) It's another name for a constellation.

(B) It's part of the four corners of the Great Square of Pegasus.

(C) The author suggests that it is a type of comet.

(D) No clear definition is provided.

(E) It is a named star pattern.

634. Which of the following statements is most correct?

(A) An asterism can be part of a constellation, but a constellation cannot be part of an asterism.

(B) An asterism may straddle several different constellations.

(C) Most constellations also contain an asterism.

(D) There are at least 88 asterisms.

(E) Asterisms are not as easy to pick out of the sky with an unaided eye as a constellation is.

Questions 635 through 640 are based on the following passage.

The earth formed 4.5 billion years ago. Evolutionary biologists believe that single-celled prokaryotic life (cells without a cell nucleus) appeared on earth less than one billion years after that. **What's remarkable about this date is that geophysicists believe this was the earliest point at which the planet had cooled enough to sustain life.** In other words, life appeared almost the instant (in geological time) that it was possible. For unknown reasons, it took more than another billion years for Eukaryotic life (cells with nuclei) to appear, another billion years for multicellular life to evolve from eukaryotic cells, and another billion years for humans to appear — which we did less than a million years ago. The processes that lead to multicellular life all took place in the earth's oceans.

Neuroscience For Dummies by Frank Amthor

635. Which of the following statements would the author of the passage be most likely to agree with?

(A) The reasons why Eukaryotic life took so long to appear will never be known to us.

(B) Humans took longer to develop because we are so complex.

(C) The ocean was vitally important to the development of multicellular life.

(D) Multi-cellular life cannot be studied with the complexity it deserves.

(E) The Earth took 4.5 billion years to form.

636. Which of the following statements most accurately captures the main point of the passage?

(A) It has been a long and winding road to the development of multicellular life.

(B) The development of multicellular life took an inconceivably long time.

(C) Since the earth's formation 4.5 billion years ago, the development of life has been a complex process.

(D) No one knows when multicellular life developed.

(E) It is startling to realize how quickly life began to develop after the earth's crust cooled.

637. According to the passage, cells without a cell nucleus are called which of the following?

(A) Multicellular life forms

(B) Human beings

(C) Eukaryotic life

(D) Cells without a cell nucleus

(E) Prokaryotic cells

638. Which of the following best explains the author's tone in the passage?

(A) Hostile, probing

(B) Disbelief, incredulity

(C) Worshipful, hagiographic

(D) Intrigued, informative

(E) Reductive, dismissive

639. According to the passage, how long did it take for humans to appear after cells with nuclei existed?

(A) 2 billion years

(B) 1 billion years

(C) 3 billion years

(D) 1 million years

(E) 4 billions years

640. Which of the following statements can be reasonably inferred, based on the bolded sentence?

(A) Life began at the earliest point at which the planet had cooled enough to sustain it.

(B) The planet cooled extremely rapidly.

(C) Life did not have to begin at the moment it was sustainable.

(D) Life needs to be studied in more depth to understand its origins.

(E) Life as we know it could exist on other planets.

Questions 641 through 646 are based on the following passage.

In 1879, inventor Thomas A. Edison came up with a practical electric light bulb. **Over the next 20 years, America began to wire up.** At first, direct current (DC) was used, but DC didn't work over distances of more than a few miles. Then a man named George Westinghouse began using alternating current (AC), which allowed high voltage to be sent long distances through transformers and then reduced to safer levels as it entered buildings. **Switching from steam engines to electricity made factories safer and more efficient, too.**

U.S. History For Dummies, 3rd Edition, by Steve Wiegand

641. Which of the following statements would most likely conclude the passage as presented?

(A) Thomas A. Edison went on to invent many other important things.

(B) Innovations in electrical safety continue to be developed by Americans.

(C) America is known for innovations in other fields as well.

(D) The rock band AC/DC took its name from the differing types of electricity.

(E) In conclusion, that is how Thomas A. Edison invented electricity.

642. According to the passage, what does the term *DC* stand for in electrical wiring?

(A) Direct Charge

(B) District of Columbia

(C) Distinct Current

(D) Distinct Charge

(E) Direct Current

643. Which of the following, if fully written, would present a logical structure similar to the passage?

(A) A paragraph that begins with the innovation of an Egyptian inventor and goes on to explain how she develops her ideas.

(B) A biographical sketch of an important Iranian architect.

(C) A passage exploring the history of containing nuclear power, beginning with a brief look at the first time it was safely processed.

(D) An editorial about the dangers of allowing children to play near live electrical wires.

(E) A review of notable achievements by American inventors in all fields.

644. What can safely be inferred about steam engines from the passage?

(A) Steam engines were responsible for a significant portion of factory accidents before electrical engines were put into use.

(B) Steam engines were cheaper to produce than electrical engines, but less safe.

(C) Steam engines and electrical engines were developed simultaneously.

(D) Steam engines are more difficult to operate than electrical engines.

(E) It's impossible to predict whether a steam engine will run safely or not.

645. Which of the following would be the best substitute for the word *practical* as used in the first sentence?

(A) Sensible

(B) Legal

(C) Reversible

(D) Unusual

(E) Serviceable

646. What is the connection between the two bolded sentences?

(A) The first puts forth an argument; the second refutes it.

(B) The first makes a general statement about events; the second offers evidence that proves that statement.

(C) The first is a metaphor for historical events; the second is the extension of that metaphor.

(D) The first is an ideological statement; the second is proof of that statement.

(E) The first is the evidence that an argument is needed; the second is the argument restated.

Questions 647 through 652 are based on the following passage.

Color is, first, a sensory event. Every color experience begins as a physiological response to a stimulus of light. Colors of light are experienced in two very different ways. The colors on a monitor screen are seen as direct light. The colors of the real world— of printed pages, physical objects, and the surrounding environment— are seen as reflected light.

The perception of colors seen as direct light is straightforward: wavelengths of light reach the eye directly from a light source. The experience of real-world color is a more complex event. Real-world colors are seen indirectly, as light reflected from a surface. For tangible objects and printed pages, light is the cause of color, colorants (like paints, inks, or dyes) are the means used to generate color, and the colors that are seen are the effect.

Understanding Color: An Introduction for Designers by Linda Holtzschue

647. Which of the following statements most accurately captures the main point of the passage?

   (A) Colors are a sensory event.

   (B) Light and color are important.

   (C) The way light interacts with color profoundly affects the way we see.

   (D) Colors shape our world.

   (E) Without light, there would be no color.

648. According to the passage, an example of a colorant would be which of the following?

   (A) Blue ink

   (B) A clear paint gloss

   (C) A beam of refracted light

   (D) A polish

   (E) An optical illusion

649. Which of the following situations is most likely to result in seeing colors in direct light, according to the passage?

   (A) Viewing a painting under a harsh florescent light.

   (B) Using a flashlight to see around a dark path in the forest.

   (C) Turning a dim lamp higher to a brighter light.

   (D) Watching a streaming service on a laptop.

   (E) Using multiple lights to create a warm feeling in a room.

650. Who is the most likely intended audience for this passage?

   (A) A group of elementary-aged children who are learning about the five senses.

   (B) Students in an Introduction to Painting class at a local college.

   (C) Scientists who work with color and light as part of their clinical trials protocol.

   (D) Attendees at a design conference, attending a workshop on choosing colors for their graphic work.

   (E) Secondary education students in an astronomy club.

651. According to the passage, what are the two ways colors of light are seen?

   (A) Reflected and unreflected

   (B) Direct and indirect

   (C) Indirect and unreflected

   (D) Direct and unreflected.

   (E) Reflected and direct

652. The first sentence plays what role in the passage?

   (A) It provides evidence to prove the thesis.

   (B) It is the thesis of the passage.

   (C) It is an anecdote that bolsters the thesis.

   (D) It is the anticipated counter-argument to the thesis.

   (E) It introduces a key concept in understanding light but is not the thesis.

Indeed, the whole concept of "politics" changes during the latter half of the twentieth century. Early on, United States politics in regard to literature was a more limited reflection of European dissatisfactions, played out in the inevitable, and usually clamorous, battles of "left" and "right." In literary circles, the bleak influence of European existentialism changed the priorities of, particularly, drama, but also led to worldwide recognition of such fiction writers as William Faulkner, Nelson Algren, James Agee, Ralph Ellison, Richard Wright, and John Steinbeck. European opinion colored the critical reception of much United States writing.

By the later twentieth century, however, after the furor of the challenging 1960s rights movements in both race and gender, "politics" took on a much more inclusive definition. Rather than being rooted in governmental policies, it stemmed from the deepest dichotomy possible: that of the human being set in opposition to the non-human.

A History of American Literature, 1950 to the Present by Linda Wagner-Martin

653. Which of the following would be the most likely next sentence in this passage?

(A) Fiction was no longer of any interest.

(B) The era of human vs. robot had begun.

(C) Also, writers were very concerned about the class of their characters.

(D) Although, existentialism continued to be a trend.

(E) American literature remained a mirror of European concerns.

654. The author incorporates the names of several famous authors for what likely purpose?

(A) To provide a reading list for interested librarians who want to put together a display about European existentialist writers.

(B) To provide a list of a-political writers.

(C) To show that existentialism was far more influential on novelists than dramatists.

(D) To back up her point with a list of examples that prove it.

(E) To work a favorite author into her book.

655. Which of the following statements most accurately captures the main point of the passage?

(A) The idea of "politics" in American literature changes in the second half of the 20th century.

(B) European existentialism played a heretofore unrecognized role in influencing American fiction writers.

(C) American writers were obsessed with robots.

(D) The word "politics" has a nebulous, ever-changing meaning when it comes to literature.

(E) The style of American literature is not as standardized as some many think.

656. According to the passage, a poor review in a major European newspaper of a new American novel could lead to which of the following?

(A) Poor sales in America for that novel.

(B) Poor sales in Europe for that novel.

(C) American critical reception that was influenced by the poor review from Europe.

(D) The publishing company abandoning the novel.

(E) The end of the writer's career.

In February 1819, the territory of Missouri petitioned Congress to be admitted as a state. At the time, America consisted of 11 slave and 11 free states, so the question was whether Missouri, with 10,000 slaves, should be admitted as a slave state or be forced to free its slaves before it was allowed into the fold. Debate on the issue raged across the country. Finally, Henry Clay crafted a compromise in March 1820. Under the aptly named Missouri Compromise, Missouri was admitted as a slave state, and the territory of Maine came in as a free state, keeping a balance of 12 slave and 12 free. Congress also deemed that slavery would be excluded from any new states or territories above latitude 36 degrees, 30 minutes.

U.S. History For Dummies, 3rd Edition, by Steve Wiegand

657. Which of the following would be the best title for the passage above?

(A) Who Was Henry Clay?

(B) 11 Became 12

(C) Maine's Entry into the U.S.

(D) What Was the Missouri Compromise?

(E) A Major Event Before the Civil War

658. According to the passage, how did the Missouri Compromise affect the entry of new states or territories into the United States?

(A) New states located above a certain latitude could not practice slavery.

(B) New states below a certain latitude could not practice slavery.

(C) Slavery was banned in all new entering states.

(D) The Missouri Compromise outlawed slavery in the United States.

(E) Every new state was allowed to follow the practice of slavery, or its stance against slavery, from before it joined the country.

659. The author's tone towards Missouri's practice of slavery could best be described as which of the following?

(A) Sneering condemnation

(B) Skeptical acceptance

(C) Repenting admittance

(D) Calm statement of fact

(E) Breezy confidence

Chapter 6

Verbal: Sentence Completion

The Sentence Completion section on the GMAT is about 12 questions in the Verbal section of the GMAT. These questions will be mixed in with the Reading Comprehension and Critical Reasoning questions, but the directions specifically for each type of question will be presented each time they appear. In the Sentence Completion section, you are presented with a sentence that may contain a grammatical error in the underlined portion. The first answer choice presents the underline portion as written, while the following answer choices make corrections in some way.

The Problems You'll Work On

When working through the Reading Comprehension questions presented here, be prepared to

>> Read the entire sentence to determine what type of sentence it is, and look for errors.

>> Focus on the underlined portion of the sentence and locate the error.

>> Be familiar with common types of grammatical errors, including in subject-verb agreement; pronoun usage; language about amount or size; placement of phrases; and more.

>> Determine the correct answer and make sure it fits in the sentence as a whole.

What to Watch Out For

Try to avoid these common traps:

>> Errors that are not in the underlined portion; you can't fix those.

>> Sentences that are written in a complicated fashion but are actually correct.

>> Small errors in subject-verb agreement, which are easy to miss.

660. Although Manny can't always decipher it, Lori <u>can always differentiate between the three signatures.</u>

(A) can always differentiate between the three signatures.

(B) can always differentiate between all of the three signatures.

(C) can always differentiate among the three signatures.

(D) can often differentiate between the three signatures.

(E) can usually differentiate between the three signatures.

661. "We can ask everyone who participated in the contest," Mariah said, "<u>but until we know what she thinks, we can't move forward.</u>"

(A) but until we know what she thinks, we can't move forward.

(B) but until we know what they think, we can't move forward.

(C) but until we know what she think, we can't move forward.

(D) but until we know what he thinks, we can't move forward.

(E) but until we know what they think, moving forward is not what we can do.

662. Alexander Graham Bell was a gifted inventor, <u>but they did not know how his invention of the telephone would change the world.</u>

(A) but they did not know how his invention of the telephone would change the world.

(B) but they did not know how his invention of the telephone would change the world back then.

(C) but he did not know how his invention of the telephone would change the world at that time.

(D) but neither he nor anyone else knew the how his invention of the telephone would change the world.

(E) but not gifted enough to see his invention was going to change the world with the invention he made that was the telephone.

663. The National Honor Society meeting <u>dissolved into a debate over</u> which of the women should serve as president.

(A) dissolved into a debate over

(B) dissolved for a debate over

(C) dissolving into a debate over

(D) dissolved into a debate around

(E) dissolves into a debate regarding

664. Beth went to the school <u>for speaking with</u> Mr. Huon.

(A) for speaking with

(B) to speak among

(C) to speak with

(D) to speak around

(E) to speak

665. Being that she was the first to arrive at the cabin, Bey didn't hear the stories we told in the car.

(A) Being that she was the first to arrive at the cabin,

(B) Because she was the first to arrive at the cabin,

(C) Being that Bey was the first to arrive at the cabin,

(D) Being that she was the first to arrive upon the cabin,

(E) Being that she would have been the first to arrive at the cabin,

666. Either the Pirates or the Orioles are the winners; we'll have to check the score to be sure.

(A) Either the Pirates or the Orioles are the winners;

(B) Either the Pirates or the Orioles will be the winners;

(C) Either Pirates or Orioles are winners;

(D) Either the Pirates or the Orioles is the winner;

(E) Either the Pirates or the Orioles is the winners;

667. Because Bobbie doesn't like liver, she would rather than cook it for her children.

(A) rather than

(B) rather but

(C) then rather

(D) but not also

(E) rather not

668. A mountain forming the perfect backdrop, Adil went for a run yesterday morning.

(A) A mountain forming the perfect backdrop, Adil went for a run yesterday morning.

(B) With a mountain forming the perfect backdrop, Adil went for a run yesterday morning.

(C) Adil, who went for a run yesterday morning, had a mountain forming the perfect backdrop.

(D) With a mountain as a backdrop, which was perfect, Adil went for a run yesterday morning.

(E) Running, Adil saw the perfect backdrop of a mountain on yesterday morning.

669. Who do you think is the better dancer, Monique or Enrique?

(A) Who do you think is the better dancer,

(B) Who do you think is the best dancer,

(C) Who do you think is a good dancer,

(D) Who do you think dances well,

(E) Who do you find to be the best dancer,

670. Liu felt that the exhaust fan in the first examination room was more effective than the second.

(A) more effective than the second.

(B) more effective than the exhaust fan in the second examination room.

(C) more effective that she expected.

(D) the most effective exhaust fan.

(E) more effective than what she had noticed in the second examination room.

671. <u>Running to catch the train,</u> the people on the platform stared at Suzie as she screamed for the conductor to wait.

   (A) Running to catch the train,

   (B) Running as she was to catch the train,

   (C) As they ran to catch the train,

   (D) As she ran to catch the train,

   (E) Seeing her running to catch the train,

672. If that group of lacrosse players <u>don't quiet down,</u> they will be asked to leave the restaurant!

   (A) don't quiet down

   (B) don't quiets down

   (C) quiets down

   (D) doesn't quiet down

   (E) quiet down

673. <u>To claim that Andrew likes ice cream is understating the truth!</u>

   (A) To claim that Andrew likes ice cream is understating the truth!

   (B) To claim that Andrew likes ice cream was understating the truth!

   (C) Andrew likes ice cream, and it's not an understatement to say that!

   (D) To say that Andrew will like ice cream is saying that the case is understated!

   (E) To say that Andrew likes ice cream is to understate the truth!

674. Bonita asked the preschool class <u>to quietly wait by the door</u> before lunch; of course, they did not.

   (A) to quietly wait by the door

   (B) to wait quietly by the door

   (C) to wait by the quiet door

   (D) to quietly go to the door and wait

   (E) to quietly by the door wait

675. Juan and Almanzo often ask me which of them <u>is the best ballplayer.</u>

   (A) is the best ballplayer.

   (B) is the bestest ballplayer.

   (C) is the better ballplayer.

   (D) is the better ballplayer of the two of them.

   (E) is, of the two of them, the best.

676. <u>Xu wishes she could join us,</u> but her Bio exam is tomorrow.

   (A) Xu wishes she could join us,

   (B) Xu wish she could join us,

   (C) Xu wishes she could joins us,

   (D) Xu, wishing she could join us,

   (E) Xu wishes she would join us,

677. <u>The dispute around who owned the land affected five generations of the Longfellow family.</u>

   (A) The dispute around who owned the land affected five generations of the Longfellow family.

   (B) The dispute in regards to who owned the Longfellow land affected five generations of the Longfellow family.

   (C) The dispute re: who owned the land affected five generations of the Longfellow family.

   (D) The dispute over who owned the land affected five generations of the Longfellow family.

   (E) The dispute over who owned the land affected five generations' of the Longfellow family.

678. The cookies in my lunch are smaller than Justin's lunch.

(A) The cookies in my lunch are smaller than Justin's lunch.

(B) The cookies in my lunch are smaller than those in Justin's lunch.

(C) The cookies in my lunch are smaller than the cookies.

(D) Justin's lunch has more cookies than in my lunch.

(E) As to the cookies in my lunch, they are smallest.

679. On her first visit to Paris, Parah wanted to visit the Louvre, walk by the Seine and shopping in the Latin Quarter.

(A) On her first visit to Paris, Parah wanted to visit the Louvre, walk by the Seine and shopping in the Latin Quarter.

(B) On her first visit to Paris, Parah visits the Louvre, walks by the Seine and shopping in the Latin Quarter.

(C) On her first visit to Paris, Parah wanted to visiting the Louvre, walking by the Seine and shopping in the Latin Quarter.

(D) On her first visit to Paris, Parah made time for to visit the Louvre, walking by the Seine, and shopping in the Latin Quarter.

(E) On her first visit to Paris, Parah wanted to visit the Louvre, walk by the Seine and shop in the Latin Quarter.

680. The girls and their coach eats together after the game.

(A) The girls and their coach eats together after the game.

(B) The girls and their coach eat together after the game.

(C) The girls and their coach, after the game, eats.

(D) After the game, the girls and their coach eats.

(E) Eating after the game is the way for the coach and the girls.

681. Wandering through the trees, the scenery was spectacular to us.

(A) Wandering through the trees, the scenery was spectacular to us.

(B) Wandering through the trees, the scenery, to us, was spectacular.

(C) Wandering as we were through the trees, spectacular scenery.

(D) As we wandered through the trees, we saw spectacular scenery.

(E) The scenery was spectacular, wandering through the trees.

682. The first and only person I thought of was you.

(A) The first and only person I thought of was you.

(B) The first and only person I thought of were you.

(C) The first and only person of whom I thought was you.

(D) The first and only person I thought about were you.

(E) You was the first and only person I thought of.

683. Belle, like many cows, eat a great deal of grass.

(A) eat a great deal of grass.

(B) eat a lot of grass.

(C) eat quite a bit of grass.

(D) eats a great deal of grass

(E) eat grass, a great deal.

684. The McCutcheons or the Jacksons were the first people to welcome us to the neighborhood.

(A) The McCutcheons or the Jacksons were

(B) The McCutcheons or the Jacksons was

(C) The McCutcheons or the Jacksons was

(D) The McCutcheons or the Jacksons was or were

(E) It were the McCutheons or the Jacksons who

685. Either Brenda or Xiu might likes to tell that story.

(A) Either Brenda or Xiu might likes to tell that story.

(B) Either Brenda or Xiu might likes to tell the story.

(C) Either Brenda or Xiu might like to tell that story.

(D) Either Brenda or perhaps Xiu might likes to tell that story.

(E) Either Brenda nor Xiu might like to tell that story.

686. The audience were euphoric upon receiving their prizes.

(A) The audience were euphoric upon receiving their prizes.

(B) The audience was euphoric upon receiving their prizes.

(C) Upon receiving their prizes, the audience were euphoric.

(D) Upon receiving the audience's prizes, they were euphoric.

(E) The audience and their prizes were euphoric upon receipt.

687. Nobody want more dessert.

(A) Nobody want more dessert.

(B) No body want more dessert.

(C) Nobody wants more desserts.

(D) Nobody want much dessert.

(E) Nobody wants more dessert.

688. Boopsie gave Charles a key to the store after he would stop by.

(A) after he would stop by.

(B) after he was stopping by.

(C) after he stopped by.

(D) after he be stopping by.

(E) after she would stop by.

689. Dennis wanted to take Neil shopping for his birthday gift, but he wasn't available on Tuesday.

(A) Dennis wanted to take Neil shopping for his birthday gift, but he wasn't available on Tuesday.

(B) Dennis wanted to take Neil shopping for a birthday gift but he wasn't available on Tuesday.

(C) Dennis wanted to take Neil shopping for a birthday gift but Neil wasn't available on Tuesday.

(D) Dennis wanted to take him shopping for a birthday gift, but he wasn't available on Tuesday.

(E) Dennis wanted to take him shopping for his birthday gift, but he wasn't available on Tuesday.

690. Annie asked Bill if he would tell her the truth.

(A) Annie asked Bill if he would tell her the truth.

(B) Annie asked Bill if Bill would tell her the truth.

(C) Annie asked Bill if he would tell Annie the truth.

(D) Annie asked Bill if Bill would tell Annie the truth.

(E) Annie asked him if he would tell Bill the truth.

691. Sunny and warm, Takeya couldn't wait to get to the beach.

(A) Sunny and warm, Takeya couldn't wait to get to the beach.

(B) Takeya couldn't wait to get to the beach, sunny and warm.

(C) Sunny and warm, Takeya couldn't wait to get to the beach the morning that it was sunny and warm.

(D) Because it was sunny and warm that morning, Takeya couldn't wait to get to the beach.

(E) Because Takeya was going to the beach that morning, it was sunny and warm.

692. A weaver with a fine sense of color, the throws made by Jade were exquisite.

(A) A weaver with a fine sense of color, the throws made by Jade were exquisite.

(B) Jade was a weaver with a fine sense of color, so her throws were exquisite.

(C) Jade, a weaver with a fine sense of color, wove throws that were exquisite in their use of color.

(D) A weaver with a fine sense of color, her throws were exquisite.

(E) Jade wove with a fine sense of color and Jade's throws were exquisite.

693. I brought three things to work that morning: my lunch bag, my laptop, and a copy of the report.

(A) I brought three things to work that morning: my lunch bag, my laptop, and a copy of the report.

(B) I brought three things to work that morning, my lunch bag, my laptop, and a copy of the report.

(C) I brought three things to work that morning: my lunch bag and my laptop, and a copy of the report.

(D) I brought three things to work that morning: my lunch bag and my laptop and my copy of the report.

(E) I brought three things — my lunch bag, my laptop, and a copy of the report — to work with me that morning.

694. A large creature with snowy white hair, Richard stared at the swimming polar bear in wonder.

(A) A large creature with snowy white hair, Richard stared at the swimming polar bear in wonder.

(B) The polar bear stared at Richard, a large creature with snowy white hair, in wonder.

(C) In wonder, Richard stared at the polar bear, the large creature with snowy white hair.

(D) Richard stared in wonder at the polar bear, which was a large creature with snowy white hair.

(E) In wonder, a large creature with snowy white hair, Richard stared at the polar bear.

695. Choose among the optional colors, please.

(A) Choose among

(B) Choose about

(C) Choose

(D) Choose from

(E) Choose near

696. The winner will be determined with the general election.

(A) The winner will be determined with

(B) The winner will be determined by

(C) The winner determines

(D) With the winner will be

(E) The winner will be determined among

697. Rather with buy food at the ballpark, we brought our own snacks.

(A) Rather with

(B) Rather but

(C) Rather against

(D) To rather with

(E) Rather than

698. We have to determine the winner among the two semi-finalists.

(A) We have to determine the winner among the two semi-finalists.

(B) We have to determine a winner among the two semi-finalists.

(C) We have to determine a winner between the two semi-finalists.

(D) We have to determine a winner between one semi-finalist and the other.

(E) We have to determine a winner among the semi-finalists: two of them.

699. The costumes for the musical are more elaborate than last year's.

(A) The costumes for the musical are more elaborate than last year's.

(B) The costumes for the musical are most elaborate than last year's.

(C) The costumes for the musical are more elaborate than last year's less elaborate ones.

(D) The costumes for the musical are more elaborate than those of the musical last year.

(E) The costumes for the musical are more elaborate compared to last year's.

700. I'm trying to determine the better of the two routes suggested, because I want to find the best way to travel to Dublin.

(A) I'm trying to determine the better of the two routes suggested, because I want to find the best way to travel to Dublin.

(B) I'm trying to determine the best of the two routes suggested, because I want to find the best way to travel to Dublin.

(C) I'm trying to determine the best of the two routes suggested, because I want to find the very best way to travel to Dublin.

(D) I'm trying to determine the better of the two routes suggested, because I want to find the better way to travel to Dublin.

(E) I'm trying to determine the best of the two routes suggested, because I want to find the better way to travel to Dublin.

701. I prefer the second of the two flavors of ice cream the most.

(A) I prefer the second of the two flavors of ice cream the most.

(B) I prefer the second of the two flavors of the ice cream the most.

(C) I prefer the second two flavors of ice cream the most.

(D) I prefer the second of the two flavors of ice cream more.

(E) I prefer the second most, of the two flavors of ice cream.

702. Jim was the least entertaining person at the party.

(A) Jim was the least entertaining person at the party.

(B) Jim was the less entertaining person at the party.

(C) Of the people at the party, Jim was the one who was not entertaining.

(D) Less than anyone else at the party, Jim was the least entertaining.

(E) At the party, Jim entertained the least.

703. A number of people stopped by my table to ask if I was OK after I tripped in front of the entire restaurant.

(A) A number of people stopped by my table to ask if I was OK

(B) An amount of people stopped by my table to ask if I was OK

(C) A quantity of people stopped by my table to ask if I was OK

(D) The people who stopped by my table to ask if I was OK were a numerous amount

(E) Asking if I was OK, people stopped by my table

704. Many of the food was thrown out after five days, but we kept the cookies that had been frozen.

(A) Many of the food was thrown out after five days,

(B) Many of the food was thrown away after five days,

(C) After five days, many of the food was thrown out,

(D) Much of the food was thrown out after five days,

(E) Much of the food was thrown away, five days after,

705. Bria gave Ebron less cookies than she gave Nadine.

(A) Bria gave Ebron less cookies than she gave Nadine.

(B) Bria gave Ebron fewer cookies than she gave Nadine.

(C) Bria gave Ebron fewer cookies than the cookies she gave to Nadine.

(D) Bria gave Ebron less cookies than the amount she gave to Nadine.

(E) Briad gave Ebron less cookies than Nadine.

706. It took me more time than I expected, but I was able to buy more towels at the sale.

(A) It took me more time than I expected, but I was able to buy more towels at the sale.

(B) It took me more time than I expected, but I was able to buy more of the towels I wanted to buy at the sale.

(C) It took me much time than I expected, but I was able to buy more towels at the sale.

(D) It took me much time than I expected, but I was able to buy much towels at the sale.

(E) It took me more time than I expected, but I was about to buy much towels at the sale.

707. It took Sally less time at the doctor than she expected, and she was able to buy less pills to complete her treatment.

(A) It took Sally less time at the doctor than she expected, and she was able to buy less pills to complete her treatment.

(B) It took Sally less time at the doctor than she expected, and she was able to buy fewer pills to complete her treatment.

(C) It took Sally fewer time at the doctor than she expected and she was able to buy fewer pills to complete her treatment.

(D) It took Sally less time at the doctor, and she expected to be able to buy fewer pills for her treatment.

(E) At the doctor, Sally took fewer minutes than she had expected the appointment to take, and she was able to buy less pills to complete her treatement.

708. Bob missed much of the discussion, and much of the key points.

(A) Bob missed much of the discussion, and much of the key points.

(B) Bob missed most of the discussion, and most of the key points.

(C) Bob missed much of the discussion, and many of the key points.

(D) Bob missed many of the discussion, and many of the key points.

(E) Bob missed many of the discussion, and much of the key points.

709. Ma started to carefully pick her way over the stones.

(A) Ma started to carefully pick her way over the stones.

(B) Ma started to carefully pick her way through the stones.

(C) Ma started to pick her carefully way through the stones.

(D) Ma started to pick her way carefully through the stones.

(E) Ma started to carefully pick her way across the stones.

710. Too many people think they can start to angrily complain about the poor service after one mistake.

(A) Too many people think they can start to angrily complain about the poor service after one mistake.

(B) Too many people think they can start to complain angrily about the poor service after one mistake.

(C) Too many people think they can start to angrily complain about the poor service they receive after one mistake.

(D) After one mistake, too many people think they can start to angrily complain about the poor service.

(E) After one mistake and poor service, too many people think they can start to angrily complain.

711. If Shelly was a nice person, she would have asked for my permission.

(A) If Shelly was a nice person,

(B) If Shelly were a nice person,

(C) If a nice person was Shelly,

(D) If a nice person were Shelly,

(E) If Shelly, a nice person, was

712. <u>That's my professor.</u>

(A) That's my professor.

(B) My professor, that is.

(C) That were my professor.

(D) Thats my professor.

(E) My professor is that.

713. <u>I found it's match in the pile of socks.</u>

(A) I found it's match in the pile of socks.

(B) I found it is match in the pile of socks.

(C) I found its matches in the pile of socks.

(D) In the pile of socks, I found it's match.

(E) I found its match in the pile of socks.

714. My GPS isn't working, <u>but I know it's just up the road.</u>

(A) but I know it's just up the road.

(B) but I know its just up the road.

(C) but it is just up the road, I know it.

(D) but it — the place we're going — is just up the road, I know.

(E) but its just up the road, I know.

715. <u>Being as she's the CEO, Maya likes to get to the construction site early.</u>

(A) Being as she's the CEO, Maya likes to get to the construction site early.

(B) Being as Maya's the CEO, she likes to get to the construction site early.

(C) Being as Maya's the CEO, Maya likes to get to the construction site early.

(D) Because she's the CEO, Maya likes to get to the construction site early.

(E) Beyond being the CEO, Maya likes to get to the construction site early.

716. Johann paced the waiting room floor, <u>being that he was nervous about his wife's delivery.</u>

(A) being that he was nervous about his wife's delivery.

(B) being that Johann was nervous about his wife's delivery.

(C) because Johann was nervous about his wife's delivery.

(D) because he was nervous about his wife's delivery.

(E) so nervous was he about his wife's delivery.

717. Manuel needs to drop off his tax information, pick up his son from daycare, <u>and also a meeting with his staff.</u>

(A) and also a meeting with his staff.

(B) and a meeting with his staff.

(C) and hold a meeting with his staff.

(D) also meet with his staff.

(E) and also meet with his staff.

718. <u>Kate, like many vet technicians, work very long hours.</u>

(A) Kate, like many vet technicians, work very long hours.

(B) Kate, like many vet technicians, works very long hours.

(C) Like many vet technicians, working very long hours, is Kate.

(D) Working many long hours, Kate is a vet technician.

(E) Kate, like many vet technicians working long hours, works long hours.

719. <u>I'm not sure why you was so upset by the phone call.</u>

   (A) I'm not sure why you was so upset by the phone call.

   (B) I'm not sure why, by the phone call, you was so upset.

   (C) You was upset by the phone call, but I'm not sure why.

   (D) I'm not sure why you were so upset by the phone call.

   (E) I'm not sure why you were so upset, by the phone call.

720. Once Xian realized that <u>the penguin wasn't going to emerge to find it's food again</u>, she left the aquarium.

   (A) the penguin wasn't going to emerge to find it's food again

   (B) the penguin wasn't going to emerge to find its food again

   (C) the penguin wasn't going to emerge to find their food again

   (D) the penguin wasn't going to emerge in order to find it's food again

   (E) the penguin wasn't going to emerge to finding food again

721. From what Melissa told me, Robert and Susan Faith took David to the zoo, <u>but he got bored and wanted to go home.</u>

   (A) but he got bored and wanted to go home.

   (B) but he got bored and he wanted to go home.

   (C) but he got bored and Robert wanted to go home.

   (D) but David got bored and wanted to go home.

   (E) but she got bored and wanted to go home.

722. <u>Screaming for the goalie to block the net, Security escorted Tom from the stadium.</u>

   (A) Screaming for the goalie to block the net, Security escorted Tom from the stadium.

   (B) Screaming for the goalie to block the net, Tom escorted Security from the stadium.

   (C) Screaming for the goalie to block the net, as Security escorted him from the stadium.

   (D) The goalie screamed as Security escorted Tom from the stadium.

   (E) As he screamed for the goalie to block the net, Tom was escorted from the stadium by Security.

723. <u>If she were taller, Shakiya could have been a ballerina.</u>

   (A) If she were taller, Shakiya could have been a ballerina.

   (B) If she was taller, Shakiya could have been a ballerina.

   (C) If she was tall, Shakiya could have been a ballerina.

   (D) If she were tall, Shakiya could have been a ballerina.

   (E) Shakiya could have been a ballerina, but only if she was taller.

724. Melissa tried her best to win the baking contest, <u>but they did not realize her oven was broken.</u>

   (A) but they did not realize her oven was broken.

   (B) but no one, including Melissa and the judges, did not realize her oven was broken.

   (C) but they realized that her oven was broken too late.

   (D) but too late was it realized that her oven was broken.

   (E) but neither she nor anyone else in attendance realized her oven was broken.

725. I had to choose <u>from the best of two schools' offers</u> when it was time to start a fellowship.

(A) from the best of two schools' offers

(B) from the better of two schools' offers

(C) from the best of two school's offers

(D) from the better of two school's offers

(E) from between the best of two schools' offers

726. <u>To say that Acadia National Park is a beautiful place is understating the truth!</u>

(A) To say that Acadia National Park is a beautiful place is understating the truth!

(B) To say that Acadia National Park is a beautiful place is to understate the truth!

(C) The truth is, it can be said that Acadia National Park is a beautiful place!

(D) To say that Acadia National Park is understating the case!

(E) To say Acadia National Park is to say that it is a beautiful place.

727. <u>I asked Mo'chelle and her brothers to help with the fair.</u>

(A) I asked Mo'chelle and her brothers to help with the fair.

(B) I asked Mo'chelle and also her brothers to help with the fair.

(C) I ask Mo'chelle and her brothers to help with the fair.

(D) I asking Mo'chelle and her brothers to help with the fair.

(E) Asking Mo'chelle and her brothers to help with the fair.

728. <u>I were the last to leave the testing center.</u>

(A) I were the last to leave the testing center.

(B) I were the last to be leaving the testing center.

(C) Being the last to leave the testing center.

(D) I was the last to leave the testing center.

(E) The testing center; I were the last to leave it.

729. <u>The clowns, even Dani, was not the children's favorite act.</u>

(A) The clowns, even Dani, was not the children's favorite act.

(B) The clowns, even Dani, was not the childrens' favorite act.

(C) The childrens' favorite act were not the clowns, even Dani.

(D) The clowns, except for Dani, was not the children's favorite act.

(E) The clowns, even Dani, were not the children's favorite act.

730. <u>Despite Elsie's reluctance, her family is asking for donations.</u>

(A) Despite Elsie's reluctance, her family is asking for donations.

(B) Despite Elsie's reluctance, she is asking her family for donations.

(C) For donations, Elsie is reluctant, yet her family is asking for them.

(D) Elsie is reluctantly asking her family for donations.

(E) For donations, her family is asking for the reluctant Elsie.

731. <u>You lifts me up as a class.</u>

(A) You lifts me up as a class.

(B) You lift me up as a class.

(C) You, class, lifts me up.

(D) You, class, lift me up.

(E) Up is where you lift me, class.

732. Either Renee or Todd will takes you to the appointment.

 (A) Either Renee or Todd will takes you

 (B) Either Renee or Todd will taking you

 (C) You will be taken by Renee or either Todd

 (D) Either Renee or Todd will take you

 (E) Renee or Todd, either will take you

733. Nobody want to go to that club again.

 (A) Nobody want to go to that club again.

 (B) Nobody want to go to the club again.

 (C) Nobody wants to go to that club again.

 (D) Nobody want to go that club again.

 (E) Nobody wants to go to that club to again.

734. Everybody love music.

 (A) Everybody love music.

 (B) Everybody loves music.

 (C) Music is loved, by everybody.

 (D) Everybody loves the music.

 (E) Everybody and the music loves.

735. We will plays when the field is dry, but for now, we'll wait.

 (A) We will plays when the field is dry,

 (B) We will plays when the field's dry,

 (C) We plays when the field is dry,

 (D) When the field is dry we plays

 (E) We will play when the field is dry,

736. I learned more complicated ideas in college after I would learn the basics in high school.

 (A) after I would learn the basics in high school.

 (B) after I learned the basics in high school.

 (C) after, in high school, I would learn the basics.

 (D) after high school, where I would learn the basics.

 (E) after high school, where learning the basics.

737. Ida fixed Bruce's bike chain after he asked her to help.

 (A) Ida fixed Bruce's bike chain after he asked her to help.

 (B) Ida fixed Bruce's bike chain after he was asking her to help.

 (C) Ida fixes Bruce's bike chain after he asks her to help.

 (D) To help, Bruce asked Ida to fix his bike chain.

 (E) Bruce's bike chain was fixed by Ida after he asks her to help.

738. I should be the last person you ask.

 (A) I should be the last person you ask.

 (B) I should be the last of the people you ask to ask.

 (C) I ask you to ask me last.

 (D) I am the last person you ask.

 (E) I will be the last person you ask.

739. I asked Miguel if Lilly would be late.

 (A) I asked Miguel if Lilly would be late.

 (B) I asked Miguel if she would be later.

 (C) I asked Miguel if he would be late.

 (D) I ask Miguel if he would be late.

 (E) I asked Miguel if he knew if she would be late.

740. Bram Stoker wrote *Dracula* after extensively researching vampires, publishing several other books and also several early drafts.

 (A) after extensively researching vampires, publishing several other books and also several early drafts.

 (B) after extensively researching vampires, and publishing several other books, and also writing several early drafts.

 (C) after extensively researching vampires, he published several other books and also several early drafts.

 (D) after extensively researching vampires, publishing several other books, and crafting several early drafts.

 (E) after several early drafts.

741. I'll leave for the interview on Tuesday, <u>subject for her availability.</u>

    (A) subject for her availability.

    (B) subject at her availability.

    (C) subject near her availability.

    (D) subject due to her availability.

    (E) subject to her availability.

742. <u>As great for the diner's breakfast is,</u> I'm going to sleep in this morning.

    (A) As great for the diner's breakfast is,

    (B) As great as the diner's breakfast is,

    (C) As great by the diner's breakfast is,

    (D) The diner's breakfast is great

    (E) Breakfast at the diner is great

743. <u>Because he is in danger of failing, Gomez went to tutoring.</u>

    (A) Because he is in danger of failing, Gomez went to tutoring.

    (B) Because he is danger to failing, Gomez went to tutoring.

    (C) Failing is a danger, Gomez went to tutoring.

    (D) Gomez, in danger to fail, went to tutoring.

    (E) Because he is of danger of failing, Gomez went to tutoring.

744. <u>This argument is different as what we've seen before.</u>

    (A) This argument is different as what we've seen before.

    (B) This argument is different by what we've seen before.

    (C) This argument is different from what we've seen before.

    (D) This argument is different to what we've seen before.

    (E) This argument is different near to what we've seen before.

745. <u>Western Pennsylvania is usually defined by Pittsburgh and further west.</u>

    (A) Western Pennsylvania is usually defined by Pittsburgh and further west.

    (B) Western Pennsylvania is usually defined to Pittsburgh and further west.

    (C) Western Pennsylvania is usually defined to be Pittsburgh and further west.

    (D) Western Pennsylvania is usually defined as Pittsburgh and further west.

    (E) Western Pennsylvania is usually defined being as Pittsburgh and further west.

746. <u>Gretel and I agreed that the pink bubble tea tasted better than the blue bubble tea.</u>

    (A) Gretel and I agreed that the pink bubble tea tasted better than the blue bubble tea.

    (B) Gretel and I agreed that the pink bubble tea tasted better than the blue bubble tea tasted.

    (C) Gretel and I agreed that the pink bubble tea we tasted was better than the blue bubble tea.

    (D) Gretel and I agreed that the pink bubble tea tasted best than the blue bubble tea.

    (E) Gretel and me agreed that the pink bubble tea tasted better than the blue bubble tea.

747. The sign warned that swimmers <u>were prohibited from diving.</u>

    (A) were prohibited from diving.

    (B) were prohibited on diving.

    (C) were prohibited to diving.

    (D) were prohibited for diving.

    (E) were prohibited by diving.

748. The eggs we gathered from the coop <u>were larger than the other coop.</u>

(A) were larger than the other coop.

(B) were larger than the other coop's.

(C) were larger than the eggs gathered in the other coop.

(D) were larger than the eggs.

(E) are larger than the other coop.

749. Janelle would like to stay home <u>rather by going out to eat.</u>

(A) rather by going out to eat.

(B) rather but going out to eat.

(C) rather to going out to eat.

(D) rather than going out to eat.

(E) rather with going out to eat.

750. <u>Marie wanted to slowly circle the block until we found a parking spot.</u>

(A) Marie wanted to slowly circle the block until we found a parking spot.

(B) Marie wanted to slowly circle the block, looking for a parking spot.

(C) Marie wanted to circle the block, slowly looking for a spot to parking in.

(D) Marie, slowly circling the block, wanted to look for a parking spot.

(E) Marie wanted to circle the block slowly until we found a parking spot.

751. <u>George Washington had to choose the better of two men when selecting a personal secretary.</u>

(A) George Washington had to choose the better of two men when selecting a personal secretary.

(B) George Washington had to choose between the best of two men when selecting a personal secretary.

(C) When selecting a personal secretary, George Washington had to select a man.

(D) When selecting a personal secretary, George Washington had to choose the best of two men.

(E) The better of two men was what George Washington had to choose when selecting a personal secretary.

752. <u>That's the worse of it.</u>

(A) That's the worse of it.

(B) That is the worse of it.

(C) That will the worst of it.

(D) That's the worst of it.

(E) The worse of it, that is.

753. Marcos felt that the last movie of the trilogy <u>was the less interesting.</u>

(A) was the less interesting.

(B) was the interesting one.

(C) was the least interesting.

(D) was interesting.

(E) wasn't as interesting.

754. Many more people signed up for the class than I expected.

    (A) Many more people signed up for the class than I expected.

    (B) Many people signed up for the class than I expected.

    (C) Much people signed up for the class than I expected.

    (D) Much more people signed up for the class than I expected.

    (E) Many people signed up for the class.

755. The physician asked the family for permission to do the surgery a large quantity of times.

    (A) a large quantity of times.

    (B) a number of times.

    (C) an amount of times.

    (D) much times.

    (E) a quantity of times.

756. Booker T. Washington is much admired today because of a lot of his achievements.

    (A) because of a lot of his achievements.

    (B) because of his many achievements.

    (C) because he achieved a lot of things.

    (D) because his achievements are much.

    (E) because of much of his achievements.

757. I seen the play you're talking about.

    (A) I seen the play you're talking about.

    (B) I seen a play you're talking about.

    (C) I seen the play you're speaking about.

    (D) I seen the play about which you speak.

    (E) I saw the play you're talking about.

758. The squirrel dropped its birdseed when we startled it.

    (A) The squirrel dropped its birdseed when we startled it.

    (B) The squirrel dropped it's birdseed when we startled it.

    (C) The squirrel dropped its birdseed when we startled its.

    (D) The squirrel dropped it's birdseed when we startled its.

    (E) The squirrel dropped it's birdseed when we startled it's.

759. It takes a long time to walk Hadrian's Wall, but its worth it.

    (A) It takes a long time to walk Hadrian's Wall, but its worth it.

    (B) It takes a long time to walk Hadrian's Wall. But its worth it.

    (C) It takes a long time to walk Hadrian's Wall. But it is worth it.

    (D) It takes a long time to walk Hadrian's wall, but its worth it.

    (E) It takes a long time to walk Hadrian's Wall, but it's worth it.

760. Its about time that Carolyn realizes its dangerous.

    (A) Its about time that Carolyn realizes its dangerous.

    (B) It's about time that Carolyn realizes its dangerous.

    (C) It's about time that Carolyn realizes it's dangerous.

    (D) Its about time that Carolyn realizes it's dangerous.

    (E) Its about time Carolyn realizes its dangerous.

761. <u>Being that he was the only nominee, it's not surprising</u> that Ben won the contract.

   (A) Being that he was the only nominee, it's not surprising

   (B) Being that he was the only nominee, its not surprising

   (C) Being that he was the only nominee and it's not surprising

   (D) Although he was the only nominee, it's not surprising

   (E) Given that he was the only nominee, it's not surprising

762. <u>From what we could see, Jill's team lost points for lack of originality, they weren't on the beat, and starting too late.</u>

   (A) From what we could see, Jill's team lost points for lack of originality, they weren't on the beat, and starting too late.

   (B) From what we could see, Jill's team lost points for lack of originality, not being on the beat, and starting too late.

   (C) From what we could see, Jill's team lost points for they weren't original, they weren't on the beat, and starting too late.

   (D) Starting too late, Jill's team lost points for they were original and they weren't on the beat.

   (E) They weren't on the beat, they weren't original and starting too late were the reasons Jill's team lost points from what we could see.

763. <u>The pipes hisses when water runs through them.</u>

   (A) The pipes hisses when water runs through them.

   (B) The pipe hisses when water runs through them.

   (C) The pipes hiss when water runs through them.

   (D) The pipes hiss when water run through them.

   (E) The pipes hiss when water runs through it.

764. <u>They are her best friends</u>, despite all of the fights the four of them have had over the years they've know each other.

   (A) They are her best friends

   (B) They are her bestest friends

   (C) They were her best friends

   (D) They is her best friend

   (E) They are her best friend

765. <u>Carlos, like many science teachers, explain evolution very clearly.</u>

   (A) Carlos, like many science teachers, explain evolution very clearly.

   (B) Carlos, like most science teachers, explain evolution very clearly.

   (C) Carlos, like many science teachers, explain evolution clearly.

   (D) Carlos, like many science teachers, explains evolution very clearly.

   (E) Like many science teachers, Carlos explain evolution very clearly.

766. You, despite the other qualified candidate, is my first pick for the job.

(A) You, despite the other qualified candidate, is my first pick for the job.

(B) You, despite the other qualified candidate, are my first pick for the job.

(C) Despite the other qualified candidates, you is my first pick for the job.

(D) You is my first pick for the job, despite the other qualified candidate.

(E) Despite the other qualified candidates, you are my first pick for the job.

767. Beverley's choice is the green, Mindy choose the gold.

(A) Beverley's choice is the green, Mindy choose the gold.

(B) Beverley's choice is the green; Mindy chose the gold.

(C) Beverley choose the green, while Mindy choose the gold.

(D) Beverley's choice is the green. Mindy gold.

(E) Beverley's choice is the green; Mindy gold.

768. Penelope, as is the case with many researchers, love the library.

(A) Penelope, as is the case with many researchers, love the library.

(B) As is the case with many researchers, Penelope love the library.

(C) Penelope, as is the case with many researchers, loves the library.

(D) Like many researches who love the library, Penelope is.

(E) Many researchers love the library; Penelope also loves the library.

769. If the diagnostic procedure doesn't work, either Susan or Daveed decide to perform the surgery.

(A) either Susan or Daveed decide to perform the surgery.

(B) either Susan or Daveed decides to perform the surgery.

(C) either Susan or Daveed decides to performs the surgery.

(D) either Susan or Daveed decide to performs the surgery.

(E) either the surgery will be decided to be performed.

770. Nobody understand the directions, so please go over them again.

(A) Nobody understand the directions, so please go over them again.

(B) Nobody understand the direction, so please went over them again.

(C) Nobody understanded the directions, so please go over them again.

(D) Nobody understands the directions, so please go over them again.

(E) Nobody understands the directions, so please goes over them again.

771. Monica sent Rachel an invitation before Rachel would be complaining about it.

(A) Monica sent Rachel an invitation before Rachel would be complaining about it.

(B) Monica sent Rachel an invitation before Rachel would complain about it.

(C) Monica sent Rachel an invitation before Rachel complained about it.

(D) Monica would send Rachel an invitation before Rachel would complain about it.

(E) Before Rachel would complain about it, Monica sent Rachel an invitation.

772. Despite trying everything she could, the patient could not be saved by Dr. Geller.

   (A) Despite trying everything she could, the patient could not be saved by Dr. Geller.

   (B) Despite trying everything she could, Dr. Geller could not save the patient.

   (C) Despite trying everything she could, the patient could not save Dr. Geller.

   (D) The patient, despite trying everything she could, could not be saved by Dr. Geller.

   (E) Dr. Geller could not save the patient who tried everything she could.

773. An astronaut with seven missions under her belt, the next mission was still exciting to Rhonda.

   (A) An astronaut with seven missions under her belt, the next mission was still exciting to Rhonda.

   (B) After being an astronaut with seven missions under her belt, the next mission was still exciting to Rhonda.

   (C) Despite being an astronaut with seven missions under her belt, the next mission was still exciting to Rhonda.

   (D) Despite being an astronaut with seven missions under her belt, Rhonda still felt excited about the next one.

   (E) The next mission, despite being an astronaut with seven missions, was under the belt exciting for Rhonda.

774. Before swimming the required laps, a hearty breakfast was enjoyed by the team.

   (A) Before swimming the required laps, a hearty breakfast was enjoyed by the team.

   (B) Before swimming the required laps, the team enjoyed a hearty breakfast.

   (C) The required laps before swimming, a hearty breakfast was enjoyed by the team.

   (D) The team enjoyed, before swimming the required laps, a hearty breakfast.

   (E) A hearty breakfast was enjoyed by the required laps before swimming by the team.

775. That old man is acting like a child!

   (A) That old man is acting like a child!

   (B) That old man is acting as a child!

   (C) The old man is acting as a child!

   (D) Like a child, the old man is acting!

   (E) An old man, acting as a child!

776. Not everyone can learn to bake like my mom does.

   (A) Not everyone can learn to bake like my mom does.

   (B) Not everyone can learn to bake the way my mom does.

   (C) Not everyone can learn to bakes like my mom.

   (D) No one can learn to bake like my mom.

   (E) No one can learn to bake as my mom.

777. Sad and scared, the campsite appeared welcoming to the hikers.

    (A) Sad and scared, the campsite appeared welcoming to the hikers.

    (B) Sad and scared, the campsite did appear welcoming to the hikers.

    (C) The campsite, sad and scared, appeared welcoming to the hikers.

    (D) To the hikers, the welcoming campsite appeared sad and scared.

    (E) The campsite appeared welcoming to the sad and scared hikers.

778. Aiyanna is a respected artist, known for her use of color, strong lines and she uses collage in her work.

    (A) known for her use of color, strong lines and she uses collage in her work.

    (B) known for her use of color, strong lines, and collage in her work.

    (C) known for her use of color, her use of strong lines and her use of collage in her work.

    (D) known, in her work, for her use of color, strong lines, and collage.

    (E) known for her use of color in her work as well as her use of strong lines and her use of collage.

779. In his work, Ricardo is required to design products, create mock-ups for review, and approve the samples for production.

    (A) Ricardo is required to design products, create mock-ups for review, and approve the samples for production.

    (B) Ricardo is required to design, mock-up and approve products.

    (C) Ricardo is required to design products, create mock-ups of those products for review, and approve the samples of the mock-ups of the products he's designed for production.

    (D) for production, Ricardo is required to design products, create mock-ups for review, and approve the samples for production.

    (E) Ricardo is required to design products, mock-up for review, and approve the samples for production.

780. To say that Ronald was an excellent dad is giving credit where it is due.

    (A) To say that Ronald was an excellent dad is giving credit where it is due.

    (B) To say that Ronald was an excellent dad is credit given where credit is due.

    (C) Ronald was an excellent dad, which is giving credit where credit is due.

    (D) Credit due, Ronald was an excellent dad.

    (E) To say that Ronald was an excellent dad is to give credit where it is due.

781. Because Joni doesn't like football, she would prefer tickets to the Pirates <u>rather from the Steelers.</u>

(A) rather from the Steelers.

(B) rather than the Steelers.

(C) rather by the Steelers.

(D) rather through the Steelers.

(E) rather near the Steelers.

782. <u>The race course will be defined as</u> the loop from the park to the municipal building.

(A) The race course will be defined as

(B) The race course will be defined by

(C) The race course will be defined to

(D) The race course will be defined

(E) The race course will be defined before

783. <u>I can conclude to your expression that your team won.</u>

(A) I can conclude to your expression that your team won

(B) I can conclude for your expression that your team won.

(C) I can conclude between your expression that your team won.

(D) I can conclude from your expression that your team won.

(E) I can conclude as to your expression that your team won.

784. <u>A debate around</u> where to eat lunch dominated the rest of the car ride.

(A) A debate around

(B) A debate under

(C) A debate of

(D) A debate in

(E) A debate over

785. Pierre doesn't think it's a good idea on a rainy day, but he will not <u>prohibit them by</u> swimming in the lake.

(A) prohibit them by

(B) prohibit them to

(C) prohibit them at

(D) prohibit them from

(E) prohibit them for

786. <u>The play that has always been attributed to</u> Christopher Marlowe, may, in fact, have been written by William Shakespeare.

(A) The play that has always been attributed to

(B) The play that has always been attributed as

(C) The play that has always been attributed for

(D) The play that has always been attributed by

(E) The play that has always been attributed past

787. <u>The entrée was different by what I expected,</u> but it was still delicious.

(A) The entrée was different by what I expected

(B) The entrée was different by what was expected

(C) The entrée was different for what was expected

(D) The entrée was different than what I expected

(E) The entrée was different

788. As great for Brooklyn is, Benji prefers Pittsburgh.

(A) As great for Brooklyn is, Benji prefers Pittsburgh.

(B) As great Brooklyn is, Benji prefers Pittsburgh.

(C) As great as Brooklyn is, Benji prefers Pittsburgh.

(D) Great as Brooklyn, Benji prefers Pittsburgh.

(E) As great as Brooklyn is, Benji is in the position of preferring Pittsburgh.

789. Dr. Huardo felt the results were the better she's seen in 8 years of performing this experiment.

(A) Dr. Huardo felt the results were the better she's seen

(B) Dr. Huardo felt the results were the better of those she has seen

(C) Dr. Huardo felt the results were the better of the results she's seen

(D) Dr. Huardo felt the results were the best she's seen

(E) Dr. Huardo felt the results are the better she's seen

790. Among the two of us, I was hoping for more information about the job offer.

(A) Among the two of us,

(B) Between the two of us,

(C) In the midst of the two of us,

(D) About the two of us,

(E) Around the two of us,

791. The reports have been printed for over a week, at the end.

(A) The reports have been printed for over a week, at the end.

(B) The reports have been printed for over a week, for the end.

(C) The reports have been printed for over a week, at least.

(D) The reports have been printed for over a week, at end.

(E) The reports have been printed for over a week, at is.

792. The recommendations from the customer service department are more helpful than the human resources department.

(A) The recommendations from the customer service department are more helpful than the human resources department.

(B) The recommendations from customer service are more helpful than the human resources.

(C) The recommendations from the customer service department are found to be more helpful than the human resources department.

(D) The recommendations from the customer services department are most helpful than the human resources department.

(E) The recommendations from the customer services department are more helpful than those from the human resources department.

793. Its easy to find the answer when you're looking for it.

    (A) Its easy to find the answer when you're looking for it.

    (B) It's easy to find the answer when your looking for it.

    (C) It's easy to find the answer when you're looking for it.

    (D) Its easy to find the answer when your looking for it.

    (E) Its easy to find the answer; when you're looking for it.

794. Liu was forced to agree that the cars traveled more quickly on the highway than the buses.

    (A) Liu was forced to agree that the cars traveled more quickly on the highway than the buses.

    (B) Liu, forced to agree, said that the cars traveled more quickly on the highway than the buses.

    (C) Forced to agree, Liu concurred that the cars traveled more quickly on the highway than the buses.

    (D) Liu was forced to agree that the cars traveled more quickly on the highway than the buses on the highway.

    (E) Liu was forced to agree that the cars traveled more quickly on the highway than the buses traveled.

795. Their the ones asking for a replay.

    (A) Their the ones asking for a replay.

    (B) Their the people asking for a replay.

    (C) They're the those asking for a replay.

    (D) They're the ones asking for a replay.

    (E) A replay is what their asking for.

796. Most orchid growers worry obsessively over their plants.

    (A) Most orchid growers worry obsessively over their plants.

    (B) More orchid growers worry obsessively over their plants.

    (C) Many orchid growers worry obsessively over their plants.

    (D) Many orchid growers worry over their plants obsession.

    (E) Most orchid growers obsessively worry over their plants.

797. A number of laptops were missing from the cart, despite Irina's careful watch over the class.

    (A) A number of laptops were missing from the cart,

    (B) An amount of laptops went missing from the cart,

    (C) A quantity of laptops went missing from the cart,

    (D) A quantity of laptops went missing from the cart,

    (E) An amount of laptops were missing from the cart,

798. Jovan applied to five colleges and now has to choose among two of them.

    (A) Jovan applied to five colleges and now has to choose among two of them.

    (B) Jovan applied to five colleges and now has to choose between two of them.

    (C) Jovan applied to five college and now chooses among two of them.

    (D) Jovan, having applied to five colleges, now chooses among two of them.

    (E) Having applied to five college, Jovan now chooses among two of them.

799. Much of the project was scrapped, but our division kept all of the blueprints.

(A) Much of the project was scrapped, but our division kept all of the blueprints.

(B) Much of the project, scrapped, but our division kept all of the blueprints.

(C) All of the blueprints were kept by our division, despite the scrapping of the project.

(D) The kept blueprints by our division after the project was scrapped.

(E) Many of the project was scrapped, but our division kept all of the blueprints.

800. We saw far fewer of an increase than we were expecting after the new logo was unveiled.

(A) We saw far fewer of an increase than we were expecting after the new logo was unveiled.

(B) We saw far little of an increase than we were expecting after the new logo was unveiled.

(C) We saw less of an increase than we were expecting after the new logo was unveiled.

(D) We saw a decrease after the new logo was unveiled.

(E) After the new logo was unveiled, the increase was far fewer than we expected.

801. The drive took less time than Maddie expected, so she arrived early for the meeting.

(A) The drive took less time than Maddie expected, so she arrived early for the meeting.

(B) The driver took less time than Maddie expected, so she arrived early for the meeting.

(C) The drive took fewer time than Maddie expected, so she arrived early for the meeting.

(D) As she arrived for the meeting, Maddie expected the drive to take less time.

(E) To take less time, Maddie drove to the meeting earlier than she expected.

802. You didn't take the time to carefully read the instructions before installing the software?

(A) You didn't take the time to carefully read the instructions

(B) You didn't take time to carefully read the instructions

(C) You did not take time to carefully read the instructions

(D) You did not take time to read the instructions carefully

(E) You carefully did not take time to read the instructions

803. If Jim was a nice guy, he would have asked for forgiveness.

(A) If Jim was a nice guy, he would have asked for forgiveness.

(B) If Jim were a nice guy, he would have asked for forgiveness.

(C) If Jim was a nice guy, he would have forgiven.

(D) If Jim was a nice guy, he could have asked for forgiveness.

(E) If Jim were a nice guy, he could had asked for forgiveness.

804. The shopping trip took Tony and Deven less time than they expected, but they ended up buying less shoes at the sale.

(A) The shopping trip took Tony and Deven less time than they expected, but they ended up buying less shoes at the sale.

(B) The shopping took Tony and Deven fewer time than they expected, but they ended up buying less shoes at the sale.

(C) The shopping trip took Tony and Deven fewer time than they expected, but they ended up buying less shoes at the sale.

(D) The shopping trip took Tony less time than expected, but Deven ended up buying fewer shoes at the sale.

(E) The shopping trip took Tony and Deven less time than they expected, but they ended up buying fewer shoes at the sale.

805. Delores called the theater to angrily complain about the audio issues after she got home.

(A) Delores called the theater to angrily complain about the audio issues

(B) Delores called the theater angrily to complain about the audio issues

(C) Delores called the theater to complain angrily about the audio problems

(D) Delores called the theater to complain about the angry audio problems

(E) Delores called the theater to complain about the audio issues

806. The cow chewed through its rope when we left it unattended.

(A) The cow chewed through its rope

(B) The cow chewed through it's rope

(C) The cow chewed thru its rope

(D) The cow chewed thru it's rope

(E) Through it's rope, the cow chewed

807. Helen, the most affluent of my friends, give lavish gifts.

(A) Helen, the most affluent of my friends, give lavish gifts.

(B) Helen, the most affluent of my friends give lavish gift.

(C) The most affluent of my friends, Helen, give lavish gifts.

(D) Helen, the most affluent of my friends, gives lavish gifts.

(E) Lavish gifts gives by Helen, the most affluent of my friends.

808. After selecting Joseph, John, and Marni to lead the project, Sam regretted choosing him.

(A) Sam regretted choosing him.

(B) Sam regretted choosing them.

(C) Sam regretted choosing her.

(D) Sam regretted choosing John.

(E) Sam regretted choosing.

809. I didn't like the colors offered, but I had to pick one, so I chose them.

(A) I didn't like the colors offered, but I had to pick one, so I chose them.

(B) I didn't like the colors offered, but I had to pick one, so I chose it.

(C) I didn't like the colors offered, but I had to pick one, so I chose one of the colors offered.

(D) I didn't like the colors offered, but I had to pick one, so I chose her.

(E) I didn't like the colors offered, but I had to pick one, so I chooses one.

810. Excited and happy, the gloomy day didn't deter the soon-to-be graduates.

(A) Excited and happy, the gloomy day didn't deter the soon-to-be graduates.

(B) Excited and happy, the gloomy day did not deter the soon-to-be-graduates.

(C) Because they were excited and happy, the soon-to-be graduates were not deterred by the gloomy day.

(D) The gloomy day, excited and happy, did not deter the soon-to-be graduates.

(E) The soon-to-be day was not deterred by the excited and happy graduates.

811. A nurse with a background in chemistry, the patient's records were easily understood by Becca.

(A) A nurse with a background in chemistry, the patient's records were easily understood by Becca.

(B) As a nurse with a background in chemistry, the patient's records were easily understood by Becca.

(C) The patient's records, for a nurse with a background in chemistry, were easily understood by Becca.

(D) Easily understood by Becca were the patient's records for a nurse with a background in chemistry.

(E) As a nurse with a background in chemistry, Becca easily understood the patient's records.

812. Before leaving for the picnic, the lunch was prepared by Jean.

(A) Before leaving for the picnic, the lunch was prepared by Jean.

(B) Before leaving for the picnic, Jean prepared the lunch.

(C) Jean, leaving for the picnic, prepared the lunch.

(D) Jean prepared the lunch, leaving for the picnic.

(E) Having prepared the lunch, Jean left for the picnic.

813. The skills we're looking for in our new hire are excellent customer service experience, a willingness to brainstorm, and a background in finance.

(A) excellent customer service experience, a willingness to brainstorm, and a background in finance.

(B) excellent customer service experience, a willingness to brainstorm, and backgrounds in finance.

(C) excellent customer service experiencing, a willingness to brainstorming, and a background in finance.

(D) serving customers excellently, willingly brainstorming and a background in finance.

(E) a background in finance, customer service and brainstorming.

814. Dax, an outstanding researcher, often takes his staff to lunch, gives plenty of vacation days, and he is sure to remember birthdays as well.

(A) Dax, an outstanding researcher, often takes his staff to lunch, gives plenty of vacation days, and he is sure to remember birthdays as well.

(B) An outstanding researcher, Dax often takes his staff to lunch, gives plenty of vacation days, and he is sure to remember birthdays as well.

(C) Dax, an outstanding researcher, often takes his staff to lunch, gives plenty of vacation days, and is sure to remember birthdays as well.

(D) Dax often takes his staff to lunch, gives plenty of vacation days, and he is sure to remember birthdays as well, as an outstanding researcher.

(E) Dax, an outstanding researcher, often takes his staff to lunch, he gives plenty of vacation days, and is sure to remember birthdays as well.

815. If you are in danger for failing, please see the professor after class.

(A) If you are in danger for failing,

(B) If you are in danger of failing,

(C) If you are in danger to failing,

(D) If in danger you are failing,

(E) If you are in danger at failing,

816. We can conclude from the results that the marketing campaign was successful.

(A) We can conclude from the results

(B) We can conclude to the results

(C) We can conclude for the results

(D) We can conclude at the results

(E) We can conclude against the results

817. The statistics appear by show that profits are stable.

(A) The statistics appear by

(B) The statistics appear

(C) The statistics appearing to

(D) The statistics appear to

(E) The statistics is

818. We will need to return to the main office because for the regulations.

(A) because for the regulations.

(B) because since the regulations.

(C) because to the regulations.

(D) because of the regulations.

(E) because at the regulations

819. Maura asked if Bridget had anything else to contribute for the discussion.

(A) to contribute for the discussion.

(B) to contribute to the discussion.

(C) contributable to the discussion.

(D) in contribution for the discussion

(E) to contribute as the discussion.

820. The temperature in Austin is higher than in Dallas today.

(A) The temperature in Austin is higher than in Dallas today.

(B) The temperature in Austin is higher than in Dallas, today.

(C) The temperature — in Austin — is higher than in Dallas today.

(D) The temperature in Austin is higher than the temperature in Dallas today.

(E) The temperature in Austin are higher than in Dallas today.

821. The questions on the GMAT are more challenging than the questions on the SAT.

(A) The questions on the GMAT are more challenging than the questions on the SAT.

(B) The questions on the GMAT are most challenging that the questions on the SAT.

(C) The questions on the GMAT are more challenging than the SAT.

(D) The questions on the GMAT are more challenging than that of the SAT.

(E) The questions on the GMAT is more challenging than the questions on the SAT.

822. We don't know yet if its a boy or a girl.

(A) We don't know yet if its a boy or a girl.

(B) We do not know yet if its a boy or a girl.

(C) No one knows yet if its a boy or a girl.

(D) We don't know yet if it's a boy or a girl.

(E) We don't know yet if it's a boy or it's a girl.

823. The penguins swim more gracefully than the polar bears.

(A) The penguins swim more gracefully than the polar bears.

(B) The penguins swim most gracefully than the polar bears.

(C) The penguins, more than the polar bears, swim more gracefully.

(D) More gracefully, the penguins swim the polar bears.

(E) The penguins swim more gracefully than the polar bears swim.

824. Think of your assignment as an opportunity, despite your misgivings.

(A) Think of your assignment as an opportunity,

(B) Think about your assignment to be an opportunity,

(C) Thinking of your assignment and opportunity,

(D) Thinking upon your assignment as an opportunity,

(E) Thinks of your assignment for opportunity,

825. To admit you've erred is admitting you're human.

(A) To admit you've erred is admitting you're human.

(B) To admit you've erred is to admit your human.

(C) To admit you've erred is to admit you're human.

(D) To admit you are in error is admitting you are human.

(E) Admit you're in error, admit you're human.

826. Anna tried to carefully pick her away through the glass shards.

(A) Anna tried to carefully pick her way through the glass shards.

(B) Anna carefully tried to pick her way through the glass shards.

(C) Through the glass shards, Anna tried to carefully pick her way.

(D) Anna, trying to carefully pick her way through the glass shards.

(E) Anna, through the glass shards, tried to carefully pick her way.

827. To begin paying quickly, Louis will need to bring a check to the signing.

(A) To begin paying quickly,

(B) To quickly begin payments,

(C) To pay quickly,

(D) To quickly pay,

(E) For making the payments quickly,

828. Mary and Rick took Takeya and Leroy to the store, but he didn't want to buy anything.

(A) Mary and Rick took Takeya and Leroy to the store, but he didn't want to buy anything.

(B) Mary and Rick took Takeya and Leroy to the store, but she didn't want to buy anything.

(C) Mary and Rick took Takeya and Leroy to the store but they didn't want to buy anything.

(D) Mary and Rick took Takeya and Leroy to the store, but Leroy didn't want to buy anything.

(E) Mary and Rick took Takeya and Leroy to the store, but Takeya and Leroy didn't want to buy anything.

829. Yelling that even he could see that the ball was fair, Mom took Bobby away from the field.

(A) Yelling that even he could see that the ball was fair, Mom took Bobby away from the field.

(B) Yelling that even she could see that the ball was fair, Mom took Bobby away from the stadium.

(C) Yelling that even she could see that the ball was fair, Bobby took Mom away from the stadium.

(D) As he yelled that even he could see that the ball was fair, Bobby was taken away from the stadium by Mom.

(E) Because he could not stop yelling that the ball was fair, Mom took Bobby away from the stadium.

830. The audience, already amazed by the first act, gasp when the curtain rises on the new set for the second act.

(A) gasp when the curtain rises

(B) gasps when the curtain rose

(C) gasp when the curtain rise

(D) gasps when the curtain rises

(E) gasp at the rising of the curtain

831. Despite our invitation, you seems surprised that we're having a party.

(A) Despite our invitation, you seems surprised

(B) Despite our invitation, you seems surprising

(C) Despite our invitation, you seems surprise

(D) Despite our invitation, you seemed surprised

(E) Despite our invitation, you seem surprised

832. Mitchell, like many nurses, work long hours.

(A) work long hours.

(B) works long hours.

(C) work longer hours.

(D) works longer hours.

(E) work for long hours.

833. Before the wedding, Vanisha needs to buy a wedding gift, resole her dancing shoes, and the visit to her dentist needs to be rescheduled.

(A) and the visit to her dentist needs to be rescheduled.

(B) and visiting her dentist needs to be rescheduled for another day.

(C) and reschedule her visit to her dentist.

(D) and dentist's visit needs to be rescheduled.

(E) and visit her dentist.

834. Maureen asked the visitors to quietly wait by the door before entering; of course, they did so.

(A) to quietly wait by the door before entering

(B) to, before entering, quietly wait by the door

(C) to by the door wait quietly before entering

(D) to wait before the door, quietly entering

(E) to wait quietly by the door before entering

835. This is its cage, but it's hiding.

(A) This is its cage, but it's hiding.

(B) This is it's cage, but it's hiding.

(C) This is it's cage, but its hiding.

(D) This is its case, but its hiding.

(E) This is its cage; but its hiding.

836. Less classmates came to the show than Rick was expecting, which disappointed him; he thought at least half of his class of 10 would show up.

(A) Less classmates came to the show

(B) Fewer classmates came to the show

(C) Lesser classmates came to the show

(D) Less classmates coming to the show

(E) Few classmates came to the show

837. If I was younger, I'd take a trip around the world.

(A) If I was younger

(B) If I was young

(C) If I could be young

(D) If I were younger

(E) If I was young once more

838. Among you and me, this is the end of the section.

(A) Among you and me,

(B) Among you and I,

(C) Between you and I,

(D) Between you and me,

(E) Among the both of us

Chapter 7

Verbal: Critical Reasoning

The Critical Reasoning section on the GMAT consists of about 12 questions in the Verbal section of the GMAT. These questions will be mixed in with the Reading Comprehension and Sentence Completion questions, but the directions specifically for each type of question will be presented each time they appear.

In Critical Reasoning, you are shown a passage that presents an argument of some kind (often dealing with a business, government, or education topic). Some passages have multiple questions. You must choose the answer that best answers the question based on your understanding of the logic in the passage.

The Problems You'll Work On

When working through the Reading Comprehension questions presented here, be prepared to

>> Read the entire passage and be able to summarize the logical argument presented there.

>> Understand what the question is asking for you to do, which will often be to find a way to strengthen or weaken the argument.

>> Choose the answer that best fits with what the question is asking.

What to Watch Out For

Try to avoid these common pitfalls:

>> Answers that fix the argument in the passage but do not answer the question posed.

>> Attempts to make you take leaps forward in inferring. Instead, take small hops in logic.

>> Answers that play to your natural assumptions. Instead, look clearly at the passage's logic.

>> Dialogues: They seem like conversations, but they still present arguments.

Hunter: **Most people blame hunters for the decline of deer in Keystone State Park over the last 10 years.** However, hunters aren't the only threat to deer. Keystone has seen a surge in deer's natural predator, the coyote, in the past 10 years as well.

839. In the hunter's argument, the portion in bold plays which of the following roles?

(A) It is a finding the argument seeks to explain.

(B) It is an explanation as to why the argument is correct.

(C) It is the conclusion of the argument.

(D) It provides evidence in support of the main conclusion of the argument.

(E) It introduces a premise that the argument goes on to oppose.

840. Which of the following, if true, would present the best support for the argument?

(A) Hunters alone aren't the problem.

(B) The large-mouth bass population in Keystone State Park has also declined.

(C) Hunting coyotes is illegal in Keystone State Park.

(D) Coyotes do not exclusively kill and eat deer.

(E) Autopsies of coyotes killed by cars or found in dead in Keystone State Park revealed that nearly all of them had recently consumed deer meat.

Two years ago, the rate of inflation was about 0.5%. Last year, it was 2%. We can conclude that the rate of inflation is on an upward trend and will be as high as 4% by the close of this year.

841. Which of the following, if true, most seriously weakens the conclusion?

(A) The inflation rate was calculated using a selection of relevant data rather than all data available for prior years.

(B) Two years ago, a dip in home mortgages dropped inflation temporarily below its stable level of 2% in recent years.

(C) Intervention by the Federal Reserve cannot affect the rate of inflation to any significant degree.

(D) Increases in the pay of some workers are tied to the inflation level, which only increases inflation.

(E) The 0.5% rate of inflation from two years ago represented a 10-year low.

842. If the argument is true, what must also be true?

(A) Inflation will continue to rise steadily at 2% per year.

(B) In two years' time, the inflation rate will be higher than 4%.

(C) The rate of inflation always doubles every year.

(D) 0.5% is an unexpectedly low rate of inflation.

(E) At some point, the rate of inflation must decrease.

Ryan is a student at a local college. In order to improve his grade point average, he's decided to study for an additional hour every night and to take a protein supplement.

843. Which of the following statements, if true, weakens Ryan's likelihood of success?

(A) The college's campus closes on weekends, including the library.

(B) Ryan has partial custody of his young daughter, but does not see her on a fixed schedule.

(C) Ryan often turns in his assignments late.

(D) Taking a protein supplement has been shown to hurt, not improve, memory.

(E) Ryan wants a 4.0 GPA.

844. Which of the following, if true offers the strongest support for Ryan's plan?

(A) Ryan's dad followed the same plan while he was at college 20 years ago.

(B) Ryan will lose his athletic scholarship if he drops below a 2.5 GPA.

(C) Ryan's Physician's Assistant suggested the protein supplement based on her observation of its success for other student-athletes at Ryan's college.

(D) Ryan has also decided to keep his planner up to date.

(E) The protein supplement is available at several drug stores close to campus.

845. If the statements in the passage are true, what must also be true?

(A) It's possible to bottle milk without preservatives in a way that still makes it safe to drink.

(B) Preservatives cause cancer.

(C) Lange Farms must be an organic dairy.

(D) Preservatives have been shown to cause harm.

(E) Scientific studies must be carefully interpreted.

846. What would most seriously weaken the argument?

(A) The term "preservatives" is vague.

(B) Lange Farms faced near bankruptcy in 1998.

(C) Several stores will no longer carry Lange Farm milk because customers have returned too many bottles in which the milk spoiled several days before the "Sell by" date stamped on the lid.

(D) Scientific studies must be compared for an accurate conclusion to be drawn.

(E) Lange Farms' bottles are stamped with a date 10 days after bottling. Many dairies stamp with a date 14 days after bottling.

Questions 845 through 846 are based on the following passage.

It's been shown in countless scientific studies that preservatives can be harmful when added to milk. Here at Lange Farms, all our milk is produced and bottled without preservatives. There's no need to be concerned about preservatives when you buy from Lange Farms! Buy a bottle of our milk today, and it will be good — and tasty — for at least a week after!

Questions 847 through 848 are based on the following passage.

Bohlburg has three major post offices, including two which are open 24 hours a day. There are also several shops in town that sell postal stamps, where more people buy stamps than at the post offices. That's an odd choice by the people of Bohlburg.

847. Which of the following is an assumption made in drawing the conclusion?

(A) The people of Bohlburg must not need many stamps.

(B) There are no advantages to buying stamps at a shop instead of a post office.

(C) Bohlburg is a large city.

(D) The post offices are difficult to reach by public transportation and do not have adequate parking.

(E) Bohlburg needs more than three post offices.

848. Which of the following should be studied in order to evaluate the validity of the conclusion presented in the passage?

(A) What reason do the citizens of Bohlburg give when asked why they prefer to buy stamps in shops instead of the post office?

(B) What is the distance between the post offices?

(C) What services and products can be purchased at the post office besides stamps?

(D) How many stamps does the average citizen of Bohlburg buy at one time?

(E) What goods and services are often purchased at small shops at the same time as stamps?

Questions 849 through 850 are based on the following passage.

It costs more to produce plastic planters in Country X because of a tariff on exports there that is more than 5% of the cost of each planter. Country Y does not have a tariff on exports. However, the business that produces the planters has chosen to remain in County X.

849. If the statement is true, which of the following best supports the company's decision to remain in Country X?

(A) The company has been in Country X for over 100 years.

(B) Country Y does not buy much of the company's product.

(C) The company's workforce in Country X can be paid 15% less than the anticipated workforce in Country Y.

(D) Moving a company to another country is a time-consuming and expensive proposition.

(E) Country X facilitates paperwork on behalf of its exporting companies.

850. Assuming the statement is true, which of the following statements below most weaken the company's resolve to stay in Country X?

(A) Country Y will offer incentives for companies seeking to relocate there.

(B) Much of the workforce in Country X is approaching retirement age.

(C) The 5% tariff will increase by 1% every year until it reaches 10%, at which point, it will surpass the company's savings on workforce cost by remaining in Country X.

(D) A significant portion of Country Y's population owns one of the company's products.

(E) Country Y offers a lower per-capita cost of living.

Questions 851 through 852 are based on the following passage.

Pineapple farmers earn a higher price when the fruit is more difficult to find in grocery stores. When the crop is plentiful, the price drops. Therefore, it makes sense that when a large pineapple crop comes in, farmers should hold back a portion of it in refrigerated warehouses, hoping that future crops will be less plentiful, and driving up the price.

851. Which of the following, if true, best supports the argument made?

(A) Avocado farmers already use this plan to keep the price of their product high.

(B) Pineapples are difficult to keep from spoiling, even in refrigerated warehouses.

(C) Pineapples grow in a three-year cycle, in which one heavy harvest is following by two less abundant harvests.

(D) Pineapple sells better at certain times of the year.

(E) Most pineapple farmers in the U.S. are concentrated in just a few states.

852. Which of the following, if true, most seriously weakens the conclusion presented?

(A) Pineapples can be kept in refrigerated warehouses for a month to six weeks at maximum.

(B) The price per pound of pineapples varies widely across the United States.

(C) Not everyone likes pineapple.

(D) The growing cycle of a pineapple takes more than a year.

(E) Pineapples sell better in warmer climates.

Since 2000, Bettyville has flooded every spring on the east side of town. The neighborhood that floods most frequently is comprised of a few residential homes, the Living Oak Nursing Home, and the abandoned J & B Warehouse. Bettyville is currently pursuing litigation against J & B Warehouse's parent company in order to force it to stabilize the river bank against future flooding.

853. In the preceding passage, which of the following is an assumption made by the town in order to pursue litigation against J & B Warehouse?

(A) It is natural for river waters to rise as the winter snows melt.

(B) Other parts of Bettyville do not flood on a yearly basis.

(C) The Living Oak Nursing Home is not as culpable as J & B Warehouse.

(D) J & B Warehouse left its facility in good shape.

(E) Stabilizing the riverbank in the area that belongs to J & B Warehouse would help to counteract the yearly floods.

Questions 854 through 855 are based on the following passage.

Jen: I'm not going to buy that brand of soda anymore.

Vic: Why not?

Jen: I've noticed that I always get sick a few hours after drinking it. I'm not going to risk that again.

854. What evidence, if true, most weakens Jen's logic in the statements?

(A) Jen is a hypochondriac.

(B) Vic does not feel sick after drinking that brand of soda.

(C) Jen often drinks that soda while indulging in fried foods.

(D) Jen has been served that brand of soda at her favorite restaurant for years without realizing that she was consuming it, and has never felt sick afterwards.

(E) That brand of soda is currently under investigation by the FDA for possible mislabeling.

855. If Vic wanted to offer evidence to show Jen that she agrees with her assumption, which of the following, if true, would be the best support?

(A) "You haven't bought that brand of soda lately."

(B) "I just read a study that shows that all soda is bad for you."

(C) "That will teach you to buy the cheapest brand of soda."

(D) "Come to think of it, in my journal, I noted that you often complained of a stomachache after we ate at restaurants that served you that brand of soda."

(E) "What other proof can you offer?"

I think that must be the most popular restaurant in town. Its parking lots is always full, and everyone I know says it's a terrific place for breakfast, lunch, or dinner. They could charge twice what they do now and people would still go there in droves!

856. In the passage preceding, the sentence in bold plays which of the following roles?

(A) It is evidence that proves the premise.

(B) It is a premise that will be proven by the rest of the argument.

(C) It is evidence that disproves the premise of the argument.

(D) It provides evidence in support of the main conclusion of the argument.

(E) It introduces a premise that the argument goes on to oppose.

Questions 857 through 858 are based on the following passage.

A few days before a local mayoral election, a local news channel polled registered voters in the area to ask them which candidate they planned to vote for. **3 percent of registered voters were polled,** and 48 percent said that they would vote for Michael Stewin, the current Mayor. Based on the poll results, the news channel presented a story that Michael Stewin would win the election, but, in fact, his opponent, Jane Alexie, won.

857. Which of the following was the most significant flaw in the news channel's logic in predicting Stewin as the likely winner?

(A) The news channel assumed that Stewin would win because he is the incumbent.

(B) The news channel failed to notice that 48 percent is not a majority.

(C) The news channel based its conclusion on only 3 percent of registered voters' responses.

(D) The news channel predicted Stewin would win.

(E) The news channel failed to ask poll responders what they thought of Jane Alexie.

858. In the passage, what role does the portion in boldface play?

(A) It is a conclusion that must be proven for the argument to be valid.

(B) It provides evidence to support a premise of the argument.

(C) It is a premise used to support the argument.

(D) It is an assumption that does not provide support for the conclusion of the argument.

(E) It provides evidence to support the new channel's conclusion.

A zoologist who's spent his career studying the Hitchjaw eel has tracked a decline in Hitchjaw eel population in local waterways. He attempted to rally local public interest in saving the Hitchjaw eel, showing the vital role they play in preserving the local river system's ecology. However, he eventually concluded that local people could not find it in themselves to save creatures that they find so repellent.

859. The zoologist's opinion would be most strengthened by which of the following statements, if true?

    (A) The Hitchjaw eel is endangered, but not nearly as much at risk as other species of eels.

    (B) The Hitchjaw eel population has been in decline for over 10 years.

    (C) A recent Twitter survey of local people shows that they report finding Hitchjaw eels more disgusting than snakes or rats.

    (D) The zoologist lives 20 miles east of the area.

    (E) Conservation efforts to save the Hitchjaw eel have been in place since the 1970s.

860. Which of the following, if true, most clearly points to a flaw in the zoologist's reasoning?

    (A) Hitchjaw eels grow to 3 feet long.

    (B) Recent efforts by locals have helped stabilize the population of long-eared rats, a deeply disliked local pest.

    (C) Conservation efforts in the area have been ongoing since the 1970's.

    (D) The local newspaper did produce a story on the zoologist's efforts.

    (E) The zoologist has not provided a poll on his website, in which people can vote on whether they like Hitchjaw eels or not.

861. If the argument is correct, which of the following conclusions could be properly drawn from it?

    (A) The zoologist should start a campaign to help people understand and grow to admire Hitchjaw eels.

    (B) The movement to save Hitchjaw eels should be abandoned.

    (C) People tend to like animals they find cute.

    (D) Hitchjaw eels are lucky to have survived this long.

    (E) The zoologist should move on to another project.

Lucy wants to paint her kitchen white, but she can't spend more than $30 on paint. Her friend Danielle has offered to give her either three gallons of leftover blue paint, or a gift card for the amount of $20. The white paint that Lucy wants to buy costs $60. Therefore, Lucy most logically should . . .

862. Which of the following best completes the preceding passage?

    (A) . . . take the blue paint, because it's free and she's on a budget.

    (B) . . . take the gift card, because it would at least lower the price to $40.

    (C) . . . ask Danielle for both the blue paint and the gift card.

    (D) . . . ask Danielle for an additional $10.

    (E) . . . accept the gift card from Danielle and wait for the white paint to go on sale or to be able to pay an additional $10 for it.

Over the past five years, Luis has won several medals in running competitions. He was recently involved in a minor hiking accident, however, and as a result of his injuries, must wear a neck brace. Despite this, Luis is highly favored to win the city marathon next month.

863. Which of the following, if true, would help explain the apparent paradox described in the passage?

(A) Participation in the annual city marathon is always paltry.

(B) Luis also slightly injured his hand during the accident.

(C) The second-place winner in prior marathons has moved to a new city and no longer expects to compete.

(D) Luis has won the marathon twice in the last 4 years.

(E) Luis's neck brace will be removed next week, and he will be able to resume his training schedule without further delay.

864. If the argument is correct, which of the following would most seriously weaken its conclusion?

(A) The running competitions Luis has won in the past have always been sprints.

(B) The second-place finisher in last year's city marathon has been training hard all year.

(C) The local newspaper that made the prediction that Luis would win the annual city marathon is unaware of his injury.

(D) Luis's neck brace can be removed in 4 to 6 weeks.

(E) Participation in the city marathon is at an all-time low.

Questions 865 through 866 are based on the following passage.

A wholesale vegetable distributor, in an effort to increase its profit margins, has proposed cutting the leafy green tops off of the carrots it ships to restaurants in order to increase the number of carrots it can ship per crate.

865. Which of the following, if true, gives the strongest evidence that the vegetable distributor's plan will increase its profit margins?

(A) Carrots rot more quickly when their leafy green tops are removed.

(B) Many customers prefer to buy carrots with their leafy green tops, which can be used in cooking.

(C) Cutting the leafy green tops off of carrots is a time-consuming process which will require hiring well-trained new staff.

(D) The vegetable distributor principally ships to vegetable juice production companies that have no use for the leafy green tops.

(E) Carrots are a good source for Vitamin D.

866. What would most seriously weaken the argument, if true?

(A) Many customers prefer to buy carrots with their leafy green tops, which can be used in cooking.

(B) Carrots are a good source for Vitamin D.

(C) Carrots rot less quickly when their leafy green tops are removed.

(D) Many people find that carrots taste sweeter after having had their leafy green tops removed.

(E) Carrots are one of the fastest growing vegetables. A crop can replenish itself several times a growing season.

Questions 867 through 868 are based on the following passage.

An outdoor apparel company has submitted a new model of windbreaker that's designed to withstand the worst outdoor elements. After the conventional round of tests, 20 of the 90 windbreakers showed significant wear and/or rips. After reviewing these results, the company determined that the windbreaker was ready to be sold to consumers.

867. Which of the following, if true, would most strongly support the company's decision?

(A) When a competitor submitted a new windbreaker design for testing, 19 out of 90 windbreakers were worn or ripped by the end.

(B) Most consumers will purchase a windbreaker that promises not to rip for 2–3 years.

(C) The windbreaker will be one of the least expensive on the market.

(D) Because of the extreme stress of the testing process, any windbreaker design that has more than two-thirds of its prototypes functional at the end of the tests is considered sufficiently durable for the consumer market.

(E) The windbreaker could be redesigned to improve its chances of not being ripped.

868. What would most seriously weaken the company's decision, if true?

(A) The testing process has not been adjusted in many years, possibly causing it to be harsher on newer materials now regularly used in windbreakers.

(B) The new model of windbreaker is widely agreed to be more attractive than the company's prior design.

(C) Several other outdoor-wear manufacturers subject their products to multiple tests.

(D) Consumers of outdoor-wear demand a very high level of performance from those products.

(E) Consumers often prefer to buy windbreakers that have scored much better in the tests described.

The Dubsville Gazette experienced a major drop in subscriptions the same month it published a series of controversial opinion columns about Dubsville Mayor Annie Maylord. The Gazette also received a flurry of complaints from readers via letter, email, texts, and tweets. The Gazette's publisher, however, maintains that the negative reactions to its coverage of Mayor Maylord had nothing to do with the cancelled subscriptions.

869. Which sentence best completes the preceding passage in a way that supports its logic?

(A) The readers who wrote it were all long-time subscribers of at least 10 years.

(B) Most people in Dubsville watch the local television news as their primary source of information regarding the Mayor.

(C) The series on Mayor Maylord was the third time the Dubsville Gazette has published a series of articles on the Mayor's possible corruption.

(D) The other newspaper in city, the Dubsville Tribune, also reported a similar spate of complaints from their readers in the same month.

(E) Newspapers will publicly attribute a drop in subscription to a certain series of stories only when they receive complaints directly about that coverage.

Questions 870 through 871 are based on the following passage.

Dirk: I can't believe how long we've been waiting for them to bring us our food.

Ellen: It's very busy in this restaurant, though.

Dirk: Well, it's Saturday night! At 6:30 PM! Of course it's busy! They should have two times the number of servers working than what they have now.

Ellen: That's ridiculous. It's impossible to predict how many customers will visit a restaurant on any given day for a particular meal.

870. Which line of dialogue would most strengthen Dirk's case, if it were true?

   (A) Dirk: Saturday night is traditionally a very busy night for restaurants, Ellen.

   (B) Dirk: They should at least serve simpler foods, which would take less time to prepare.

   (C) Dirk: You know as well as I have that we've eaten here every Saturday night for years, and usually there are twice as many employees working.

   (D) Dirk: There's a motorcycle rally in town tonight, too, and that always draws a crowd.

   (E) Dirk: If we had ordered the specials, they'd have been served by now.

871. What line of dialogue, if true, could be added to Ellen's last statement in order to improve her logic?

   (A) You know this, Dirk. You've been a bartender.

   (B) We've eaten here before on a Saturday night at this time and been the only customers!

   (C) The motorcycle rally brings a lot of extra people to town.

   (D) It's important to order the correct amount of inventory without wasting much, too.

   (E) None of the other customers look as angry as you do.

Questions 872 through 873 are based on the following passage.

Houses built on a concrete foundation are likely to survive a tornado. We built our house on a concrete foundation, so it will survive any tornados that touch down here.

872. Which of the following is an assumption that enables the conclusion to be drawn?

   (A) Houses built on wooden foundations are less likely to withstand a tornado.

   (B) Houses built on a concrete foundation are likely to survive a tornado.

   (C) The additional cost of a concrete foundation is worth it.

   (D) A house built on a concrete foundation will definitely survive a tornado.

   (E) Tornados are not always accompanied by devastating storms.

873. What fact, if true, would most seriously weaken the argument?

   (A) Houses with concrete foundations are three times as likely to withstand a tornado than any other foundation.

   (B) Within five miles of the house in the passage, dozens of houses with concrete foundations were destroyed in a tornado three years ago.

   (C) Technology is constantly improving the sturdiness of concrete foundations.

   (D) Concrete foundations cost twice as much to have poured as it costs to lay a wood foundation.

   (E) It is exceedingly difficult to add a basement storm shelter to a house with a concrete foundation.

Questions 874 through 876 are based on the following passage.

The town of Muir draws drinking water from the Acadia River, which feeds Lake Onnipi. If Muir's water use continues to increase at its present rate, in about 20 years, the water level of Lake Onnipi will inevitably decrease to the point that it can no longer support its biologically fragile population of trout.

874. The prediction is based on which of the following assumptions?

(A) Muir could reverse its trend of increasing water use if it implements a water conservation program.

(B) As Muir's need for water grows, it would have no other water resources except Lake Onnipi.

(C) There are other rivers that feed into Lake Onnipi besides the Acadia River.

(D) The Lake Onnipi trout population was not always fragile.

(E) The Lake Onnipi trout population is a source of concern for many in Muir.

875. Which of the following best concludes the argument?

(A) Thus, Muir must make immediate plans to reduce water usage.

(B) Lake Onnipi is also a destination for water skiing and swimming.

(C) Plans must be made to transfer the biologically fragile population of trout to another body of water as soon as possible.

(D) The Acadia River feeds into Lake Onnipi.

(E) If the town of Muir wants to preserve the fragile trout population of Lake Onnipi, they should consider finding other sources for water in the next few years.

876. What additional evidence, if true, would most strengthen the concern expressed?

(A) Lake Onnipi is one of the largest lakes in the state.

(B) A significant portion of tourists to Muir are fishermen, interested in catching some of the Lake Onnipi trout.

(C) A recent scientific study shows a strong correlation between the increase of water consumption in Muir and the decrease in the trout population in Lake Onnipi.

(D) Acadia River is too cold for trout to survive in.

(E) The Acadia River flows into Lake Onnipi.

Questions 877 through 878 are based on the following passage.

It's often said that people should eat as many fruits and vegetables as they can. Five to seven servings per day is recommended by most nutritionists. However, eating too many carrots can lead to a disorder that can prove fatal if not treated. Therefore, nutritionists should advise that people . . .

877. If the passage is correct, finish the sentence in keeping with the logic presented.

(A) . . . avoid eating carrots.

(B) . . . avoid overconsumption of carrots.

(C) . . . only eat carrots at selected meals.

(D) . . . avoid eating carrots during he morning hours.

(E) . . . get five to seven servings of fruits and vegetables every day.

878. Assuming that the argument presented is true, which of the following would be the least logical way to conclude the paragraph?

(A) . . . avoid overconsumption of carrots.

(B) . . . limit themselves to three carrots a day.

(C) . . . read up on the fatal disease caused by overconsuming carrots.

(D) . . . avoid overconsumption of all vegetables and fruits.

(E) . . . eat carrots to excess.

Sammy is unbeaten in wrestling competitions at the college level. Last year, he won Best All-Around at the collegiate championship. Three weeks ago, Sammy broke his wrist in a bike accident, and he will need to wear a cast, then a brace, for the rest of the school year. Therefore, when the collegiate championship is held this year, _____.

879. Which of the following best completes the preceding passage?

(A) Shawn, who consistently won second place after Sammy, will likely win the collegiate championship.

(B) Sammy will definitely not win the collegiate championship in wrestling.

(C) Sammy should drop out of the competition so he does not embarrass himself or his team.

(D) It's unlikely that Sammy will win the collegiate championship this year.

(E) Sammy may not even be allowed to register for the collegiate championship.

Questions 880 through 882 are based on the following passage.

The Downintown Mayor made the following statement: "We're going to take down all of the fire alarm boxes around town. Almost 90 percent of them end up being false alarms, and besides, everyone has a cell phone now. The fire alarm boxes are more of a nuisance than help to public safety. Did you know that if the fire department is out on a false alarm, and a real fire needs to be put out, it takes the department anywhere from 10 to 40 extra minutes to get there? Let's get rid of those boxes!"

880. Which of the following, if true, would provide additional evidence that most strongly support the Mayor's argument?

(A) It costs Downintown over $5,000 to respond to a fire alarm, even if it turns out to be false.

(B) Not everyone has a cell phone.

(C) The Downintown Police Department has technology that allows it to maintain a video feed of most of the fire alarm boxes, so as to see who pulls them.

(D) The fire alarm boxes, which date from the 1960's, are widely celebrated in the design world.

(E) The fire department has tried sending out only half the available fire fighters when a questionable alarm comes in.

881. What would most seriously weaken the Mayor's argument, if true?

(A) In a recent poll, only 40 percent of the residents of Downintown owned cell phones.

(B) False alarms often come in at the rate of one a day.

(C) The fire department sometimes sends one firefighter to a suspected false alarm to see if there really is a fire before sending the entire brigade.

(D) The fire alarm boxes can malfunction and send out false alarms on their own.

(E) The fire alarm boxes look very charming in Downintown's down-town area.

882. Assuming that the Mayor's statements are correct, what would be another logical way to cut down on false alarms without removing the fire alarm boxes?

(A) The police could fine anyone caught making a false alarm.

(B) The fire alarm boxes could be fitted with locks that only a small portion of the town's citizens would have keys to open.

(C) The fire alarm boxes could be fitted with cameras that take photos of those citizens pulling them.

(D) Fire fighters could be authorized to make citizens' arrests.

(E) Downinsville could offer classes on how to use different brands of cell phones.

Questions 883 through 884 are based on the following passage.

As part of their customer rewards program, a chain of restaurants issues a paper voucher good for one free meal to customers who have eaten at the restaurant 10 times. Recently, the chain's marketing division has noticed that people are selling their vouchers online for the less than the average price of a meal at the restaurant. Therefore, the marketing department has advised that the restaurant issue vouchers marked "Non-Transferrable."

883. What assumption underlines the marketing department's logic in their plan?

(A) That customers are deliberately ordering the most expensive meals when they have a voucher to cover its cost.

(B) The customer rewards program is worth continuing, even if the chain loses some money on it.

(C) The word "Non-Transferrable" is a significant deterrent to customers who might have otherwise sold their vouchers online.

(D) The price of meals on the chain restaurant's menu varies too much.

(E) The cost of a web-based customer rewards program is too great to try.

884. Which of the following, if true, would most seriously weaken logic behind the marketing department's new plan?

(A) A competing chain found that marking their free drink coupons "Non-Transferrable" did little to change customers' habits of selling those coupons online.

(B) Surveys show that the customer rewards program is one of the reasons at least 75% of the chain's customers frequent its restaurants.

(C) It is legal to sell vouchers online.

(D) The website many people use to sell their vouchers recently filed for bankruptcy.

(E) The word "Non-Transferrable" is not legally binding.

Questions 885 through 887 are based on the following passage.

Jane wants to win a promotion. Her boss told her that if she is able to sell three houses this month, she will be eligible to be promoted to Head Realtor. Jane was able to sell four houses this month, more than her boss requested; **therefore, she is sure to be promoted.**

885. Which of the following arguments most closely follows the same logic as in the argument?

(A) Linda wants to be promoted at work. Her boss suggested that Linda develop three new client relationships this month. Linda researched possible clients and made some initial calls, but her colleague Lisa was promoted two weeks later.

(B) Xinyuan wants to earn an A in her class. Her professor told her that she should try to get As on most of her exams. Xinyuan was able to earn an A on all of her exams, and thus, expects an A in the class.

(C) Monica is a realtor who has been tasked with selling a large house in poor shape in an unpopular part of town. Monica put together a video tour of the house and was able to get it onto a local television news show. She soon had two offers for the home to choose from.

(D) Sarah's boss thinks she is capable of more hard work than she has shown so far. He told her that if she is able to beat her average sales number for the last three months this month, he will reward her with an extra vacation day.

(E) In the lab where she works, Bette is often the last person to leave. She takes on extra work and reads up on her studies relevant to her work at home. Many people predict that she will be running the lab soon.

886. What role in the argument presented does the bolded portion play?

(A) It introduces the main argument.

(B) It is a premise of the argument.

(C) It is the conclusion to the argument.

(D) It gives evidence to support the premise of the argument.

(E) It explains the need for the argument.

887. What is the most obvious error in the argument presented?

(A) It is not clear that "Head Realtor" is the promotion Jane wants.

(B) Jane's boss is not aware of her plan to sell three houses this month.

(C) Jane sold more houses than she was asked to.

(D) There might be a reason why Jane's boss wanted her to sell three, not four, houses.

(E) We don't know how much the houses Jane sold cost.

> *Questions 888 through 889 are based on the following passage.*

Yogurt is widely-agreed by nutritionists to be helpful for people struggling to maintain helpful microbes in their digestive system. Many nutritionists advise that their patients consume a cup of yogurt per day.

888. What piece of evidence, if true, could be added to the argument to best support the conclusion?

(A) Yogurt is often quite tasty.

(B) Yogurt can be consumed in other foods, such as a smoothie.

(C) Some people find the taste of yogurt unpleasantly sour.

(D) Scientific studies have consistently shown that yogurt does indeed help create a healthful environment in the digestive tract.

(E) That yogurt is so helpful to good health is a surprise since the health benefits of consuming dairy are controversial.

889. What evidence, if true, would most seriously weaken the argument?

(A) The source of the nutritionists' belief about yogurt turns out to be a widely-discredited article from the 1950s.

(B) Not everyone who eats yogurt daily sees an immediate improvement.

(C) People who eat yogurt sometimes experience improvements in their skin's health as well.

(D) Yogurt can be high in calories.

(E) Yogurt is shown to be one of the least popular foods in many consumer studies.

Questions 890 through 891 are based on the following passage.

A National Park administrator said the following in a public meeting: "Our attendance has been steadily decreasing for the last five years. I think it's because people are on their phones too much and don't want to tear themselves away from playing games or checking social media apps to appreciate our nation's natural beauty. Therefore, I'm proposing that we ban smart phones in our park."

890. What would most strengthen the administrator's argument?

(A) Cell phone reception in the park is spotty.

(B) Visitors can check email at the both of the park's visitor centers.

(C) Scientific studies show that people carrying smart phones often feel concerned that they're missing something important if they don't check their phones frequently.

(D) The decrease in the park's visitors is especially noticeable in the ages 16–25 demographics.

(E) Surveys of park visitors show that they consistently asked for a cell phone ban, writing things like "Save us from ourselves!"

891. What, if true, would most seriously weaken the argument?

(A) People prefer to be able to use their smart phones whenever they like.

(B) Three years ago, there was a widely publicized incident in the park in which a hiker was hurt and unable to call for help because he didn't have a phone with him.

(C) The park's entrance fee doubled last year.

(D) Many visitors to the park report that they felt less interest in checking their cell phones while in the park.

(E) The park in question is widely agreed to be the most beautiful in the Midwest.

Questions 892 through 893 are based on the following passage.

In a survey taken by a local high school's administration, 40 percent of the graduating seniors asked for more AP classes to be offered. Only 20 percent of the junior class and 10 percent of the freshmen class asked for the same. The administration has decided to offer five more AP classes next year.

892. What evidence, if true, would best help explain why the administration has decided to offer five more AP classes?

(A) Most of the junior class had identified themselves as "college-bound" on a recent survey.

(B) The survey was given in October, so the freshmen class most likely has little justified opinion about their course load yet.

(C) The administration noticed that the 80 seniors who had taken two or more AP classes all were accepted into their first-choice college. The colleges reported that their AP credits strongly influenced their acceptances.

(D) The high school's junior class is notoriously lazy.

(E) There may be a small financial bonus available from the state for schools which offer 10 or more AP courses.

893. Which of the following should be studied over the next year to evaluate whether the administration's decision helped to produce more college-bound seniors?

(A) A survey of the seniors polled this year, taken at the end of their freshman year in college.

(B) A comparison of the number of graduates from next year's class who got into their first choice college, and the number of graduates from this year's class who got into their first choice college.

(C) A poll of teachers who lead the new AP classes about the difficulties of teaching those courses.

(D) Test results from all five new AP classes.

(E) A follow-up survey of this year's freshmen after their sophomore year.

Questions 894 through 895 are based on the following passage.

My favorite band did not tour last summer, so they will tour this summer.

894. Which of the following is an assumption that allows the conclusion to be properly drawn?

(A) My favorite band released two new albums last year.

(B) My favorite band toured Europe this past winter.

(C) My favorite band has a strong fan base which always turns out for their concerts.

(D) My favorite band strictly follows an every-other-summer tour schedule, and have done so for over 20 years.

(E) Critics say that my favorite band are exceptionally good in concert.

895. Which of the following, if true, would most weaken the conclusion?

(A) The band has always followed a "two summers off, one summer on" touring schedule since their founding 15 years ago.

(B) The band often changes guitarists.

(C) The band's albums do not sell as well as they once did, although touring revenues remain strong.

(D) Bootlegs of my favorite's bands best shows are widely available online.

(E) The lead singer broker his foot recently.

Questions 896 through 897 are based on the following passage.

Scientists predict that the next flood to hit the area will be two times as bad as the flood of 1957, when most of Bridgeton was destroyed. Therefore, we can conclude that much of Bridgeton will be destroyed in the next flood.

896. If the argument is correct, what must also be correct?

(A) Bridgeton's system of flood levees has been ineffectual.

(B) Bridgeton has not faced any floods since 1957.

(C) "Most of Bridgeton and "much of Bridgeton" mean the same thing.

(D) No significant changes have been made to help protect Bridgeton from flooding since 1957.

(E) Bridgeton faces greater danger from tornadoes than from flooding.

897. What evidence, if true, would most seriously weaken the argument presented?

(A) Scientists can predict the next flood with 80% accuracy.

(B) Since 1957, Bridgeton has undertaken multiple steps to improve the town's protection against the next flood, including raising the river walls by three feet.

(C) Bridgeton is smaller in size today than it was in 1957.

(D) Some of the town records were destroyed in the 1957 flood.

(E) Much of the destruction in 1957 came not from the flood but from downed power lines caused by the flood.

Questions 898 through 900 are based on the following passage.

A medication called Hypoloss has been shown to be effective at helping extremely obese people lose weight. Some patients have lost over 350 pounds while on Hypoloss. Despite the success of the medication, most doctors have not embraced prescribing the medication.

898. Which of the following arguments, if true, best accounts for the lukewarm response from doctors to Hypoloss?

(A) Treatment of obesity by medication generally results in a boomerang effect, in which the patient gains back much of the weight after they stop taking the medicine.

(B) Most health insurance plans will cover the cost of Hypoloss if the patient is at risk for a heart attack or stroke as well.

(C) Obesity rates among the American population have been increasing steadily for the last three decades.

(D) Obesity contributes to the likelihood of a heart attack or stroke, two of the leading causes of death in America.

(E) Hypoloss carries a high risk of serious complications, including internal bleeding and death.

899. What piece of evidence, if true, might convince doctors to prescribe Hypoloss more frequently?

(A) Hypoloss is not regulated by the FDA.

(B) Most patients who use Hypoloss report losing significant amounts of weight.

(C) Hypoloss is carried in grocery and drug stores around the U.S.

(D) Three recent scientific studies have found that taking Hypoloss is no less dangerous to a patient than non-prescription weight loss techniques.

(E) Patients like the convenience of taking Hypoloss at breakfast.

900. What sentence would best conclude the argument?

(A) Many people who take Hypoloss find it has an unpleasant taste.

(B) Scientific studies on the safety of Hypoloss have not been conducted yet.

(C) There are other ways to lose weight.

(D) Prior weight loss medications have not proven to be safe for consumers.

(E) We'd be better off finding ways to support natural weight loss through diet and exercise.

Questions 901 through 902 are based on the following passage.

Gladys: If we leave now, we'll get there by 5:00. But if we wait an hour, we won't get there until 6:30.

Nedra: That's ridiculous! How can you know that the trip will take an extra half an hour?

901. What statement could Gladys make to best prove her argument is correct?

    (A) Gladys: It will be rush hour.

    (B) Gladys: This happened to us two years ago when we made this trip.

    (C) Gladys: Calling me names doesn't help.

    (D) Gladys: You know as well as I do that the factory on Main Street changes shifts at 5:00 p.m., and that slows traffic to a crawl every day at that time.

    (E) Gladys: It always happens at this time of day around there.

902. What is the question in bold doing in this argument?

    (A) It is a request that Gladys prove her argument.

    (B) It is the premise of the counter-argument.

    (C) It is the evidence that proves the counter-argument.

    (D) It reveals the argument that Nedra hopes to prove.

    (E) It is a request that Gladys restate her argument more broadly.

Questions 903 through 905 are based on the following passage.

A university has decided to award a scholarship to a student they have decided is the most deserving. Student A can contribute $10,000 to her education every year, while Student B can contribute $25,000 to her education every year. Student B was awarded the scholarship.

903. What can we infer from the statement?

    (A) Student B is wealthier than Student A.

    (B) The university's definition of "most deserving" is not solely based on financial need.

    (C) Universities always appreciate when a student can pay for a significant chunk of their education.

    (D) The scholarship program as described in the passage is rigged against poor people.

    (E) The scholarship program as described in the passage should be more clearly explained to its applicants.

904. What evidence would best help us understand the university's decision?

    (A) A clear explanation of how the scholarship committee defines "most deserving."

    (B) A graph showing the yearly income of prior scholarship winners.

    (C) A table which compares the amount and sources of the money Students A and B can each contribute to their educations.

    (D) A list of scholarships the university offers.

    (E) A pie chart that shows how the university allocates resources for less well-off students.

905. What statement, if true, would make the university's decision most questionable?

(A) The committee did not interview either Student A or Student B before making its decision.

(B) In the past, the university has awarded scholarships based solely on financial need.

(C) The student who won the scholarship last year was the grandson of a university trustee.

(D) The guidelines for the scholarship clearly define "most deserving" as being a student who cannot contribute more than $12,000 a year to their education.

(E) Student B is from a very wealthy family.

At our shop, 60 percent of the people who bought an ice cream cone yesterday purchased a chocolate flavor. Therefore, we can say for sure that chocolate flavors are more popular than vanilla flavors.

906. What would most seriously weaken the argument in the preceding passage?

(A) Only three people bought ice cream cones yesterday.

(B) The majority of customers bought dishes of ice cream, and 80% of those bought vanilla or a vanilla-based flavor.

(C) Ice cream is a notoriously seasonal business.

(D) Vanilla flavors were 20% off per scoop because it was National Vanilla Day.

(E) The staff of an ice cream shop are sometimes too busy to pay close attention to their customers' purchases.

Questions 907 through 908 are based on the following passage.

Li said, "I've been the manager of this bookstore for 6 years. **We've always sold more books with a green cover than any other color.** I think publishing companies should only make books with green covers!"

907. What role does the bolded sentence play in the passage?

(A) It is the premise of Li's argument.

(B) It is the conclusion of Li's argument.

(C) It is the evidence that Li uses in his argument.

(D) It is the idea of Li's argument.

(E) It is the counter-argument to Li's idea.

908. Which of the following is not an assumption behind Li's argument?

(A) Book publishers would like to sell more books.

(B) Li's six-year experience in working as a bookstore manager has given him particular insight into book selling.

(C) Customers are buying books at least partly because of the color of the cover.

(D) Publishers do not already always use green on their book covers.

(E) Green is a color people like more than red or blue.

Questions 909 through 910 are based on the following passage.

City A's dumps are so full that they've been forced to pay City B to accept their garbage. City A's selectmen have suggested offsetting the fee paid to City B by imposing a tax on manufacturing businesses in City A. Business C, the largest manufacturer in the area, protests that the tax is unfair because businesses should not have to pay for a garbage problem created by City A's homeowners.

909. Which of the following, if true, would most seriously weaken Business C's argument?

(A) Business C pays over a half a million dollars a year to City A already.

(B) Business C is on the border between City A and City B.

(C) 30% of the people of City A work at Business C's factory.

(D) Business C produced more than 80% of the waste City A had to dispose of in the last year.

(E) City B is facing a shortfall in its infrastructure budget and is hoping to use the money from City A's garbage to offset that shortfall.

910. Which of the following, if true, would most seriously strengthen Business C's argument?

(A) The people of City B won an award from the state's environmental council for reducing waste.

(B) City A's homeowners contributed 60% of the town's waste last year. The year before that, they contributed 68%.

(C) Business C has planted trees to offset its carbon emissions.

(D) City A's dumps have not been well-managed.

(E) City A and City B share a border.

Questions 911 through 912 are based on the following passage.

Wadsworth College is experiencing a high turnover rate among its creative writing faculty members. To rectify this problem, the chairperson of the creative writing program has proposed to the dean that beginning next semester, starting salaries for creative writing instructors be increased by 10 percent to provide a more competitive pay package.

911. Which statement, if true, would best support the chairperson's plan?

(A) Creative writing is one of Wadsworth College's best known programs. Many students cite it as a reason they applied to, and attend, the college.

(B) The computer technology faculty receives, on average, 15 percent more than the average creative writing faculty member's salary.

(C) Student dissatisfaction with Wadsworth College's dean is very high, according to the most recent survey.

(D) Many of the creative writing faculty members who've left Wadsworth College have continued teaching at nearby schools for higher pay.

(E) At a meeting at the beginning of the semester, the dean announced that she would be interested in receiving suggestions from department chairs.

912. Which of the following, if true, would indicate a flaw in the department chairperson's plan?

(A) Evidence for the high turnover rate among creative writing faculty is anecdotal, not statistical.

(B) Enrollment in creative writing classes has been steady at Wadsworth College since the early 2000's.

(C) The college is facing a funding crisis because of the loss of a multi-million-dollar endowment.

(D) The chemistry department recently gave all of its faculty members an 8 percent increase in pay.

(E) Exit interviews with creative writing faculty members who've left the college indicate that course assignments and inadequate health benefits were the most common reasons they left Wadsworth College.

Jackie: "If we hire two new clerks before the wedding season, I think we will have enough help."

Chip: "Are you sure? Last year, we hired two clerks a month before wedding season, and we were still overwhelmed at that time of year."

Jackie: "Sure, but those clerks were new, so they weren't able to be as fast as someone who's worked here for longer."

Chip: "But the new clerks will be just as inexperienced!"

913. What fact, if true, would be best for Jackie to use in her response?

(A) "Right, but one of the new clerks had a job in a flower shop before."

(B) "Sure, but we have five months until wedding season this time."

(C) "Yeah, but you will help me train them this time!"

(D) "Wedding season happens every year. There's nothing I can do about it."

(E) "But you haven't met them! How can you know that?"

914. What role does the bolded portion play in the argument Chip is making?

(A) It is the premise of Chip's argument.

(B) It is the point of Chip's disagreement.

(C) It is the evidence that Chip is presenting to bolster his argument.

(D) It is his restatement of Jackie's main argument.

(E) It is the premise of Jackie's argument.

Goodcare Hospital's ER sees, on average, 10 patients per hour. The hospital administrator has decided to award a bonus to any ER nurse who sees more than 10 patients per hour. The nurses' union has filed a grievance against the hospital's administrator because _____.

915. Which of the following, if true, best finishes the sentence in the preceding passage by providing a logical reason for the union's decision?

(A) An ER is no place for workers to try to move quickly.

(B) Nurses at Goodcare Hospital's ER make $3 less per hour than nurses at Samaritan Hospital, just five miles away.

(C) Nurses may be tempted to rush through treating patients in order to achieve a bonus.

(D) The "10 patients per hour" statistic is misleading because it is an average. Daytime nurses sometimes treat 15 patients per hour while night nurses may only see 5 patients per night.

(E) It is not clear what "sees" means, according to the hospital administrator's usage.

Mystique Auto, a car dealership in Rowena, has decided to offer a no-money-down-for-18-months program. Its rival, Miracle Cars, does not offer such a program. Miracle Cars' owner, Michael Sanchez, said, "I'm not worried about their offer. Our sales are always good."

916. Which of the following, if true, would give the best support for Sanchez's confidence?

(A) Mystique Auto charges a finance rate that is three times the rate charged by Miracle Cars, and customers must get their financing in-house when buying at Mystique.

(B) Mystique tends to stock newer models of cars.

(C) Miracle Cars has been in business for 20 years longer than Mystique Auto.

(D) Michael Sanchez knows the owner of Mystique Auto personally.

(E) Many people shop at several car dealerships before making their selections.

917. Which of the following, if true, would most undercut Michael Sanchez's confidence that Miracle Cars will continue to have good sales?

(A) At the end of last year, Miracle Cars experienced a slight drop in sales, which recovered after the new year.

(B) Mystique is 10 miles closer to the nearest large town.

(C) Mystique's no-money-down offer has been widely advertised.

(D) Sanchez does not know that Miracle Cars' CFO has ordered that they raise interest rates on their in-house loans, which had been well below market average.

(E) Mystique's lot has many more new cars than Miracle's.

Questions 918 through 919 are based on the following passage.

Hannah: "I couldn't get my son to fall asleep last night, so I made him a deal: If he would lay quietly for 15 minutes, I would let him get up and play for an extra half an hour if he did not fall asleep. Can you believe he didn't fall asleep? **I told him he couldn't play that late at night.**"

918. Which of the following statements most closely follows the logic that Hannah uses?

(A) Steve: "I could get my daughter to fall asleep last night, so I let her stay up an extra 15 minutes and watch TV with me. The show I was watching ended up scaring her so much, I had to let sleep with the light on!"

(B) Meghan: "My coworkers wouldn't stop asking me where I was going on vacation. I finally made them a deal: If they would stop bothering me for an hour, long enough for me to get my report written, I would tell them all about my trip. They left me alone, and when my hour was up, I told them it was none of their business where I traveled!"

(C) Bobby: "When my dogs won't stop howling during the night, I tell them that I'll give them a treat if they stop. When they finally shut up, I always give them their reward."

(D) Danielle: "The students I teach often ask me for extra help on a test question. I tell them that they can figure it out themselves, but if they really think they can't get the answer, they can ask me after waiting 10 minutes. They almost never do."

(E) Erica: "When I go to the store in my neighborhood, I always want to buy everything. My trick is to put everything I want in the cart and then tell myself I can have one thing. That usually solves my problem."

919. What role does the bolded sentence play in Hannah's argument?

(A) It is the premise of her argument.

(B) It is the introduction to her argument.

(C) It is the evidence that supports the argument.

(D) It is the counter-argument that proves the argument is true.

(E) It is the conclusion to the argument.

Many tennis players prefer a lightweight racquet, but a racquet that is too lightweight will snap during vigorous play. A new type of steel alloy reduces the weight of a typical tennis racquet by 20 percent while providing a racquet as strong as the average used now. Manufacturers expect it to sell well.

920. What would most seriously weaken the argument, if true?

(A) The new racquet costs 200 times the amount of the most expensive racquets made now.

(B) The new type of steel alloy is only made by one company.

(C) The company that manufactures the steel alloy does not currently make sports-related products.

(D) No famous player has been signed on to represent the new racquet yet.

(E) The new racquet only comes in one color.

921. Which of the following sentences, if true, could be added to the end of the passage to improve the argument?

(A) It will cost twice the amount of the most expensive racquet available today.

(B) Several people were seriously injured by snapped racquets last year.

(C) The manufacturer has secured the support of three top tennis players to act as ambassadors for the racquet. One was recently quoted as saying the racquet improved her game "more dramatically than I thought possible."

(D) The racquet comes with an attractive case.

(E) The manufacturer is offering the racquet with a money-back guarantee if you are not completely satisfied with it.

Andrew: If I can read and respond to thirty emails an hour, I will soon have an empty mailbox. I'd like to do that in as little time as possible.

Diane: You might not need to respond to every email. Do you know what's in your in-box?

Andrew: No yet, but if I plan an hour to read and respond to 30, and I only have to respond to twenty, I will save time.

Diane: Wouldn't it be more accurate to . . .

922. What would best complete Diane's argument in the preceding passage?

(A) . . . delete all of your emails without answering them?

(B) . . . time how long it takes you to read and respond to a couple of emails in your in-box and that recalculate the time you'll need?

(C) . . . count up the number of emails you have in your in-box and divide the number by the number of hours you have to take care of email?

(D) . . . read and respond to each email, keeping track of how long it takes, and then, when you're done, figure out your average?

(E) . . . only respond to the emails that seem to be critical?

In most factories, improving the technology of the assembly line increases labor productivity: the amount of goods a worker can produce per hour. In Factory A, labor productivity is 20 percent higher than in Factory B. Therefore, Factory A must be further advanced in technology than Factory B.

923. Which statement, if true, would best support the argument made in this passage?

(A) Factory A and Factory B do not work in the same industry.

(B) Factory A was recently taken over by a foreign company.

(C) Until three years ago, Factory B far outpaced Factory A.

(D) There is only one way to calculate labor productivity.

(E) A survey of Factory B's workers reveled that 78 percent would like to see technological improvements on their assembly line.

924. The argument is most vulnerable to which of the following criticisms, if true?

(A) It presents a numerical fact as a premise leading to a false conclusion.

(B) It fails to consider the other means of calculating labor productivity.

(C) It presents as fact the author's conclusion about Factory B.

(D) It presents a possible cause of a condition as the only cause of that condition without considering other causes.

(E) It presents a conclusion that ignores the facts stated in the argument.

Zero waste clothes are gaining in popularity. In this manufacturing process, clothing is designed to be cut from fabric in such a way that no waste fabric is created. However, the process is not as kind to the environment as some may think.

925. What sentence, if true, would make the argument in the preceding passage stronger if added to it?

(A) "Zero waste" is a term that is catching on in many places where fashion is celebrated.

(B) Zero waste clothing is popular with celebrities who want to show their support for environmental causes while on the red carpet.

(C) Zero waste clothing has to be meticulously designed.

(D) Chemicals used in the creation of fabrics are far more damaging to the environment than fabric scraps created in traditional clothing manufacture.

(E) Some zero waste manufacturers force their workers to be on the factory floor for 12 hours at a time.

Questions 926 through 928 are based on the following passage.

In the last 10 years, there has been a significant decrease in underage drinking. In the same period, a campaign to reduce the portrayal of underage drinking in television has also been undertaken. Therefore, the decrease in underage drinking must be caused by the decrease in the portrayal of underage drinking in television.

926. Which of the following, if true, most seriously weakens the argument?

(A) Viewership of television is at an all-time high.

(B) People who drink alcohol at a younger age are believed to be more susceptible to addiction than their peers.

(C) Teenagers are more likely to watch videos online than any other form of entertainment, including television, these days.

(D) Underage drinking has been on a steady decline for the last 25 years, long before the campaign to reduce the portrayal of it on television.

(E) Many people do not understand the real health hazards that arise from underage drinking.

927. Which of the following is an assumption on which the argument depends?

(A) Underage people who drink alcohol watch a great deal of television.

(B) Advertisements for alcohol are still widely shown on television.

(C) People who drink when underage are more easily influenced than those who do not.

(D) The quality of television shows has not been affected by the movement to remove portrayals of underage drinking from them.

(E) There is a direct correlation between seeing an activity on television and taking part in that activity.

928. The argument could be strengthened with the addition of which of the following sentences, if true?

(A) Underage drinking is rarely shown on television, at least on network shows.

(B) When underage drinking is portrayed on television, it is often shown as leading to bad consequences for the drinkers.

(C) In a poll of graduating high school seniors, 60 percent reported that they did not drink alcohol on a regular basis because of negative portrayals of the same in television and movies.

(D) Teenagers generally don't like to be told what to do.

(E) Drinking alcohol can cause many problems in the future.

Questions 929 through 930 are based on the following passage.

The art of writing an essay is no longer valued. These days, people can click on dozens of poorly written articles online if they want something to read.

929. The argument apparently assumes what?

(A) Readers are not interested in distinguishing between a well written essay and a hastily written short article.

(B) No one reads anymore.

(C) No one bothers to handwrite a longer piece before typing it up anymore.

(D) There are no good online sites worth reading.

(E) Essays are less important than fiction.

930. What fact, if true, would most seriously weaken the argument?

    (A) Because many articles on the internet are free, people are more likely to read them.

    (B) Subscriptions to print-based journals that publish long, well written essays are at an all-time high.

    (C) Most Americans learn how to write a good essay in high school.

    (D) Online journals are popular because you can read them on many different devices.

    (E) Many people prefer the smell of old books.

Questions 931 through 932 are based on the following passage.

Use of a new drug has decreased the reoccurrence of thyroid cancer in 60% of patients studied. In the next round of tests, the dosage of the new drug will be doubled. It is expected that the reoccurrence rate will be cut in half.

931. What would most seriously weaken the assumption?

    (A) When the dosage of the drug was half of what was used in the latest round of tests, the reoccurrence rate was still 60%.

    (B) The doubled dosage of the drug has not been tested for safety.

    (C) When the dosage was doubled in an animal tests, the rate of reoccurrence dropped too.

    (D) The initial tests have not been replicated for verification yet.

    (E) Thyroid cancer has a low reoccurrence rate even without medication.

932. All of the following, if true, support the argument, except for which one?

    (A) Thyroid cancer is considered a relatively small impact disease. Most patients who have it recover.

    (B) The new drug was tested at a lower dosage, and the reoccurrence rate was higher than 60% after that test.

    (C) In an animal trial, a direct correlation between upping the dosage and lowering the recurrence rate was seen.

    (D) A rival lab was able to achieve the same results while testing the new drug.

    (E) Doubling the dosage does not pose any danger to the patients.

The business owners of Mitford have protested plans by the state highway commission to build a new bypass. The owners say that the bypass will cause a severe decline in their businesses which are currently on a highway used by many commuters. Those commuters will most likely take the new bypass.

933. What would most seriously weaken the argument in the preceding passage?

    (A) Construction of the new bypass has not been approved yet.

    (B) A similar bypass, built in the next town over, has not affected the income of local businesses there.

    (C) People prefer to return to the same businesses over and over.

    (D) The bypass will have a speed limit of over 70 miles per hour, far faster than the highway's speed limit.

    (E) Construction of the bypass is controversial, and most town residents have signed a pledge not to use it.

Sam: I am going to buy two sodas, since the offer is two for $3.00.

Halle: But will you be able to drink them both tonight?

Sam: That doesn't matter. **The price of just one is $1.75,** so buying two is a saving.

Halle: I don't understand how that can be if you only drink one.

934. What would be the most helpful thing for Sam to say next in order to demonstrate to Halle what his logic is?

(A) "A savings is a savings! I'll save 50 cents!"

(B) "Sure, 50 cents doesn't sound like much, but if I invest it. . . ."

(C) "Because the soda won't go bad, I can drink it tomorrow. I'm paying a little more for two sodas today, but I won't pay anything for tomorrow's soda."

(D) "If I get thirsty again later, I'll have the second soda."

(E) "It's a good idea to have something saved up for later."

935. What role does the bolded portion play in Sam's argument?

(A) It is the conclusion to his argument.

(B) It is the introduction to his argument.

(C) It is the premise of his argument.

(D) It is evidence that supports the premise of his argument.

(E) It is the counter-argument that he is deflecting.

"The color blue has a soothing effect on humans and animals, according to the book I'm reading," said Tyronicah. "I'm going to paint my bedroom blue to help soothe both me and my dog, Sparky. He has been barking a lot lately."

936. Which of the following, if true, would be likely decrease the hoped-for effects of Tyronicah's plan?

(A) Many different shades of blue exist.

(B) It will cost Tyronicah a lot of money to paint her bedroom.

(C) Home improvement projects are regularly shown to be very stressful for those completing them.

(D) Tyronicah didn't finish the entire book before embarking on her plan to paint her bedroom.

(E) The book is incorrect. Not all animals, including dogs, can see colors.

937. Which of the following pieces of evidence, if true, would most support Tyronicah's plan?

(A) The author of the book has a PhD from a prestigious university.

(B) Sparky is an unusually intelligent dog, who is able to do five or six tricks in a row.

(C) Tyronicah's friend Lesley painted her living room blue recently, and she reports that her cat seems calmer now.

(D) Sparky began barking a lot after Tyronicah painted her bedroom red.

(E) Blue is widely agreed to be a soothing color.

In recent years, there has been a significant increase in accidents caused by the car's driver texting while operating the vehicle. **In fact, the percentage of accidents caused by texting has increase 200 percent since 2005.** Therefore, lawmakers in this state have proposed legislation to make texting while driving illegal and punishable by jail time.

938. What role does the sentence in bold play in the passage?

(A) It is the argument's conclusion.

(B) It is evidence that supports the premise.

(C) It is the counter-argument.

(D) It is the premise of the argument.

(E) It is an anecdote that supports the argument.

939. Which of the following is the most reasonable inference from the argument?

(A) Lawmakers in this state never text while driving themselves.

(B) Texting while driving is the biggest killer of young people in this state.

(C) This law would not apply to drivers of trucks and other commercial vehicles as well as cars.

(D) The lawmakers assume that the threat of jail time would be a deterrent for those who might have contemplated texting while driving.

(E) Some people will text while driving no matter what the possible punishment for doing so is.

Many psychologists have studied the aftermath of a traumatic event in an attempt to understand why some people develop Post-Traumatic Stress Disorder (PTSD), while others do not. **Some have suggested that the PTSD develops when the patients are unable to take time to process their feelings and responses after the event, while those that do are less likely to develop PTSD, even though they may be disturbed by the event.** Several recent studies explain this is greater detail. **However, my colleague and I have recently discovered a link between the impact of the event and the patient which may provide a better explanation.**

940. How do the two sentences in bold relate to each other?

(A) The first sentence presents evidence, and the second sentence refutes that evidence.

(B) The first sentence presents evidence, while the second sentence explains that evidence in greater detail.

(C) The first sentence presents a course of action, and the second shows the results of following that course.

(D) The first sentence presents a theory about a topic, while the second sentence introduces the a more recent theory about that topic.

(E) The first tells an anecdote about that topic, while the second cautions against using anecdotal evidence.

941. What would be most likely to follow the last sentence in the passage?

    (A) An explanation of why the theory that PTSD develops when patients are unable to take time to process their responses is wrong.

    (B) An explanation of what PTSD is.

    (C) Evidence to support the new theory.

    (D) An explanation of what the new theory about the link between the impact and the patient is.

    (E) Suggestions about where those battling PTSD may find help.

942. Which of the following is an assumption the writers of this argument have made about their readers?

    (A) They already know what PTSD stands for.

    (B) They are interested in reading new theories about PTSD.

    (C) They suffer from PTSD.

    (D) They are doctors who may treat someone with PTSD.

    (E) They are people who have doubts PTSD is a real disorder.

Questions 943 through 944 are based on the following passage.

Luke: I'm leaning towards selling my house myself.

Bridget: I wouldn't do that. A real estate agent can be a big help. When we sold our house, we were so glad to work with Katrina, our agent. She made the entire process so much easier.

Luke: Sure, but they take a big profit from the sale.

943. Which of the following could Bridget say next in hopes of convincing Luke?

    (A) Bridget: But agents also are able to set the price accurately. When you sell your home yourself, you run the risk of underpricing it. And keep in mind that you still have to pay for much of what the agency would cover, such as listing and closing costs.

    (B) Bridget: Katrina and I got along really well, so I feel like I made a new friend as well as sold our house.

    (C) Bridget: I hate dealing with money and that stuff, so it was so much easier to let someone else do it.

    (D) Bridget: We had a friend who sold her house by herself and it took her ages, maybe three years?

    (E) Bridget: I don't know that I'd call 20 percent a "big profit"!

944. What role is Luke's response in bold playing in this argument?

    (A) It is the premise of Luke's argument.

    (B) It is evidence that Luke is presenting.

    (C) It is an assumption Luke has made to support his argument.

    (D) It is the reason for Luke's argument.

    (E) It is the conclusion to Luke's argument.

Questions 945 through 946 are based on the following passage.

Vlad said, "I really don't understand the obsession Londoners have with American food. I've been here three days, and I've walked by dozens of restaurants serving American food. What has happened to the traditional British food I've always loved to eat here? I can't believe how badly Londoners' tastes have declined!"

945. Which of the following pieces of evidence, if true, would most seriously weaken Vlad's argument as presented?

(A) There is no such like as "traditional British food."

(B) Most Londoners go to pubs, not traditional restaurants, when they want British food.

(C) Vlad has only walked around in neighborhoods that cater to the large number of American tourists who visit the city each year.

(D) London actually has more Indian restaurants than any other cuisine.

(E) Vlad tried to visit a restaurant he remembered from a prior trip but it had moved.

946. Which of the following pieces of evidence, if true, would best add support to Vlad's argument?

(A) London has a wide variety of cuisines available in many restaurants.

(B) There were more Chinese tourists than American tourists in London last year.

(C) "American food" is a term so broad as to be unhelpful.

(D) A London daily newspaper recently polled its readers on their favorite cuisine when dining out. "American" won by 30 percent.

(E) Vlad doesn't care for American food himself.

Questions 947 through 948 are based on the following passage.

Polls of viewers overwhelmingly show that news anchors who wear glasses are perceived as more intelligent. Yet, Nancy Stigart, who is WVDG's evening anchorperson, declines to wear glasses, claiming that to do so would be a lie since her eyesight is perfect.

947. What argument could a producer at WVDG make to Nancy to try to convince her to wear glasses?

(A) He could argue that the weatherman for the broadcast wears glasses and thus might be perceived as smarter than Nancy.

(B) He could argue that the practice of wearing glasses with non-prescription lenses is very common these days, citing a statistic that 25 percent of glasses–wearers do not actually need them.

(C) He could point out that glasses come in a wide variety of styles these days.

(D) He could accuse Nancy of vanity because she doesn't want to wear glasses on the air.

(E) He could argue that viewers will not know that Nancy does not actually need the glasses.

948. What fact, if true, could Nancy Stigart use to bolster her case most effectively?

(A) Polls show that viewers prefer for their news anchors to be attractive people.

(B) Most people who think someone who wears glasses is more intelligent are making that assumption subconsciously.

(C) Studies show that when a news anchor feels she is lying, it is perceivable by viewers in her body language.

(D) Glasses tend to create a glare on camera.

(E) Nancy does use a cane, which she has occasionally been shown using on the air.

A publisher wants to reissue a novel by an author who died 20 years ago. The author's estate has been slow to communicate, and the copyright on the novel will lapse in two years. The publisher has suggested that his house go ahead and release a reissue of the novel next year, because by the time the author's estate realizes this has happened, the book will go into the public domain.

949. All of the following are assumptions that the publisher is making except for which of the following?

   (A) The author's estate is unlikely to renew the novel's copyright before it expires.

   (B) The author's estate is not paying attention to what publishing companies are releasing.

   (C) The author's novel will become a best-seller.

   (D) A court case would not use the fact that the novel was republished while under copyright and not with the author's estate's permission against the publishing company.

   (E) The publishing company's lawyers won't block this plan.

950. Which of the following, if true, would most seriously weaken the argument?

   (A) It is illegal to publish a book without permission from the copyright holder.

   (B) People who repeatedly violate copyright law can go to jail.

   (C) The author's estate was recently taken over by a law firm capable of practicing much closer diligence.

   (D) The book is unlikely to sell well because of its dated dialogue.

   (E) The publisher has not actually read the book himself.

90 percent of all likely voters have been polled about their likely votes. A majority, 53 percent, say they will vote for Candidate A. The remaining voters, 47 percent, will vote for Candidate B. A writer for the local news website wants to share a predication that Candidate A will win, but the website's editor has told him no.

951. Which of the following is the most likely reason why the website's editor has said no in the preceding passage?

   (A) The margin of error for the poll is greater than the difference in support between the candidates.

   (B) News organizations should not be in the business of making electoral predictions.

   (C) Predications can suppress voter turnout.

   (D) Another nearby local news website made an incorrect prediction a few years ago and people remember that.

   (E) Anyone reading the website should be able to figure out that Candidate A is likely to win.

Ben: "I've decided to stop donating to that organization. From what I can see, all of their money goes to throwing lavish fundraisers instead of helping people in need. **Just last week, I got another invitation for a huge party they are throwing, with an expensive ticket price. From now on, I'll give my money to organizations that will actually use it to help others.**"

952. What piece of information, if true, could best argue against Ben's decision and convince him to continue supporting the organization in question?

(A) A list of all of the organizations that throw lavish fundraisers.

(B) Written proof that the fundraisers for this organization were paid for by generous donors so that the money raised could go to people in need.

(C) A slide show of five people in need receiving help from the organization.

(D) A discount on the price of the ticket to the latest fundraiser.

(E) A testimonial from another organization by a supporter who explained she would give less if the parties were less lavish.

953. What fact, if true, could Ben use to most effectively support his argument?

(A) Over 40 percent of the organization's budget is dedicated to fundraising.

(B) 60 percent of people who attend the fundraisers give less than $1,000 a piece.

(C) The local economy is so poor that it's actually quite inexpensive to help a person in need buy a home.

(D) The organization throws one big fundraiser a year.

(E) The local newspaper always carried extensive coverage of the fundraisers.

954. Two sentences are bolded in the passage. What is the relationship between them?

(A) The first sentence is a premise, and the second is a reason why Ben doesn't believe in the premise.

(B) The first sentence is one reason why Ben won't support the group, and the second sentence is a second reason.

(C) The first is the argument presented by the organization, and the second is the counter-argument that Ben is making.

(D) The first sentence is evidence that Ben is using to support the argument he is making, and the second is the conclusion to his argument.

(E) The first sentence is an anecdote to support his argument, and the second sentence is his rebuttal to that anecdote.

Questions 955 through 956 are based on the following passage.

Suzie says, "My mom always told me not to go swimming until an hour has passed after eating. Well, I've never gone swimming after eating for at least an hour, and I've never gotten a cramp while swimming!"

955. Which of the following would most seriously weaken Suzie's argument?

(A) Suzie is a vegetarian and does not eat meat, which is difficult to digest.

(B) Suzie's mother was a doctor.

(C) Suzie's best friend nearly drowned from a cramp while swimming when they were kids.

(D) Most people are unlikely to wait an hour after eating before swimming if they are at a pool.

(E) Scientific studies have conclusively proven that there's no truth to this advice.

956. Which of the following sentences, if added to Suzie's argument, would provide the best support for it?

(A) "Many other people avoid swimming soon after eating, and they don't get cramps either!"

(B) "I asked my doctor, and she said that this was a good policy to follow. Cramps are often caused by eating followed by vigorous exercise."

(C) "Of course, I don't exert myself much while swimming."

(D) "My older brother is prone to cramps, so my mom was concerned."

(E) "Cramps can come on very suddenly."

Questions 957 through 958 are based on the following passage.

In order to study the effect of environmental factors on attitudes and behaviors, students at a local high school were given a survey in their Sociology class. The results of that survey indicated that students who spend a minimum of two hours on social media like Twitter are more likely to indulge in online bullying. The study concluded that . . .

957. Which of the following best completes the passage?

(A) . . . students should not bully.

(B) . . . online bullying is a real threat to students' well-being.

(C) . . . Twitter is morally indefensible.

(D) . . . students should be encouraged to think about whether spending time on social media is affecting their decision-making about bullying behaviors.

(E) . . . Twitter does not cause bullying.

958. Which of the following is an assumption that enables the conclusion presented to be drawn?

(A) Most teenagers use social media.

(B) A sociology class in a high school is principally made up of teenagers.

(C) There is a direct link between the use of social media and the likelihood that the user is an online bully.

(D) Social media brings out the worst instincts in people.

(E) People who not bully in real life are willing to do so online.

Questions 959 through 961 are based on the following passage.

A manufacturer of dressy raincoats has decided to cease production. Sales have been steadily declining, and now the cost of maintaining the factory and workforce is great than the expected profit.

959. Which of the following, if true, would be a helpful piece of evidence to include to support the manufacturer's decision.

(A) The manufacturer plans to reopen next year with the factory making a new product.

(B) People still dress up for important occasions.

(C) The loss of a major contract with a hotel corporation has also contributed to the manufacturer's decline.

(D) Most manufacturers are reporting losses this year.

(E) The workforce has volunteered to take a 10 percent pay cut.

960. Which of the following, if true, would most seriously weaken the decision to close the factory?

(A) The manufacturer recently secured a large, multi-year contract with a restaurant chain.

(B) The factory could be improved with a costly remodel.

(C) Much of the workforce is willing to take a 10 percent pay cut.

(D) The neighborhood where the factory is located has become mostly residential.

(E) Most raincoats are now produced overseas.

961. Which of the following is most like the argument in its logical structure?

(A) A local restaurant has decided to close. The neighborhood where it is located has become too expensive.

(B) A local manufacturer of flower pots has decided to move its operations to another state where the workforce will be cheaper.

(C) The agricultural community in this state is in decline. Many people prefer to buy organic products, and few farmers here can afford the expensive certification to be classified as organic.

(D) The factory that has employed 40 percent of the workforce in town has closed. The union is attempting to see if the owners will sell the building to a co-operative of workers.

(E) A beauty salon has decided to close. Few women need a weekly hairstyling session, and the products used in styling hair are very expensive. Thus, the salon is putting more money into products than its making back in sales.

Questions 962 through 963 are based on the following passage.

The Danielsville Fire Department is holding a silent auction to raise funds. The Danielsville Police Department has decided to hold an auction on the same day, at the same time. The Fire Chief told the firefighters, "I'm not worried about turnout. We'll have a lot of people at our event."

962. Which of the following sentences, if true, could the Fire Chief add to her argument in order to provide more evidence that it is true?

(A) "Our event costs twice what the Police Department's event does."

(B) "I just think people appreciate firefighters more."

(C) "My gut tells me that our silent auction offerings are better."

(D) "I've been to the Police Department's event before and it was fine, but nothing great."

(E) "As you know, the Police Department is next door, and we're going to offer a discounted admission to people who present a ticket from that auction."

963. Which of the following sentences, if true, would be the strongest counter-argument to the Fire Chief's statement.

(A) "The Police Department's event has three times the number of items up for auction and admission is free!"

(B) "The Police Department just announced that they will start their event one hour earlier."

(C) "The Danielsville quilting guild is also holding their annual meeting that day!"

(D) "Last year's silent auction event was rained out!"

(E) "But these events are being held on the same day, and at the same time!"

Questions 964 through 965 are based on the following passage.

The Federal Reserve recently set the rate of inflation at 1 percent. **For the past eight years, the rate was not raised.** Therefore, we can conclude that the rate of inflation will not be raised again for another eight years.

964. The argument is most vulnerable to which of the following statements?

(A) The rate of inflation is on an upward trend.

(B) The last 20 years have shown a widely varying rate of inflation.

(C) Most people don't understand how the rate of inflation is calculated.

(D) The prior eight years are incidental, not prophetic.

(E) The rate of inflation can be changed more than twice in a year.

965. What role is the sentence in bold playing in the argument?

(A) It is the premise of the argument being made.

(B) It is the conclusion to the argument being made.

(C) It explains the historical context for why the counter-argument is being made.

(D) It is the counter-argument that is being refuted.

(E) It is evidence that supports the argument being made.

Questions 966 through 967 are based on the following passage.

A recent scientific study concluded that preservatives can be harmful to consumers when added to food. Here at Marr Foods, we avoid the use of preservatives in the production of our food. It's our pleasure to provide healthy food for you and your family.

966. If the statements are true, which of the following must also be true?

(A) Scientific studies are open to interpretation.

(B) It is possible to produce food without preservatives that is safe to consume.

(C) Marr Foods is an organic food producer.

(D) Marr Foods uses natural preservatives.

(E) Preservatives in food can cause health issues to those who consume them.

967. Which of the following, if true, most seriously weaken the argument presented?

(A) Marr Foods does not employ a food scientist on their staff.

(B) Marr Foods received a report of numerous health code violations two years ago.

(C) Several other scientific studies found that preservatives were in no way harmful to those who consumed food with them.

(D) The idea that preservatives are chemicals and all chemicals are bad for humans to consume is too broad.

(E) Marr Foods products have a relatively short shelf life.

Questions 968 through 970 are based on the following passage.

Neighbor A would like to set up a sprinkler to water his lawn, which would run from 7:00 a.m. to 11:00 a.m. every day. Neighbor B has suggested that it would be better to run the sprinkler from 10:00 a.m. to 2:00 p.m. when the sun is higher in the sky and the grass is drier. **Neighbor A refused, saying Neighbor B's plan was too expensive.**

968. Which of the following if true, is most likely explanation for Neighbor A's stance?

(A) Neighbor A has invested several thousand dollars in lawn care recently.

(B) Neighbor B lives in a home that cost $25,000 more than Neighbor A.

(C) Neighbor A is on a plan from the water authority that provides a lower rate on water in the morning hours.

(D) Neighbor B has a rain collection system and uses that to water his lawn.

(E) The people who owned Neighbor A's house before him maintained a lawn of wild native plants.

969. What is an assumption that Neighbor B is making in the passage?

(A) That Neighbor A is inflexible about his habits.

(B) That Neighbor A overwaters his lawn.

(C) That the sun is higher in the sky in the early afternoon than in the morning.

(D) That Neighbor A doesn't have a good reason for watering his lawn in the morning.

(E) That plants like grass need watering.

970. How are the two bolded sentences connected?

(A) The first sentence is a premise to an argument, and the second sentence is a response to a counter-argument.

(B) Both sentences are conclusions to their respective arguments.

(C) The first sentence is a premise, and the second sentence is a second premise.

(D) The first sentence is a premise, and the second sentence is evidence that supports that premise.

(E) The first sentence is a premise, and the second sentence is the conclusion to that argument.

In order to increase revenues, a cell-phone company has decided to change from a flat rate of $30 a month and $0.10 for every minute over 150 minutes to a $50 per month for unlimited usage plan.

971. Which of the following, if true, would most clearly offer evidence to support the company's plan in the preceding passage?

(A) Most customers use between 150 and 300 minutes of cell time a month.

(B) Customers have repeatedly asked the company to offer an unlimited usage plan, which many other cell service providers already offer.

(C) The company began by advertising itself as a provider of low-cost cell service.

(D) Many cell service providers charge $0.20 per minute for extra minutes.

(E) The unlimited service will not include charges incurred while traveling in some foreign countries.

Questions 972 through 973 are based on the following passage.

A school's basketball team often makes it to the state semi-final tournament but has not made it to the finals since 1968. The coach has decided to look at the playbook, notes, and other materials from the 1968 season and try to copy what was done then. This, **she assures her team, means that they will definitely make it to the final game.**

972. Which of the following arguments is most like the in its logical structure?

(A) The players on a football team who are frustrated that they never have a winning season have asked their owner to fire the head coach.

(B) A woman who wants to win an equestrienne title has decided to review the techniques of other riders who have won the title.

(C) A woman who is remodeling her house has gone back to the original plans for the building and reviewed them for ideas about how to decorate. The house was built in 1968.

(D) A mock trial team that often makes it to the final round of competition but rarely wins is frustrated. They've decided to interview the members of the 2002 team, which won the state competition. Using those techniques, they're sure, will put them over the top to win.

(E) A bookseller who's frustrated at low sales in his store has decided to review the *New York Times* bestseller list and choose a few of those books to feature in his store.

973. What role does the sentence in bold play in the passage?

(A) It concludes the coach's argument.

(B) It reveals what the team must do to win.

(C) It shows the flaw in looking at the 1968 playbook and other materials.

(D) It reveals the author's true opinion of the coach's plan.

(E) It creates a template for the team to follow.

A representative noticed that attendance at events in his district had declined, so he ordered his staff to conduct a poll to find out why. It was soon revealed that his events were often scheduled during the daytime, when many people were at work. Because the representative wants a variety of his constituents at his events, he further instructed his staff to . . .

974. Which of the following best completes the preceding passage?

(A) . . . continue scheduling events as usual.

(B) . . . continue scheduling events as usual but conduct another poll to find out if people would come to events held at different times.

(C) . . . look for opportunities to schedule events before or after typical working hours and on weekends.

(D) . . . review the schedules of other members of Congress to see how they handle daytime events.

(E) . . . personally approach people at upcoming events and ask them to come to more events.

Questions 975 through 976 are based on the following passage.

It's difficult to win playing the slots at a casino. Sheila has a foolproof plan, though. She watches others playing the slots until she sees someone who has played the same machine many times but not won. After that person gives up, Sheila plays at that machine. She often wins.

975. If we can assume that the slot machines Sheila is playing are fair, which of the following facts or observations, if true, would most reveal a fallacy in her logic?

(A) Even if this plan works, Sheila will inevitably lose her won funds by further gambling.

(B) If there was a way to predict when slot machines were going to cash out, everyone would play the slot machines following that plan.

(C) The probability of a certain slot machine cashing out on any given day is very low.

(D) There's no "build up" in playing the slot machines. Each game is new and not tied to the game before it.

(E) Slot machines require very little skill to play.

976. Which of the following, if true, would be the best evidence to support Sheila's theory?

(A) Sheila often wins when playing the slot machines.

(B) A scientific study, based on the observation of 500 slot machines at a Las Vegas casino, showed that machines that are played repeatedly are three times more likely to cash out.

(C) Sheila is willing to spend 8 hours per day playing the slot machines when in Las Vegas.

(D) Gambling tricks, such as card counting, are illegal in most casinos is the U.S.

(E) No one has ever published a comprehensive and accurate guide to winning at slot machines.

Questions 977 through 978 are based on the following passage.

Jane: I prefer to go to the beach when it's less crowded.

Jake: Oh? When do you go?

Jane: Usually before 8:00 a.m. or after 3:00 p.m.

Jake: **Isn't it crowded in the evening?**

Jane: Yes, but I just put on my earbuds and ignore everyone.

977. Which of the following conclusions could be properly drawn from the information in the dialogue?

(A) Jane is not very intelligent.

(B) Jake and Jane do not know each other well.

(C) The beach is less crowded in the evenings than it is during the day.

(D) When Jane says that she prefers to go to the beach when it is less crowded, she may not mean that there are actually fewer people on the beach than at any other time of the day.

(E) Jane listens to music whenever she is on the beach.

978. In the bolded sentence, what is Jake asking Jane for?

(A) Evidence to persuade him of the merits of her argument.

(B) An explanation of an apparent discrepancy in her argument.

(C) A conclusion to her argument.

(D) A consideration of his counter-argument.

(E) A premise to validate her argument.

In order to prevent the recurrence of avalanches on its property, a ski resort has installed a new type of fencing that is guaranteed to reduce the impact of an avalanche by 50 percent. The marketing company suggests advertising the resort as "50 percent less likely to have an avalanche than our neighbors!"

979. Which of the following, if true, would be the best reason for the resort's owner to reject this advertising campaign?

(A) It's not a good idea to bring up something as terrible as an avalanche in an advertisement.

(B) The new type of fencing has not actually been tested by an avalanche on a ski slope.

(C) Studies show that most visitors to a ski resort spend less than 60 percent of their time there actually skiing.

(D) The fencing is nearly invisible to the naked eye and thus will not make much of an impact visually.

(E) Reducing an avalanche's impact by 50 percent is not the same as reducing the likelihood of an avalanche by 50 percent.

980. What fact, if true, would most strengthen the argument made by the marketing company?

(A) Neighboring properties are higher up on the mountains than this resort.

(B) The properties on either side of the ski resort are not ski resorts.

(C) When the impact of an avalanche is reduced, the avalanche is less likely to travel further down the mountain and affect skiers.

(D) The fencing company has a money-back guarantee.

(E) There are warning signs posted around the resort that caution skiers to be alert for avalanches.

Company K can produce 80 widgets per minute. **Company L can produce 100 widgets per minute.** The owner of Company K studied Company L's methods and decided to implement two changes to how Company K makes widgets. After the improvements were complete, Company K can now make 90 widgets per minute. **Company K's owner has decided not to make any more changes.**

981. Which of the following, if true, would best provide support for Company K's owner?

(A) Company K sells five time the number of widgets that Company L sells.

(B) Company L faced bankruptcy last year.

(C) Company K employs 200 fewer employees than Company L, and pays them $0.50 more an hour.

(D) Company L's speed at producing widgets has repeatedly caused accidents that ultimately cost the company more money than producing at a lower rate.

(E) Company K and Company L produce virtually the same product.

982. Which of the following, if true, would most seriously weaken the logic behind Company K's owner?

(A) Because Company K's production line was already more efficient than Company L's, a few more small changes should allow Company K to produce widgets at a rate of 150 a minute.

(B) The two changes that were implemented by Company K were very expensive.

(C) Global demand for widgets has declined severely over the past three years as the market is saturated.

(D) Company L did not reveal all of the methods it uses for faster widget-making to Company K's owner.

(E) Worker satisfaction at Company K is very high.

983. What is the relationship between the two sentences in bold in the passage?

(A) The first sentence is a conclusion of the argument, and the second sentence gives evidence for the conclusion.

(B) The first sentence is evidence used in building the argument, and the second sentence is the conclusion of the argument.

(C) Both sentences are premises of the argument.

(D) Both sentences are evidence in the argument.

(E) The first sentence is an argument, and the second sentence is a counter-argument.

Questions 984 through 985 are based on the following passage.

A law firm is experiencing a high turnover rate among its second-year associates. Many are recruited by a rival firm. To rectify this problem, the firm's board has proposed instituting a clause in all new hires' contracts, which would require them to work for the firm for five years.

984. Which of the following facts, if true, would most seriously weaken the argument?

(A) The contracts would continue to provide a generous pay raise for every year of service to the firm.

(B) In a poll of recent law school graduates, "job fluidity" — that is, the ability to change positions and firms — was one of the top three qualities new lawyers wanted in their first jobs.

(C) Only a handful of junior associates will eventually become partner.

(D) The law firm publishes its salaries, so a rival firm would be able to easily figure out how much to offer second-year associates whom they want to poach.

(E) The contracts already contain a clause which forbids first-year associates from leaving the firm for any reason besides illness or a move.

985. Which of the following is most likely to yield significant information which would help the board decide whether to institute the clause or not?

(A) A survey of former second-year associates who have left the firm for other law offices.

(B) Tracking salary data for the last five years for all of the city's law firms' second-year associates.

(C) A review of the legal precedents in contractual law.

(D) Poll data collected from current first-year associates about whether they would have taken the job if such a clause was included in their contracts.

(E) A head count of the firm's board's members, to find out who would vote for the new contractual clause.

Questions 986 through 987 are based on the following passage.

"The recipe says to bake this cake at 350 degrees for 30 minutes. I will bake it at 400 degrees for 15 minutes!"

986. Which of the following is an assumption that allows the conclusion of the argument to be reached?

(A) Increasing the temperature at which a cake is baked also increases the time for which a cake must be baked.

(B) It's possible to correctly bake a cake at a higher temperature so long as the time the cake is in the oven is reduced.

(C) Recipes are essentially instructions for scientific experiments.

(D) An increase in temperature will have no effect on the amount of time a cake should bake in the oven.

(E) The person speaking probably grew up in a country where the Celsius temperature system is used.

987. What of the following, if true, most clearly points to a flaw in the speaker's plan?

(A) The mathematical calculation in the argument is incorrect.

(B) A cake is unlikely to bake thoroughly at any temperature if only left in the oven for 15 minutes.

(C) The speaker has confused the concept of baking and broiling.

(D) Most ovens are slightly above or below the temperature to which they are set; this is why professional bakers recommend using an oven thermometer.

(E) Baking is a chemical reaction dictated by the recipe that cannot be sped up by setting the oven temperature higher.

Questions 988 through 989 are based on the following passage.

Providing adequate public health–care facilities is a crucial task in Davis County, where more than 60 percent of the household incomes are below the poverty line. Davis County has recently opened a free health care clinic on weekday afternoons. A county supervisor suggested that the clinic be offered every day from 8:00 a.m. to 4:00 p.m., but her suggestion was not approved.

988. Which if the following, if true, provides the best rationale for why the supervisors did not vote to open the clinic from 8:00 a.m. to 4:00 p.m. every weekday?

(A) The supervisors feel that several new businesses which plan to open in Davis County will provide more jobs to the people currently using the clinic.

(B) It's hard to maintain patient confidentiality at a clinic.

(C) The majority of people who need the services would prefer that the clinic open in the evening hours.

(D) The majority of volunteers who staff the clinic are doctors and nurses with full-time jobs, and they are often scheduled for hospital rounds and surgery in the morning hours.

(E) The clinic does not take health insurance.

989. Which of the following facts, if true, would most strengthen the suggestion of the Davis County supervisors who wants to open the clinic during morning hours?

(A) There are fewer than 40 doctors in Davis County.

(B) The majority of patients at the clinic do not have access to health insurance and cannot afford anything higher than a $15 fee.

(C) Morning hours would allow the clinic to see, on average, 20 additional patients per day.

(D) Many people in Davis County rely on the clinic for basic health care services, such as vaccinations.

(E) Lyme Disease has been on the rise in Davis County over the last year.

The owner of a store in Fernville says, "If we want to save our downtown shopping area, we need to protest the opening of a CheapDeals on the outskirts of our town! CheapDeals is a menace. They opened a store in St. Barbara last year, and 20 percent of the stores in that town filed for bankruptcy! St. Barbara didn't protest the arrival of CheapDeals, but we're not going to make the same mistake here in Fernville!"

990. The conclusion to the argument presented is based on which of the following assumptions?

(A) Bankruptcy is an unfortunate but likely part of running a business.

(B) People tend to support local businesses when they know the store owners.

(C) CheapDeals does not want bad publicity.

(D) More people would shop in Fernville's downtown if they knew more about the stores there.

(E) CheapDeals won't build in a town where they have been clearly told they are not welcome.

991. The store owner quoted could strengthen his argument with which of the following facts, if true?

(A) CheapDeals often undercuts the price of local competitors.

(B) The downtown shopping area is a historical landmark.

(C) CheapDeals tries to keep a low-profile; the publicity from a protest has kept the company from setting up shop in other towns.

(D) St. Barbara's shop owners held several protests against CheapDeals.

(E) The land CheapDeals is looking to purchase is not actually in what is considered downtown.

An exhibit of the Royal jewels is planned for the museum's upcoming season. In deciding insurance costs, the director the museum said, "We do not need to insure the smaller items. Insuring the larger jewels, such as the tiaras and crowns, will be sufficient. If the larger pieces are stolen, the amount we will receive will more than cover the cost of all the jewels."

992. What of the following facts, if true, would most seriously weaken the director's logic?

(A) The insurance company may not allow the larger jewels to be insured for more than they're worth.

(B) If the jewels were to be stolen, thieves might target the smaller items, which will be displayed less securely, rather than the larger items.

(C) Some of the smaller jewels have quite large stones.

(D) The jewels will be displayed in several rooms.

(E) The museum's security system was recently overhauled and is now widely agreed to be among the best in the world.

993. The logical flaw in the reasoning is most similar to that in which of the following statements?

(A) "I'm not going to buy insurance on my boat because we rarely have flooding or typhoons here."

(B) "Let's try all of the flavors before deciding on which one we want to have for our cake."

(C) "I'm going to reserve the most expensive dining room, which will be big enough to hold all of us. If some of the group doesn't come along, we can move to a smaller room."

(D) "I put on sunscreen before leaving the house, but I didn't bother with insect repellent. The sunblock should be strong enough to keep away any mosquitos that show up."

(E) "The jewelry case needs to be as far back from the window as possible. That's the only way I can think of to protect it if someone hurls a rock or a brick through the window."

Questions 994 through 995 are based on the following passage.

"If the student body wants to have more parking spots at our school," Principal Lavine said, "**they need to raise the money to buy the field in front of the school building so that it can be turned into a parking lot.** We're out of options since the faculty parking lot takes up the property behind the building, and Lake Matteo is on one side, while parking for visitors and parents is on the other."

994. What role does the portion of the passage in bold play in the argument?

(A) It is an inference used in the creation of the argument.

(B) It is an assumption that feeds the argument.

(C) It presents facts in support of the argument.

(D) It presents a premise upon which the argument is based.

(E) It is the conclusion of the argument.

995. Which of the following facts, if true, would most weaken the argument presented?

(A) The field in front of the school building is prohibitively expensive.

(B) The parking for visitors and parents is rarely used, so 30 empty spaces are often available next to the school but forbidden to the students.

(C) Turning a field into a parking lot is not an easy task.

(D) Lake Matteo often floods in the springtime.

(E) The student government has been asking for more parking for the last three years because the majority of students drive to school.

Questions 996 through 998 are based on the following passage.

Julian noticed a strange discrepancy when he visited the city of New Winchester. The city has numerous corner stores that sell candy and other small purchases, but there are well-stocked grocery stores around town that sell the same products for far less money.

996. Which of the following would prove least helpful for Julian to study in order to find the reason for the discrepancy?

    (A) A map of New Winchester, marking the location of all corner stores and grocery stores.

    (B) A list of the most purchased items at a corner store.

    (C) A survey of New Winchester shoppers about their buying preferences.

    (D) A historical map showing the growth of neighborhoods in New Winchester.

    (E) A spreadsheet of the average purchases at a corner store in New Winchester.

997. What fact, if true, could help explain the discrepancy that Julian has noted?

    (A) New Winchester's grocery stores are not as numerous as its corner stores.

    (B) The grocery stores are located on the outskirts of town, whereas the corner stores are in residential areas.

    (C) Most people prefer fewer choices.

    (D) The grocery stores publish lavish sales bills, which are left around town for people to pick up.

    (E) The corner stores often lower the price by a few cents if a customer does not have exact change.

998. Which of the following is a logical conclusion for Julian to make?

    (A) There must be something appealing about the corner stores that make people willing to spend slightly more money there than at the grocery store.

    (B) New Winchester citizens are very loyal shoppers.

    (C) The grocery stores must provide terrible customer service.

    (D) The corner stores must offer some sort of frequent shopper incentive.

    (E) There must be racial/ethnic reasons why people shop where they do.

Questions 999 through 1,000 are based on the following passage.

The small country of Mapple could, in theory, be the world's largest exporter of lettuce, but it isn't. The explanation is that 75 percent of Mapple's farmland is owned by the government. This hurts Mapple's lettuce production because the government doesn't have the flexibility necessary for efficient lettuce farming that private industry possesses.

999. The answer to which of the following questions would be most relevant to evaluating the adequacy of the explanation?

    (A) Who owns the 15 percent of the farmland that isn't owned by the government?

    (B) How does lettuce production from Mapple's government-owned farmland compared to production from farmland owned by private industries?

    (C) Would a larger country be better suited to producing lettuce than Mapple?

    (D) What percentage of Mapple's lettuce is consumed domestically?

    (E) Has the government stated any plans to sell farmland to private industry, provided that the price is fair?

1000. Which of the following, if true, would most seriously weaken the argument?

(A) Mapple's lettuce production is still five times what it was 10 years ago.

(B) Lettuce is a hardy crop and can withstand a great deal of fluctuation in water and sunlight.

(C) There's no discernable difference in the amount of lettuce produced per acre by the government's farmland and by farmland owned by private industry.

(D) Many of the non-government owners of farmland in Mapple once worked for the government's agricultural department.

(E) Private industry has fewer restrictions placed on it in terms of treatment of worker and working conditions than the government's regulations.

The McAllister Bridge was supposed to relieve traffic congestion in the town of Allegheny, but even though the bridge opened last year, congestion has increased. To relieve the traffic problems in Allegheny, therefore, the traffic commission should order the McAllister Bridge closed.

1001. Which of the following, if true, most weakens to the conclusion presented in the passage?

(A) Ship captains have complained that the McAllister Bridge disrupts shipping on the river it spans, hurting the local economy.

(B) The bridge is only open from 6:00 to 8:00 a.m. on weekdays.

(C) The increased traffic in Allegheny is largely because of a new shopping center that opened for business in the town shortly after the McAllister Bridge was opened.

(D) The McAllister Bridge allows inhabitants of Allegheny to reach downtown Pittsburgh in less than 40 minutes, as opposed to the two hours the trip required before the bridge opened.

(E) The bridge's toll is so low that it will take over 100 years for the bridge to pay for itself.

2

The Answers

IN THIS PART . . .

Review the answers to all 1,001 questions.

Study the answer explanations to better understand the concepts being covered.

Chapter 8

The Answers

Chapter 1

1.

A well written sample essay that will score well on the GMAT exam is shown below:

The speaker, perhaps in an attempt to make an argument that battles persistent and unfair stereotypes about young people who enjoy playing role playing games, makes a leap in logic that leads to a flawed argument. Her premises are flawed, and thus, her conclusion (that more people should play role playing games) is unsupported.

To begin with, let's consider the premises of the argument. The speaker states one stereotype about RPG players that is undoubtedly persistent and unfair, the idea that they are "nerds without social skills." But in order to refute this idea, she provides a statistic from a survey that states that young adults who play RPGs value social skills and courtesy more than those who were surveyed 10 years ago. There are two essential flaws in the premise of that argument.

First, the speaker fails to recognize that the survey she is using asked the same group — young people who play RPG's — ten years apart. Suggesting that RPGs are the reason the young people value social skills and courtesy now fails to recognize that, according to the survey, 10 years ago, young people who play RPGs did not value social skills and courtesy. It's clear that what has changed cannot be the playing of RPGs, which the group that is being surveyed does as a precondition of being part of the group.

The second essential flaw is that the speaker fails to connect the results of the survey, which indicate that young people who play RPGs "value" social skills and courtesy, with her interpretation, which is that the evidence suggests that role playing games "are actually promoting social interaction and friendship." The logic is stretched too far. One can value something without promoting it. It's also worth noting that "promoting" an ideal and "practicing" an ideal are not the same thing. By conflating these three distinct ideas, the speaker weakens her already flawed argument. It would be better if she stated that those who value a quality will often seek to practice it themselves.

Additionally, whether or not RPG players value, promote, or practice social skills and courtesy, this is a strange premise to support the idea that more people should play RPGs. There are many more qualities about RPGs that might make them alluring to new players, and these qualities have nothing to do with whether their co-players are courteous or have good social skills, or whether their own social skills will be improved by playing RPGs. These include an interest in the created narrative and the enjoyment in feeling like one is immersed in a fantastical world.

It's admirable of this speaker to try to eradicate a tired cliché about young people who participate in role-playing games. The statistic that she provides, however, is not well used in making this argument. Instead of her current flawed logic, the speaker might point out that the change in valuing "social skills and courtesy" over the last 10 years among RPG players shows that they have become increasingly aware of their false reputation and wish to show that they do not fit the stereotype. The idea that they "value" these qualities most likely goes hand in hand with practicing them themselves, and thus welcome new players. The speaker might also suggest other, more compelling reasons for new players to try RPGs. It's likely that the speaker would do better to find a different statistic or anecdotal proof to make her case. As the argument stands now, it is too flawed to carry much weight.

This essay would likely score a 6 (out of 6) on the GMAT. It fulfills the prompt by considering and explaining the questionable assumptions that underline the speaker's principal argument, and showing how or why those assumptions are likely misinterpretations. The essay is well organized and moves smoothly, with plenty of transitions between ideas. The writer also proposes alternative evidence that could help the speaker strengthen her argument. Finally, the tone throughout is notably even. The writer of this essay praises the speaker's assumed good will and is gentle in rebuking her flawed ideas.

2.

A well written sample essay that will score well on the GMAT exam is shown below:

Most of us have faced a so-called "hard sell," when a salesperson reaches too far and acts too aggressively in a desperate attempt to secure our business. Unfortunately, that's what's happened with the Stipesville Business Directory's mailing as shown in the prompt. The advertisement uses faulty logic to make a flawed argument that may ultimately turn potential advertisers away from the Directory, instead of increasing sales.

The premise is wrong from the first line, which states that "one of the best ways to reach new customers is also one of the cheapest." This line of thinking is doesn't make much sense, as no facts or figures are provided to show that the Business Directory is an inexpensive choice compared to other means of alerting potential customers about one's business. It also assumes that local business owners value "cheapness," which may not be true.

The ad continues to make a flawed argument with the statement that "local business owners" who bought ads in the Directory in past years will testify that doing so is "one of the best" ways to reach new customers. This argument has no meat to it since no testimonials from local business owners are included. It's possible that the Directory is more helpful for businesses like repair shops, which rely on serving customers faced with emergencies, than businesses like hair salons, which rely on repeat customers and word of mouth. But that argument is not considered here.

Perhaps the most glaring error in the ad is the assumption presented in the listing of "three of our town's top doctors, two of our top-five caterers, and several of our top dog groomers" who bought ads last year. There's no means provided of understanding what "top" means here: Are these businesses the top in a local newspaper's customer satisfaction survey or the top in money earned or some other means of measuring their success? And by what means is their success, however it is measured, tied to their participation in the business Directory? This information is not explained and thus equates participation in the Stipesville Business Directory with success as a business in a way that is not at all clear.

Additionally, this flawed logic continues with an anecdote about an unnamed hairdresser who apparently attributes her 5% drop in business to not purchasing an ad in the Stipesville Business Directory. This is flimsy evidence, and without knowing more about the hairdresser, we cannot be sure that the drop in her business is related to her failure to place an ad in the Directory. Her business might be located in an area of Stipesville where construction has taken place over several months, causing a decrease in visitors. Or she might have taken a vacation of a month or more, during which time her business would obviously see a decrease in earnings.

The shoddiness of the arguments presented ends up making the Stipesville Business Directory seem like an organization that's overaggressive and abrasive, which is unfortunate. The inclusion of more detailed testimonials from satisfied local business owners who bought ads would provide more convincing, if anecdotal, evidence. The Directory's compilers might also try to accrue more convincing figures, perhaps by surveying local businesses before and after they've placed ads. This sort of information, presented coherently, would ultimately be much more convincing to local business who are on the fence about placing an ad in the Stipesville Business Directory.

This essay would likely score a 6 (out of 6) on the GMAT. It fulfills the prompt by considering and explaining the questionable assumptions that underline the speaker's principal argument, and showing how or why those assumptions are unconvincing in a piece of writing that seeks, above all, to convince. The essay is well organized and moves smoothly, using transitions between ideas well, working down the advertisement in a way that makes natural sense. The writer also proposes alternative ways that the ad could be written to make it more convincing. While the tone of this essay borders on being too harsh, the case made here is very convincing.

3.

A well written sample essay that will score well on the GMAT exam is shown below:

Imagine telling a group of high school seniors that their prom, senior trip, senior work day, and the school musical have been cancelled. Why? They need to focus on raising their test scores on a standardized test that in no way benefits them, but only helps the school from which they will soon graduate — the very school that just cancelled all their senior activities. If the school board member quoted in the argument gets his way, that's exactly what will happen.

The argument he makes is not just cruel but deeply flawed. To begin with, he does not prove his opening premise, that the students at Richmeade Senior High School (RSHS) are scoring poorly on their standardized test. He fails to point out that the only standardized test given in June is an exit test for graduating high school seniors, and that RSHS has never required students to sit for it unlike Richmeade Prep. It's also possible that, as is typical for a private school, Richmeade Prep has a smaller class than Richmeade Senior High School.

It would be most practical to simply make taking the test mandatory for all graduating RSHS seniors. That would significantly improve the scores. But instead of suggesting that, the school board member presents another flawed argument. He points out that Richmeade Prep School doesn't offer any extracurricular or special activities during the month before the test is given and suggests that RSHS try the same thing. He mentions but fails to grasp the important fact that Richmeade Prep School gives the test in May, after they may have had a two-week break for spring break and/or spring holidays, which is typical for American high schools. Thus, the students are only required to focus on the test for two weeks instead of a month.

But more importantly, there is faulty logic at work here. The elimination of extracurricular and special activities does not automatically lead to an uptick in students' studying for their standardized tests. Indeed, even if students react without the rancor suggested in the first paragraph, there's no reason to think that they'll spend more time in test preparation. The standardized tests do not benefit the students taking them, even if their scores are very high.

There are ideas that might do better to increase students' desire to both sit for and do well on the tests. A program might be presented which demonstrates to students how high scores on the test would benefit the younger students in the school, for example. Or the RSHS might move the testing forward to the same timeframe as Richmeade Prep, and thus make the senior activities a reward for doing well on it. A discount on Senior Prom tickets might be given to any senior who takes the test. Finally, simply requiring that students at Richmeade Senior High School take the test, the way that Richmeade Prep does, will go a long way toward solving the problem.

No matter what other ideas are tried, it's clear that the connection between Richmeade Prep's test scores and the RSHS is tangential at best. There are financial reasons for a school to want to do well on a standardized test, so it may be worthwhile to develop a new plan. But this will require far greater research, and a better understanding of logical cause and effect, to avoid the disaster suggested in the opening paragraph.

This essay would likely score a 6 (out of 6) on the GMAT. It fulfills the prompt by considering and explaining the questionable assumptions that underline the speaker's principal argument. The writer unpacks the lengthy series of false assumptions that the speaker has made in a well-organized way. It transitions clearly from one idea to the next. The writer validates the concern the speaker has but shows alternative ways for the concern to be addressed. Finally, the writer opens with a gripping idea that should propel readers to continue.

4.

A well written sample essay that will score well on the GMAT exam is shown below:

The article in a conventional cosmetic industry newsletter makes one case for why a customer might not need to buy organic makeup products. The author of this article is writing on behalf of the conventional cosmetics industry and clearly wants to undercut the growing movement towards buying organic cosmetics. However, the argument presented here is not convincing and might even drive more business into organic cosmetics!

The author relies on selected facts from a study of the chemical class Zbt, mentioning that chemical class Zbt has never been shown to cause scarring on human test subjects. While this fact may be true, using it reveals that it has been shown to cause scarring in animal studies. This begs the question as to whether any studies have been done on human subjects at all! Clearly, this is poor logic. In a situation in which a conventional cosmetic industry employee is trying to convince a potential customer to buy their product using this fact, many potential customers would not be convinced. They might ask not only if tests were ever done on human subjects, but whether the scarring on animals was so severe that tests on humans were not allowed. Even if customers don't ask, the idea that chemical class Zbt causes scarring in animal studies will remain a vivid picture in their minds. That's not going to improve sales.

It would be better for the conventional cosmetic industry employee to use nearly any other argument than the one presented here, which ends up begging too many questions that are not answered. A better argument is briefly alluded to at the end of the column, when it is mentioned that "searching out organic cosmetics" is a "hassle." Pursuing this line of thought would be more convincing because many consumers would respond well to the idea that they are too busy to specially search out certain items that are not widely available. In addition, you can build a case around the expense of organic cosmetics, which are often twice or even three times as expensive as conventional cosmetics. Organic makeup can be both difficult to find and expensive to purchase, and reminding customers of these facts will not beg any questions about the likelihood of scarring. This argument is not well-reasoned, but another, better, argument is available.

This essay would likely score a 6 (out of 6) on the GMAT. While it is shorter than other example essays, it fulfills the prompt by considering and explaining the questionable assumptions that underline the speaker's principal argument, and showing how the argument would be picked apart by the very people it hopes to convince. In a tone that is fair-minded, the author also suggests several alternative arguments that could be made to amplify the stance of the article while rejecting the argument made at this time.

5.

A well written sample essay that will score well on the GMAT exam is shown below:

In his zeal to cut costs and increase profits, the bank executive quoted here employs dubious logic. Let's take a look at how his arguments fall apart.

To begin, consider the comparison he makes between the profits of today's six locations versus the profits of a single location. The executive says — without any statistical proof — that the main location was once more profitable than the combined profit from the six locations that North Bank offers today. He then attributes the loss in profitability to having six locations, without ever quite explaining what he means. It's not clear if he feels that six locations are more expensive to operate, or if customer usage has somehow declined, or how, exactly, the increase in locations means a decrease in profits. It's counter-intuitive — although not impossible — that a bank with one location would do less business than a bank with six. More explanation is needed.

It's also worth noting that the executive doesn't give a timeframe for when the single bank was more profitable. With more information, the story could be clearer. It's possible, for example, that he refers to a time when North Bank not only had but one location, but was also the only bank in town. A monopoly on the town's business would surely increase profits. Logically, the bank cannot be expected to meet the same profit margin today that it could many years ago when that was so.

While there is more to say about the first premise, let's move on to the second premise. The executive claims that customers will enjoy the "nostalgic feel" of having to use one North Bank location for their business. This does not match up with any easily seen trends in banking, in which more and more people prefer to use ATMs and online banking instead of traveling several miles to do their banking in person. But even if the case could be made that, for some reason, North Bank's customers are not following the trends, proof is needed but not provided. Believing the logic here requires the acceptance of a premise that is unproven and goes against common observation.

Perhaps there is a logical case to be made for reducing North Bank to one location. The executive could, for example, provide evidence that shows five branches bring in less money that they spend in salary and building costs. But that is not the argument he makes here, and thus, this argument must be rejected as illogical and unconvincing.

This essay would likely score a 6 (out of 6) on the GMAT. The writer does a good job of exposing the two assumptions the executive made in his comments and showing why they are not logically sound. The writer also makes good use of transitions and moves logically and clearly from one point to the next, closing by making a suggestion of what a more convincing case would be before soundly rejecting this case.

Chapter 2

6.1. A. Yes

6.2. B. No

6.3. B. No

For 6.1, sort by Kind of Business. Under Column 4, the combined sales of the six kinds of businesses in March 2016 was

$$29,628 + 21,242 + 57,406 + 17,278 + 56,337 + 92,140 = 274,031$$

Under Column 2, the combined sales of the six kinds of businesses in March 2017 was

$$30,864 + 21,504 + 59,583 + 17,618 + 56,466 + 96,423 = 282,458$$

The percent change is

$$\frac{282,458 - 274,031}{274,031} \times 100\% = \frac{8,427}{274,031} \times 100\% \approx 3.1\%$$

Note: The symbol "$\approx$" means "approximately equal to." Therefore, the answer is Yes.

For 6.2, sort by Inventories March 2017. The business with the highest March 2017 inventory is motor vehicle and parts dealers. Re-sort by Inventories/Sales Ratios March 2017. The business with the highest March 2017 Inventories/Sales Ratio is clothing stores. Therefore, the answer is No.

For 6.3, sort by Kind of Business. Under Column 8, the inventories/sales ratio for general merchandise stores for March 2017 is 1.43, indicating that this business has more than one month's worth of merchandise on hand. Therefore, the answer is No.

7.1. **B. Greater than or equal to median**

7.2. **A. Less than median**

7.3. **A. Less than median**

For 7.1, sort by Stock. Under Column 4, the volume quote for Company B is 2,315. Re-sort by Volume. The median for the 20 companies is halfway between 2,290 and 2,315. Thus, the volume quote for Company B is greater than or equal to the median.

For 7.2, sort by Stock. Under Column 7, the close quote for Company G is 39.65. Re-sort by Close. The median for the 20 companies is halfway between 55.27 and 56.45. Thus, the close quote for Company G is less than the median.

For 7.3, sort by Stock. Under Column 8, the net change quote for Company L is 0.23. Re-sort by Net Change. The median for the 20 companies is halfway between 0.32 and 0.67. Thus, the net change quote for Company L is less than the median.

8.1. **A. Yes**

8.2. **A. Yes**

8.3. **B. No**

For 8.1, sort by the average number of daily sales in January. The median is 144. Re-sort by the average number of daily sales in March. The median is 140. The median in January is greater. Therefore, the answer is Yes.

For 8.2, sort by the Total Sales Amount, Feb. Store A is the store with the highest total sales in February. Re-sort by the average number of daily sales in February. Store A is the store with the highest average number of daily sales in February. Therefore, the answer is Yes.

For 8.3, sort by Total Sales Amount, Feb. Count the number of stores for which the total sales amount in February exceeds the total sales amount in March. Only 7 of the 15 stores reported February total sales amounts that exceed March's total sales amounts. Therefore, the answer is No.

9.1. D. 250

9.2. C. 200

Let x = the rate of increase for company X, and y = the rate of increase for company Y. Given that the number of components in inventory for the two companies will be equal in 20 months, set up an equation and solve for x in terms of y.

$$15,000 + 20x = 16,000 + 20y$$
$$20x = 20y + 16,000 - 15,000$$
$$20x = 20y + 1,000$$
$$x = y + 50$$

This result tells you that company X's rate is 50 greater than company Y's rate. The only selections in the table where company X's rate is 50 greater than company Y's is 250 and 200, respectively.

10.1. B. two

10.2. D. four

For 10.1, according to condition (b), if item 1 is selected, then two cases are possible. Case I. Suppose item 1 and item 3 are selected. Given that item 4 is not selected, then, according to condition (c), item 2 must be selected. Neither condition (a), (d), nor (e) requires that additional items must be selected. Thus, if item 1 and item 3 are selected, a total of three items must be selected. Case II. Suppose item 1 and item 4 are selected. Then none of conditions (a) through (e) requires that additional items must be selected. Thus, if item 1 and item 4 are selected, a total of two items must be selected. Therefore, the minimum number of items that must be selected if item 1 is selected is two.

For 10.2, if item 5 is selected, then only two cases that satisfy all conditions are possible. Case I. Item 5, item 1, item 3, and item 2 are selected. This combination does not violate any of the conditions (a) through (e). Item 4 cannot be selected because of condition (b), and item 6 cannot be selected because of condition (e). Thus, if item 5, item 1, item 3, and item 2 are selected, then the maximum possible number of items that can be selected is four. Case II. Item 5, item 6, item 4, and item 2 are selected. This combination does not violate any of the conditions (a) through (e). Item 3 cannot be selected because of condition (d), and item 1 cannot be selected because of condition (e). Note that item 4 and item 2 can both be selected. Condition (c) applies only if item 4 is not selected. Thus, if item 5, item 6, item 4, and item 2 are selected, the maximum possible number of items that can be selected is four. Therefore, the maximum possible number of items that can be selected if item 5 is selected is four.

11.1. D. $120.00

11.2. C. $117.50

For 11.1, Ace Company's chain discounts of 20% and 5% are equivalent to the single discount rate of

$$100\% - (100\% - 20\%)(100\% - 5\%) = 100\% - (80\%)(95\%) = 100\% - 76\% = 24\%$$

$$\text{discount} = \text{list price} \times \text{discount rate} = \$500 \times 24\% = \$500 \times 0.24 = \$120.00$$

For 11.2, Deuce Company's chain discounts of 15% and 10% are equivalent to the single discount rate of

$$100\% - (100\% - 15\%)(100\% - 10\%) = 100\% - (85\%)(90\%) = 100\% - 76.5\% = 23.5\%$$

$$\text{discount} = \text{list price} \times \text{discount rate} = \$500 \times 23.5\% = \$500 \times 0.235 = \$117.50$$

12.1. E. Anyone who likes swimming likes the ocean

12.2. A. Anyone who likes the ocean likes swimming

For 12.1, the correct choice is the statement for which Aziz and Presley are both committed to believing is true. Aziz's second statement that "anyone who does not like the ocean, does not like swimming" is logically equivalent to "anyone who likes swimming likes the ocean." Presley's second statement that "liking the ocean is a necessary condition for liking swimming" is also logically equivalent to "anyone who likes swimming likes the ocean." Thus, they both agree on statement E.

For 12.2, the correct choice is the statement for which one of the two people, Aziz or Pressley, is committed to believing is true, and the other person is committed to believing is false. Aziz's first statement that "Anyone who does not like swimming must not like the ocean either" is logically equivalent to "Anyone who likes the ocean likes swimming." Thus, Aziz believes statement A is true. Pressley's first statement, "That's not true. I do not like swimming, but I do like the ocean" refutes statement A and gives a counterexample. Thus, Aziz and Pressley disagree on statement A.

Statements B, C, and D are all logically equivalent to "anyone who likes the ocean does not like swimming," which Pressley does not express a committed opinion on.

13.1. C. $30R - B$

13.2. E. $\dfrac{FC \times \$100}{B}$

For 13.1, the finance charge is the difference between the sum of payments and the amount borrowed, which is $30R - B$.

For 13.2, the finance charge per $100 borrowed is

$$FC \div \dfrac{B}{\$100} = FC \times \dfrac{\$100}{B} = \dfrac{FC \times \$100}{B}$$

14.1. D. 22

14.2. A. 11

Solve $\dfrac{X(30) + Y(45)}{X + Y} = 35$ for X in terms of Y.

$$\dfrac{X(30) + Y(45)}{X + Y} = 35$$

$$35(X + Y) = 30X + 45Y$$

$$35X + 35Y = 30X + 45Y$$

$$35X - 30X = 45Y - 35Y$$

$$5X = 10Y$$

$$X = 2Y$$

Thus, the value of X is twice the value of Y. The only values in the table that satisfy this relationship are X equal to 22 and Y equal to 11.

15.1. **D.** 36

15.2. **B.** 18

Let x equal the time (in hours) it will take machine X, working alone, to finish the job, and let $y = 2x$ equal the time (in hours) it will take machine Y, working alone, to finish the job. The portion of the job that machine X can complete in one hour is $\frac{1}{x}$ and the portion of the job that machine Y can complete in one hour is $\frac{1}{2x}$. The portion of the job that the two machines, working together, can complete in one hour is $\frac{1}{12}$. Thus, $\frac{1}{x} + \frac{1}{2x} = \frac{1}{12}$. Solve this equation for x and $2x$:

$$\frac{1}{x} + \frac{1}{2x} = \frac{1}{12}$$
$$\frac{2+1}{2x} = \frac{1}{12}$$
$$\frac{3}{2x} = \frac{1}{12}$$
$$2x = 36$$
$$x = 18$$

Therefore, the time for machine X, working alone, is 18 hours, and the time for machine Y, working alone, is 36 hours.

16.1. **B. negative**

16.2. **B.** 140,000

For 16.1, the line of best fit indicates that weekly fuel consumption and weekly average hourly temperature tend to move in a linear pattern, with higher fuel consumption being associated with lower temperatures, and conversely. Therefore, the relationship between weekly fuel consumption and weekly average hourly temperature is best described as negative.

For 16.2, using (39, 10.0) and (46, 9.0), an estimate of the slope of the line of best fit is $\frac{9.0-10.0}{46-39} = -\frac{1}{7}$. Therefore, when the weekly average hourly temperature increases by 1 degree, the mean (average) weekly fuel consumption decreases (because the slope is negative) by $\frac{1}{7}(1\text{ MMcf}) = \frac{1}{7}(1,000,000\text{ ft}^3) \approx 140,000\text{ ft}^3$.

17.1. B. 2

17.2. C. 300

For 17.1, percentages for question 2 are plotted on the vertical axis. Vertically, the center of disk A is at 20%, and the center of disk B is at 40%, which is twice as much.

For 17.2, given that the diameter of disk D is twice the diameter of disk A, then the area of disk D is 4 times the area of disk A. Let $a\%$ = the percentage of customers who would recommend restaurant A to their friends. Then the percentage of customers who would recommend restaurant D to their friends is $4a\%$, which equals $a\% + 3a\% = 100\%(a\%) + 300\%(a\%)$. Therefore, the percentage of customers who would recommend restaurant D to their friends is 300% greater than the percentage of customers who would recommend restaurant A to their friends.

18.1. C. $\frac{1}{3}$

18.2. B. $\frac{3}{8}$

For 18.1, The diagram shows there are four ways for exactly one of the two marbles drawn to be red: BR, which has probability $\frac{5}{12} \cdot \frac{1}{6} = \frac{5}{72}$; GR, which has probability $\frac{1}{3} \cdot \frac{1}{6} = \frac{1}{18}$; RB, which has probability $\frac{1}{4} \cdot \frac{2}{3} = \frac{1}{6}$; and RG, which has probability $\frac{1}{4} \cdot \frac{1}{6} = \frac{1}{24}$. Therefore, the probability that exactly one of the two marbles drawn is red is $\frac{5}{72} + \frac{1}{18} + \frac{1}{6} + \frac{1}{24} = \frac{1}{3}$.

For 18.2, The diagram shows there are three ways for both marbles to be the same color: BB, which has probability $\frac{5}{12} \cdot \frac{2}{3} = \frac{5}{18}$; GG, which has probability $\frac{1}{3} \cdot \frac{1}{6} = \frac{1}{18}$; and RR, which has probability $\frac{1}{4} \cdot \frac{1}{6} = \frac{1}{24}$. Therefore, the probability that both marbles drawn will be the same color is $\frac{5}{18} + \frac{1}{18} + \frac{1}{24} = \frac{3}{8}$.

19.1. B. less than

19.2. D. 72.75

For 19.1, the histogram shows an imbalance created by the one low score between 25.5 and 40.5. The result of this imbalance is that the mean of the scores will be influenced by this low score, but the median will not. As a result, the mean of the 20 exam scores is less than the median of the 20 exam scores.

For 19.2, because of the grouping of the scores into intervals, the exact scores are not shown in the histogram. However, from the question information, you know that each score is a multiple of 5. Thus, the possible scores between 25.5 and 40.5 are 30, 35, and 40; between 55.5 and 70.5 are 60, 65, and 70; between 70.5 and 85.5 are 75, 80, and 85; and between 85.5 and 100.5 are 90, 95, and 100. There were no scores between 40.5 and 55.5, meaning there were no scores of 45, 50, or 55. The least possible mean score corresponds to the case where each student scored the minimum score in the interval in which the score falls. That is, 1 score of 30, 5 scores of 60, 9 scores of 75, and 5 scores of 90. Therefore, the least possible value for the mean (arithmetic average) score on the exam is

$$\frac{1(30) + 5(60) + 9(75) + 5(90)}{20} = \frac{1,455}{20} = 72.75$$

20.1. B $\frac{4}{13}$

20.2. A $\frac{3}{16}$

For 20.1, the diagram shows that 130 of the seniors have a home computer. Out of this 130, 40 have Wi-Fi access. Therefore, the probability that the person selected has Wi-Fi access at home, given that the person has a home computer is $\frac{40}{130} = \frac{4}{13}$.

For 20.2, out of the 160 senior citizen, 30 have Wi-Fi access, but no computer at home. Therefore, the probability that the person selected has Wi-Fi access, but no computer at home is $\frac{30}{160} = \frac{3}{16}$.

21.1. A. positive

21.2. C. 66

For 21.1, the graph shows that median annual earnings increase as educational attainment increases. This pattern is consistent from left to right across the table. Therefore, the relationship between educational attainment and median annual earnings in 2014 is best described as positive.

For 21.2, the median annual earnings in 2014 of those whose highest educational attainment was a bachelor's degree were close to 66 percent higher than the median annual earnings in 2014 of those whose highest educational attainment was high school completion. This is true because

$$\frac{\$49,900 - \$30,000}{\$30,000} \times 100\% = \frac{\$19,900}{\$30,000} \times 100\% \approx 66\%$$

22.1. B. No

22.2. B. No

22.3. A. Yes

For 22.1, the statement is not supported by the information provided. Chen provided guidance; and, given she is Allmedia's CFO, she likely expects the incentive program to yield a net profit. However, there is no information indicating that this outcome is of *primary* importance to her. Therefore, the correct answer is No.

For 22.2, Talley has concerns about the incentive program, but having these concerns does not necessarily mean that he thinks the program should be discontinued. He might just want modifications to be made to the program. Therefore, the correct answer is No.

For 22.3, from Talley's concern in his memo to Chen about the incentive program possibly leading some clients to buy advertising they don't need, you can reasonably conclude that Talley is uncomfortable with WXXX being involved with clients in that way. Therefore, the correct answer is Yes.

23.1. A. Yes

23.2. A. Yes

23.3. B. No

For 23.1, according to Talley's memo to Chen, the radio station needed $17,000 in additional monies from each incentive program participant to break even. According to Table 1, there were 12 program participants. To break even, a total of $17,000 \times 12 = $204,000$ in additional monies was needed from these clients. The table shows that the station obtained a total of $202,000 in additional monies from these 12 clients, resulting in a deficit of $204,000 - $202,000 = 2000. Therefore, the statement is true, and the correct answer is Yes.

For 23.2, Talley's memo states the radio station needed $17,000 in additional monies from each incentive program participant to break even. Table 1 shows that only four of the 10 current clients met that minimum. Therefore, the statement is true, and the correct answer is Yes.

For 23.3, the median amount of additional advertising purchased by current clients participating in the incentive program was $14,500, not $16,000. Therefore, the statement is false, and the correct answer is No.

24. **E. From a business standpoint, offering incentives to advertisers builds solid client relationships.**

Eliminate choices (A), (C), and (D) because each of these statements would indicate an unfavorable attitude toward continuing the program. Between choices (B) and (E), choice (E) would indicate more directly that Chen is in favor of continuing the program.

25.1. **A. Yes**

25.2. **B. No**

25.3. **A. Yes**

For 25.1, the statement is inferable because the superintendent begins his memo with an enthusiastic statement about the campaign. Therefore, the correct answer is Yes.

For 25.2, the superintendent's memo states that a board of trustee member will serve on the campaign committee, but there is no indication that the board member will serve as chairperson. Therefore, the correct answer is No.

For 25.3, the superintendent's memo states that the committee has already obtained federal and state authorization for the campaign. This information implies that the DW Campaign is in compliance with federal and state policies. Therefore, the correct answer is Yes.

26.1. **A. Yes**

26.2. **A. Yes**

26.3. **A. Yes**

For 26.1, the model shows funding as an input. This information assumes that funding for the campaign can be secured. Therefore, the statement is a reasonable assumption, and the correct answer is Yes.

For 26.2, the model shows the logical connections that flow from inputs to outputs to outcomes. The outcomes include short-, intermediate-, and long-term behavior outcomes related to students. This information assumes that students can and will be motivated to change. Therefore, the statement is a reasonable assumption and the correct answer is Yes.

For 26.3, the model shows that local celebrities/athletes will be enlisted to promote the campaign. This information assumes that local celebrities/athletes can be recruited to do that. Therefore, the statement is a reasonable assumption, and the correct answer is Yes.

27. **D. 53,000**

As reported in the superintendent's memo (according to the dental hygienist's presentation), nationally, 63 percent of youth consume at least one sugar-sweetened beverage daily. The superintendent's memo gives the number of students in the district as 84,000. If these students follow the national trend, then $63\%(84,000) = 52,920$ students consume at least one sugar-sweetened beverage on a given day. This number is closest to Choice (D).

Chapter 3

28. **D. 329**

Substitute 165 for C in the equation, and then solve the equation for F:

$$C = \frac{5}{9}(F - 32)$$

$$165 = \frac{5}{9}(F - 32)$$

$$\frac{9}{5} \cdot \frac{165}{1} = \frac{9}{5} \cdot \frac{5}{9}(F - 32)$$

$$\frac{9}{\cancel{5}} \cdot \frac{\cancel{165}^{33}}{1} = \frac{\cancel{9}}{\cancel{5}} \cdot \frac{\cancel{5}}{\cancel{9}}(F - 32)$$

$$297 = (F - 32)$$

$$297 = F - 32$$

$$297 + 32 = F - 32 + 32$$

$$329 = F$$

29.   B. 0.27

Let N = the total number of members in the university orchestra. The probability of randomly selecting a senior band member equals the number of senior band members in the orchestra divided by N. Choose a convenient value for N. Given that you are working with percentages, let $N = 100$. Then the number of senior orchestra member is 60%(100) = 0.6(100) = 60. Of that number, 45% are band members, so there are 45%(60) = 0.45(100) = 27 senior band members in the orchestra. Therefore, the probability of randomly selecting a senior band member is $\frac{27}{N} = \frac{27}{100} = 0.27$.

30.   B. $8 - 2\sqrt{10}$

Square the expression, and then simplify the result:

$$\left(\sqrt{4+\sqrt{6}} - \sqrt{4-\sqrt{6}}\right)^2$$
$$= \left(\sqrt{4+\sqrt{6}}\right)^2 - 2\sqrt{4+\sqrt{6}}\sqrt{4-\sqrt{6}} + \left(\sqrt{4-\sqrt{6}}\right)^2$$
$$= 4 + \sqrt{6} - 2\sqrt{16-6} + 4 - \sqrt{6}$$
$$= 8 - 2\sqrt{10}$$

31.   C. 45

This is a combination counting question. You can answer the question by finding the combination of 10 items (teams) taken 2 at a time. Using the combination formula, you have

$$_{10}C_2 = \frac{10!}{2!(10-2)!} = \frac{10!}{2!(8)!} = \frac{10 \cdot 9 \cdot 8 \cdot 7 \cdot 6 \cdot 5 \cdot 4 \cdot 3 \cdot 2 \cdot 1}{(2 \cdot 1)(8 \cdot 7 \cdot 6 \cdot 5 \cdot 4 \cdot 3 \cdot 2 \cdot 1)} =$$

$$\frac{\cancel{10}^5 \cdot 9 \cdot \cancel{8} \cdot \cancel{7} \cdot \cancel{6} \cdot \cancel{5} \cdot \cancel{4} \cdot \cancel{3} \cdot \cancel{2} \cdot \cancel{1}}{\cancel{2} \cdot 1 \cdot \cancel{8} \cdot \cancel{7} \cdot \cancel{6} \cdot \cancel{5} \cdot \cancel{4} \cdot \cancel{3} \cdot \cancel{2} \cdot \cancel{1}} = 45$$

Thus, there are 45 games in the season. (*Note:* Recall that $n!$ (read "n factorial") is the product of all positive integers descending down from n to 1.)

32.   B. 134

Illustrate the problem with a Venn diagram to answer the question. Use three overlapping circles, one for each course. Fill in the diagram using the information in the question. Start with intersections. None of the students are enrolled in both mathematics and psychology, so put 0s in the intersection of mathematics and psychology. It follows that none of the 12 students enrolled in both mathematics and English are enrolled in psychology. Those 12 students are represented in the region corresponding to mathematics and English only. Similarly, none of the 22 students enrolled in psychology and English are enrolled in mathematics. Those 12 students are represented in the region corresponding to psychology and English only. With the numbers in the intersections completed, you can determine that $52 - 12 = 40$ students are enrolled in mathematics only; $52 - 22 = 30$ students are enrolled in psychology only; and $64 - (12 + 22) = 64 - 34 = 30$ students are enrolled in English only.

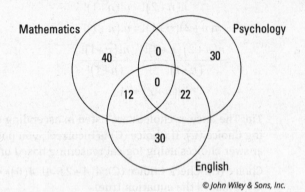

© John Wiley & Sons, Inc.

Therefore, according to the diagram, $40 + 30 + 30 + 12 + 22 = 134$ students are enrolled in at least one of these courses.

---

33. **A. 7**

Recall that $n!$ (read "n factorial") is the product of all positive integers descending down from n to 1. Given that $n!$ is divisible by 840, then it must be divisible by the factors in the prime factorization of 840. The prime factorization of 840 is $2 \cdot 3 \cdot 4 \cdot 5 \cdot 7$. Therefore, $n!$ must have factors of 2, 3, 4, 5, and 7. The least positive value of n such that $n!$ contains these factors is 7 (because $7! = 7 \cdot 6 \cdot 5 \cdot 4 \cdot 3 \cdot 2 \cdot 1$).

---

34. **D. 34**

$15! = 15 \cdot 14 \cdot 13 \cdot 12 \cdot 11 \cdot 10 \cdot 9 \cdot 8 \cdot 7 \cdot 6 \cdot 5 \cdot 4 \cdot 3 \cdot 2 \cdot 1$. Thus, any number ≤ 15 is a factor of 15! Eliminate Choice (A) because 14 is a factor of 15! Eliminate Choice B because 22 is a factor of 15! (given that $22 = 2 \cdot 11$). Eliminate Choice (C) because 19 is a prime number. Choice (D) is not a prime number and $34 = 2 \cdot 17$ is not a factor of 15! Thus, 34 is the least integer that satisfies the requirements given in the question. You do not have to check Choice (E) because $34 < 38$.

35.   C. 4

Using your knowledge that the factorial of a positive integer k is the product of all positive integers descending down from k to 1, simplify the equation. Next, check the answer choices to find a value for n that makes the simplified equation true.

$$n(n+2)! = n!(n+1)!$$
$$n(n+2)(n+1)! = n!(n+1)!$$
$$\frac{n(n+2)\cancel{(n+1)!}}{\cancel{(n+1)!}} = \frac{n!\cancel{(n+1)!}}{\cancel{(n+1)!}}$$
$$n(n+2) = n!$$

Tip: The answer choices are listed in ascending order, so start by checking Choice (C). If Choice (C) is incorrect, you possibly can eliminate other answer choices using logical reasoning based on the result obtained with Choice (C). Check Choice (C): $4(4+2)\overset{?}{=}4!$; $4(6)\overset{?}{=}4\cdot3\cdot2\cdot1$; $24\overset{\checkmark}{=}24$. Thus, $n = 4$ makes the equation true.

36.   E. 20

Let t = the time (in hours) it would take Melora, working alone, to paint the room. The portion of the room Melora, working alone, can paint in one hour is $\frac{1}{t}$. The portion of the room Kyra and Sage, working together, can paint in one hour is $\frac{1}{5}$. The portion of the room the three of them, working together, can paint in one hour is $\frac{1}{4}$. Therefore, $\frac{1}{t}+\frac{1}{5}=\frac{1}{4}$. Solve the equation:

$$\frac{1}{t}+\frac{1}{5}=\frac{1}{4}$$
$$\frac{1}{t}=\frac{1}{4}-\frac{1}{5}$$
$$\frac{1}{t}=\frac{5}{20}-\frac{4}{20}$$
$$\frac{1}{t}=\frac{1}{20}$$
$$t = 20$$

Melora would take 20 hours, working alone, to paint the room.

37.   A. 10π

An angle inscribed in a semicircle is a right angle. Thus, triangle PQR is a right triangle with legs of lengths 16 and 12. The length, PR, of the hypotenuse is $\sqrt{16^2+12^2} = \sqrt{256+144} = \sqrt{400} = 20$. Thus, the diameter of the semicircle is 20. The length of the arc PQR is half the circumference of the circle that contains the semicircle. This length is $\frac{1}{2}\pi d = \frac{1}{2}\pi(20) = 10\pi$.

38. D. $2A - 16$

The sum, S, of all 20 numbers divided by 20 equals A; that is, $\frac{S}{20} = A$. Hence, $S = 20A$. Similarly, the sum of the 10 numbers whose average is 16 equals $(10)(16) = 160$. Therefore, the sum of the remaining 10 numbers is $S - 160 = 20A - 160$. The average of these 10 numbers is $\frac{20A - 160}{10} = 2A - 16$.

39. C. $1,200

Let x = the amount (in dollars) allocated for utilities, $3x$ = the amount (in dollars) allocated for food, and $5x$ = the amount (in dollars) allocated for home mortgage payment. Solve the equation for x, and then determine $3x$, the amount allocated for food.

$$5x + 3x + x = \$3,600$$
$$9x = \$3,600$$
$$x = \$400$$
$$3x = \$1,200$$

The amount allocated for food is $1,200.

40. A. $500 - c - d + b$

Illustrate the problem with a Venn diagram to answer the question. Use two overlapping circles, labeled C for cat ownership and D for dog ownership. Fill in the diagram using the information in the question. Start with the intersection. There are b students in the intersection. It follows that $c - b$ students are cat only owners and $d - b$ students are dog only owners.

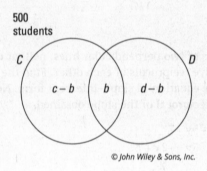

© John Wiley & Sons, Inc.

Therefore, according to the diagram, the number of students who own neither a cat nor a dog is

$$500 - \big[(c - b) + b + (d - b)\big] = 500 - \big[c - b + b + d - b\big] =$$
$$500 - c + b - b - d + b = 500 - c - d + b$$

41. E. 21

The second plant grew 6 inches plus 250% of 6 inches, which is

$6 \text{ in} + 250\% (6 \text{ in}) = 6 \text{ in} + 2.5(6 \text{ in}) = 6 \text{ in} + 15 \text{ in} = 21 \text{ in}$

42. B. II only

Because 15! is the product all positive integers descending down from 15 to 1, 13 (II) is a factor of 15! Also, 13 is a factor of 13. Hence, 13 is a common factor of 15! and 13, so it is a factor of the sum $(15! + 13)$. Thus, the correct answer choice must include II. Eliminate Choice (A). If you assume 11 (I) is a factor of $(15! + 13)$, then given that 11 is also a factor of 15!, it would follow that 11 is a factor of $(15! + 13) - 15! = 15! + 13 - 15! = 13$. But 11 is not a factor of 13 which implies that your assumption is false, meaning 11 is not a factor of $(15! + 13)$. In a similar manner, you can show that 15 (III) also is not a factor of $(15! + 13)$. Eliminate choices (C), (D), and (E), leaving Choice (B), II only, as the correct answer choice.

43. E. 12

Simplify the expression using scientific notation and the rules for exponents.

$$(0.00005)(0.0005)(0.005) \times 10^p = (5 \times 10^{-5})(5 \times 10^{-4})(5 \times 10^{-3}) \times 10^p = 125 \times 10^{p-12}$$

Thus, the product $125 \times 10^{p-12}$ is an integer. Given that 125 is an integer, then 10^{p-12} must be an integer as well. Thus, $p - 12 \geq 0$. Therefore, the least possible value of $p - 12$ is 0, which implies that the least possible value of p is 12.

44. E. 2.5

The slopes of two perpendicular lines, neither of which is a vertical line, are negative reciprocals of each other. Find the slope of the given line by writing its equation in slope–intercept form. Next, determine the negative reciprocal of the slope obtained.

$$2x + 5y = 7$$
$$5y = -2x + 7$$
$$y = -\frac{2}{5}x + \frac{7}{5}$$

The slope of the given line is $-\frac{2}{5}$. The negative reciprocal of this slope is $\frac{5}{2} = 2.5$.

45. D. 9,515

Let N = the attendance on the final day of the festival. Solve the equation:

$$N + 20\%N = 11,418$$
$$N + 0.2N = 11,418$$
$$1.2N = 11,418$$
$$\frac{1.2N}{1.2} = \frac{11,418}{1.2}$$
$$N = 9,515$$

The attendance on the final day was 9,515.

46. D. 3.6

Let t = the time (in hours) it would take if both inlet pipes are opened simultaneously. The portion of the cistern's capacity that the first inlet pipe can fill in one hour is $\dfrac{\left(\frac{1}{3}\right)}{3} = \dfrac{1}{3} \times \dfrac{1}{3} = \dfrac{1}{9}$. The portion of the cistern's capacity that the second inlet pipe can fill in one hour is

$\dfrac{\frac{3}{4}}{4.5} = \dfrac{\frac{3}{4}}{4\frac{1}{2}} = \dfrac{\frac{3}{4}}{\frac{9}{2}} = \dfrac{\cancel{3}^1}{\cancel{4}^2} \times \dfrac{\cancel{2}^1}{\cancel{9}^3} = \dfrac{1}{6}$. If both pipes are opened simultaneously, the

portion of the cistern's capacity they can fill in one hour is $\dfrac{1}{t}$. Therefore, $\dfrac{1}{6} + \dfrac{1}{9} = \dfrac{1}{t}$. Solve the equation:

$$\frac{1}{6} + \frac{1}{9} = \frac{1}{t}$$
$$\frac{3}{18} + \frac{2}{18} = \frac{1}{t}$$
$$\frac{5}{18} = \frac{1}{t}$$
$$5t = 18$$
$$t = 3.6$$

It will take 3.6 hours to fill the tank.

47. C. 90

Let N = the number of marbles in the box. The fraction of N that are yellow is

$$1 - \left(\frac{1}{2} + \frac{1}{3} + \frac{1}{10}\right) = 1 - \left(\frac{15}{30} + \frac{10}{30} + \frac{3}{30}\right) = 1 - \frac{28}{30} = \frac{2}{30} = \frac{1}{15}$$

Therefore, $\dfrac{1}{15}N = 6$, which implies $N = 15 \cdot 6 = 90$.

48. A. 60

Let W = the garden's width (in feet) and $L = 2W$ = the garden's length (in feet). The formula for the perimeter of a rectangle is $2(L+W)$, where L is the rectangle's length and W is its width. Substitute into the formula and solve for W, and then find $2W$, the garden's length.

$$2(L+W) = 180$$
$$2(2W+W) = 180$$
$$2(3W) = 180$$
$$6W = 180$$
$$W = 30$$
$$L = 2W = 60$$

The garden's length is 60 feet.

49. B. –1.25

Solve the equation:

$$\left(2 - 2\frac{4}{5}\right)x = 1$$
$$-\frac{4}{5}x = 1$$
$$x = -\frac{5}{4}$$
$$x = -1.25$$

50. D. I and II only

The expression in I is rational because $\dfrac{\sqrt{46}\sqrt{46}}{(46)^2} = \dfrac{46}{46^2} = \dfrac{1}{46}$,

which is rational. The correct answer must contain I, so eliminate choices (B), (C), and (E). The expression in II is rational because $\left(\sqrt{46} + \sqrt{46}\right)^2 = \left(2\sqrt{46}\right)^2 = 4 \cdot 46 = 184$, which is rational. The correct answer must contain II. Eliminate Choice (A). Therefore, I and II only is the correct answer. Just to verify, the expression in III is not rational because it is the product of a rational number, 46, and an irrational number, $\sqrt{46}$.

51. B. $N + 562$

Using the distributive property, $(562)(9k+1) = (562)(9k) + 562$. Substitute $N = (562)(9k)$ to obtain $(562)(9k) + 562 = N + 562$.

52. D. 50

Let N = the minimum number of seeds that should be planted. According to the question information, $60\%N = 30$. Solve the equation:

$$60\%N = 30$$
$$\frac{3}{5}N = 30$$
$$\frac{\cancel{5}}{\cancel{3}} \cdot \frac{\cancel{3}}{\cancel{5}}N = \frac{5}{\cancel{3}} \cdot \cancel{30}^{10}$$
$$N = 50$$

53. D. 4,000

Let A = the size (in acres) of the original field. Then $90\%A$ = the size (in acres) of the cleared land. The percent of the cleared land planted in gooseberry plants is $100\% - (50\% + 40\%) = 100\% - 90\% = 10\%$. Therefore, $10\%(90\%A) = 360$. Solve the equation:

$$10\%(90\%A) = 360$$
$$0.10(0.90A) = 360$$
$$0.09A = 360$$
$$A = 4,000$$

The size of the original field is 4,000 acres.

54. C. $\frac{1}{12}$

Simplify the expression:

$$\frac{1}{\left(\frac{1}{2}-2\right)} + \frac{1}{\left(\frac{4}{3}\right)} = \frac{1}{\frac{1}{2}-\frac{4}{2}} + \frac{1}{\frac{4}{3}} = \frac{1}{-\frac{3}{2}} + \frac{1}{\frac{4}{3}} = -\frac{2}{3} + \frac{3}{4} = -\frac{8}{12} + \frac{9}{12} = \frac{1}{12}$$

55. A. 8:1

Let n = the number of triangles; then $2n$ = the number of circles; and $4(2n) = 8n$ = the number of squares. The ratio of the number of squares to the number of triangles is $\frac{8n}{n} = \frac{8}{1}$ or 8:1.

56.   D. 360

Let x = the number of students who like only one of the juices, y = the number of students who like exactly two of the juices, and z = the number of students who like exactly three of the juices. Then $x + y + z = 600$ because all of the participants like at least one of these juices. From the question information $y = 35\%(600) = 210$, which implies that $x + z = 600 - 210 = 390$. Now, let O = the number of students who like orange juice, A = the number of students who like apple juice, and G = the number of students who like grape juice. From the question information:

$$O = 75\%(600) = 0.75(600) = 450$$

$$A = 40\%(600) = 0.40(600) = 240$$

$$G = 30\%(600) = 0.30(600) = 180$$

The sum of O, A, and G will count x exactly one time, y exactly two times, and z exactly three times. Thus,

$$x + 2(210) + 3z = O + A + G$$
$$x + 2(210) + 3z = 450 + 240 + 180$$
$$x + 420 + 3z = 870$$
$$x + 3z = 450$$

Solve $x + z = 390$ and $x + 3z = 450$ simultaneously. Solving $x + z = 390$ for z yields $z = 390 - x$. Substituting this result *into* $x + 3z = 450$ yields

$$x + 3(390 - x) = 450$$
$$x + 1{,}170 - 3x = 450$$
$$-2x = -720$$
$$x = 360$$

Therefore, 360 survey participants like only one of the juices.

57.   D. $\frac{1}{4}$

For each equation, set each factor equal to 0 and solve for x. For the first equation $(2x + 1) = 0$ implies $x = -\frac{1}{2}$ and $(4x - 1) = 0$ implies $x = \frac{1}{4}$. For the second equation $(5x - 1) = 0$ implies $x = \frac{1}{5}$ and $\left(x - \frac{1}{4}\right) = 0$ implies $x = \frac{1}{4}$. Therefore, the simultaneous solution is $x = \frac{1}{4}$.

58. **A. 15**

Let N = the number of nonfiction books last year and F = the number of fiction books last year. Then $\frac{N}{F} = \frac{1}{30}$ and $\frac{N+5}{F+50} = \frac{1}{25}$. Solve these two equations simultaneously. Solving $\frac{N}{F} = \frac{1}{30}$ for F yields $F = 30N$.

Substituting this result into $\frac{N+5}{F+50} = \frac{1}{25}$ yields

$$\frac{N+5}{30N+50} = \frac{1}{25}$$
$$(30N+50)(1) = (25)(N+5)$$
$$30N+50 = 25N+125$$
$$5N = 75$$
$$N = 15$$

The number of nonfiction books last year was 15.

59. **C.** $\left(\dfrac{1-a}{1+a}\right)^2$

Find $f\left(\dfrac{1}{a}\right)$ and simplify.

$$f(x) = \left(\frac{x-1}{x+1}\right)^2$$

$$f\left(\frac{1}{a}\right) = \left(\frac{\frac{1}{a}-1}{\frac{1}{a}+1}\right)^2 = \left(\frac{a\left(\frac{1}{a}-1\right)}{a\left(\frac{1}{a}+1\right)}\right)^2 = \left(\frac{1-a}{1+a}\right)^2$$

60. **D. 30**

First find the prime factorization of 5,880 using a systematic approach similar to the one shown here:

$$5,880 = 2 \times 2,940 = 2 \times 2 \times 1,470 =$$
$$2 \times 2 \times 2 \times 735 = 2 \times 2 \times 2 \times 3 \times 245 =$$
$$2 \times 2 \times 2 \times 3 \times 5 \times 49 = 2 \times 2 \times 2 \times 3 \times 5 \times 7 \times 7 =$$
$$2^3 \times 3 \times 5 \times 7^2$$

To be a perfect square, the prime factors of $5,880k$ must have even exponents. Therefore, k must contain at least one factor each of 2, 3, and 5. Hence, the least value of k is $2 \times 3 \times 5 = 30$.

61. D. $1 : \sqrt{3}$

Consecutive interior angles of a rhombus are supplementary, so the measure of $\angle D = 180° - 120° = 60°$. The diagonals of a rhombus are perpendicular bisectors of each other and bisect the angles of the rhombus. Construct the diagonals of the rhombus. Label the intersection E. Thus, triangle AED below is a 30°-60°-90° right triangle, with hypotenuse $\overline{AD}$ and legs $\overline{AE}$ and $\overline{DE}$.

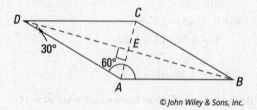

© John Wiley & Sons, Inc.

Given that the diagonals bisect each other, the length of $\overline{AC}$ is twice the length of $\overline{AE}$, and the length of $\overline{DB}$ is twice the length of $\overline{DE}$. Hence, the ratio of the length of $\overline{AC}$ to the length of $\overline{DB}$ is the same as the ratio of the length of $\overline{AE}$ to the length of $\overline{DE}$. The lengths of the sides of a 30°-60°-90° right triangle are in the ratio $\frac{1}{2} : \frac{\sqrt{3}}{2} : 1$. Therefore, the ratio of the length of $\overline{AC}$ to $\overline{DB}$ equals the ratio of the length of $\overline{AE}$ to $\overline{DE}$ equals $\frac{1}{2} : \frac{\sqrt{3}}{2}$, which is $1 : \sqrt{3}$ in simplified form.

62. C. Four

If $\frac{n}{5}$ = the square of a prime number, then $n = 5($the square of a prime number$)$. For each of the first five prime numbers (2, 3, 5, 7, and 11), compute 5 times its square to obtain the following values:

$$5\left(2^2\right) = 20, \ 5\left(3^2\right) = 45, \ 5\left(5^2\right) = 125, \ 5\left(7^2\right) = 245, \ 5\left(11^2\right) = 605$$

Only four of these values (20, 45, 125, and 245) lie between 15 and 250; and, thus, are possible values of n. Therefore, there are four possible values of n for which $\frac{n}{5}$ is the square of a prime number.

63. B. 0.032

The probability of guessing correctly is $\frac{1}{5} = 0.2$. Then the probability of guessing incorrectly is $\frac{4}{5} = 0.8$. Each guess is independent of the next, so the probability that the player's turn ends after three guesses is the product of the probability of guessing correctly twice followed by guessing incorrectly once. This product is $(0.2)(0.2)(0.8) = 0.032$.

64. D. 60%

Let $P(A)$ = the probability that team A wins the tournament and $P(B)$ = the probability that team B wins the tournament. Then according to the question information, $P(A) = 1 - 80\% = 20\%$ and $P(B) = 1 - 60\% = 40\%$. Given that there is only one tournament winner, the event that team A wins the tournament and the event that team B wins are mutually exclusive, meaning they cannot occur at the same time. Therefore, the probability that team A or team B wins the tournament equals $P(A) + P(B) = 20\% + 40\% = 60\%$.

65. B. 9

Determine the number of factors of 3 that are contained in 21!. As shown below, 21! is the product of all positive integers descending down from 21 to 1.

$$21! = 21 \cdot 20 \cdot 19 \cdot 18 \cdot 17 \cdot 16 \cdot 15 \cdot 14 \cdot 13 \cdot 12 \cdot 11 \cdot 10 \cdot 9 \cdot 8 \cdot 7 \cdot 6 \cdot 5 \cdot 4 \cdot 3 \cdot 2 \cdot 1$$

In this product, $21 (= 3 \times 7)$ has 1 factor of 3, $18 (= 2 \times 3 \times 3)$ has 2 factors of 3, $15 (= 3 \times 5)$ has 1 factor of 3, $12 (= 2 \times 2 \times 3)$ has one factor of 3, $9 (= 3 \times 3)$ has 2 factors of 3, $6 (= 2 \times 3)$ has 1 factor of 3, and $3 (= 1 \times 3)$ has 1 factor of 3. None of the other factors in 21! has a factor of 3. Thus, the total number of factors of 3 in 21! is $1 + 2 + 1 + 1 + 2 + 1 + 1 = 9$. Therefore, the greatest integer p for which 3^k is a factor of 21! is 9.

66. E. 27

Square both sides of the equation and then determine x.

$$\sqrt{\frac{x}{3}} = 3$$

$$\left(\sqrt{\frac{x}{3}}\right)^2 = 3^2$$

$$\frac{x}{3} = 9$$

$$x = 27$$

67. D. 270

According to the figure, triangles ABC and DEC are right triangles, segments $\overline{AB}$ and $\overline{DE}$ are parallel (because they are both perpendicular to the same line), and the measure of $\angle A$ is 55°. The measure of $\angle CDE$ is 55° (because $\angle A$ and $\angle CDE$ are corresponding angles of parallel lines). Thus, $x° = 180° - 55° = 125°$. Also, $y° = 90° + 55° = 145°$ (because the measure of an exterior angle of a triangle equals the sum of the measures of the nonadjacent interior angles). Therefore, $x + y = 125 + 145 = 270$.

68. **A.** $\dfrac{4k-12}{k(k-4)}$

Each of the three circles is divided into k equal parts, so each part is $\dfrac{1}{k}$ of a circle. The fourth circle is divided into $k-4$ equal parts, so each part is $\dfrac{1}{k-4}$ of a circle. The child colored one of the k parts in each of the three circles, and one of the $k-4$ parts in the fourth circle. Thus, the total fraction of a whole circle that the child colored is

$$3\left(\dfrac{1}{k}\right)+\dfrac{1}{k-4}=\dfrac{3}{k}+\dfrac{1}{k-4}=\dfrac{3(k-4)}{k(k-4)}+\dfrac{k\cdot1}{k(k-4)}=$$

$$\dfrac{3k-12}{k(k-4)}+\dfrac{k}{k(k-4)}=\dfrac{3k-12+k}{k(k-4)}=\dfrac{4k-12}{k(k-4)}$$

69. **B. 36**

In a 5-digit number there are five place values to fill. If there were no restrictions on the placement of the two 3s, the number of ways to select two locations for the two 3s from the five place value slots is the combination of 5 things taken 2 at a time. This number is

$$_5C_2=\dfrac{5!}{2!3!}=\dfrac{5\cdot4\cdot3\cdot2\cdot1}{(2\cdot1)(3\cdot2\cdot1)}=\dfrac{5\cdot\cancel{4}^2\cdot\cancel{3}\cdot\cancel{2}\cdot\cancel{1}}{\cancel{2}\cdot1\cdot\cancel{3}\cdot\cancel{2}\cdot\cancel{1}}=10.$$

However, you must remove from this number, the number of ways for the two 3s to be adjacent to each other. There are four ways for the two 3s to be adjacent to each other as illustrated here with ? marks taking the place of the other three digits: 33???, ?33??, ??33?, and ???33. Therefore, the number of ways to select the location for the two 3s is the number of ways to select two of the five place value locations minus the four ways in which the two selected locations would be adjacent. This number is $10-4=6$. Now, for each of these 6 ways, there are $3\cdot2\cdot1=6$ ways to arrange the other three digits. This is true because there are 3 ways to select the first digit; and, for each of these ways, there are 2 ways to select the next digit; and, for each of these ways, there is just 1 way to select the last digit. Therefore, there are $6\cdot6=36$ ways to arrange the given digits into a 5-digit number so that the two occurrences of the digit 3 are separated by at least one other digit.

70. **D. 32**

Let L be the length of the patio (in feet), then $\dfrac{3.5}{2}=\dfrac{L}{18}$. Solve the equation:

$$\dfrac{3.5}{2}=\dfrac{L}{18}$$
$$2L=(3.5)(18)$$
$$2L=63$$
$$L=31.5$$

The length is closest to 32.

71.   C. 16%

The curve is symmetric about M, so 50% of the scores are above M (and 50% are below). Again, due to symmetry about M, $\frac{68\%}{2} = 32\%$ of the scores are between M and $M + S$. Therefore, $50\% - 32\% = 16\%$ of the scores are greater than $M + S$.

72.   D. 50

For the estimated time, $RT = 800$; and for the actual time, $(T + 4)(R - 10) = 800$. Solve these two equations simultaneously. Solving $RT = 800$ for T yields $T = \frac{800}{R}$. Substituting this result into $(T + 4)(R - 10) = 800$ yields

$$\left(\frac{800}{R} + 4\right)(R - 10) = 800$$

$$800 - \frac{8,000}{R} + 4R - 40 = 800$$

$$-\frac{8,000}{R} + 4R - 40 = 0$$

$$R\left(-\frac{8,000}{R} + 4R - 40\right) = R \cdot 0$$

$$-8,000 + 4R^2 - 40R = 0$$

$$4R^2 - 40R - 8,000 = 0$$

$$\frac{1}{4}\left(4R^2 - 40R - 8,000\right) = \frac{1}{4} \cdot 0$$

$$R^2 - 10R - 2,000 = 0$$

$$(R + 40)(R - 50) = 0$$

$$(R + 40) = 0 \text{ or } (R - 50) = 0$$

$$R = -40 \text{ (reject) or } R = 50$$

Reject $R = -40$ because the rate cannot be negative. Therefore, the painter's regular rate is $50 per hour. *Note:* In this problem, you are permitted to divide and multiply both sides of an equation by R because the question information implies that $R > 0$.

73.   B. 7

Because $27 = 3^3$, rewrite the given equality as $\left(3^3\right)^p > 3^{18}$, which simplifies to $3^{3p} > 3^{18}$. It follows that p is the least integer such that $3p > 18$ or, equivalently, $p > 6$, which is 7.

74. B. 11

From the question information, $M = x \oplus y = 10x + y$ and $N = y \oplus x = 10y + x$. Hence,

$$M + N = (10x + y) + (10y + x) = 10x + y + 10y + x = 11x + 11y = 11(x + y)$$

Given that x and y are positive integers, then $(x + y)$ is an integer, which implies that 11 must be a factor of $M + N$. None of the other answer choices must be a factor of $M + N$.

75. D. 0.05

Use your knowledge of square roots to simplify the expression.

$$\sqrt{\sqrt{0.00000625}} = \sqrt{0.0025} = 0.05$$

76. C. 19

Use logical reasoning to determine the solution. The difference (in years) between the mother's age and the son's age is $37 - 9 = 28$. Therefore, when the son is 28 years old, the mother will be $2(28 \text{ years}) = 56$ years old. The son is 9 years old, so in 19 years (because $28 - 9 = 19$), he will be 28 years old and his mother will be 56 years old, twice his age.

77. E. 60

Lupita's schedule (in days) is 12, 24, 36, 48, **60**, and so on. Vin's schedule (in days) is 15, 30, 45, **60**, and so on. The number of days until the next time both will swim at that same gym is 60, which is the least common multiple of 12 and 15.

78. A. $\dfrac{3x + 5y}{xy}$

Combine the two fractions algebraically by using a common denominator of xy.

$$\frac{5}{x} + \frac{3}{y} = \frac{5y}{xy} + \frac{3x}{xy} = \frac{5y + 3x}{xy} = \frac{3x + 5y}{xy}$$

79. E. $\dfrac{1}{\sqrt{s^2 + 9}}$

Use your knowledge of exponents and algebraic manipulation to simplify the expression.

$$(s^2 + 9)^{-\frac{1}{2}} = \frac{1}{(s^2 + 9)^{\frac{1}{2}}} = \frac{1}{\sqrt{s^2 + 9}}$$

80. B. $5^k\left(2^k+1\right)$

Use your knowledge of exponents and algebraic manipulation to simplify the expression.

$$10^k + 5^k = \left(5\cdot2\right)^k + 5^k = 5^k \cdot 2^k + 5^k = 5^k\left(2^k + 1\right)$$

81. D. I and III only

Because m and n are positive integers, their sum, $m+n$, is a positive integer. Given that m is three times n, let $m=3n$. Then $m+n=3n+n=4n$. This result implies that $m+n$ is divisible by 4. A number is divisible by 4 if and only if its last two digits form a number that is divisible by 4. Of the Roman choices given, only 314 (II) fails the test for divisibility by 4 (because the last two digits of 314 are 14, which is not divisible). Therefore, $m+n$ could be 216 (I) or 1,048 (III) only.

82. C. 900

From the figure, $\triangle ABC$ is a right triangle. To find the area of a right triangle, you find $\frac{1}{2}$ the product of the lengths of the two legs. To find the area of $\triangle ABC$, First, determine CA, the length of leg $\overline{CA}$. Next, determine BC, the length of leg $\overline{BC}$. Then find the area of $\triangle ABC$ by calculating $\frac{1}{2}bh = \frac{1}{2}(CA)(BC)$. First, find CA by adding the lengths of the two segments, $\overline{CE}$ and $\overline{EA}$: $CA = 40$ ft $+ 20$ ft $= 60$ ft. Next, to find BC, observe that right triangles ABC and ADE are similar triangles because they have the acute angle A in common. Using properties of similar triangles,

$$\frac{BC}{60 \text{ ft}} = \frac{\overset{1}{\cancel{10}} \text{ ft}}{\underset{2}{\cancel{20}} \text{ ft}}$$
$$2BC = 60 \text{ ft}$$
$$BC = 30 \text{ ft}$$

Thus, the area of $\triangle ABC$ is $\frac{1}{2}bh = \frac{1}{2}(CA)(BC) = \frac{1}{2}(60 \text{ ft})(30 \text{ ft}) = 900 \text{ ft}^2$.

83. C. 20

The pole, the wire, and the ground form a right triangle. The wire is the hypotenuse of a right triangle that has legs of lengths 16 and 12, in feet. Use the Pythagorean theorem to find the length of the hypotenuse, denoted by c.

$$c^2 = 16^2 + 12^2$$
$$c^2 = 256 + 144$$
$$c^2 = 400$$
$$c = \sqrt{400} = 20$$

(*Note:* −20 is also a solution, but it is rejected because length is positive.)

The length of the wire is 20 feet.

84.   E. 20,000

Divide 8×10^2 by 4×10^{-2}.

$$\frac{8 \times 10^2}{4 \times 10^{-2}} = \frac{\overset{2}{\cancel{8}} \times 10^2}{\underset{1}{\cancel{4}} \times 10^{-2}} = 2 \times 10^{2-(-2)} = 2 \times 10^{2+2} = 2 \times 10^4 = 20,000$$

The number of grams of sugar in solution Y is 20,000 times the number of grams of sugar in solution X.

85.   E. 840

The number of different arrangements to seat four spectators in four of seven empty stadium seats that are all in the same row is the number of ways to select the four seats times the number of different arrangements of four spectators in four seats. First, consider selection of four of the seven empty stadium seats. Because different orderings of the seat selection does not produce different arrangements, the number of ways to select four of seven seats is the combination of 7 items taken 4 at a time, which is

$$_7C_4 = \frac{7!}{4!3!} = \frac{7 \cdot 6 \cdot 5 \cdot 4 \cdot 3 \cdot 2 \cdot 1}{(4 \cdot 3 \cdot 2 \cdot 1)(3 \cdot 2 \cdot 1)} = \frac{7 \cdot \cancel{6} \cdot 5 \cdot \cancel{4} \cdot \cancel{3} \cdot \cancel{2} \cdot \cancel{1}}{\cancel{4} \cdot \cancel{3} \cdot \cancel{2} \cdot 1 \cdot \cancel{3} \cdot \cancel{2} \cdot \cancel{1}} = 35$$

Next, consider the arrangement of the four spectators in the four seats. Because different orderings of the spectators results in different arrangements, the number of different arrangements to seat the four spectators in four seats is $4 \cdot 3 \cdot 2 \cdot 1 = 24$. This is true because there are 4 ways to seat someone in the first seat. And for each of these ways, there are 3 ways to seat a person in the second seat, and so on. Therefore, The number of different arrangements to seat four spectators in four of seven empty stadium seats in the same row is $35 \cdot 24 = 840$.

86.   E. $\frac{11}{20}$

This question asks you to find a conditional probability; that is, you are to find the probability when you already know that the student is a seventh grader. Thus, when computing the probability, the number of possible students under consideration is no longer 300, but is reduced to the total number of seventh graders, which is 100. According to the table, 55 of the 100 seventh graders own a cell phone. Therefore, the probability a randomly selected student owns a cell phone given that the student is a seventh grader equals $\frac{55}{100} = \frac{11}{20}$.

87. **B. 15%**

Fill in the missing probabilities.

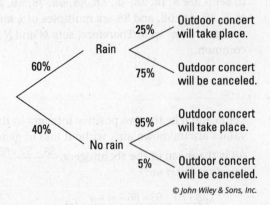

© John Wiley & Sons, Inc.

With probability tree diagrams, you multiply along the branches to determine the probability of the outcome at the end of the branch. Therefore, the probability that the concert takes place given that it rains is $(60\%)(25\%) = (0.60)(0.25) = 0.15 = 15\%$.

88. **D. $(26^2)(10^4)$**

There are six slots to be filled, so to speak, on the license plate. There are 26 possible choices for each of the two letters, and there are 10 possible choices for each of the four digits, which means the total number of possible license plate alphanumeric codes is $26 \cdot 26 \cdot 10 \cdot 10 \cdot 10 \cdot 10 = (26^2)(10^4)$.

89. **E. 5.4**

To find the rate of gallons per day, change 15 hours to days, and then divide $3\frac{3}{8}$ gallons by the result.

$$15\ hr \times \frac{1\ day}{24\ hr} = \frac{\cancel{15}^{5}\ \cancel{hr}}{1} \times \frac{1\ day}{\cancel{24}^{8}\ \cancel{hr}} = \frac{5}{8}\ day$$

$$\frac{3\frac{3}{8}\ gal}{\frac{5}{8}\ day} = \frac{\frac{27}{8}}{\frac{5}{8}} \cdot \frac{gal}{day} = \frac{\cancel{8}\left(\frac{27}{8}\right)}{\cancel{8}\left(\frac{5}{8}\right)} \cdot \frac{gal}{day} = \frac{27}{5}\ \frac{gal}{day} = 5.4\ gal/day$$

The motor's fuel consumption rate is 5.4 gallons per day.

90. **C. Five**

The integers in set M are 4, 8, 12, 16, 20, 24, 28, and so on. The integers in set N are 8, 18, 28, 38, 48, 58, 68, 78, 88, and 98. Of the integers in set N, 8, 28, 48, 68, and 88 are multiples of 4 and therefore these integers are in set M as well. Therefore, sets M and N have five numbers in common.

91. **D. 161**

Let m and n be the two positive integers in the list of six integers whose values are unknown and, without loss of generality, let $m > n$. Given that 68 is the mean of the six integers, $\dfrac{38+57+65+86+m+n}{6} = 68$. Solve this equation for $m+n$:

$$\frac{38+57+65+86+m+n}{6} = 68$$
$$38+57+65+86+m+n = 6(68)$$
$$38+57+65+86+m+n = 408$$
$$246+m+n = 408$$
$$m+n = 162$$

Because m and n are positive integers, the least that n can be is 1. Therefore, the greatest that m can be is 161.

92. **A. 114**

Of the 75 students who are enrolled in a science course, 34 are not enrolled in a sociology course. It follows that $75 - 34 = 41$ students are enrolled in both a science course and a sociology course. Of the 52 students who are enrolled in a sociology course, $52 - 41 = 11$ students are enrolled in a sociology course only. Sketch a Venn diagram to illustrate the information.

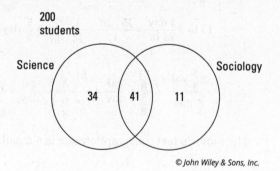

© John Wiley & Sons, Inc.

The entire rectangle represents the 200 students. The region that is outside the two intersecting circles represents the students who are enrolled in neither a science course nor a sociology course. From the diagram, this number is

$$200 - (34 + 41 + 11) = 200 - 86 = 114.$$

93.   D. $20 + 12\sqrt{5}$

The perimeter of $\triangle PQR = PQ + QR + PR$. From the information given, $PR = PS + RS = 16 + 4 = 20$. Now, determine PQ and QR to find the perimeter. The length of the altitude to the hypotenuse of a right triangle is the geometric mean of the lengths of the two segments into which it separates the hypotenuse. Let x = the altitude's length. Then $\frac{PS}{x} = \frac{x}{RS}$. Substitute $PS = 16$ and $RS = 4$, and then solve for x.

$$\frac{16}{x} = \frac{x}{4}$$
$$x^2 = 64$$
$$x = 8$$

(*Note:* The number -8 is also a solution, but it is rejected because length is positive.). Use the Pythagorean theorem to solve for PQ and QR.

$$PQ = \sqrt{16^2 + 8^2} = \sqrt{256 + 64} = \sqrt{320} = \sqrt{64 \cdot 5} = 8\sqrt{5}$$

and

$$QR = \sqrt{4^2 + 8^2} = \sqrt{16 + 64} = \sqrt{80} = \sqrt{16 \cdot 5} = 4\sqrt{5}$$

Therefore, the perimeter of $\triangle PQR = 20 + 8\sqrt{5} + 4\sqrt{5} = 20 + 12\sqrt{5}$.

94.   D. $\frac{7}{11}$

Let F = the number of female students enrolled a year ago and M = the number of male students enrolled a year ago. Then the enrollment a year ago is $F + M$ and the number of students currently enrolled =

$$(F + M) + 10\%(F + M) = (F + M) + 0.10(F + M) =$$
$$1.10(F + M) = 1.10F + 1.10M$$

The number of female students currently enrolled = $F + 5\%F = F + 0.05F = 1.05F$ and the number of male students currently enrolled = $M + 20\%M = M + 0.20M = 1.20M$. It follows that $1.05F + 1.20M = 1.10F + 1.10M$, which implies that $0.10M = 0.05F$, or equivalently, $2M = F$.

This result tells you that a year ago, there were twice as many female students as male students at the private school. Pick convenient values for M and F that satisfy this relationship. For example, let $M = 100$ and $F = 200$. With these hypothetical values, the total enrollment a year ago is 300. Therefore, the fraction of the current enrollment at the private school that is female students is $\frac{1.05(200)}{1.10(300)} = \frac{210}{330} = \frac{7}{11}$.

95. A. I only

$\frac{1}{4}x < 150 < \frac{1}{3}x$ implies that $12\left(\frac{1}{4}x\right) < 12(150) < 12\left(\frac{1}{3}x\right)$, which is equivalent to $3x < 1{,}800 < 4x$. Check for Roman choices that satisfy this double inequality. Check I: $3(500) = 1{,}500 < 1{,}800$ and $1{,}800 < 4(500) = 2{,}000$, so 500 satisfies the double inequality. The correct answer contains I, so eliminate choices (C) and (E).

Check II: $3(600) = 1{,}800 \not< 1{,}800$, so 600 does not satisfy the double inequality. Reject II, and eliminate Choice (B). Check III: $3(700) = 2{,}100 \not< 1{,}800$ so 700 does not satisfy the double inequality. Reject III, and eliminate Choice (D). Thus, Choice (A), I only, is the correct answer. (*Note:* Eliminating fractions at the outset simplifies the calculations for this problem.)

96. A. $k - 1$

Simplify the equation. Then determine n.

$$\frac{1}{5^n} = \frac{1}{5^k} + \frac{1}{5^k} + \frac{1}{5^k} + \frac{1}{5^k} + \frac{1}{5^k}$$

$$\frac{1}{5^n} = \frac{5}{5^k}$$

$$\frac{1}{5^n} = \frac{1}{5^{k-1}}$$

This result implies that $n = k - 1$.

97. D. 47

For the recursive formula given, you will need to find a_2 and a_3 before you can find a_4. Using the formula, $a_2 = 2a_1 + 1 = 2(5) + 1 = 10 + 1 = 11$; $a_3 = 2a_2 + 1 = 2(11) + 1 = 22 + 1 = 23$; and $a_4 = 2a_3 + 1 = 2(23) + 1 = 46 + 1 = 47$.

98. D. 52

For each vehicle, divide 1,200 miles by its average miles per gallon of gasoline performance. Then find the difference in the amount of gasoline used. The truck averages 12 miles per gallon of gasoline, so for 1,200 miles, it will use $\frac{1{,}200 \text{ miles}}{12 \text{ miles/gal}} = 100$ gal. The car averages 25 miles per gallon of gasoline, so for 1,200 miles, it will use $\frac{1{,}200 \text{ miles}}{25 \text{ miles/gal}} = 48$ gal. The difference is 100 gal – 48 gal = 52 gal.

99. **D. I and II only**

Statement I is true because $x < y < z$ implies $z > x$, which implies $\frac{1}{z} < \frac{1}{x}$. Given that $y > 0$, then $y \cdot \frac{1}{z} < y \cdot \frac{1}{x}$ or, equivalently, $\frac{y}{z} < \frac{y}{x}$. The correct answer choice must include I. Eliminate choices (B), (C), and (E). Statement II is true because $x < y < z$ implies $z > y$. Given that $x > 0$, then $xz > xy$. The correct answer choice must include II. Eliminate Choice (A). Therefore, Choice (D), I and II only, is the correct answer. You do not have to check statement III, but it is not necessarily true. If, for example, $x = 2$, $y = 7$, and $z = 8$, $8 \not> 2 + 7 = 9$.

100. **B. $\frac{1}{4}$**

The number of integers from 101 to 500 is $(500 - 101) + 1 = 399 + 1 = 400$. Of these 400 integers, the number that have a hundreds digit of 3 is $(399 - 300) + 1 = 99 + 1 = 100$. Therefore, the probability that a randomly selected integer from a list of consecutive integers from 101 to 500 will have a hundreds digit of 3 is $\frac{100}{400} = \frac{1}{4}$.

101. **D. 14.25**

The average weight, kilograms, of the 20 boxes is

$$\frac{8(12.75) + 12(15.25)}{20} = \frac{285}{20} = 14.25.$$

102. **C. 112**

Let $2x$ = the number of pennies in the collection, $3x$ = the number of nickels, $5x$ = the number of dimes, and $6x$ = the number of quarters. Thus, the total number of coins in the collection is $2x + 3x + 5x + 6x = 16x$. You know the number of coins of one of the denomination is 30, so check each denomination in turn to determine the possible values for $16x$. If $2x = 30$, then $x = 15$ and $16x = 16(15) = 240$, so Choice (E) is a possible value for $16x$. If $3x = 30$, then $x = 10$ and $16x = 16(10) = 160$, so Choice (D) is a possible value for $16x$. If $5x = 30$, then $x = 6$ and $16x = 16(6) = 96$, so Choice (B) is a possible value for $16x$. If $6x = 30$, then $x = 5$ and $16x = 16(5) = 80$, so choice (A) is a possible value for $16x$. Therefore, Choice (C) cannot be the total number of coins in the collection.

103. **A. 25%**

The price reduction is $\$800 - \$600 = \$200$. This amount represents a percent reduction of $\frac{200}{800} = \frac{1}{4} = 25\%$.

104. **C. III only**

Substitute the values of x and y from each given ordered pair to determine whether the values satisfy the equation for every possible value of m. The ordered pair in I yields $m(2)+4(0)=8$, which is true for only one value of m: $m=4$. Reject I, and eliminate choices (A), (D), and (E). The ordered pair in II yields $m(2)+4(2)=8$, which is true for only one value of m: $m=0$. Reject II, and eliminate Choice (B). Thus, Choice (C), III only, is the correct answer. You do not have to check it, but the ordered pair yields $m(0)+4(2)=8$, which is always true regardless of the value of m.

105. **C. 26**

If K is neither the least nor the greatest of the six numbers, then the range of the six numbers would be $28-6=22$, which is not consistent with the question information that the range is 24. It follows that K is either the least of the six numbers or the greatest of the six numbers. If K is the least of the six numbers then $28-K=24$, which implies that $K=4$. If K is the greatest of the six numbers then $K-6=24$, which implies that $K=30$. Hence, the two possible values for K are 30 and 4, from which you have 30 is 26 greater than 4.

106. **C. III only**

The equation $a+b=2$ implies $b=2-a$. Given that b is positive, this result implies that $a<2$ (because otherwise, b would be 0 or negative). Substitute $b=2-a$ into $50a-100b$ to obtain $50a-100b=50a-100(2-a)=50a-200+100a=150a-200$. Now check the Roman choices. For I, $150a-200=150$ implies $a=\frac{350}{150}=\frac{7}{3}=2\frac{1}{3}$. This result contradicts $a<2$. Reject I, and eliminate choices (A) and (D). For II, $150a-200=100$ implies $a=\frac{300}{150}=2$. This result contradicts $a<2$. Reject II, and eliminate choices (B) and (E). Therefore, Choice (C), III only, is the correct answer, so move on to the next question. However, to verify, $150a-200=50$ implies $a=\frac{250}{150}=\frac{5}{3}=1\frac{2}{3}$ and $b=2-a=2-1\frac{2}{3}=\frac{1}{3}$.

107. **A. 4 to 5**

The desired ratio is $\frac{A}{C}$. From the question information you have three proportions: $\frac{A}{B}=\frac{3}{4}$, $\frac{B}{D}=\frac{8}{5}$, and $\frac{C}{D}=\frac{3}{2}$. From the first proportion, $A=\frac{3}{4}B$. From the second proportion, $B=\frac{8}{5}D$. From the third proportion, $D=\frac{2}{3}C$. Thus, $A=\frac{3}{4}B=\frac{3}{4}\left(\frac{8}{5}D\right)=\frac{3}{4}\left(\frac{8}{5}\left(\frac{2}{3}C\right)\right)=\frac{\cancel{3}}{\cancel{4}}\cdot\frac{\cancelto{2}{8}}{5}\cdot\frac{2}{\cancel{3}}C=\frac{4}{5}C$, which implies $\frac{A}{C}=\frac{4}{5}$. Therefore, the ratio of A to C is 4 to 5.

108. D. 10

Let H = the number of hardcover books purchased and P = the number of paperback books purchased. Then, $7H + 5P = 56$. You have one equation and two variables, so without additional information, finding specific values for H and P is problematic. However, the question scenario implies that H and P are both positive integers. Keeping this additional information in mind, solve the equation for P.

$$7H + 5P = 56$$
$$5P = 56 - 7H$$
$$P = \frac{56 - 7H}{5}$$
$$P = \frac{7(8 - H)}{5}$$

Knowing that P has to be a positive integer implies that $(8 - H)$ is positive and that it is divisible by 5. For $(8 - H)$ to be positive H could be 1, 2, 3, 4, 5, 6, or 7. For each of these values, the corresponding values for $(8 - H)$ are 7, 6, 5, 4, 3, 2, and 1, respectively. Of these values, only 5, which corresponds to $H = 3$, is divisible by 5. Thus, $H = 3$ and $P = \frac{7(8 - H)}{5} = \frac{7(8 - 3)}{5} = \frac{7(\cancel{5})}{\cancel{5}} = 7$. Therefore, the customer purchased a total of $3 + 7 = 10$ books.

109. E. 72π

The formula for the area of a circle is $A = \pi r^2$, where r is the circle's radius. The value of r^2 is the square of the distance between the center $(-4,1)$ and the point $(2,-5)$, which lies on the circle. Use the formula for the distance between two points in the xy-plane:

$$r^2 = \left(2 - (-4)\right)^2 + (-5 - 1)^2 = (6)^2 + (-6)^2 = 36 + 36 = 72$$

Therefore, $A = \pi(72) = 72\pi$.

110. B. $400 + 0.06V$

Given that the total votes cast by seniors was 40%V, then the total votes cast by juniors was 60%V. The candidate received 10% of the total votes cast by juniors. Thus, the candidate received $10\%(60\%V) = 0.1(0.6V) = 0.06V$ votes cast by juniors. Therefore, the candidate received $400 + 0.06V$ votes in the election.

111. C. 30

The ratio of red to white quinoa is $\frac{6}{16} = \frac{3}{8}$. Let $3x$ = the amount (in ounces) of red quinoa in the 110-ounce mixture and $8x$ = the amount (in ounces) of white quinoa in the mixture. Then, $3x + 8x = 110$. Solve this equation for x, and then find $3x$, the amount of red quinoa in the mixture.

$$3x + 8x = 110$$
$$11x = 110$$
$$x = 10$$
$$3x = 30$$

The chef puts 30 ounces of red quinoa in the 110-ounce mixture.

112. C. Four

Determine the prime factorization of 3,080 using a systematic approach similar to the one shown here.

$$3,080 = 2 \times 1,540 = 2 \times 2 \times 770 = 2 \times 2 \times 10 \times 77 =$$
$$2 \times 2 \times (2 \times 5) \times (7 \times 11) = 2^3 \times 5 \times 7 \times 11$$

Therefore, 3,080 has four distinct prime factors: 2, 5, 7, and 11.

113. B. $240 + \dfrac{K-1}{2}$

For an odd number of data values, the median is the middle number when the values are put in ascending order as are the consecutive integers in this problem. Furthermore $\frac{K-1}{2}$ of the data values are below the median and $\frac{K-1}{2}$ are above the median. Because K is an odd number, 240 is the middle value in the list of numbers and there are $\frac{K-1}{2}$ consecutive integers above 240. Therefore, the greatest integer in the list is $240 + \dfrac{K-1}{2}$.

114. C. 81

Express $99X$ as $(100-1)X$. Substitute $X = 0.\overline{81}$ into this expression and simplify.

$$99X = (100-1)X = (100-1)(0.\overline{81}) =$$
$$(100)(0.\overline{81}) - (1)(0.\overline{81}) = 81.\overline{81} - 0.\overline{81} = 81$$

115. D. $\dfrac{5}{2}\sqrt[3]{\dfrac{V}{15}}$

Let $6x$ = the length of the box, $4x$ = the width of the box, and $5x$ = the height of the box. Then $V = (6x)(4x)(5x) = 120x^3$. Solve $120x^3 = V$ for x and then find $5x$, the height of the box:

$$120x^3 = V$$
$$x^3 = \frac{V}{120}$$
$$x = \sqrt[3]{\frac{V}{120}}$$
$$x = \sqrt[3]{\frac{V}{8 \cdot 15}}$$
$$x = \frac{1}{2}\sqrt[3]{\frac{V}{15}}$$
$$5x = 5\left(\frac{1}{2}\sqrt[3]{\frac{V}{15}}\right)$$
$$5x = \frac{5}{2}\sqrt[3]{\frac{V}{15}}$$

116. C. $3\dfrac{1}{3}S$

Use logical reasoning to determine the solution. Sofi has half as many game cards as her brother, so her brother has $2S$ game cards. She has three times as many game cards as her sister, so her sister has $\frac{1}{3}S$ game cards. Therefore, the three siblings have a total of $S + 2S + \frac{1}{3}S = 3\frac{1}{3}S$ game cards.

117. A. 7

The mean of N numbers is their sum divided by N. Let S = the sum of the list of K numbers. Then $S + 180$ = the sum of the list of $K + 1$ numbers. From the question information, you can write two equations: $\frac{S}{K} = 100$ and $\frac{S + 180}{K + 1} = 110$. Solve these two equations simultaneously. Solving $\frac{S}{K} = 100$ for S yields $S = 100K$. Substituting this result into $\frac{S + 180}{K + 1} = 110$ yields

$$\frac{100K + 180}{K + 1} = 110$$
$$110(K + 1) = 100K + 180$$
$$110K + 110 = 100K + 180$$
$$10K + 110 = 180$$
$$10K = 70$$
$$K = 7$$

118. B. 10^5

Given that $a_{n+1} = 10a_n$, then $a_1 = a_1$, $a_2 = 10a_1$, $a_3 = 10a_2 = 10 \cdot 10a_1 = 10^2 a_1$, $a_4 = 10a_3 = 10 \cdot 10^2 a_1 = 10^3 a_1$, and so on. You have the pattern $a_1, 10a_1, 10^2 a_1, 10^3 a_1$, and so on. Thus, in general, $a_n = 10^{n-1} a_1$. Using this formula, $a_8 = 10^{8-1} a_1 = 10^7 a_1$. From the previous calculations, $a_3 = 10^2 a_1$. Therefore, $\dfrac{a_8}{a_3} = \dfrac{10^7 \cancel{a_1}}{10^2 \cancel{a_1}} = 10^5$, which shows a_8 is 10^5 times greater than a_3.

119. E. II and III only

Check the Roman choices. For I, $x < y$ implies $y > x$, which implies $\dfrac{y}{x} > 1$. Thus, $\sqrt{\dfrac{y}{x}}$ cannot be less than 1. Reject I, and eliminate (A) and (D). For II, $x < y$ implies $x^2 < y^2$, which implies $x^2 - 100 < y^2 - 100$. Thus, $\dfrac{x^2 - 100}{y^2 - 100} < 1$. The correct answer must include II. Eliminate Choice (C). For III, $x < y$ implies $\dfrac{x}{y} < 1$. The correct answer must include III. Eliminate Choice (B), leaving Choice (E), II and III only, as the correct answer.

120. A. 0

The six positive numbers are in ascending order, so the median is the average of the middle pair of numbers, which is

$$\frac{(k+4)+(k+8)}{2} = \frac{2k+12}{2} = k+6$$

The mean is the sum of the numbers divided by 6, which is

$$\frac{k+k+3+k+4+k+8+k+9+k+12}{6} = \frac{6k+36}{6} = k+6$$

The mean and the median both equal $k+6$, so the difference is 0.

121. B. 15

Let x = the amount (in milliliters) of the 1% sulfuric acid solution that must be added. Then $x + 60$ = the amount (in milliliters) in the final 5% sulfuric acid solution. Make a table to organize the information given.

When?	Percent sulfuric acid strength	Amount (in milliliters)	Amount of sulfuric acid (in milliliters)
Before	1%	x	1%x
	6%	60	6%(60)
After	5%	$x + 60$	5%($x + 60$)

Using the table, write an equation based on the following fact: The amount of sulfuric acid before mixing equals the amount of sulfuric acid after mixing.

$$1\%x + 6\%(60) = 5\%(x+60)$$
$$0.01x + 0.06(60) = .05(x+60)$$
$$0.01x + 3.6 = .05x + 3$$
$$3.6 = 0.04x + 3$$
$$0.6 = 0.04x$$
$$15 = x$$

The amount of the 1% sulfuric acid solution to be added is 15 milliliters.

122.   B. 3.5

Use logical reasoning to determine the solution. The combined distance that the two vehicles must travel is 455 miles. They will cover that distance at a combined speed of 70 mph + 60 mph = 130 mph. Therefore, the time it will the two vehicles to be 455 miles apart is $\dfrac{455 \text{ miles}}{130 \frac{\text{miles}}{\text{hour}}} = 3.5$ hours.

123.   A. 0

Follow the order of operations and simplify the expression:

$$\frac{5}{16} + \frac{\left(\frac{3}{8}\right)\left(\frac{2}{3}\right)}{4} - \frac{3}{8} = \frac{5}{16} + \frac{\left(\frac{\cancel{3}}{{}_4\cancel{8}}\right)\left(\frac{2^1}{\cancel{3}}\right)}{4} - \frac{3}{8} =$$

$$\frac{5}{16} + \frac{\frac{1}{4}}{4} - \frac{3}{8} = \frac{5}{16} + \frac{1}{16} - \frac{6}{16} = 0$$

124.   D. II and III only

Factor $5^8 - 2^8$ completely and then simplify the factors.

$$5^8 - 2^8 = \left(5^4 - 2^4\right)\left(5^4 + 2^4\right) = \left(5^2 - 2^2\right)\left(5^2 + 2^2\right)\left(5^4 + 2^4\right) =$$
$$(5-2)(5+2)\left(5^2 + 2^2\right)\left(5^4 + 2^4\right) = (3)(7)(29)(641)$$

Therefore, of the choices given, only 3 (II) and 7 (III) are prime factors of $5^8 - 2^8$.

Note: The prime numbers 29 and 641 are also prime factors of $5^8 - 2^8$, but that information is not needed to correctly answer the question.

125. E. 14

Let W = the width (in feet) of the rectangle and $L = 2W + 4$ = the length (in feet) of the rectangle. Given the area (in feet^2) of the rectangle is 70, solve the following equation for W, and then determine $2W + 4$, which is the length of the rectangle.

$$W(2W + 4) = 70$$
$$2W^2 + 4W = 70$$
$$2W^2 + 4W - 70 = 0$$
$$\frac{1}{2}(2W^2 + 4W - 70) = \frac{1}{2} \cdot 0$$
$$W^2 + 2W - 35 = 0$$
$$(W + 7)(W - 5) = 0$$
$$W + 7 = 0 \text{ or } W - 5 = 0$$
$$W = -7(\text{reject}) \text{ or } W = 5$$
$$2W + 4 = 2(5) + 4 = 10 + 4 = 14$$

(*Note:* The number –7 is rejected because length is positive.) The length of the rectangle is 14 feet.

126. C. III only

First determine the values of x, x^2, and x^3. $x = -\frac{1}{20}$, $x^2 = \left(-\frac{1}{20}\right)^2 = \frac{1}{400}$, and $x^3 = \left(-\frac{1}{20}\right)^3 = -\frac{1}{8000}$. Thus, $-\frac{1}{20} < -\frac{1}{8000} < \frac{1}{400}$. Therefore, only the double inequality in III is true, so the correct answer is Choice (C), III only.

127. A. 188

Let L = the amount of money (in dollars) that Loyce has initially and T = the amount of money (in dollars) Tiara has initially. Then according to the question information, $L + T = 278$ and $L - 8 = 2T$. Solve these two equations simultaneously. Solving $L + T = 278$ for T yields $T = 278 - L$. Substituting this result into $L - 8 = 2T$ yields

$$L - 8 = 2(278 - L)$$
$$L - 8 = 556 - 2L$$
$$3L - 8 = 556$$
$$3L = 564$$
$$L = 188$$

Loyce has $188 initially.

128. E. 5,832

First, determine the volume of one 3-inch cube. Next, multiply the result by 216, the number of cubes, to determine the volume of the crate. The volume, in cubic inches, of a 3-in cube is $3^3 = 27$. Therefore, the volume, in cubic inches, of the crate is $27 \times 216 = 5{,}832$.

129. A. 15

Let M = the number of months of membership at which Merida and Jude will have paid the same amount. Solve the following equation.

$$40 + 20M = 70 + 18M$$
$$2M + 40 = 70$$
$$2M = 30$$
$$M = 15$$

After 15 months of membership, Merida and Jude will have paid the same total amount.

130. E. 0.8

The median of the 20 times shown in the dot plot is the average of the middle pair of times, which, in minutes, is $\frac{14+15}{2} = \frac{29}{2} = 14.5$. The mean of the 20 times is their sum divided by 20, which, in minutes, is

$$\frac{5 + 2(8) + 2(10) + 12 + 2(13) + 2(14) + 5(15) + 2(17) + 2(19) + 20}{20} = \frac{274}{20} = 13.7$$

The difference, in minutes, between the median and the mean is $14.5 - 13.7 = 0.8$.

131. D. $\frac{21}{41}$

Use logical reasoning to determine the solution. There are $(100 - 60) + 1 = 40 + 1 = 41$ integers in the sequence. The sequence starts and ends with an even integer, so the number of even integers in the sequence is 1 more than the number of odd integers. Subtracting 1 from 41 leaves 40 integers, of which 20 (half) are even and 20 (half) are odd. Thus, there are $20 + 1 = 21$ even integers. Therefore, the probability that the randomly selected integer is even is $\frac{21}{41}$.

The outcome of the drawing from one bag has no effect on the outcome of the drawing from the other bag, so the drawings from the two bags are independent. For either bag, let B represent the outcome "the chip drawn is blue," G represent the outcome "the chip drawn is gold," and R represent the outcome "the chip drawn is red."

Bag 1 contains 24 chips. For this bag, $P(\text{B}) = \frac{10}{24} = \frac{5}{12}$, $P(\text{G}) = \frac{8}{24} = \frac{1}{3}$, and $P(\text{R}) = \frac{6}{24} = \frac{1}{4}$.

Bag 2 contains 12 chips. For this bag, $P(\text{B}) = \frac{8}{12} = \frac{2}{3}$, $P(\text{G}) = \frac{2}{12} = \frac{1}{6}$, and $P(\text{R}) = \frac{2}{12} = \frac{1}{6}$.

Make a tree diagram to illustrate the situation.

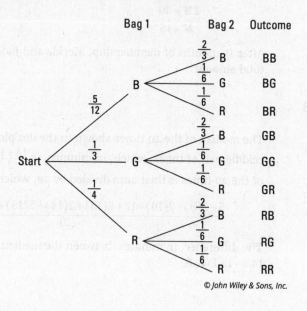

© John Wiley & Sons, Inc.

With probability tree diagrams, you multiply along a branch to determine the probability of the outcome at the end of the branch. Thereafter, if the probability of two or more end outcomes is desired, their probabilities are added to obtain a total probability.

According to the tree diagram, there are four end outcomes for which neither chip is gold: BB, which has probability $\frac{5}{12} \cdot \frac{2}{3} = \frac{5}{18}$; BR, which has probability $\frac{5}{12} \cdot \frac{1}{6} = \frac{5}{72}$; RB, which has probability $\frac{1}{4} \cdot \frac{2}{3} = \frac{1}{6}$; and RR, which has probability $\frac{1}{4} \cdot \frac{1}{6} = \frac{1}{24}$. Therefore, the probability neither chip is gold is

$$P(\text{BB or BR or RB or RR}) =$$
$$P(\text{BB}) + P(\text{BR}) + P(\text{BR}) + P(\text{RR}) =$$
$$\frac{5}{18} + \frac{5}{72} + \frac{1}{6} + \frac{1}{24} = \frac{5}{9}$$

133.

E. 36

The greatest length, in feet, for each side of the square plots is the greatest common factor of 18 and 30. Because $18 = 2 \cdot 3 \cdot 3$ and $30 = 2 \cdot 3 \cdot 5$, the greatest common factor of 18 and 30 is 6 $(= 2 \cdot 3)$. Therefore, the greatest area, in square feet, for each of the square plots is $6 \cdot 6 = 36$.

134.

E. 8

Determine the answer by identifying a pattern in the units digits of 2^n, for n, a positive integer. If the units digit of an integer m is 2, then the units digits of $m^1, m^2, m^3, m^4, m^5, m^6, m^7, m^8 \ldots$, in the order given, have a 4-digit repeating pattern of 2, 4, 8, 6, 2, 4, 8, 6, and so on. Thus, if n is a nonzero multiple of 4, the units digit of 2^n is 6. Also, for some $k \geq 0$, if n has the form $4k + 1$, the units digit of 2^n is 2; if n has the form $4k + 2$, the units digit of 2^n is 4; and if n has the form $4k + 3$, the units digit of 2^n is 8. In this question, $n = 99$, which has the form $4(24) + 3$. Thus, the units digit of 2^{99} is 8.

135.

A. 51 to 31

First, find the total amount of fruit juice. Next, find the total amount of water and cinnamon sugar. Then, find the ratio of the total amount of fruit juice to the total amount of water and cinnamon sugar.
The total amount, in cups, of fruit juice is $2\frac{3}{4} + 1\frac{1}{2} = \frac{11}{4} + \frac{3}{2} = \frac{11}{4} + \frac{6}{4} = \frac{17}{4}$.
The total amount, in cups, of water and cinnamon sugar is
$2\frac{1}{3} + \frac{1}{4} = \frac{7}{3} + \frac{1}{4} = \frac{28}{12} + \frac{3}{12} = \frac{31}{12}$. Therefore, the ratio of the total amount of fruit juice to the total amount of water and cinnamon sugar is

$$\frac{\frac{17}{4}}{\frac{31}{12}} = \frac{\cancel{12}^3}{1} \cdot \frac{17}{\cancel{4}} = \frac{51}{31} \text{ or, equivalently, 51 to 31.}$$

136.

B. $\frac{25}{3}$

Express $\frac{m}{n+p}$, in terms of p, and then simplify. $\frac{n}{p} = 5$ implies $n = 5p$ and $\frac{m}{n} = 10$ implies $m = 10n = 10(5p) = 50p$. Therefore, $\frac{m}{n+p} = \frac{50p}{5p+p} = \frac{50\cancel{p}}{6\cancel{p}} = \frac{25}{3}$.

137. C. 20

The formula for the perimeter of a rectangle is $2(L+W)$, where L is the rectangle's length and W is its width. Substitute into the formula and solve the equation that follows for x. Next, determine $\dfrac{10}{x}$ and $\dfrac{8}{x}$, the rectangle's dimensions, in feet. Then determine its area, in square feet.

$$2\left(\frac{8}{x}+\frac{10}{x}\right)=18$$

$$2\left(\frac{18}{x}\right)=18$$

$$\frac{36}{x}=18$$

$$18x=36$$

$$x=2$$

$$\frac{10}{x}=\frac{10}{2}=5$$

$$\frac{8}{x}=\frac{8}{2}=4$$

The rectangle has dimensions 5 feet by 4 feet. Its area, in square feet, is $5\times4=20$.

138. D. 13% profit

Given that $144 is 20% greater than the initial cost of a microwave oven, it follows that the initial cost for each microwave oven was $\dfrac{\$144}{120\%}=\dfrac{\$144}{1.2}=\$120$. The total revenue is the amount obtained from the sale of $45(=50-5)$ microwave ovens at $144 each plus the amount from the refund of $60 $(=50\%$ of $120)$ for each of the 5 microwaves that were returned. This total revenue is $45(\$144)+5(\$60)=\$6,480+\$300=\$6,780$. The total initial cost of the 50 microwave ovens was $50(\$120)=\$6,000$. The difference between total revenue and cost is $\$6,780-\$6,000=\$780$, which is a profit because it's positive. The profit as a percent of the total initial cost is $\dfrac{\$780}{\$6,000}\times100\%=0.13\times100\%=13\%$.

139. B. Two

$$\frac{1}{X}=\frac{1}{625,000}=\frac{1}{625}\times\frac{1}{1000}=\frac{1}{5^4}\times\frac{1}{10^3}=\left(\frac{1}{5}\right)^4\times10^{-3}=$$

$$(0.2)^4\times10^{-3}=(0.0016)\times10^{-3}=0.0000016$$

Therefore, the decimal representation of $\dfrac{1}{X}$ has two nonzero digits.

140. C. $\frac{6}{11}$

Initially, the box contains 3 defective remote controls and 9 non-defective remote controls. The probability that the first remote control selected is non-defective is $\frac{9}{12} = \frac{3}{4}$. Thereafter, the box contains 3 defective and 8 non-defective remote controls, so the probability that the second remote control selected is non-defective is $\frac{8}{11}$. Therefore, the probability that neither of the first two remote controls tested is defective is $\frac{3}{4} \cdot \frac{8}{11} = \frac{3}{\cancel{4}} \cdot \frac{\cancel{8}^2}{11} = \frac{6}{11}$.

141. D. $230

Let A = Richard's average gratuity per day for the last four of the past 10 workdays. Then his total gratuities in dollars for those four days is $4A$. His total gratuities for the previous 6 days was $6(\$180) = \$1,080$. Given that his average gratuity for the 10 workdays is $200, solve the following equation:

$$\frac{\$1,080 + 4A}{10} = \$200$$
$$\$1,080 + 4A = \$2,000$$
$$4A = \$920$$
$$A = \$230$$

Richard's average gratuity per day for the last four of the past 10 workdays is $230.

142. C. $\frac{1}{16}$

Use rules of exponents to determine the solution.

$$x^{-4} = x^{-2} \cdot x^{-2} = \frac{1}{4} \cdot \frac{1}{4} = \frac{1}{16}$$

143. B. 1

Rewrite the expression using the product rule for exponents.

$(13)^{25}(17)^{25} = (13 \cdot 17)^{25}$. The product $13 \cdot 17$ has a units digit of 1 (because $3 \cdot 7 = 21$). Thus, every power of $(13 \cdot 17)$ has a units digit of 1. Therefore, the units digit of $(13 \cdot 17)^{25}$ is 1, which implies the units digit of $(13)^{25}(17)^{25}$ is 1 as well.

144. B. $22.50

First, determine the cost of the meal before the gratuity was added. Next, divide the result by 20. Let C = the cost of the meal before the gratuity was added. Solve the following equation:

$$C + 18\%C = \$531.00$$
$$C + 0.18C = \$531.00$$
$$1.18C = \$531.00$$
$$C = \$450.00$$

Thus, the cost of the meal before the gratuity was added is $450. Therefore, the average price of the meal per person not including the gratuity or sales tax is $\dfrac{\$450.00}{20} = \$22.50$.

145. E. 200

First, in the given expression, rewrite 80 in prime factored form. Next, apply the exponent 50 to the factored form. You have $80^{50} = \left(2^4 \cdot 5\right)^{50} = 2^{200} \cdot 5^{50}$. Thus, 2^{200} is the highest power of 2 that is a factor of 80^{50}. Therefore, $p = 200$.

146. B. $3\sqrt{2}$

Let r = the radius of the circle. A radius from the center of circle to a tangent of the circle is perpendicular to the tangent. Thus, the circle's center is located at (r,r). Using the distance formula, solve the following equation:

$$r^2 + r^2 = 6^2$$
$$2r^2 = 36$$
$$r^2 = 18$$
$$r = \sqrt{18} = \sqrt{9 \cdot 2} = 3\sqrt{2}$$

Therefore, the circle's radius is $3\sqrt{2}$.

147. C. 14,400

In going from point A to point E, there are 4 different ways to go from A to B, 2 different ways to go from B to C, 6 different ways to go from C to D, and 5 different ways to go from D to E. In returning from point E to point A, because the player cannot retrace a previous path taken, there are 4 different ways to go from E to D, 5 different ways to go from D to C, 1 way to go from C to B, and 3 different ways to go from B to A. Therefore, there are $4 \cdot 2 \cdot 6 \cdot 5 \cdot 4 \cdot 5 \cdot 1 \cdot 3 = 14{,}400$ different ways for the player to move from point A to point E and back without retracing a previous path taken.

148. C. $7,000

To calculate the per capita expenditure, divide $9.8 billion by 1.4 million.

$$\frac{\$9.8 \text{ billion}}{1.4 \text{ million}} = \frac{9.8 \times 10^9}{1.4 \times 10^6} = \left(\frac{9.8}{1.4}\right) \times 10^{9-6} = 7 \times 10^3 = \$7,000$$

The government's per capita expenditure is $7,000.

149. A. $\left|x - \frac{1}{2}\right| < \frac{7}{2}$

From your knowledge of solving inequalities, you know the open circles at −3 and 4 mean that −3 and 4 are not included in the solution set. Thus, the inequality symbol in the answer must be either < or >, so eliminate choices (C) and (D).

Test a number from the interval shown in the graph in each of the inequalities given in choices (A), (B), and (E). For convenience and ease of calculation, select 0 as your test number. For Choice (A) when $x = 0$,
$\left|x - \frac{1}{2}\right| = \left|0 - \frac{1}{2}\right| = \left|-\frac{1}{2}\right| = \frac{1}{2} < \frac{7}{2}$, which is true. Thus, $\left|x - \frac{1}{2}\right| < \frac{7}{2}$ is the correct answer.

You have determined the correct answer, so there is no need to check the remaining answer choices. However, you can easily see that $x = 0$ does not satisfy the inequalities in choices (B) and (E) because $\frac{1}{2} \not< \frac{7}{2}$ and $1 \not< \frac{7}{2}$, respectively.

150. D. 20%

Given that both sales totals are expressed in millions, the percent increase from the previous year to the current year is

$$\left(\frac{768 - 640}{640}\right) \times 100\% = \left(\frac{128}{640}\right) \times 100\% = 0.2 \times 100\% = 20\%$$

151. D. 53%

Given that you're working with percentages, for convenience and ease of calculation, assume the number of attendees at the party was 100. Then $62\%(100) = 62$ attendees were friends of the bride and $47\%(100) = 47$ attendees were friends of the bridegroom. Use logical reasoning to determine the solution. Because $62 + 47 = 109$, which is greater than 100 (the total number of attendees), logically, you can conclude that the excess $109 - 100 = 9$ attendees were friends of both the bride and bridegroom. Thus, $62 - 9 = 53$ attendees were friends of the bride, but not friends of the bridegroom. This number represents $\frac{53}{100} \times 100\% = 53\%$ of the attendees.

152. **E. 25**

Solve the following equation for $\frac{x}{y}$. Then multiply the result by 15.

$$20\%x = 33\frac{1}{3}\%y$$
$$\frac{1}{5}x = \frac{1}{3}y$$
$$15\cdot\frac{1}{5}x = 15\cdot\frac{1}{3}y$$
$$3x = 5y$$
$$\frac{x}{y} = \frac{5}{3}$$

Therefore, $15\left(\dfrac{x}{y}\right) = 15\cdot\dfrac{5}{3} = 25$.

153. **C. 6.25%**

Given that Amiel lost $\frac{1}{2}$ pound each week for 30 weeks, he lost a total of $30\left(\frac{1}{2}\text{ pound}\right) = 15\text{ pounds}$ during this period. This amount represents

$\dfrac{15}{240}\times100\% = 0.0625\times100\% = 6.25\%$ of Amiel's original weight.

154. **D. 8,000**

Evaluate the quantity:

$$\sqrt{6.4\times10^7} = \sqrt{64\times10^6} = 8\times10^3 = 8,000$$

155. **D. 6**

Solve the two equations. For the first equation,

$$m^2 - 2m - 15 = 0$$
$$(m-5)(m+3) = 0$$
$$m-5 = 0 \text{ or } m+3 = 0$$
$$m = 5 \text{ or } m = -3$$

For the second equation,

$$n^2 - 3n - 10 = 0$$
$$(n-5)(n+2) = 0$$
$$n-5 = 0 \text{ or } n+2 = 0$$
$$n = 5 \text{ or } n = -2$$

Given that $m \neq n$, $m = -3$ and $n = -2$. Therefore, the product of m and n is $(-3)(-2) = 6$.

156. D. 15

Solve the given equation for x and then determine $3x$.

$$\frac{1}{x} = \frac{1}{2} + \frac{2}{5} + \frac{1}{3} - \frac{5}{6} + \frac{1}{4} - \frac{9}{20}$$

$$\frac{1}{x} = \frac{30}{60} + \frac{24}{60} + \frac{20}{60} - \frac{50}{60} + \frac{15}{60} - \frac{27}{60}$$

$$\frac{1}{x} = \frac{30 + 24 + 20 - 50 + 15 - 27}{60}$$

$$\frac{1}{x} = \frac{12}{60}$$

$$\frac{1}{x} = \frac{1}{5}$$

$$x = 5$$

$$3x = 15$$

157. E. 12NCP

Each crate has $C \times 12 = 12C$ boxes, each of which yields P cents profit. The total profit, in cents, for each case is $12C \times P = 12CP$. Therefore, the total profit, in cents, for N crates is $N \times (12CP) = 12NCP$.

158. C. 55%

Given that you're working with percentages, for convenience and ease of calculation, assume the total distance for the round trip is 100 miles. Upon arrival at City B, the motorist has driven $50\%(100 \text{ miles}) = 50 \text{ miles}$. It follows that the drive back to City A is also 50 miles. At the service station, the motorist has completed $10\%(50 \text{ miles}) = 5 \text{ miles}$ of the trip from City B to City A. Thus, at that point, the motorist has completed $50 \text{ miles} + 5 \text{ miles} = 55 \text{ miles}$, which is $\frac{55}{100} \times 100\% = 55\%$ of the round trip.

159. D. 5

Given that the graph is symmetric about the vertical line at $x = 3$, x values that are the same horizontal distance from 3 will have the same y values on the graph. From the graph, observe that 1 is 2 units to the left of 3, and 5 is 2 units to the right of 3. Therefore, the y value when $x = 5$ is the same as the y value when $x = 1$, which is 5.

160. E. $247.50

Compute the difference. $\frac{1}{10}(\$2,500) - \frac{1}{10}\%(\$2,500) = 0.1(\$2,500) - 0.1\%(\$2,500) = 0.1(\$2,500) - 0.001(\$2,500) = \$250.00 - \$2.50 = \$247.50$

Therefore, the difference is $247.50.

161. B. 200

Let M = the number of 25-cent coins in the jar. Then $640 - M$ = the number of 10-cent coins in the jar. In dollars, the face value of each 25-cent coin is $0.25, and the face value of each 10-cent coin is $0.10. Given that the total face value of the coins is $94, solve the following equation:

$$0.25M + 0.10(640 - M) = 94$$
$$0.25M + 64 - 0.10M = 94$$
$$0.15M = 30$$
$$M = 200$$

Therefore, there are 200 25-cent coins in the jar.

162. B. 22

The mean of the four integers is their sum divided by 4. Solve the following equation:

$$\frac{6 + 30 + 64 + 2K}{4} = 36$$
$$6 + 30 + 64 + 2K = 4(36)$$
$$6 + 30 + 64 + 2K = 144$$
$$2K + 100 = 144$$
$$2K = 44$$
$$K = 22$$

163. D. $18,000

Let $3x$ = the amount, in dollars, the youngest grandchild received, $4x$ = the amount, in dollars, the middle grandchild received, and $6x$ = the amount, in dollars, the oldest grandchild received. Solve the following equation for x, and then determine $3x$, the amount, in dollars, that the youngest grandchild received.

$$3x + 4x + 6x = \$78,000$$
$$13x = \$78,000$$
$$x = \$6,000$$
$$3x = \$18,000$$

Therefore, the youngest grandchild received $18,000.

164.   B. 800

Let M = the school's previous enrollment. Solve the following equation:

$$M + 15\%M = 920$$
$$M + 0.15M = 920$$
$$1.15M = 920$$
$$M = 800$$

There were 800 students enrolled the previous year.

165.   B. $\dfrac{S}{(1.02)^3}$

Each year the value of the investment increases by a factor of 1.02 ($=1+2\%$) over the previous year. Let P = the amount of the initial investment. At the end of the first year, the value of the investment is $1.02P$. At the end of the second year, the value of the investment is $1.02(1.02P) = (1.02)^2 P$. At the end of the third year, the value of the investment is $1.02(1.02P) = (1.02)^3 P$. Solve the following equation for P:

$$(1.02)^3 P = S$$
$$P = \frac{S}{(1.02)^3}$$

In terms of S, the amount of the initial investment is $\dfrac{S}{(1.02)^3}$.

166.   D. 20%

The royalty percentage to number of copies ratio for the first 10,000 copies is

$$\frac{10\%}{10,000} = \frac{0.10}{10,000} = \frac{10}{1,000,000} = \frac{1}{100,000}$$

The royalty percentage to number of copies ratio for the next 15,000 copies is

$$\frac{12\%}{15,000} = \frac{0.12}{15,000} = \frac{12}{1,500,000} = \frac{4}{500,000}$$

The percent decrease in the ratios is

$$\left| \frac{\frac{4}{500,000} - \frac{1}{100,000}}{\frac{1}{100,000}} \right| \times 100\% = \left| \frac{\frac{100,000}{1}\left(\frac{4}{500,000} - \frac{1}{100,000}\right)}{\frac{100,000}{1}\left(\frac{1}{100,000}\right)} \right| \times 100\% =$$

$$\left| \frac{\frac{4}{5} - 1}{1} \right| \times 100\% = \left| \frac{-\frac{1}{5}}{1} \right| \times 100\% = \frac{1}{5} \times 100\% = 20\%$$

Therefore, the ratio of the royalty percentage to number of copies decreases by 20% from the first 10,000 copies to the next 15,000 copies.

167.   C. 96%

Translating the statements into algebraic symbolism yields
$X = Y + 60\%Y = Y + 0.6Y = 1.6Y$ and $Y = Z - 40\%Z = 1 - .4Z = 0.6Z$. It follows
that $X = 1.6Y = 1.6(0.6Z) = 0.96Z = 96\%Z$.

168.   A. $\dfrac{X+100}{60}$

Finn drove $X\%(100 \text{ miles}) = X$ miles at 30 miles per hour. It follows that
Finn drove $(100 - X)$ miles at 60 miles per hour. Use the formula, $T = \dfrac{D}{R}$,
where D is the distance traveled at a constant rate of speed, R, for a given
time T, to determine the time for each portion of the trip.

The time, in hours, it took Finn to drive X miles at 30 miles per hour
is $\dfrac{X}{30}$, and the time, in hours, it took Finn to drive $(100 - X)$ miles at
60 miles per hour is $\dfrac{(100 - X)}{60}$. Therefore, the total time, in hours, for the
trip equals

$$\frac{X}{30} + \frac{(100 - X)}{60} = \frac{2X}{60} + \frac{(100 - X)}{60} = \frac{2X + 100 - X}{60} = \frac{X + 100}{60}$$

169.   B. 1,275K

The sum of the first 50 multiples of K equals

$$K + 2K + 3K + \cdots + 49K + 50K = K(1 + 2 + 3 + \cdots + 49 + 50)$$

Thus, the sum is the product of K and the sum of the 50 consecutive
integers from 1 to 50. The formula for the sum of the N consecutive
integers from 1 to N is $\dfrac{(N)(N+1)}{2}$. Therefore, the sum of the first
50 multiples of K equals $K\left(\dfrac{50 \cdot 51}{2}\right) = 1,275K$.

170.   A. 21

Together, the girls have less than P colored markers, so $(P - 2) + (P - 20) < P$,
which implies that $P < 22$. Given that each girl has at least one colored
marker, $P - 2 \geq 1$ and $P - 20 \geq 1$, which implies, $P \geq 21$. Hence, $21 \leq P < 22$.
Therefore, $P = 21$ because the situation in the question implies P is a positive
integer.

171.   B. $\frac{1}{7}$

Because the pens are randomly drawn from the box, each draw is independent of the other draws. After three non-defective pens have been drawn, there are only seven pens left in the box, one of which is defective. Therefore, the probability that the next pen drawn is defective is $\frac{1}{7}$.

172.   B. II only

The expression in I is not factorable over the real numbers, so $a+b$ is not a factor of this expression. Reject I, and eliminate choices (A) and (D). The expression in II can be factored as $(a+b)(c+d)$, so $a+b$ is a factor of this expression. The correct answer must include II. Eliminate Choice (C). Expanding the expression in III yields $a+bc+bd$, which does not contain $a+b$ as a factor. Reject III, and eliminate Choice (E). Therefore, Choice (B), II only, is the correct answer.

173.   B. –2

Solve the two equations simultaneously using the elimination method. To eliminate m, multiply the second equation by –2, and add the result to the first equation. Then solve for n.

$$4m = 10 - 5n$$
$$\underline{-4m = -6n - 32}$$
$$0 = -11n - 22$$
$$11n = -22$$
$$n = -2$$

174.   C. III only

The mean of the first three major exams is $\frac{80+95+92}{3} = 89$.
Let F = the student's score on the fourth major exam. Check the Roman choices using the following expression: $60\%(89) + 40\%F$.
Check I: $60\%(89) + 40\%(90) = 53.4 + 36 = 89.4$, which is less than 90.0. Thus, reject I, and eliminate choices (A) and (E). Check II: $60\%(89) + 40\%(91) = 53.4 + 36.4 = 89.8$, which is less than 90.0. Thus, reject II and eliminate choices (B) and (D). Therefore, the correct answer is Choice (C), III only. You do not have to check III, but to verify, $60\%(89) + 40\%(92) = 53.4 + 36.8 = 90.2$, which is greater than 90.0.

175. D. 150

The angles that measure $x°$ and $y°$ are angles formed when parallel lines are cut by a transversal. The angle that measures $y°$ and the angle above line n and adjacent to the angle that measures $x°$ are congruent because they are alternate interior angles of parallel lines. Thus, the angles that measure $x°$ and $y°$ are supplementary angles. Recall that the sum of supplementary angles is $180°$. Thus, $x + y = 180$. It is given that $x = 5y$, so $5y + y = 180$. Solve this equation for y, and then determine $5y$, the value of x.

$$5y + y = 180$$
$$6y = 180$$
$$y = 30$$
$$5y = 5(30) = 150$$

Therefore, the value of x is 150.

176. B. 125

Let P = the population of horned lizards in the park. The proportion of tagged lizards in the second group should equal the proportion of tagged lizards in the whole population, P. Set up a proportion and solve for P.

$$\frac{4}{20} = \frac{25}{P}$$
$$P = \frac{(20)(25)}{4}$$
$$P = 125$$

The best estimate of the horned lizard population in the park is 125.

177. C. $\frac{3}{2}$

According to the graph, 45 students chose 5 or higher as a response (because 30 chose 5, 5 chose 6, and 10 chose 7) and 30 students chose 3 or lower as a response (because 10 chose 3, 15 chose 2, and 5 chose 1). Therefore, the ratio of the number of students who chose 5 or higher to the number of students who chose 3 or lower is $\frac{45}{30} = \frac{3}{2}$.

178. B. 11

Use logical reasoning to determine the solution. Because $47 + 40 = 87$, which is greater than 76 (the total number of customers), you can conclude that the excess $87 - 76 = 11$ is the number of customers who bought both a washer and a dryer.

179.

A. $\dfrac{\text{lb} \cdot \text{ft}}{\text{sec}^2}$

Plug the units into the lift formula and simplify as you would for variable quantities.

$$C_L\left(\frac{dAV^2}{2}\right) = C_L\left(\frac{\frac{\text{lb}}{\text{ft}^3} \cdot \text{ft}^2 \cdot \left(\frac{\text{ft}}{\text{sec}}\right)^2}{2}\right) =$$

$$C_L\left(\frac{\frac{\text{lb}}{\text{ft}^3} \cdot \text{ft}^2 \cdot \frac{\text{ft}^2}{\text{sec}^2}}{2}\right) = \frac{1}{2}C_L\left(\frac{\text{lb} \cdot \text{ft}}{\text{sec}^2}\right)$$

Given that C_L has no units, the lift of an airplane has units of $\dfrac{\text{lb} \cdot \text{ft}}{\text{sec}^2}$.

180.

E. I, II, and III

The sum of the lengths of any two sides of a triangle must be greater than the third side. It follows that given two sides of lengths 14 and 31, the length of the third side must be greater than $31 - 14 = 17$ and less than $14 + 31 = 45$; that is, $17 <$ third side < 45. Select Choice (E) (I, II, and III) because each satisfies the double inequality.

181.

A. $\dfrac{91}{216}$

The probability of 50 appearing on the up face at least once in three tosses of the number cube is 1 minus the probability of no 50 appearing in three tosses. The probability that 50 appears on the up face in one toss of the number cube is $\frac{1}{6}$. Thus, the probability of no 50 in one toss of the number cube is $1 - \frac{1}{6} = \frac{5}{6}$. The probability of no 50 in three tosses is $\frac{5}{6} \cdot \frac{5}{6} \cdot \frac{5}{6} = \frac{125}{216}$. Therefore, the probability of at least one 50 in three tosses of the number cube is $1 - \frac{125}{216} = \frac{91}{216}$.

182.

C. 4

The equation $y = 4(x - 2) + 9$ is equivalent to $y = 4x + 1$. The rate of change for this equation is 4. Therefore, for every 1–unit increase in x, there is a 4–unit increase in y.

183.

C. $1,365

The armoire's original price was 70% of $1,500, which is $70\%(\$1,500) = 0.7(\$1,500) = \$1,050$. The armoire's selling price was 130% of $1,050, which is $130\%(\$1,050) = 1.3(\$1,050) = \$1,365$.

184. D. 11

Given that k is an integer, then $(14k+13)$ and $(7k+1)$ are integers as well. Because n is a factor of both $(14k+13)$ and $(7k+1)$, then $(14k+13)=an$ and $(7k+1)=bn$ for positive integers a and b. Hence, as shown here, n is a factor of $an-2(bn)=an-2bn=n(a-2b)$, which implies, by substitution, that n is a factor of $(14k+13)-2(7k+1)=14k+13-14k-2=11$. The only factors of 11 are 1 and 11. Given that n is prime, it follows that n equals 11.

185. D. 9

Expand the right side of the equation, and then set corresponding coefficients equal to each other to determine c.

$$4x^2+12x+c=(2x+k)^2=4x^2+4kx+k^2$$

Thus, $4k=12$, which implies $k=3$; and $c=k^2$. Therefore, $c=k^2=3^2=9$.

186. A. $\frac{1}{18}$

The prism is composed of 36 cubes: three 3×4 layers of 12 cubes each. After the prism is submerged in paint, the 24 cubes that make up the top and bottom layers will have paint on them. In the middle layer, 10 cubes will have paint on them: the 3 cubes on each of the two ends of the middle layer and the 2 cubes in the center on each side of the middle layer. Hence, $24+10=34$ cubes will have paint on them. Thus, only $36-34=2$ cubes will have no paint on them. Therefore, the fraction of small cubes that will not have any paint on them is $\frac{2}{36}=\frac{1}{18}$.

187. B. $\frac{7}{16}$

The probability that the token is red or black, denoted $P(R \text{ or } B)$, is the probability that the token is red, denoted $P(R)$, plus the probability that the token is black, denoted $P(B)$. First, determine the number of red or black tokens in the bag. Then calculate the necessary probabilities. Let G = the number of green tokens, $2G$ = the number of red tokens, $G+6$ = the number of black tokens, and $2(G+6)$ = the number of white tokens. Solve the following equation for G and then determine $2G$ and $G+6$:

$$G+2G+(G+6)+2(G+6)=48$$
$$G+2G+G+6+2G+12=48$$
$$6G+18=48$$
$$6G=30$$
$$G=5$$
$$2G=10$$
$$G+6=11$$

Thus, the number of red tokens is 10 and the number of black tokens is 11. Therefore, the probability that the token drawn is red or black is

$$P(R \text{ or } B) = P(R) + P(B) = \frac{10}{48} + \frac{11}{48} = \frac{21}{48} = \frac{7}{16}$$

188. **B. 4**

Rewrite $5^{-p} < 0.0025$ as $\frac{1}{5^p} < \frac{1}{400}$, which implies that $5^p > 400$. Substitute values for p to determine the least one that makes this inequality true: $5^2 = 25, 5^3 = 125, 5^4 = 625$. Therefore, $p = 4$ is the least positive integer that satisfies the inequality.

189. **E. 16**

You can list the factors of 1,000 (1, 2, 4, 5, etc.), or you can use the following theorem: If the prime factorization of a positive integer n is $p_1^{k_1} p_2^{k_2} \cdots p_n^{k_n}$, where each p_i is a distinct positive prime number and k_i is its corresponding exponent, then the number of positive factors of n is the product $(k_1 + 1)(k_2 + 1) \cdots (k_n + 1)$. The prime factorization of 1,000 is $2^3 \cdot 5^3$. Therefore, 1,000 has $(3+1)(3+1) = 16$ positive factors.

190. **D. 612**

Given that the units digit is $\frac{1}{3}$ times the hundreds digit, then the hundreds digit can be only 3, 6, or 9. Thus, the units digit can be only 1, 2, or 3. The units digit is twice the tens digit, so the units digit must be even. Thus, the units digit is 2, which makes the tens digit 1. Therefore, the number is 612.

191. **E. 8**

Perform the indicated operations:

$$(4e3)e(5e4) = \left(\frac{1}{3} - \frac{1}{4}\right)e\left(\frac{1}{4} - \frac{1}{5}\right) = \left(\frac{4}{12} - \frac{3}{12}\right)e\left(\frac{5}{20} - \frac{4}{20}\right) =$$

$$\left(\frac{1}{12}\right)e\left(\frac{1}{20}\right) = 20 - 12 = 8$$

192. **E. 18**

The possible remainders for division by a positive integer D are $0, 1, 2, \dots, (D-1)$. Given that 9 is the remainder when w is divided by x, then $x > 9$. Similarly, given that 7 is the remainder when z is divided by y, then $y > 7$. Therefore, the least value of $x + y$ is $10 + 8 = 18$.

193. D. $\frac{1}{\sqrt{2}}$

The ratio of AB to CD is

$$\frac{6\frac{1}{2} - 6\frac{1}{4}}{\frac{3\sqrt{2}}{2} - \frac{5\sqrt{2}}{4}} = \frac{6.5 - 6.25}{1.5\sqrt{2} - 1.25\sqrt{2}} = \frac{0.25}{0.25\sqrt{2}} = \frac{1}{\sqrt{2}}$$

194. A. $\frac{x+1}{x-3}$

Simplify the expression:

$$\left(2x^2 + 7x + 3\right)\left(2x^2 - 3x - 2\right)^{-1}\left(x^2 - 9\right)\left(x^2 - x - 2\right)$$

$$= \frac{(2x^2 + 7x + 3)(x^2 - x - 2)}{(2x^2 - 3x - 2)(x^2 - 9)}$$

$$= \frac{(2x+1)(x+3)(x+1)(x-2)}{(2x+1)(x-2)(x+3)(x-3)}$$

$$= \frac{\cancel{(2x+1)}\cancel{(x+3)}(x+1)\cancel{(x-2)}}{\cancel{(2x+1)}\cancel{(x-2)}\cancel{(x+3)}(x-3)}$$

$$= \frac{x+1}{x-3}$$

195. E. 15

Let t = the time (in hours) it will take to fill the tank if both valves are open. The portion of the tank that is being filled per hour when both valves are open is $\frac{1}{t}$. The portion of the tank that the input valve is filling per hour is $\frac{1}{6}$. The portion of the tank that the output valve is emptying per hours is $\frac{1}{10}$. Thus, because the valves are working counter to each other, the net portion that is being filled per hour when both valves are open is $\frac{1}{6} - \frac{1}{10} = \frac{5}{30} - \frac{3}{30} = \frac{2}{30} = \frac{1}{15}$. Thus, $\frac{1}{t} = \frac{1}{15}$, which implies $t = 15$. Therefore, the time to fill the tank to capacity if both valves are open is 15 hours.

196. B. 0.2

The probability that the house next door will be sold if the model home is sold first is a conditional probability. If M is the event that the model home will be sold and N is the event that the house next door will be sold, then the probability that the house next door will be sold if the model home is sold first is

$$P(N \text{ given } M \text{ has already occurred}) = \frac{P(M \text{ and } N)}{P(M)}.$$

Looking at this formula, you are given $P(M) = 0.5$, but you are not given $P(M \text{ and } N)$, which is the probability that both houses will be sold, regardless which is sold first. Using the formula for the probability that two events occur at the same time and the question information, you have

$$P(M \text{ and } N) = P(M) + P(N) - P(M \text{ or } N) = 0.5 + 0.4 - 0.8 = 0.1$$

Note: $P(M \text{ or } N)$ is the probability that at least one of the two houses will be sold, which is given as 0.8 in the question information.

Therefore

$$P(N \text{ given } M \text{ has already occurred}) = \frac{P(M \text{ and } N)}{P(M)} = \frac{0.1}{0.5} = 0.2$$

197. C. 8

The angle bisector of an angle of a triangle divides the opposite side in the ratio of the two sides that form the angle bisected, with each of these sides corresponding to the segment to which it is adjacent. Thus, solve $\frac{12}{x} = \frac{6}{4}$:

$$\frac{12}{x} = \frac{6}{4}$$

$$x = \frac{\cancel{12}^{2} \cdot 4}{\cancel{6}}$$

$$x = 8$$

198. E. I, II, and III

$\sqrt{ab} = 14$ implies $ab = 14^2 = 196$. Make an organized table in which each column contains two factors whose product is 196 in the first two rows and their sum in the third row.

factor	1	2	4	7	14
factor	196	98	49	28	14
sum	197	100	53	35	28

The possible sums for two-factor combinations are 197 (not a choice), 100 (III), 53 (II), 35 (I), and 28 (not a choice). Therefore, Choice (E) (I, II, and III) is the correct answer.

199.   A. 400

Show the possible products in a table.

		Spinner 1			
		10	**20**	**30**	**40**
Spinner 2	10	100	200	300	400
	20	200	400	600	800
	30	300	600	900	1,200
	40	400	800	1,200	1,600

The table shows that the product 400 occurs three times, which is more often than the occurrence of any other product. Therefore, the product most likely to occur is 400.

200.   D. II and III only

The square root symbol $\left(\sqrt{}\right)$ always returns the principal square root, which is nonnegative, so the solution set of $x = \sqrt{4}$ (I) is 2. Thus, the correct answer does not contain I. Eliminate choices (A) and (E). The solution set of $x^2 = 4$ is 2 and -2. The correct answer contains II. Eliminate Choice (C). The solution set of $x^4 = 16$ contains 2 and -2. Eliminate Choice (B). Therefore, the correct answer is Choice (D), II and III only.

201.   C. $\frac{47}{113}$

The number of patrons who chose nonfiction genres is $44 + 50 = 94$, and the number who chose fiction genres is $320 - 94 = 226$. Therefore, the ratio of the number of patrons who chose nonfiction genres to the number who chose fiction genres is $\frac{94}{226} = \frac{47}{113}$.

202.   C. 420

First determine T, the time, in hours, that it will take for the two machines working simultaneously to produce 1,050 components. The portion of the 1,050 components that Machine A can produce per hour is $\frac{1}{5}$, and the portion of the 1,050 components that Machine B can produce per hour is $\frac{1}{7\frac{1}{2}} = \frac{1}{\frac{15}{2}} = \frac{2}{15}$. Thus, the number of components the two machines together can produce per hour is

$$\frac{1}{5}(1,050) + \frac{2}{15}(1,050) = 210 + 140 = 350$$

Thus,

$$T = 1{,}050 \text{ components} \div 350 \frac{\text{components}}{\text{hour}} = 3 \text{ hours}$$

Therefore, at the end of 3 hours, because Machine B produces 140 components per hour, Machine B has produced $3(140) = 420$ components.

203.   A. $25\left(2 + \sqrt{6} + \sqrt{2}\right)$

The perimeter of triangle SQT is $50 + ST + QT$. Make a sketch. Extend $\overline{ST}$ to $\overline{PQ}$. Label the point of intersection K.

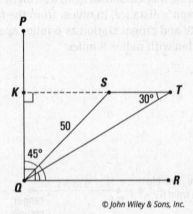

© John Wiley & Sons, Inc.

Given that $\overline{ST}$ and $\overline{QR}$ are parallel, $\overline{ST}$ is perpendicular to $\overline{PQ}$ (because a line perpendicular to one of two parallel lines is perpendicular to the other one as well). Angle KQS is a 45° angle because its measure is $90° - 45° = 45°$. Given that $\overline{ST}$ and $\overline{QR}$ are parallel and $\angle TQR = 30°$, $\angle KTQ$ is a 30° angle (because alternate interior angles of parallel lines are congruent). Find KQ and KS, the lengths of the legs of the 45°-45°-90° right triangle SKQ, which has hypotenuse of length 50. The length of the sides of a 45°-45°-90° right triangle are in the ratio $\frac{1}{\sqrt{2}} : \frac{1}{\sqrt{2}} : 1$. Hence,

$$KQ = KS = 50\left(\frac{1}{\sqrt{2}}\right) = \frac{50}{\sqrt{2}} = \frac{50 \cdot \sqrt{2}}{\sqrt{2} \cdot \sqrt{2}} = \frac{\overset{25}{\cancel{50}} \cdot \sqrt{2}}{\cancel{2}} = 25\sqrt{2}.$$

Use KQ to find both QT, which is the length of the hypotenuse of the 30°-60°-90° right triangle TKQ; and KT, which is the length of the side opposite the 60° angle. The lengths of the sides of a 30°-60°-90° right triangle are in the ratio $1 : \sqrt{3} : 2$. So $QT = (KQ)(2) = \left(25\sqrt{2}\right)(2) = 50\sqrt{2}$ and $KT = (KQ)\left(\sqrt{3}\right) = \left(25\sqrt{2}\right)\left(\sqrt{3}\right) = 25\sqrt{6}$. Use KT and KS to find ST, which is $KT - KS = 25\sqrt{6} - 25\sqrt{2}$. Therefore, the perimeter of triangle SQT is

$$50 + ST + QT = 50 + \left(25\sqrt{6} - 25\sqrt{2}\right) + 50\sqrt{2} =$$

$$50 + 25\sqrt{6} - 25\sqrt{2} + 50\sqrt{2} = 50 + 25\sqrt{6} + 25\sqrt{2} = 25\left(2 + \sqrt{6} + \sqrt{2}\right)$$

204.   B. 1

Absolute value is always nonnegative, so $|19-3x| \geq 0$. Thus, the least possible value for $|19-3x|$ is 0. This equation has solution $x = \frac{19}{3} = 6\frac{1}{3}$. Given that x is an integer, the integer value of x for which $|19-3x|$ is least is the integer that is closest to $6\frac{1}{3}$. Therefore, x is 6, which yields $|19-3x| = |19-3\cdot6| = |19-18| = 1$.

205.   C. I and II only

Do not assume that Carson went in a straight line in one direction. Let D = Carson's distance, in miles, from the family RV. Make a sketch. Show the RV and ranger station as 6 miles apart. Construct a circle at the ranger station with radius 8 miles.

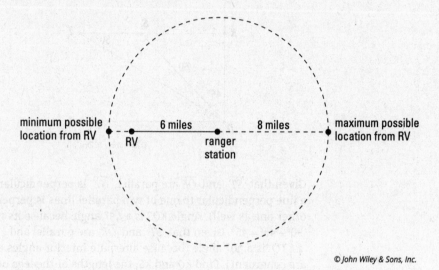

From the sketch, you can determine that $2 \leq D \leq 14$. Select I and II because each falls in this interval. Eliminate III because it is too far. Therefore, the correct answer is Choice (C), I and II only.

206.   A. $\frac{3}{64}$

The probability that Rory will *not* get a job offer is $1 - \frac{5}{8} = \frac{3}{8}$. Therefore, the probability that Katie and Ace will get job offers, but not Rory is $\frac{1}{4} \cdot \frac{1}{2} \cdot \frac{3}{8} = \frac{3}{64}$.

207. **C. 12**

The three constraint inequalities define a region in the xy-plane that represents their intersections. The region's boundary equations are $x = y$, $3x - y = 1$, and $3x + y = 5$. The maximum value of P will occur at one of the intersections of these three linear equations. To find the maximum value of P, systematically pair the three equations and solve for their intersections. Solving $x = y$ and $3x - y = 1$ by substitution yields

$$3x - x = 1$$
$$2x = 1$$
$$x = \frac{1}{2}$$
$$y = x = \frac{1}{2}$$

Thus, the intersection of $x = y$ and $3x - y = 1$ is $\left(\frac{1}{2}, \frac{1}{2}\right)$. Solving $x = y$ and $3x + y = 5$ by substitution yields

$$3x + x = 5$$
$$4x = 5$$
$$x = \frac{5}{4}$$
$$y = x = \frac{5}{4}$$

Thus, the intersection of $x = y$ and $3x + y = 5$ is $\left(\frac{5}{4}, \frac{5}{4}\right)$. Solving $3x - y = 1$ and $3x + y = 5$ by elimination yields

$$3x - y = 1$$
$$\underline{3x + y = 5}$$
$$6x = 6$$
$$x = 1$$
$$y = 5 - 3x = 5 - 3(1) = 5 - 3 = 2$$

Thus, the intersection of $3x - y = 1$ and $3x + y = 5$ is $(1,2)$. Substitute the intersection points into $P = 2x + 5y$ to find the maximum. For $\left(\frac{1}{2}, \frac{1}{2}\right)$, $P = 2 \cdot \frac{1}{2} + 5 \cdot \frac{1}{2} = 1 + 2.5 = 3.5$. For $\left(\frac{5}{4}, \frac{5}{4}\right)$, $P = 2 \cdot \frac{5}{4} + 5 \cdot \frac{5}{4} = 2.5 + 6.25 = 8.75$. For $(1,2)$, $P = 2 \cdot 1 + 5 \cdot 2 = 2 + 10 = 12$. Therefore, subject to the given constraints, the maximum value of P is 12, which occurs at $(1,2)$.

208. **B. $33\frac{1}{3}$% decrease**

If b increases by 50% of its value to $b + 50\%b = b + \frac{1}{2}b = \frac{3}{2}b$, then a must decrease to $\frac{2}{3}a$, which is $a - \frac{1}{3}a$, so that the product $\left(\frac{2}{3}a\right)\left(\frac{3}{2}b\right) = ab = c$ remains constant. Thus, if b increases by 50% of its value, then a should decrease by $\frac{1}{3} = \frac{1}{3} \times 100\% = 33\frac{1}{3}\%$ of its value to keep the equation a true statement.

209.   B. 128

The area of square $ABCD$ is s^2. Right angle DAB is an inscribed angle. Thus, the degree measure of arc DB is 180° (because the degree measure of an inscribed angle is half the degree measure of its intercepted arc), so $\overline{DB}$ is a diameter of the circle. Let D = the length of the diameter, $\overline{DB}$. Then, $\pi D = 16\pi$, which implies $D = 16$. It follows that 16 is the length of the hypotenuse of right triangle DAB, which has congruent legs of length s. Use the Pythagorean theorem to determine s^2, the area of the square.

$$s^2 + s^2 = (16)^2$$
$$2s^2 = 256$$
$$s^2 = 128$$

The square's area is 128.

210.   A. I only

$y = \dfrac{x^2 - 3x - 10}{x + 2}$ is undefined when $x = -2$ because the denominator $x + 2$ equals zero when $x = -2$. Simplified, $y = \dfrac{x^2 - 3x - 10}{x + 2} = \dfrac{(x+2)(x-5)}{(x+2)} = x - 5$,

whose graph is defined for all real numbers except $x = -2$. Thus, its graph, which, otherwise, would be the graph of the line $y = x - 5$ does not contain the point $(-2, -7)$. The graph of $y = 3x - 1$ passes through the

point $(-2, -7)$ but it does not intersect $y = \dfrac{x^2 - 3x - 10}{x + 2}$ because $x = -2$ is

excluded from the domain of the latter function. Hence, $y = \dfrac{x^2 - 3x - 10}{x + 2}$

and $y = 3x - 1$ have zero points of intersection. Therefore, Choice (A), I only, is the correct answer.

211.   B. 20%

Let x = the number of coins at A, $2x$ = the number of coins at B, $3x$ = the number of coins at C, $4x$ = the number of coins at D, and $5x$ = the number of coins at E. The minimum number of coins needed to win is 50% of the combined number of coins in locations A, B, and C (because these locations have the fewest number of coins). This minimum number is $50\%(x + 2x + 3x) = 0.5(6x) = 3x$. The total number of coins is. $x + 2x + 3x + 4x + 5x = 15x$. Therefore, the minimum percent to win is $\dfrac{3x}{15x} \times 100\% = \dfrac{1}{5} \times 100\% = 20\%$.

212. **E. 720**

For any two positive integers, their product equals their greatest common factor times their least common multiple. Therefore, the product of p and $q = 6 \times 120 = 720$.

213. **D. 16**

Use logical reasoning to determine the solution. The machines are identical, so if two machines can complete the job in 40 hours, then it should take twice as long for one machine to complete the same job. So one machine can complete the job in 80 hours. If five such machines do the job together, they should take $\frac{1}{5}$ as long as it takes for one machine. Therefore, five machines can complete the same job in $\frac{1}{5}(80 \text{ hours}) = 16$ hours.

214. **D. 24**

The greatest number of packets that the teacher can make is the greatest common factor of 72 and 48, which is 24. In each of the 24 packets there will be 5 pens: 3 black pens and 2 red pens. No pens will be left over because 24×5 pens = 120 pens.

215. **C. Two**

The equation $y = \dfrac{x^4 - 81}{x^2 + x - 12}$ is undefined when its denominator equals zero. Set the denominator equal to zero and solve for x.

$$x^2 + x - 12 = 0$$
$$(x+4)(x-3) = 0$$
$$x + 4 = 0 \text{ or } x - 3 = 0$$
$$x = -4 \text{ or } x = 3$$

Therefore, there are two values of x for which $y = \dfrac{x^4 - 81}{x^2 + x - 12}$ is undefined.

216. **E. 5 to 17**

Half of the 400 multiples of 5 are odd, and half are even. All of the multiples of 4 are even including $\frac{1}{5}(600) = 120$ that are multiples of 5. Thus, the total number of odd numbers is 200 and the total number of distinct even numbers is $200 + 600 - 120 = 680$. The ratio of odd to even is $\dfrac{200}{680} = \dfrac{5}{17}$ or 5 to 17.

217.   C. 3 to 1

Write and simplify the ratio:

$$\frac{\dfrac{2^{-16}+2^{-17}+2^{-18}+2^{-19}}{\frac{1}{4}(5)}}{2^{-17}} = \frac{\dfrac{2^{-16}+2^{-17}+2^{-18}+2^{-19}}{2^{-2}\cdot 5}}{\dfrac{1}{2^{17}}} =$$

$$\frac{\dfrac{2^{-14}+2^{-15}+2^{-16}+2^{-17}}{2^{2}\cdot 5}}{\dfrac{1}{2^{17}}} = \frac{\dfrac{2^{17}}{1}\left(\dfrac{2^{-14}+2^{-15}+2^{-16}+2^{-17}}{5}\right)}{\dfrac{2^{17}}{1}\left(\dfrac{1}{2^{17}}\right)} =$$

$$\frac{\dfrac{2^{3}+2^{2}+2^{1}+1}{5}}{1} = \frac{8+4+2+1}{5} = \frac{15}{5} = \frac{3}{1}$$

Therefore, the ratio is 3 to 1.

218.   D. I and III only

Factoring the expression on the right side yields $y = (x-a)(x-b)(x-c)(x-d)$. Thus, y is zero when x is a, b, c, or d; and y is negative when it has one or three negative factors. Make a sign chart showing where y has positive and negative values.

	$x < a$	$a < x < b$	$b < x < c$	$c < x < d$	$x > a$
$x-a$	–	+	+	+	+
$x-b$	–	–	+	+	+
$x-c$	–	–	–	+	+
$x-d$	–	–	–	–	+
y	+	–	+	–	+

The chart shows that when x lies to the left of a value that makes a factor zero, that factor is negative, and when x lies to the right of the value, that factor is positive. According to the sign chart, y is negative in the interval $a < x < b$ (I) because it has three negative factors in that interval; y is positive in the interval $b < x < c$ (II) because it has two negative factors in that interval; and y is negative in the interval $c < x < d$ (III) because it has one negative factor in that interval. Therefore, the correct answer is Choice (D), I and III only.

219.   E. $66\frac{2}{3}\%$

Let A = the amount (by weight) of the 25% brown rice mixture (Mixture A) in the blend; let B = amount (by weight) of the 40% brown rice mixture (Mixture B) in the blend; and $A + B$ = the amount (by weight) of the 30% brown rice blend. Make a table to organize the information given.

When?	Percent brown rice	Amount (by weight)	Amount of brown rice (by weight)
Before	25%	A	25%A
	40%	B	40%B
After	30%	$A + B$	30%($A + B$)

Using the table, write an equation based on the following fact: The amount of brown rice before mixing equals the amount of brown rice after mixing.

$$25\%A + 40\%B = 30\%\left(A + B\right)$$
$$0.25A + 0.40B = .30\left(A + B\right)$$
$$0.25A + 0.40B = .30A + .30B$$
$$0.10B = 0.05A$$
$$10B = 5A$$
$$2B = A$$

Therefore, the percent by weight of mixture A in the blend is

$$\frac{A}{A+B} \times 100\% = \frac{2B}{2B+B} \times 100\% = \frac{2\cancel{B}}{3\cancel{B}} \times 100\% = 66\frac{2}{3}\%$$

220.   B. $\left(\frac{1}{a}\right)^{-11}$

Simplify the expression:

$$\left(\frac{1}{a}\right)^{-3}\left(\frac{1}{a^2}\right)^{-2}\left(\frac{1}{a^4}\right)^{-1} = \left(a^{-1}\right)^{-3}\left(a^{-2}\right)^{-2}\left(a^{-4}\right)^{-1} = a^3 a^4 a^4 = a^{11}$$

This result is equivalent to $\left(\frac{1}{a}\right)^{-11}$.

221. D. $\dfrac{ab}{a+b}$

Solve the equation for x.

$$\frac{1}{a}+\frac{1}{b}=\frac{1}{x}$$

$$\frac{b}{ab}+\frac{a}{ab}=\frac{1}{x}$$

$$\frac{a+b}{ab}=\frac{1}{x}$$

$$\frac{ab}{a+b}=x$$

222. A. -2

Let x = the tens digit and y = the units digit of the original number. Solve the following equation for $x-y$:

$$(10y+x)=(10x+y)+18$$

$$10y+x=10x+y+18$$

$$10y-y-10x+x=18$$

$$9y-9x=18$$

$$9(y-x)=18$$

$$y-x=2$$

$$x-y=-2$$

223. E. 1:15 p.m.

Use logical reasoning to determine the solution. After $1\frac{1}{2}$ hours (= 1 hour and 30 minutes), the van has traveled

$$\frac{50\text{ miles}}{\text{hour}}\times1\frac{1}{2}\text{ hour}=\frac{\overset{25}{\cancel{50}}\text{ miles}}{\cancel{\text{hour}}}\times\frac{3}{\cancel{2}}\text{ }\cancel{\text{hour}}=75\text{ miles}$$

Thus, when the car starts out at 9:30 a.m., the van is 75 miles ahead. The car is traveling 20 miles per hour faster than the van (because $70-50=20$). To overtake the van, the car will have to make up the 75-mile difference at an average speed, relative to the van, of 20 miles per hour. Thus, the time, in hours, for the car to overtake the van is $\frac{75}{20}=3.75$ hours, which is 3 hours and 45 minutes. Therefore, the car will overtake the van at 9:30 a.m. plus 3 hours and 45 minutes, which is 1:15 p.m.

224.   B. 12

Given that point O is the origin, point A is located on the positive y-axis, and point B is located on the positive x-axis, triangle AOB is a right triangle with legs of lengths a and 8 and area of 48. Solve the following equation for a:

$$\frac{1}{2}(a)(8) = 48$$
$$4a = 48$$
$$a = 12$$

225.   B. 144

There are 8 ways to select the first digit; 2 ways to select the second digit, and 9 ways to select the third digit. Therefore, there are $8 \cdot 2 \cdot 9 = 144$ different possible codes.

226.   C. 14

N is an odd integer because the remainder is 1 when N is divided by 2. Given the remainder is 4 when N is divided by 5, N has the form $5q + 4$ where $q \geq 0$. The expression $5q + 4$ generates the integers 4, 9, 14, 19, 24, 29, etc. These integers show a pattern of ending in 4 or 9. Then, because N is odd, its units digit must be 9. Because the remainder is 2 when N is divided by 3, N cannot equal 9 or any other multiple of 3. Thus, N must have at least two digits. Two-digit candidates for N are 19, 29, 49, 59, 79 and 89. Of these, only 59 has remainder 2 when divided by 3 and remainder 3 when divided by 4. Thus, the least possible value of N is 59. And the sum of its digits is 14.

227.   E. Five

The least possible product will be negative. Therefore, it must contain an odd number of negative factors. The least negative product possible is -5^{10}, which can be obtained in five ways using the expression $(-5)^p (5)^{10-p}$, where p is 1, 3, 5, 7, or 9. For example, when p is 3, $(-5)^p (5)^{10-p} = (-5)^3 (5)^{10-3} = (-5)^3 (5)^7 = -5^3 \cdot 5^7 = -5^{10}$

228.   B. 49

Let $p, q\ r, M, x, y$, and G be the seven integers, listed from least to greatest. From the question information, $M = 42$ and $G = 2p + 7$. The greatest value of G will occur when p has a maximum value, which will occur only if $p = q = r$. Thus, from least to greatest, the integers are $p, p, p, 42, x, y$, and $G = 2p + 7$. The integers x, y, and G are listed on the right of the median 42. Thus, G will have it maximum value when x and y have their least possible values, which, in this case, is $x = y = 42$. Then, from least to greatest, the integers are $p, p, p, 42, 42, 42$, and $G = 2p + 7$. Solve the following equation for p, then determine $G = 2p + 7$:

$$\frac{p + p + p + 42 + 42 + 42 + (2p + 7)}{7} = 34$$
$$p + p + p + 42 + 42 + 42 + 2p + 7 = (7)(34)$$
$$5p + 133 = 238$$
$$5p = 105$$
$$p = 21$$
$$G = 2p + 7 = 2(21) + 7 = 49$$

Therefore, the maximum possible value for the greatest of the seven integers is 49.

229.   A. $6.25

Mani's total savings, in dollars, for the six months is

$$S + \frac{1}{2}S + \frac{1}{2} \cdot \frac{1}{2}S + \frac{1}{2} \cdot \frac{1}{2} \cdot \frac{1}{2}S + \frac{1}{2} \cdot \frac{1}{2} \cdot \frac{1}{2} \cdot \frac{1}{2}S + \frac{1}{2} \cdot \frac{1}{2} \cdot \frac{1}{2} \cdot \frac{1}{2} \cdot \frac{1}{2}S =$$
$$S + \frac{1}{2}S + \frac{1}{4}S + \frac{1}{8}S + \frac{1}{16}S + \frac{1}{32}S$$

Solve the following equation for S, and then determine $\frac{1}{32}S$, the amount saved the sixth month:

$$S + \frac{1}{2}S + \frac{1}{4}S + \frac{1}{8}S + \frac{1}{16}S + \frac{1}{32}S = \$393.75$$
$$32\left(S + \frac{1}{2}S + \frac{1}{4}S + \frac{1}{8}S + \frac{1}{16}S + \frac{1}{32}S\right) = 32(\$393.75)$$
$$32S + 16S + 8S + 4S + 2S + S = \$12,600$$
$$63S = \$12,600$$
$$S = \$200$$
$$\frac{1}{32}S = \frac{1}{32}(\$200) = \$6.25$$

Therefore, Mani saves $6.25 in the sixth month.

230. B. 22

Let F = the number of pages Rose read on the first day. Solve the following equation:

$$F + (F + 20) + (F + 2 \cdot 20) + (F + 3 \cdot 20) = 208$$
$$F + F + 20 + F + 40 + F + 60 = 208$$
$$4F + 120 = 208$$
$$4F = 88$$
$$F = 22$$

Rose read 22 pages on the first day.

231. D. II and III only

First, determine values of x that satisfy $|2x + 1| < 3$.

$$|2x + 1| < 3$$
$$-3 < 2x + 1 < 3$$
$$-4 < 2x < 2$$
$$-2 < x < 1$$

Given that x is an integer, only $x = -1$ or 0 satisfy the inequality. Substitute each of these values into $x^3 + 2x^2 + 5x + 10$ and evaluate. For $x = -1$,

$$x^3 + 2x^2 + 5x + 10 = (-1)^3 + 2(-1)^2 + 5(-1) + 10 = -1 + 2 - 5 + 10 = 6$$

Thus, the correct answer must include II. Eliminate Choice (A). For $x = 0$, by inspection, $x^3 + 2x^2 + 5x + 10 = 10$. Thus, the correct answer must include III. There are no other possible values for x, so Choice (D), II and III only, is the correct answer.

232. D. 12

The integers a and b are even because each contains at least one factor of 2. Thus, there exists integers m and n such that $a = 2m$ and $b = 2n$. Then by substitution,

$$K = 3(2m)^2 + 6(2n)^2 = 3(4m^2) + 6(4n^2) = 12m^2 + 24n^2 = 12(m^2 + 2n^2)$$

Thus, 12 is the greatest even number that must be a factor of K.

233.   C. $\frac{2}{11}$

First, determine the initial number of bus riders. $25\%(4{,}800) = \frac{1}{4}\left(\cancel{4{,}800}^{\,1{,}200}\right) = 1{,}200$
bus riders in the school district. Next, determine how many bus riders transferred.
$33\frac{1}{3}\%(1{,}200) = \frac{1}{3}\left(\cancel{1{,}200}^{\,400}\right) = 400$. The number of students remaining in the school
district is $4{,}800 - 400 = 4{,}400$. The number of bus riders remaining in the school
district is $1{,}200 - 400 = 800$, which represents $\frac{800}{4{,}400} = \frac{2}{11}$ of the students remaining
in the school district.

234.   D. I and II only

The lowest score the student can make is $S = C - \frac{1}{4}B = 0 - \frac{1}{4}(8) = -2$. The
highest score the student can make is $S = C - \frac{1}{4}B = 42 - \frac{1}{4}(8) = 40$. Thus,
$-2 \le S \le 40$. Any score in this range is possible. Eliminate III because it is
too high. Therefore, Choice (D), I and II only, is the correct answer.

235.   B. 10

First simplify Z:

$$Z = N\left(\frac{1}{1+N^{-1}}\right)^{-1} = N\left(\frac{1+N^{-1}}{1}\right) = N\left(1+\frac{1}{N}\right) = N+1$$

Then $\frac{10Z}{N+1} = \left(\frac{10}{\cancel{N+1}}\right)\left(\cancel{N+1}\right) = 10$.

236.   E. 130

$2x + 60 = y$ (because vertical angles of intersecting lines are congruent);
and $3x + 25 = y$ (because corresponding angles of parallel lines are congruent). Solve the following equation for x, then determine either
$y = 2x + 60$ or $y = 3x + 25$:

$$2x + 60 = 3x + 25$$
$$60 = x + 25$$
$$35 = x$$
$$y = 2x + 60 = 2(35) + 60 = 70 + 60 = 130$$

237.   E. 16

When a positive integer is divided by 8, the possible remainders are
0, 1, 2, 3, 4, 5, 6, and 7. Thus, any nonnegative integer has the form
$8k$, $8k+1$, $8k+2$, $8k+3$, $8k+4$, $8k+5$, $8k+6$, or $8k+7$. Given that N is not
divisible by 2 or 4, then N has the form $8k+1$, $8k+3$, $8k+5$, or $8k+7$.
Therefore, the sum of the possible remainders when N is divided by 8 is
$1+3+5+7 = 16$.

238. **C. 102%**

Because you're working with percentages, you can pick a convenient value for the original price of the jacket. Let $100 = the jacket's original price. Then the 15%–off sale price is $85\%(\$100) = 0.85(\$100) = \$85$. After the sale, this sale price is increased to $120\%(\$85) = 1.2(\$85) = \$102$.

Therefore, the final price of the jacket is $\dfrac{\$102}{\$100} \times 100\% = 102\%$ of its original price.

239. **D.** $\pm\sqrt{\dfrac{6A}{5y}}$

Solve for x:

$$y = \frac{6A}{5x^2}$$
$$y\left(5x^2\right) = 6A$$
$$5yx^2 = 6A$$
$$x^2 = \frac{6A}{5y}$$
$$x = \pm\sqrt{\frac{6A}{5y}}$$

240. **D. 80**

Triangle PQR is isosceles (because $PQ = PR$). The angle at R measures 50° (because base angles of an isosceles triangle are congruent). The sum of the measures of the interior angles of a triangle is 180°. Therefore, $y = 180 - 2(50) = 180 - 100 = 80$.

241. **E. 6 to 1**

For convenience, suppose initially the solution weighs 100 grams. The percent water by weight in the initial solution is $100\% - 10\% = 90\%$. Then it would contain 10 grams (= 10% of 100) of salt and 90 grams (= 90% of 100) of water. After evaporation, the amount of salt, in grams, is still 10. This now represents 40% of the evaporated solution by weight. Write the following percent equation and solve for S, the new weight, in grams, of the solution (after evaporation):

$$40\%S = 10$$
$$0.4S = 10$$
$$S = 25$$

Subtract the weight of the salt to obtain the final weight, in grams, of water in the evaporated solution. $25 - 10 = 15$. Therefore, the ratio of the initial weight to the final weight of water in the solution is $\frac{90}{15} = \frac{6}{1}$, which is 6 to 1.

242.   C. 13

Use the "3-D" Pythagorean theorem to determine the answer. Therefore, the length of the space diagonal is $\sqrt{3^2 + 4^2 + 12^2} = \sqrt{9 + 16 + 144} = \sqrt{169} = 13$.

243.   D. $192\sqrt{3}$

Equilateral triangles are equiangular, so each angle is 60°. The altitude of an equilateral triangle bisects the angle at the vertex from which it is drawn, and it bisects the side to which it is drawn. Let $2x$ = the length of a side of the equilateral triangle. Make a sketch to illustrate the situation.

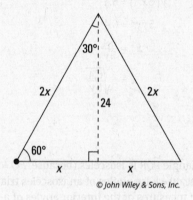

© John Wiley & Sons, Inc.

The altitude shown is the leg opposite the 60° angle in a 30°-60°-90° right triangle. The sides of a right triangle are in the ratio $1 : \sqrt{3} : 2$. Solve the following proportion for x, then determine $2x$:

$$\frac{x}{1} = \frac{24}{\sqrt{3}}$$

$$x = \frac{24 \cdot \sqrt{3}}{\sqrt{3} \cdot \sqrt{3}} = \frac{24\sqrt{3}}{3} = 8\sqrt{3}$$

$$2x = 2\left(8\sqrt{3}\right) = 16\sqrt{3}$$

Therefore, the area of the triangle is $\frac{1}{2}\left(16\sqrt{3}\right)(24) = 192\sqrt{3}$

244. E. 16

In a circle, a radius that is perpendicular to a chord bisects the chord. Let x = one-half the length of the chord. Then $2x$ = the length of the chord. Make a sketch, filling in the question information.

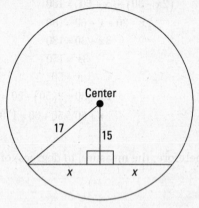

Center

17   15

x x

Using the Pythagorean theorem, solve for x, then determine $2x$, the chord's length:

$$x^2 = 17^2 - 15^2$$
$$x^2 = 289 - 225$$
$$x^2 = 64$$
$$x = \sqrt{64}$$
$$x = 8$$
$$2x = 16$$

Therefore, the length, in centimeters, of the chord is 16.

245. B. 80%

Because you're working with percentages, you can pick a convenient value for the price of season tickets last year. Let $100 = the price of season tickets last year. Then the price of season tickets this year is $100 + 25\%(\$100) = \$100 + 0.25(\$100) = \$100 + \$25 = \$125$. Therefore, last year's price represents the following percent of this year's price:

$$\frac{\$100}{\$125} \times 100\% = \frac{\$100^4}{\$125_5} \times 100\% = 80\%$$

246. C. 70

Consecutive angles of a parallelogram are supplementary (that is, their sum is 180°). Write an equation and solve for x. Then determine $2x - 30$ and $x + 60$:

$$(2x - 30) + (x + 60) = 180$$
$$2x - 30 + x + 60 = 180$$
$$3x + 30 = 180$$
$$3x = 150$$
$$x = 50$$
$$2x - 30 = 2(50) - 30 = 100 - 30 = 70$$
$$x + 60 = 50 + 60 = 110$$

Therefore, the measure, in degrees, of the smaller angle is 70.

247. D. 23

Find all the positive integers that leave a remainder of 2 when you divide 17 by the integer. Test positive integers less than 17 by mentally dividing and checking whether the remainder is 2. Only when 17 is divided by 3, 5, or 15, is the remainder 2 each time. Therefore, the sum of all possible values of K is 23.

248. A. 3,600

To determine the number of different meal combinations, find the product of the number of options for each selection. This product is $10 \cdot 12 \cdot 5 \cdot 6 = 3,600$. Therefore, there are 3,600 different meal combinations.

249. C. 0.64

The probability that Jayma will receive an acceptance letter from at least one of the two universities, denoted $P(A \text{ or } B)$, is the probability she will receive an acceptance letter from university A, denoted $P(A)$, plus the probability she will receive an acceptance letter from university B, denoted $P(B)$, minus the probability she will receive an acceptance letter from both universities, denoted $P(A \text{ and } B)$. This probability is

$$P(A \text{ or } B) = P(A) + P(B) - P(A \text{ and } B) = 0.45 + 0.36 - 0.17 = 0.64$$

250. B. 24

The people are not assigned to particular seats but are arranged relative to one another only. Two arrangements are considered different only when the positions of the people are different relative to each other. Thus, given that the chairs are identical, the five different ways the first person can be seated are indistinguishable. It follows that the number of different seating arrangements equals the number of ways to fill the other four chairs once the first person's position is fixed somewhere around the circular pattern. Therefore, there are 4 ways to seat the second person, 3 ways to seat the third person, 2 ways to seat the fourth person, and 1 way to seat the fifth person, for a total of $4 \cdot 3 \cdot 2 \cdot 1 = 24$ different seating arrangements.

251. D. $a^{\frac{3}{4}}$

Write the radicals using fractional exponents, then multiply the exponents and simplify:

$$\left(\sqrt[4]{\sqrt[3]{\sqrt{a}}}\right)^{18} = \left(\left(\left((a)^{\frac{1}{2}}\right)^{\frac{1}{3}}\right)^{\frac{1}{4}}\right)^{18} = a^{\frac{1}{2} \cdot \frac{1}{3} \cdot \frac{1}{4} \cdot \frac{18}{1}} = a^{\frac{6}{8}} = a^{\frac{3}{4}}$$

252. A. One

Solve the inequality:

$$|4n - 3| \le 2$$
$$-2 \le 4n - 3 \le 2$$
$$1 \le 4n \le 5$$
$$\frac{1}{4} \le n \le \frac{5}{4}$$

The only integer that satisfies this double inequality is the integer 1. Therefore, the answer is one.

253. B. $\frac{1}{x^2}$

Simplify the expression using the rules of exponents:

$$\left(\frac{x^{-7}}{x^{-11}}\right)^{-\frac{1}{2}} = \left(x^{-7+11}\right)^{-\frac{1}{2}} = \left(x^4\right)^{-\frac{1}{2}} = x^{-2} = \frac{1}{x^2}$$

254. D. 1

To solve the equation, use the technique of squaring both sides of the equation, as necessary, to eliminate radicals.

$$\sqrt{2x}-1=\sqrt{2x-1}$$
$$\left(\sqrt{2x}-1\right)^2=\left(\sqrt{2x-1}\right)^2$$
$$2x-2\sqrt{2x}+1=2x-1$$
$$-2\sqrt{2x}+1=-1$$
$$-2\sqrt{2x}=-2$$
$$\sqrt{2x}=1$$
$$\left(\sqrt{2x}\right)^2=1^2$$
$$2x=1$$

255. C. −1

Observe that the numbers 4, 8, and 128 are powers of 2. Substitute powers of 2 into the given equation and let $y=3$ to obtain $\left(\left(2^2\right)^x\right)\left(\left(2^3\right)^3\right)=2^7$. Simplifying this equation yields $2^{2x}2^9=2^7$, which implies $2x+9=7$. Solve this equation for x:

$$2x+9=7$$
$$2x=-2$$
$$x=-1$$

256. B. 5

When two chords intersect within a circle, the products of their segments are equal. Chords $\overline{AB}$ and $\overline{CD}$ intersect at point E. Thus, solve the following equation for x:

$$(5)(4x+1)=(3)(6x+5)$$
$$20x+5=18x+15$$
$$2x+5=15$$
$$2x=10$$
$$x=5$$

257. A. $\frac{13}{15}$

For convenience, let 15 (a common denominator for 3 and 5), be the number of student surveyed. Then the number of participants who answered "Strongly Agree" to both questions is $\left(\frac{1}{5}\right)\left(\frac{2}{3}(15)\right)=2$. Thus, $15-2=13$ did not answer "Strongly Agree" to both questions. Therefore, the portion of the survey participants who did not answer "Strongly Agree" to both questions is $\frac{13}{15}$.

258. **D. I and III only**

The situation in the question implies that B and J are positive integers. According to the question, $B = 3J + 7$, then $J = \dfrac{B-7}{3}$. Thus, J is an integer only if $B-7$ is divisible by 3. Because $10-7=3$, which is divisible by 3, the correct answer must include I. Eliminate choices (B) and (C). Because $18-7=11$, which is not divisible by 3, eliminate Choice (E). Because $49-7=42$, which is divisible by 3, the correct answer must include III. Therefore, the correct answer is Choice (D), I and III only.

259. **D. 61**

Start with the angles for which you can find the measure by using the given information. The sum of the degree measures of the interior angles of a triangle is $180°$, so $x + 45 + 60 = 180$, which implies $x = 75$. Then, $75 + 68 + y = 180$ (because these angles form a straight angle) implies $y = 37$. Therefore, $z + 82 + 37 = 180$, which implies $z = 61$.

260. **C. 16**

The possible remainders when an integer is divided by 7 are 0, 1, 2, 3, 4, 5, and 6; and the possible remainders when an integer is divided by 11 are 1, 2, 3, 4, 5, 6, 7, 8, 9, and 10. Therefore, the greatest value for $x + y$ is $6 + 10 = 16$.

261. **B.** $-\dfrac{1}{2}$

First, substitute $x = 3$ into the equation and solve for k:

$$2(3)^2 - 5(3) + k = 2$$
$$2(9) - 15 + k = 2$$
$$18 - 15 + k = 2$$
$$3 + k = 2$$
$$k = -1$$

Next, substitute $k = -1$ into the equation and solve for x:

$$2x^2 - 5x - 1 = 2$$
$$2x^2 - 5x - 3 = 0$$
$$(2x + 1)(x - 3) = 0$$
$$2x + 1 = 0 \text{ or } x = 3$$
$$x = -\frac{1}{2} \text{ or } 3$$

Chapter 4

262. **A. Statement (1) ALONE is sufficient, but statement (2) alone is not sufficient.**

From the question information $x \geq 1$ and $y \geq 1$ because both are positive integers. From (1) $xy = 300y$, which, because $y \geq 1$, implies $xy \geq 300$ (and so implies $xy \geq 250$), yielding an answer of Yes to the question posed. Thus, (1) is sufficient.

According to (2) $50 < y < 100$, so it's possible for $xy < 250$ (if say $x = 1$ and $y = 75$) or for $xy > 250$ (if say $x = 4$ and $y = 80$). So (2) is not sufficient to give a definite Yes or No answer to the question posed. Therefore, statement (1) alone is sufficient.

263. **B. Statement (2) ALONE is sufficient, but statement (1) alone is not sufficient.**

From the question information, the total time for the trip is 4 hours $\left(1\frac{1}{2} + 2\frac{1}{2} = 4\right)$. And the total distance traveled $d = \left(1\frac{1}{2}\right)x + \left(2\frac{1}{2}\right)y = 1.5x + 2.5y$.

Thus, the average speed, call it s, in terms of x and y, is $s = \frac{d}{4} = \frac{1.5x + 2.5y}{4}$.

Using (1), substitute $x = y + 10$ into $s = \frac{1.5x + 2.5y}{4}$ to obtain

$$s = \frac{1.5x + 2.5y}{4} = \frac{1.5(y+10) + 2.5y}{4} = \frac{1.5y + 15 + 2.5y}{4} = \frac{4y + 15}{4}$$

You have two variables, s and y, and only one equation $s = \frac{4y + 15}{4}$, so (1) is not sufficient.

Using (2), gives $s = \frac{d}{4} = \frac{255}{4}$, so (2) is sufficient. Therefore, statement (2) alone is sufficient.

264. **C. Both statements TOGETHER are sufficient, but NEITHER statement ALONE is sufficient.**

From (1) you can conclude that x and y have the same sign because their product is positive, but without additional information you cannot determine whether $xz < 0$. Thus, (1) is not sufficient.

From (2) you can conclude that y and z have opposite signs because their product is negative, but without additional information, you cannot determine whether $xz < 0$.

Taking (1) and (2) together, if y is positive, then x is also positive, and z is negative, so $xz < 0$. If y is negative, then x is also negative, and z is positive, so $xz < 0$. Therefore, in either case, you can answer Yes to the question posed. Therefore, both statements together are sufficient, but neither statement alone is sufficient.

265. **B. Statement (2) ALONE is sufficient, but statement (1) alone is not sufficient.**

From (1), if n is a prime number, then the answer to the question is No, because there are no prime number factors k such that $1 < k < n$. However, if n is not a prime number (for example, if $n = 15$), the prime number factor k could be 3 or 5, so then the answer to the question is Yes. You have no way of knowing whether n is prime or not, so (1) is not sufficient.

Using (2), 10! is the product of all positive integers descending down from 10 to 1. Then n is one of the nine integers from $(10! + 2)$ to $(10! + 10)$. Note that any prime number $p < 10$ is a factor of 10!. Thus, 2 is a factor of $(10! + 2)$, $(10! + 4)$, $(10! + 6)$, $(10! + 8)$, and $(10! + 10)$; 3 is a factor of $(10! + 3)$ and $(10! + 9)$; 5 is a factor of $(10! + 5)$; and 7 is a factor of $(10! + 7)$. Thus, for each integer n from $(10! + 2)$ to $(10! + 10)$, there is a prime number factor k of n. So the answer to the question posed is Yes. Thus, (2) is sufficient. Therefore, statement (2) alone is sufficient.

266. **C. Both statements TOGETHER are sufficient, but NEITHER statement ALONE is sufficient.**

Let P = the selling price, in dollars, of one tee shirt. From (1), the amount expected to be denoted is $1,000P$, which you cannot determine because P is unknown. Thus, (1) is not sufficient.

From (2), the expected amount plus an additional $500P$ is \$30,000. Thus, the expected amount to be denoted is $\$30,000 - 500P$, which you cannot determine because P is unknown. Thus, (2) is not sufficient.

Taking (1) and (2) together gives $1,500P = \$30,000$, from which you can determine P; and, thereafter, compute $1,000P$, the amount the organization expected to denote. Therefore, both statements together are sufficient, but neither statement alone is sufficient.

267. **E. Statements (1) and (2) TOGETHER are NOT sufficient.**

From (1) you have the length of the shelf, but without additional information, you cannot give a definite Yes or No answer to the question posed.

From (2), you can determine that the greatest length that is needed to accommodate the 25 books is $25 \times 1\frac{1}{2}$ inches $= 37\frac{1}{2}$ inches, but without additional information, you cannot give a definite Yes or No answer to the question posed.

Taking (1) and (2) together, if the average thickness of the books is, for instance, exactly $1\frac{1}{2}$ inches, then the answer to the question posed is No (because $25 \times 1\frac{1}{2}$ inches $= 37\frac{1}{2}$ inches, which is greater than 36). However, if the average thickness is say 1 inch, then the answer is Yes (because 25×1 inches $= 25$ inches, which is less than 36 inches). Therefore, statements (1) and (2) together are not sufficient.

268. **C. Both statements TOGETHER are sufficient, but NEITHER statement ALONE is sufficient.**

Let D = the current number of Josephine's dolls. From (1), $D + 2 \geq 14$, which implies $D \geq 12$. Thus, D cannot be less than 12, but without further information you cannot determine an exact value of D. Thus, (1) is not sufficient.

From (2), $D - 3 < 10$, which implies $D < 13$. Thus, D can be any number from 1 to 12, but without further information, you cannot determine an exact value of D.

Taking (1) and (2) together gives $12 \leq D < 13$, which implies that $D = 12$. Therefore, both statements together are sufficient, but neither statement alone is sufficient.

269. **D. Each statement ALONE is sufficient.**

If you multiply (or divide) both sides of an inequality by a negative number, you must reverse the direction of the inequality symbol. From (1) $-x^3 > 0$ implies $x^3 < 0$. Thus, $x < 0$ because the cube root of a negative number is negative. So the answer to the question posed is Yes. Thus, (1) is sufficient.

From (2), $-3x > 0$ implies $x < 0$, which yields an answer of Yes to the question posed. Thus, (2) is sufficient. Therefore, each statement alone is sufficient.

270. **D. Each statement ALONE is sufficient.**

Let P = the number of pepper plants in the garden. Using the question information and (1) gives the proportion $\frac{32}{P} = \frac{8}{3}$, which you can solve for P. Thus, (1) is sufficient.

Using the question information and (2) gives the proportion $\frac{36}{P} = \frac{3}{1}$, which you can solve for P. Therefore, each statement alone is sufficient.

271. **C. Both statements TOGETHER are sufficient, but NEITHER statement ALONE is sufficient.**

Let A = the number of avocados sold today, and P = the number of pineapples sold today. From (1), $A = 2P + 20$, which is one equation with two unknowns. Without additional information, you cannot determine an exact value of A. For example, if $P = 5$, then $A = 30$. But if $P = 10$, then $A = 40$. Thus, (1) is not sufficient.

From (2), $1.50A + 2.00P = 155.00$, which is one equation with two unknowns. Without additional information, you cannot determine an exact value of A. For example, if $P = 1$, then $A = 102$. But if $P = 4$, then $A = 98$. Thus, (2) is not sufficient.

Taking (1) and (2) together, yields a system of two equations, $A - 2P = 20$ and $1.50A + 2.00P = 155.00$, with two variables, A and P. The system has a unique solution because $\frac{1}{1.50} \neq \frac{-2}{2}$. Thus, you can determine a unique value of A. Therefore, both statements together are sufficient, but neither statement alone is sufficient.

272.

C. Both statements TOGETHER are sufficient, but NEITHER statement ALONE is sufficient.

Let R = the number of red chips. From (1), the total number of chips is 48, and the number of black chips is 16. But additional information is needed to determine the number of red chips.

From (2), the number of green chips is half the number of total chips, but additional information is needed to determine the number of red chips.

Taking (1) and (2) together, $R + 16 + \frac{1}{2}(48) = 48$, which you can solve for R. Therefore, both statements together are sufficient, but neither statement alone is sufficient.

273.

D. Each statement ALONE is sufficient.

From (1), $a^{\frac{1}{8}} = 16$ implies $\left(a^{\frac{1}{8}} \right)^4 = (16)^4$, which implies $a^{\frac{1}{2}} = 16^4$. Thus, (1) is sufficient.

From (2), $a^{\frac{1}{32}} = 2$ implies $\left(a^{\frac{1}{32}} \right)^{16} = 2^{16}$, which implies $a^{\frac{1}{2}} = 2^{16}$. Note that (1) and (2) give the same result because $16^4 = \left(2^4 \right)^4 = 2^{16}$. Therefore, each statement alone is sufficient.

274.

D. Each statement ALONE is sufficient.

From (1), $15\%B = 0.15B = 375$, from which you can solve for B; and, thereafter, determine $20\%B$.

From (2), $B = 40\%(6,250) = 0.40(6,250)$, from which you can solve for B; and, thereafter, determine $20\%B$. Therefore, each statement alone is sufficient.

275.

B. Statement (2) ALONE is sufficient, but statement (1) alone is not sufficient.

From (1), $m = n$ implies $x = z$ (because base angles of an isosceles triangle are congruent). However, without additional information, you cannot determine the value of x or z. Thus, (1) is not sufficient.

From (2), because the measure of an exterior angle of a triangle equals the sum of the measures of the nonadjacent interior angles, $88 = 54 + z$, which you can solve for z. Thus, (2) is sufficient. Therefore, statement (2) alone is sufficient.

276.

E. Statements (1) and (2) TOGETHER are NOT sufficient.

The formula for the slope m of a line is $\frac{y_2 - y_1}{x_2 - x_1}$, where (x_1, y_1) and (x_2, y_2) are two points on the line. This formula indicates that two points are needed to find a line's slope. From (1), you have one point on line p, but another point on line p is needed to determine the slope and whether it is negative.

From (2), you have one point on line q, but another point on line q is needed to determine the slope and whether it is negative.

Taking (1) and (2) together yields no additional useful information. Therefore, statements (1) and (2) together are not sufficient.

277.

B. Statement (2) ALONE is sufficient, but statement (1) alone is not sufficient.

Let B = the number of students enrolled at Sunshine Elementary School who ride the ride the bus to school. From (1), $100\% - 10\% = 90\%$ of the students enrolled at Sunshine Elementary School do not walk to school. However, not all of the non-walkers are necessarily bus riders. Some students may get to school by other means of transportation. Thus, (1) is not sufficient to determine a definite Yes or No answer to the question posed.

Using (2), if X is the number of students enrolled at Sunshine Elementary School who do not ride the bus to school, then $B = 3X$. Thus, the percent of the students enrolled at Sunshine Elementary School who ride the bus to school is

$$\frac{B}{B + X} \times 100\% = \frac{3X}{3X + X} \times 100\% = \frac{3X}{3X + X} \times 100\% = \frac{3X}{4X} \times 100\% = 75\%$$

So you have a response of Yes to the question posed. Thus, (2) is sufficient. Therefore, statement (2) alone is sufficient.

278.

D. Each statement ALONE is sufficient.

Recall that even $\pm$ even = even, odd $\pm$ odd = even, and even $\pm$ odd (or odd $\pm$ even) = odd. From (1), if $5k + 2$ is even, then $5k$ is even. Given that 5 does not contain a factor of 2, it follows that k is an even integer, yielding an answer of Yes to the question posed.

From (2), if $k^2 + 1$ is odd, then k^2 is even. Given that square roots of even numbers are even, it follows that k is an even integer, yielding an answer of Yes to the question posed. Therefore, each statement alone is sufficient.

279.

D. Each statement ALONE is sufficient.

Let P = Hollis's current gross hourly pay in dollars, and $P + \$2$ = Hollis's gross hourly pay after an increase of \$2 per hour. From (1), the increase in Hollis's gross hourly pay is $\frac{1}{9}$ of her current gross hourly pay. Thus, $\$2 = \frac{1}{9}P$, which implies $P = \$18$ and $P + \$2 = \$20$. The number of hours Hollis could work each week and earn the same gross weekly pay is

$$\frac{(\$18 \text{ per hour})(40 \text{ hours})}{(\$20 \text{ per hour})} = \frac{(\$18 \text{ per hour})(40 \text{ hours})}{(\$20 \text{ per hour})} = 36 \text{ hours}$$

This result is 4 hours fewer than 40 hours. Thus, (1) is sufficient.

From (2), $P = \frac{\$720}{40} = \$18$ and $P + \$2 = \$20$. This information is the same as that obtained from statement (1) and will yield the same result. Thus, (2) is sufficient. Therefore, each statement alone is sufficient.

280.

D. Each statement ALONE is sufficient.

From (1), $abc = 1$ implies $b = \frac{1}{ac} = (ac)^{-1}$, yielding an answer of Yes to the question posed. Thus, (1) is sufficient. Note that $abc = 1$ implies none of the factors a, b, or c is 0.

From (2), $(abc)^{-1} = 1$ implies $\frac{1}{abc} = 1$, which implies $abc = 1$ and $b = \frac{1}{ac} = (ac)^{-1}$, yielding an answer of Yes to the question posed. Note that $\frac{1}{abc} = 1$ implies none of the factors a, b, or c is 0. Therefore, each statement alone is sufficient.

281.

D. Each statement ALONE is sufficient.

Given that $54k^2 + 93k + 40 = (9k + 8)(6k + 5)$, then $54k^2 + 93k + 40 = (9k + 8)(6k + 5)$ will equal M, the least common multiple of $9k + 8$ and $6k + 5$, only if the greatest common factor of $9k + 8$ and $6k + 5$ is 1. Thus, by inspection, (1) is sufficient to determine the answer to the question posed.

To use (2), express $6k + 5$ as $6k + 5 = 6k + 6 - 1 = 2(3k + 3) - 1$. Given D is a factor of $6k + 5$, then because D is a factor of $3k + 3$, D must also be a factor of -1. The factors of -1 are 1 and -1. It follows that D is 1 because it is the greatest common factor of $9k + 8$ and $6k + 5$. Thus, (2) is sufficient to determine the answer to the question posed. Therefore, each statement alone is sufficient.

282. **A. Statement (1) ALONE is sufficient, but statement (2) alone is not sufficient.**

To use (1), express $\dfrac{4a-3b}{a-2b}$ as

$$\frac{4a-3b}{a-2b}=\frac{3a-b+a-2b}{a-2b}=\frac{3a-b}{a-2b}+\frac{a-2b}{a-2b}=\frac{3a-b}{a-2b}+1$$

Then, because $\dfrac{3a-b}{a-2b}=1$, $\dfrac{4a-3b}{a-2b}=1+1=2$. Thus, (1) is sufficient.
From (2), $a-b=3$ implies $a=b+3$. Substituting into $\dfrac{4a-3b}{a-2b}$ yields
$\dfrac{4(b+3)-3b}{(b+3)-2b}=\dfrac{4b+12-3b}{b+3-2b}=\dfrac{b+12}{3-b}$. The value of this expression varies
depending on the value of b. For example, $\dfrac{b+12}{3-b}=4$ if $b=0$ and $\dfrac{b+12}{3-b}=14$
if $b=2$. Thus, (2) is not sufficient. Therefore, statement (1) alone is
sufficient.

283. **B. Statement (2) ALONE is sufficient, but statement (1) alone is not sufficient.**

From (1), given that the units digit of $2K$ is 6, it follows that the units
digit of K is 3 or 8. But without additional information, you cannot determine a single value for the units digit. Thus, (1) is not sufficient.

From (2), given that the hundreds digit of $100K$ is 8, then the units digit of
K is 8 because the hundreds digit of $100K$ is always equal to the units digit
of K. Thus, (2) is sufficient. Therefore, statement (2) alone is sufficient.

284. **B. Statement (2) ALONE is sufficient, but statement (1) alone is not sufficient.**

From (1), $m=n^4+n^5$ implies $\sqrt[6]{m+n^4}=\sqrt[6]{n^4+n^5+n^4}=\sqrt[6]{2n^4+n^5}$. Without
knowing n, you cannot determine whether this expression is an integer.
For example, if $n=2$, then $\sqrt[6]{2n^4+n^5}=\sqrt[6]{2(16)+32}=\sqrt[6]{32+32}=\sqrt[6]{64}=2$,
which is an integer. But if $n=1$, $\sqrt[6]{2n^4+n^5}=\sqrt[6]{2(1)+1}=\sqrt[6]{3}$, which is not an
integer. Thus, (1) is not sufficient.

From (2), because n is positive, $m=n^4\left(n^2-1\right)$ implies

$$\sqrt[6]{m+n^4}=\sqrt[6]{n^4\left(n^2-1\right)+n^4}=\sqrt[6]{n^6-n^4+n^4}=\sqrt[6]{n^6}=n$$

This result is an integer, yielding an answer of Yes to the question posed.
Thus, (2) is sufficient. Therefore, statement (2) alone is sufficient.

285. **D. Each statement ALONE is sufficient.**

The decimal equivalent of $\dfrac{3}{7}$ is approximately 0.429. From (1) $\dfrac{m}{n}<0.42$
implies $\dfrac{m}{n}<\dfrac{3}{7}$ because $\dfrac{m}{n}<0.42<0.429$. Thus, (1) is sufficient to answer
the question posed.

From (2), $\left(\dfrac{m}{n}\right)^{-1}>2.5$ implies $\dfrac{m}{n}<\dfrac{1}{2.5}=0.4$. So $\dfrac{m}{n}<\dfrac{3}{7}$ because
$\dfrac{m}{n}<0.4<0.429$. Thus, (2) is sufficient to answer the question posed.
Therefore, each statement alone is sufficient.

286.

E. Statements (1) and (2) TOGETHER are NOT sufficient.

Using (1), let S = the amount, in dollars, of the sales clerk's total weekly sales last week. Then the sales clerk earned 2% of $S = 2\%(S)$ as commission on last week's total sales. Without knowing S, you cannot determine the amount of the sales clerk's commission. Thus, (1) is not sufficient.

Using (2), you can determine neither the amount of last week's total sales nor the commission rate, both of which are needed to determine the sales clerk's commission. Thus, (2) is not sufficient.

Taking (1) and (2) together, you have the commission rate, but not the amount of last week's total sales, which is needed to determine the sales clerk's commission. Therefore, statements (1) and (2) together are not sufficient.

287.

B. Statement (2) ALONE is sufficient, but statement (1) alone is not sufficient.

Let B = the price of one banana and N = the price of one navel orange. Then Chiaki paid $B + 2N$. From (1), $B = \frac{\$1}{4} = \$0.25$, but without additional information, you cannot determine $B + 2N$. Thus, (1) is not sufficient.

From (2), $3B + 6N = \$6.15$. Dividing both sides of this equation by 3 yields $B + 2N = \$2.05$. Thus, (2) is sufficient. Therefore, statement (2) alone is sufficient.

288.

C. Both statements TOGETHER are sufficient, but NEITHER statement ALONE is sufficient.

The area of the triangle is $\frac{1}{2}ab$.

From (1), $a + b = 14$ implies $a = 14 - b$. Substituting into $\frac{1}{2}ab$ yields $\frac{1}{2}(14 - b)b = 7b - \frac{b^2}{2}$. The value of this expression varies. For example, $b = 2$ gives $7(2) - \frac{2^2}{2} = 14 - 2 = 12$; and $b = 4$ gives $7(4) - \frac{4^2}{2} = 28 - 8 = 20$. Thus, (1) is not sufficient.

From (2), $b = 6$ because the Pythagorean theorem applies to the sides of the triangle. Substituting into $\frac{1}{2}ab$ yields $\frac{1}{2}a(6) = 3a$. The value of this expression varies depending on the value of a.

Taken (1) and (2) together, you can substitute $b = 6$ into $7b - \frac{b^2}{2}$ and obtain the area. Thus, (2) is sufficient. Therefore, both statements together are sufficient, but neither statement alone is sufficient.

289. **A. Statement (1) ALONE is sufficient, but statement (2) alone is not sufficient.**

From (1), $x = 10y$ implies $A = \dfrac{7x}{5y} = \dfrac{7\left(\overset{2}{\cancel{10}}y\right)}{\cancel{5}\cancel{y}} = 14$. Thus, (1) is sufficient.

From (2), $x = \dfrac{5}{7}$ implies $A = \dfrac{7\left(\dfrac{5}{7}\right)}{5y} = \dfrac{\cancel{5}^{1}}{\cancel{5}y} = \dfrac{1}{y}$, which varies depending on the value of y. For example, $y = 2$ gives $A = \dfrac{1}{2}$; and $y = \dfrac{1}{4}$ gives $A = 4$.

Thus, (2) is not sufficient. Therefore, statement (1) alone is sufficient.

290. **D. Each statement ALONE is sufficient.**

From the question information, given that the mean of the eight numbers is 60, then the sum of the eight numbers is $8(60) = 480$. From (1), if none of the eight numbers is less than 60, then suppose n of the numbers are greater than 60 and $(8 - n)$ of the numbers equal 60. For the n numbers that are greater than 60, let p_1 = the positive difference between the first number and 60, p_2 = the positive difference between the second number and 60, and so on to p_n = the positive difference between the nth number and 60. Let p = the sum of the n p_i differences. where $i = 1, 2, \ldots n$. Then the sum of the eight numbers is

$$(8 - n)(60) + n(60) + p = 480 - 60n + 60n + p = 480 + p$$

This result indicates that the sum of the eight numbers is greater than 480, which contradicts the fact the sum of the eight numbers equals 480. Thus, n must be 0, which implies each of the eight numbers equals 60. Thus, (1) is sufficient.

From (2), if none of the eight numbers is greater than 60, then suppose k of the numbers are less than 60 and $(8 - k)$ of the numbers equal 60. For the k numbers that are less than 60, let d_1 = the positive difference between 60 and the first number, d_2 = the positive difference between 60 and the second number, and so on to d_k = the positive difference between 60 and the kth number. Let d = the sum of the k d_i differences, where $i = 1, 2, \ldots k$. Then the sum of the eight numbers is

$$(8 - k)(60) + k(60) - d = 480 - 60k + 60k - d = 480 - d$$

This result indicates that the sum of the eight numbers is less than 480, which contradicts the fact the sum of the eight numbers equals 480. Thus, k must be 0, which implies each of the eight numbers equals 60. Thus, (2) is sufficient. Therefore, each statement alone is sufficient.

291. **E. Statements (1) and (2) TOGETHER are NOT sufficient.**

Given that you're working with percentages, for convenience, let 100 = the number of members in the organization who are over 40. Statement (1) leads to inexact results. For example, if 50 of the 100 members are female and 50 are male, then $24\%(50) = 12$ is the number of female members who are over 40 and have college degrees; and $16\%(50) = 8$ is the number of male members who are over 40 and have college degrees. These results indicate that $\frac{12+8}{100} \times 100\% = \frac{20}{100} \times 100\% = 20\%$ of the organization members who are over 40 have college degrees. So in this case, the answer to the question posed is Yes. However, if, for example, 25 of the 100 members are female and 75 are male, then $24\%(25) = 6$ is the number of female members who are over 40 and have college degrees; and $16\%(75) = 12$ is the number of male members who are over 40 and have college degrees. These results indicate that $\frac{6+12}{100} \times 100\% = \frac{18}{100} \times 100\% = 18\%$ of the organization members who are over 40 have college degrees. So in this case, the answer to the question posed is No. Thus, (1) is not sufficient.

Statement (2) is not sufficient because it provides no information about the members who are over 40. Taking (1) and (2) together provides no additional useful information. You cannot assume that 55% of the membership over 40 is female. Therefore, statements (1) and (2) together are not sufficient.

292. **E. Statements (1) and (2) TOGETHER are NOT sufficient.**

Statement (1) gives inexact results. For example, $A = 6$ and $B = 18$ satisfy $A + 20 < 2B$ because $26 < 36$. Substituting these values into $|20 - A| < |20 - B|$ yields $14 < 2$, which is false, meaning the answer to the question posed is No. However, $A = 12$ and $B = 36$ also satisfy $A + 20 < 2B$ because $32 < 72$. Substituting these values into $|20 - A| < |20 - B|$ yields $8 < 16$, which is true, meaning the answer to the question posed is Yes. Thus, (1) is not sufficient.

Statement (2) also gives inexact results. You can use $A = 6$ and $B = 18$, which satisfy $B = 3A$, to obtain a No answer to the question posed. Or $A = 12$ and $B = 36$, which also satisfy $B = 3A$, to obtain a Yes answer. Thus, (2) is not sufficient.

Taking (1) and (2) together gives inexact results as well because, for example, both the pair $A = 6$ and $B = 18$ and the pair $A = 12$ and $B = 36$ satisfy the conditions in both (1) and (2) but lead to opposite results. Therefore, statements (1) and (2) together are not sufficient.

293.

C. Both statements TOGETHER are sufficient, but NEITHER statement ALONE is sufficient.

From (1), N could be 9, 18, 27, 36, 45, and so on. $\frac{36}{N}$ is an integer for 9, 18, and 36 but is not an integer for any other multiple of N. Thus, (1) is not sufficient.

From (2), N could be could be any of the consecutive integers from 10 to 26. $\frac{36}{N}$ is an integer for 12 and 18 but is not an integer for any of the other possible values of N. Thus, (2) is not sufficient.

Taking (1) and (2) together, only $N = 18$ satisfies all conditions given, and it yields an answer of Yes to the question posed. Therefore, both statements together are sufficient, but neither statement alone is sufficient.

294.

D. Each statement ALONE is sufficient.

Given that x and y are both positive, $\frac{x}{y} > \frac{y}{x}$ is equivalent to $x^2 > y^2$, which will be true only if $x > y$. From (1) $\frac{4y}{x} = 5$ implies $\frac{4}{5}y = x$. This result indicates that $y > x$ yielding an answer of No to the question posed. Thus, (1) is sufficient.

From (2) $x + 4 = y$ implies $y > x$, which yields an answer of No to the question posed. Thus, (2) is sufficient. Therefore, each statement alone is sufficient.

295.

A. Statement (1) ALONE is sufficient, but statement (2) alone is not sufficient.

The ratio of $\frac{x}{6}$ to $\frac{y}{7}$ is $\dfrac{\left(\dfrac{x}{6}\right)}{\left(\dfrac{y}{7}\right)} = \frac{7x}{6y}$. From (1), $7x = 6y$ implies $\frac{7x}{6y} = \frac{6y}{6y} = 1$. Thus (1) is sufficient.

From (2), $x = 6$ implies $\frac{7x}{6y} = \frac{7(6)}{6y} = \frac{7}{y}$. The value of this expression varies depending on the value of y. Thus, (2) is not sufficient. Therefore, statement (1) alone is sufficient.

296. **E. Statements (1) and (2) TOGETHER are NOT sufficient.**

Consider the Venn diagram below, where C is the number of seniors enrolled in AP calculus only, S is the number of seniors enrolled in AP statistics only, and x is the number of seniors enrolled in both AP calculus and AP statistics.

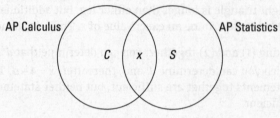

AP Calculus   AP Statistics

C x S

From (1), you have $C = 45 - x$, which is one equation with two unknowns. Without additional information, you cannot determine an exact value of x. Thus, (1) is not sufficient.

From (2), you have $C + x + S = 60$, which implies $x = 60 - C - S$, but additional information is needed to determine an exact value of x. Thus, (2) is not sufficient.

Taking (1) and (2) together, you have $(45 - x) + x + S = 60$, which implies $S = 60 - 45 = 15$ and $(45 - x) + x + 15 = 60$. More than one value of x makes this equation true. For example, if $x = 10$, $C = 45 - x = 45 - 10 = 35$, $S = 15$ and $C + x + S = 35 + 10 + 15 = 60$. But if $x = 20$, $C = 45 - x = 45 - 20 = 25$, $S = 15$ and $C + x + S = 25 + 20 + 15 = 60$. Therefore, statements (1) and (2) together are not sufficient.

297. **B. Statement (2) ALONE is sufficient, but statement (1) alone is not sufficient.**

Let P = Micah's take-home pay last month. From (1) Micah saved $300 and paid $3(\$300) = \$900$ for rent. This information tells you that

$P \geq \$300 + \$900 = \$1,200$, but additional information is needed to determine an exact value of P. Thus, (1) is not sufficient.

From (2), you have

$$25\%(P - 50\%P) = 25\%(50\%P) = \frac{1}{4}\left(\frac{1}{2}P\right) = \frac{1}{8}P = \$300$$

From this equation, you can determine an exact value of P. Thus, (2) is sufficient. Therefore, statement (2) alone is sufficient.

298. **C. Both statements TOGETHER are sufficient, but NEITHER statement ALONE is sufficient.**

From the figure, $x = a + d$. From (1), $x = 4 + d$, which is one equation with two unknowns, so without additional information you cannot determine an exact value of x. Thus, (1) is not sufficient.

From (2), you can determine only that $d < 4\sqrt{2}$ because the hypotenuse of a right triangle is longer than either leg. But additional information is needed to determine an exact value of x. Thus, (2) is not sufficient.

Taking (1) and (2) together, you can determine that $d^2 = \left(4\sqrt{2}\right)^2 - 4^2$, from which you can determine d; and, thereafter, $x = 4 + d$. Therefore, both statements together are sufficient, but neither statement alone is sufficient.

299. **C. Both statements TOGETHER are sufficient, but NEITHER statement ALONE is sufficient.**

Let F = the first term of the sequence and L = the last term of the sequence. Given that 2 is the common difference between terms, the number of terms in the arithmetic sequence is $N = \dfrac{L - F}{2} + 1$. From (1), $N = \dfrac{L - 18}{2} + 1$, which is one equation with two unknowns. Without additional information, you cannot determine an exact value of N. Thus, (1) is not sufficient.

From (2), $N = \dfrac{70 - F}{2} + 1$, which is one equation with two unknowns. Without additional information, you cannot determine an exact value of N. Thus, (2) is not sufficient.

Taking (1) and (2) together, $N = \dfrac{70 - 18}{2} + 1 = \dfrac{52}{2} + 1 = 26 + 1 = 27$. Therefore, both statements together are sufficient, but neither statement alone is sufficient.

300. **A. Statement (1) ALONE is sufficient, but statement (2) alone is not sufficient.**

Let x = the amount (in cups) of flaxseed in the mixture and $4x$ = the amount (in cups) of cornmeal in the mixture. Then $5x$ = the total amount (in cups) in the mixture. From (1), $5x = 15$, which you can solve for x, the amount, in cups, of flaxseed in the mixture. Thus, (1) is sufficient.

From (2) you can determine that $5x$ = the total amount (in cups) in the mixture, which you already knew. So additional information is needed to determine x. Thus, (2) is not sufficient. Therefore, statement (1) alone is sufficient.

301.

E. Statements (1) and (2) TOGETHER are NOT sufficient.

The fifth term of a geometric sequence is given by $a_5 = a_1 r^{5-1} = a_1 r^4$, where a_1 is the first term of the geometric sequence, and r is the common ratio between a term and the term preceding it. From (1), $a_2 = a_1 r^{2-1} = a_1 r^1 = 12$. This result implies that $a_5 = a_1 r^4 = (a_1 r^1) r^3 = 12 r^3$. Without knowing r, you cannot determine an exact value of a_5. For example, if $r = 2$ (which implies $a_1 = 6$), then $a_5 = (12)(2^3) = (12)(8) = 96$. But if $r = 3$ (which implies $a_1 = 4$), then $a_5 = (12)(3^3) = (12)(27) = 324$. Thus, (1) is not sufficient.

From (2), $a_4 = a_1 r^{4-1} = a_1 r^3 = 432$. This result implies that $a_5 = a_1 r^4 = (a_1 r^3) r^1 = 432 r$. Without knowing r, you cannot determine an exact value of a_5. For example, if $r = 2$ (which implies $a_1 = \dfrac{432}{2^3} = \dfrac{432}{8} = 54$), then $a_5 = (432)(2) = 864$. But if $r = 3$ (which implies $a_1 = \dfrac{432}{3^3} = \dfrac{432}{27} = 16$), then $a_5 = (432)(3) = 1{,}296$. Thus, (2) is not sufficient.

Taking (1) and (2) together yields $12 r^3 = 432 r$, which implies $r^2 = 36$. Thus, r is 6 or –6. If r is 6, then $a_5 = 432r = 432(6) = 2{,}592$. If r is –6, then $a_5 = 432r = 432(-6) = -2{,}592$. Therefore, statements (1) and (2) together are not sufficient.

302.

D. Each statement ALONE is sufficient.

From (1), $x^{-4} = (x^{-2})(x^{-2}) = (225)(225)$. Thus, (1) is sufficient.

From (2), $x^{-4} = \dfrac{1}{x^4} = \dfrac{1}{\frac{1}{50,625}}$. Thus, (2) is sufficient. Therefore, each statement alone is sufficient.

303.

D. Each statement ALONE is sufficient.

Let P = the initial value (purchase price) of the certificate of deposit (CD). The value of the investment increases by 2% (=0.02) each year. Thus, the value of the CD at the end of the fifth year is $P(1.02)(1.02)(1.02)(1.02)(1.02) = P(1.02)^5$ and the interest earned at the end of the fifth year is $P(1.02)^5 - P$. From (1), $P(1.02) = \$5{,}100$, from which you can determine P; and, thereafter, $P(1.02)^5 - P$. Thus, (1) is sufficient.

From (2), $P(1.02)^3 = \$5{,}306.04$, from which you can determine P; and, thereafter, $P(1.02)^5 - P$. Thus, (2) is sufficient. Therefore, each statement alone is sufficient.

304.

A. Statement (1) ALONE is sufficient, but statement (2) alone is not sufficient.

Using the quadratic formula, the two roots of $x^2 + bx + c = 0$ are

$$x = \frac{-b + \sqrt{b^2 - 4(1)c}}{2(1)} = \frac{-b}{2} + \frac{\sqrt{b^2 - 4c}}{2} \text{ and } x = \frac{-b - \sqrt{b^2 - 4(1)c}}{2(1)} = \frac{-b}{2} - \frac{\sqrt{b^2 - 4c}}{2}.$$

Adding the roots yields $\frac{-b}{2} + \frac{\sqrt{b^2 - 4c}}{2} + \frac{-b}{2} - \frac{\sqrt{b^2 - 4c}}{2} = \frac{-2b}{2} = -b$. Hence, the

sum of the roots of $x^2 + bx + c = 0$ equals $-b$. From (1) $b < 0$ implies $-b > 0$, so the sum of the roots is positive. Thus, (1) is sufficient to answer the question posed.

From (2), $c < 0$ implies that the product of the two roots is negative, indicating that the two roots have opposite signs. However, without additional information, you cannot determine whether the sum is positive. For instance, the sum of the roots of $x^2 - 2x - 15 = 0$, which has roots 3 and -5, is -2. This result yields an answer of No to the question posed. But the sum of the roots of $x^2 + 2x - 15 = 0$, which has roots 5 and -3 is 2. This result yields an answer of Yes to the question posed. Thus, (2) is not sufficient. Therefore, statement (1) alone is sufficient.

305.

C. Both statements TOGETHER are sufficient, but NEITHER statement ALONE is sufficient.

From (1), the rate, in gallons per minute, that the inlet pipe is pumping water into the cistern is

$$\frac{7 \text{ gallons}}{30 \text{ seconds}} = \frac{7 \text{ gallons}}{\frac{1}{2} \text{ minute}} = 14 \text{ gallons per minute}$$

But without knowing the rate at which water is being pumped out of the cistern, the rate at which the amount of water in the cistern is increasing cannot be determined.

From (2), the rate, in gallons per minute, that the outlet pipe is pumping water out of the cistern is

$$\frac{12 \text{ gallons}}{1 \text{ minute } 30 \text{ seconds}} = \frac{12 \text{ gallons}}{1\frac{1}{2} \text{ minute}} = 8 \text{ gallons per minute}$$

But without knowing the rate at which water is being pumped into the cistern, the rate at which the amount of water in the cistern is increasing cannot be determined.

Taking (1) and (2) together, the rate at which water in the cistern is increasing is

$$14 \text{ gallons per minute} - 8 \text{ gallons per minute} = 6 \text{ gallons per minute}$$

Therefore, both statements together are sufficient, but neither statement alone is sufficient.

306. **D. Each statement ALONE is sufficient.**

Let B = the number of black cars, and W = the number of white cars. From the question information, $B + W = 70$. The ratio of the number of black cars to the number of white cars in the fleet is $\frac{B}{W}$. From (1), $B = 2W + 10$, which implies $B + W = (2W + 10) + W = 70$, which you can solve for W; and, thereafter, determine $\frac{B}{W} = \frac{2W + 10}{W}$. Thus, (1) is sufficient. From (2), $\frac{B}{70} = \frac{W}{70} + \frac{3}{7}$, which implies $\frac{B}{70} = \frac{W}{70} + \frac{30}{70}$, from which it follows that $B - W = 30$. Solve this equation simultaneously with the equation $B + W = 70$ to obtain exact values for B and W; and, thereafter, determine $\frac{B}{W}$. Thus, (2) is sufficient. Therefore, each statement alone is sufficient.

307. **E. Statements (1) and (2) TOGETHER are NOT sufficient.**

From (1), $n = 5$ or -5, which implies $m - n$ equals $m - 5$ or $m + 5$. Without additional information, you cannot determine an exact value of $m - n$. Thus, (1) is not sufficient.

From (2), $m = 7$ or -7, which implies $m - n$ equals $7 - n$ or $-7 - n$. Without additional information, you cannot determine an exact value of $m - n$. Thus, (2) is not sufficient.

Taking (1) and (2) yields inexact results because $n = 5$ or -5 and $m = 7$ or -7, so $m - n$ can equal $7 - 5 = 2$ or $7 + 5 = 12$ or $-7 - 5 = -12$ or $-7 + 5 = -2$. Therefore, statements (1) and (2) together are not sufficient.

308. **B. Statement (2) ALONE is sufficient, but statement (1) alone is not sufficient.**

The percent increase in the sale price is

$$\frac{\text{the amount of the increase in the sale price, in dollars}}{\$250} \times 100\%$$

From (1), you cannot determine the amount of the increase in the sale price. Thus, (1) is not sufficient.

From (2), The percent increase in the sale price is $\frac{\$50}{\$250} \times 100\%$, which you can compute. Thus, (2) is sufficient. Therefore, statement (2) alone is sufficient.

309. **E. Statements (1) and (2) TOGETHER are NOT sufficient.**

From (1), $p = 6x$ implies $pq = (6x)q = 6xq$, where x is a prime number and q is a positive integer. If $x = 2$ and $q = 1$, then $pq = 6xq = 6(2)(1) = 12$ is not a multiple of 36. But if $x = 3$ and $q = 4$, then $pq = 6xq = 6(3)(4) = 72$ is a multiple of 36. Thus, (1) is not sufficient to determine a definite Yes or No answer to the question posed.

From (2), $q = 15y$ implies $pq = p(15y) = 15py$, where p and y are positive integers. If $p = 1$ and $y = 1$, then $pq = 15(1)(1) = 15$ is not a multiple of 36. But if $p = 3$ and $y = 4$, then $pq = 15(3)(4) = 180$ is a multiple of 36. Thus, (2) is not sufficient to determine a definite Yes or No answer to the question posed.

Taking (1) and (2) together yields $pq = (6x)(15y) = 90xy$, where x is a prime number and y is a positive integer. If $x = 2$ and $y = 1$, then $pq = 90xy = 90(2)(1) = 180$ is a multiple of 36; but if $x = 3$ and $y = 1$, then $pq = 90xy = 90(3)(1) = 270$ is not a multiple of 36. Therefore, statements (1) and (2) together are not sufficient to answer the question posed.

310. **D. Each statement ALONE is sufficient.**

From (1), the remainder when $1,000a + 100b + 10c + d$ is divided by 3 is the same as the remainder when the sum of its digits is divided by 3. Hence, the remainder when $1,000a + 100b + 10c + d$ is divided by 3 equals 2 because $17 = 5 \cdot 3 + 2$. Thus, (1) is sufficient.

From (2), $(1,000a + 100b + 10c + d) - 2$ is divisible by 3 implies $(1,000a + 100b + 10c + d) - 2 = 3M$, where M is an integer. This result implies $(1,000a + 100b + 10c + d) = 3M + 2$. Hence, the remainder when $1,000a + 100b + 10c + d$ is divided by 3 equals 2 because $(1,000a + 100b + 10c + d) = M \cdot 3 + 2$. Thus, (2) is sufficient. Therefore, each statement alone is sufficient.

311. **C. Both statements TOGETHER are sufficient, but NEITHER statement ALONE is sufficient.**

From (1), x can take on a range of values. If $x = \frac{1}{2}$, $x^2 = \left(\frac{1}{2}\right)^2 = \frac{1}{4}$, which yields an answer of No to the question posed. But if $x = -2$, $x^2 = (-2)^2 = 4$, which yields an answer of Yes to the question posed. Without additional information, you cannot give a definite Yes or No answer to the question posed. Thus, (1) is not sufficient.

From (2), x can take on a range of values. If $x = -\frac{1}{2}$, $x^2 = \left(-\frac{1}{2}\right)^2 = \frac{1}{4}$, which yields an answer of No to the question posed. But if $x = 2$, $x^2 = (2)^2 = 4$, which yields an answer of Yes to the question posed. Without additional information, you cannot give a definite Yes or No answer to the question posed. Thus, (2) is not sufficient.

Taking (1) and (2) together gives $-1 < x < 1$, which implies that $|x| < 1$. It follows that $x^2 < 1$, yielding an answer of No to the question posed. Therefore, both statements together are sufficient, but neither statement alone is sufficient.

312. **D. Each statement ALONE is sufficient.**

Let M = the marked-down price. The customer pays $M + 8\%M = M + 0.08M = 1.08M$ for the marked-down shoes, including sales tax. From (1), you have $\left(\$170 + 8\%(\$170)\right) - 1.08M = \$36.72$, which you can solve for an exact value of M; and, thereafter, compute $1.08M$. Thus, (1) is sufficient.

From (2), you have $8\%M = 0.08M = \$10.88$, which you can solve for an exact value of M, and, thereafter, compute $1.08M$. Thus, (2) is sufficient. Therefore, each statement alone is sufficient.

313. **C. Both statements TOGETHER are sufficient, but NEITHER statement ALONE is sufficient.**

From the question information, $n = 3$, 4, 5, 6, or 7. From (1), $n = 3$ or 5 because the units digit of $(3+1)^2$ is 6 $\left(4^2 = 16\right)$ and the units digit of $(5+1)^2$ is 6 $\left(6^2 = 36\right)$.

From (2), $n = 5$ or 7 because the units digit of $(5-1)^2$ is 6 $\left(4^2 = 16\right)$ and the units digit of $(7-1)^2$ is 6 $\left(6^2 = 36\right)$. Taking (1) and (2) together yields $n = 5$ as the only one of the possible values of n that satisfies all conditions given. So 5 is the units digit of $n^2 \left(5^2 = 25\right)$. Therefore, both statements together are sufficient, but neither statement alone is sufficient.

314. **D. Each statement ALONE is sufficient.**

Let M = Mayte's present age, then $M + 5$ = Mayte's age in 5 years. From (1), $M + 10 = 1\frac{1}{2}M$, which you can solve for M; and, thereafter, determine $M + 5$. Thus, (1) is sufficient. From (2), $M - 5 = \frac{3}{4}M$, which you can solve for M; and, thereafter, determine $M + 5$. Thus, (2) is sufficient. Therefore, each statement alone is sufficient.

315. **C. Both statements TOGETHER are sufficient, but NEITHER statement ALONE is sufficient.**

In (1), no information about y is given, so additional information is needed to answer the question posed. Thus, (1) is not sufficient.

In (2), no information about x is given, so additional information is needed to answer the question posed. Thus, (2) is not sufficient.

Taking (1) and (2) together, $x = \frac{1}{7}\left(91^{25}\right) = \frac{1}{7}(91)\left(91^{24}\right) = 13\left(91^{24}\right) = y$, which yields an answer of No to the question posed. Therefore, both statements together are sufficient, but neither statement alone is sufficient.

316. **B. Statement (2) ALONE is sufficient, but statement (1) alone is not sufficient.**

Let $A = 2x$, $B = 3x$, and $C = 5x$. Then the sum of the three integers is $A + B + C = 2x + 3x + 5x = 10x$. From (1), $A + B = C$ implies $2x + 3x = 5x$, which you already know, so additional information is needed. Thus, (1) is not sufficient.

From (2), $C - A = 24$ implies $5x - 2x = 3x = 24$. You can solve this equation for an exact value of x, and, thereafter, determine $10x$, the sum of A, B, and C. Thus, (2) is sufficient. Therefore, statement (2) alone is sufficient.

317. **A. Statement (1) ALONE is sufficient, but statement (2) alone is not sufficient.**

From (1), $x^2 - 6x = 16$ implies $x^2 - 6x + 9 = 16 + 9$, from which you have $(x - 3)^2 = 25$. It follows that $|x - 3| = 5$. Thus, (1) is sufficient.

From (2), $-3 < x < 9$ implies $-6 < x - 3 < 6$, from which you have $|x - 3| < 6$, but additional information is needed to determine an exact value of $|x - 3|$. Thus, (2) is not sufficient. Therefore, statement (1) alone is sufficient.

318. **A. Statement (1) ALONE is sufficient, but statement (2) alone is not sufficient.**

Let L = the larger integer. Then $21 - L$ = the smaller integer. From (1), $L(21 - L) = 104$. Solving this equation yields

$$L(21 - L) = 104$$
$$21L - L^2 = 104$$
$$-L^2 + 21L - 104 = 0$$
$$L^2 - 21L + 104 = 0$$
$$(L - 13)(L - 8) = 0$$
$$L = 13 \text{ and } 21 - L = 8$$
$$\text{or } L = 8 \text{ and } 21 - L = 13 \text{ (reject because } L \text{ is the larger integer)}$$

Thus, (1) is sufficient.

Statement (2) yields inexact results. For example, $L = 19$ and $21 - L = 2$ satisfy the condition. And $L = 17$ and $21 - L = 4$ also satisfy the condition. Thus, (2) is not sufficient. Therefore, statement (1) alone is sufficient.

319. **C. Both statements TOGETHER are sufficient, but NEITHER statement ALONE is sufficient.**

Let Q = the number of quarters in the coin bank, and D = the number of dimes in the bank. From (1), $D = 2Q$, but additional information is needed to determine an exact value of Q.

From (2) $0.25Q + 0.10D = \$9.90$, which is one equation with two unknowns, so additional information is needed to determine an exact value of Q.

Taking (1) and (2) together, you have $0.25Q + 0.10(2Q) = \$9.90$, which you can solve for an exact value of Q. Therefore, both statements together are sufficient, but neither statement alone is sufficient.

320. **C. Both statements TOGETHER are sufficient, but NEITHER statement ALONE is sufficient.**

The average of R, S, and T is $\frac{R + S + T}{3}$. Statement (1), gives inexact results because the values of R, S, and T can vary. For instance, $R = S = T = 5$ (which satisfy the equation) yield an average of 5. But $R = 15$, $S = 0$, and $T = 5$ (which satisfy the equation) yield an average of $\frac{20}{3}$. Thus, (1) is not sufficient.

From (2), $3R = 90 - (2S + T)$ implies $3R + 2S + T = 90$, which gives inexact results because the values of R, S, and T can vary. For instance, $R = S = T = 15$ (which satisfy the equation) yield an average of 15. But $R = 20$, $S = 0$, and $T = 30$ (which satisfy the equation) yield an average of $\frac{50}{3}$. Thus, (2) is not sufficient.

Taking (1) and (2) together and adding the two equations yields $4R + 4S + 4T = 120$, which implies $R + S + T = 30$, from which you can determine an exact value of $\frac{R + S + T}{3} = \frac{30}{3}$. Therefore, both statements together are sufficient, but neither statement alone is sufficient.

321. **D. Each statement ALONE is sufficient.**

From (1), $x^3 + 8 < 0$ implies $x^3 < -8$, from which you have $x < -2$, yielding an answer of Yes to the question posed. Thus, (1) is sufficient.

From (2), $-\left(\frac{1}{4}x + 3\right) > 0$ implies $\left(\frac{1}{4}x + 3\right) < 0$, from which you have $\frac{1}{4}x < -3$, so $x < -12$, yielding an answer of Yes to the question posed. Thus, (2) is sufficient. Therefore, each statement alone is sufficient.

322. **B. Statement (2) ALONE is sufficient, but statement (1) alone is not sufficient.**

Simplify the expression:

$$\left(a\sqrt{5}+b\sqrt{5}\right)^2 = \left(\sqrt{5}(a+b)\right)^2 = \left(\sqrt{5}\right)^2(a+b)^2 = 5(a+b)^2$$

From (1), $a-b=5$ leads to inexact results. For example, $a=10$ and $b=5$ satisfy the condition and result in

$$5(a+b)^2 = 5(10+5)^2 = 5(15)^2 = 5(225) = 1{,}125$$

But $a=15$ and $b=10$ satisfy the condition and result in

$$5(a+b)^2 = 5(15+10)^2 = 5(25)^2 = 5(625) = 3{,}125$$

Thus, (1) is not sufficient.

From (2), $a(a+b) = 81-b(b+a)$ implies $a^2+ab = 81-b^2-ab$, from which you have $a^2+2ab+b^2 = 81$. Factoring yields $(a+b)^2 = 81$. Hence, $5(a+b)^2 = 5(81)$. Thus, (2) is sufficient. Therefore, statement (2) alone is sufficient.

323. **B. Statement (2) ALONE is sufficient, but statement (1) alone is not sufficient.**

From the question, you know that each machine will do $\frac{1}{6}$ of the work. From (1), each machine produces 200 of the 1,200 components. This amount is $\frac{200}{1{,}200} = \frac{1}{6}$ of the work, which you already knew, so additional information is needed. Thus, (1) is not sufficient.

From (2), if it takes $4\frac{1}{2}$ hours for two such machines to produce 1,200 components, then one such machine will take twice as long, or 9 hours. Six such machines will take $\frac{1}{6}$ as long as one machine takes, or $\frac{1}{6}(9 \text{ hours})$. Thus, (2) is sufficient. Therefore, statement (2) alone is sufficient.

324. **C. Both statements TOGETHER are sufficient, but NEITHER statement ALONE is sufficient.**

Let t = the time, in hours, it will take the two vehicles to be 405 miles apart. Then

$$t = \frac{405 \text{ miles}}{\text{combined speeds of the two vehicles (in miles per hour)}}$$

From (1), you have the speed of the truck, but you need the speed of the van also to compute t. Thus, (1) is not sufficient.

From (2), you have the speed of the van, but you need the speed of the truck also to compute t. Thus, (2) is not sufficient.

Taking (1) and (2) together yields $t = \dfrac{405 \text{ miles}}{(70+65)\text{ miles per hour}}$, from which you can compute an exact value of t. Therefore, both statements together are sufficient, but neither statement alone is sufficient.

325. **A. Statement (1) ALONE is sufficient, but statement (2) alone is not sufficient.**

From (1), $\dfrac{3}{4x} + \dfrac{k}{3x} = \dfrac{1}{x}$ implies $\dfrac{9}{12x} + \dfrac{4k}{12x} = \dfrac{12}{12x}$. It follows that $9 + 4k = 12$, which you can solve for an exact value of k. Thus, (1) is sufficient.

From (2), $\dfrac{k}{x} = 2$ implies $k = 2x$. Without additional information, you cannot determine an exact value of k. Thus, (2) is not sufficient. Therefore, statement (1) alone is sufficient.

326. **C. Both statements TOGETHER are sufficient, but NEITHER statement ALONE is sufficient.**

From the question information, $a_{51} = a_1 + (50)d$. From (1) $a_{11} = a_1 + (10)d = 25$, which yields one equation with two unknowns. Without additional information, you cannot determine an exact value of $a_{51} = a_1 + (50)d$. Thus, (1) is not sufficient.

From (2) $a_{21} = a_1 + (20)d = 45$, which yields one equation with two unknowns. Without additional information, you cannot determine an exact value of $a_{51} = a_1 + (50)d$. Thus, (2) is not sufficient.

Taking (1) and (2) together, you have two linear equations with two unknowns. You can solve the two equations simultaneously to obtain exact values for a_1 and d, and, thereafter, determine an exact value of $a_{51} = a_1 + (50)d$. Therefore, both statements together are sufficient, but neither statement alone is sufficient.

327. **A. Statement (1) ALONE is sufficient, but statement (2) alone is not sufficient.**

From the question information, make a table of possible paired values of m and n.

m	1	2	3	4	5	6	7	8
n	8	7	6	5	4	3	2	1

Using the information in (1) and checking through the possible paired values of m and n, only one pair ($m = 2$ and $n = 7$) satisfies the double inequality $39 < 3m + 5n < 43$. With these values, you can compute an exact value of mn. Thus, (1) is sufficient.

Using the information in (2), six of the possible paired values of m and n satisfy the double inequality. These six pairs result in three different values (8, 14, and 18) for mn. Thus, (2) is not sufficient. Therefore, statement (1) alone is sufficient.

328. **B. Statement (2) ALONE is sufficient, but statement (1) alone is not sufficient.**

From (1), $|x+y| = 11$ implies $(x+y) = 11$ or -11. Without additional information, you cannot determine an exact value of $x + y$. Thus, (1) is not sufficient.

From (2), $\sqrt{44(x+y)} = 22$ implies $44(x+y) = 22^2$, from which you can determine an exact value of $x + y$. Thus, (2) is sufficient. Therefore, statement (2) alone is sufficient.

329. **D. Each statement ALONE is sufficient.**

Simplify the inequality:

$$\frac{4^{x+5}}{2^{12}} > 1$$

$$4^{x+5} > 2^{12}$$

$$4^x 4^5 > 2^{12}$$

$$4^x \left(2^2\right)^5 > 2^{12}$$

$$4^x 2^{10} > 2^{12}$$

$$4^x > 2^2$$

$$4^x > 4$$

Hence, the answer to the question posed is Yes if $4^x > 4$ and No, otherwise. From (1), given that $x > 1$, then $4^x > 4$ is true. Thus, (1) is sufficient.

Simplifying (2) yields

$$2^{2x-2} > 1$$

$$2^{2x}2^{-2} > 1$$

$$\frac{\left(2^2\right)^x}{2^2} > 1$$

$$\frac{4^x}{4} > 1$$

$$4^x > 4$$

Thus, (2) is sufficient. Therefore, each statement alone is sufficient.

330. **D. Each statement ALONE is sufficient.**

From (1), $\sqrt{x^2+4}=x+2$. Squaring both sides yields $x^2+4=x^2+4x+4$, which implies $4x=0$, from which you have $x=0$. Thus, (1) is sufficient.

From (2), $h=2$ or -2. Square both sides of $\sqrt{x^2+4}=x+h$ to obtain $x^2+4=x^2+2hx+h^2$. Substituting $h^2=4$ yields $x^2+4=x^2+2hx+4$, which implies $2hx=0$, from which you have $x=0$ (because $h\neq0$). Thus, (2) is sufficient. Therefore, each statement alone is sufficient.

331. **E. Statements (1) and (2) TOGETHER are NOT sufficient.**

Let Max = the maximum value and Min = the minimum value of the 15 numbers. Then the range of the 15 numbers is $Max - Min$. From (1), you know only that five $\left(=\frac{1}{3}\cdot15\right)$ of the 15 numbers equal 25, but you need additional information to determine the range. Thus, (1) is not sufficient.

From (2), you have the range equals $Max - Min = Max - \frac{1}{4}Max = \frac{3}{4}Max$. This result can vary depending on the value of Max.

Taking (1) and (2) together provides no additional information that will lead to an exact value of the range. For example, a Max and Min of 100 and 25, respectively, satisfy all conditions and yield a range of 75. While a Max and Min of 80 and 20, respectively, satisfy all conditions and yield a range of 60. Therefore, statements (1) and (2) together are not sufficient.

332. **E. Statements (1) and (2) TOGETHER are NOT sufficient.**

If x and y have opposite signs, the answer to the question posed is Yes; otherwise, the answer is No. Statement (1) indicates that x could be negative, but it does not have to be. Further, there is no information about y given. Thus, (1) is not sufficient.

From (2), y is positive, but there is no information about x given. Thus, (2) is not sufficient.

Taking (1) and (2) together, x could be negative, in which case $xy<0$ (yielding an answer of Yes to the question posed) or x could be positive, in which case $xy>0$ (yielding an answer of No to the question posed). Therefore, statements (1) and (2) together are not sufficient.

333. **A. Statement (1) ALONE is sufficient, but statement (2) alone is not sufficient.**

From (1), $3^x4^x=144$ implies $12^x=12^2$, from which you have $x=2$. Thus, (1) is sufficient.

From (2) $\left(10^x\right)^x=10{,}000$ implies $10^{x^2}=10^4$, from which you have $x^2=4$. So $x=2$ or -2, not an exact value. Thus, (2) is not sufficient. Therefore, statement (1) alone is sufficient.

334. **C. Both statements TOGETHER are sufficient, but NEITHER statement ALONE is sufficient.**

$\frac{a}{b} > \frac{c}{d}$ will be true if $ad > bc$. From (1), $a - c > 0$ implies $a > c$, from which you can obtain $ad > cd$ (because $d > 0$), but additional information is needed to determine whether $ad > bc$. Thus, (1) is not sufficient.

From (2), $b - d < 0$ implies $b < d$ or, equivalently, $d > b$, from which you can obtain $cd > bc$ (because $c > 0$), but additional information is needed to determine whether $ad > bc$. Thus, (2) is not sufficient.

Taking (1) and (2) together, $ad > cd$ and $cd > bc$ implies $ad > bc$, yielding an answer of Yes to the question posed. Therefore, both statements together are sufficient, but neither statement alone is sufficient.

335. **A. Statement (1) ALONE is sufficient, but statement (2) alone is not sufficient.**

From (1), $\frac{c}{d} = \frac{5}{1}$, which implies $c = 5d$. Substituting into $\frac{c+d}{c-d}$ yields $\frac{5d+d}{5d-d} = \frac{6d}{4d} = \frac{3}{2}$. Thus, (1) is sufficient.

From (2), you have a range of possible values for $\frac{c+d}{c-d}$. For instance, both $\frac{c+d}{c-d} = \frac{5}{4}$ and $\frac{c+d}{c-d} = \frac{7}{4}$ satisfy the condition given. Thus, (2) is not sufficient. Therefore, statement (1) alone is sufficient.

336. **C. Both statements TOGETHER are sufficient, but NEITHER statement ALONE is sufficient.**

From (1), Given k is a prime such that $k < 5$, then $k = 2$ or 3. Without additional information, you cannot determine an exact value of k. Thus, (1) is not sufficient.

Statement (2) implies that all the positive factors of k are odd (because odd + 1 = even, but even + 1 = odd). So k is a positive integer that has only odd factors. The list of such integers (1, 3, 5, 7, 9, 11, 15, . . .) continues indefinitely. Without further information, you cannot determine an exact value of k. Thus, (2) is not sufficient.

Taking (1) and (2) together indicates $k = 3$, which satisfies all conditions given. Therefore, both statements together are sufficient, but neither statement alone is sufficient.

337. **A. Statement (1) ALONE is sufficient, but statement (2) alone is not sufficient.**

From (1), $\dfrac{14 + 6x + x^2 + 19}{4} = 6$. Solve this equation for x:

$$\frac{14 + 6x + x^2 + 19}{4} = 6$$
$$14 + 6x + x^2 + 19 = 24$$
$$x^2 + 6x + 33 = 24$$
$$x^2 + 6x + 9 = 0$$
$$(x + 3)^2 = 0$$
$$x + 3 = 0$$
$$x = -3$$

Thus, (1) is sufficient.

From (2), x is either the least of the four numbers are the greatest (because $15 - 4 \neq 18$). Case I: If x is the least, then $15 - x = 18$, which implies $x = -3$. Case II: If x is the greatest, then $x - 4 = 18$, which implies $x = 22$. Without further information, you cannot determine an exact value of x. Thus, (2) is not sufficient. Therefore, statement (1) alone is sufficient.

338. **D. Each statement ALONE is sufficient.**

Let M = the number of teachers who have masters degrees. Then $90 - M$ = the number of teachers who do not have masters degrees. From (1), $90 - M = \dfrac{1}{5}M$, which you can solve for an exact value of M. Thus, (1) is sufficient.

From (2), $M = (90 - M) + 60$, which you can solve for an exact value of M. Thus, (2) is sufficient. Therefore, each statement alone is sufficient.

339. **D. Each statement ALONE is sufficient.**

Substituting from (1) yields $(-2)^2 - 3(-2) + k = -30$, which you can solve for an exact value of k. Thus, (1) is sufficient.

Substituting from (2) yields $(5)^2 - 3(5) + k = -30$, which you can solve for an exact value of k. Thus, (2) is sufficient. Therefore, each statement alone is sufficient.

340. **D. Each statement ALONE is sufficient.**

From (1), given that 18, the sum of N's digits, is divisible by 9, then N is divisible by 9. Thus, (1) is sufficient.

From (2), given that $N + 432$ is divisible by 9, then $N + 432 = 9m$, where m is an integer. Then, $N = 9m - 432 = 9(m - 48)$, which implies N is divisible by 9. Thus, (2) is sufficient. Therefore, each statement alone is sufficient.

341. **D. Each statement ALONE is sufficient.**

The perimeter of the triangle is $P = a + 5.6 + c$. Substituting (1) into the Pythagorean theorem yields $a = \sqrt{7.0^2 - 5.6^2}$. So $P = \sqrt{7.0^2 - 5.6^2} + 5.6 + 7.0$. Thus, (1) is sufficient.

Substituting (2) into the Pythagorean theorem yields $c = \sqrt{4.2^2 + 5.6^2}$. So $P = 4.2 + 5.6 + \sqrt{4.2^2 + 5.6^2}$. Thus, (2) is sufficient. Therefore, each statement alone is sufficient.

342. **A. Statement (1) ALONE is sufficient, but statement (2) alone is not sufficient.**

By the triangle inequality $x < y + z$. Substituting (1) into $x < y + z$ yields $x < y + y = 2y$. So the answer to the question posed is No. Thus, (1) is sufficient.

From (2), you have a range of possible values of x. For $x = 9$, $y = 4$, and $z = 6$ (values that satisfy the triangle inequality), the answer to the question posed is Yes. But for $x = 7$, $y = 5$, and $z = 5$ (values that satisfy the triangle inequality), the answer to the question posed is No. Thus, (2) is not sufficient. Therefore, statement (1) alone is sufficient.

343. **C. Both statements TOGETHER are sufficient, but NEITHER statement ALONE is sufficient.**

Let H = the number of tiles along each of the horizontal boundaries of the wall area, and V = the number of tiles along each of the vertical boundaries of the wall area. Then the perimeter of the wall area is $P = 2(H)(9 \text{ inches}) + 2(V)(9 \text{ inches})$. From (1), you know the number of tiles is 48, but without knowing the configuration of the 48 tiles, you cannot determine an exact value of P. For example, $H = 16$ and $V = 3$ yields $P = 2(16)(9 \text{ inches}) + 2(3)(9 \text{ inches}) = 342$ inches, but $H = 12$ and $V = 4$ yields $P = 2(12)(9 \text{ inches}) + 2(4)(9 \text{ inches}) = 288$ inches. Thus, (1) is not sufficient.

From (2) $H = 3V$ implies $P = 2(3V)(9 \text{ inches}) + 2(V)(9 \text{ inches}) = (8V)(9 \text{ inches})$, but further information is needed to determine an exact value of P. Thus, (2) is not sufficient.

Taking (1) and (2) together, you have $(3V)(V) = 48$, or equivalently, $V^2 = 16$, from which you can determine an exact value of V (because the question situation implies that V is a positive integer). Thereafter, you can determine an exact value of $P = (8V)(9 \text{ inches})$. Therefore, both statements together are sufficient, but neither statement alone is sufficient.

344. **A. Statement (1) ALONE is sufficient, but statement (2) alone is not sufficient.**

From the figure $kx < 180$ (because the sum of the measures of the interior angles of a triangle is 180°) and $kx > 90$ (because an exterior angle of a triangle is greater than either of the remote interior angles of the triangle). Thus, $90 < kx < 180$. From (1), $90 < 6x < 180$, which implies $15 < x < 30$. So the answer to the question posed is Yes. Thus, (1) is sufficient.

From (2), $x > 15$ implies $kx > 15k$, from which it follows that $15k < 180$. So $k < 12$, which gives a range of possible values for k. But without additional information, you cannot determine an exact value of x. Thus, (2) is not sufficient. Therefore, statement (1) alone is sufficient.

345. **C. Both statements TOGETHER are sufficient, but NEITHER statement ALONE is sufficient.**

From the question information, $x + y + z = 180$ (because the sum of the measures of the interior angles of a triangle is 180°). From (1), $y = z$ (because base angles of an isosceles triangle have equal measure). Substituting into $x + y + z = 180$ yields $x + 2y = 180$. But without additional information, you cannot determine an exact value of x.

From (2), $x + 65 + z = 180$. But without additional information, you cannot determine an exact value of x.

Taking (1) and (2) together, you have $x + 2(65) = 180$, which you can solve for an exact value of x. Therefore, both statements together are sufficient, but neither statement alone is sufficient.

346. **E. Statements (1) and (2) TOGETHER are NOT sufficient.**

Let R miles per hour = the speed, at which Tek travels to and from work. Let D_1 = the distance to and from work via route 1, and D_2 = the distance to and from work via route 2. The difference is $D_1 - D_2$. From (1), $D_1 = (R \text{ miles per hour})(1 \text{ hour}) = R$ miles. Without additional information, you cannot determine an exact value of $D_1 - D_2$. Thus, (1) is not sufficient.

From (2), because 40 minutes equals $\frac{2}{3}$ hour, $D_2 = (R \text{ miles per hour})$ $\left(\frac{2}{3} \text{ hour}\right) = \frac{2}{3}R$ miles. Without additional information, you cannot determine an exact value of $D_1 - D_2$. Thus, (2) is not sufficient.

Taking (1) and (2) together, $D_1 - D_2 = R \text{ miles} - \frac{2}{3}R \text{ miles} = \frac{1}{3}R \text{ miles}$, which varies depending on the value of R. For example, if $R = 60$, the difference is 20 miles, but if $R = 45$, the difference is 15 miles. Therefore, statements (1) and (2) together are not sufficient.

347.

A. Statement (1) ALONE is sufficient, but statement (2) alone is not sufficient.

From (1), if 80 houses do not have four bedrooms, and they make up 40 percent of the houses in the neighborhood, then there are $200 \left(= \frac{80}{40\%} \right)$ houses in the neighborhood. 50% of these houses, or 100, are over 30 years old, which means there are also 100 houses that are 30 years old or under. 75% of the 100 houses over 30 years old have four bedrooms, so 25% of 100, or 25, do not. Because 80 houses do not have four bedrooms and 25 are over 30 years old, the remaining 55 without four bedrooms must be 30 years old or under. Thus, (1) is sufficient.

From (2), you have $25\%(60\%) = 15\%$ of the houses having four bedrooms are two story houses that are more than 30 years old. But further information is needed to determine the total number of houses 30 years or under that do not have four bedrooms. Thus, (2) is not sufficient. Therefore, statement (1) alone is sufficient.

348.

B. Statement (2) ALONE is sufficient, but statement (1) alone is not sufficient.

From (1), $r = 3(s+1)$ implies $\frac{r}{s} = \frac{3(s+1)}{s} = \frac{3s+3}{s}$. This result will vary depending on the value of s. For example, if $s = 1$, then $\frac{r}{s} = \frac{3(s+1)}{s} = \frac{3s+3}{s} = \frac{6}{1}$. But $s = 3$, so then $\frac{r}{s} = \frac{3s+3}{s} = \frac{12}{3} = \frac{4}{1}$. Thus, (1) is not sufficient.

From (2), $\frac{1.2r}{3.6s} = \frac{3}{2}$ implies $\frac{r}{3s} = \frac{3}{2}$, from which you have $\frac{r}{s} = \frac{9}{2}$. Thus, (2) is sufficient. Therefore, statement (2) alone is sufficient.

349.

A. Statement (1) ALONE is sufficient, but statement (2) alone is not sufficient.

From (1), the only way $x, y,$ and z can have a mean of 2 is if they have the values 1, 2, and 3, respectively. The range is $3 - 1 = 2$. So the answer to the question posed is Yes. Thus, (1) is sufficient.

From (2), given that the median is 2, then x and y must have the values 1 and 2, respectively. If $z = 3$, the range is $3 - 1 = 2$. So the answer to the question posed is Yes. But if, for example, $z = 5$, the range is $5 - 1 = 4 \neq 2$. So the answer to the question posed is No. Thus, (2) is not sufficient. Therefore, statement (1) alone is sufficient.

350.

A. Statement (1) ALONE is sufficient, but statement (2) alone is not sufficient.

Recall that odd $\pm$ odd = even and even $\pm$ odd = odd. Because 425,371 is odd, $n + 425,371$ is odd only if n is even. Hence, the answer to the question posed is Yes if n is even and No otherwise.

From (1), because 268,865 is odd, then n must be even given that $n - 268,865$ is odd. This result yields an answer of Yes to the question posed. Thus, (1) is sufficient.

From (2), because 890,214 is even, then $890,214n$ is even regardless whether n is even or odd. So you cannot answer definitely Yes or No to the question posed. Thus, (2) is not sufficient. Therefore, statement (1) alone is sufficient.

351. **C. Both statements TOGETHER are sufficient, but NEITHER statement ALONE is sufficient.**

From (1), let $10x$ = the amount, in grams, of ingredient A, $5x$ = the amount, in grams, of ingredient B, $4x$ = the amount, in grams, of ingredient C, and $2x$ = the amount, in grams, of ingredient D. Then ingredient A is $10x - 2x$ more than ingredient D. This amount can vary depending on the value of x. Thus, (1) is not sufficient.

From (2), you are not given information about A or D. Thus, (2) is not sufficient.

Taking (1) and (2) together, you have $5x = 4x + 4$, from which you can determine an exact value of x; and, thereafter, determine an exact value of $10x - 2x$. Therefore, both statements together are sufficient, but neither statement alone is sufficient.

352. **D. Each statement ALONE is sufficient.**

From (1), given that a number is divisible by 4 if its tens and units digit form a number that is divisible by 4, K is divisible by 4 because 36 is divisible by 4. Thus, (1) is sufficient.

From (2), 12 is a factor of K, which implies that 3 and 4 are factors of K, so K is divisible by 4. Thus, (2) is sufficient. Therefore, each statement alone is sufficient.

353. **D. Each statement ALONE is sufficient.**

From (1), you have a negative number raised to a negative power. The result will be the reciprocal of a negative number. So the answer to the question posed is No. Thus, (1) is sufficient.

From (2), $x^3 + 64 = 0$ implies $x^3 = -64$, so $x = -4$. With this result you can determine that $(-4)^{(-4)^3}$ is negative, yielding an answer of No to the question posed. Thus, (2) is sufficient. Therefore, each statement alone is sufficient.

354. **A. Statement (1) ALONE is sufficient, but statement (2) alone is not sufficient.**

Simplifying (1) yields

$$36a^2 + 5a + 49b^2 - 5b = \left(6a\right)^2 + \left(7b\right)^2 + 20$$
$$36a^2 + 5a + 49b^2 - 5b = 36a^2 + 49b^2 + 20$$
$$5a - 5b = 20$$
$$a - b = 4$$

Thus, (1) is sufficient.

From (2), $\sqrt{a^2 - b^2} = 8$ implies $a^2 - b^2 = 64$, from which you have $(a-b)(a+b) = 64$. Without additional information, you cannot determine an exact value of $a - b$. For example, $a = 17$ and $b = 15$ satisfy the condition (because $17^2 - 15^2 = 289 - 225 = 64$) and yield a value of $a - b = 17 - 15 = 2$. But $a = 10$ and $b = 6$ also satisfy the condition (because $10^2 - 6^2 = 100 - 36 = 64$) and yield a value of $a - b = 10 - 6 = 4$. Thus, (2) is not sufficient. Therefore, statement (1) alone is sufficient.

355. **B. Statement (2) ALONE is sufficient, but statement (1) alone is not sufficient.**

Let P = the value of the pendant in 2013. Then $50\%P = 0.5P$ is the value of the pendant in 2015. From (1), you have the value of the pendant in 2014, but you cannot assume that the value of the pendant changed the same amount each year. It's possible that the value of the pendant may have increased from 2013 to 2014 and then decreased from 2014 to 2013 to $0.5P$. So additional information is needed to determine an exact value of P. Thus, (1) is not sufficient.

From (2), you have $125\%\left(0.5P\right) = \$3,125$, which you can solve for an exact value of P. Thus, (2) is sufficient. Therefore, statement (2) alone is sufficient.

356. **E. Statements (1) and (2) TOGETHER are NOT sufficient.**

From (1), $a = 24$, 28, or 36. You need additional information to determine an exact value of a. Thus, (1) is not sufficient.

From (2), $a = 24$, 33, or 36. You need additional information to determine an exact value of a. Thus, (2) is not sufficient.

Taking (1) and (2) together, $a = 24$ or 36. Without additional information, you cannot determine an exact value of a. Therefore, statements (1) and (2) together are not sufficient.

357. **A. Statement (1) ALONE is sufficient, but statement (2) alone is not sufficient.**

The sum of the measures of the interior angles of a triangle is 180°. A triangle is equilateral if the measure of each of its angles is 60°. From (1), $x + x + 60 = 180$, which implies $2x = 120$. So $x = y = 60$, indicating that Yes, the triangle is an equilateral triangle. Thus, (1) is sufficient.

From (2), $x + y = 120$, which you already knew because the third angle measures 60°. Without additional information, you cannot determine definite values for x and y. For example, $x = 80$ and $y = 40$ satisfy the condition and yield an answer of No to the question posed. But $x = 60$ and $y = 60$ satisfy the condition and yield an answer of Yes to the question posed. Thus, (2) is not sufficient.

Therefore, statement (1) alone is sufficient.

358. **C. Both statements TOGETHER are sufficient, but NEITHER statement ALONE is sufficient.**

From (1), $m = n + 8$, which implies $\frac{m}{n} = \frac{n+8}{n}$. Without additional information, you cannot determine an exact value of $\frac{m}{n}$. For example, if $n = 4$, then $\frac{m}{n} = \frac{4+8}{4} = 3$. But if $n = -4$, then $\frac{m}{n} = \frac{-4+8}{-4} = -1$. Thus, (1) is not sufficient.

From (2), $(m+n)(m-n) = 0$ implies $m^2 - n^2 = 0$ or, equivalently, $m^2 = n^2$. Although the squares of m and n are equal, m and n are not necessarily equal. For example, $m = 4$ and $n = 4$ yield $\frac{m}{n} = \frac{4}{4} = 1$. But $m = 4$ and $n = -4$ yield $\frac{m}{n} = \frac{4}{-4} = -1$. Thus, (2) is not sufficient. Taking (1) and (2) together yields $(n+8)^2 = n^2$, which implies $n^2 + 16n + 64 = n^2$. From this result, you have $16n = -64$, so $n = -4$ and $\frac{m}{n} = \frac{-4+8}{-4} = -1$. Therefore, both statements together are sufficient, but neither statement alone is sufficient.

359. **D. Each statement ALONE is sufficient.**

Factoring (1) yields

$$Kx + x - Ky - y = 0$$
$$Kx - Ky + x - y = 0$$
$$K(x-y) + (x-y) = 0$$
$$(K+1)(x-y) = 0$$

Given that $x \neq y$, this result implies $K + 1 = 0$, so $K = -1$. Thus, (1) is sufficient.

From (2), $\left(\frac{x}{y}\right)^K = \frac{y}{x}$ implies $K = -1$. Thus, (2) is sufficient. Therefore, each statement alone is sufficient.

360.

C. Both statements TOGETHER are sufficient, but NEITHER statement ALONE is sufficient.

From (1), the exterior angle that is adjacent to angle Y equals $180° - 60° = 120° \neq 140°$. Without additional information, you cannot determine whether one of the other exterior angles measures $140°$. Thus, (1) is not sufficient.

From (2), the exterior angle that is adjacent to angle Z equals $180° - 70° = 110° \neq 140°$. Without additional information, you cannot determine whether one of the other exterior angles measures $140°$. Thus, (2) is not sufficient.

Taking (1) and (2) together, neither of the exterior angles adjacent to angles Y and Z equals $140°$. The third exterior angle equals the sum of the measures of the two non-adjacent interior angles. So the measure of the third exterior angle is $60° + 70° = 130° \neq 140°$, yielding an answer of No to the question posed. Therefore, both statements together are sufficient, but neither statement alone is sufficient.

361.

B. Statement (2) ALONE is sufficient, but statement (1) alone is not sufficient.

From (1), $x = \dfrac{15}{y}$. Substituting into $5x - 3y$ yields $5\left(\dfrac{15}{y}\right) - 3y$, which simplifies to $\dfrac{75 - 3y^2}{y}$, which will equal zero if $75 - 3y^2 = 0$.

If $y = 5$, $75 - 3(5)^2 = 0$, yielding an answer of Yes to the question posed. But if $y = 3$, $75 - 3(3)^2 = 48$, yielding an answer of No to the question posed. Thus, (1) is not sufficient.

From (2), $20x = 12y$ implies $5x = 3y$, from which you have $5x - 3y = 0$, yielding an answer of Yes to the question posed. Thus, (2) is sufficient. Therefore, statement (2) alone is sufficient.

362.

B. Statement (2) ALONE is sufficient, but statement (1) alone is not sufficient.

The question is asking whether $1.08P$ dollars $> S$ dollars. From (1), $1.08P$ dollars $= 1.08(\$405) = \$437.40$. But without information about S, you cannot determine whether $1.08P$ dollars $> S$ dollars. Thus, (1) is not sufficient.

From (2), $1.08P$ dollars $= 1.08(0.9S)$ dollars $= 0.972S$ dollars, yielding an answer of No to the question posed. Thus, (2) is sufficient. Therefore, statement (2) alone is sufficient.

363. **B. Statement (2) ALONE is sufficient, but statement (1) alone is not sufficient.**

From (1), y could be a range of values. For example, y could be 0, which is less than 1 or y could be 2, which is greater than 1. Thus, (1) is not sufficient.

From (2), given that $xy < 10$, $x > 10$ implies that $0 \le y < 1$ or y is negative. Either way, $y < 1$, yielding an answer of Yes to the question posed. Thus, (2) is sufficient. Therefore, statement (2) alone is sufficient.

364. **C. Both statements TOGETHER are sufficient, but NEITHER statement ALONE is sufficient to answer the question asked.**

Recall that even $\pm$ even = even, odd $\pm$ odd = even, and even $\pm$ odd (or odd $\pm$ even) = odd. From (1), given that $n + 95$ is odd and 95 is odd, it follows that n is even. Without additional information, you cannot determine whether n is a prime number. For example, n could be 2, which is the only even prime, or n could be 4, which is not prime. Thus, (1) is not sufficient.

From (2), you have a range of values of n, some that are prime and some that are not prime. For example, n could be 3 which is prime, or n could be 4, which is not prime. Thus, (2) is not sufficient.

Taking (1) and (2) together, n is not prime because there are no even prime numbers that satisfy $2 < n < 12$. Therefore, both statements together are sufficient, but neither statement alone is sufficient.

365. **E. Statements (1) and (2) TOGETHER are NOT sufficient.**

From (1), the customer buys $4 \times 6 = 24$ cans of tomatoes, but you need the original price and the sale price to determine the savings. Thus, (1) is not sufficient.

From (2), the sale price per can of the store-brand tomatoes is $\frac{\$1}{4} = \$0.25$, but you need the original price and the number of cans purchased to determine the savings. Thus, (2) is not sufficient.

Taking (1) and (2) together yields 24 cans × $0.25 per can = $6 as the sale price of the six-month supply, but you need the original price of the canned tomatoes to determine the savings. Therefore, statements (1) and (2) together are not sufficient.

366. **C. Both statements TOGETHER are sufficient, but NEITHER statement ALONE is sufficient.**

From (1), the time for the trip from city A to City B is $\dfrac{288 \text{ miles}}{72 \text{ miles per hour}} = 4$ hours. Without additional information, you cannot determine the time Adwoa left city A. Thus, (1) is not sufficient.

From (2), you know the time at which Adwoa arrived in city B, but without additional information, you cannot determine the time Adwoa left city A. Thus, (2) is not sufficient.

Taking (1) and (2) together, you can determine that Adwoa left city A at 10 a.m., 4 hours before 2 p.m. Therefore, both statements together are sufficient, but neither statement alone is sufficient.

367. **C. Both statements TOGETHER are sufficient, but NEITHER statement ALONE is sufficient.**

From (1), section C accounts for $1 - \dfrac{8}{9} = \dfrac{1}{9}$ of the total area. But additional information is needed to determine the portion of the total area represented by section A. Thus, (1) is not sufficient.

From (2), let b = the portion of the total area corresponding to section B. Then b = 3 times the portion of the total area corresponding to section C. But without additional information, you cannot determine the portion of the total area represented by section A. Thus, (2) is not sufficient.

Taking (1) and (2) together yields $b = 3\left(\dfrac{1}{9}\right) = \dfrac{3}{9}$ of the total area. So the portion of the total area corresponding to section A is $\dfrac{8}{9} - \dfrac{3}{9} = \dfrac{5}{9}$. Therefore, both statements together are sufficient, but neither statement alone is sufficient.

368. **C. Both statements TOGETHER are sufficient, but NEITHER statement ALONE is sufficient.**

From (1), $\dfrac{x+y}{2} = 55$ implies $x + y = 110$. You need additional information about z to determine the value of $x - z$. Thus, (1) is not sufficient.

From (2), $\dfrac{y+z}{2} = 80$ implies $y + z = 160$. You need additional information about x to determine the value of $x - z$. Thus, (2) is not sufficient.

Taking (1) and (2) together, subtract the equation in (2) from the equation in (1) to obtain

$$
\begin{aligned}
(x+y) &= 110 \\
-(y+z) &= -160 \\
\hline
x+y-y-z &= -50 \\
x-z &= -50
\end{aligned}
$$

Therefore, both statements together are sufficient, but neither statement alone is sufficient.

369. **D. Each statement ALONE is sufficient.**

From (1), $10 < p - 3 < 16$ implies $13 < p < 19$, from which you have $p = 17$ because 17 is the only prime number in the interval given. Thus, (1) is sufficient.

From (2), $p^2 = 289$ implies $p = 17$ because -17 is not a prime number. Thus, (2) is sufficient. Therefore, each statement alone is sufficient.

370. **D. Each statement ALONE is sufficient.**

From (1), $\frac{2}{3} \times 1{,}380 = 920$ spectators are residents of the town. Then, because $\frac{3}{4}$ of the spectators who are residents of the town are close relatives of players in the game, $\frac{1}{4} \times 920 = 230$ of the spectators who are residents of the town are not close relatives of players in the game. Thus, (1) is sufficient.

From (2), let n = the number of spectators at the game, then because $\frac{2}{3}$ of the spectators are residents of the town, then $\frac{1}{3}n = 460$, which implies $n = 3 \times 460 = 1{,}380$. Thus, (2) is sufficient because you can complete it as shown in (1). Therefore, each statement alone is sufficient.

371. **C. Both statements TOGETHER are sufficient, but NEITHER statement ALONE is sufficient.**

When the $M + N$ integers are ordered from least to greatest, the median is located at position $\frac{(M+N)+1}{2}$. From (1), $M + N = 25 + N$, and the median is located at position $\frac{(25+N)+1}{2} = \frac{26+N}{2}$. If $M = N$, the median is located at position $\frac{25+26}{2} = \frac{51}{2} = 25.5$, so the median equals the arithmetic average of 400 and 475, which is 475.5. If $M \neq N$, say, for example, $N = 10$, the median is located at position $\frac{(25+10)+1}{2} = \frac{36}{2} = 18$, which indicates the median is an integer and, therefore, cannot equal 475.5. Thus, (1) gives inconclusive results, so it is not sufficient.

From (2), $M + N = M + 24$, and the median is located at position $\frac{(M+24)+1}{2} = \frac{M+25}{2}$. If $M = N$, the median is located at position $\frac{24+25}{2} = \frac{49}{2} = 24.5$, so the median equals the arithmetic average of 400 and 475, which is 475.5. If $M \neq N$, when say, for example, $M = 3$, so the median is located at position $\frac{(3+24)+1}{2} = \frac{28}{2} = 14$, which indicates the median is an integer and, therefore, cannot equal 475.5. Thus, (2) gives inconclusive results, so it is not sufficient.

Taking (1) and (2) together, the median is located at position $\frac{(25+24)+1}{2} = \frac{50}{2} = 25$, which indicates the median is 400. Therefore, both statements together are sufficient, but neither statement alone is sufficient.

372. D. Each statement ALONE is sufficient.

When the numbers are ordered from least to greatest, the median is b. Hence, the question posed can be stated as follows: Is $b = \frac{a+b+c}{3}$, or, equivalently, is $2b = a + c$? From (1), $c - a = 2(c - b)$, which implies $c - a = 2c - 2b$, from which you have $2b = a + c$. Thus, (1) is sufficient.

From (2), you have $a + b + c = 3a$, $a + b + c = 3b$ or $a + b + c = 3c$. Case I: If $a + b + c = 3a$, then $(b - a) + (c - a) = 0$. Because $(b - a) > 0$ and $(c - a) > 0$, their sum cannot equal zero. So reject $a + b + c = 3a$. Case II: If $a + b + c = 3b$, then $(a - b) + (c - b) = 0$. Because $(a - b) < 0$ and $(c - b) > 0$, their sum can equal zero. So do not reject $a + b + c = 3b$. Case III: If $a + b + c = 3c$, then $(a - c) + (b - c) = 0$. Because $(a - c) < 0$ and $(b - c) < 0$, their sum cannot equal zero. So reject $a + b + c = 3c$. Hence, it must be the case that $a + b + c = 3b$, which implies $a + c = 2b$. Thus, (2) is sufficient. Therefore, each statement alone is sufficient.

373. E. Statements (1) and (2) TOGETHER are NOT sufficient.

From (1), set A contains 4 numbers and thus, set B contains at least 4 numbers. This information leads to inconclusive results. For example, if $A = \{1, 2, 3, 4\}$ and $B = \{0, 1, 2, 3, 4\}$, then the range of B (which is $4 - 0 = 4$) is greater than the range of A (which is $4 - 1 = 3$). But if $A = \{0, 2, 3, 4\}$ and $B = \{0, 1, 2, 3, 4\}$, then the range of B (which is $4 - 0 = 4$) equals the range of A (which is $4 - 0 = 4$). Thus, (1) is not sufficient.

From (2), set B contains 5 numbers and thus, set A contains no more than 5 numbers. The same examples given in (1) can be used to show that this information leads to inconclusive results. Thus, (2) is not sufficient.

Taking (1) and (2) together, the examples given in (1) can be used to show that it cannot be determined whether the range of set A is less than the range of set B. Therefore, statements (1) and (2) together are not sufficient.

374. B. Statement (2) ALONE is sufficient, but statement (1) alone is not sufficient.

Statement (1) gives inconclusive results. For example, $r = 100$ and $s = 80$ yield

$$(1 + 0.01(100))(1 - 0.01(80)) = (1 + 1)(1 - 0.8) = (2)(0.2) = 0.4 \not> 1$$

But $r = 100$ and $s = 20$ yield $(1 + 0.01(100))(1 - 0.01(20)) = (1 + 1)(1 - 0.2) = (2)(0.8) = 1.6 > 1$

Thus, (1) is not sufficient.

Simplify (2) as follows:

$$0.01rs < r - s$$
$$0.0001rs < 0.01r - 0.01s$$
$$0.01r - 0.01s > 0.0001rs$$
$$0.01r - 0.01s - 0.0001rs > 0$$
$$0.01r - 0.01s - 0.0001rs + 1 > 0 + 1$$
$$1 + 0.01r - 0.01s - 0.0001rs > 1$$
$$(1 + 0.01r) - 0.01s(1 + 0.01r) > 1$$
$$(1 + 0.01r)(1 - 0.01s) > 1$$

This result yields an answer of Yes to the question posed. Thus, (2) is sufficient. Therefore, statement (2) alone is sufficient.

---

375. **D. Each statement ALONE is sufficient.**

Recall that a circle with radius r has circumference equal to $2\pi r$ and area equal to πr^2. From (1), in circle Y, $\pi r^2 = 100\pi$ ft^2 implies $r^2 = 100$ ft^2, so r, the radius of circle Y, is 10 feet. Then given that the circumference of circle X equals $\frac{1}{2}$ the circumference of circle Y, the circumference of circle X is $\frac{1}{2} \times 2\pi(10 \text{ ft}) = 10\pi$ ft, which implies the radius of circle X is 5 feet and its area is $\pi(5 \text{ ft})^2$. Thus, (1) is sufficient.

From (2), you know from (1) that if the circumference of circle Y is known, you can proceed as in (1) to determine circle X's area. Thus, (2) is sufficient. Therefore, each statement alone is sufficient.

---

376. **D. Each statement ALONE is sufficient.**

The triangle is a right triangle, so $x^2 + y^2 = 20^2 = 400$. The perimeter of the triangle is $P = 20$ in $+ x$ in $+ y$ in. From (1), given that the area of the triangle is 96, then $\frac{1}{2}xy = 96$, which implies $xy = 192$. Because $(x + y)^2 = x^2 + 2xy + y^2 = x^2 + y^2 + 2xy$, then $(x + y)^2 = x^2 + y^2 + 2xy = 400 + 2(192)$. So $(x + y) = \sqrt{400 + 2(192)}$ and the exact value of the perimeter is $P = 20$ in $+ \sqrt{400 + 2(192)}$ in. Thus, (1) is sufficient.

From (2), $x^2 + y^2 = x^2 + (x + 4)^2 = 20^2$, which implies $2x^2 + 8x - 386 = 0$ or, equivalently, $x^2 + 4x - 192 = 0$. Because −192 is negative, the two roots of this quadratic equation have opposite signs. You can solve the equation for the positive root x, and then determine y; and, thereafter, the exact value of the perimeter, $P = 20$ in $+ x$ in $+ y$ in. Thus, (2) is sufficient. Therefore, each statement alone is sufficient.

377.

B. Statement (2) ALONE is sufficient, but statement (1) alone is not sufficient.

From the question, $y = ax$ and $x = bz$ implies $y = a(bz) = (ab)z$. From (1), $\frac{1}{2} = b(60)$, which implies $b = \frac{1}{120}$. But without additional information, you cannot determine an exact value of $y = (ab)75$. Thus, (1) is not sufficient.

From (2), $2 = (ab)50$, which implies $ab = \frac{1}{25}$. Hence, when $z = 75$, $y = (ab)z = \frac{1}{25}(75)$. Thus, (2) is sufficient. Therefore, statement (2) alone is sufficient.

378.

D. Each statement ALONE is sufficient.

The triangle is a right triangle, so $a^2 + b^2 = c^2$. The area of the triangle is 24, so $\frac{1}{2}(ab) = 24$. From (1), $b = \sqrt{225} = 15$. Then given $\frac{1}{2}(ab) = 24$, $\frac{1}{2}(a)(15) = 24$ implies $a = \frac{16}{5}$. Then $c^2 = \left(\frac{16}{5}\right)^2 + 15^2$, from which you can obtain an exact value of c. Thus, (1) is sufficient.

From (2), $a = \sqrt{\frac{256}{25}} = \frac{16}{5}$. Then given $\frac{1}{2}(ab) = 24$, $\frac{1}{2}\left(\frac{16}{5}\right)(b) = 24$ implies $b = 15$. Then $c^2 = \left(\frac{16}{5}\right)^2 + 15^2$, from which you can obtain an exact value of c.

Thus, (2) is sufficient. Therefore, each statement alone is sufficient.

379.

C. Both statements TOGETHER are sufficient, but NEITHER statement ALONE is sufficient.

Let h = the height that is 2 standard deviations greater than the mean height. Then $h = \text{mean} + 2(\text{standard deviation})$. From (1), $h = 32.8 \text{ cm} + 2(\text{standard deviation})$. Without knowing the standard deviation, you cannot determine an exact value of h. Thus, (1) is not sufficient.

From (2), $h = \text{mean} + 2(2.4 \text{ cm})$. Without knowing the mean, you cannot determine an exact value of h. Thus, (2) is not sufficient.

Taking (1) and (2) together, $h = 32.8 \text{ cm} + 2(2.4 \text{ cm})$, which you can calculate to determine an exact value of h. Therefore, both statements together are sufficient, but neither statement alone is sufficient.

380.

C. Both statements TOGETHER are sufficient, but NEITHER statement ALONE is sufficient.

Let x = the amount, in grams, of Brand X cat food that Sergio's cat receives each day. Then $500 - x$ = the amount, in grams, of Brand Y cat food that Sergio's cat receives each day. The amount of fat that Sergio's cat receives each day from x grams of Brand X cat food plus the amount of fat that Sergio's cat receives each day from $(500 - x)$ grams of Brand Y cat food is 103 grams. From (1), the amount of fat that Sergio's cat receives each day from Brand X cat food is $35\%x = 0.35x$. But without information about the amount of fat from Brand Y cat food, you cannot determine an exact value of x. Thus, (1) is not sufficient.

From (2), the amount of fat that Sergio's cat receives each day from Brand Y cat food is $11\%(500-x)=0.11(500-x)$. But without information about the amount of fat from Brand X cat food, you cannot determine an exact value of x. Thus (2) is not sufficient.

Taking (1) and (2) together yields $0.35x+0.11(500-x)=103$, which you can solve to determine an exact value of x. Therefore, both statements together are sufficient, but neither statement alone is sufficient.

381. **C. Both statements TOGETHER are sufficient, but NEITHER statement ALONE is sufficient.**

Let L = the length, in feet, of the floor, and W = the width, in feet, of the floor. The area of the floor is $A=L\times W$. From (1), $L=W+4$, then $A=L\times W=(W+4)W=W^2+4W$, which is one equation with two unknowns. Without additional information, you cannot determine an exact value of A. Thus, (1) is not sufficient.

From (2), $2(L+W)=56$, which implies $L+W=28$, from which you have $L=28-W$ and $A=L\times W=(28-W)W=28W-W^2$, which is one equation with two unknowns. Without additional information, you cannot determine an exact value of A. Thus, (2) is not sufficient.

Taking (1) and (2) together yields $W^2+4W=28W-W^2$, which implies $W^2-12W=0$ or, equivalently, $W(W-12)=0$. Given that $W\neq0$ (because it's a measurement of the floor), you can determine an exact value of W and $L=W+4$; and, thereafter, determine an exact value of A. Therefore, both statements together are sufficient, but neither statement alone is sufficient.

382. **E. Statements (1) and (2) TOGETHER are NOT sufficient.**

Let V = the number of vehicles in the parking lot. From (1), you have that $V\geq5$, but additional information is needed to determine an exact value of V. Thus, (1) is not sufficient.

From (2), $60\%V=0.6V$ is the number of sedans in the parking lot, but additional information is needed to determine an exact value of V. Thus, (2) is not sufficient.

Taking (1) and (2) together, you know that 40 percent of the vehicles in the parking lot are not sedans, and that 5 of those vehicles are pickup trucks. But you cannot assume that only pickup trucks and sedans are in the parking lot. Therefore, statements (1) and (2) together are not sufficient.

383. **C. Both statements TOGETHER are sufficient, but NEITHER statement ALONE is sufficient.**

From the triangle inequality, $z - y < x < z + y$. From (1), $z - 5 < x < z + 5$. But additional information is needed to determine the least value of k in $j < x < k$. Thus, (1) is not sufficient.

From (2), $17 - y < x < 17 + y$. But additional information is needed to determine the least value of k in $j < x < k$. Thus, (1) is not sufficient. Taking (1) and (2) together, $z - y < x < z + y = 17 - 5 < x < 17 + 5 = 5 < x < 22$, which implies 22 is the least value of k. Therefore, both statements together are sufficient, but neither statement alone is sufficient.

384. **A. Statement (1) ALONE is sufficient, but statement (2) alone is not sufficient.**

From (1), $m^5 + n^5 < 1,200$ implies that n assumes its greatest value when $m^5 = 0$. Substituting possible values for n yields $3^5 = 243$; $4^5 = 1,024$; and $5^5 = 3,125$. So the greatest possible value of n is 4. Thus, (1) is sufficient.

Statement (2) provides no information about n, so it is not sufficient. Therefore, statement (1) alone is sufficient.

385. **D. Each statement ALONE is sufficient.**

Let S = the number of decorated one-layer cakes sold, and L = the number of decorated two-layer cakes sold. Then $S + L$ = the total number of decorated one-layer and two-layer cakes sold. From the question information, $\$40S + \$75L = \$13,900$. From (1), $S = 2L - 40$. So $\$40(2L - 40) + \$75(L) = \$13,900$, which you can solve for L and $S = 2L - 40$; and, thereafter, determine an exact value of $S + L$. Thus, (1) is sufficient.

From (2), $L = S - 60$. So $\$40(S) + \$75(S - 60) = \$13,900$, which you can solve for S and $L = S - 60$; and, thereafter, determine an exact value of $S + L$. Thus, (2) is sufficient. Therefore, each statement alone is sufficient.

386. **C. Both statements TOGETHER are sufficient, but NEITHER statement ALONE is sufficient.**

Let C = the number of chess club members only, and S = the number of swim team members only. Then $C + S$ = the number of students who belong to either the chess club or the swim team, but not both. Statement (1) tells you only that $C \leq 24$. Without additional information, you cannot determine an exact value of either C or S. Thus, (1) is not sufficient.

Statement (2) tells you only that $S \leq 20$. Without additional information, you cannot determine an exact value of either C or S. Thus, (2) is not sufficient.

Taking (1) and (2) together, $24 + 20 = 44$. This result is 13 more than 31, the total number of students who belong to the chess club or the swim team or both. The excess of 13 is the number of members who belong to both the chess club and the swim team. So $C = 24 - 13 = 11$, $S = 20 - 13 = 7$, and $C + S = 11 + 7$. Therefore, both statements together are sufficient, but neither statement alone is sufficient.

387. **B. Statement (2) ALONE is sufficient, but statement (1) alone is not sufficient.**

Using (1), the answer to the question posed can be No or Yes, depending on the values of x and y. For example, if $x = 7.5$ and $y = 2.5$, then $xy = (7.5)(2.5) = 18.75 \not< 16$, in which case the answer is No. But if $x = 7$ and $y = 2$, then $xy = (7)(2) = 14 < 16$, in which case the answer is Yes. Thus, (1) is not sufficient.

From (2), $x^3 < 8$ implies $x < 2$ and $y - 8 < 0$ implies $y < 8$. So $xy < (2)(8) = 16$. Thus, (2) is sufficient. Therefore, statement (2) alone is sufficient.

388. **D. Each statement ALONE is sufficient.**

From (1), because alternate interior angles of parallel lines are congruent, $w = 125$ implies $5y = 125$, from which you can determine an exact value of y. Thus, (1) is sufficient.

From (2), because corresponding angles of parallel lines are congruent, $z = 55$ implies $x = 55$, Then, because consecutive angles of a parallelogram are supplementary, $5y = 180 - 55 = 125$, from which you can determine an exact value of y. Thus, (2) is sufficient. Therefore, each statement alone is sufficient.

389. **B. Statement (2) ALONE is sufficient, but statement (1) alone is not sufficient.**

From (1), $\Diamond$ could represent multiplication or division because $1 \times 1 = 1$ and $1 \div 1 = 1$. Thus, (1) is not sufficient.

From (2), $\Diamond$ can only represent multiplication because $1 \times 3 = 3$, while $1 \div 3 \neq 3$, $1 + 3 \neq 3$, and $1 - 3 \neq 3$. So $2 \Diamond 5 = 10$. Thus, (2) is sufficient. Therefore, statement (2) alone is sufficient.

390. **C. Both statements TOGETHER are sufficient, but NEITHER statement ALONE is sufficient.**

Let M = the number of math majors in Professor X's physics class, and N = the number of non-math majors in Professor X's physics class. From (1), $\frac{N}{M+10} = \frac{5}{4}$, which is one equation with two unknowns. So without additional information, you cannot determine an exact value of M. Thus, (1) is not sufficient.

Statement (2) provides no information about M. Thus, (2) is not sufficient. Taking (1) and (2) together yields $\dfrac{25}{M+10} = \dfrac{5}{4}$, which you can solve for an exact value of M. Therefore, both statements together are sufficient, but neither statement alone is sufficient.

391. **C. Both statements TOGETHER are sufficient, but NEITHER statement ALONE is sufficient.**

Let P = the current membership of the photography club. From (1), $2P \geq 34$, which implies $P \geq 17$. This result gives a range of values of P. For example, P could equal 17 or any integer greater than 17. Thus, (1) is not sufficient.

From (2), $P - 5 < 13$, which implies $5 \leq P < 18$. This result gives a range of values of P. For example, P could equal 17 or any integer such that $5 \leq P \leq 17$. Thus, (2) is not sufficient.

Taking (1) and (2) together, $17 \leq P \leq 17$, from which it follows that $P = 17$. Therefore, both statements together are sufficient, but neither statement alone is sufficient.

392. **E. Statements (1) and (2) TOGETHER are NOT sufficient.**

Because $xyz \neq 0$, none of the factors are zero. The product xyz will be greater than 0 if it has exactly zero or exactly two negative factors. From (1), $xz < 0$ implies that x and z have different signs. Hence, xyz cannot have exactly zero negative factors. If $y < 0$, then xyz has exactly two negative factors and $xyz > 0$ is true, indicating a Yes response to the question posed. But if $y > 0$, then xyz has exactly one negative factors and $xyz < 0$ is true, indicating a No response to the question posed. Thus, (1) is not sufficient.

From (2), $x + y + z = 0$ implies that x, y, and z do not all have the same sign. Hence, xyz cannot have exactly zero negative factors. If there are exactly two negative factors among the three numbers, then $xyz > 0$ is true, indicating a Yes response to the question posed. If there is exactly one negative factor among the three numbers, then $xyz < 0$ is true, indicating a No response to the question posed.

Taking (1) and (2) together, xyz cannot have exactly zero negative factors, but additional information is needed to determine whether the product has exactly two negative factors. Therefore, statements (1) and (2) together are not sufficient.

393. **D. Each statement ALONE is sufficient.**

From (1), $6 < k - 0.6 < 7$ implies $6.6 < k < 7.6$. It follows that $13.2 < 2k < 15.2$, indicating an answer of Yes to the question posed. Thus, (1) is sufficient.

From (2), if $6.7 \le k < 7.7$ then $7.5 \le k + 0.8 < 8.5$, which implies that $k + 0.8$ rounded to the nearest integer is 8. It follows that $13.4 \le 2k < 15.4$, indicating an answer of Yes to the question posed. Thus, (2) is sufficient. Therefore, each statement alone is sufficient.

394. **E. Statements (1) and (2) TOGETHER are NOT sufficient.**

From (1), $k^2 < 10$ implies $k = 1$, 2, or 3. Thus, (1) is not sufficient.

From (2), $k^5 > 30$ implies $k = 2$ or any integer greater than 2. Thus, (2) is not sufficient.

Taking (1) and (2) together, $k = 2$ or 3 satisfies all conditions given. Therefore, statements (1) and (2) together are not sufficient.

395. **C. Both statements TOGETHER are sufficient, but NEITHER statement ALONE is sufficient.**

Let P_0 = the initial population of the bacteria. Given that the population doubles every m minutes, in 4 hours, the number of times the population doubles is 4 hours $\div \dfrac{m \text{ minutes}}{60 \text{ minutes per hour}} = \dfrac{240}{m}$ times. So in four hours, the population of the bacteria colony equals $P_0 \times 2^{\frac{240}{m}}$.

From (1), in 1 hour, the number of times the population doubles is 1 hour $\div \dfrac{m \text{ minutes}}{60 \text{ minutes per hour}} = \dfrac{60}{m}$ times. So $P_0 \times 2^{\frac{60}{m}} = 20{,}000$. This is one equation with two unknowns, so additional information is needed to determine an exact value of $P_0 \times 2^{\frac{240}{m}}$. Thus, (1) is not sufficient.

From (2), in 3 hour, the number of times the population doubles is 3 hours $\div \dfrac{m \text{ minutes}}{60 \text{ minutes per hour}} = \dfrac{180}{m}$ times. So $P_0 \times 2^{\frac{180}{m}} = 320{,}000$. This is one equation with two unknowns, so additional information is needed to determine an exact value of $P_0 \times 2^{\frac{240}{m}}$. Thus, (2) is not sufficient.

Taking (1) and (2) together, you have two equations and two unknowns that you can solve simultaneously to determine exact values of m and P_0; and, thereafter, compute an exact value of $P_0 \times 2^{\frac{240}{m}}$. You do not have to actually work out the solution. However, for the purpose of clarity, proceed as follows: $\dfrac{P_0 \times 2^{\frac{180}{m}}}{P_0 \times 2^{\frac{60}{m}}} = \dfrac{320{,}000}{20{,}000}$, which implies $2^{\frac{120}{m}} = 16$ or, equivalently, $2^{\frac{120}{m}} = 2^4$. It follows that $\dfrac{120}{m} = 4$ or $m = 30$. Substituting $m = 30$ into $P_0 \times 2^{\frac{60}{m}} = 20{,}000$ yields $P_0 \times 2^2 = 20{,}000$, from which you have $P_0 = 5000$. So in four hours, the population of the bacteria colony is $P_0 \times 2^{\frac{240}{m}} = 5000 \times 2^{\frac{240}{30}}$. Therefore, both statements together are sufficient, but neither statement alone is sufficient.

396. **B. Statement (2) ALONE is sufficient, but statement (1) alone is not sufficient.**

From (1), $|y| > 1$ implies $y < -1$ or $y > 1$. If $y < -1$, then $y < 0$, yielding an answer of No to the question posed. But if $y > 1$, then $y > 0$, yielding an answer of Yes to the question posed. Thus, (1) is not sufficient.

From (2), $\dfrac{y^2 + y}{y^2} > 1$ implies $1 + \dfrac{y}{y^2} > 1$, from which you have $\dfrac{y}{y^2} > 0$ or equivalently, $y > 0$, yielding an answer of Yes to the question posed. Thus, (2) is sufficient. Therefore, statement (2) alone is sufficient.

397. **E. Statements (1) and (2) TOGETHER are NOT sufficient.**

From (1), n divisible by 12 implies $n = k(12)$, where k is a positive integer. If k is even, then n is divisible by 24, yielding an answer of Yes to the question posed. But, if k is odd, then n is not divisible by 24, yielding an answer of No to the question posed. Thus, (1) is not sufficient.

From (2), n could be any even number such as 20, which is not divisible by 24, or 72, which is divisible by 24. Thus, (2) is not sufficient.

Taking (1) and (2) together is not sufficient because the possibilities for n are the same as described for statement (1). Therefore, statements (1) and (2) together are not sufficient.

398. **C. Both statements TOGETHER are sufficient, but NEITHER statement ALONE is sufficient.**

Let y = the price of one 64-ounce container of Brand Y ice cream, and x = the price of one 48-ounce container of Brand X ice cream. From (1), $y + 2x = \$15$. This is one equation with two unknowns. Without additional information, you cannot determine an exact value of y. Thus, (1) is not sufficient.

From (2), you have two possibilities because 192-ounces is either 3 times 64 ounces or 4 times 48 ounces. No other combination using 64 ounces and 48 ounces will sum to 192 ounces. Case I: The customer bought 4 48-ounce containers of Brand X ice cream for $18. So $x = \dfrac{\$18}{4} = \$4.50$. Case II: The customer bought 3 64-ounce containers of Brand Y ice cream for $18. So $y = \dfrac{\$18}{3} = \$6$. Without additional information, you cannot determine the value of y. Thus, (2) is not sufficient.

Taking (1) and (2) together, you have two cases. Case I: $x = \$4.50$. Substituting into $y + 2x = \$15$ yields $y + 2(\$4.50) = \$15$, which implies $y = \$6$. Case II: $y = \$6$. In either case, $y = \$6$. Therefore, both statements together are sufficient, but neither statement alone is sufficient.

399. **D. Each statement ALONE is sufficient.**

Let m = the number of students who are taking mathematics only, and p = the number of students who are taking physics only. Then the percent of students who are taking only mathematics or only physics and no other class is $\frac{m+p}{400} \times 100\%$. From (1), $(m+p)+20 = 400-240 = 160$. You can solve this equation for $(m+p)$; and, thereafter, obtain $\frac{m+p}{400} \times 100\%$. Thus, (1) is sufficient.

From (2), $m = 190-20-30-50 = 90$ and $p = 140-20-30-40 = 50$. Then $(m+p) = 90+50$, from which you can determine $\frac{m+p}{400} \times 100\%$. Thus, (2) is sufficient. Therefore, each statement alone is sufficient.

400. **E. Statements (1) and (2) TOGETHER are NOT sufficient.**

Solving the equation in (1) yields

$$x^2 + x - 12 = 0$$
$$(x+4)(x-3) = 0$$
$$x = -4 \text{ or } 3$$

Without additional information, you cannot determine and exact value of x. Thus, (1) is not sufficient.

From (2), $x^2 < 25$ implies $|x| < 5$. This result indicates that x can be any number such that $-5 < x < 5$. Thus, (2) is not sufficient.

Taking (1) and (2) together is not sufficient because either -4 or 3 satisfies all conditions given. Therefore, statements (1) and (2) together are not sufficient.

401. **E. Statements (1) and (2) TOGETHER are NOT sufficient.**

From (1), you have $r - p = 260$, which is one equation with two unknowns. Without additional information, you cannot determine an exact value of q. Thus, (1) is not sufficient.

From (2), you have $r - q = 170$, which is one equation with two unknowns. Without additional information, you cannot determine an exact value of q. Thus, (2) is not sufficient.

Taking (1) and (2) together, you have two equations and three unknowns. Without additional information, you cannot determine an exact value of q. Therefore, statements (1) and (2) together are not sufficient.

402. D. Each statement ALONE is sufficient.

Let D = the total distance, in miles, that Rylon drove, and T = the total time, in hours, that Rylon drove. Then Rylon's average speed, in miles per hour, was $\frac{D}{T}$. From (1), because 1 hour 48 minutes is 1.8 hours,

$\frac{D}{T} = \frac{100 \text{ miles}}{1.8 \text{ hours}} \approx 55.6$ miles per hour, which is greater than 55 miles per hour. Thus, (1) is sufficient to answer the question posed.

From (2), $D = 60 \text{ miles} + 40 \text{ miles} = 100 \text{ miles}$ and $T = \frac{60 \text{ miles}}{60 \text{ miles per hour}} + \frac{40 \text{ miles}}{50 \text{ miles per hour}} = 1.8$ hours, so $\frac{D}{T}$ is the same as in (1). Thus, (2) is sufficient to answer the question posed. Therefore, each statement alone is sufficient.

403. D. Each statement ALONE is sufficient.

From (1), $x^2 + 2xy = 12y + 36$ implies $x^2 + 2xy + y^2 = y^2 + 12y + 36$ or, equivalently, $(x+y)^2 = (y+6)^2$. This result gives $x = 6$. Thus, (1) is sufficient.

From (2), given that $y > 0$, $y(x^3 - 216) = 0$ implies $x^3 - 216 = 0$ or, equivalently, $x^3 = 216$. This result gives $x = 6$. Thus, (2) is sufficient. Therefore, each statement alone is sufficient.

404. D. Each statement ALONE is sufficient.

Let S = the cost of the sweater, excluding sales tax. Then the total amount of Vinod's purchase, including sales tax, is $(\$100 + 6\%(\$100)) + (S + 6\%S) = (\$100 + 0.06(\$100)) + (S + 0.06S) = \$106 + 1.06S$. From (1), $0.06S = \$19.20$, from which you can determine S; and, thereafter, determine an exact value of $\$106 + 1.06S$. Thus, (1) is sufficient.

From (2), $0.06(\$100 + S) = \$25.20$, from which you can determine S; and, thereafter, determine an exact value of $\$106 + 1.06S$. Thus, (2) is sufficient. Therefore, each statement alone is sufficient.

405. C. Both statements TOGETHER are sufficient, but NEITHER statement ALONE is sufficient.

Let a_1 = the first term of sequence A, and a_{100} = the hundredth term of sequence A. From (1), $a_1 = -10$. But without additional information, you cannot determine subsequent terms, including an exact value of a_{100}. Thus, (1) is not sufficient.

From (2), $a_1 = a_1$, $a_2 = a_1 + 15$, $a_3 = a_1 + (2)(15)$, $a_4 = a_1 + (3)(15)$, and so on. Hence, $a_{100} = a_1 + (99)(15)$. But without additional information, you cannot determine an exact value of a_{100}. Thus, (2) is not sufficient.

Taking (1) and (2) together, the exact value of the 100th term is $a_{100} = (-10) + (99)(15)$. Therefore, both statements together are sufficient, but neither statement alone is sufficient.

406. E. Statements (1) and (2) TOGETHER are NOT sufficient.

Create a two-way table to organize the information. Put variable expressions in empty cells:

	on-campus	off-campus	Total
senior	x	50	$x + 50$
junior	y	z	$y + z$
Total	$x + y$	$50 + z$	S

From (1), $x + 50 = 80$, which implies $x = 30$. Use this information to update the table:

	on-campus	off-campus	Total
senior	30	50	80
junior	y	z	$y + z$
Total	$30 + y$	$50 + z$	S

From the table, $S = 80 + y + z$. This is one equation with three unknowns. Without additional information, you cannot determine an exact value of S. Thus, (1) is not sufficient.

From (2), $50 + z = 120$, which implies $z = 70$. Use this information to update the table:

	on-campus	off-campus	Total
senior	x	50	$x + 50$
junior	y	70	$y + 70$
Total	$x + y$	120	S

From the table, $S = x + y + 120$. This is one equation with three unknowns. Without additional information, you cannot determine an exact value of S. Thus, (2) is not sufficient.

Taking (1) and (2) together, you have the following updated table:

	on-campus	off-campus	Total
senior	30	50	80
junior	y	70	$y+70$
Total	$30+y$	120	S

From the table, $S = 150 + y$. Without knowing y, the number of juniors who live on campus, you cannot determine an exact value of S. Therefore, statements (1) and (2) together are not sufficient.

407.

C. Both statements TOGETHER are sufficient, but NEITHER statement ALONE is sufficient.

From (1), $wz(x+y) = (+\text{odd})(z)((+\text{odd})+(+\text{odd})) = (+\text{odd})(z)(+\text{even}) = (z)(+\text{even})$ This result implies $wz(x+y)$ is even. However, without additional information, you cannot determine whether it is positive or negative. If z is positive, then $wz(x+y)$ is a positive even integer. But if z is negative, then $wz(x+y)$ is a negative even integer. Thus, (1) is not sufficient.

From (2), $wz(x+y) = w(-\text{even})(x+y)$. This result implies $wz(x+y)$ is even. However, without additional information, you cannot determine whether it is positive or negative.

Taking (1) and (2) together, given z is negative, then $wz(x+y)$ is a negative even integer. Therefore, both statements together are sufficient, but neither statement alone is sufficient.

408.

C. Both statements TOGETHER are sufficient, but NEITHER statement ALONE is sufficient.

From (1), $0.01R(\$300,000) = \$1,500$, which implies $R = \dfrac{\$1,500}{0.01(\$300,000)} = \dfrac{\$1,500}{\$3,000} = \dfrac{1}{2}$.

Substitute into $RX > \$2,000$. Then the question asks: is $\frac{1}{2}X > \$2,000$? or, equivalently, is $X > \$4000$? Without additional information about X, you cannot determine a definite Yes or No response to the question posed. Thus, (1) is not sufficient.

From (2), $\frac{1}{4}\%(X) = \$12.50$, which implies $X = \dfrac{\$12.50}{\frac{1}{400}} = (\$12.50)(400) = \$5000$.

Substitute into $RX > \$2,000$. Then the question asks, is $R(\$5000) > \$2,000$? or, equivalently, is $R > \frac{2}{5}$? Without additional information about R, you cannot determine a definite Yes or No response to the question posed. Thus, (2) is not sufficient.

Taking (1) and (2), together, you have $R = \frac{1}{2}$ and $X = \$5000$. So you can compute RX; and, thereafter, determine a definite Yes or No response to the question of whether $RX > \$2,000$? Therefore, both statements together are sufficient, but neither statement alone is sufficient.

409.

D. Each statement ALONE is sufficient.

Make a sketch.

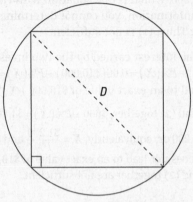

The figure shows that the diagonal of the square is the diameter of the circle (because the measure of the inscribed angle of 90° is $\frac{1}{2}$ the measure of the arc that it subtends). Because the radius of the circle is $r = \frac{1}{2}(D)$, the area of the circle is $A = \pi r^2 = \pi \left(\frac{D}{2}\right)^2$. From (1), because the area of a square is $\frac{1}{2}$ the square of the length of its diagonal, $\frac{1}{2}D^2 = 18$, which implies $D^2 = 36$. It follows that $D = 6$ and $A = \pi \left(\frac{6}{2}\right)^2$. Thus, (1) is sufficient.

From (2), because the circumference of the circle is π times its diameter, $6\pi = \pi D$, which implies $D = 6$ and $A = \pi \left(\frac{6}{2}\right)^2$. Thus, (2) is sufficient.

Therefore, each statement alone is sufficient.

410.

D. Each statement ALONE is sufficient.

Let M = the number of men at the ceremony and W = the number of women at the ceremony. Then $\frac{M}{W}$ = the ratio of the number of men to the number of women at the ceremony. From (1), $W = 3M$, so $\frac{M}{W} = \frac{M}{3M} = \frac{1}{3}$. Thus, (1) is sufficient.

From (2), $W = \frac{3}{4}(W + M)$, which implies $W = \frac{3}{4}W + \frac{3}{4}M$ or, equivalently, $\frac{1}{4}W = \frac{3}{4}M$. It follows that $\frac{M}{W} = \frac{1}{3}$. Thus, (2) is sufficient. Therefore, each statement alone is sufficient.

411. **E. Statements (1) and (2) TOGETHER are NOT sufficient.**

Let X = the amount invested at P percent simple annual interest. Then the total amount invested is $\$10,000 + X$. From (1) $R\%(\$10,000) + P\%(X) = \$1,800$, which is one equation with two unknowns. Without additional information, you cannot determine an exact value of $\$10,000 + X$. Thus, (1) is not sufficient.

From (2), the interest earned by the two investments in one year is $6\%(\$10,000) + P\%(X) = 0.06(\$10,000) + P\%(X) = \$600 + P\%(X)$. This result does not lead to an exact value of $\$10,000 + X$. Thus, (2) is not sufficient.

Taking (1) and (2) together, $\$600 + P\%(X) = \$1,800$, which implies $P\%(X) = \$1,200$ or, equivalently, $X = \dfrac{\$1,200}{P\%}$ and $\$10,000 + X = \$10,000 + \dfrac{\$1,200}{P\%}$. This result does not lead to an exact value of $\$10,000 + X$. Therefore, statements (1) and (2) together are not sufficient.

412. **B. Statement (2) ALONE is sufficient, but statement (1) alone is not sufficient.**

From (1), h could be 5, 6, 7, 8, or 9 because each of 0.458, 0.468, 0.478, 0.488, and 0.498 rounded to the nearest tenth is 0.5. Thus, (1) is not sufficient.

From (2), when $X = 0.4h8$ is rounded to the nearest hundredth, because 8 is the digit in the thousandths place, the digit in the hundredths place increases by 1. So $h + 1 = 7$, which implies $h = 6$. Thus, (2) is sufficient. Therefore, statement (2) alone is sufficient.

413. **D. Each statement ALONE is sufficient.**

Recall that even $\pm$ even = even, odd $\pm$ odd = even, and even $\pm$ odd (or odd $\pm$ even) = odd. And even $\times$ even = even, odd $\times$ odd = odd, and even $\times$ odd (or odd $\times$ even) = even. From (1), because $m + 1$ is odd, then m is even. It follows that mn is even. Thus, (1) is sufficient.

From (2), because $m + n$ is odd, then m and n cannot both be odd (because odd + odd = even). It follows that at least one of m and n is even, so mn is even. Thus, (2) is sufficient. Therefore, each statement alone is sufficient.

414. **B. Statement (2) ALONE is sufficient, but statement (1) alone is not sufficient.**

It is given that net proceeds increase as the number of tickets sold increases. From (1), you know only that net proceeds exceeded $\$40,000$ on 4,000 tickets sold. But because you have no way of knowing how net proceeds increase as a function of tickets sold, you cannot assume that net proceeds exceeded $\$80,000$ on 7,600 tickets sold. Thus, (1) is not sufficient.

From (2), given that the net proceeds on 7,000 tickets sold exceeded $100,000, then, because net proceeds increase as the number of tickets sold increases, sales of $7,000 + 600 = 7,600$ tickets will also have a profit exceeding $100,000, which is greater than $80,000. Thus, (2) is sufficient. Therefore, statement (2) alone is sufficient.

415.

A. Statement (1) ALONE is sufficient, but statement (2) alone is not sufficient.

It is given that x and y are integers such that $0 < x < y$. From (1), $\sqrt{x} = 4 - \sqrt{y}$ and $\sqrt{y} = 4 - \sqrt{x}$. These results imply that $\sqrt{y} < 4$ and $\sqrt{x} < 4$. Hence, $y \le 9$ and $x \le 9$. Given that $\sqrt{x} + \sqrt{y} = 4$, which is a rational number, neither x nor y can equal 2, 3, 5, 6, 7, or 8 because the square roots of these integers are positive irrational numbers. The sum of a positive irrational number and a positive rational number or the sum of two positive irrational numbers is irrational. Hence, given $0 < x < y$, the possible values of x are 1 or 4, and the possible values of y are 4 or 9. Only the values $x = 1$ and $y = 9$ will satisfy $0 < x < y$ and $\sqrt{x} + \sqrt{y} = 4$. So $xy = 1 \cdot 9 = 9$. Thus, (1) is sufficient.

From (2), given $0 < x < y$, the possible values of x and y are the pairs 1 and 9; 2 and 8; 3 and 7; or 4 and 5; respectively. Without additional information, you cannot determine an exact value of xy. Thus, (2) is not sufficient. Therefore, statement (1) alone is sufficient.

416.

A. Statement (1) ALONE is sufficient, but statement (2) alone is not sufficient.

Let P = the original price of the computer and D = the discounted price of the computer. Then the percent discount is $\frac{P-D}{P} \times 100\%$. From (1), $P = D + 25\%D = 125\%D = 1.25D$. Substitute this result into $\frac{P-D}{P} \times 100\%$ to obtain $\frac{1.25D - D}{1.25D} \times 100\% = \frac{0.25D}{1.25D} \times 100\% = \frac{0.25}{1.25} \times 100\%$. Thus, (1) is sufficient.

From (2), $D = P - \$148$, which implies $P - D = \$148$. Substitute this result into $\frac{P-D}{P} \times 100\%$ to obtain $\frac{\$148}{P} \times 100\%$. Without additional information about P, you cannot determine an exact value of $\frac{\$148}{P} \times 100\%$. Thus, (2) is not sufficient. Therefore, statement (1) alone is sufficient.

417.

C. Both statements TOGETHER are sufficient, but NEITHER statement ALONE is sufficient.

Let F = the number of favorable responses from former customers and P = the number of favorable responses from potential customers. Then the percent of favorable responses is $\frac{F+P}{300+700} \times 100\% = \frac{F+P}{1,000} \times 100\%$. From (1), $F = 30\%(300) = 90$, which you can substitute into $\frac{F+P}{1,000} \times 100\%$ to obtain $\frac{90+P}{1,000} \times 100\%$. The value of this quantity can vary, so without additional information, you cannot determine an exact value of $\frac{F+P}{1,000} \times 100\%$. Thus, (1) is not sufficient.

From (2), $P = 20\%(700) = 140$, which you can substitute into $\dfrac{F+P}{1,000} \times 100\%$ to obtain $\dfrac{F+140}{1,000} \times 100\%$. The value of this quantity can vary, so without additional information, you cannot determine an exact value of $\dfrac{F+P}{1,000} \times 100\%$. Thus, (2) is not sufficient.

Taking (1) and (2) together, $\dfrac{90+140}{1,000} \times 100\%$. Therefore, both statements together are sufficient, but neither statement alone is sufficient.

418. **A. Statement (1) ALONE is sufficient, but statement (2) alone is not sufficient.**

From (1), $33\frac{1}{3}\%A = 25\%B$. Multiply both sides of this equation by 3 to obtain $3\left(33\frac{1}{3}\%A\right) = 3(25\%B)$, which implies $100\%A = 75\%B$. Thus, (1) is sufficient.

From (2), $A + B = 175$ implies $A = 175 - B$ and $\dfrac{A}{B} \times 100\% = \dfrac{175-B}{B} \times 100\%$. The value of this result will vary. Without additional information, you cannot determine an exact value of $\dfrac{A}{B} \times 100\%$. Thus, (2) is not sufficient. Therefore, statement (1) alone is sufficient.

419. **D. Each statement ALONE is sufficient.**

Let a = the number of components produced by machine A in 20 minutes, and b = the number of components produced by machine B in 20 minutes. Then $a + b = 50$. From (1), $a = b - 10$. Solving this equation simultaneously with $a + b = 50$ yields $a = 20$ and $b = 30$. Hence, machine B works at a constant rate of $\dfrac{30 \text{ components}}{20 \text{ minutes}} = 1.5$ components per minute So working alone, machine B would have taken $\dfrac{50 \text{ components}}{1.5 \text{ components per minute}} = 33\frac{1}{3}$ minutes. Thus, (1) is sufficient.

From (2), given that machine B's rate is 150% of machine A's rate, then $b = 1.5a$. Solving this equation simultaneously with $a + b = 50$ yields $a = 20$ and $b = 30$, which leads to the same result as obtained in (1). Thus, (2) is sufficient. Therefore, each statement alone is sufficient.

420. **D. Each statement ALONE is sufficient.**

You can answer the question by solving $\dfrac{1}{6} + kx^2 \geq \dfrac{5}{6}$ for the least positive value of x. From (1), substitute $k = \dfrac{1}{5,400}$ into $\dfrac{1}{6} + kx^2 \geq \dfrac{5}{6}$ to obtain $\dfrac{1}{6} + \dfrac{1}{5,400}x^2 \geq \dfrac{5}{6}$, which you can solve for the least positive value of x that makes the inequality true. Thus, (1) is sufficient.

You can solve (2) for k, substitute the result into $\dfrac{1}{6} + kx^2 \geq \dfrac{5}{6}$, and then solve for the least positive value of x that makes the inequality true. Thus, (2) is sufficient. Therefore, each statement alone is sufficient.

421.

B. Statement (2) ALONE is sufficient, but statement (1) alone is not sufficient.

From (1), $x^2 - y^2 < 0$ implies $x^2 < y^2$, from which it follows that $|x| < |y|$. Additional information is needed to determine an exact value of xy. For example, if $x = 3$ and $y = -5$, then $xy = -15$. But if $x = 2$ and $y = -4$, then $xy = -8$. Thus, (1) is not sufficient.

From (2), there are only two pairs of integer values for which $x^y = \frac{1}{16}$. These are $x = 2$ and $y = -4$ $\left(\text{because } 2^{-4} = \frac{1}{16}\right)$ and $x = 4$ and $y = -2$ $\left(\text{because } 4^{-2} = \frac{1}{16}\right)$. In either case, $xy = -8$. Therefore, statement (2) alone is sufficient.

422.

E. Statements (1) and (2) TOGETHER are NOT sufficient.

From (1), $\frac{a+b}{2} = 55$ implies $a + b = 110$. Without additional information about c, you cannot determine an exact value of $a + c$. Thus, (1) is not sufficient.

From (2), $\frac{b+c}{2} = 70$ implies $b + c = 140$. Without additional information about a, you cannot determine an exact value of $a + c$. Thus, (2) is not sufficient.

Taking (1) and (2) together, you can eliminate b from the two equations by subtracting $a + b = 110$ from $b + c = 140$ to obtain $c - a = 30$. But without additional information, you cannot determine an exact value of $a + c$. For example, $a = 50$, $b = 60$, and $c = 80$ satisfy all conditions given and yield $a + c = 50 + 80 = 130$. But $a = 40$, $b = 70$, and $c = 70$ satisfy all conditions given and yield $a + c = 40 + 70 = 110$. Therefore, statements (1) and (2) together are not sufficient.

423.

D. Each statement ALONE is sufficient.

To use (1), first write $\frac{x}{3}$ divided by $\frac{y}{5}$ as follows: $\dfrac{\frac{x}{3}}{\frac{y}{5}} = \dfrac{\frac{x}{3} \cdot \frac{3}{3}}{\frac{y}{5}} = \dfrac{\frac{3x}{9}}{\frac{y}{5}}$. Next,

substitute $3x = 5y$ and simplify $\dfrac{\frac{3x}{9}}{\frac{y}{5}} = \dfrac{\frac{5y}{9}}{\frac{y}{5}} = \dfrac{\cancel{45}^5 \cdot \frac{5y}{\cancel{9}}}{\cancel{45}^9 \cdot \frac{y}{\cancel{5}}} = \dfrac{25y}{9y} = \dfrac{25}{9}$. Thus, (1) is sufficient.

To use (2), first write $\frac{x}{3}$ divided by $\frac{y}{5}$ as follows: $\dfrac{\frac{x}{3}}{\frac{y}{5}} = \dfrac{15 \cdot \frac{x}{3}}{15 \cdot \frac{y}{5}} = \dfrac{5x}{3y}$.

Then, $\sqrt{\dfrac{5x}{3y}} = \dfrac{5}{3}$ implies $\dfrac{5x}{3y} = \dfrac{25}{9}$. Thus, (2) is sufficient. Therefore, each statement alone is sufficient.

424.

C. Both statements TOGETHER are sufficient, but NEITHER statement ALONE is sufficient.

Let S = the number of restaurants that serve shrimp; let C = the number of restaurants that serve crab; and let B = the number of restaurants that serve both shrimp and crab. Then the number of restaurants in the city that serve shrimp but not crab is $(S - B)$, and the number of restaurants in the city that serve crab but not shrimp is $(C - B)$. Hence, the number of restaurants in the city that serve neither shrimp nor crab is $220 - ((S - B) + (C - B) + B) = 220 - (S + C - B)$. From (1), $220 - (S + C - B) = 220 - (94 + 72 - B)$. The value of this quantity will vary, depending on the value of B. If $B = 0$, then the number of restaurants that serve neither shrimp nor crab is $220 - (94 + 72) = 54$. But if $B = 20$, then the number of restaurants that serve neither shrimp nor crab is $220 - (94 + 72 - 20) = 74$. From (2), $220 - (S + C - B) = 220 - (S + C - 42) = 262 - (S + C)$. The value of this quantity will vary depending on the values of S and C. Thus, (2) is not sufficient.

Taking (1) and (2) together, $220 - (S + C - B) = 220 - (94 + 72 - 42)$, which you can calculate to determine an exact value of the number of restaurants in the city that serve neither shrimp nor crab. Therefore, both statements together are sufficient, but neither statement alone is sufficient.

425.

C. Both statements TOGETHER are sufficient, but NEITHER statement ALONE is sufficient.

It is given that b is an integer. From (1), $a + b$ is an integer implies a is an integer (because b is an integer). Additional information is needed because the number of values of b that satisfy $a < b < c$ can vary. For example, if $a = -5$ and $c = 0$, then four values of b satisfy $a < b < c$. But if $a = -5$ and $c = 5.5$, then nine values of b satisfy $a < b < c$. Thus, (1) is not sufficient.

From (2), $c - a = 6.5$ implies $c = a + 6.5$. Additional information is needed because the number of values of b that satisfy $a < b < c$ can vary. For example, if $a = -5$ and $c = 1.5$, then six values of b satisfy $a < b < c$. But if $a = 1.8$ and $c = 8.3$, then seven values of b satisfy $a < b < c$. Thus, (2) is not sufficient.

Taking (1) and (2) together implies that only six values of b satisfy $a < b < c$. Therefore, both statements together are sufficient, but neither statement alone is sufficient.

426. **C. Both statements TOGETHER are sufficient, but NEITHER statement ALONE is sufficient.**

From (1), Let T = the total of the selling prices of the 21 home security systems. Then Nio's compensation is $21(\$25) + 15\%T = \$525 + 0.15T$. This quantity will vary depending on the value of T. Without additional information, you cannot determine an exact value of $\$525 + 0.15T$. Thus, (1) is not sufficient.

From (2), you know only that the total of the selling prices of the 21 home security systems is $52,500. But you need additional information about how Nio's compensation is determined to answer the question. Thus, (2) is not sufficient.

Taking (1) and (2) together, Nio's compensation is $\$525 + 0.15(\$52,500)$, which you can calculate to answer the question. Therefore, both statements together are sufficient, but neither statement alone is sufficient.

427. **B. Statement (2) ALONE is sufficient, but statement (1) alone is not sufficient.**

From (1), $X + 50 = Y - 50$ implies $Y - X = 100$, which establishes that $X < Y$. But additional information is needed to determine whether $X < \frac{1}{4}Y$. For example, if $X = 25$ and $Y = 125$, then $\frac{X}{Y} = \frac{25}{125} = \frac{1}{5}$, which implies $X = \frac{1}{5}Y < \frac{1}{4}Y$, yielding an answer of Yes to the question posed. But if $X = 400$ and $Y = 500$, then $\frac{X}{Y} = \frac{400}{500} = \frac{4}{5}$, which implies $X = \frac{4}{5}Y \not< \frac{1}{4}Y$, yielding an answer of No to the question posed. Thus, (1) is not sufficient.

From (2), $X + Y = 1.2Y$ implies $X = 0.2Y = \frac{1}{5}Y < \frac{1}{4}Y$, yielding an answer of Yes to the question posed. Thus, (2) is sufficient. Therefore, statement (2) alone is sufficient.

428. **A. Statement (1) ALONE is sufficient, but statement (2) alone is not sufficient.**

Recall that even $\pm$ even = even, odd $\pm$ odd = even, and even $\pm$ odd (or odd $\pm$ even) = odd. And even $\times$ even = even, odd $\times$ odd = odd, and even $\times$ odd (or odd $\times$ even) = even. From (1), $K + K + 20 + K + 25 = 3K + 45$ is even. This result implies $3K$ is odd, so K must be odd, yielding an answer of No to the question posed. Thus, (1) is sufficient.

From (2), $K - 15 + K + K + 23 + K + 24 = 4K + 32$, which is even regardless whether K is odd or even. Thus, (2) is not sufficient. Therefore, statement (1) alone is sufficient.

429. **E. Statements (1) and (2) TOGETHER are NOT sufficient.**

From (1), the percent increase in Nayeli's salary is $\frac{\$48,300 - \$46,000}{\$46,000} \times 100\% = \frac{\$2,300}{\$46,000} \times 100\% = 5\%$. But without information to determine Tristan's percent increase, you cannot answer the question. Thus, (1) is not sufficient.

From (2), without knowing Tristan's salary last year, you cannot determine Tristan's percent increase. Further, without information to determine Nayeli's percent increase, you cannot answer the question.

Taking (1) and (2) together, Nayeli's percent increase is 5 percent, but you do not have sufficient information to determine Tristan's increase to make the comparison required to answer the question. Therefore, statements (1) and (2) together are not sufficient.

430. **C. Both statements TOGETHER are sufficient, but NEITHER statement ALONE is sufficient.**

Let C = the country's current national debt in dollars, and I = the amount the national debt increases each day. Then $C + (I \text{ per day})(30 \text{ days})$ is the country's national debt in 30 days. From (1), the country's national debt in 30 days is $C + (\$120 \text{ million per day})(30 \text{ days})$. This quantity will vary depending on the value of C. Thus, (1) is not sufficient.

From (2), the country's national debt in 30 days is $50 \text{ billion} + (I \text{ per day})(30 \text{ days})$. This quantity will vary depending on the value of I. Thus, (2) is not sufficient.

Taking (1) and (2) together, the country's national debt in 30 days is $50 \text{ billion} + (120 \text{ million per day})(30 \text{ days})$, which you can calculate to answer the question. Therefore, both statements together are sufficient, but neither statement alone is sufficient.

431. **C. Both statements TOGETHER are sufficient, but NEITHER statement ALONE is sufficient.**

Let V = the value of the stock fund. Then $50\%V = \frac{1}{2}V$ = the amount invested in U.S. companies. From (1), $12.5\%\left(\frac{1}{2}V\right) = \frac{1}{8}\left(\frac{1}{2}V\right) = \frac{1}{16}V$ = the amount invested in Texas companies. Without additional information, you cannot determine an exact value of V. Thus, (1) is not sufficient.

From (2), you can determine that $\frac{1}{2}V \geq \$20$ million. But additional information is needed to determine an exact value of V. Thus, (2) is not sufficient.

Taking (1) and (2) together, $\frac{1}{16}V = \$20$ million, which you can solve for an exact value of V. Therefore, both statements together are sufficient, but neither statement alone is sufficient.

432. **B. Statement (2) ALONE is sufficient, but statement (1) alone is not sufficient.**

From (1), $k^2 < 16$ implies $|k| < 4$. So k could equal $-3, -2, -1, 0, 1, 2,$ or 3. Thus, (1) is not sufficient.

From (2), because $(-4)^3 = -64$, $(-3)^3 = -27$, and $(-2)^3 = -8$, only $k = -3$ satisfies $-60 < k^3 < -20$. Thus, (2) is sufficient. Therefore, statement (2) alone is sufficient.

433.

A. Statement (1) ALONE is sufficient, but statement (2) alone is not sufficient.

From (1), $1 + t + 5 < 10$ implies $t < 4$. Hence, t could be 0, 1, 2, or 3, all of which would result in $X = 0.01$ when rounded to the nearest hundredth. Thus, (1) is sufficient.

From (2), X could be, for example, 0.0135 or 0.0175. In the first case, $X = 0.01$ when rounded to the nearest hundredth. But in the second case, $X = 0.02$ when rounded to the nearest hundredth. Thus, (2) is not sufficient. Therefore, statement (1) alone is sufficient.

434.

D. Each statement ALONE is sufficient.

Let D = the flight distance, in kilometers, from city A to city B. From (1), $D = \left(270 \text{ kilometers per hour}\right)\left(6\frac{2}{3} \text{ hours}\right)$, which you can calculate to determine an exact value of D.

From (2), $\dfrac{D \text{ kilometers}}{270 \text{ km per hour}} = \dfrac{D \text{ kilometers}}{300 \text{ km per hour}} + \dfrac{2}{3}$ hour, which you can solve for an exact value of D. Thus, (2) is sufficient. Therefore, each statement alone is sufficient.

435.

D. Each statement ALONE is sufficient.

Let R = the length of the radius of the larger circle, and r = the length of the radius of the smaller circle. From (1), $R = r + 300\%r = r + 3r = 4r$, which implies that the ratio of R to r is 4 to 1. Hence, the ratio of the area of the smaller circle to the area of the larger circle is $1\left(= 1^2\right)$ to $16\left(= 4^2\right)$. It fol-

lows that the total area of the smaller circle is $\dfrac{1}{16} \times 100\%$ of the total area of the larger circle. Thus, (1) is sufficient.

From (2), the ratio of R to r is 4 to 1. You can complete (2) as shown in (1). Thus, (2) is sufficient. Therefore, each statement alone is sufficient.

436.

E. Statements (1) and (2) TOGETHER are NOT sufficient.

Let X = the value of products labeled gluten-free in the grocery in 2015, and Y = the value of products labeled gluten-free in the grocery in 2017. Then the percent increase in value from 2015 to 2017 is $\dfrac{Y - X}{X} \times 100\%$. From (1), if V is the value of all products sold in the grocery store in 2015, then $X = 2.4\%V$. But without additional information, you cannot determine an exact value of $\dfrac{Y - X}{X} \times 100\%$. Thus, (1) is not sufficient.

From (2), if W is the value of all products sold in the grocery store in 2017, then $Y = 7.2\%W$. But without additional information, you cannot determine an exact value of $\dfrac{Y - X}{X} \times 100\%$. Thus, (2) is not sufficient.

Taking (1) and (2) together, $\frac{Y-X}{X} \times 100\% = \frac{7.2\%W - 2.4\%V}{2.4\%V} \times 100\%$.

This expression gives inconclusive results. For example, if $V = W$, then $\frac{7.2\%W - 2.4\%W}{2.4\%W} \times 100\% = \frac{4.8\%W}{2.4\%W} \times 100\% = 200\%$. But if $V = 2W$, then

$\frac{7.2\%W - 2.4\%(2W)}{2.4\%(2W)} \times 100\% = \frac{2.4\%W}{4.8\%W} \times 100\% = 50\%$. Therefore, statements (1)

and (2) together are not sufficient.

---

437. **C. Both statements TOGETHER are sufficient, but NEITHER statement ALONE is sufficient.**

It is given that Hachi read for 15 days. From (1), Hachi read $22 \times 10 = 220$ pages during the first 10 days. But without additional information, you cannot determine the average number of pages read for 15 days. Thus, (1) is not sufficient.

From (2), Let x = the average number of pages Hachi read during the first 10 of the 15 days, and y = the average number of pages Hachi read during the last 5 of the 15 days. Then $x = 2y + 2$ and the average number of page read for 15 days is $\frac{(2y+2)(10) + (y)(5)}{15} = \frac{25y + 20}{15}$. This expression gives inconclusive results, depending on the value of y. For example, if $y = 4$, $\frac{25y + 20}{15} = \frac{120}{15} = 8$. But if $y = 10$, $\frac{25y + 20}{15} = \frac{270}{15} = 18$. Thus, (2) is not sufficient.

Taking (1) and (2) together, $22 = 2y + 2$, from which you can determine y; and, thereafter, an exact value of $\frac{25y + 20}{15}$. Therefore, both statements together are sufficient, but neither statement alone is sufficient.

---

438. **C. Both statements TOGETHER are sufficient, but NEITHER statement ALONE.**

Recall that if $p_1^{k_1} \cdot p_2^{k_2} \cdots p_n^{k_n}$ is the prime factorization of a non–prime integer Z, then the number of positive factors of Z is the product $(k_1 + 1)(k_2 + 1) \cdots (k_n + 1)$. From (1), $X = 4p = 2^2 p$ implies that X has $(2+1)(1+1) = (3)(2) = 6$ factors. But no information about Y is given. Thus, (1) is not sufficient to answer the question posed.

From (2), $Y = 8p = 2^3 p$ implies that Y has $(3+1)(1+1) = (4)(2) = 8$ factors. But no information about X is given. Thus, (2) is not sufficient to answer the question posed.

Taking (1) and (2) together, given that $Y = 8p = 2(4p) = 2X$, then every positive factor of X is a factor of Y. Because Y has two more factors than X does, two positive factors of Y are not factors of X. Therefore, both statements together are sufficient, but neither statement alone is sufficient.

439. B. **Statement (2) ALONE is sufficient, but statement (1) alone is not sufficient.**

Given that $a - 2b + 3c > a + 2b - 3c$ is equivalent to $-2b + 3c > 2b - 3c$, the question asks: is $3c - 2b > 2b - 3c$?

From (1), information about a is not helpful because a can be eliminated from the inequality given in the question without altering its meaning. Thus, (1) is not sufficient.

From (2), $b < c$ implies $2b < 2c$. It follows that $2b < 3c$. Hence, $3c - 2b > 0$ and $2b - 3c < 0$. So $3c - 2b > 2b - 3c$, yielding an answer of Yes to the question posed. Thus, (2) is sufficient. Therefore, statement (2) alone is sufficient.

440. C. **Both statements TOGETHER are sufficient, but NEITHER statement ALONE is sufficient.**

Let A = the number of workers over the age of 40 at company X, and B = the number of works age 40 years and younger at company X. From (1), $16\%B$ and $29\%(A + B)$ have 401(k) accounts. But without additional information, you cannot determine whether the percent of the workers over the age of 40 years who have 401(k) accounts is at least 40 percent. Thus, (1) is not sufficient.

From (2), $B > A$. But without additional information, you cannot determine whether the percent of the workers over the age of 40 years who have 401(k) accounts is at least 40 percent. Thus, (2) is not sufficient.

Taking (1) and (2) together, consider, for a moment, the implications if A and B were equal, then $29\%A$ = the number of workers over the age of 40 who have 401(k) accounts and $29\%B$ = the number of workers age 40 years and younger who have 401(k) accounts. But it's given in (1) that 16% of B have 401(k) accounts. This percent is $13\%(= 29\% - 16\%)$ below the average of 29%. So in the hypothetical case of $A = B$, the percent of A that have 401(k) must be $42\%(= 29\% + 13\%)$ to maintain an overall average of 29%. It's given in (2) that $B > A$, from which you can infer that more than 42% of workers over the age of 40 years must have 401(k) accounts in order to pull up the average for all workers to 29%. Therefore, both statements together are sufficient, but neither statement alone is sufficient.

441. A. **Statement (1) ALONE is sufficient, but statement (2) alone is not sufficient.**

It is given that $r > 120\%s = 1.2s$. From (1), $s > 60$ implies $1.2s > 1.2(60) = 72$. Hence, because $r > 1.2s$, then $r > 72$, yielding an answer of Yes to the question posed. Thus, (1) is sufficient.

From (2), $r - s = 40$ gives inconclusive results. For example, $r = 110$ and $s = 70$ yield an answer of Yes to the question posed $\left(\text{because } r > 1.2(70) > 70\right)$. But $r = 60$ and $s = 20$ yield an answer of No to the question posed $\left(\text{because } r > 1.2(20) \not> 70\right)$. Thus, (2) is not sufficient. Therefore, statement (1) alone is sufficient.

442.

C. Both statements TOGETHER are sufficient, but NEITHER statement ALONE is sufficient.

Let R = the number of red chips in the box initially, and B = the number of black chips in the box initially. From (1), $\frac{R}{B} = \frac{3}{25}$, which is one equation with two variables. Without additional information, you cannot determine an exact value of B. Thus, (1) is not sufficient.

From (2), $\frac{(R-12)}{(R-12)+(B-80)} = \frac{1}{11}$, which is one equation with two variables. Without additional information, you cannot determine an exact value of B. Thus, (2) is not sufficient.

Taking (1) and (2) together, because $\frac{R}{B} = \frac{3}{25}$, let $R = 3x$ and $B = 25x$. Then substitute into $\frac{(R-12)}{(R-12)+(B-80)} = \frac{1}{11}$ to obtain $\frac{(3x-12)}{(3x-12)+(25x-80)} = \frac{1}{11}$, which you can solve for x; and, thereafter, obtain an exact value of $B = 25x$. Therefore, both statements together are sufficient, but neither statement alone is sufficient.

443.

C. Both statements TOGETHER are sufficient, but NEITHER statement ALONE is sufficient.

From (1), $m = -\left(\frac{1}{-5}\right) = \frac{1}{5}$ because if two non-vertical lines are perpendicular, their slopes are negative reciprocals of each other. Hence, $y = \frac{1}{5}x + b$.

Without additional information, you cannot determine whether $y = \frac{1}{5}x + b$ contains the point $(3,1)$. Thus, (1) is not sufficient.

Substituting (2) into $y = mx + b$ yields $\frac{2}{5} = m(0) + b$ or, simply, $b = \frac{2}{5}$.

Hence, $y = mx + \frac{2}{5}$. Without additional information, you cannot determine whether $y = mx + \frac{2}{5}$ contains the point $(3,1)$. Thus, (2) is not sufficient.

Taking (1) and (2) together $y = \frac{1}{5}x + \frac{2}{5}$ and $(1) = \frac{1}{5}(3) + \frac{2}{5}$, confirming that the line contains the point $(3,1)$. Therefore, both statements together are sufficient, but neither statement alone is sufficient.

444.

D. Each statement ALONE is sufficient.

From (1), of the $76(=100-24)$ beads remaining in the bag, half or 38, are blue. Thus, (1) is sufficient.

From (2), let x = the number of blue beads removed, and $3x$ = the number of pink beads removed. Then $x + 3x = 24$ or, equivalently, $4x = 24$. Hence, $x = 6$ and $44 - 6 = 38$ blue beads are left in the jar. Thus, (2) is sufficient. Therefore, each statement alone is sufficient.

445. **C. Both statements TOGETHER are sufficient, but NEITHER statement ALONE is sufficient.**

Let h = the number of hours that Cerenity and Jas rented the jet ski, x = the rental fee for the first hour, and y = the rental fee for each additional hour. It is given that $x > y$ and $\$16.50 = x + (h-1)y$. From (1), $\$10.50 = x + y$, which implies $\$10.50 - y = x$. Substituting into $\$16.50 = x + (h-1)y$ yields $\$16.50 = (\$10.50 - y) + (h-1)y$ or, equivalently, $\dfrac{\$6.00}{(h-2)} = y$. This equation

eliminates $h = 2$ as a possible value of x because division by 0 is undefined. And it eliminates $h = 3$ as a possible value for h because $y = \$6$ implies $x = \$10.50 - \$6 = \$4.50$, which contradicts $x > y$. Hence, $h > 3$. But without additional information, you cannot determine an exact value of h. Thus, (1) is not sufficient.

From (2), because you have no way of knowing how many hours came before the last three hours, you cannot determine an exact value of h. Thus, (2) is not sufficient.

Taking (1) and (2) together, because $h > 3$, the last three hours does not include the first hour. Hence, $\$9 = 3y$, which implies $y = \$3$. Substituting into $\dfrac{\$6.00}{(h-2)} = y$ yields $\dfrac{\$6.00}{(h-2)} = \$3$, which you can solve for an exact value of h. Therefore, both statements together are sufficient, but neither statement alone is sufficient.

446. **A. Statement (1) ALONE is sufficient.**

It is given that k is a prime number. From (1), you have that the common factors of 24 and 36 are 1, 2, 3, 4, 6, and 12. Because k is prime, $3k \geq 6$, the only common factors to consider are 6 and 12. Of these factors, only $3k = 6$, or $k = 2$, results in a prime number value for k. Thus, (1) is sufficient.

From (2), k could be 2 or 3. Without additional information, you cannot determine an exact value of k. Thus, (2) is not sufficient. Therefore, statement (1) alone is sufficient.

447. **B. Statement (2) ALONE is sufficient, but statement (1) alone is not sufficient.**

Let x = the cost of one item of type 1, and y = the cost of one item of type 2. To answer the question posed, determine whether $x < y$. From (1), $6x + 4y < 4x + 8y$, which implies $2x < 4y$, or, equivalently, $x < 2y$. This inequality does not necessarily guarantee that $x < y$. For example, if $x = 1$ and $y = 2$ then $x < 2y$ and $x < y$. But if $x = 6$ and $y = 4$ then $x < 2y$ and $x \not< y$. Thus, (1) is not sufficient to answer the question posed.

From (2), $5x + 4y < 4x + 5y$, which implies $x < y$, yielding an answer of Yes to the question posed. Therefore, statement (2) alone is sufficient.

448. **A. Statement (1) ALONE is sufficient, but statement (2) alone is not sufficient.**

It is given that the arithmetic average cost of the three items is $25. Hence, the total cost of the three items is $3($25) = 75. From (1), one item cost $50. The remaining two items cost a total of $25(= $75 - $50)$ and thus were not taxed (because each would have a cost less than $40). Only the $50 is taxed, resulting in a total sales tax of $8\%($50)$. Thus, (1) is sufficient.

From (2), one item is $5. The remaining two items cost a total of $70(= $75 - $5)$. Without additional information, you cannot determine an exact value of the sales tax on the three items. For example, if the remaining two items cost $35 and $35, then none of the items is taxed, resulting in a total of $0 tax on the three items. But if the three items cost $5, $60, and $10, then the total sales tax on the three items is $8\%($60)$. Thus, (2) is not sufficient. Therefore, statement (1) alone is sufficient.

449. **C. Both statements TOGETHER are sufficient, but NEITHER statement ALONE is sufficient.**

Let $P(\text{both})$ = the probability Harper will get a job offer from both companies, $P(\text{exactly one})$ = the probability Harper will get a job offer from exactly one of the two companies, and $P(\text{neither})$ = the probability that Harper will get a job offer from neither company. Given that one of these three events is certain to happen, then $P(\text{both}) + P(\text{exactly one}) + P(\text{neither}) = 1$, from which you have $P(\text{both}) = 1 - P(\text{exactly one}) - P(\text{neither})$. From (1) $P(\text{both}) = 1 - 0.6 - P(\text{neither})$. Without additional information, you cannot determine an exact value of $P(\text{both})$. Thus, (1) is not sufficient.

From (2), $P(\text{both}) = 1 - P(\text{exactly one}) - 0.1$. Without additional information, you cannot determine an exact value of $P(\text{both})$. Thus, (2) is not sufficient.

Taking (1) and (2) together, $P(\text{both}) = 1 - 0.6 - 0.1 = 0.3$. Therefore, both statements together are sufficient, but neither statement alone is sufficient.

450. **A. Statement (1) ALONE is sufficient, but statement (2) alone is not sufficient.**

Standard deviation is a statistical measure that is used to quantify the amount of deviation from the mean in a set of data values. If all the values of a data set are equal, the standard deviation is 0; otherwise, the standard deviation is positive. From (1), x is 0 because all the data values equal 50. Two cases for y are possible. Case I: If $y = 0$, then $x > y$ is false because $0 > 0$ is false. Case II: If $y > 0$, then $x > y$ is false because $0 \not> y$, a positive number. Therefore, statement (1) alone is sufficient.

From (2), $y > 0$ because the values in the data set are not all equal. But without additional information, you cannot determine whether $x > y$. Thus, (2) is not sufficient. Therefore, statement (1) alone is sufficient.

451. **A. Statement (1) ALONE is sufficient, but statement (2) alone is not sufficient.**

From (1), it is given that the probability is $\frac{1}{2}$ that the chip drawn will be green or red, meaning $\frac{1}{2}$ of the chips are green or red. Hence, $\frac{1}{2}$ of the chips are black or blue. So the probability that the chip drawn is black or blue is $\frac{1}{2}$. Thus, (1) is sufficient.

From (2), it is given that the probability is $\frac{1}{3}$ that the chip drawn will be black, meaning $\frac{1}{3}(24)=8$ of the chips are black. However, there is no information about how many of the remaining 16 chips are blue, green, or red. Without additional information, you cannot determine an exact value of the probability that the chip drawn is black or blue. Therefore, statement (1) alone is sufficient.

452. **D. Each statement ALONE is sufficient.**

From (1), given $a=3b$ and $a+b=180$ (because consecutive angles of a parallelogram are supplementary), then $3b+b=180$, which you can solve for b; and, thereafter, determine an exact value for $a=3b$. Thus, (1) is sufficient.

From (2), given $a+c=270$ and $a=c$ (because opposite angles of a parallelogram have the same measure), then $a+a=270$, which you can solve for an exact value of a. Thus, (2) is sufficient. Therefore, each statement alone is sufficient.

453. **A. Statement (1) ALONE is sufficient, but statement (2) alone is not sufficient.**

Let P = the original price of the computer, and N = the new price of the computer. Then $N-P$ = the increase in price, which as a percent of the new price is $\frac{N-P}{N}\times100\%$. From (1), $N-P=25\%P=0.25P$, which implies that $N=1.25P$. Substituting into $\frac{N-P}{N}\times100\%$ yields $\frac{0.25P}{1.25P}\times100\%=\frac{1}{5}\times100\%$. Thus, (1) is sufficient.

From (2), $N=\$1{,}200$ and $\frac{\$1{,}200-P}{\$1{,}200}\times100\%$. The value of this expression will vary, depending on the value of P. Without additional information, you cannot determine an exact value of $\frac{N-P}{N}\times100\%$. Thus, (2) is not sufficient. Therefore, statement (1) alone is sufficient.

454. **C. Both statements TOGETHER are sufficient, but NEITHER statement ALONE is sufficient.**

Let M = Makayla's current age, and G = Gilbert's current age. From (1), $2M=G-2$, which is one equation with two unknowns, so additional information is needed to determine an exact value of M. Thus, (1) is not sufficient.

From (2), $M + 4 = G$, which is one equation with two unknowns, so additional information is needed to determine an exact value of M. Thus, (2) is not sufficient.

Taking (1) and (2) together, you can solve $2M = G - 2$ and $M + 4 = G$ for an exact value of M. Therefore, both statements together are sufficient, but neither statement alone is sufficient.

455. **D. Each statement ALONE is sufficient.**

It is given that $x = \dfrac{a}{2} = 3b$. Hence, $a = 2x$, $b = \dfrac{x}{3}$, and $a^2 - b^2 = (2x)^2 - \left(\dfrac{x}{3}\right)^2$.

From (1), $\dfrac{x^3}{27} = -1$ implies $x^3 = -27$, so $x = -3$. You can substitute this value into $(2x)^2 - \left(\dfrac{x}{3}\right)^2$ to determine an exact value of $a^2 - b^2$. Thus, (1) is sufficient.

From (2), $|x| = 3$ implies $x = 3$ or -3. Substituting either of these values into $(2x)^2 - \left(\dfrac{x}{3}\right)^2$ will lead to the same results for the value of $a^2 - b^2$. Thus, (2) is sufficient. Therefore, each statement alone is sufficient.

456. **B. Statement (2) ALONE is sufficient, but statement (1) alone is not sufficient.**

From (1), t could be 5, 6, 7, 8, or 9 because each of 0.5658, 0. 5668, 0.5678, 0.5688, and 0.5698 rounded to the nearest hundredth is 0.57. Thus, (1) is not sufficient.

From (2), when $N = 0.56t8$ is rounded to the nearest thousandths, because 8 is the digit in the ten-thousandths place, the digit in the thousandths place increases by 1. So $t + 1 = 8$, which implies $t = 7$. Thus, (2) is sufficient. Therefore, statement (2) alone is sufficient.

457. **E. Statements (1) and (2) TOGETHER are NOT sufficient.**

From (1), in terms of ordered pairs, (r, s) could be $(1, 15)$, $(15, 1)$, $(3, 5)$, or $(5, 3)$. Thus, (1) is not sufficient.

From (2), in terms of ordered pairs, (r, s) could be $(1, 7)$, $(2, 6)$, $(3, 5)$, $(4, 4)$, $(5, 3)$, $(6, 2)$, or $(7, 1)$. Thus, (2) is not sufficient.

Taking (1) and (2), together, there are still two possibilities for (r, s). These are $(3, 5)$ or $(5, 3)$, meaning $\dfrac{r}{s}$ could be $\dfrac{3}{5}$ or $\dfrac{5}{3}$. Therefore, statements (1) and (2) together are not sufficient.

458. **D. Each statement ALONE is sufficient.**

From (1), the car is traveling $5 (= 70 - 65)$ miles per hour faster than the van. Given that the car is already 4 miles ahead of the van, the time it will take the car to be 10 miles ahead of the van is $\dfrac{10 \text{ miles} - 4 \text{ miles}}{5 \text{ miles per hour}} = \dfrac{6 \text{ miles}}{5 \text{ miles per hour}} = 1.2$ hours. Thus, (1) is sufficient.

From (2), the car gained $5(=1+4)$ miles on the van in 1 hour, so it is traveling 5 miles per hour faster than the van. This result leads to the same calculations as performed in (1) to obtain a time of 1.2 hours for the car to be 10 miles ahead of the van. Thus, (2) is sufficient. Therefore, each statement alone is sufficient.

459. **B. Statement (2) ALONE is sufficient, but statement (1) alone is not sufficient.**

From (1), given that one apartment has more than three occupants, you know only that there are 39 apartments left to accommodate the remaining occupants. But without additional information, you cannot determine how many occupants are left to distribute among the 39 apartments. Thus, (1) is not sufficient.

From (2), the apartment manager and family account for 1 apartment and 4 occupants, leaving 39 apartments to accommodate 79 occupants. The only way to distribute 79 occupants among the 39 apartments is 38 apartments with 2 occupants and 1 apartment with 3 occupants. So there is a total of 2 apartments that have more than two occupants (the apartment manager's apartment being one of those two). Thus, (2) is sufficient. Therefore, statement (2) alone is sufficient.

460. **A. Statement (1) ALONE is sufficient, but statement (2) alone is not sufficient.**

It's given that $X = \frac{a}{2^2} + \frac{b}{2^3} + \frac{c}{2^5}$. From (1), there are only 8 possible values of X, depending on the possible values of the ordered triples (a,b,c). The possible values for (a,b,c) are $(0, 0, 0)$, $(0, 0, 1)$, $(0, 1, 0)$, $(0, 1, 1)$, $(1, 0, 0)$, $(1, 0, 1)$, $(1, 1, 0)$, and $(1, 1, 1)$. Hence, X can equal only the values 0, $\frac{1}{32}$, $\frac{4}{32}$, $\frac{5}{32}$, $\frac{8}{32}$, $\frac{9}{32}$, $\frac{12}{32}$, or $\frac{13}{32}$. Given that $\frac{5}{16} = \frac{10}{32}$ is not among this list, then the answer to the question posed is No. Thus, (1) is sufficient.

From (2), given that $\frac{5}{16} = \frac{10}{32}$ is less than $\frac{13}{32}$, additional information is needed to rule this value out as a possible value of X. Thus, (2) is not sufficient. Therefore, statement (1) alone is sufficient.

461. **C. Both statements TOGETHER are sufficient, but NEITHER statement ALONE is sufficient.**

From (1), $(k-2)^2 = 64$ implies $|k-2| = 8$, from which you have $k = 10$ or -6. This result yields $k-4$ equal to 6 or -10. Thus, (1) is not sufficient.

From (2), $(k+2)^2 = 144$ implies $|k+2| = 12$, from which you have $k = 10$ or -14. This result yields $k-4$ equal to 6 or -18. Thus, (2) is not sufficient. Taking (1) and (2) together, $k = 10$ satisfies all conditions given, resulting in $k-4 = 6$. Therefore, both statements together are sufficient, but neither statement alone is sufficient.

462. **B. Statement (2) ALONE is sufficient, but statement (1) alone is not sufficient.**

Statement (1) is not sufficient because all of the possible fractions given are less than 0.5.

From (2), $\frac{p}{q} = \frac{2}{5}$ because, of the possible fractions given, only $\frac{2}{5} = 0.4$ is greater than 0.25. Therefore, statement (2) alone is sufficient.

463. **E. Statements (1) and (2) TOGETHER are NOT sufficient.**

From (1), $4x + 7 > y$ leads to inconclusive results. Without additional information, you cannot determine a definite Yes or No answer to the question posed because there are multiple values for x and y that satisfy this condition. For example, $x = 2$ and $y = 12$ yield a Yes response. But $x = 3$ and $y = 4$ yield a No response. Thus, (1) is not sufficient.

From (2), $y > 15$ is inconclusive because no information about x is given. Without additional information, you cannot answer the question posed. Thus, (2) is not sufficient.

Taking (1) and (2) together yields inconclusive results. For example, $x = 3$ and $y = 16$ yield a Yes response. But $x = 4$ and $y = 16$ yield a No response. Therefore, statements (1) and (2) together are not sufficient.

464. **B. Statement (2) ALONE is sufficient, but statement (1) alone is not sufficient.**

It is given that $6 < X < 7$. From (1), you cannot determine a definite Yes or No answer to the question posed because, for example, X could be $6.6 \ldots$, which yields a No answer to the question posed, or X could be $6.8 \ldots$, which yields a Yes answer to the question posed. Thus, (1) is not sufficient.

From (2), $X + 0.28 > 7$ implies $X > 7 - 0.28 = 6.72$, which yields a Yes answer to the question posed. Thus, (2) is sufficient. Therefore, statement (2) alone is sufficient.

465. **D. Each statement ALONE is sufficient.**

It is given that $x^3 = y^4$. Hence, $x = \sqrt[3]{y^4}$. From (1), $y^3 = -64$ implies $y = -4$, from which you have $x = \sqrt[3]{(-4)^4}$. Thus, (1) is sufficient.

From (2), given $y^2 = 16$, then $x = \sqrt[3]{y^4} = \sqrt[3]{y^2 \cdot y^2} = \sqrt[3]{16 \cdot 16}$. Thus, (2) is sufficient. Therefore, each statement alone is sufficient.

466. **A. Statement (1) ALONE is sufficient, but statement (2) alone is not sufficient.**

From (1), given $AD = BD = CD$, then triangles ADB, ADC, and BDC are isosceles. Given that base angles of isosceles triangles have equal measure, $m\angle DAB = 20°$, $m\angle DCB = 40°$, and $m\angle DCA = x°$. Note: $m\angle X$ denotes the measure of angle X. Given that the sum of the measures of the interior angles of a triangle is 180°, $\angle BDA = 180° - 2(20°) = 140°$ and $\angle BDC = 180° - 2(40°) = 100°$. Also, $m\angle BDA + m\angle BDC + m\angle ADC = 360°$, so $140° + 100° + m\angle ADC = 360°$, which implies $m\angle ADC = 120°$. Hence, $120° + 2x° = 180°$, from which you can determine that $x = 30$. Thus, (1) is sufficient.

From (2), given $y = 140$, $\angle DAB = 180° - 140° - 20° = 20°$. But additional information is needed to determine an exact value of x. Thus, (2) is not sufficient. Therefore, statement (1) alone is sufficient.

467. **B. Statement (2) ALONE is sufficient, but statement (1) alone is not sufficient.**

It is given that $224 < k < 256$ for the integer k. Hence, $14 < \frac{k}{16} < 16$. From (1), $\sqrt{k} < 16$ implies $k < 16^2 = 256$, which you already knew. Thus, (1) is not sufficient.

From (2), k is divisible by 16 implies $\frac{k}{16}$ is an integer. Given that $14 < \frac{k}{16} < 16$, then $k = 15$. Thus, (2) is sufficient. Therefore, statement (2) alone is sufficient.

468. **A. Statement (1) ALONE is sufficient, but statement (2) alone is not sufficient.**

From (1), because $\sqrt{49m} = \sqrt{49}\sqrt{m} = 7\sqrt{m}$ is an integer, then $\sqrt{m}$ is an integer. Thus, (1) is sufficient.

From (2), $\sqrt{7m} = \sqrt{7}\sqrt{m}$. Without additional information, you cannot determine whether $\sqrt{m}$ is an integer because, for example, if $m = 4$, $\sqrt{m}$ is an integer. But if $m = 3$, $\sqrt{m}$ is not an integer. Thus, (2) is not sufficient. Therefore, statement (1) alone is sufficient.

469. **A. Statement (1) ALONE is sufficient, but statement (2) alone is not sufficient.**

From (1), $-5x^{99} > 0$ implies $x^{99} < 0$. Because an odd root of a negative number is negative, then $x < 0$, yielding an answer of Yes to the question posed. Thus, (1) is sufficient.

From (2), $-5x^{100} < 0$ implies $x^{100} > 0$. This result is true regardless whether x is positive or negative, leading to inconclusive results. Thus, (2) is not sufficient. Therefore, statement (1) alone is sufficient.

470. **C. Both statements TOGETHER are sufficient, but NEITHER statement ALONE is sufficient.**

It is given that the total amount of the bonuses is $5,600. Let B = the amount of Benjamin's bonus. From (1), Let X = the amount of Sian's bonus = the amount of Lin's bonus. Then $2X + B = \$5,600$, which implies $B = \$5,600 - 2X$. This is one equation with two unknowns. Without additional information, you cannot determine an exact value of B. Thus, (1) is not sufficient.

From (2), if X = amount of Sian's bonus, then $B = \frac{1}{3}X$, which is one equation with two unknowns. Without additional information, you cannot determine an exact value of B. Thus, (2) is not sufficient.

Taking (1) and (2) together, $\frac{1}{3}X = \$5,600 - 2X$, which you can solve for X; and, thereafter, determine an exact value of B. Therefore, both statements together are sufficient, but neither statement alone is sufficient.

471. **A. Statement (1) ALONE is sufficient, but statement (2) alone is not sufficient.**

From (1), $m^k < 0$ implies that k must be odd. This is true because the only way that m^k can be negative is if m is a negative integer raised to an odd power. Otherwise, if k is even and m is negative or positive, $m^k > 0$. Thus, (1) is sufficient.

From (2), $4k - 5$ is odd leads to inconclusive results. This is true because (2) would be true for both odd and even values of k. Thus, (2) is not sufficient. Therefore, statement (1) alone is sufficient.

472. **E. Statements (1) and (2) TOGETHER are NOT sufficient.**

From (1), $xy = 36$ leads to inconclusive results because $x + y$ could be the sum of any two factors whose product is 36. For example, if $x = 1$ and $y = 36$, then $x + y = 1 + 36 = 37$. But if $x = 2$ and $y = 18$, then $x + y = 2 + 18 = 20$. Thus, (1) is not sufficient.

From (2), $y \geq x + 6$ leads to inconclusive results because $x + y$ could be the sum of any two integers that satisfy the inequality. For example, if $x = 4$ and $y = 20$, then $x + y = 4 + 20 = 24$. But if $x = 2$ and $y = 18$, then $x + y = 2 + 18 = 20$. Thus, (2) is not sufficient.

Taking (1) and (2) together also leads to inconclusive results because both $x = 2$ and $y = 18$ and $x = 3$ and $y = 12$ satisfy all conditions given, yet yield different values of $x + y$. Therefore, statements (1) and (2) together are not sufficient.

473. **D. Each statement ALONE is sufficient.**

It is given that a, b, and c are positive integers and $a^2 + b^2 = c^2$. Thus, a, b, and c constitute a Pythagorean triple. From (1), given $a = 3$, then $b = 4$ and $c = 5$ because there is no other positive integer solution of $3^2 + b^2 = c^2$. Hence, $\frac{a}{c} = \frac{3}{5}$. Thus, (1) is sufficient.

From (2), given $c = 5$, then $a = 3$ and $b = 4$ because there is no other positive integer solution of $a^2 + b^2 = 5^2$. Hence, $\frac{a}{c} = \frac{3}{5}$. Thus, (2) is sufficient. Therefore, each statement alone is sufficient.

474. **D. Each statement ALONE is sufficient.**

Let H = the number who have lived in their current home for at least 10 years. Then $160 - H$ = the number of homeowners who have <u>not</u> lived in their current home for at least 10 years. From (1), $160 - H = 3H$, which you can solve for an exact value of H. Thus, (1) is sufficient.

From (2), $160 - H = H + 80$, which you can solve for an exact value of H. Thus, (2) is sufficient. Therefore, each statement alone is sufficient.

475. **E. Statements (1) and (2) TOGETHER are NOT sufficient.**

Let x, y, and z be the costs, in dollars, of the individual shirts; and, for convenience, let $x \leq y \leq z$. Then $x + y + z = \$210$. From (1), either $z = 2x$, in which case $x + y + 2x = \$210$; $y = 2x$, in which case $x + 2x + z = \$210$; or $z = 2y$, in which case $x + y + 2y = \$210$. Either way, you have one equation with two unknowns. Without additional information, you cannot determine an exact value of z. Thus, (1) is not sufficient.

From (2), either $x = \frac{1}{2}y$, in which case $\frac{1}{2}y + y + z = \$210$; $x = \frac{1}{2}z$, in which case $\frac{1}{2}z + y + z = \$210$; or $y = \frac{1}{2}z$, in which case $x + \frac{1}{2}z + z = \$210$. Either way, you have one equation with two unknowns. Without additional information, you cannot determine an exact value of z. Thus, (2) is not sufficient.

Taking (1) and (2) together leads to inconclusive results. For example, if $x = \frac{1}{2}y$ and $z = 2y$ are true, then $\frac{1}{2}y + y + 2y = \$210$, which you can solve for y; and, thereafter, determine an exact value of z. But if $x = \frac{1}{2}y$ and $y = 2x$ are true, then $\frac{1}{2}y + y + z = \$210$, from which you cannot determine an exact value of z. Therefore, statements (1) and (2) together are not sufficient.

476.

D. Each statement ALONE is sufficient.

From (1), $xy = 3x^2$ implies $y = 3x$, which, in turn, implies $\frac{x}{y} = \frac{1}{3}$. Thus, (1) is sufficient.

From (2), you have $\dfrac{\frac{1}{4}x}{2y} = \dfrac{1}{24}$, which implies $6x = 2y$, which, in turn, implies $\frac{x}{y} = \frac{1}{3}$. Thus, (2) is sufficient. Therefore, each statement alone is sufficient.

477.

A. Statement (1) ALONE is sufficient, but statement (2) alone is not sufficient.

Note: $m\angle C$ denotes the measure of $\angle C$. From (1), $2(x + y) = 180$ implies $(x + y) = 90$. Given that the sum of the measures of the interior angles of a triangle is 180°, $m\angle C$ equals $180° - 90° = 90°$. Hence, triangle ABC is a right triangle, and, by the Pythagorean theorem, $a^2 + b^2 = 53^2$. Thus, (1) is sufficient.

From (2), given that the sum of the measures of the interior angles of a triangle is 180°, $x° + y° + m\angle C = 2x° + m\angle C = 180°$, which implies $m < C = 180° - 2x°$, which is one equation with two unknowns. Without additional information, you cannot determine an exact value of $a^2 + b^2$. Thus, (2) is not sufficient. Therefore, statement (1) alone is sufficient.

478.

A. Statement (1) ALONE is sufficient, but statement (2) alone is not sufficient.

Simplify the equation in (1) as follows:

$$(x - y)(x + y) = xz$$
$$x^2 - y^2 = xz$$
$$x^2 - xz = y^2$$
$$x(x - z) = y^2$$
$$x = \frac{y^2}{x - z}$$

This result yields an answer of Yes to the question posed. Thus, (1) is sufficient.

From (2), $y^2 \geq x - z$ implies $\dfrac{y^2}{x - z} \geq 1$. This result is not sufficient to answer the question posed. Thus, (2) is not sufficient. Therefore, statement (1) alone is sufficient.

479. **C. Both statements TOGETHER are sufficient, but NEITHER statement ALONE is sufficient.**

From (1), $p = 2q$ leads to inconclusive results because no information is given about r. Thus, (1) is not sufficient.

From (2), $4q = 11r$ leads to inconclusive results because no information is given about p. Thus, (2) is not sufficient.

Taking (1) and (2) together, $p = 2q$ implies $2p = 4q$. Hence, $2p = 4q = 11r$. Because p, q, and r are positive integers, you can determine a solution for $2p = 4q = 11r$ by finding the least common multiple of 2, 4, and 11, which is 44. Let $2p = 4q = 11r = 44$, which yields $p = 22$, $q = 11$, and $r = 4$. Thus, the least possible value of $p + q + r$ is $22 + 11 + 4 = 37$. Therefore, both statements together are sufficient, but neither statement alone is sufficient.

480. **E. Statements (1) and (2) TOGETHER are NOT sufficient.**

Let A = the amount, in gallons, of water added to the barrel, and let B = the barrel's capacity, in gallons. Then $\frac{1}{4}B$ = the amount, in gallons, of water already in the barrel. From (1), $B = 2A$, implies $A = \frac{1}{2}B$, which is one equation with two unknowns. Without additional information, you cannot determine an exact value of B. Thus, (1) is not sufficient.

From (2), $A = 2\left(\frac{1}{4}B\right) = \frac{1}{2}B$, which is equivalent to $B = 2A$, the same equation as in (1). Thus, (2) is not sufficient.

Taking (1) and (2) together results in $B = 2A$, which leads to the same conclusions as in (1) and (2). Therefore, statements (1) and (2) together are not sufficient.

481. **E. Statements (1) and (2) TOGETHER are NOT sufficient.**

Let M = the number of math teachers in the group of 9 teachers, then $\frac{M}{9} \times 100\%$ is the percent of math teachers in the group. From (1), $9 > M \geq 2$, which leads to inconclusive results because you can't assume there are only two math teachers in the group. So M could be a range of values. Thus, (1) is not sufficient.

Statement (2) provides no information about M. Thus, (2) is not sufficient.

Taking (1) and (2) together leads to inconclusive results because you cannot determine an exact value of M from the information given. Therefore, statements (1) and (2) together are not sufficient.

482. **B. Statement (2) ALONE is sufficient, but statement (1) alone is not sufficient.**

From (1), $x^2 + y^2 = 169$ leads to inconclusive results. For example, if $x^2 = 25$ and $y^2 = 144$, then $x^2 < y^2$ is true, yielding answer of Yes to the question posed. But if $x^2 = 144$ and $y^2 = 25$, then $x^2 < y^2$ is false, yielding answer of No to the question posed. Thus, (1) is not sufficient.

From (2), $y - x = 7$ implies $y > x$. Hence, $x^2 < y^2$ is true, yielding an answer of Yes to the question posed. Thus, (2) is sufficient. Therefore, statement (2) alone is sufficient.

483. **E. Statements (1) and (2) TOGETHER are NOT sufficient.**

Let D = the number of people in the group who own a dog, and C = the number of people in the group who own a cat. Then $(D \text{ or } C)$ = the number of people in the group who own either a dog or a cat or both, $(D \text{ and } C)$ = the number of people in the group who own both a dog and a cat, and $100 - (D \text{ or } C)$ = the number of people in the group who own neither a dog nor a cat. From (1), $(D \text{ or } C) < 100$ implies $100 - (D \text{ or } C) \geq 1$. But without additional information, you cannot determine an exact value of $100 - (D \text{ or } C)$. Thus, (1) is not sufficient.

From (2), $(D \text{ and } C) = 30$ implies $100 - (D \text{ or } C) \leq 70$. But without additional information, you cannot determine an exact value of $100 - (D \text{ or } C)$. Thus, (1) is not sufficient.

Taking (1) and (2) together, you have $1 \leq 100 - (D \text{ or } C) \leq 70$. So without additional information, you cannot determine an exact value of $100 - (D \text{ or } C)$. Therefore, statements (1) and (2) together are not sufficient.

484. **D. Each statement ALONE is sufficient.**

From (1), $x^{-2} = \dfrac{1}{36}$ implies $x^{-6} = \left(x^{-2}\right)^3 = \left(\dfrac{1}{36}\right)^3$. Thus, (1) is sufficient.

From (2), $x^6 = 46{,}656$ implies $x^{-6} = \dfrac{1}{46{,}656}$. Thus, (2) is sufficient.

Therefore, each statement alone is sufficient.

485. **B. Statement (2) ALONE is sufficient, but statement (1) alone is not sufficient.**

From (1), $5m - mn = 3$ implies $m(5 - n) = 3$, or, equivalently, $m = \dfrac{3}{5 - n}$. Given that m and n are positive integers, $n < 5$; otherwise, m would be negative. To assure that m is an integer, the possible values for n are 2 and 4, in which case $m = 1$ or 3, respectively. Hence, $m + n = 3$ or $m + n = 7$. Thus, (1) is not sufficient.

From (2) $m(m+2n)+4=13-n^2$ implies $m^2+2mn+4=13-n^2$ or, equivalently, $m^2+2mn+n^2=9$. Hence, $(m+n)^2=9$, which implies $m+n=3$. (It cannot equal -3 because m and n are both positive). Thus, (2) is sufficient. Therefore, statement (2) alone is sufficient.

486.

B. Statement (2) ALONE is sufficient, but statement (1) alone is not sufficient.

Let g_1 = the first term of sequence G, g_n = the nth term of sequence G, and g_{51} = the 51st term of sequence G. From (1), $g_1=5$. But without further information, you cannot determine an exact value of g_{51}. Thus, (1) is not sufficient.

From (2), because $g_1=g_1$, $g_2=g_1(2)^1$, $g_3=g_1(2)^2$, and so on, then $g_7=g_1(2)^6=320$, from which you have $g_1=\dfrac{320}{64}=5$. Hence, $g_{51}=5(2)^{50}$. Thus, (2) is sufficient. Therefore, statement (2) alone is sufficient.

487.

E. Statements (1) and (2) TOGETHER are NOT sufficient.

From (1), $ab^8<0$ implies $a<0$. Without knowing whether b is positive or negative, you cannot give a definite Yes or No answer to the question posed. If $b<0$, then $ab>0$, yielding an answer of No to the question posed. But if $b>0$, then $ab<0$, yielding an answer of Yes the question posed. Thus, (1) is not sufficient.

From (2), $a+b^8=12$ leads to inconclusive results. If $a=11$ and $b=-1$, then $ab<0$, yielding a Yes answer to the question posed. But if $a=11$ and $b=1$, then $ab>0$, yielding a No answer to the question posed. Thus, (2) is not sufficient.

Taking (1) and (2) together, the examples in (2) satisfy all conditions given and lead to inconclusive results. Therefore, statements (1) and (2) together are not sufficient.

488.

D. Each statement ALONE is sufficient.

From (1), $\dfrac{6+4}{2m}=\dfrac{10}{2m}=\dfrac{1}{5}$, which implies $m=25$. Thus, (1) is sufficient.

From (2), because 4 members left team B, $m=21+4=25$. Thus, (2) is sufficient. Therefore, each statement alone is sufficient.

489. **E. Statements (1) and (2) TOGETHER are NOT sufficient.**

From (1), $X < \frac{1}{2}$ implies that X's tenths digit is 0, 1, 2, 3, or 4. Thus, (1) is not sufficient.

From (2), $X > \frac{1}{3}$ implies that X's tenths digit is 3, 4, 5, . . . , or 9. Thus, (2) is not sufficient.

Taking (1) and (2) together, $\frac{1}{3} < X < \frac{1}{2}$ implies X's tenths digit can be 3 or 4. Therefore, statements (1) and (2) together are not sufficient.

490. **D. Each statement ALONE is sufficient to answer the question.**

It is given that $x < y < z$ and $x + y + z = 45$. From (1), $z - x = 4$ implies $z - 4 = x$. Because $x < y < z$ implies x, y, and z are three different odd integers, then $z - 2 = y$. Hence, $(z - 4) + (z - 2) + z = 45$, which you can solve for an exact value of z. Thus, (1) is sufficient.

From (2), given that $x + y + z = 45$, then $y = \frac{45}{3} = 15$ and $z = 15 + 2 = 17$. Thus, (2) is sufficient. Therefore, each statement alone is sufficient.

491. **A. Statement (1) ALONE is sufficient, but statement (2) alone is not sufficient.**

From (1), $r^3 > 0$ implies $r > 0$. Because any number raised to an even power is positive, $s^{10} > 0$. Hence, $r + s^{10} > 0$, yielding an answer of Yes to the question posed. Thus, (1) is sufficient.

From (2), $s > 0$ leads to inconclusive results. For example, $r + s^{10}$ can be positive if, say, $r = 2$ and $s = 1$. Or $r + s^{10}$ can be negative if, say, $r = -2$ and $s = 1$. Thus, (2) is not sufficient. Therefore, statement (1) alone is sufficient.

492. **D. Each statement ALONE is sufficient.**

From (1), $a < b$ implies $ab < b^2$. Given $ab = 25$, then $25 < b^2$. Similarly, $a < b$ implies $a^2 < ab$. Given $ab = 25$, then $a^2 < 25$. Hence, $a^2 < 25 < b^2$. Because a and b are both positive this equation implies $\sqrt{a^2} < \sqrt{25} < \sqrt{b^2}$ or, equivalently, $a < 5 < b$, yielding a Yes answer to the question posed.

From (2), $a^2 < 25 < b^2$ leads to the same results as shown in (1). Thus, (2) is sufficient. Therefore, each statement alone is sufficient.

493. **B. Statement (2) ALONE is sufficient, but statement (1) alone is not sufficient.**

Let x, y, and z be the prices of the three chairs. And, for convenience, let $x \leq y \leq z$. From (1), $z > \$300$ implies $x + y + z > \$300$. This inequality leads to inconclusive results. The prices of the chairs can be under $600, yielding a No response to the question posed, if $x = \$100$, $y = \$100$, and $z = \$350$. And the prices of the chairs can be over $600, yielding a Yes response to the question posed, if $x = \$100$, $y = \$100$, and $z = \$500$. Thus, (1) is not sufficient.

From (2), $x > \$200$ implies $x + y + z > 3(\$200) = \$600$, yielding a Yes response to the question posed. Thus, (2) is sufficient. Therefore, statement (2) alone is sufficient.

494. **C. Both statements TOGETHER are sufficient, but NEITHER statement ALONE is sufficient.**

Let B = the number of tokens that Blake has, and K = the number of tokens that Kylie has. Then $B + K$ equals the total number of tokens that Blake and Kylie have. From (1), $B = 1\frac{1}{2}K = 1.5K$. Hence, $B + K = 1.5K + K = 2.5K$. The value of this quantity will vary, depending on the value of K. Thus, (1) is not sufficient.

From (2), $19 < B + K < 25$, which implies $B + K$ could be 20, 21, 22, 23, or 24.

Taking (1) and (2) together, if $B + K = 2.5K = 20$, then $K = 8$ and $B = 1.5K = 1.5(8) = 12$. None of the other possible values for $B + K$ yield integer values for B, K, and $B + K$. Therefore, both statements together are sufficient, but neither statement alone is sufficient.

495. **A. Statement (1) ALONE is sufficient, but statement (2) alone is not sufficient.**

It is given that machines A, B, and C, working together, can complete the job in 24 hours. Thus, the portion of the job the three machines, working together, can complete in 1 hour is $\frac{1}{24}$. Let T = the time it would take machine A to complete the job, working alone. Hence, the portion of the job that machine A can do in 1 hour is $\frac{1}{T}$. From (1), given machines B and C, working together, can complete the job in 36 hour, the portion of the job they can do in 1 hour, when working together, is $\frac{1}{36}$. It follows that $\frac{1}{T} + \frac{1}{36} = \frac{1}{24}$, which you can solve for an exact value of T. Thus, (1) is sufficient.

From (2), given machines A and C, working together, can complete the job in 48 hour, the portion of the job they can do in 1 hour, when working together, is $\frac{1}{48}$. Let K = the time it would take machine C to complete the job, working alone. Then $\frac{1}{T} + \frac{1}{K} = \frac{1}{48}$, which is one equation with two unknowns. Without additional information, you cannot determine an exact value of T. Thus, (2) is not sufficient. Therefore, statement (1) alone is sufficient.

Chapter 5

496. **B. Literature in the United States changed dramatically in the second half of the 20th century.**

> Essentially, you're looking for the thesis of the passage, so it will most likely be fairly broad, but be careful not to select an answer [like Choice (A)] that's too broad. Choice (B) walks the line between capturing the entirely of the passage but also being specific to the two paragraphs here. It's the best choice.

497. **A. The aftermath of the war.**

> The last sentence is a complicated one with many clauses, which is why the GMAT test-makers have chosen it to ask this question, hoping you will read through it too quickly and choose the wrong answer. However, a careful read reveals that Choice (A) is the main subject of the sentence, and other choices describe what happened during the aftermath. It's the best choice.

498. **D. An emphasis on plain character and plain language.**

> The answer to this question is factual. You need only find it in the passage itself. Choice (D) is taken directly from the passage.

499. **A. . . . historical events in each country radically changed their writers in non-analogous ways.**

> Inference questions are tricky. Simply answering with a fact isn't enough. You must find the step beyond what's said in the passage. Here, Choice (B) is a fact from the passage, while Choices (C) and (D), whether true or not, are factual responses. Choice (A) is best here because it points to a trend that is hinted at but not explicitly stated in the passage.

500. **E. To recognize as different or unique**

> Even if you can't figure out what the word means, it is clearly used as a verb in the sentence, and only Choice (E) is a verbal definition.

501. **D. It provides a turn from the topic of the first paragraph, clarifying what the purpose of the passage will be.**

> The word "however" in the second paragraph should be a hint that it's contradicting or turning away (even slightly) from the first paragraph. A careful read shows that the second paragraph clarifies what the passage will be about, as it turns slightly away from the premise of the opening. Choice (D) is thus the best.

502. **B. While an incandescent lamp may produce heat, many people will continue to use them because the light is familiar and comforting.**

With an inference question, you always want to make a short jump, not a long leap. Choice (D) represents a long leap — it may be true, but it's not implied in the passage. Choice (B), however, is a very small hop that even uses words from the passage, making it the best choice.

503. **D. It provides additional factual information about the topic of the passage.**

The topic of the passage is the incandescent lamp. The last sentence provides additional information about the light given off by such lamps. Choice (D) is best.

504. **C. About 95 percent**

So long as you read the question carefully and take a moment to a brief calculation, you'll choose correctly. If 5 percent or less of the lamp's energy is given to producing light, that means that 95 percent or more is given to other tasks. Choice (C) is best.

505. **C. Despite their inefficiencies, there are reasons why incandescent lamps remain popular.**

The passage is not a screed against incandescent lamps. In fact, suggesting that they be eliminated isn't even suggested. Choice (C) is the closest to capturing the real point of the passage.

506. **A. Visible, obvious**

The best definition of *apparent* as used here is Choice (A). The whiteness is visible or obvious.

507. **E. The first paragraph describes Fischer's prowess in chess at the height of his career, and the second paragraph describes the fall he experienced.**

The answer here is fairly obvious if you've read the passage, but the question is designed to keep you reading for as long as possible. Choice (E) is ultimately the best answer.

508. **B. He finds Fischer's ultimate fate tragic, but also finds fault with Fischer.**

Only Choice (B) fits the tone of the passage. Fischer's withdrawal is described as "tragic" but the use of the word "unfortunately" hints at the idea that the author thinks the chess master should have made different decisions.

509. **D. José Rail Capablanca was also a successful chess player with a high degree of self-confidence.**

> Choice (D) is best here. The author's reference to Capablanca means that he sees a connection between Fishcer and the other chess player. It's not too much of a stretch to infer that they shared some characteristics, as seen in Choice (D).

510. **C. Anxiety about playing a match against Fischer that was so extreme that it causes physical illness.**

> This is a factual question, so don't try to infer what the symptoms of the "fever" are, beyond what the passage describes. That's best captured in Choice (C).

511. **B. Crafting characters and structures, and gathering resources.**

> The answer is in the passage — you just need to take the time to read it and the answer choices carefully to find one that matches. Choice (B) is correct. Remember not to bring your outside knowledge into the game. You might play Minecraft, but you can only respond based on what the passage says.

512. **D. An overview of the game of Minecraft, aimed at those who might want to try playing it.**

> The author is seeking to explain how to play the game. It is clear from the first sentence, which explains Minecraft in extremely simple terms, that her audience is intended to be people who are not very familiar with the game. Choice (D) is best.

513. **A. Minecraft is a game that allows players to change in their focus the more they play it.**

> The inference of the last sentence is that the game will change as you play it, because it will be "less about surviving" and "more about building. . . . " Choice (A) is a logical step in inferring — the game can become what the player wants.

514. **B. Creating a physical object or a representation of a physical object**

> Choice (B) is best here. Choice (A) is a type of craft, which is not the same thing. Choice (D) has some merit, but in a virtual world "sculpting" is less likely to be the meaning as Choice (B). Choices (C) and (D) represent ways to craft, but they're not quite right for this question. People playing Minecraft would not need to program computer code.

515. **E. Some Stars Aren't What You Think!**

> The best title captures some understanding of the main point of the passage, which is that the Evening and Morning Stars are not actually stars at all. Choice (E) is the best of the answers here.

516. **B. Mercury and Venus**

> This is a factual question, so all you need to do is read the passage to find the correct information carefully. Choice (B) is the right answer.

517. **D. Many Americans may have ideas about the sky that show their interest but lack of understanding about astronomy.**

> The only reasonably inference you can make about the writer has to be rooted in what he's written here. Choice (D) is a safe assumption — it's clear from the passage that the writing is correcting misapprehensions, but in a friendly way.

518. **C. A group of people on a boat spot what they think is a pack of dolphins in the ocean in the distance, but the captain informs them they're actually looking at buoys bouncing in the water.**

> The passage describes mistaking one thing for another, which is clarified by an expert (in that case, the author). Choice (C) describes a similar phenomenon.

519. **E. Wrong names**

> The best alternative for *misnomer* is *incorrect names*. It is incorrect to name a meteor a "shooting star," making Choice (E) the best answer. Notice that Choice (A) is correct but too broad. A misnomer is a kind of mistake — Choice (E) explains which kind.

520. **C. Allowing one of the branch of the government to be tied to a hereditary monarch and aristocrats.**

> It is strongly implied in the passage that the Americans saw the British monarchy and hereditary aristocrats to be a flaw that kept their government from being a true republic. Choice (C) is best.

521. **D. Factual and learned**

> You may be thinking "What tone?" because the author here has avoided a strong personal tone. The best answer, therefore, is Choice (D) because the passage sticks to the facts intelligently.

522.   **D. It provides historical proof of the assertion the author has made earlier.**

> The bolded portion is factual, and a careful reading shows that the facts are included to provide support for the idea mentioned in the sentence before it: "Most did not last very long." Choice (D) is best.

523.   **B. The American who set up the country's government tried to do something uniquely long-lasting yet based in the historical example of republics that came before.**

> Choice (B) best captures the main idea of this long passage. The Americans who set up the government the country still uses were aware of republics that came before, as well as the government of Britain, and created their new government in response to those examples.

524.   **D. A dictatorship**

> As clearly stated in the passage, the republic was followed by a dictatorship, making Choice (D) correct.

525.   **E. Landowners**

> The passage states that "Large landowners controlled the House of Commons" so Choice (E) is best.

526.   **D. Including video elements in a website is increasingly common, and may be a good choice for your site.**

> The passage suggests (but does not insist upon) including video on one's website. Choice (D) thus expresses the main idea of the passage the best.

527.   **C. Business owners who are deciding what elements to include in their web pages.**

> The passage is clearly aimed at business owners, but the emphasis is not on those who are deciding about whether to have an online presence, as in Choice (A), but rather those who have decided to have one and now want to figure out what to include. That makes Choice (C) the best answer.

528.   **A. It increases.**

> The passage includes the following: "Research supports the idea that video increases customer engagement. . . . " That makes the answer Choice (A).

529. **D. Video should be used carefully on a website, as it can work against the site's accessibility and enjoyment.**

> In the last sentence of the passage, it is suggested that website owners should "weigh the pros and cons of video" and use it in a way that "supports, rather than detracts." That points out the correct answer as Choice (D).

530. **D. The ever-increasing interest in YouTube**

> This is an unusual variation on this type of question, but you might see it on the test. The point is for you to find a phrase that best matches the original phrase in meaning. Here, Choice (D) is best because it means something akin to "soaring popularity."

531. **B. Swollen and damaged**

> The last section of the passage, in the bullet points, answers this question. The passage advises avoiding cans that are swollen and damaged. Choice (B) is right.

532. **E. They provide a helpful list of characteristics to look for that is drawn from the main paragraph.**

> In this case, the bullet points flow from the main paragraph, adding more information, not contradicting or repeating it. In this case Choice (E) is thus the best.

533. **A. Botulism is a serious health hazard, but there are steps you can take to avoid the risk of mistakenly consuming it.**

> The correct answer is Choice (A) which captures the main idea of the entire passage in a tone that is factual.

534. **C. Anhydration**

> The passage defines *anaerobic* to show that *an-* means without. Applying this rule (and knowing that *hydration* must be the other part because it is in every answer), the correct answer must be Choice (C).

535. **E. Poison**

> Even if you are not familiar with the word *toxin*, its use in the passage makes it clear that it is a type of *poison*, so Choice (E) is correct.

536. **C. Carefully check cans for swelling, damage, rust or deep dents, and do not consumer the food therein if you notice any of these.**

The answer is in the passage, but you must take the time to read it carefully, not just skim it. Choice (C) is best.

537. **C. Personal Real Estate Is Not a Foolproof Investment**

Choice (C) best gets to the tone of the piece, which suggests that individual real estate can plummet in price. That hints at the idea of the title, that real estate is not a foolproof investment because it can sour.

538. **D. Both towns were sites of carcinogenic toxic waste contamination.**

Here, you're asked to find the factual information as listed in the passage. It's clear that Choice (D), which includes language taken directly from the passage, is the best answer.

539. **B. Pursued legal action against the real estate agencies that did not disclose known contaminants to them before selling them property in the towns.**

In an inference question, you want to make a small step away from facts and into supposition. The trick is not to wander too far away from what is already known. Here, the best choice is Choice (B), because it can be inferred from the final sentence of the passage that legal action was most likely taken. All of the other choices might be true, but there is not as much justification in the choices as in Choice (B).

540. **A. Cautious and factual**

The author's tone here is cautious, as is clear from the first sentence when he points out the pitfalls of individual real estate property as an investment. In the rest of the passage, he provides facts to prove his point. That makes Choice (A) the best selection.

541. **D. It clarifies that some property owners were eventually compensated for their losses.**

The best choice here is Choice (D) because the bolded sentence offers clarification about information presented in the passage. It suggests that while the property owners did lose money on their investment, they were eventually compensated for at least part of the lost money.

542. **E. It summarizes attempts to fix a problem before asserting that the problem is not yet fixed.**

The best choice here is clear: Choice (E). The passage explains a problem in "the world of intellectual property" as well as attempts to fix that problem, but concludes that the problem is not yet resolved.

543. **B. By producing guides to initial patent application.**

It's clearly stated in the passage that the Patent Offices "have recently intensified their efforts to be more accessible" by publishing "guides to initial patent application." Thus, Choice (B) is the best answer.

544. **D. Intellectual property management must do a better job of connecting legal procedure with technological development and business strategy.**

In this main idea question, the trick is to avoid choosing an answer that identifies an idea from the passage, but not the main idea. Choice (D) is the only one here that correctly explains the main idea of the passage.

545. **C. Of a whole, more than the sum of its parts**

In the sentence from the passage, *holistic* is used in its standard meaning, to suggest *more than the sum of its parts*. Choice (C) is correct.

546. **D. They will have further suggestions about how intellectual property management can be approached.**

The passage reads like the opening to a longer piece of writing about intellectual property management. It seems clear that further suggestions will come, making Choice (D) the most accurate of those offered here.

547. **A. Zoos are not very well understood. Zookeepers, administrators, and veterinarians have to work together at a zoo, but often they are unable to see how their efforts appear to visitors to the zoo, even after making efforts to make the zoo accessible. Their efforts need to be combined better.**

The passage identifies an area where three groups must work together, which is difficult. They've made improvements, but the overall picture is still very hard to see, and they must improve. That's the same logic as we see in Choice (A).

548. **D. The author is gently teasing readers about the items that they might be storing on their kitchen counters instead of using them for cooking.**

Choice (D) is the best answer here. The author's tone is gentle and humorous, suggesting that these items don't belong on a kitchen counter. It's too much to think the author is suggesting you get rid of these items permanently or should never have owned them at all.

549. **C. Cleaning Off Your Counter Gets Your Ready to Cook!**

The best answer here is Choice (C), which is neither too narrow, as in Choice (B), nor too broad, as in Choice (A). It captures the main idea of the passage.

550. **B. Unsure about keeping their deep fryer on their kitchen counter, even though they only use it once a month.**

The advice in the second paragraph specifically urges people to store their seldom-used appliances off their counters. Thus Choice (B) is best.

551. **E. Maintaining a clutter-free kitchen so it is usable whenever cooking inspiration strikes.**

The answer choices provided read like a list of commonly asserted ideas from cooks and cookbook writers, so it's easy to get confused. However, if you pay attention the passage, only Choice (E) is truly justified as an inference. The authors write "A clean, clear counter space can inspire the creation of a great meal."

552. **D. Not specified, but not on a kitchen counter.**

This is a supporting idea question. You just need to read the passage carefully to find the answer. Here, no system is advocated, except that the kitchen counter should not be used, so Choice (D) is best.

553. **E. A compiled language.**

The last sentence of the passage reads, "Software you install on your computer . . . are coded using compiled language." Choice (E) is thus the best.

554. **C. As the speed advantage that compiled languages have continues to decline, both languages will offer equal incentives to be used.**

Choice (C) is just a small extension from the passage, which points out that the "speed advantage compiled languages have is starting to fade in importance." If that is true, it is safest to say that the languages will be continue to be equally appealing for different reasons.

555. **B. There are two types of programming languages, and each offers advantages and disadvantages.**

Choice (B) best captures the main idea of the passage: There are two main types of languages, and each has distinct characteristics to recommend them.

556. **C. Factual and helpful**

The choice between Choice (C) and Choice (E) is a little tricky here. Keep in mind the somewhat negative meaning of *rote,* which is typically used to describe going through the motions. *Disinterested* also implies a lack of true engagement with the topic. That's hard to prove here, so Choice (C) is better. The tone is definitely factual and helpful.

557. **C. A computer translates the code into an executable file, and then it is distributed via the internet, CD-ROMs, or other media.**

Choice (C) is correct. The language is taken directly from the passage, but the test-taker must carefully read both the passage and the answer choices to make the correct pick.

558. **D. Javascript, Ruby, and C++**

A half-dozen high-level programming languages are listed in the passage. Choice (D) collates three of them into a list and thus is the best choice.

559. **E. The first paragraph provides an overview of how beneficial bees are to our world, so as to make the impact of losing them clearer when presented later.**

The best choice here is Choice (E). The opening paragraph can be summed up in this sentence: "You may not have thought much about the role honey bees play in our everyday food supply." The rest of the paragraph works to prove that point, so that the next paragraph's concern about the loss of honeybees has more of an impact.

560. **B. Beef and dairy**

It's certainly possible that all of the food products mentioned here could be negatively affected by the decline of bees. However, the passage makes specific reference to "meat and dairy" as well as "cattle" so Choice (B) is the best of the answers here.

561. **A. The health of honey bees has been so compromised in recent years that a spring without them is a possibility.**

> The passage mentions that honey bees have been compromised and then goes on to mention a "spring without bees" that could endanger our food supply. Choice (A) makes a reasonable inference that a spring without bees is therefore a possibility.

562. **C. Concerned and alert**

> While the author is neither scheming nor hysterical, he does seem to be both concerned and alert, to judge from the tone of the second paragraph, so Choice (C) is best.

563. **D. Scientists who have been studying bees should provide suggestions about how the rest of us can help, including keeping hives.**

> In this inference question, the author's tone is key. It is too urgent for Choice (A) and too calm for Choice (B). Choice (E) is not justified by the text, and Choice (C) seems like the exact opposite of what the author wants. Choice (D), therefore, is correct.

564. **E. To expose to danger in some way**

> In any sentence with a bolded word, you must look carefully at the context in which it is used. Here, several accurate definitions of the word *compromise* are offered, but only Choice (E) is a verb version that makes sense in the sentence.

565. **A. Cerro Tololo in the Chilean Andes**

> The passage notes that at Cerro Tololo you "can see even more stars" than the other places listed in the passage, so Choice (A) is right. Notice that the question is not asking for the best place in the world, but the best place mentioned in the passage.

566. **C. The sky is a busy place, and no matter where you watch it from, you can see interesting things.**

> Choice (C) sums up the two main points of the passage the best. First, there are many interesting sights in the night-time sky, and secondly, no matter where you watch, you'll be able to see something worth your time.

567.   **B. The Hubble Space Telescope**

The passage specifically states that space satellites, like the Hubble Space Telescope, and airliners can be mistaken for each other. Notice that while it's certainly possible that any of the choices provided could also fool an amateur, the passage is specifically referring to this comparison, so Choice (B) is right.

568.   **C. It explains the phenomenon mentioned in the sentence before it.**

The bolded sentence explains what the "beautiful pearly swath across the heavens" is, as mentioned in the sentence before it. That makes Choice (C) the best.

569.   **C. "Starry Night" may have been painted in an area that the author would deem a "great observation place" like Cerro Tololo.**

Choice (C) is the best inference of those offered here, because it connects to the text of the passage. "Starry Night" is mentioned as depicting a scene that is similar to what one might see at a place like Cerro Tololo, so Choice (C) makes sense.

570.   **E. Average adults interested in learning more about the night sky.**

The passage is clearly aimed at people who do not already know quite a bit about the night sky, which eliminates Choices (A), (B), and (C). The students mentioned in Choice (D) are too young to understand language of this complexity, so Choice (E) makes the most sense.

571.   **E. America's Democratic Republic System**

Choice (E) is best here. The passage explains why America is not a democratic republic in a factual tone.

572.   **A. They are democracies.**

The example of a New England town meeting is used in the passage as an example of a vestige of democracy, so Choice (A) is the right one.

573.   **D. It turns the paragraph back to the main topic after a series of sentences that provided exceptions to the topic under discussion.**

Choice (D) is best because the passage seeks to build an argument that America is a democratic republic. In order to do so fairly, several examples of a true democracy are offered, and the bolded sentence acknowledges them before turning the paragraph back to the topic.

574. B. Referendum; Democracy

A silly question, perhaps, but one you'll need to double-check the passage to make sure you've chosen the correct answer for. It's stated that the ballot initiative is "also called the referendum" so Choice (B) gets it right.

575. C. The Board of Trustees, chosen by election, vote on the next steps for an insurance company.

You're looking for a situation similar to what is explained within the passage, where a group of people elect a smaller group to make decisions for them. Choice (C) presents such an example.

576. D. To alert readers that something paradoxical has been noted.

The author makes use of the phrase *In contradictory* language to note that she is aware of what readers will surely notice: the paradox between the rise in temperature measurements and the colors we perceive them in. Choice (D) is best.

577. E. Yellow

Choice (E) is correct, which follows the statement in the passage that "Temperatures around 2,700 – 3,000 K . . . are perceived as warm in color, tilting toward yellow and red."

578. B. Colloquial language about light often reflects actual observation about the color of hot things.

The end of the passage notes that the "heat-light-color relationship is recognized in colloquial language." The safest inference, then, is that it has been observed closely. Choice (B) is best.

579. D. The relationship between heat, light, and color is sometimes counter-intuitive.

The best answer notes the relationship between heat, light, and color [not just heat and color, as in Choice (A)], as well as some characteristic of that relationship that is expressed in the passage. Choice (D) is best.

580. B. Metal burning "white-hot."

The type of item burning doesn't matter; the passage states that something burning "white-hot" is hotter than something burning "red-hot" so Choice (B) is best.

581. **C. A brief biography of a memorable American.**

Choice (C) is the best answer. The passage gives a very brief biography of Huey Long.

582. **D. Polls showed he would secure enough of the Democratic vote to swing the election to the Republican party.**

According to the passage, the principal reason that the Democratic party would have been concerned was Long's likelihood of splitting the vote. Choice (D) is the best answer.

583. **A. Long's policies hurt some of the people who he was supposed to represent as an elected official.**

The safest inference is to take the words of the last sentence — that Long had "ruined" the family of the man who shot him — and draw a conclusion that he had hurt people whom he was supposed to help. Choice (A) is best.

584. **E. "Kingfish"**

The question is simple, so long as you read the passage for the answer. Huey Long was called "Kingfish."

585. **C. Reminds or informs readers that Long did some good things on the way to his eventual demagoguery.**

The use of the word "actually" is key here. It has a tone of revelation, teaching readers that Long did good things as well as bad. Choice (C) is thus the correct answer.

586. **D. Wealthy people with annual incomes of over $1,000,000**

It's not a guess: The passage states that Long's "Share Our Wealth" program would redistribute wealth of people with an annual income of over $1,000,000. It's a logical inference that those people would dislike Long.

587. **C. Enthusiastic and supportive**

The authors strike a tone of enthusiasm and support, as can best be seen in the last sentence of the passage: "Why shouldn't one of those people be you?" Thus, Choice (C) is the best offered.

588. **E. It develops the main idea beyond the initial example to show another way it applies.**

Choice (E) is the best answer here. The bolded sentence adds an additional idea to the support the thesis that "an Internet-based business model has proven to be a worthwhile investment."

589. **D. Consider Starting an Online Business**

The purpose of the passage is to explain why starting an online business might be a good choice for readers. Choice (D) is the best pick to capture that idea.

590. **D. Smartphones**

The passage specifically refers to smartphones as a technology that has made shopping online "as easy as ever." Choice (D) is thus the best.

591. **E. It invites readers to give an Internet-based business a try.**

The use of a sentence at the end of the passage can create several different effects. It could be rhetorical, as in Choice (A), or suspenseful, as in Choice (D). But here, the question serves as an invitation to read and explore more about the topic, so Choice (E) is correct.

592. **D. Businesses of all sizes**

The passage includes this sentence: "Increasingly, businesses of all sizes are also buying products and services online." That makes Choice (D) the best answer.

593. **A. To set up a contrast between the appealing smell of apple pie baking and the less pleasant smell of cruciferous vegetables being cooked.**

Here, you must look at the context of the sentence in bold. Notice how it is followed by the word "But . . . " in the next sentence. You can tell that it is setting up a contrast from that alone. Choice (A) is best.

594. **C. Sulfur Is the Smell of Cruciferous Vegetables Cooking**

Of the choices presented here, Choice (C) is the best. It refers to a main idea of the passage, which is that cruciferous vegetables release a sulfurous scent.

595. **D. Plexin**

> Choice (D), Plexin, is not listed in the passage, so it is the best choice. Remember to read the question carefully — so you know you're looking for the name that is NOT a sulfur compound — and also check the passage for the right answer.

596. **B. The *crucifix* at the front of the sanctuary.**

> The word *crux* is defined in the passage as "the Latin word meaning cross." Thus, the best answer here is one that uses the prefix in the same way, as in Choice (B).

597. **D. Interested in one of their distinctive characteristics**

> Choice (D) is correct. The author is pointing out an interesting characteristic of this type of vegetable, not dismissing them or discouraging use of them.

598. **E. The smell of sulfurous compounds in cruciferous vegetables is heightened by heat.**

> The passage indicates but never explicitly states that heating cruciferous vegetables makes the sulfuric smell worse. (It states that the smells "are liberated" but you must infer the rest). That makes Choice (E) the best.

599. **D. Carrots**

> Choice (D) is best because carrots are not in the passage's list of cruciferous vegetables.

600. **C. The brain's minicolumns are key to how it works, as are the inputs it receives.**

> While Choices (D) and (E) contain factual information from the passage, they don't represent the main idea of the passage. Choice (C) is better at that.

601. **A. A repeated neural circuit in the brain**

> You're presented with two choices that are correct — Choices (A) and (C). A quick review of the question asked, though, reveals that you're to find the "most specific" answer, which must be Choice (A).

602.

D. It supplies further details and information about a general concept presented in the first paragraph.

The second paragraph develops the idea of the first paragraph, providing more information about how minicolumns work in the neocortex of the brain, the main idea presented in the introduction. Thus, Choice (D) is the best.

603.

E. Auditory

The context gives you the clues you need to understand this unusual usage of *audition.* It's used here as opposing *vision,* indicating that it's an adjective too. That makes Choice (E), *auditory,* also an adjective relating to hearing, the best.

604.

B. A phone system is built out of a single type of wire which adjusts to respond to the location of the call being placed.

Choice (B) most closely mimics the idea presented in the second paragraph: The brain is not build out of differing structures of minicolumns; instead, the input received and the output sent by the minicolumn defines its role.

605.

D. Respond differently to different inputs from vision or hearing.

Choice (D) gets at a reasonable inference from reading the passage. If, as the passage suggests, minicolumns are the same in the brain and respond to become part of a certain area because of the input from a different sense, it stands to reason that they might also be able to change based on those inputs. Thus, it is correct.

606.

D. Factual and explanatory

The author may feel wonder or be aggrieved, but that's not clear from this passage. It's factual and full of information, so Choice (D) is best.

607.

B. It's important to find a balance between your work life and your personal life.

Choice (B) is the best conclusion. The paragraph develops the idea that even people who really love their work sometimes neglect other aspects of their lives. Choice (B) finishes that thought well.

608. **C. To introduce in an interesting way an idea the author intends to develop.**

This type of question is really an inference question: you need to infer why the author might use a quotation at this point in the passage. Here, the most likely answer is Choice (C) because the author wants to capture the attention of readers and use the quotation to introduce the main point of the passage.

609. **B. An excessive amount of time for a small-business owner to work.**

Choice (B) is best here. It's possible that the author feels that several other choices here are also true, but in a GMAT inference question, you always want to choose the small hop in logic, not a leap.

610. **E. You may want to consider hiring an employee to help with the business.**

Choice (E) is best here. The passage states, "You may need to start hiring people." Choice (D) seems like a good idea, but an accountant is not specifically referred to in the passage, so it cannot be correct.

611. **E. A thoughtful exploration about finding a balance between a rewarding small business and a personal life.**

Choice (E) is best. The passage does include a quotation and seems slightly discouraging of putting too much effort into business, but Choices (A) and (D) are too extreme. The passage mostly seems to be about finding a balance between work and personal life.

612. **C. Enterprising**

The use of *inventive* in the passage suggests a person who is *enterprising*, so Choice (C) here is best.

613. **D. Baked**

The passage suggest that kale is "traditionally sautéed, baked, or simmered," so a restaurant that prepares it in a traditional way would serve it baked, as in Choice (D).

614. **E. Kale, which has several types, can be prepared in a myriad of ways, including an innovative new form.**

Choice (E) is best. The passage does indeed indicate that there are several kinds of kale as well as a multitude of ways to prepare and serve it.

615. **A. It is less fibrous and grassy tasting that curly kale.**

A close re-read of the passage will remind you that the authors state, "Lacinato is less fibrous and grassy tasting than curly kale." Choice (A) is thus correct.

616. **D. Competing in a chess tournament can be emotionally grueling for children, but doing so can also teach them resilience and other valuable lessons.**

The author's position is that "Chess is a good was to help children deal with" loss and similar issues, and that crying after a grueling loss is natural. Thus, he is most likely to agree with the sentence in Choice (D).

617. **B. At any age so long as the child is ready.**

According to the passage, "Kids begin competing at all ages. When a child is ready for individual or team competition depends on many factors." Thus, Choice (B) is closest to what the author believes.

618. **A. Straightforward, gently leading**

The test-makers have provided answer choices with higher-level vocabulary in hopes of confusing you. Don't fall for it. The tone of the passage is best described by Choice (A): straightforward and gently leading.

619. **C. The child is reacting to a loss in a natural way.**

The author states that crying is a "natural response to loss." Therefore, the correct answer is Choice (C).

620. **D. Chess Will Teach Children Valuable, If Sometimes Painful, Lessons**

Choice (D) best gets at the author's main purpose in this passage, which is to convince parents that playing competitive chess may be hard on their child but still worth their time.

621. **C. They do not produce pollen and thus do not attract bees.**

The passage states "Watch out for the hybrid that is pollenless because it is of little use to the bees." That means that Choice (C) is correct.

622. **D. The widely-loved sunflower is more complex than you may know.**

Of the choices given here, Choice (C) is the best. It's clear that the passage is about sunflowers, but a couple of the choices — (A) and (C) — are too specific. Choice (B) is an opinion that goes further than the passage itself, and Choice (E) is never actually stated. That leaves Choice (D), which aptly explains the main idea of the passage.

623. **B. A principal reason for maintaining a garden is to provide pollen for bees.**

> The most reasonable inference is to extend the author's statement to "watch out for" hybrid sunflowers that are pollenless and provide "little use" to the bees. It is not too far a jump to assume, therefore, that the author thinks garden should provide pollen for bees. Choice (B) is correct.

624. **A. The author feels that they are an important part of the ecosystem.**

> Choice (A) is best here. It is clear that the author feels bees are important enough in the ecosystem that plants which do not support them should be avoided. Notice that while Choice (D) feels like it is likely true (especially given the source of the passage as stated), there's no actual proof that it is correct in the passage itself. Choice (A) is the more justified and thus, correct, choice.

625. **B. The author's experience in trying to transplant sunflowers has taught him that using peat pots is a smart move.**

> The general tone of the passage is to give advice, which indicates that the author is an expert in his field. Choice (B) makes the most sense here: The author is giving advice he's learned, perhaps the hard way. The context of the sentence supports this idea.

626. **C. To show how the concept of a republic is an ancient ideal.**

> The use of the term *res publica* is most likely to show how the idea of a republic is an ancient one, which gives it greater meaning and esteem. Choice (C) is the best.

627. **D. The concept of a republic now used in America has been developed for thousands of years.**

> The passage essentially traces the historical precedent of the American concept of a republic, so Choice (D) is best.

628. **E. It was felt that short terms of office reduced the likelihood of corruption.**

> Choice (E) is taken directly from the passage: "No one held office for a long period of time, because when citizens rotate in and out of office they avoid corrupting influences."

629. **A. Virtue**

> The passage states that "virtue" was "the highest ideal a republican citizen could achieve." Choice (A) is best.

630. **C. The American republic grew out of a number of historical precedents.**

We may hope that the author believes Choice (E) and suspect that he thinks Choice (A), but Choice (C) is the safest answer. It is reasonable to assume that the author believes the American republic grew out of a number of historical forbearers.

631. **D. What Is an Asterism?**

There are other choices here that point out facts mentioned in the passage, but only Choice (D) gets at the main point of it: explaining what an asterism is and where readers might encounter them.

632. **A. It provides an example so that readers can relate to the main idea of the passage.**

Choice (A) best reveals the purpose of the first sentence: It gives an example of an asterism, the main topic of the passage, to set up the idea that the rest of the passage will explain what an asterism is.

633. **E. It is a named star pattern.**

The passage reads, "An asterism is a named star pattern that's not identical to one of the 88 recognized constellations." Choice (E) is thus the best.

634. **B. An asterism may straddle several different constellations.**

Reviewing the passage, Choice (B) is clearly supported by the ideas within it, so it is the best choice. Other answer may be correct, but Choice (B) is definitely correct.

635. **C. The ocean was vitally important to the development of multicellular life.**

Refer to the last sentence of the passage: "The processes that lead to multicellular life all took place in the earth's oceans." It is a reasonable inference to say that the author agrees, as Choice (C) suggests, making it the best answer.

636. **C. Since the earth's formation 4.5 billion years ago, the development of life has been a complex process.**

Of the choices provided, Choice (C) combines specificity (in the 4.5 billion years figure) with the general outline of the passage. It's the best answer here, beating out Choice (A), which is correct but also very broad.

637. **E. Prokaryotic cells**

It's clear from the passage that another term for cells without a cell nucleus is "prokaryotic cells." Choice (E) is thus the best.

638. **D. Intrigued, informative**

The author is intrigued by his topic, as the phrase "What's remarkable is . . . " alone indicates. But the author is also well-informed. That makes Choice (D) the best.

639. **A. Two billion years**

If you follow the passage's math, it took two billion years for humans to develop after Eukaryotic life (cells with nuclei) appeared. Choice (A) is right.

640. **C. Life did not have to begin at the moment it was sustainable.**

If it's "remarkable" that life began at the earliest moment it could on our planet, the possibility that life did not have to start at that exact moment must also be true. Thus, Choice (C) is the best answer.

641. **B. Innovations in electrical safety continue to be developed by Americans.**

The passage begins with mention of Edison, but isn't actually about the man. The rest of the passage focuses on the development of electrical safety, and Choice (B) captures that the best.

642. **E. Direct Current**

The passage clearly defines DC as "direct current"; a careful read of the passage and answer choices will keep you from choosing any answer but Choice (E), the correct choice.

643. **C. A passage exploring the history of containing nuclear power, beginning with a brief look at the first time it was safely processed.**

Choice (C) best captures the flow of the passage: It begins with an innovation that increased the safety of the power source, and it then chronicles additional innovations that increased safety. The original passage does this as well.

644. **A. Steam engines were responsible for a significant portion of factory accidents before electrical engines were put into use.**

The safest inference is that steam engines were the cause of a significant portion of factory accidents, because the final sentence of the passage states that electrical engines improved safety on factory floors. Thus, Choice (A) is the best.

645. **E. Serviceable**

We're used to hearing the word *practical* as meaning something similar to Choice (A), *sensible.* But the word has another meaning, used here. Choice (E) captures that.

646. **B. The first makes a general statement about events; the second offers evidence that proves that statement.**

The first sentence is an overview of what the rest of the passage — including the second bolded sentence — will prove. Choice (B) is best.

647. **C. The way light interacts with color profoundly affects the way we see.**

Some of the answer choices provided here are on the right track, but are too broad, as in Choice (A) and Choice (B). Choice (C) does a better job of capturing the general point of the passage without being so broad as to be almost meaningless.

648. **A. Blue ink**

The passage lists colorants "like paints, inks, or dyes" so Choice (A) makes the most sense here.

649. **D. Watching a streaming service on a laptop.**

Reading the passage carefully will allow you to note the sentence "The colors on a monitor screen are seen as direct light." Whether you under-stand the science involved or not, you can tell that only Choice (D) offers a similar situation to that one.

650. **D. Attendees at a design conference, attending a workshop on choosing colors for their graphic work.**

The material presented here is introductory, so a group of scientists [Choice (C)] would be unlikely to need to know it. But it's too complex for a group of children, as in Choice (A). That makes Choice (D) the most likely audience.

651. **E. Reflected and direct**

The passage mentions direct and reflected light as the two colors of light. Choice (E) is thus correct.

652. **E. It introduces a key concept in understanding light but is not the thesis.**

The first sentence is often assumed to be the thesis of a passage, but that's not true here. Instead, Choice (E) is correct: The first sentence sets boundaries for the discussion about light but isn't the main point to be proven by the passage.

653. **B. The era of human vs. robot had begun.**

Only Choice (B) presents a continuation of the idea in the second paragraph: that of a human in opposition to a non-human. It's the best choice.

654. **D. To back up her point with a list of examples that prove it.**

Although it may seem quite obvious, the truth is that in this inference question, the safest answer is Choice (D) — to provide examples that prove her point. It's the best answer.

655. **A. The idea of "politics" in American literature changes in the second half of the 20th century.**

Choice (A) is best. The passage is difficult to follow, but the overarching point is clear from the first sentence.

656. **C. American critical reception that was influenced by the poor review from Europe.**

Remember than in an inference question, the idea is not to wander too far down the path from the passage. Choice (C) goes just a bit further than the passage itself and thus is the best choice.

657. **D. What Was the Missouri Compromise?**

Choice (D) captures the topic of the passage best. Choice (E) is a little too vague to work — it could refer to many different events — while Choice (D) is specific to this topic.

658. **A. New states located above a certain latitude could not practice slavery.**

As the last sentence makes clear, "slavery would be excluded from any new states or territories above latitude 36 degrees, 30 minutes," so Choice (A) is best.

659. D. Calm statement of fact

The author is not sneering or accepting — he merely restates the historical facts. Thus, the only answer that fits here is Choice (D).

Chapter 6

660. C. can always differentiate among the three signatures.

The correct answer is Choice (C). When the sentence involves two choices *between* is correct. Here, there are three signatures, so *among* is correct, which is only found in Choice (C). Notice that Choices D and E change the meaning of the sentence, and Choice (B) adds in an unnecessary word.

661. B. but until we know what they think, we can't move forward.

The best answer is Choice (B), because it matches the correct pronoun *(they)* with *everyone*, and the verb is correct as well. Choices A and D do not use the correct pronoun (and Choice (C) doesn't use the correct verb for that incorrect pronoun, anyway). Choice (E) needlessly makes the sentence more complicated by changing the word order of a common phrase.

662. D. but neither he nor anyone else knew the how his invention of the telephone would change the world.

This is a question about pronoun choices, so ignore those answers which do not address this, including Choice (B) and Choice (E). The sentence as is contains a pronoun error: *they* does not refer back to *Alexander Graham Bell* correctly. Choice (C) matches the pronouns correctly, but changes the meaning of the sentence, which refers to how Bell's invention would go on to change the world in the future. Choice (D) does the best job of matching the pronoun and making it clear (by the addition of the phrase *nor anyone else*) that the sentence is meant to show that no one, including Bell, foresaw how his invention would change the world.

663. A. dissolved into a debate over

The sentence is correct the way it's written, so Choice (A) is best. The idiomatic expression is *debate over* and the test always wants you to choose the most standard English language expression, even if other choices sound fine.

664. C. to speak with

Choice (C) is the only answer that uses a common English idiom, *to speak with*. Choices A, B, and D do not render the idiom correctly, and Choice (E) lacks the needed preposition.

665. B. Because she was the first to arrive at the cabin,

Choice (B) is the best, because the *being* construction shown in every other choice is wrong. *Being* is only properly used as a verb.

666. A. Either the Pirates or the Orioles are the winners;

The original sentence is correct, so Choice (A) is the best. When *either . . . or* is used with plural nouns, the verb in the sentence must match the noun closest to it. In this case, that's *Orioles*, which is plural, making *are* the best choice. Choice (B) changes the meaning of the sentence.

667. E. rather not

Choice (E) presents the idiom correctly as commonly used in the English language. No other choice makes sense in the sentence.

668. B. With a mountain forming the perfect backdrop, Adil went for a run yesterday morning.

Choice (B) is the best of the sentence options offered, since it add a preposition *(with)* to make the phrase *a mountain forming the perfect backdrop* work as the introduction. The original sentence allows it to modify Adil, making him the mountain! Choice (D) is technically correct but is less streamlined than Choice (B).

669. A. Who do you think is the better dancer,

Choice (A) is correct because the sentence is correctly written. When the options are only two (*Monique or Enrique*) you must use the word *better* not *best*, which is reserved for three or more options. Choices C and D are written correctly but change the meaning of the sentence slightly.

670. B. more effective than the exhaust fan in the second examination room.

Of the choices provided, Choice (B) is the best. It clarifies that the comparison is between the exhaust fans in two examining rooms, whereas the original leaves it unclear as to what *the second* is referring to.

671. **E. Seeing her running to catch the train,**

> Because you can only modify the first, underlined, part of the sentence, Choice (E) is the best. It makes clear that the people on the platform were watching Suzie, not running themselves.

672. **D. doesn't quiet down**

> Because *of lacrosse players* is a prepositional phrase, it is not the subject of the sentence. The subject is *group* which is singular and thus needs a singular form of the verb, which is only found in Choice (D). Choice (C) changes the meaning of the sentence.

673. **E. To say that Andrew likes ice cream is to understate the truth!**

> Choice (E) is the best because it balances *To claim* with *to understate*, which is the error in the original sentence. The test makers are hoping that you will think the mistake is with the verb, so it offers a few choices in that realm in Choices B and C.

674. **B. to wait quietly by the door**

> Never split an infinitive verb, which in this case is *to wait*. Only Choice (B) puts the adverb (*quietly*) after the verb phrase. It is the only correct choice.

675. **C. is the better ballplayer.**

> Remember, when you have two nouns being compared (in this case, *Juan and Almanzo*) you can only choose the better of them. Three or more allows you to choose the *best*. With this rule in mind, only Choices C and D can be considered, and Choice (D) repeats unnecessary information with the addition of *of the two of them*. That makes Choice (C) the best.

676. **A. Xu wishes she could join us,**

> Choice (A) is correct. The sentence is fine as it is.

677. **D. The dispute over who owned the land affected five generations of the Longfellow family.**

> The popular idiom is *the dispute over* as in Choice (D). Notice that Choice (E) offers incorrect punctuation — there's no need for a possessive — and Choice (C) misuses *re:* in a sentence.

678. **B. The cookies in my lunch are smaller than those in Justin's lunch.**

The sentence as is presents a false comparison by comparing *the cookies* to *Justin's lunch*. Choice (B) fixes this problem by comparing the two sets of cookies.

679. **E. On her first visit to Paris, Parah wanted to visit the Louvre, walk by the Seine and shop in the Latin Quarter.**

Balancing phrases with the same verb is the issue in this sentence. In the original, the last phrase *(shopping in the Latin Quarter)* doesn't match the first two. You can see the problem if you put the sentence together without the first two phrases: *On her first visit to Paris, Parah shopping in the Latin Quarter.* Choice (E) is the only rewrite that makes sense.

680. **B. The girls and their coach eat together after the game.**

Choice (B) matches the verb *eat* to the subject *The girls and their coach* correctly. Remember that even though *coach* is a singular noun, it is combined with *The girls* with the conjunction *and*, making the subject plural.

681. **D. As we wandered through the trees, we saw spectacular scenery.**

The best answer is Choice (D), which re-words the sentence so that the subject is *we*. The original sentence implies that *the scenery* was *wandering* through *the trees*, which, of course, does not make sense. Only Choice (D) fixes the problem.

682. **A. The first and only person I thought of was you.**

The sentence is correct as written, so Choice (A) is right. The test-makers are hoping that you might remember the rule to always use the plural form of a verb with *you*. But in this case, the subject of the sentence is *The first and only person* so the verb must be the singular *was*.

683. **D. Belle, like many cows, eats a great deal of grass.**

This is a subject-verb matching question. It's natural to match the word *cows* to the verb *eat*, but the subject of the verb is *Belle*, not *cows*. That makes Choice (D) the only correct answer.

684. **A. The McCutcheons or the Jacksons were**

The sentence is correct as written, so Choice (A) is appropriate. The subject is joined by the conjunction *or*, but both parts of the subject are plural, so the plural noun *were* is still correct.

685. C. **Either Brenda or Xiu might like to tell that story.**

The problem in the original sentence is that a plural verb, *might likes*, is paired with a singular subject in *Either Brenda or Xiu*. A simple way to tell what to do is to eliminate the names and consider *Either* on its own. It's clearly singular and should get a singular verb. This makes Choice (C) the best.

686. B. **The audience was euphoric upon receiving their prizes.**

Choice (B) is correct because *The audience* is a collective noun. These are almost always treated as a singular noun on the test. Choice (D) seems like it could be correct because the sentence has been reworded. However, notice that *they* no longer clearly refers to *the audience*.

687. E. **Nobody wants more dessert.**

This the type of question the GMAT throws at you sometimes in hopes that utterly confusing you will make you guess wrong. Don't fall for it! The sentence is incorrect, eliminating Choice (A), and the only fix for it is to change the verb to match a singular noun. That makes Choice (E) correct because it makes the verb *wants*. Choice (C) was close, but there's no need to make *dessert* plural.

688. C. **after he stopped by.**

This is a verb tense agreement question. The problem with the original sentence is that the first verb *gave* is in past tense, while the second verb *would stop* is in conditional tense. The best fix is to make both verbs past tense, and Choice (C) does that.

689. C. **Dennis wanted to take Neil shopping for a birthday gift, but Neil wasn't available on Tuesday.**

The original sentence has several pronoun errors: It's not clear whose birthday gift they're going shopping for, nor it is clear who isn't available on Tuesday. While Choice (B) partially fixes this problem, Choice (C) is the best choice. It makes the sentence much more clear. Notice that Choice (D) and Choice (E) don't eliminate the confusion but make it worse.

690. A. **Annie asked Bill if he would tell her the truth.**

The sentence is correct as written. Because the original sentence involves a man and a woman, the pronouns *he* and *her* are correct as written. While it's possible that *tell her the truth* is referring to a woman who is not *Annie*, you can assume by the answer choices that this is not correct. All of the answer choices only involve *Annie* and *Bill*.

691. **D. Because it was sunny and warm that morning, Takeya couldn't wait to get to the beach.**

> The modifier of the original sentence, *sunny and warm*, needs to be properly placed. It's a slightly confusing that either *the beach* or *Takeya* could be described as *sunny and warm*, so reading the other choices is necessary. That makes it clear that beach is being described making Choice (D) the best. Notice that while Choice (E) makes a simple, clear sentence, it isn't logical: the beach isn't sunny and warm because Takeya's going to it!

692. **B. Jade was a weaver with a fine sense of color, so her throws were exquisite.**

> Choice (B) fixes the problem in the original sentence: the adjectival phrase, *a weaver with a fine sense of color*, is modifying *the throws* instead of *Jade*. No other choice fixes this problem.

693. **A. I brought three things to work that morning: my lunch bag, my laptop, and a copy of the report.**

> The sentence is correct as written, so Choice (A) is the best choice. Choice (E) is very close to being correct, but notice that it adds an unnecessary phrase (*with me*) that is already clear and does not need to be restated. Choice (C) similarly adds in an extra *my* which isn't needed.

694. **C. In wonder, Richard stared at the polar bear, the large creature with snowy white hair.**

> The original sentence has a misplaced adjectival phrase, making it seem that *the large creature with snowy hair* is *Richard*. Choice (C) fixes that problem and is the only choice to do so without adding in extra words as Choice (D) does.

695. **D. Choose from**

> The idiomatic expression is *Choose from*, so even if other choices seem reasonable, Choice (D) is correct.

696. **B. The winner will be determined by**

> The idiomatic expression is *determined by*. Choice (B) is thus the best choice. Notice that Choice (C) changes the meaning of the sentence.

697. **E. Rather than**

> The standard idiomatic expression is *Rather than*, making Choice (E) the correct choice.

698. **C. We have to determine a winner between the two semi-finalists.**

The best answer is Choice (C) because it follows the grammatical rule than when the quantity in question is two (*two semi-finalists*) the correct phrasing is *between*. Choice (D) also uses *between* but needlessly complicates the rest of the sentence.

699. **D. The costumes for the musical are more elaborate than those of the musical last year.**

This is the rare instance in which making a sentence more wordy is correct. The problem with the original is that it compares *The costumes for the musical* with *last year*. Only Choice (D) makes it clear that the comparison is between two musicals.

700. **A. I'm trying to determine the better of the two routes suggested, because I want to find the best way to travel to Dublin.**

The original sentence, for all its complexity, is correct, so Choice (A) works well here. Remember that *better* is used when determining between two nouns, while *best* is used when there are more than two (including an indeterminate amount such as *way*).

701. **D. I prefer the second of the two flavors of ice cream more.**

Choice (D) is the only suggestion that correctly uses the grammatical rule. When only two things are being compared, the correct wording is *more*. *Most* can only be used when three or more things are being compared.

702. **A. Jim was the least entertaining at the party.**

To choose the correct answer, you have to infer that the party had more than two people. That seems a safe bet, which means that Jim could be *the least entertaining* person, not just *the less* entertaining person. So Choice (A) is correct. Choices (C) and (D) are correct sentences, but they slightly change the meaning in each case, making Choice (A) the best.

703. **A. A number of people stopped by my table to ask if I was OK**

The sentence is fine as it is, so Choice (A) is correct. *A number of* is the correct term for a countable group of people, and it's safe to presume that in a restaurant, the speaker could count the number of people who stopped by. Notice that Choice (B) and (C) sound wrong — that's not always a good hint on the GMAT, but in this case, it is.

704. **D. Much of the food was thrown out after five days,**

> Choice (D) is the best choice. In the original sentence, *Many of the food* is incorrect. When the amount is uncountable, it's grammatically correct to use *Much* instead, as Choice (D) does. While Choice (E) also makes this switch, *after five days* is also changed incorrectly.

705. **B. Bria gave Ebron fewer cookies than she gave Nadine.**

> Choice (B) is the best of those offered. The original sentence misuses *less cookies,* which should be *fewer cookies.* Both Choice (B) and Choice (C) correct for this error, but Choice (C) is needlessly repetitive. That makes Choice (B) the best.

706. **A. It took me more time than I expected, but I was able to buy more towels at the sale.**

> The sentence is correct as written, so there's no need to make any changes. Choice (A) is correct. Don't be fooled into not following your gut!

707. **B. It took Sally less time at the doctor than she expected, and she was able to buy fewer pills to complete her treatment.**

> The key question here is whether there is an error in the original sentence and, if so, whether it's in *less time* or *less pills.* If you remember that we use *fewer* when the amount is countable — as presumably pills would be — that makes Choice (B) clearly the correct one.

708. **C. Bob missed much of the discussion, and many of the key points.**

> Choice (C) is the best choice, because it fixes the error in the original sentence. When writing about a countable amount (as in *the key points*), we use *many of* . . . not *much of* . . . Notice that Choice (B) is a correctly composed sentence, but it slightly changes the meaning of the original sentence. That makes Choice (C) the better choice.

709. **D. Ma started to pick her way carefully through the stones.**

> Choice (D) is the best, because it fixes the error in the main sentence. That's a split infinitive — *to carefully pick.* Choice (C) might have fooled you, but notice that it moved the adverb, *carefully,* to the wrong place.

710. **B. Too many people think they can start to complain angrily about the poor service after one mistake.**

> The sentence is a mess, but the main error in the original version is the split infinitive: *to angrily complain.* Only Choice (B) fixes it by moving *angrily* to after the infinitive phrase.

711. B. If Shelly were a nice person,

This is a very tricky question. It makes use of the subjunctive mood verb tense. What you must remember about this sentence is that the subjunctive verb form of *to be* is always *were* even if the subject (*Shelly*) is singular. That makes Choice (B) correct. Choice (D) also employs *were* but changes the meaning of the sentence to nonsense.

712. A. That's my professor.

There's nothing wrong with this sentence. It uses a possessive correctly (*That's*). That makes Choice (A) the best because it correctly replaces the missing letter with an apostrophe. Although it sounds very strange, Choice (E) could be considered grammatically correct, but it's obviously not the best answer.

713. E. I found its match in the pile of socks.

Choice (E) is correct, because it fixes the apostrophe error in the original sentence. When using *its* as a possessive (that is, belong to *it*), there's no need for an apostrophe. It's not replacing a letter.

714. A. but I know it's just up the road.

The sentence is correct as written. Choice (A) correctly uses an apostrophe in *it's* because the word is replacing *it is*. Whether the meaning is that the destination is *just up the road*, or that the GPS is *just up the road*, the punctuation would remain the same.

715. D. Because she's the CEO, Maya likes to get to the construction site early.

The error in the original sentence is the use of *Being*. Unless it is being used in a phrase like *human being* or *state of being*, it's almost always incorrect. In Choice (D), that error is fixed by replacing *Being* with *Because*.

716. D. because he was nervous about his wife's delivery.

Choice (D) fixes the incorrect use of *being* in the sentence. Choice (C) replaces the pronoun *he* with *Johann*, but that's unnecessary. It's clear in the sentence who *he* refers to.

717. C. and hold a meeting with his staff.

Choice (C) is the best answer. The original sentence doesn't balance phrases: *drop off* and *pick up* are both verb phrases, and *also a meeting* is a noun phrase. It needs to be changed to a verb phrase as well, and the word *also* isn't needed.

718. B. Kate, like many vet technicians, works very long hours.

> The prepositional phrase *like many vet technicians* is meant to trip you up, since it is plural. But the subject of this sentence, *Kate*, is singular, and should be matched with a singular verb, as in Choice (B).

719. D. I'm not sure why you were so upset by the phone call.

> The original question mismatches the subject, *you*, to the verb, *was*. *You* is always matched with a plural verb even when being used as a singular pronoun.

720. B. the penguin wasn't going to emerge to find its food again

> Choice (B) fixes the error in the sentence. The original uses *it's* when *its* is correct.

721. D. but David got bored and wanted to go home.

> The fixed sentence is less than ideal, but remember that on the test, you can only fix the underlined portion of the sentence. Given that constraint, Choice (D) is the best because it makes clear that *he* is referring to *David*.

722. E. As he screamed for the goalie to block the net, Tom was escorted from the stadium by Security.

> Choice (E) is the best because it clarifies that Tom was escorted from the stadium while *he screamed*, while the original sentence implies that Security was screaming.

723. A. If she were taller, Shakiya could have been a ballerina.

> The sentence, which is in that tricky subjective mood, is correct as written. We choose Choice (A) because it uses a plural verb, *were*, which is always correct with the subjective mood.

724. E. but neither she nor anyone else realized her over was broken.

> Choice (E) fixes the main problem in the original sentence, which is that the pronoun *they* is unclear. By substituting *neither she nor anyone else in attendance*, Choice (E) makes clear who exactly did not *realize her oven was broken*.

725. **B. from the better of two schools' offers**

Choice (B) fixes the error in the original sentence. Remember, you can only choose between *the better* of two options. And Choice (B) maintains the correct possessive form of *schools* from the original. Choice (E) needlessly adds in the word *between*.

726. **B. To say that Acadia National Park is a beautiful place is to understate the truth.**

Choice (B) fixes the error in the original, which is not balanced. It begins with a *to* statement: *To say that . . .* and thus needs to be balance with another *to* statement, as in *to understate the truth!*

727. **A. I asked Mo'chelle and her brothers to help with the fair.**

There is no error in the original sentence, so Choice (A) is the best. It's typical for sentences that are completely correct to appear as if they must have errors after working on questions like these. Stay focused!

728. **D. I was the last to leave the testing center.**

The original sentence contains a subject/verb agreement error, because *I* should not be paired with *were*. Choice (D) fixes this mistake.

729. **E. The clowns, even Dani, were not the children's favorite act.**

Choice (E) fixes the error in the original sentence. *The clowns* is plural, but the verb in the sentence is *was*, which is singular. The correct choice is *were*. Remember that *even Dani* is a phrase, not the subject of the sentence.

730. **A. Despite Elsie's reluctance, her family is asking for donations.**

There's no error in the original sentence. The use of the phrase *her family* makes clear how the subject is connected to the introductory phrase *Despite Elsie's reluctance*. Choice (A) is best.

731. **B. You lift me up as a class.**

The key issue here is matching the subject, *You*, with the correct verb. In Choice (B), *You* is correctly treated as a plural verb, which makes it the best choice. There's no need to alter anything else in the sentence as in Choice (D).

732. **D. Either Renee or Todd will take you**

Choice (D) is the best offered here because it fixes the subject/verb agreement issue. Remember *Either* always makes the noun singular, so it must be used with *will take.*

733. **C. Nobody wants to go to that club again.**

Choice (C) correct fixes the subject/verb agreement problem in the original sentence. *Nobody* is a singular, collective pronoun and must be matched with *wants.*

734. **B. Everybody loves music.**

Choice (B) corrects the mistaken subject/verb agreement to *Everybody loves. Everybody* is a singular, collective noun. Note that Choice (D) is a correctly composed sentence but does not have quite the same meaning as the original.

735. **E. We will play when the field is dry,**

Choice (E) is the only one here that correctly fixes the subject/verb agreement error. *We*, which is plural, should be matched with *will play.*

736. **B. after I learned the basics in high school.**

The original cannot be correct because learning in *high school* must have come before learning in *college* chronologically. The conditional tense (*would learn*) cannot be paired with the past tense (*learned*). Choice (B) fixes this error.

737. **A. Ida fixed Bruce's bike chain after he asked her to help.**

Choice (A) is correct because there aren't any errors in the sentence. Both verbs — *fixed* and *asked* — are in past tense.

738. **A. I should be the last person you ask.**

Choice (A) is correct. There's no need to change anything in the sentence. While Choices (D) and (E) are both acceptable sentences, they slightly change the meaning of the original and are thus incorrect.

739. **A. I asked Miguel if Lilly would be late.**

There's no error in the original sentence. Choice (A) is therefore correct. Choice (B) might seem like the better choice, but do make sure to read the entire sentence: *late* has been changed to *later.*

740. **D. after extensively researching vampires, publishing several other books, and crafting several early drafts.**

Choice (D) fixes the parallelism error of the original sentence. While *after extensively researching vampires* and *publishing several other books* are both verb phrases, *and also several early drafts* is a noun phrase. Choice (D) changes it to a verb phrase.

741. **E. subject to her availability.**

Choice (E) is the best sentence. The common idiom is *subject to,* and that is what the test-makers are looking for you to know.

742. **B. As great as the diner's breakfast is,**

Choice (B) correctly renders the idiomatic phrase, *As great as* so it is the best choice. Notice that Choice (D) and (E) can be eliminated because they do not include the proper punctuation.

743. **A. Because he is in danger of failing, Gomez went to tutoring.**

The original sentence renders the idiomatic phrase *in danger of* correctly. Choice (A) is correct.

744. **C. This argument is different from what we've seen before.**

Choice (C) correctly places the idiomatic expression *different from* in the sentence.

745. **D. Western Pennsylvania is usually defined as Pittsburgh and further west.**

Choice (D) correctly uses the idiomatic expression *defined as* in the sentence.

746. **B. Gretel and I agreed that the pink bubble tea tasted better than the blue bubble tea tasted.**

Choice (B) is the best because it matched the comparison in a correct parallelism. The phrase *the pink bubble tea tasted* must not be matched to just *the blue bubble tea* but to *the blue bubble tea tasted.*

747. **A. were prohibited from diving.**

There aren't any errors in the original sentence, so Choice (A) is correct. The common phrase is *prohibited from.*

748. **C. were larger than the eggs gathered in the other coop.**

The original sentence has a false comparison. It compares *The eggs* to *the other coop.* Choice (C) fixes this problem by making it clear that *The eggs* are being compared to *the eggs gathered in the other coop.*

749. **D. rather than going out to eat.**

The correct idiomatic expression is *rather than,* and only Choice (D) uses it.

750. **E. Marie wanted to circle the block slowly until we found a parking spot.**

The original sentence splits the infinitive phrase *to circle* by inserting an adverb, *slowly.* Only Choice (E) fixes the error in a sentence that is grammatically correct.

751. **A. George Washington had to choose the better of two men when selecting a personal secretary.**

The sentence is correct as written, so Choice (A) is the best choice. Remember that when selecting between two choices, *better* is the correct word.

752. **D. That's the worst of it.**

The sentence incorrectly uses *worse.* Because *of it* implies more than two — or an uncountable number — *worst* is the correct choice, as found in Choice (D).

753. **C. was the least interesting.**

Choice (C) is best because the three movies are compared in the original sentence. When three or more things are compared, it's appropriate to use *least.* Do note that Choice (E) makes a false comparison because it doesn't complete the idea of what *the last movie* is being compared to, while Choice (D) makes a correct sentence but changes the meaning.

754. **A. Many more people signed up for the class than I expected.**

There is no error in the original sentence, so Choice (A) is correct. When writing about a countable number, the use of *many* is correct, and it can be assumed that the number of people who signed up for the class is countable. Note that Choice (E) is an acceptable sentence but does not convey the same meaning as the original.

755. **B. a number of times.**

When the amount is countable — as we can presume *the physician* asking *the family* was, it's proper to use the word *amount.* That makes Choice (B) correct. *Quantity* and *amount* are for non-countable things.

756. **B. because of his many achievements.**

The error in the underlined phrase is not the appearance of *a lot,* which is so controversial that the GMAT will never present it as a usage error, but in awkwardness of the phrase. Choice (B) is simpler and much more elegant. Remember that Washington's achievements are countable, so *many* is used.

757. **E. I saw the play you're talking about.**

The error in the original sentence is easy to spot: *seen* had been substituted for *saw.* That makes Choice (E) the correct one. Don't be thrown off by Choice (D), which "fixes" a prepositional mistake which is not always considered an error anymore.

758. **A. The squirrel dropped its birdseed when we startled it.**

The original sentence is correct, so Choice (A) is the best. The use of *its* without an apostrophe is correct because it is a possessive, not replacing *it is.*

759. **E. It takes a long time to walk Hadrian's Wall, but it's worth it.**

The error in the original sentence is the substitution of *its* when *it's* is needed. Choice (E) fixes the error. Remember that *it's,* with the apostrophe, is the correct substitute for *it is.*

760. **C. It's about time that Carolyn realizes it's dangerous.**

Choice (C) makes clear that both *it's* in the sentence are substituting for *it is* and thus should have an apostrophe. The easiest way to figure this out is to substitute *it is* into the sentence. In this case, it would read: *It is about time that Carolyn realizes it is dangerous,* which is correct.

761. **E. Given that he was the only nominee, it's not surprising**

The error in the original sentence is not with its use of *it's,* but in the use of *Being,* which is almost never correct. Choice (E) fixes this error. Notice that Choice (D) doesn't make sense — the word *although* doesn't work with *it's not surprising.*

762. **B. From what we could see, Jill's team lost points for lack of originality, not being on the beat, and starting too late.**

Choice (B) best fixes the parallelism problem in the original sentence by changing *they weren't on the beat* to *not being on the beat* so that the phrases match.

763. **C. The pipes hiss when water runs through them.**

The original sentence has an error in how the subject, *pipes*, matches with the verb, *hisses*. Only Choice (C) fixes this error. Notice that Choice (B) is a correct sentence but changes the meaning of the original, which involved *pipes*, not one *pipe*.

764. **A. They are her best friends**

You may feel that the second part of the sentence, *despite all of the fights the four of them had had over the years they've known each other* is poorly written — and we wouldn't disagree — but there are no errors in the first part, so Choice (A) works best! Notice that the comma is not underlined, so its placement, whether correct or not, cannot be part of the solution to the problem.

765. **D. Carlos, like many science teachers, explains evolution very clearly.**

Despite how the answer choices may mislead you, the problem in this sentence is in the subject/verb agreement. The subject is *Carlos*, and that must be matched with *explains*. Choice (D) does this correctly. That the subject ends in −*s* and that the sentence includes a plural phrase, *like most science teachers*, doesn't change the answer.

766. **B. You, despite the other qualified candidate, are my first pick for the job.**

Choice (B) is correct. *You* is always matched with a plural verb. Notice that while Choice (E) does so, it also uses the word *candidates*, although the original sentence mentions only one *candidate*.

767. **B. Beverley's choice is the green; Mindy chose the gold.**

Choice (B) best fixes the error in the original sentence, which substitutes a comma for a semi-colon. Semi-colons are used when two sentences that could stand independently are linked together.

768. **C. Penelope, as is the case with many researchers, loves the library.**

There's most likely an even better way to phrase this sentence, but of the choices offered here, Choice (C) is the best. It matches the subject of the sentence, *Penelope*, to the verb, *loves*, correctly. Notice that while Choice (E) is a correctly formed sentence, it changes the meaning of the original, making it not entirely clear that Penelope is a researcher herself.

769. **B. either Susan or Daveed decides to perform the surgery.**

The use of *either* in the original sentence means that the subject is rendered singular, and the verb must agree with a singular noun. Thus, Choice (B) is the best, with the verb *decides*.

770. **D. Nobody understands the directions, so please go over them again.**

Choice (D) is the best. Remember that a collective noun like *nobody* is almost always (and always on the GMAT) treated as a singular noun.

771. **C. Monica sent Rachel an invitation before Rachel complained about it.**

Choice (C) best reconciles the unmatched verbs in the original sentence, *sent*, which is past tense, and *would be complaining*, which is in the conditional tense. Choice (C) puts both verbs in the past tense with *sent* and *would complain*.

772. **B. Despite trying everything she could, Dr. Geller could not save the patient.**

The original sentence features a misplaced modifier: *Despite trying everything she could* should modify *Dr. Geller*, not *the patient*. Choice (B) is the only option that fixes this effectively.

773. **D. Despite being an astronaut with seven missions under her belt, Rhonda still felt excited about the next one.**

Choice (D) best fixes the misplaced adjectival phrase in the original sentence, which implies that *An astronaut with seven missions under her belt* describes *the next mission*, not Rhonda.

774. **B. Before swimming the require laps, the team enjoyed a hearty breakfast.**

In the original sentence, a misplaced participial phrase means that *Before swimming the required laps*, is modifying *a hearty breakfast*. Choice (B) fixes the error so that the phrase correctly modifies *the team*.

775. **A. That old man is acting like a child!**

Choice (A) is correct. This sentence preys on uneasiness about whether to use *like* or *as*. Remember that when two things are compared (*man* to *child*), the best choice is *like*.

776. **B. Not everyone can learn to bake the way my mom does.**

In the original sentence, the sentiment is expressed in the way we commonly speak. But to be grammatically correct, the sentence cannot include *like* because there is a verb after the words *my mom*.

777. **E. The campsite appeared welcoming to the sad and scared hikers.**

Choice (E) fixes the misplaced adjectives in the original sentence, making it clear that *sad and scared* modify *the hikers*, not *the campsite*.

778. **B. known for her use of color, strong lines, and collage in her work.**

The original sentence fails to use parallelism correctly in the three phrases. Choice (B) best fixes this error, correcting *she uses collage in her work* to *collage in her work*. This makes all three phrases match.

779. **A. Ricardo is required to design products, create mock-ups for review, and approve the samples for production.**

There are no errors in the original sentence so Choice (A) is best. Notice that while Choices (D) and (E) are tempting, Choice (D) misplaces the phrase *for production*, while Choice (E) incorporates a parallelism mistake.

780. **E. To say that Ronald was an excellent dad is to give credit where it is due.**

Choice (E) best fixes the error in the original sentence, which fails to balance the phrases in a parallelism structure. *To say* must be balanced with *to give credit*.

781. **B. rather than the Steelers.**

Choice (B) uses the idiomatic expression *rather than* correctly, so it is the best choice.

782. **A. The race course will be defined as**

The sentence renders the idiomatic phrase, *defined by*, correctly, so Choice (A) is correct.

783. **D. I can conclude from your expression that your team won.**

The idiomatic phrase is *conclude from*, so Choice (D) is the best.

784. **E. A debate over**

Choice (E) renders the idiomatic expression *A debate over* correctly, so it is the best choice.

785. **D. prohibit them from**

Choice (D) is the only option that correctly renders the common phrase *prohibit them* from, making it the correct answer.

786. **A. The play that has always been attributed to**

The original sentence correctly uses the idiomatic expression *attributed to*, so Choice (A) should be chosen.

787. **D. The entrée was different than what I expected**

The original sentence contains an idiomatic expression error. The correct expression is *different than* not *different by*. Choice (D) fixes this mistake. Choice (E) forms a correct sentence, but the meaning is changed with the phrase *than what I expected* is dropped.

788. **C. As great as Brooklyn is, Benji prefers Pittsburgh.**

The idiomatic expression is *as great as*, and only Choice (C) uses it correctly.

789. **D. Dr. Huardo felt the results were the best she's seen**

The error in the sentence is in *the better*, which is only used when comparing two items. Since the experiment has been performed for 8 years, we can assume that more than two results are being compared, and we can use *the best she's seen* construction, which you'll only find in Choice (D).

790. **B. Between the two of us,**

Choice (B) is the best choice because the correct phrasing is *Between the two of us*. When speaking of two items, we use the *between* construction instead of the *among* construction.

791. **C. The reports have been printed for over a week, at least.**

The idiomatic expression is *at least*, which is correctly used in Choice (C), making it the best answer.

792. **E. The recommendations from the customer service department are more helpful than those from the human resources department.**

The original sentence contains a false comparison by comparing *The recommendations from the customer service department* to *the human resources department*. Choice (E) fixes this error by adding in the clarifying phrase *those from*.

793. **C. It's easy to find the answer when you're looking for it.**

The original sentence contains a mistake in *Its*, which is substituting for *It is* and thus should have an apostrophe. Choice (C) fixes the mistake without changing the correct *you're* to the incorrect *your*.

794. **E. Liu was forced to agree that the cars traveled more quickly on the highway than the buses traveled.**

The flaw with the original sentence is a false comparison: *the cars traveled more quickly* is compared to *the buses*. Choice (E) makes it clear that *the buses traveled*. It's the best choice.

795. **D. They're the ones asking for a replay.**

The error in the original sentence is replacing *They're* with *Their*. Choice (D) fixes the problem. Remember that *they're = they are*.

796. **E. Most orchid growers obsessively worry over their plants.**

The error in the original sentence is in the misplacement of an adverb, *obsessively*. It should not split the phrase *worry over*. There's no problem in using *Most*, so Choice (E) is the best fix.

797. **A. A number of laptops were missing from the cart,**

The sentence is correct as written, so Choice (A) is best. When writing about a countable number — and presumably the *laptops* that *were missing* is a countable number — it is correct to use *A number* instead of *An amount* or *A quantity*.

798. **B. Jovan applied to five colleges and now has to choose between two of them.**

Choice (B) is the best answer. The original sentence uses *among* when *between* is the correct choice, as it is used for when two things are being compared.

799. **A. Much of the project was scrapped, but our division kept all of the blueprints.**

There is no error in the original sentence. It's correct to use *Much* in this context, when the number is not countable. *The project* is not a countable number. Choice (A) is the best.

800. **C. We saw less of an increase than we were expecting after the new logo was unveiled.**

Choice (C) is the best here because it uses the wording *less of an increase*, which is correct for an uncountable number. Notice that while Choice (D) is a correctly worded sentence, it changes the original sentence's meaning. *Far less of an increase* is not the same as *a decrease*.

801. **A. The drive took less time than Maddie expected, so she arrived early for the meeting.**

Choice (A) is correct. The sentence does not have any errors: *less time* is the correct phrasing.

802. **D. You did not take time to read the instructions carefully**

The original sentence splits the infinitive *to read* with the adverb *carefully*. Choice (D) fixes that error.

803. **B. If Jim were a nice guy, he would have asked for forgiveness.**

The sentence uses the subjunctive mood, expressing something that the writer wishes was true, but is not. In that tense, the verb is always *were*, even if the subject is singular, like *Jim*. Choice (B) is the only one that renders that correctly.

804. **E. The shopping trip took Tony and Deven less time than they expected, but they ended up buying fewer shoes at the sale.**

Choice (E) is the only one available that fixes the error at the end of the sentence. When writing about a countable number (such as *shoes*), it's correct to use *fewer*, not *less*.

805. **C. Delores called the theater to complain angrily about the audio problems**

There are several issues with this sentence, but in the underlined portion, the biggest error is splitting the infinitive *to complain* with *angrily*. Choice (C) fixes this mistake.

806. **A. The cow chewed through its rope**

The original sentence correctly spells *through*, as well as uses the possessive form of *its*. *It's* would only be used if substituting for *it is*. Thus, Choice (A) is correct.

807. **D. Helen, the most affluent of my friends, gives lavish gifts.**

The original sentence involves a subject–verb agreement error, since the subject of the sentence is *Helen* (not *friends*). Choice (D) fixes the verb to *gives* which correctly matches *Helen*.

808. **D. After selecting Joseph, John, and Marni to lead the project, Sam regretted choosing John.**

The original sentence contains a pronoun error: It's unclear whether *Sam regretted choosing* Joseph or John. Choice (D) clarifies which *him* is meant. Notice that while Choices (B), (C) and (D) all form correct sentences, they slightly change the meaning of the original and thus cannot be the best choice.

809. **B. I didn't like the colors offered, but I had to pick one, so I chose it.**

Choice (B) is the best of the answer choices offered. It correctly uses the pronoun *it* as a substitute for *one of the colors*. The error in the original sentence is to replace that phrase with *them*.

810. **C. Because they were excited and happy, the soon-to-be graduates were not deterred by the gloomy day.**

The original sentence contains a misplaced set of adjectives, *Excited and happy*. The way the sentence is worded makes it appear that the gloomy day is also *excited and happy*. Reorganizing the sentence and making the subject *the soon-to-be graduates* appear shortly after the adjectives solves this problem. Choice (C) does that.

811. **E. As a nurse with a background in chemistry, Becca easily understood the patient's records.**

> The original sentence has a misplaced adjectival phrase. *A nurse with a background in chemistry* modifies *Becca*, but appears to be connected to *the patient's records* in the original. Choice (E) rewords the sentence to be clearer, so it is correct.

812. **E. Having prepared the lunch, Jean left for the picnic.**

> Choice (E) best fixes the mistake in the original, a participial phrase that's misplaced. *Before leaving for the picnic* modifies *Jean,* not *the lunch.*

813. **A. The skills we're looking for in our new hire are excellent customer service experience, a willingness to brainstorm, and a background in finance.**

> Choice (A) is the best because there aren't any errors in the original sentence. It balances the parallelism correctly, since all three phrases are nouns. Notice that while Choice (E) also forms a complete sentence, it changes the meaning of the original, so it cannot be the correct choice.

814. **C. Dax, an outstanding researcher, often takes his staff to lunch, gives plenty of vacation days, and is sure to remember birthdays as well.**

> The original sentence contains an error in parallelism: Two of the phrases (*often takes his staff to lunch, gives plenty of vacation days*) are verb phrases, while *he is sure to remember birthdays* is a noun phase with the subject *he*. Choice (C) fixes this error by making all three verb phrases, so they are parallel.

815. **B. If you are in danger of failing,**

> The original sentence does not correctly use a common idiom, *in danger of*. Choice (B) fixes that error.

816. **A. We can conclude from the results**

> The original sentence is correct: The idiom is *conclude from*. Thus, Choice (A) is best.

817. **D. The statistics appear to**

> The original sentence does not use an idiom correctly. It is common to write *appear to*, which is what Choice (D) offers. Thus, it is correct.

818. **D. because of the regulations.**

> Only Choice (D) uses the correct idiomatic expression: *because of.* Thus, it is correct.

819. **B. to contribute to the discussion.**

> Choice (B) uses the idiomatic expression *contribute to* correctly, which makes it the best choice.

820. **D. The temperature in Austin is higher than the temperature in Dallas today.**

> This is a false comparison question. In the original sentence, *The temperature in Austin* is falsely compare to *in Dallas.* Choice (D) fixes the sentence so that *The temperature in Austin* is compared to *the temperature in Dallas.* The comparison is no longer false.

821. **A. The questions on the GMAT are more challenging than the questions on the SAT.**

> The original sentence correctly uses a comparison by comparing *The questions on the GMAT* and *the questions on the SAT.* Thus, Choice (A) is best, since no changes are needed.

822. **D. We don't know yet if it's a boy or a girl.**

> The original sentence contains *its,* which is used incorrectly. When replacing *it is,* use the version with an apostrophe: *it's.* Choice (D) does this without making any other changes, so it is correct.

823. **E. The penguins swim more gracefully than the polar bears swim.**

> The original sentence contains a false comparison: How *the penguins swim* is compared to *the polar bears.* In Choice (E), the comparison is corrected so that how each animal *swims* is compared. It's the best choice.

824. **A. Think of your assignment as an opportunity,**

> The original sentence uses the common idiom construction *Think of . . . as* correctly, so it does not need to be changed. Choice (A) is best.

825. **C. To admit you've erred is to admit you're human.**

> The original sentence contains a parallelism error. The phrase *To admit you've erred* requires another *to . . .* phrase to balance the sentence. Only Choice (C) does so.

826. **B. Anna carefully tried to pick her way through the glass shards.**

Choice (B) fixes the error in the original sentence: a split infinitive. *To pick* should not be split by the adverb *carefully.*

827. **A. To begin paying quickly,**

In this case, the infinitive — *To begin paying* — is not split by an adverb because *quickly* appears after it in the sentence. This is correct, so Choice (A) is also correct.

828. **D. Mary and Rick took Takeya and Leroy to the store, but Leroy didn't want to buy anything.**

Choice (D) best fixes the error in the original sentence, which is the unclear use of the pronoun *he.* It could refer to *Leroy* or *Rick* in the original. Choice (D) shows that *Leroy* is meant. Don't be fooled by the fact that Choice (B), Choice (C) and Choice (E) form what appear to be correct sentence: They change the meaning of the original.

829. **D. As he yelled that even he could see that the ball was fair, Bobby was taken away from the stadium by Mom.**

In the original sentence, the phrase *Yelling that even he could see that the ball was fair* is misplaced because it appears to modify *Mom,* not *Bobby.* Choice (D) fixes the mistake.

830. **D. gasps when the curtain rises**

Remember that collective nouns like *the audience* are almost always treated as singular. The original sentence does not do that, but Choice (D) does. Notice, too, that there is no error in *the curtain rises.*

831. **E. Despite our invitation, you seem surprised**

Remember that *you* is always treated as a plural noun, even when referring to one person. Thus, it should be paired with *seem.* Choice (D) forms a correct sentence, but changed the verb to the past tense, which is not in line with the original. Choice (E) is the best choice.

832. **B. works long hours.**

Choice (B) best fixes the issue in the original sentence, which mistakes the subject as *nurses.* In fact, the subject is *Mitchell,* which needs the verb *works.*

833. **C. and reschedule her visit to her dentist.**

Choice (C) best fixes the parallelism error in the original sentence: *buy a wedding gift* and *resole her dancing shoes* are both verb phrases, while *and the visit to her dentist needs to be rescheduled* is a noun phrase. You can't change the first two because they are not underlined, so you're left fixing the last phrase. Choice (E) is tempting, but doesn't convey the idea *needs to be rescheduled*.

834. **E. to wait quietly by the door before entering**

The complicated sentence structure should not fool you into failing to notice the split infinitive: *to quietly wait*. Fixing it, as in Choice (E) means moving the adverb to after the phrase: *to wait quietly*.

835. **A. This is its cage, but it's hiding.**

There's no error in the sentence. The first *its* is correctly possessive: The *cage* belongs to it. The second *it's* replaces *it is*. Thus Choice (A) is correct.

836. **B. Fewer classmates came to the show**

Choice (B) is correct because we use *fewer* when considering a countable number of *classmates*. Since the rest of the sentence tells you that it was a *class of 10*, it seems reasonable that Roberto would be able to count the number of classmates exactly.

837. **D. If I were younger,**

Remember that when a sentence employs the subjunctive mood, expressing something that the speaker or writer wishes were true but is not, we always use the *were* form of the verb *to be*, even if only one person makes up the subject. Thus, Choice (B) is correct.

838. **D. Between you and me,**

The original sentence uses *among* when *between* is the correct choice for a sentence that compares two things. Choice (D) is correct. By the way, *Between you and I* is not how the idiomatic phrase is correctly rendered.

Chapter 7

839.   **E. It introduces a premise that the argument goes on to oppose.**

The bolded portion of the passage is a premise that the rest of the argument goes on to contradict, or prove wrong. Only Choice (E) shows itself as a premise, and must be the correct answer.

840.   **E. Autopsies of coyotes killed by cars or found in dead in Keystone State Park revealed that nearly all of them had recently consumed deer meat.**

Choice (E) is the best answer because the evidence it reveals helps to support the idea that coyotes have contributed the decline of the deer population in the park. Choice (A) merely restates the argument, while Choice (D) argues against it.

841.   **B. Two years ago, a dip in home mortgages dropped inflation temporarily below its stable level of 2% in recent years.**

In order to weaken the conclusion in the argument, you have to find a reason for it to not be, or come, true. Choice (B) does that the best here because it provides information that indicates the rate of inflation from two years ago was a one-time blip, and that inflation has already returned to as steady rate of 2% per year.

842.   **B. In two years' time, the inflation rate will be higher than 4%.**

This question is tricky because it's asking you nearly the reverse of the question before it. You must throw out the arguments made in that question and look only at the initial reading passage. If you do so, you'll see that if the passage is true, it must also be true that the inflation rate will rise to greater than 4% in two years' time, which is Choice (B). There's nothing in the argument that suggests the rate of inflation, which eliminates Choices (A) and (C). While Choices (D) and (E) might seem to intuitively true, we don't have proof of them from the initial passage.

843.   **D. Taking a protein supplement has been shown to hurt, not improve, memory.**

The question asks you to find the reason that will weaken Ryan's chance of success. Only Choice (D) does that. While Choice (C) is not likely to earn him that 4.0, which Choice (E) says he wants, neither of these weaken his likelihood of success. Choice (A) might, but we don't learn if he prefers to study in the library. In Choice (B), we see a possible reason why his plan might now work, but we are not given enough information. Choice (C) is a bad habit, but Choice (D) shows a direct contradiction to his plan: He plans to take a protein supplement in order to help him improve his grades, but if Choice (D) is true, it's clear that they may not help, and, in fact, hurt his plan.

844. **C. Ryan's Physician's Assistant suggested the protein supplement based on her observation of its success for other student-athletes at Ryan's college.**

> The best answer is Choice (C) because it provides evidence from a medical professional that a similar plan has recently worked for students very like Ryan.

845. **A. It's possible to bottle milk without preservatives in a way that still makes it safe to drink.**

> If everything in the argument is true, then Choice (A) must be inferred. A dairy that has eliminated preservatives must have found a way to bottle milk without them. The other choices are either a leap in logic that are not supported by the argument, as in Choices (B) and (C), or restate elements of the argument, as in Choice (D), or are simply too broad to be inferred from the argument, as in Choice (E).

846. **C. Several stores will no longer carry Lange Farm milk because customers have returned too many bottles in which the milk spoiled several days before the "Sell by" date stamped on the lid.**

> The basic premise of the argument is that Lange Farms says that their milk will be good and tasty for at least a week after it is bottled. Choice (C) shows that they have not been able to guarantee that their milk will not spoil without preservatives. It is thus the best choice.

847. **B. There are no advantages to buying stamps at a shop instead of a post office.**

> The argument states that the people of the town are making an odd choice. In order to make that argument, it must be assumed that there are no advantages to buying stamps at a shop instead of post office, which is Choice (C). Choice (D) is a good reason to argue against the premise, but that's not what the question asks you to do.

848. **A. What reason do the citizens of Bohlburg give when asked why they prefer to buy stamps in shops instead of the post office?**

> The conclusion that must be supported is that it's odd for the people of Bohlburg to buy their stamps at shops instead of the post office. The only question that will provide helpful information is Choice (A) because it directly asks why this is so. The other choices make assumptions about why people don't go to the post office — because of the distance or because certain products aren't offered there — but without input from the people of the town, these are not justified assumptions.

849. **C. The company's workforce in Country X can be paid 15% less than the anticipated workforce in Country Y.**

> Choice (C) is best because it shows the financial logic that could justify remaining in Country X. While Choice (A) and Choice (D) might be important to the company, these are not logical reasons to stay in Country X. Choice (B) has no merit since the company exports its product, and Choice (E) is helpful but not a better reason than Choice (C).

850. **C. The 5% tariff will increase by 1% every year until it reaches 10%, at which point, it will surpass the company's savings on workforce cost by remaining in Country X.**

> In a question like this one, it's worth your time to seek out the answer that most directly addresses the premise of the statement. Choice (C) does that here, but taking the one number in the question — 5% — and building on it to create a scenario in which the company would be foolish to stay. All the other answer choices are far too vague to be correct.

851. **C. Pineapples grow in a three-year cycle, in which one heavy harvest is followed by two less abundant harvests.**

> The question asks you to support the argument that farmers should hold back a portion of an over-abundant harvest. Choice (C) best supports that particular line of logic by showing that any given pineapple farmer is sure to have two years of lean harvests after a flush one. Holding back the plentiful harvest will even out their supply.

852. **A. Pineapples can be kept in refrigerated warehouses for a month to six weeks at maximum.**

> The question asks you to weaken the conclusion presented. To do that, you'll need to find the argument that presents the best roadblock to the idea of keeping extra pineapples in refrigerated warehouses to drive up the price. Choice (A), if true, shows that this plan is not likely to work because the pineapples will spoil. It is the best answer.

853. **E. Stabilizing the riverbank in the area that belongs to J & B Warehouse would help to counteract the yearly floods.**

> The concern here is not why the flooding is happening, but why the town of Bettyville has decided to pursue litigation against J & B Warehouse for their role in the flooding. Choice (E) best suggests an assumption that must have been made: J & B Warehouse is particularly culpable for the flooding and their property must be stabilized.

854. **D. Jen has been served that brand of soda at her favorite restaurant for years without realizing that she was consuming it, and has never felt sick afterwards.**

> Choice (D) most weakens Jen's argument, which is that the brand of soda makes her feel sick. If she was correct, she should feel ill after consuming the soda whether she knows she is doing so or not. Choice (D) shows that this is not the case.

855. **D. "Come to think of it, in my journal, I noted that you often complained of a stomachache after we ate at restaurants that served you that brand of soda."**

> Dialogue questions, while a little strange, do occasionally appear on the GMAT. Here, you need to think of finding the best evidence to support Jen's assumption. Vic offers her own evidence, as in Choice (D), that strengthens Jen's assumption. That's the best choice.

856. **B. It is a premise that will be proven by the rest of the argument.**

> The bolded portion of the passage is a premise that the rest of the argument goes on to prove. That means that Choice (B) must be correct. Notice that it cannot be the evidence, since it does not provide any. It must be a premise or idea.

857. **C. The news channel based its conclusion on only 3 percent of registered voters' responses.**

> Here, you're asked to find the most significant mistake in the news channel's logic — in other words, where did they most go wrong with their prediction? Choice (C) is the best answer because it reminds us that the news channel polled a very small portion of registered voters. Choice (B) is a mistake as well, but less important than the extrapolating a town-wide result from 3 percent of its population.

858. **B. It provides evidence to support a premise of the argument.**

> The bolded portion of the passage is evidence that supports the premise of the argument. The news channel's argument was that Stewin would win, premised on the poll results. Therefore, the registered voters polled provided evidence to support that premise. That's Choice (B). Notice that this is true even if the argument is wrong or flawed: The news channel was incorrect, but its argument was supported by a premise and evidence.

859. **C. A recent Twitter survey of local people shows that they report finding Hitchjaw eels more disgusting than snakes or rats.**

> The best choice is Choice (C). The argument presented in the reading is that the zoologist thinks local people won't help to save the Hitchjaw eel because they find it off-putting. Choice (C) give evidence to support that idea, in showing that people do, indeed, find them disgusting.

860. **B. Recent efforts by locals have helped stabilize the population of long-eared rats, a deeply disliked local pest.**

The premise of the argument is that people haven't helped to save the Hitchjaw eel because they don't like them. Choice (B) points to a recent effort by locals to preserve another animal that they don't like, which argues against their logic in the passage. It best disproves the passage.

861. **A. The zoologist should start a campaign to help people understand and grow to admire Hitchjaw eels.**

The conclusion must logically flow from the argument presented. Here, the zoologist has concluded that people won't help animals that they find off-putting. However, if he was able to convince people that Hitchjaw eels are not off-putting — as in Choice (A) — public interest might turn toward helping them. That makes Choice (A) the best choice. Notice that Choice (C) is essentially restating the zoologist's conclusion in the passage.

862. **E. . . . accept the gift card from Danielle and wait for the white paint to go on sale or to be able to pay an additional $10 for it.**

In this question, the GMAT test-makers hope that you'll get confused by the choices. But the premise of the argument is clear: Lucy can't spend more than $30. If that is true, only Choice (E) is a logical choice because it recognizes that premise. Choice (A) might seem like a good choice, but the other premise of the argument is that Lucy wants to paint her kitchen white and it is in no way indicated that that premise is less important.

863. **E. Luis's neck brace will be removed next week, and he will be able to resume his training schedule without further delay.**

In this question, test-takers must find a premise that would help the argument make sense. In this case, Choice (E) does that because it provides an explanation that directly shows how Luis could still be the favorite. Choices (A) and (C) hint toward other reasons why he would be, but they are not as clear or convincing as Choice (E).

864. **C. The local newspaper that made the prediction that Luis would win the annual city marathon is unaware of his injury.**

The best way to weaken this argument is to attack the conclusion that Luis will win. If it can be shown, as in Choice (C), that the prediction is not based on a full understanding of Luis' situation, that would seriously weaken the conclusion. It is the correct choice.

865. **D. The vegetable distributor principally ships to vegetable juice production companies that have no use for the leafy green tops.**

To improve profits is the ultimate goal of the logic in the passage. In order to achieve that goal, only Choice (D) is helpful, providing a clear reason why eliminating the leafy green tops of the carrots would be helpful to the company buying the most carrots.

866. **A. Many customers prefer to buy carrots with their leafy green tops, which can be used in cooking.**

The question asks you to find the evidence that would most weaken the plan to cut the leafy green tops off of carrots before selling them. Choice (A) does that the best by providing evidence that carrots without their leafy green tops would be less desirable to many consumers.

867. **D. Because of the extreme stress of the testing process, any windbreaker design that has more than two-thirds of its prototypes functional at the end of the tests is considered sufficiently durable for the consumer market.**

The company's decision is based on logic that is not clear to readers. Choice (D) best provides an explanation that shows why the company decided to put the windbreaker on sale. If the test process is so extreme that it is typical for one-third of the products tested to be ruined, that only 20 windbreakers were ruined shows this product to be superior to the average.

868. **E. Consumers often prefer to buy windbreakers that have scored much better in the tests described.**

To weaken the logic behind the company's plan to put their windbreakers on sale despite the poor test results, it must be shown that those test results can weaken the potential sales. Only Choice (E) does that by showing that potential customers may be reluctant to buy windbreakers which have not scored well on such tests.

869. **D. The other newspaper in city, the Dubsville Tribune, also reported a similar spate of complaints from their readers in the same month.**

That another newspaper in the same city experienced a similar drop in subscriptions at the same time best supports the newspaper's case, so Choice (D) is best. Keep in mind that you may find the newspaper's case dubious, but you're asked to complete its logic, not attack the premises.

870. **C. Dirk: You know as well as I have that we've eaten here every Saturday night for years, and usually there are twice as many employees working.**

You want to complete the dialogue in a way that proves Dirk's point as logically as possible. If he has prior evidence that the restaurants is frequently busy on Saturday nights and usually has more staff at work, his case that they can plan for a particularly busy night is stronger. That's Choice (C).

871. **B. We've eaten here before on a Saturday night at this time and been the only customers!**

You want to improve Ellen's logic. Choice (B) does this best, by offering evidence that proves her thesis: that there is no way to predict how many people will visit the restaurant on a given Saturday night.

872. **D. A house built on a concrete foundation will definitely survive a tornado.**

The argument presented in the passage moves from a "likely" premise (the house is likely to survive) to a "definite" premise (the house will survive any tornados.) This is only possible if the assumption is that likely really means definitely, which is best expressed in Choice (D).

873. **B. Within five miles of the house in the passage, dozens of houses with concrete foundations were destroyed in a tornado three years ago.**

In order to weaken the argument, it must be shown that the assumption that a concrete foundation renders a house impervious to a tornado isn't true. Choice (B) supplies direct evidence to counteract that assumption.

874. **B. As Muir's need for water grows, it would have no other water resources except Lake Onnipi.**

In order for the argument in the passage to make logical sense, it's necessary for Lake Onnipi to be the only water resource available to the town of Muir. That argument is presented in Choice (B). If the town could access any other water supply, the concern over Lake Onnipi would be lessened.

875. **E. If the town of Muir wants to preserve the fragile trout population of Lake Onnipi, they should consider finding other sources for water in the next few years.**

Choice (E) is the best choice. The key in choosing between Choices (A) and (E) is the time frame. The passage tells you that the trout population will be affected in 20 years. Therefore, the rush to curb water usage "immediately," as in Choice (A), seems too rash. Choice (E) presents a more appropriate time frame.

876. **C. A recent scientific study shows a strong correlation between the increase of water consumption in Muir and the decrease in the trout population in Lake Onnipi.**

> The question asks you to extend the argument presented. What further information would make the argument stronger? In this case, Choice (C) does so by presenting a scientific study that connects the overuse of water and the decrease of trout. It's the best answer.

877. **B. . . . avoid overconsumption of carrots.**

> This question seems very simple, and it is. The best choice is Choice (B). People should avoid overconsumption of carrots. No other advice is justified by the passage, and Choice (E) merely repeats a statement in the passage.

878. **E. . . . eat carrots to excess.**

> Here, you're tasked with finding a conclusion that most poorly finishes the paragraph's logic. If the paragraph is building a logical case for nutritionists to warn people not to eat too many carrots, Choice (E) is the most illogical conclusion. It encourages people to eat carrots.

879. **D. It's unlikely that Sammy will win the collegiate championship this year.**

> While we can look at the situation as given and perceive that Sammy most likely won't win the championship, we do not know enough about the situation to absolutely predict that or to make predictions about the probably winner. Thus, Choice (D) is the best answer.

880. **C. The Downintown Police Department has technology that allows it to film most of the fire alarm boxes and see who pulled them.**

> To support the Mayor's argument with evidence, you need to know what it is: He or she is proposing that the fire alarm boxes be removed because they're a nuisance that keep fire fighters from responding to real emergencies. The best evidence to support that is Choice (C), which would provide actual evidence of people pulling the alarms without reason. The cost of a false alarm, Choice (A), could be a nuisance, but the Mayor has not mentioned anything about the monetary cost of a false alarm so it's not as good a choice.

881. **A. In a recent poll, only 40 percent of the residents of Downintown owned cell phones.**

> The Mayor's entire argument is premised on the idea that citizens of Downintown won't need to use fire alarm boxes because they'll be able to call for help on their cell phones. Choice (A) is a direct rebuttal to this idea, making it clear that the majority of citizens do not have a cell phone to use. It's the strongest argument against the Mayor's plan.

882. **C. The fire alarm boxes could be fitted with cameras that take photos of those citizens pulling them.**

Of the choices provided, Choice (C) is the best. It provides a selection of data that could be sorted into helpful photos of people pulling false alarms. Choice (A) is a step after Choice (C): First the perpetrators need to be caught before they can be fined. Choices (B) and (D) are not logically consistent, and Choice (E) not direct enough to solve this problem.

883. **C. The word "Non-Transferrable" is a significant deterrent to customers who might have otherwise sold their vouchers online.**

The logic shown by the marketing department is that marking the vouchers as "Non-Transferrable" will be, by itself, a significant deterrent. Thus, Choice (C) is the best answer.

884. **A. A competing chain found that marking their free drink coupons "Non-Transferrable" did little to change customers' habits of selling those coupons online.**

The chain does not want to pursue a court case against people who sell the vouchers. From the passage, it's clear that they just want to keep the vouchers from being sold as often as possible. The plan to mark the vouchers "Non-Transferrable" hits a snag if Choice (A) is true, as it's direct evidence that marking coupons "Non-Transferrable" did little to stop the practice of selling them.

885. **B. Xinyuan wants to earn an A in her class. Her professor told her that she should try to get As on most of her exams. Xinyuan was able to earn an A on all of her exams, and thus, expects an A in the class.**

This kind of question is rare on the GMAT, but you'll probably get one of them. Instead of asking you to look at the argument itself, it asks you to think through the logic used in the argument and then find another argument that most resembles the passage. Here, that's Choice (B). Even though the setting is a college instead of a workplace, the logic shown is the same (and as equally flawed, by the way), as in the main passage.

886. **C. It is the conclusion to the argument.**

This is an easy one. Choice (C) is correct because the bolded portion is the conclusion to the argument.

887. **D. There might be a reason why Jane's boss wanted her to sell three, not four, houses.**

It seems likely that if Jane was tasked with selling three houses in order to get a promotion, four houses would be even better. However, we don't know that for sure, and Jane has changed the criteria under which she was to be promoted. As Choice (D) suggests, there might be a reason that was a bad idea.

888. **D. Scientific studies have consistently shown that yogurt does indeed help create a healthful environment in the digestive tract.**

The argument presented is that yogurt if helpful to maintain microbes a person's digestive system. Only Choice (D) provides evidence — in the form of scientific studies — that help to prove that argument is correct. It's thus the only good choice.

889. **A. The source of the nutritionists' belief about yogurt turns out to be a widely-discredited article from the 1950s.**

If the argument is that nutritionists are recommending yogurt because it will be helpful to patients' digestive systems, that needs to be scientifically validated. Choice (A) shows that, in fact, the advice is based on a scientifically invalid piece of evidence. It most weakens the argument.

890. **E. Surveys of park visitors show that they consistently asked for a cell phone ban, writing things like "Save us from ourselves!"**

The basic premise of the argument is that people are avoiding the park because they can't tear themselves away from their cell phones long enough to enjoy being there. The administrator suggests that by banning cell phones, people may return to the park in greater numbers. The logic here is shaky, but Choice (E) best supports the idea that people want to spend time in a place where their smart phones must be put away.

891. **B. Three years ago, there was a widely publicized incident in the park in which a hiker was hurt and unable to call for help because he didn't have a phone with him.**

To attack the argument, one must find reasons why the administrator's logic is flawed, so you can either find another reason why attendance is down or find a reason why people would want to have their phones with them in the park. Choice (B) does both, so it beats Choices (A) and (C), which answer one or the other need.

892. **C. The administration noticed that the 80 seniors who had taken two or more AP classes all were accepted into their first-choice college. The colleges reported that their AP credits strongly influenced their acceptances.**

Here, you must find evidence to support the administration's decision to add five more AP classes. Choice (C) is the best answer because it shows why the administration would add courses that are not widely requested by the student body. Choice (A) makes a similar point, but with less specificity and no actual proof. Choice (E) presents another reason to add AP courses, but is likely to be less convincing than Choice (C).

893. **B. A comparison of the number of graduates from next year's class who got into their first choice college, and the number of graduates from this year's class who got into their first choice college.**

The most helpful evidence would be a comparison of the rate of getting into one's first choice colleges between this year's senior class and next year's, so Choice (B) is best. Notice that both Choices (D) and (E) are too vague and can be eliminated immediately.

894. **D. My favorite band strictly follows an every-other-summer tour schedule, and have done so for over 20 years.**

Despite appearing to be about music, this short passage is really about logic. In order to make the argument true, you have to find logic that would support the idea that if the band didn't tour last summer, they will this summer. Choice (D) best does that, by showing the pattern: if they don't tour one summer, they do the next.

895. **A. The band has always followed a "two summers off, one summer on" touring schedule since their founding 15 years ago.**

Choice (A) is the clearest evidence that the band won't tour this summer: It's not in their well-established pattern. Notice that Choice (E) is misleading: Since you know nothing about the band, the lead singer's injury may or may not be a factor. You can't tell for sure.

896. **D. No significant changes have been made to help protect Bridgeton from flooding since 1957.**

The argument made in the passage can only be true if nothing much has changed since the last time the town faced a flood. That makes Choice (D) the best answer.

897.   **B. Since 1957, Bridgeton has undertaken multiple steps to improve the town's protect against the next flood, including raising the river walls by three feet.**

In order to attack the argument, it's necessary to show that the premise that the flood will be more destructive is unlikely to be true. Choice (B) does that best by showing that the town is less vulnerable to a flood than it used to be.

898.   **E. Hypoloss carries a high risk of serious complications, including internal bleeding and death.**

Notice that most of the choices explain why obesity is a risk factor, but the argument is about why doctors won't prescribe Hypoloss. Choice (E) best gives a reason why that may be. The drug itself carries a "high risk" of serious complications, even death. That's most likely why doctors are reluctant to prescribe it.

899.   **D. Three recent scientific studies have found that taking Hypoloss is no less dangerous to a patient than non-prescription weight loss techniques.**

It's most likely that doctors, who are scientists, would be most convinced by scientific evidence that argues for a medication that they found dubious. Choice (D) best provides that evidence.

900.   **B. Scientific studies on the safety of Hypoloss have not been conducted yet.**

Doctors wouldn't want to prescribe a medication that may not prove safe to their patients. Choice (B) indicates that the jury is still out on that question.

901.   **D. Gladys: You know as well as I do that the factory on Main Street changes shifts at 5:00 p.m., and that slows traffic to a crawl every day at that time.**

Gladys needs to present the best evidence she can to prove her argument is correct. Choices (A) and (B) provide evidence, but they're slimmer than Choice (D), which provides much more clear and convincing evidence.

902.   **A. It is a request that Gladys prove her argument.**

Although it sounds like a sentence one might hear in a disagreement, the bolded sentence does have a role to play: It is a request that Gladys provide evidence to prove her argument that they will not get there until 6:30. Thus, Choice (A) is best.

903. **B. The university's definition of "most deserving" is not solely based on financial need.**

Since we are told almost nothing about the university's scholarship program, we can only use the information we've been given. Choice (B) best does that. Notice that all of the other choices make assumptions that we might be sure are correct, but which are not justified by the language of the passage.

904. **A. A clear explanation of how the scholarship committee defines "most deserving."**

The missing evidence that is most needed here is an understanding of how the university defines "most deserving." If given that, we might better understand the choice that was made. Choice (A) is the best answer.

905. **D. The guidelines for the scholarship clearly define "most deserving" as being a student who cannot contribute more than $12,000 a year to their education.**

For the decision to be weakened, evidence showing that the scholarship committee chose to award a student who should not have received the scholarship. Choice (D) demonstrates that the committee ignored one of the terms of the scholarship's rules.

906. **B. The majority of customers bought dishes of ice cream, and 80% of those bought vanilla or a vanilla-based flavor.**

While Choice (A) has some merit in weakening the argument, the best choice is Choice (B), because it provides evidence that the argument presented is not comprehensive enough. If the idea is to find out whether chocolate flavors are more popular than vanilla flavors overall (and not just in scoop form), Choice (B) gives the best evidence to be considered.

907. **C. It is the evidence that Li uses in his argument.**

The information in the bolded sentence is the evidence Li presents in order to support his argument, so Choice (C) is correct. Whether or not we think that the argument is a good one, that is the evidence Li is presenting to support it.

908. **E. Green is a color people like more than red or blue.**

Every answer except Choice (E) is an assumption that Li makes. With Choice (E), however, the assumption may not be correct. Li states that people buy more books with a green cover than any other color, but he doesn't indicate that he believes people like green more than any other color.

909. **D. Business C produced more than 80% of the waste City A had to dispose of in the last year.**

Don't get distracted! Business C's assertion that it should not have to pay a tax to help offset the fee paid to City B is the premise here. The best argument against it is Choice (D) which makes it clear that Business C does, in fact, produce far more garbage than City A's homeowners.

910. **B. City A's homeowners contributed 60% of the town's waste last year. The year before that, they contributed 68%.**

Business C needs to prove that homeowners in City A are contributing more to the trash problem than it is in order for the argument to work. Choice (B) does that best.

911. **D. Many of the creative writing faculty members who've left Wadsworth College have continued teaching at nearby schools for higher pay.**

Here, you want to find a reason to support the chairperson's plan. Choice (D), which indicates that creative writing faculty are leaving Wadsworth College because they can do the same work for more pay elsewhere, supports the plan the best.

912. **E. Exit interviews with creative writing faculty members who've left the college indicate that course assignments and inadequate health benefits were the most common reasons they left Wadsworth College.**

The idea here is to find the flaw in the chairperson's logic, not merely find a reason why his or her plan is not likely to be approved, as in Choice (C). Choice (E) is the best answer because it indicates that faculty members may not be more likely to stay merely because of a pay increase.

913. **B. "Sure, but we have five months until wedding season this time."**

The basic premise of the argument Chip is making is that inexperienced clerks do not help during the wedding season. But Jackie is arguing that they will have more time to train the new clerks this time. Choice (B) best shows that she's right because there is more time to train new clerks this year.

914. **C. It is the evidence that Chip is presenting to bolster his argument.**

The bolded portion is evidence that Chip is presenting to strengthen his argument against Jackie. Thus, Choice (C) is the best.

915. **D. The "10 patients per hour" statistic is misleading because it is an average. Daytime nurses sometimes treat 15 patients per hour while night nurses may only see 5 patients per night.**

> The nurses' union's grievance attacks the premise of the administrator's offer. If all of the ER nurses do not actually see 10 patients per hour, some will be much more likely to earn a bonus than others. Choice (D) shows that this is true.

916. **A. Mystique Auto charges a finance rate that is three times the rate charged by Miracle Cars, and customers must get their financing in-house when buying at Mystique.**

> Michael Sanchez can feel confident if he has a tangible reason in mind as to why customers would want to shop at his auto dealership instead of Mystique Auto. Only Choice (A) gives a clear, compelling reason why consumers would choose his dealership and thus justifies his belief. It is the best answer.

917. **D. Sanchez does not know that Miracle Cars' CFO has ordered that they raise interest rates on their in-house loans, which had been well below market average.**

> Sanchez makes his statement with the assumption that nothing will change at Miracle Cars, so they remain in good standing, even when compared to Mystique's new offer. But Choice (D) shows that Sanchez does not have all of the information and that there is good reason to feel less confidence.

918. **B. Meghan: "My coworkers wouldn't stop asking me where I was going on vacation. I finally made them a deal: If they would stop bothering me for an hour, long enough for me to get my report written, I would tell them all about my trip. They left me alone, and when my hour was up, I told them it was none of their business where I traveled!"**

> Here, you're asked to figure out the logic in an argument in the passage. Hannah's logic seems to run as follows: If I want A, I promise B if he does C. He did C, but I took away B. The closest mirror to this logic is in Choice (B), where Meghan employs the same logic. Notice that Choice (A) seems appealing because it's about a similar situation, but Steve does not use the same logic.

919. **E. It is the conclusion to the argument.**

> The bolded sentence shows how the argument concluded, so it is the conclusion, as stated in Choice (E).

920. **A. The new racquet costs 200 times the amount of the most expensive racquets made now.**

All of the choices presented could weaken the expectation that the new racquet will sell well, but Choice (A) is the largest threat. It practically guarantees that the racquet will sell poorly because the price difference is so large. It is the best choice.

921. **C. The manufacturer has secured the support of three top tennis players to act as ambassadors for the racquet. One was recently quoted as saying the racquet improved her game "more dramatically than I thought possible."**

The manufacturer wants to support the idea that the racquet will sell well. Their confidence would like be well-placed if Choice (C) is correct, and several top players are endorsing the product so vociferously.

922. **B. . . . time how long it takes you to read and respond to a couple of emails in your in-box and that recalculate the time you'll need?**

The point of Andrew's argument is that he wants to empty his email in-box in as little time as possible, but he does not know how long it will take do so. Choice (B) is the best suggestion Diane can make. Following it would allow Andrew to make a reasonable guess on how long it will take him to empty his email box while also responding as needed.

923. **E. A survey of Factory B's workers reveled that 78 percent would like to see technological improvements on their assembly line.**

Choice (E) best supports the argument that Factory A is more advanced than Factory B. If the workers of Factory B want to see improvement that will be similar to what is already in place at Factory A, that's good evidence to support the argument as stated in the passage.

924. **D. It presents a possible cause of a condition as the only cause of that condition without considering other causes.**

The argument is clearly flawed, but figuring out where the major flaw is located is tricky. Choice (D) is best because the argument's biggest error is using one reason to explain why Factory B's output us lower than Factory A's. It may well be because of the technology of the assembly line, but that is not proven yet.

925. **D. Chemicals used in the creation of fabrics are far more damaging to the environment than fabric scraps created in traditional clothing manufacture.**

The premise of the argument is that zero waste manufacturing of clothing is not as kind to the environment as some might think it is. The best facts to support that premise is in Choice (D), which shows that a major environmental problem in manufacturing is not addressed by zero waste clothing.

926. **D. Underage drinking has been on a steady decline for the last 25 years, long before the campaign to reduce the portrayal of it on television.**

> The argument that reducing the portrayal of underage drinking in films can be tied to the reduction of the same in real life becomes questionable if underage drinking has been on a steady decline for many years. Thus, Choice (D) most seriously weakens the argument.

927. **E. There is a direct correlation between seeing an activity on television and taking part in that activity.**

> As strange as it may seem, there indeed must be a belief that there's a direct correlation between the portrayal of underage drinking and the rise of underage drinking to make the argument work, so Choice (D) is the best.

928. **C. In a poll of graduating high school seniors, 60 percent reported that they did not drink alcohol on a regular basis because of negative portrayals of the same in television and movies.**

> Poll results are the kind of evidence that provide figures to boost an argument. Choice (C) does that for this argument.

929. **A. Readers are not interested in distinguishing between a well written essay and a hastily written short article.**

> The basic premise of the argument holds that people cannot or will not distinguish between quality writing and poor writing, so long as something is provided for them to read. That makes Choice (A) the best answer.

930. **B. Subscriptions to print-based journals that publish long, well written essays are at an all-time high.**

> The fact that people are buying more journals that publish essays would seriously weaken the argument that people do not care what they read. Thus, Choice (B) is best.

931. **A. When the dosage of the drug was half of what was used in the latest round of tests, the reoccurrence rate was still 60%.**

> The assumption is that upping the dosage will also lower the rate of reoccurrence. Choice (A) demonstrates that there's no connection between the dosage and the reoccurrence rate. That's where the assumption is.

932. **A. Thyroid cancer is considered a relatively small impact disease. Most people recover from it.**

Choice (A) may be true, but the impact thyroid cancer has on people who have it is not a factor in the plan to double the dosage.

933. **E. Construction of the bypass is controversial, and most town residents have signed a pledge not to use it.**

Of these choices, Choice (E) provides the clearest argument for why the businesses may be wrong. If local residents have pledged not to use the bypass, it is less likely to be used, which would mean that traffic would continue as normal, passing the local businesses.

934. **C. "Because the soda won't go bad, I can drink it tomorrow. I'm paying a little more for two sodas today, but I won't pay anything for tomorrow's soda."**

The fact that the soda isn't perishable is the key to Sam's logic. Choice (C) explains that he will be able to consume the soda tomorrow and thus spread the savings into the next day.

935. **D. It is evidence that supports the premise of his argument.**

Sam's argument is that it's better to buy two sodas now instead of one soda each day because he will save money. The bolded portion is evidence that supports the premise that he will save money. Choice (D) is best.

936. **E. The book is incorrect. Not all animals, including dogs, can see colors.**

If Sparky can't see that the room is blue, it is unlikely to have a soothing effect on him. Thus, Choice (E) is best.

937. **D. Sparky began barking a lot after Tyronicah painted her bedroom red.**

However unlikely to work we may find Tyronicah's plan, the best support for it would show that Sparky is apparently affected by the color of the bedroom. Choice (D) does that.

938. **B. It is evidence that supports the premise.**

The use of statistics is almost always a presentation of evidence. Here, the sentence in bold is a statistic that is used as evidence to support the premise that there has been a significant increase in accidents. Thus, Choice (B) is best.

939. **D. The lawmakers assume that the threat of jail time would be a deterrent for those who might have contemplated texting while driving.**

While Choice (E) is likely true, it's not an inference drawn from this argument itself. The better answer is Choice (D), which looks at the specifics of this argument: Jail time is more likely to deter texting while driving than a fine.

940. **D. The first sentence presents a theory about a topic, while the second sentence introduces the a more recent theory about that topic.**

The connection between the two sentences is clear. The first explains what some scientists have put forward as a theory about PTSD, while the second seeks to replace that theory with a new idea. Choice (D) explains this well.

941. **D. An explanation of what the new theory about the link between the impact and the patient is.**

In a well written passage — which one must assume this is — the most logical next sentence would explain what the new theory is, exactly. That makes Choice (D) the best.

942. **B. They are interested in reading new theories about PTSD.**

In a question like this, the GMAT test-makers know that you're being asked to speculate. The answer will therefore be simple. In this case, the best choice is Choice (B), which is indeed so obvious as to be almost overlooked. It is the best choice because it is the only assumption of those offered that can be very safely made.

943. **A. Bridget: But they also are able to set the price accurately. When you sell your home yourself, you run the risk of underpricing it. And keep in mind that you still have to pay for much of what the agency would cover, such as listing and closing costs.**

Luke's concern is that using a real estate agent will be expensive because they take a big profit from the sale of a house. If Bridget responds with Choice (A), she is most directly speaking to that particular concern, so it's the best choice.

944. **C. It is an assumption Luke has made to support his argument.**

The sentence Luke says isn't detailed enough to be evidence: He doesn't provide any supporting information. He is using it to support his argument, but it is an assumption he is making. Choice (C) is thus the best answer.

945. **C. Vlad has only walked around in neighborhoods that cater to the large number of American tourists who visit the city each year.**

> If Vlad is making his argument based on insufficient or biased evidence, the argument cannot be valid. Choice (C) presents a situation in which that would be the case: He isn't getting an accurate sampling of London's restaurant scene, and he's collecting evidence in an area that's biased towards a certain kind of patron.

946. **D. A London daily newspaper recently polled its readers on their favorite cuisine when dining out. "American" won by 30 percent.**

> Evidence is best presented in quantifiable form, so far as the GMAT is concerned. Choice (D) does so with a figure that supports the idea that American food is increasingly popular in London.

947. **B. He could argue that the practice of wearing glasses with non-prescription lenses is very common these days, citing a statistic that 25 percent of glasses-wearers do not actually need them.**

> Nancy refuses to wear glasses because she does not need them, and feels doing so would mislead her viewers. The best counter-argument presented here is Choice (B), which effectively points out that viewers may not assume that Nancy needs the glasses.

948. **C. Studies show that when a news anchor feels she is lying, it is perceivable by viewers in her body language.**

> Nancy's argument is that wearing glasses would be a lie, which would affect her performance and/or her relationship with the audience of the show. Choice (C) most clearly speaks to that idea.

949. **C. The author's novel will become a best-seller.**

> The assumption least likely to be in use here is that the novel will become a best seller. We don't know why the publisher wants to re-release this novel, and certainly have no reason to think he expects it to be a best seller. Thus, Choice (C) is the best bet.

950. **C. The author's estate was recently taken over by a law firm capable of practicing much closer diligence.**

> The publisher's argument is based on the premise that the author's estate is not paying attention to what happens to the author's works. However, Choice (C) would indicate that the estate is now capable of paying far closer to attention, which would ruin the publisher's plan. It's the best answer.

951. **A. The margin of error for the poll is greater than the difference in support between the candidates.**

It's good to remember that the question has asked for the "most likely" reason, not "a plausible" reason. There are several plausible reasons, but Choice (A) is the most likely reason: It is factual and would be an immediate disincentive to publish a prediction if true.

952. **B. Written proof that the fundraisers for this organization were paid for by generous donors so that the money raised could go to people in need.**

Because Ben's specific concern seems to be that the organization is putting a great deal of money into lavish fundraisers instead of helping people in need, proof that the organization is not paying for those fundraisers would be most helpful in convincing him. Thus, Choice (B) is the right answer.

953. **A. Over 40 percent of the organization's budget is dedicated to fundraising.**

To support Ben's argument, it's necessary to find a evidence that the organization bankrolls fundraising far more than helping people in need. Choice (A) would help with that. 40 percent is a significant portion of any size budget.

954. **D. The first sentence is evidence that Ben is using to support the argument he is making, and the second is the conclusion to his argument.**

In the first bolded sentence, Ben is sharing evidence to support his argument (that the organization spends too much on lavish fundraisers). The second sentence is his conclusion: He states what he will do instead of supporting the organization. Choice (D) is best.

955. **E. Scientific studies have conclusively proven that there's no truth to this advice.**

Suzie's argument is that her mother's advice must be correct because she's followed it and never had a cramp while swimming. The best argument against this is to show that the connection is coincidental, not casual. Thus, Choice (E) is best because it provides factual proof that Suzie's argument does not make sense.

956. **B. "I asked my doctor, and she said that this was a good policy to follow. Cramps are often caused by eating followed by vigorous exercise."**

Suzie's argument is weak because it relies on what could be coincidence. It can be improved with some sort of evidence. The closest to doing that here is Choice (B), in which a scientist puts her weight behind Suzie's argument.

957. D. . . . students should be encouraged to think about whether spending time on social media is affecting their decision-making about bullying behaviors.

> Most of the choices here are too broad to have been derived from the study. Choice (A) is the sort of obvious response that is a societal goal, not the result of a study. Choice (D) gives the best take-away from the study, presenting a reasonable response not a broad statement.

958. C. There is a direct link between the use of social media and the likelihood that the user is an online bully.

> Without the assumption in Choice (C) — that social media's usage and bullying are interconnected — the argument does not make logical sense. Thus, it is the best choice.

959. C. The loss of a major contract with a hotel corporation has also contributed to the manufacturer's decline.

> The manufacturer's argument is an attempt to show how that the factory can no longer be profitable. To do this, showing that business will not pick up is helpful. Choice (C) gives more evidence suggesting the factory's decline.

960. A. The manufacturer recently secured a large, multi-year contract with a restaurant chain.

> A contract with a lucrative customer would argue against ceasing production. That the contract is "multi-year" is particularly compelling. Choice (A) is the best choice.

961. E. A beauty salon has decided to close. Few women need a weekly hairstyling session, and the products used in styling hair are very expensive. Thus, the salon is putting more money into products than its making back in sales.

> The connection between a hair salon and a raincoat manufacturer may be less obvious, but the argument — essentially that supply far outpaces demand — is essentially the same. Thus, Choice (E) is correct.

962. E. "As you know, the Police Department is next door, and we're going to offer a discounted admission to people who present a ticket from that auction."

> This question is fairly easy; you just need to find the sentence that provides actual evidence. Choice (E) does that the best, if you recognize that Choice (A) would weaken the argument, not strengthen it.

963. **A. "The Police Department's event has three times the number of items up for auction and admission is free!"**

Choice (A) provides a reasonable counter-argument: If the other event has more items and is free, people are indeed more likely to attend it. Notice that Choices (B) and (D) might provide counter-arguments if they were given more context, but without more information, Choice (A) is stronger.

964. **D. The prior eight years are incidental, not prophetic.**

The question is essentially asking you to find the biggest flaw in the argument. Here, the assumption that the rate of inflation follows a fixed pattern is the largest flaw, and Choice (D) points that out. Other choices point to flaws, but not as large as Choice (D).

965. **E. It is evidence that supports the argument being made.**

The bolded sentence presents evidence that supports the argument being made, so Choice (E) is best. Choice (C) would have been a good guess if it was about the argument, not the counter-argument.

966. **B. It is possible to produce food without preservatives that is safe to consume.**

For the passage to be true, it must also be true that Marr Foods is able to make products that are safe to consume and do not have chemicals. That makes Choice (B) the best.

967. **C. Several other scientific studies found that preservatives were in no way harmful to those who consumed food with them.**

The basic premise of the argument is preservatives are harmful to those who consume them. If that is not true, the rest of the argument falls apart. Choice (C) makes a strong argument that the scientific study presented by Marr Foods is not representative of the common consensus.

968. **C. Neighbor A is on a plan from the water authority that provides a lower rate on water in the morning hours.**

The key here it to identify the correct argument that you need to find support for. Neighbor A's chief concern is the cost of watering his lawn later in the day. Choice (C) points to why that is: He is able to save money by watering the lawn earlier.

969. **D. That Neighbor A doesn't have a good reason for watering his lawn in the morning.**

> To choose the answer correctly, you need to be alert to the difference between facts and assumptions. Choices (C) and (E) are facts; Choice (D) is an assumption that Neighbor B is making about Neighbor A. Given the wording of the question, Choice (D) is thus best.

970. **A. The first sentence is a premise to an argument, and the second sentence is a response to a counter-argument.**

> The first sentence presents Neighbor A's argument, and the second sentence shows that Neighbor A is rejecting Neighbor B's counter-argument. Choice (A) is correct.

971. **B. Customers have repeatedly asked the company to offer an unlimited usage plan, which many other cell service providers already offer.**

> If customers do not like the new plan, it will not do well. If they do, it will do well and revenues will increase, regardless of any other detail. That makes Choice (B) the best offered.

972. **D. A mock trial team that often makes it to the final round of competition but rarely wins is frustrated. They've decided to interview the members of the 2002 team, which won the state competition. Using those techniques, they're sure, will put them over the top to win.**

> The logical structure in the original passage is a flawed plan to use the idiosyncratic success of a past group of people to improve the chances of another unique group of people in winning the same title. Choice (D) best follows that logical scale.

973. **A. It concludes the coach's argument.**

> The best answer is Choice (A). If the team follows the coach's plan, it will conclude in making it to the final game. Remember that the merits of the argument are not the question here. You may find it flawed, and it is, but that's not the point of the question. Avoid Choice (C).

974. **C. . . . look for opportunities to schedule events before or after typical working hours and on weekends.**

> All of the choices here are possible, so you need to focus on choosing the one that best completes the passage. The need for further information, as in Choices (B) and (D) seems unnecessary. Choice (A) doesn't address the problem, and Choice (E) addressed the problem with the wrong people. That leaves Choice (C), the most direct response to the problem, and the best choice.

975. **D. There's no "build up" in playing the slot machines. Each game is new and not tied to the game before it.**

> Sheila's theory is based on the idea that slot machines must be primed to cash out, and thus watching someone else lose repeatedly is priming the machine for her take-over and win. If Choice (D) is true, it means that her plan is meritless: Slot machines are not primed.

976. **B. A scientific study, based on the observation of 500 slot machines at a Las Vegas casino, showed that machines that are played repeatedly are three times more likely to cash out.**

> The best evidence would show help to prove Sheila's theory that slot machines that have been played frequently are primed to cash out. Choice (B) provides scientific evidence that proves that, in at least one case, Sheila's theory is true.

977. **D. When Jane says that she prefers to go to the beach when it is less crowded, she may not mean that there are actually fewer people on the beach than at any other time of the day.**

> The trick with this question is to understand that the logic it is seeking is not Jane's internal logic, but rather, how Jane's choice can be justified logically. Choice (D) does that best because it explains what Jane is most likely thinking.

978. **B. An explanation of an apparent discrepancy in her argument.**

> Jake is presenting a discrepancy between what Jane says she prefers and what she actually does. He's found an error and wants her to explain it. Choice (B) is correct.

979. **E. Reducing an avalanche's impact by 50 percent is not the same as reducing the likelihood of an avalanche by 50 percent.**

> The answer here is obvious if you take the time to read through everything presented to find it. Any reduction in an avalanche's impact is not the same as being less likely to have an avalanche. Thus, Choice (E) is the best answer.

980. **C. When the impact of an avalanche is reduced, the avalanche is less likely to travel further down the mountain and affect skiers.**

> The main problem with the argument made by the marketing company is that it conflates the impact of an avalanche with having an avalanche at all. Choice (C) provides further evidence to solve the problem, making it the right choice.

981. **D. Company L's speed at producing widgets has repeatedly caused accidents that ultimately cost the company more money than producing at a lower rate.**

Here, you're looking for a reason why the owner of Company K would not fully embrace Company L's methods. Choice (D) provides the best evidence why this would be true: Company L's methods are both dangerous and costly.

982. **A. Because Company K's production line was already more efficient than Company L's, a few more small changes should allow Company K to produce widgets at a rate of 150 a minute.**

In order to attack the argument presented, you need to find a reason why Company K shouldn't stop at just two improvements. Choice (A), which reveals that the Company could soon be producing 150 widgets a minute, is the best choice.

983. **B. The first sentence is evidence used in building the argument, and the second sentence is the conclusion of the argument.**

Choice (B) is best here. The first sentence presents evidence that helps to build the argument (even if it seems to be countering the main argument), while the second sentence presents the conclusion of the argument, using the evidence from the first sentence.

984. **B. In a poll of recent law school graduates, "job fluidity" — that is, the ability to change positions and firms — was one of the top three qualities new lawyers wanted in their first jobs.**

To argue against the board's idea, you need to find reasons to show that the potential pool of applicants would not like having to sign a five-year contract. Choice (B) provides evidence that this would be disliked.

985. **D. Poll data collected from current first-year associates about whether they would have taken the job if such a clause was included in their contracts.**

The best answer here is Choice (D). First-year associates at the firm are in the best position to evaluate whether the contract — which they have recently signed themselves — would be as sought-after if they had to commit themselves to five years at the firm.

986. **B. It's possible to correctly bake a cake at a higher temperature so long as the time the cake is in the oven is reduced.**

The cake baker in the argument is making an (incorrect) assumption that baking a cake at a higher temperature will work out find so long as the time the cake is in the oven is reduced. That makes Choice (B) the best answer.

987. **E. Baking is a chemical reaction dictated by the recipe that cannot be sped up by setting the oven temperature higher.**

This is the kind of argument that is so clearly flawed that it can be difficult to figure out exactly what the flaw is. Choice (E), which points out that the argument has no scientific merit, is the best bet.

988. **D. The majority of volunteers who staff the clinic are doctors and nurses with full-time jobs, and they are often scheduled for hospital rounds and surgery in the morning hours.**

The argument here is not about whether the clinic is a good idea, or even if it is needed. Instead, the question is asking you why the supervisors would decline to open the clinic in the morning. Choice (D) provides the best answer. Choice (C) has some merit but is really making a separate argument for evening hours, not arguing against opening the clinic during morning hours.

989. **C. Morning hours would allow the clinic to see, on average, 20 additional patients per day.**

Don't get confused by the question. The Davis County supervisor wants to extend hours into the morning at the clinic. Choices (A), (B) and (D) support the existence of a clinic more broadly and do not offer any particular support for morning hours. Only Choice (C) does that, making it the correct answer.

990. **E. CheapDeals won't build in a town where they have been clearly told they are not welcome.**

The argument is to support the idea of protesting the arrival of CheapDeals. The assumption presented in Choice (E) — that CheapDeals won't build where they're not welcome — is the assumption behind the protest.

991. **C. CheapDeals tries to keep a low-profile; the publicity from a protest has kept the company from setting up shop in other towns.**

To support the argument that they should protest, the store owner needs to show that a protest could be effective. Choice (C) best shows how that could be true by offering evidence that protests against this company have worked before.

992. B. **If the jewels were to be stolen, thieves might target the smaller items, which will be displayed less securely, rather than the larger items.**

> The director's argument is flawed, but the key to this question is figuring out where the greatest flaw is. Choice (B) points out one of the problems with his logic: He's assuming that thieves would choose to take the larger jewels, but there's actually no reason to think that is likely.

993. D. **"I put on sunscreen before leaving the house, but I didn't bother with insect repellent. The sunblock should be strong enough to keep away any mosquitos that show up."**

> The best answer here is Choice (D). While the topic here is different from the original argument, the logic is the same. By buying one kind of protection, the speaker hopes that other protections will fall into place even though steps have not been taken to secure them.

994. E. **"I put on sunscreen before leaving the house, but I didn't bother with insect repellent. The sunblock should be strong enough to keep away any mosquitos that show up."**

> Remember, the conclusion of an argument doesn't always have to arrive at the end of the passage. Here, Principal Lavine proposes his solution before presenting evidence that explains why the solution must be what it is. That's Choice (E).

995. B. **The parking for visitors and parents is rarely used, so 30 empty spaces are often next to the school but forbidden to the students.**

> Choice (B) is best because it argues against the premise the principal puts forward in his argument: There is no alternative for expanding student parking except to convert a field into a parking lot. Choice (B) implies that, in fact, the visitor and parent parking could be converted without much difficulty.

996. D. **A historical map showing the growth of neighborhoods in New Winchester.**

> It's probably possible to rank these from most to least helpful, but surely Choice (D) would prove to be of little help. It's not clear how understanding the past growth of neighborhoods in the city would shed any light on the paradox Julian has noted.

997. B. **The grocery stores are located on the outskirts of town, whereas the corner stores are in residential areas.**

> The discrepancy must be addressed here: What would cause people to routinely pay more for an item that they could get less at a grocery store? Choice (B) provides the best answer: The corner stores are geographically more convenient than the grocery stores.

998. **A. There must be something appealing about the corner stores that make people willing to spend slightly more money there than at the grocery store.**

Choice (A) seems so simple as to be obvious, but it's really the only choice one can logically conclude from the passage. Notice that the question asks for a "logical conclusion" — that's the key that Choice (A) must be right.

999. **B. How does lettuce production from Mapple's government-owned farmland compared to production from farmland owned by private industries?**

In order to evaluate this argument, you must look for a question that gets to the heart of it: Why is private industry's farmland more productive than farmland owned by the government? Choice (B) is the best evaluation question here because it would allow for the collection of data comparing the two types of farmland.

1,000. **C. There's no discernable difference in the amount of lettuce produced per acre by the government's farmland and by farmland owned by private industry.**

The basic premise of the argument is that there is a significant difference between the amount of lettuce produced on government farmland and the amount produced on farmland owned by private industry. If this is not true, as in Choice (C), the argument is severely weakened.

1,001. **B. The bridge is only open from 6:00 to 8:00 a.m. on weekdays.**

If Choice (B) is true, it implies that the problem with the bridge is not that it should be closed down, but rather, that it is not open enough.

Index

A

Abraham, Nikhail (author)
  Coding For Dummies, 155–156
AC (alternating current), 173–174
adding fractions, 35
advertising, buying, 8
algebra
  in Data Sufficiency section, 71
  in Problem Solving section, 31
alternating current (AC), 173–174
American Constitutional History (Fruchtman),
    147–148, 159–160, 170–171
Amthor, Frank (author)
  Neuroscience For Dummies, 165–166, 172–173
Analytical Writing Assessment
  about, 7
  answers, 259–265
  problem types for, 7
  questions, 8–10
  tips for, 7
angles, finding, 58, 67, 69, 76, 96, 100, 101, 107,
    109, 127, 131
answers, to example questions
  Analytical Writing Assessment, 259–265
  Critical Reasoning section, 470–498
  Data Sufficiency section, 344–419
  Integrated Reasoning (IR) section, 265–275
  Problem Solving section, 275–343
  Reading Comprehension section, 420–444
  Sentence Completion section, 444–469
arc length, finding, 33
area

finding, 40, 47, 103
  finding of a circle, 44, 105, 115
  finding of a rectangle, 107
  finding of a square, 61
  finding of a triangle, 67, 80
arithmetic average
  calculating, 21–22
  finding, 33, 49, 54, 72, 89, 123
asterism, 171–172
astronomy, 158–159, 171–172
Astronomy For Dummies (Maran), 146–147,
    158–159, 171–172
average
  calculating, 21–22
  finding, 33, 49, 54, 72, 89, 123

B

basic math
  in Data Sufficiency section, 71
  in Problem Solving section, 31
Beekeeping For Dummies (Blackiston), 156–157,
    169–170
bees, 156–157
Belew, Shannon (author)
  Starting an Online Business, 148–149, 162–163
Big Dipper, 171–172
Blackiston, Howland (author)
  Beekeeping For Dummies, 156–157, 169–170
botulism, 149–151
brain, 165–166
budgets, calculating, 33
Building a Minecraft City (Guthals), 145–146

C

Venn diagram, 25, 112

video, 148–149

Visual Basic, 155–156

volume, finding, 46

W

Wagner-Martin, Linda (author)

A History of American Literature, 1950 to the Present, 142–143, 176

water consumption, 28–30

website design, 148–149

websites

Cheat Sheet, 2

Dummies, 2, 3

Technical Support, 3

weight, finding, 43

Wiegand, Steve (author)

U. S. History For Dummies, 3rd Edition, 161–162, 173–174, 177

word problems

in Data Sufficiency section, 71

in Problem Solving section, 31

Notes

Notes

About the Authors

Sandra Luna McCune, PhD, is professor emeritus and a former Regents professor at Stephen F. Austin State University in Nacogdoches, Texas, where she was honored with the Distinguished Professor Award. She now is a full-time author and resides in Dripping Springs, Texas.

Shannon Reed is a Visiting Lecturer at the University of Pittsburgh, where she teaches composition, creative writing, and professional writing courses for the English Department. Shannon has also taught in the Slavic Department at Pitt, and as a high school English and Theatre teacher in Brooklyn and Queens, New York. She's proud to be a playwriting teaching artist at Pittsburgh's City Theatre, and her writing has appeared in *The New Yorker, McSweeney's Internet Tendency,* and *Buzzfeed,* among many other venues.

Authors' Acknowledgements

I'd like to thank my past and present students and colleagues at the University of Pittsburgh, as well as my coauthor Sandra McClune. I'm also grateful to our agent, Grace Freedson, and Lindsay Lefevere and Tim Gallan at Wiley for their steadfast support of this project. Thanks also to Gloria Reed, Justin and Kate Reed, Andrew Hansen, Christine Marr, Melissa Ellington, and Melissa and Eric Stoller. —Shannon Reed

Dedication

With immeasurable love, Sandra Luna McCune dedicates her work on this project to her grand-children: Richard, Rose, Jude, Sophia, Josephine, Myla, and Micah.

This book is for all high school and college students dreaming of furthering their education by getting an MBA. I hope it helps you! —Shannon Reed

Publisher's Acknowledgments

Executive Editor: Lindsay Sandman Lefevere

Project Editor: Tim Gallan

Production Editor: Antony Sami

Cover Image: © phototechno/iStockphoto

Leverage the power

Dummies is the global leader in the reference category and one of the most trusted and highly regarded brands in the world. No longer just focused on books, customers now have access to the dummies content they need in the format they want. Together we'll craft a solution that engages your customers, stands out from the competition, and helps you meet your goals.

Advertising & Sponsorships

Connect with an engaged audience on a powerful multimedia site, and position your message alongside expert how-to content. Dummies.com is a one-stop shop for free, online information and know-how curated by a team of experts.

- Targeted ads
- Video
- Email Marketing
- Microsites
- Sweepstakes sponsorship

20 **MILLION** PAGE VIEWS EVERY SINGLE MONTH

15 MILLION UNIQUE VISITORS PER MONTH

43% OF ALL VISITORS ACCESS THE SITE VIA THEIR MOBILE DEVICES

700,000 NEWSLETTER SUBSCRIPTIONS TO THE INBOXES OF *300,000* UNIQUE INDIVIDUALS EVERY WEEK

PERSONAL ENRICHMENT

Staying Sharp
9781119187790
USA $26.00
CAN $31.99
UK £19.99

Facebook
9781119179030
USA $21.99
CAN $25.99
UK £16.99

Guitar
9781119293354
USA $24.99
CAN $29.99
UK £17.99

Investing
9781119293347
USA $22.99
CAN $27.99
UK £16.99

Beekeeping
9781119310068
USA $22.99
CAN $27.99
UK £16.99

Digital Photography
9781119235606
USA $24.99
CAN $29.99
UK £17.99

Meditation
9781119251163
USA $24.99
CAN $29.99
UK £17.99

Pregnancy
9781119235491
USA $26.99
CAN $31.99
UK £19.99

Samsung Galaxy S7
9781119279952
USA $24.99
CAN $29.99
UK £17.99

iPhone
9781119283133
USA $24.99
CAN $29.99
UK £17.99

Crocheting
9781119287117
USA $24.99
CAN $29.99
UK £16.99

Nutrition
9781119130246
USA $22.99
CAN $27.99
UK £16.99

PROFESSIONAL DEVELOPMENT

Windows 10
9781119311041
USA $24.99
CAN $29.99
UK £17.99

AutoCAD
9781119255796
USA $39.99
CAN $47.99
UK £27.99

Excel 2016
9781119293439
USA $26.99
CAN $31.99
UK £19.99

QuickBooks 2017
9781119281467
USA $26.99
CAN $31.99
UK £19.99

macOS Sierra
9781119280651
USA $29.99
CAN $35.99
UK £21.99

LinkedIn
9781119251132
USA $24.99
CAN $29.99
UK £17.99

Windows 10 All-in-One
9781119310563
USA $34.00
CAN $41.99
UK £24.99

SharePoint 2016
9781119181705
USA $29.99
CAN $35.99
UK £21.99

Fundamental Analysis
9781119263593
USA $26.99
CAN $31.99
UK £19.99

Networking
9781119257769
USA $29.99
CAN $35.99
UK £21.99

Office 2016
9781119293477
USA $26.99
CAN $31.99
UK £19.99

Office 365
9781119265313
USA $24.99
CAN $29.99
UK £17.99

Salesforce.com
9781119239314
USA $29.99
CAN $35.99
UK £21.99

Coding
9781119293323
USA $29.99
CAN $35.99
UK £21.99

dummies.com

dummies
A Wiley Brand